# SCIENCE IN RUSSIAN CULTURE

## 1861–1917

# Science in
# Russian Culture

*1861–1917*

ALEXANDER VUCINICH

\*\*

1970
*Stanford University Press*
*Stanford, California*

Stanford University Press
Stanford, California
© 1970 by the Board of Trustees of the
Leland Stanford Junior University
Printed in the United States of America
ISBN 0-8047-0738-3
LC 75-107650

To John and Andrea

# Preface

This book is divided into two parts. Part I, covering the period 1861–83, examines the changes in scientific culture produced by the rapid promulgation of, and gradual retreat from, the great reforms of the 1860's. Part II covers the period from the promulgation of the 1884 university charter, which abolished the last traces of academic autonomy, to the fall of the autocratic system in 1917. The scientists who were actively engaged in scholarly work during both periods have been treated mostly in the part covering the period of their most outstanding achievements. In some cases, I have treated them equally in both parts, particularly if they maintained an undiminished output of scholarship while significantly redirecting their research interests. I have discussed the growth of sociology as a systematic study of society only in the second part (in Chapter Fourteen); this, I feel, will best emphasize certain common themes that pervaded Russian sociological thought during both periods, while recognizing that an overwhelming majority of Russian sociologists were most active during the second period.

I am most grateful to the American Philosophical Society in Philadelphia and the Russian and East European Center at the University of Illinois, Urbana, for financial grants that helped me spend a profitable summer in the major libraries of the Soviet Union. I am particularly indebted to the American Council of Learned Societies, whose research grant enabled me to spend four months in Moscow and Leningrad. I should also like to thank the Institute of the History of the Natural Sciences and Technology (a division of the Soviet Academy of Sciences), whose scholarly aid and hospitality made my stay in Moscow and Leningrad so much more productive. Mrs. Liudmila Markova, a research associate of the Institute, was especially helpful, introducing me to many leading Soviet historians of science and exchanging ideas on the many theoretical and philosophical aspects of the history of science. To the Hoover Institution at Stanford I am indebted for a research grant and for the courtesy and professional assistance of its library staff. Finally, I am grateful to the Center for Advanced Studies at the University of Illinois, Urbana, whose grant in the spring of 1967 relieved me of my teaching duties and allowed me to devote more time to the writing of this book.

I should like to acknowledge with particular gratitude the help of my colleague Professor Laurence H. Miller, head of the Special Languages Department of the magnificent university library at Urbana. He helped me obtain numerous sources of vital information, gave me invaluable bibliographical hints, and drew my attention to important data hidden in periodical publications not primarily concerned with the history of science. I was the first beneficiary of his endeavors, which have made the University of Illinois Library the holder of one of the finest collections outside the Soviet Union of published sources on the history of Russian science.

In the preparation of the manuscript for publication, I have received extensive help from three persons, to whom I am much indebted. J. G. Bell, Editor of Stanford University Press, read the manuscript and offered voluminous suggestions that greatly improved the organization and cogency of my final draft. For further stylistic and organizational improvements I am grateful to James Trosper, assistant editor at Stanford University Press. Finally, my wife Dorothy has helped me in every phase of this book, from the collection of data to the preparation of the final draft.

A. VUCINICH

# Contents

# Introduction

This book surveys the development of scientific thought in Russia during the turbulent years from 1861 to 1917—a period characterized by the gradual modernization of technology and thought and the irreparable disintegration of the values on which the autocratic state was built. To some degree I have examined the work of individual scientists and scientific institutions. My main concern, however, is with the distinctive social and cultural attributes of Russian science, and in particular with the relationship between the values of scientists and the dominant values of Russian culture as expressed by spokesmen for the more prominent nonscientific modes of inquiry—notably theology, metaphysics, ethical philosophy, and literary criticism.

I also explore at some length the nature and consequences of the tsarist government's decidedly ambivalent attitude toward science, which was best expressed in its educational policies. On the one hand, the government saw science as indispensable to the modernization of Russia's economy, armed forces, and public services; on the other, it distrusted the scientific spirit, with its critical attitude toward authority, its relativistic interpretation of nature and social institutions, its individualistic approach to problems, and its belief in the supreme wisdom of man's rational capacities. The authorities had good reason for their distrust, since nearly all the regime's leading opponents explicitly expected science to play a major role in liberating Russia from the feudal past and introducing an age of civil liberty, social equality, and freedom of thought. Indeed, official ideologues as well as conservative religious philosophers opposed science mostly because of its democratic nature. N. A. Berdiaev spoke for many others when he described science as the ideology of democracy, and both as characteristic of decaying societies.

The concept of "science" has no precisely defined substantive, logical, or epistemological boundaries; one may study it from many different points of view. In this book I have chosen to examine science from four points of view in particular: as a specific mode of inquiry, as a unique system of knowledge built on certain basic metaphysical assumptions, as part of a specifically national culture, and as a world view.

To talk about science as a distinctive mode of inquiry is to talk about science in the most common sense of the term—the accumulation of empirically verifiable facts and the reordering of these facts into facts of a higher order of generality. The process of accumulation follows its own inner logic; new scientific facts build on other facts that logically precede them. Whether they are routine additions to empirical knowledge or grand laws of nature, they can be established only when previously accumulated knowledge makes their discovery possible.

One must accordingly be careful not to exaggerate the role of sociocultural conditions in stimulating scientific discoveries. Mendeleev, for example, discovered the periodic law of elements not because of any unique quality in his social environment, but because chemistry was sufficiently advanced by the 1860's to present a scientist of sufficient brilliance with the necessary clues. Socioeconomic conditions can interfere with the internal development of science by hampering or encouraging it; but they cannot change the logical sequence of ideas in a given line of scientific inquiry.

In brief, the growth of science cannot be explained primarily as a response of the scientific community to the dictates and needs of society at large. No competent scientist would deny the essentially utilitarian quality of scientific knowledge; but none would go on to argue that the scientific community should concern itself exclusively with solving the acute problems of the day. The inner logic of social development and the inner logic of scientific development are different.

Science is more than a unique mode of inquiry. It is also, to use an expression of Niels Bohr, an endeavor to reduce knowledge to order—to subsume an increasing flow of knowledge under a decreasing number of general laws. In "ordering" knowledge, the scientist is guided by an underlying scientific paradigm—a system of broad assumptions about the nature and behavior of the universe. Until the end of the nineteenth century the Newtonian system of mechanics was the dominant and most general paradigm; its chief elements were the concepts of continuity, external causality, the absoluteness of space and time, the indivisibility and immutability of atoms, and the ontological primacy of matter. The Newtonian paradigm was flexible enough to allow both for limited transgressions and for the emergence of subparadigms in the form of special traditions in individual sciences. In broad terms, however, it held absolute sway over the main lines of scientific development. Not only did it set the terms in which scientists went about their daily professional work, but it offered the only generally accepted criteria by which to judge new theories and findings.

The accumulation of scientific knowledge leads to increasing professional specialization among scientists; and the scientific ethos encourages this process of fission by emphasizing the fallibility of authority and the variousness of knowledge. The centrifugal effects of this process are counterbalanced by the centripetal force of scientific paradigms, which help to form and maintain a clearly defined scientific community. An amateur naturalist in Kaluga province and a professional mathematician in St. Petersburg are bound to the same community of scholars by their adherence to the same set of philosophical propositions. This intellectual unity is not the only foundation of a scientific community, but it is the most important single force in that community; and unlike the idealized norms of the scientific ethos, it encourages conservatism. As Robert Oppenheimer once remarked, "Science is not skepticism. It is not the practice of science to look for things to doubt."

If a scientist is to be accepted as a member of the scientific community, he must not stray beyond the philosophical boundaries of what Thomas Kuhn calls "normal science." Thus Mendeleev's discovery of the periodic law was a logical extension of the grand paradigm of Newtonian mechanics, as was the work of his contemporary K. A. Timiriazev, who sought to reconcile Newton's mechanicism with Darwin's historicism. But N. I. Lobachevskii, the founder of non-Euclidean geometry, died unheralded by his contemporaries because his work had challenged a sacred principle of the mechanistic view: the absoluteness of Euclidean space.

The philosophical propositions that make up a scientific paradigm are sociologically important not only because they define the internal orientation and goals of the scientific community, but also because they are the main targets for attacks by the critics of science. The intellectual unity provided by a definite paradigm allows scientists as a social group to offer a strong common defense against all kinds of external attacks. And the change of a scientific paradigm is often accompanied by changes in the ideological preferences, educational philosophies, class origins, and ethnic composition of the scientific community.

A scientist has obligations not only to his discipline as such and to the scientific community, but to society at large. He is not only a scientist but an American or German or Russian scientist. Scientific facts and theories recognize no national boundaries, and science involves the labors of professional men from all civilized countries. Yet a given society can influence the development of science in many ways. A society's needs may emphasize some sciences at the expense of others, or stimulate the rise of new sciences.

A society's dominant philosophic traditions may interact with scientific theory in different ways, and different kinds of relations may be worked out between science and various nonscientific modes of inquiry. Or a society may insist on making a value distinction between "pure science" and "applied science."

The society of Imperial Russia influenced Russian scientists in these ways and many more. For example, a cultural historian can easily link the preoccupation of many Russian mathematicians with probability theory and approximative calculation to the dismal lack of concrete statistical data on the human and natural resources of the country, particularly before the 1860's. Similarly, the emergence of soil science as a distinctively Russian discipline can be related to the great national concern with the depletion of cultivated soil, the drastic annual fluctuation in agricultural output, and the perennial threat of famine. There is an unmistakable link between the recurrence of plague and cholera epidemics and the pronounced Russian interest in microbiology. And the early flowering of Russian geography, ethnography, and comparative linguistics can be accounted for, at least in part, by the rich profusion of the empire's geographical, racial, and linguistic resources.

National differences in science have still another important source: the personal influence of the scientific genius. At the end of the nineteenth century, for example, there were two strong orientations in European physiology. One was the physico-chemical orientation, which sought to reduce the dynamics of organisms to the laws of physics and chemistry; the other was the biological orientation, which held that physiological processes could best be explained in terms of purely biological laws. Russian physiology at that time was dominated by the biological orientation—not because this approach was in any sense peculiarly Russian, but because it happened to be favored by Pavlov, the giant of Russian physiology.

Strong national scientific traditions are the backbone of a nation's scientific community, and usually produce its greatest scientific contributions. Yet they can inhibit achievement as well as foster it. Sechenov and Pavlov gave Russian neurophysiology a new theoretical direction and many new research techniques, but the enormous influence of their ideas worked against a more systematic development of social psychology in Russia. Likewise, there is no doubt that the powerful influence of A. M. Butlerov's school in structural chemistry, which had helped usher in a new age in chemistry, later prevented a rapid diffusion of the theoretical ideas and research techniques of stereochemistry in Russia; or that Mendeleev's firm belief in the indivisibility and immutability of atoms slowed the spread of modern physical chemistry.

Finally, science is an attitude, a state of mind, a world view. As such, it ceases to be the indisputable domain of scientists and becomes the province of society as a whole. According to V. I. Vernadskii, an eminent Russian geochemist, it was not until the middle of the eighteenth century, with Diderot's *Encyclopedia*, that the scientific world view became a major cultural and ideological force; in the same vein, Buckle described the French Revolution as the first major event in history attributable primarily to the spirit of science. In Russia, the growth of the intelligentsia was inseparable from the growth of the scientific world view. By the end of the eighteenth century, the Russian intelligentsia had made the connection between scientific inquiry and political modernization, with the predictable response from the tsarist government and the Orthodox church.

The study of science as a world outlook takes us outside the scientific community and into broader areas of intellectual life. In order to fully understand the nonscientists who championed the scientific attitude, we must also examine the views of the major critics of science. But we must never forget that scientific knowledge and the scientific attitude are two different things: one is a reservoir of facts and theories, the other a philosophy of life and a state of mind. As often as not, Russian scientists did not share the enthusiasms of their nonscientist admirers; and as often as not their admirers based their plans and predictions on antiquated or misunderstood scientific ideas. Yet the relationship was on the whole a fruitful one. If the scientific attitude is more a product of society than of science, it remains both a powerful instrument of social change and a valuable stimulus to the growth of science as a vocation. The growth of Russian science in the years 1861–1917 was extraordinary. But the growth of the scientific attitude in Russia in the same years was if anything more important.

# PART I

# SCIENCE IN THE AGE OF EMANCIPATION
## 1861–1883

## CHAPTER ONE

# Science and Ideology

## THE NEW SOCIETY: DREAMS AND REALITIES

The epoch of great reforms in Russia began at the end of the 1850's, reached its climax in the early 1860's, and ran its course by 1868. Short though it was, this period produced enormous changes in Russian society: the emancipation of the serfs, the reorganization of the universities, and the liberalization of local government and justice. These fundamental reforms arose from an acute awareness of the compounded burdens of the autocratic system, and from a new moral sentiment favoring a social order based on enlightenment, justice, and equality.

"This was a wonderful age," said the social critic N. V. Shelgunov, "an age when every person aspired to think, read, and study, and when every person of integrity was outspoken in expressing his commitment to these rules. Thought, previously dormant, was awakened and set to work: its impulse was forceful, and its tasks titanic. There was no concern for the present; the fate of future generations and the fate of Russia were contemplated, judged, and always related to specific reforms. This inspiring work attracted all gifted men, and brought forth a host of young journalists, literati, and scholars who will forever illumine the annals of Russian education and thought, testifying to the brilliant achievements of the 1860's, which for long gave sense and direction to the intellectual development of Russia."[1] Elsewhere, Shelgunov characterized the early 1860's as the years "when everything was blessed with overflowing energy ... when everything awakened, and when the forces of good and evil engaged in a battle that was real and truly national."[2]

V. V. Markovnikov, a professor of chemistry at St. Petersburg University and a member of the St. Petersburg Academy of Sciences, described the Reform from the vantage point of science: "Every person who had the opportunity strove to learn. On all sides, we heard the cry: We are backward! We are very backward! Everyone tried to make up for lost time. These were the years of ecstatic enthusiasm for science and learning. Recently, I happened to read the following characterization of that period: 'That was a strange epoch—an epoch of the regeneration of social life, of the yearning for truth, and of a struggle for the rights and the honor of one's weaker brother. That epoch blended passionate and energetic activity with the world of dreams, sentimentalism, and broad, youthful impracticality that so typified the young men of that age. Everything came to life. The rays of sunlight reached even the most remote and isolated corners of the land!' "[3]

Everyone sensed the colossal magnitude and true meaning of this national frenzy.* A contemporary historian stated that the second half of the 1850's marked "the end of the literary period of our social development" and the beginning of "the era of practical activity."[4] A. I. Herzen noted that the new man, the man of action, was simultaneously a prominent literary figure and a spokesman of the time; the "superfluous man" of the preceding generation had fulfilled his historical role, and "just as it was earlier *necessary* to have superfluous men, it has now become *necessary* not to have them."[5] The men of action differed in philosophical views, social origins, and aspirations. A new corps of government officials, imbued with the spirit of reform, was as much a part of this movement as were the Dostoevskii brothers in their passionate struggle against rural illiteracy, the early Populists with their schemes for voluntary work by the intelligentsia in the villages, M. E. Saltykov-Shchedrin with his eloquent plea for practical work, and Dmitrii Pisarev with his plea for an extensive popularization of scientific thought.

The growth rate of the Russian population increased greatly during the 1860's, especially in the urban areas. Industry, mining, and railroad transportation expanded significantly, and many industrial products reached the peasants for the first time. The first systematic efforts were made to lessen the constant threat of fires and epidemics, the peasants' most devastating enemies. The production of grain set new records, even though the land was not cultivated as intensively as it could have been. A network of educational institutions was established in the countryside; and in the cities, Sunday schools were set up in order to offer education to wider segments of the urban population.

* According to the Academician Nestor Kotliarevskii, the "world view" of the 1860's was formulated most precisely by N. G. Chernyshevskii in his articles in *Contemporary* from 1854 to 1861. Dedicated to a sharp break with tradition, this world view extolled "a substitution of 'anthropology' for religion, inductive method for deductive method, materialistic monism for idealistic dualism, empirical aesthetics for abstract aesthetics, and the theory of rational egotism for morality based on supersensory principles." (Nestor Kotliarevskii, No. 11, p. 275.)

In sum, this was an era of material progress, social fermentation, and the opening of new intellectual paths. In all these activities the emphasis was on "independent action" (*samostoiatel'nost'*), action untutored and unguarded by the official arm of autocratic power. As a slogan of the new age, *samosto-iatel'nost'* had two connotations: practical, socially useful work, and independent thought. Both were free of government guidance or control, and both relied on the emergence of a new public opinion, formed in the free market of ideas. Boris Chicherin felt that the formation of "many publics" was the most important single development of the 1860's.[6] Independent action was given its first great test by university students. Immediately after the Crimean War, the universities became centers of cultural activity. Students organized and sponsored public lectures, art exhibits, and music festivals. The students of St. Petersburg University published the *Students' Symposium,* which carried learned and literary articles written mostly by the students themselves.[7] In 1857, the same university organized an agency for financial assistance to needy students, and other schools of higher education followed suit. The conservatives disapproved of the many new extracurricular activities, and considered them an antithesis of the very idea of the university as a center of learning;[8] the liberals interpreted them as a mere reflection of the general conditions in the country.

A succession of government ordinances that modified the crippling decrees issued by Nicholas I during the last years of his reign greatly stimulated the new academic spirit. In 1855 the government annulled an earlier decree that had severely limited the number of students enrolled in each university. Subsequently, the compulsory teaching of "military sciences" (essentially drill and discipline) was eliminated, and the teaching of philosophy and the constitutional law of European states was reintroduced. Russian students were again allowed to study in Western European universities. Many young university professors—notably D. I. Mendeleev, A. M. Butlerov, I. M. Sechenov, and A. O. Kovalevskii—now had an opportunity to work in the leading universities of Western Europe. University halls were again made available for public lectures. The traditional right of the universities and the Academy of Sciences to purchase foreign books without prior approval from the censorship authorities, rescinded by Nicholas I, was fully reinstated in 1859.[9] Western ideas came to Russia more freely than ever, and they appealed to larger segments of the population.

The search for independent action and thought affected people far beyond the university halls. Innovations came in a constant stream, and many of them left an indelible imprint on the Russian polity. The first private daily newspapers appeared, the first commercially sponsored lecture halls were opened, and for the first time private publishers were allowed to print gymnasium and university textbooks.[10] Everywhere, it seemed, the acquisition of knowledge was inseparable from mounting demands for social and political action. The temper of the time required and supported secular wisdom, of which science formed a vital part. Secular thought made notable inroads even into the schools of theology, which by tradition trained the custodians of philosophical irrationalism. Both M. A. Antonovich and A. P. Shchapov, two of the more belligerent critics of the autocratic ideology, graduated from theological schools. They were typical of the growing ranks of young theologians who attended public lectures on scientific themes and were intimately familiar with David Strauss's *Life of Jesus* and Ludwig Büchner's *Kraft und Staff*. The 1854 graduating class of the St. Petersburg Theological Academy, of which Antonovich was a member, did not produce a single monk: work that could produce tangible results was more attractive to them than the spiritual life of monastic seclusion.[11]

The new culture had deep roots in tradition. The literature of this epoch was dominated by Turgenev, Dostoevskii, Tolstoi, Ostrovskii, and Saltykov-Shchedrin—all products of the era of Nicholas I. The scientific world was dominated by such men as the mathematician P. L. Chebyshev; the chemists N. N. Zinin, A. M. Butlerov, and D. I. Mendeleev; the physiologist I. M. Sechenov; the zoologists N. A. Severtsov and Lev Tsenkovskii; and many others who had received their academic training under Nicholas. Many great journalists, theologians, and enlightened statesmen were also products of the preceding era. Despite this unmistakable continuity, the 1860's were a unique decade; and perhaps the most important feature of this uniqueness was the fortunate blending of values and ideals that created the necessary conditions for a continuous and diverse growth of secular wisdom in general and scientific thought in particular.

The rapid growth of Russian scientific thought during the 1860's was stimulated by news from abroad. The late 1850's and the 1860's were one of the most exciting periods in the history of modern science. These were the years that witnessed the triumph of spectral analysis, structural chemistry, transformist biology, non-Euclidean geometry, experimental physiology, and many other theories and experimental complexes. There was also an extensive reorganization of social sciences on the model of the natural sciences. Above everything else, this was a period of uncompromising attacks on metaphysics and the concurrent growth of new philosophical systems. French positivism, English utilitarianism, and German materialism and neo-Kantianism had perhaps only one thing in common—an avowed compatibility with scientific thought. Such scientific giants as Hermann Helmholtz and Gustav Kirchhoff in Germany, Louis Pasteur and Claude Bernard in France, and Thomas Huxley in England were eager to break through the wall that separated scientists from the general public, and did their best to spread scientific knowledge outside the narrow academic halls. Russia, which has never been closer to Western Europe, opened its doors to all these influences. The Russian intellectual was mostly an eclectic; but he gravitated toward a philosophy that was particularly harsh on supernaturalism as a source of sanctions and justifications of the social status quo, and the idea of historical relativism occupied a prominent place in his thought. H. T. Buckle's *History of Civilization in England*, with its denial of providentialism in history and its humanistic emphasis on free will, provided particularly attractive reading for young Russians.[12]

Science can develop only in cultures that recognize man's rational capacities as the prime source of knowledge, measure the value of knowledge by its practical utility, and uphold the right of every man to interpret knowledge in his own way. These minimum conditions for scientific progress took root in Russian culture before the 1860's; but it was not until the Reform that they blended into a single powerful system of values and gained a prominent position in that culture.

The dominant ideas of the 1860's, according to one analyst, were: (1) "a striving to rationalize the way of life, to eliminate from it everything mystical, traditional, and patriarchal . . . and to build a new life based on the principle of utility"; (2) "the demand that each man be engaged in useful civic work"; (3) "a full denial of the past" in order to liberate the personality and the social system. This characterization sounds very much like Robert Merton's description of the Puritan values that stimulated the intensive growth of modern Western science; actually, it was made in 1909 by a man who knew little sociology but had deeply sensed the values and motives that guided the "men of the sixties."[13]

During the 1860's, science, the purest form of rationalist thought, ceased to occupy a peripheral place in Russian culture. Many contemporaries interpreted Turgenev's *Fathers and Sons* as literary recognition of this fact. Bazarov, Turgenev's hero, was a typical "new man" and a significant development in the impressive line of intellectuals portrayed by the great Russian novels. Before the 1850's the typical intellectual hero of fiction was a "superfluous man." For example, Pechorin, the leading character of Lermontov's *A Hero of Our Time* (1839), was definitely ready to descend to earth, but found himself short of solid knowledge embedded in a rationalist philosophy. Turgenev's Rudin, a man of the 1840's, had acquired ample knowledge of the world around him, but was unready for action; in Pisarev's words, he had knowledge but no will, in contrast to Pechorin, who had will but no knowledge.[14] Bazarov, the "new man" who appeared on the historical scene after the Crimean War, combined Pechorin's readiness for social action with Rudin's appreciation and thirst for positive knowledge.

Many conservative critics of the day preferred to regard Bazarov as a victim of exaggerated rationalist views, untempered individualism, and the corruptive influences of Western materialism and utilitarianism. They were inclined to treat him as a specimen of intellectual degeneracy, and were disturbed by Turgenev's reluctance to state clearly and forthrightly his own feeling for the hero of *Fathers and Sons*. The responsible advocates of social reform, on the other hand, greeted Bazarov as a symbol of their own ideas. In the eyes of Russian scientists, he was the harbinger of a new, healthier civilization. The plant physiologist Kliment Timiriazev compared Bazarov to Peter the Great: both men, in his estimation, urged the building of a new life by a merciless destruction of the old one, and both pursued the challenging search for scientific knowledge with hard-forged, ascetic determination.[15]

Reminiscing about the 1860's, the mathematician Sof'ia Kovalevskii noted: "We were so exalted by all these new ideas, so convinced that the present state of society could not last long—that the glorious time of liberty and general knowledge was quite near, quite certain."[16] The rationalism of the 1860's was not a mere philosophical stance, or a position in an epistemological debate. It was a *Weltanschauung* based on the belief that Russia's place in the family of civilized nations would be determined not by its mystical-irrationalist tradition but by its contributions in the fields of human endeavor that depend on man's exercise of his rational powers. It was not codified into an ordered system of thought, but flowed freely through all sorts of writings and pronouncements by the epoch's great minds.

The previous generations' philosophical pondering had centered on the relative merits of rationalism and irrationalism, viewing them as two valid but contradictory systems of thought. This struggle was very much alive in the 1860's, but this time rationalism occupied the central position, and debate was focused on its power and intellectual adequacy. Some people—

epitomized by Bazarov—believed in the unlimited power of reason, but others were more interested in its limitations. The unnamed hero of Dostoevskii's *Notes from Underground* was quite willing to exaggerate the limitations of reasoning power to achieve a dramatic effect. "I . . . want to live," said he, "in order to satisfy all my capacities for life, and not simply my capacity for reasoning, not simply one-twentieth of my capacity for life. . . . The conclusions of reason and arithmetic may be the law of logic, but not the law of humanity." He went even further by suggesting that we had better "scatter rationalism to the winds . . . send these logarithms to the devil, and . . . live once more by our own foolish will!" This unqualified attack is less a denial of rationalism than an expression of a subdued fear of scientific thought and its exacting logic.

The Orthodox Church, lost and intellectually impoverished because of its passive subservience to autocratic ideology, was the main enemy of the onrushing waves of rationalist thought. Filaret, the Metropolitan of Moscow and hence the most powerful man in the Church, ordered that a special prayer be introduced in all the churches under his jurisdiction to ward off the evils of rationalism and its social and intellectual correlates. Chernyshevskii's "The Anthropological Principle in Philosophy," a manifesto of realism dedicated to the proposition that no philosophy is sound unless it is firmly embedded in natural science, was probably the chief reason for this measure.[17]

Filaret's negative attitude did not represent all Russian theological thought of the time. The sixties produced a small group of new theologians who were willing to search for a possible meeting ground between theological thought and rationalist philosophy. This trend found its most profound expression in the writings and criticisms of P. D. Iurkevich, who taught philosophy first at the Kiev Theological Academy and then at Moscow University. In a lengthy essay devoted to "the science of the human spirit" and published in the journal of the Kiev Academy, Iurkevich acknowledged that the modern philosophy of realism, grounded in science, "has enriched many fields of culture and has given us such an exact analysis of the phenomena of the human mind that, in all probability, it will sooner or later be of great interest to theology."[18] The idea of a "rational theology," which had also appeared in seventeenth-century England as a response to the great achievements of the physical sciences, thus found its first voice in Russia. The influential *Russian Messenger* greeted Iurkevich as a new kind of religious thinker: "Expressing the spirit of our time . . . the orientation of

Iurkevich's thought is free of one-sided judgments and doctrinaire exclusiveness. We are particularly pleased to note that he fully appreciates the rigor of the scientific method as applied to subjects of philosophical relevance."[19]

Iurkevich failed to elaborate his ideas, and left little imprint on the religious thought of his time; his essay, however, did show that rationality as a source of secular wisdom had taken a firmer position in Russian culture. He presented himself as a defender of pure philosophical realism. Referring to Chernyshevskii's "The Anthropological Principle in Philosophy" he said: "[Chernyshevskii's] essay actually belongs to the philosophy of realism, which has contributed so much that is good and fruitful to science and society; but it does not acquaint us with the real conclusions of that philosophy. We do not know whether the author is familiar with the names of the philosophers of this orientation, but we know for certain that he is unfamiliar with their psychological and philosophical theories. He talks about philosophical topics by hearsay. He has heard that the philosophy of realism employs the methods of natural science, and that it itself is a sort of natural science concerned with psychic phenomena. Thus he has arrived at the idea that psychic phenomena can be explained in chemical laboratories."[20] In brief, Chernyshevskii erred not in subscribing to realism as a philosophy based on science, but in misrepresenting its fundamental principles.

Iurkevich's defense of "realism" was only a dialectical maneuver, and did not echo his philosophical orientation. He firmly rejected Chernyshevskii's materialistic monism, and instead subscribed to the monism of Christian theology, according to which "matter is a product of the spirit." He appealed to the conservative elements of society, who saw in his arguments a determined effort to protect the uninterrupted flow of theological thought into the expanding domain of psychological and social sciences. By resisting the extension of scientific knowledge and methodology to the study of society, Iurkevich actually worked against the rapidly widening horizons of science. His main enemies were the men who viewed science as a new religion dedicated to radical changes in the structure of Russian society. He recognized the role of science in the acquisition of socially useful knowledge, but he also limited the intellectual jurisdiction of the scientific quest for truth.[21]

The development of Russian religious ideas during and after the 1860's was marked by a growing rationalist element in such influential sects as the Dukhobortsy and the Molokane, and by the emergence of new sects guided by rationalist principles. In fact, sectarianism, according to V. S.

Ikonnikov, provided the only religious basis for the growth of rationalist thought in Russia.[22]  The theology of official Russian Orthodoxy never deviated from irrationalism, asceticism, and mysticism, even though some of its unofficial spokesmen, like Iurkevich, did try to accommodate modern scientific thought. The rationalist element in Russian sectarianism did not originate in theory, but in the burning social and economic questions of the Reform era. The Shtundisty, a typical "rationalist sect," blossomed in this atmosphere. It was, in a sense, a religious response to the increasing pace of modernization in Russia. In two decades the Shtundisty influence was so strong that followers of the sect were found in almost every community in southern Russia.[23]

The Shtundisty differed in several respects from Russian Orthodoxy. The Orthodox religion is a religion first of liturgy and religious drama and then of doctrine; it emphasizes an affective rather than an intellectual experience. The Shtundisty had no churches to speak of; their services were undramatic, and the emphasis was on intellectual exercise. The Russian Orthodox Church equated autocracy with justice and equality. The Shtundisty sought a way out of a social world deprived of the most elementary justice, and the liberation of the serfs gave them renewed inspiration for the development of their religious ideas. Orthodoxy stressed a pious repetition of passages from the Bible; the Shtundisty emphasized an open-minded but critical examination and modernization of biblical passages. The Shtundisty rejected not only asceticism and mysticism, but also all the saints and the church hierarchy. Whereas the Orthodox Church looked toward the past, the Shtundisty looked toward the future. Their most important difference from the Orthodox Church was in their emphasis on education as an essential prerequisite for a virtuous life and a more intelligent understanding of divine creations.[24] They did not have a precise and logically ordered theological thought; but they firmly believed that man's power lay in his rational capacities, and not in divine whims and miracles.[25]

The emphasis on rationality as a basis of wisdom went hand in hand with the emphasis on practicality of knowledge—that is, on the role of science as a repository of positive knowledge that could be translated into social welfare. This attitude was a natural result of the widespread demands for social action, and of reform plans supported by an impressive cross-section of the intelligentsia and a solid group of highly placed government officials. Never before had the Baconian dictum that knowledge is the main source of human power sounded as true and as inspiring. A. P. Shchapov noted in 1864 that throughout the country the people felt "the powerful need for a natural-scientific world view and the application of scientific knowledge to social and economic activity." "In order to engender in the masses a love and a striving for natural science," he said, "it is necessary to show them the practical utility of a knowledge of nature and its applicability to economic life."[26] To Chernyshevskii, natural science was the basis of a healthy world outlook; to Shchapov it was the key to true, realistic education. "It is extremely important for us to popularize science because until now all our theories and ideals operated outside the world of reality, outside the working masses, for whom knowledge is a real necessity and a tool of useful work."[27] Vladimir Odoevskii, who had claimed two decades earlier that "the goal of science is science itself, and it has no other, external goals," was now a great advocate of making science the guide to social reforms.[28]

The future progress of science, according to N. A. Serno-Solov'evich, would depend on both a systematic accumulation and a social utilization of exact knowledge. He was clearly impatient with contemporaries who appreciated the emancipation of science from "all metaphysical trivialities" and "old research routines" but who exalted science for science's sake. To become practically oriented, the social sciences, in his opinion, should establish closer ties with the natural sciences.[29]

According to P. L. Lavrov, scientific knowledge had passed through three stages of development. During the first stage, knowledge was essentially subjective, for it was anchored in a view that placed man at the center of the universe. During the second stage, knowledge was basically objective; it was rooted in a new view that considered man "only one of the infinite products of the immutable laws of the external world." The third, or modern, stage resulted from a dialectical synthesis of the two previous stages. Man had again become the center of the universe—not the universe as it existed in itself, however, but the universe as it was conceived by man and subordinated to human thought and goals.[30] To contemporary man, according to Lavrov, the chemical studies of albumen and Kepler's mathematically articulated astronomical laws were not only abstract knowledge, but also sources of social progress. The chemistry of albumen opened new vistas for the enrichment of food supplies, and Kepler's laws denied the idea of divine whims in the universe and brought nature closer to human control. Lavrov felt that positive knowledge could be used both to improve man's material welfare and to emancipate the human mind from the fetters of superstition. Socially useful scientific knowledge, according to him, was the motive force of cultural progress.

The utility of knowledge was also emphasized by Russian thought outside science. N. S. Tikhonravov interpreted Shakespeare as a great realist who had made literary art an active and direct part of real life, just as Bacon had done for science.[31] M. A. Antonovich wrote in a similar vein, but with more naïveté: "History supplies ample proof that art has never refused to serve various theoretical and practical tasks; poetry, in particular, has frequently popularized ideas of general usefulness, has guided its readers toward a humanistic orientation, and has intentionally and consciously satisfied the needs of its time."[32] He conceded, however, that this realistic orientation of poetry and other forms of artistic expression had been particularly valued in politically backward societies where science was not well developed. In reference to his own country, he cited the example of a poet whose reading of an ode eulogizing Lomonosov on the hundredth anniversary of his death made a profound impression on an audience that had just ignored the delivery of a mathematician's academic paper on the same theme. Antonovich wanted to impress on the literary men of his time the importance of giving their support to the growing scientific attitude in Russia.

The men of the 1860's not only worshipped rationality and utilitarianism, but also strove to affirm the individual as a moving historical force and as a philosophical principle. Among older historians, K. D. Kavelin had anticipated this spirit in the late 1840's with his unequivocal demand for an identification of the historical process with the progressive affirmation of personality. He returned to the same topic in the 1870's. In the article "Philosophy and Science in Europe and Russia," published in 1874, Kavelin stated that the relatively low status of philosophical and scientific thought in Russian culture had originated in the essentially impersonal character of Russian history, which provided very little opportunity for the individual to express his "will" and "energy." In Europe, he said, the individual was the creator of history, whereas in Russia the individual was so far out of the picture that he was hardly more than "a passive carrier of history."[33] He conceded, however, that during "the last ten to fifteen years" the cultural and social changes in Russia had provided more favorable conditions for the emergence of the individual as an active historical force.

P. L. Lavrov greeted the new epoch with the statement that progress, measured in terms of growing "truth and justice," was the essence of history. "The growth of personality in the physical, intellectual, and moral sense, as embodied in the social forms of truth and justice, provides a formula embracing everything that may be defined as progress."[34] N. K. Mikhailovskii was equally forthright in his assertion that the historical struggle for individuality was the essential process in human progress.[35] The history of human society, according to him, is the history of an expanding satisfaction of individual needs. When society becomes aware of the cultural needs and proclivities of the individual, it has created sound conditions for the development of science. To Mikhailovskii, individuality was produced by simultaneous processes of functional differentiation and cultural integration. It reflected "the principle of freedom, independence, and unfitness for a given form of society," and encouraged criticism, skepticism, and innovation, the essential conditions for scientific pursuits.

Kavelin, Lavrov, and Mikhailovskii all identified individuality with "complete personality," a force that both reflects and changes the dominant values of a society. All three described personality as the best index of the gradually unfolding idea of progress.

This general demand for the affirmation of man's individuality was a by-product of the general outburst of national energy after the Sevastopol catastrophe. It was an expression of the new concept of social justice, deeply ingrained in the Emancipation of 1861, and at the same time a specific ideological adaptation to the burgeoning modernization of economic processes. The individuality of judgment and taste—the newly discovered nobility of "unfitness"—was a bright glimpse of the future. It gave extraordinary strength to both the pioneers of the new Russian society and the founders of modern Russian science.

### NIHILISM: THE OMNIPOTENCE OF SCIENCE

Nihilism was one of the most fateful phenomena in the history of modern Russia: it signaled the inevitable disintegration of the autocratic system and the beginning of the rapid growth of scientific thought. The growth of science did not cause the downfall of the autocratic system; rather, the same social and intellectual forces that favored the growth of one led to the collapse of the other.[36]

The Nihilists, who preferred to call themselves Realists, were the most outspoken of the radical intellectuals who dominated the critical thought and anti-autocratic ideologies of the 1860's. Their struggle was a passionate one, and in defending rationalism they often approached irrationality. Science, to the Nihilists, was not only a body of applicable knowledge and theoretical principles, but also a point of view, an ideological weapon. In science they saw the wisdom without which Russia could not build a better society. The only philosophy that they considered sound was a philosophy based on science, and they treated the natural sciences as the source of the best models for the solution of social problems. According to M. E. Saltykov-Shchedrin, the Nihilists and their successors took upon themselves "the task of explaining the relationship of man to nature, of unveiling the laws governing the latter, and of eradicating the conditions unfavorable to social progress." By contrast, the "idealists" saw man as permanently dependent on the mysterious forces of nature.[37] The Nihilists were particularly interested in modern physiology, for they were convinced that scientific insights into the working of the human organism would lead to a better understanding of human society, and would be valuable in charting the future course of political institutions. They were impressed with Comte's claim that a rigorous physiological study of the brain could supply precious clues to the inner pulses of human social life.

D. I. Pisarev and other major architects of Nihilism elaborated and clarified the philosophical and ideological legacy of N. A. Dobroliubov and N. G. Chernyshevskii. These two men, together with Pisarev, gave the critical thought of the 1860's its major substance and its line of attack. All three apotheosized the intellectual power of science and the humanistic qualities of the scientific attitude.

Nikolai Dobroliubov distinguished himself particularly by his unsparing journalistic attacks on the misrepresentations of modern scientific views by university professors. He attacked the vitalistic orientation in biology and physiology, and generally condemned all similar tendencies to substitute idealistic metaphysics for modern scientific thought in universities—especially all efforts to give theology an upper hand in the interpretation of natural laws. Dobroliubov's fight against the intellectual supremacy of theological thought was part of his broader attack on the very foundations of the existing social system, which should be modernized, he felt, chiefly by applying the principles and methods of natural science. Even though Dobroliubov was not a practicing scientist, he spoke for the new generation's identification with natural science and scientific philosophy. "Today," he wrote, "young people not only treat Paracelsus's dreams as nonsense, but also find that Liebig ... was mistaken; they read Moleschott, Du Bois-Reymond, and Vogt, and do not take even these scientists on faith, but try to test and supplement the theories by their own investigations." Dobroliubov noted that young scholars combined a profound interest in modern natural science with a realistic philosophy of science; and that in their philosophical views they did not follow "Plato, Oken, or Schelling, but rather the best, the most courageous, and the most practical disciples of Hegel."[38] Impressed with the forthright materialism of Jakob Moleschott and Karl Vogt, Dobroliubov treated their work as the last word in physiology, overlooking the more modern ideas of Claude Bernard, Karl Ludwig, and Hermann Helmholtz.

Nikolai Chernyshevskii touched upon science in many of his writings, although he was not a scientist by training and his major interests were not scientific. In "The Anthropological Principle in Philosophy" he endeavored to summarize modern scientific views on the unity of the physiological and psychological endowments of man. "Physiology and medicine have established that the human organism is a very complex chemical combination, placed into an equally complex chemical process that we call life."[39] Because the physiological and the psychological were unified, Chernyshevskii claimed that the natural and social sciences should have a common methodology and epistemology. The laws of universal causality, motion, and transformation, according to him, were equally applicable to the physical order and the "moral" order. He felt that human society could be understood if one understood the functioning of the human body—that both were equally perfectible, and that social change and biological transformation both resulted in steady progress. In advocating a scientific study of the "moral" order, he spoke not as a competent scientist but as an ideologue, a man determined to provide philosophical justification for the rapidly growing demand for radical changes in Russian society. Chernyshevskii, more than Dobroliubov, made science a weapon for the foes of autocracy.

No Russian of the 1860's was more dedicated to the social functions of science than D. I. Pisarev, who identified himself fully with Turgenev's Bazarov. He reproached Saltykov-Shchedrin for the pointless and diffuse descriptions contained in that writer's *Provincial Sketches*, and urged him to dedicate himself to a popularization of science. Pisarev attached the utmost importance to the diffusion of scientific knowledge through the entire population, noting that many prejudices were widespread because even the most elementary laws of nature were beyond the knowledge of the so-called educated people. The true tempering of the new man would be achieved, in his opinion, only when the natural sciences become the basis of general education.[40] "Science, and science alone, has the power ... to awaken public opinion and to produce enlightened leaders for the nation."[41] Pisarev insisted that the concentration of science and scientists on these two problems would rapidly eliminate the pernicious wall separating the world of science from that of physical work. In the growing subordination of physical work to the "durable, rational, and beneficent influences of science" he saw the best index of modern progress.*

Writing in the early 1860's, before the vigorous upsurge of Russian science itself, Pisarev lamented his countrymen's inborn disregard for the practical value of science. He thought that the main source of this disregard was the well-known and disturbing fact that most Russian scientific studies were written in foreign languages and directed at foreign scholars rather than at practical workers in Russian industries, schools, agriculture, and other agencies that could promote social welfare. "Some *genuine* researchers, who make *real* contributions to science and belong to all mankind, live in Russian cities and often bear Russian names, but they are dead or unknown capital in our society. Our Academician Karl Ernst von Baer is regarded throughout Europe as one of the greatest embryologists of our time; Darwin, Karl Vogt, and Huxley cite his work with particular respect. In the *Physiology of Common Life*, G. H. Lewes refers to F. V. Ovsiannikov's studies of the spinal cord, and Iakubovich's of nerve cells. The French scholar Beclard mentions the experimental works of Sechenov and Botkin. But what about us? We, I dare say, have no idea that men engaged in the study of embryology and nerve cells, and in experimental work, could live in our country. We learn about these men from foreign books."[42]

Pisarev knew, indeed, that the writing of scientific papers in Russian would not by itself ensure a practical regard for science in Russia. The imported foreign scholar, he said, could and did learn Russian, but "living in Russia is equivalent to living in the Arabian desert." In order to acquire a solid place in a culture, scientific work must receive support from society; society, not science, produces the values that create the intellectual atmosphere conducive to scientific work.[43] In a moralizing mood, Pisarev added that society must support the development of science or forfeit its right to control science. And in the intellectual excitement and broad reforms of the early 1860's he sensed the emergence of a climate favoring the growth of scientific thought. He thought that the most essential prerequisite for this growth was a universal understanding of and dedication to the practical utility of knowledge.

Like other "new men," Pisarev dealt extensively with the role of individuality in emancipating modern thought from the fetters of sacred cul-

* A. I. Herzen saw in the natural sciences "the salvation of the present-day man," the backbone of true education, and the most powerful weapon against the dark forces of mysticism. (Herzen, *Polnoe sobranie sochinenii*, XII, p. 106.)

ture. In doing so, he stuck closely to the intriguing and violent character of
Turgenev's Bazarov. Like Bazarov, he was not afraid to exaggerate the role
of individuality as a source for unrestrained criticism of every value and
every moral or intellectual authority. "Bazarov's actions are always motivated by personal wishes, advantages, and convenience. Bazarov is guided
only by personal whim and personal considerations. *He recognizes no authority above or outside himself, no moral law, no principle.* He sees no
higher goals ahead, and has no higher motives; yet he senses an ascendancy
of gigantic forces. I hear from indignant readers on every side: 'He is an
immoral man! A scoundrel, a monster!' Well, you can scold this scoundrel
and monster all you want; you can haunt him with your satires and epi-
grams, with indignant lyricism and public contempt, with the scissors of
inquisition and the executioner's ax. But you will not do away with this
monster; you will not place him in a bottle full of alcohol to be observed by
a respectable public.... If *bazarovshchina* is a sickness, it is a sickness of
our age."[44]

Pisarev differed from Dobroliubov and Chernyshevskii in one important
regard: not only was he an eloquent and dedicated champion of modern
scientific ideas, but he also tried to cast them in popular terms for a wider
reading audience.[45] For example, Darwin's *Origin of the Species* was translated into Russian in 1864 by S. A. Rachinskii, a professor of plant physiology at Moscow University. The translation, however, was awkward, uninspiring, and in spots erroneous. Rachinskii did not write an introduction
to his translation, nor did he append any comments. This omission, coupled
with the fact that the translation made Darwin's work unpalatable to most
readers, prompted Pisarev to write a broad, popular essay on the significance of the idea of evolution as postulated by Darwin. The essay, "Progress
in the Animal and Vegetable Worlds," was published in *Russian Word*
in 1864. It is a rambling piece of literature, full of logical flaws and incon-
gruous bypaths. However, it is written forcefully—in places, lyrically—and
it purports to place the Darwinian idea in a broader intellectual context.
Pisarev had read Darwin carefully, and read him in English. He correlated
Darwin's work with that of Lyell, Wallace, and many other naturalists of
great repute. He wanted to acquaint his readers with one of the gigantic
ideas of modern science; but he also wanted to show the superiority of science to all other modes of inquiry. He said:

"When the readers have acquainted themselves with Darwin's ideas,
even through my weak and colorless sketch, I shall ask them whether we

are right or wrong in rejecting metaphysics, ridiculing our fantasy, and expressing complete scorn for our conventional aesthetics.... Darwin, Lyell, and thinkers like them are the philosophers, the poets, the aestheticians of our time. When human reason, in the person of its most brilliant representatives, has succeeded in rising to the heights from which it can survey the basic laws of universal life, we the ordinary people, unable to be creative in the realm of thought, owe it to our human dignity to raise ourselves at least enough to be able to understand the leading brilliant minds, to appreciate their great achievements, to love them as the ornament and the pride of our race, to live in thought in the bright and boundless realm they have opened for every thinking being."[46]

Pisarev was more a forceful and enthusiastic champion of the scientific mode of inquiry than an unimpeachable spokesman for scientific facts; but even here he was not too far off the mark. He may not have interpreted every detail of Darwin's theory correctly, but he did impress on his readers the revolutionary significance of the new scientific path opened by the great English scholar. "Darwin's ideas have brought about a complete revolution in nearly all branches of the natural sciences: botany, zoology, anthropology, paleontology, comparative anatomy and physiology, and even experimental psychology have found in his discoveries the guiding principle that will link up the numerous observations already made and will put investigators on the track of new, fruitful discoveries."[47]

Pisarev believed that it is "only in the higher spheres of scientific activity that man can develop, maintain, and ennoble all his truly human qualities and capacities; that is why we also see that science, in the real sense of the word, is developing with extraordinary speed and leaving far behind all other branches of human activity."[48] Pisarev was widely read, and many a young man acted on his advice. Ivan Pavlov noted in one of his autobiographical sketches: "Under the influence of the great minds of the 1860's, particularly that of Pisarev, our intellectual interests were directed toward natural science, and many of us decided to study the natural sciences at universities."[49] S. A. Vengerov, preparing his *Critical Biographical Dictionary of Russian Writers and Scholars* in 1889, solicited autobiographical data from many persons. Thus, he talked with authority when he said: "I learned to appreciate the real impact of Pisarev's passion for the natural sciences from many autobiographies sent to me by the naturalists who were young men at the time when the influence of Pisarev's writing was at its peak.... Most of the present-day naturalists of middling years admit that their initial interest in natural science was stimulated by Pisarev's writings, with their penetrating analyses and tantalizing suggestion that only on the basis of 'real' knowledge is it possible for us to create a truly human life."[50]

Pisarev dealt primarily with the cultural foundations of the scientific attitude and the social role of scientific knowledge. His contemporary M. A. Antonovich, however, wrestled with the ontological and epistemological problems of science. Although a critic of *bazarovshchina* and Pisarev's excessive individualism, Antonovich shared much of the Nihilist philosophy of science. In his view: "There is nothing in the world that is outside the concepts of matter and force."[51] Superimposed on Antonovich's ontological materialism are his epistemological views, which he labeled "objective empiricism." He said: "We should study phenomena in order to recognize, unveil, and enunciate laws. We do not construct phenomena, and we do not create laws. It is not our duty to devise and compose the plans and orders of nature, but to record them. We must not shut our eyes and withdraw into ourselves, but must open our eyes and directly contact the outside world."[52] Clarifying this, Antonovich stated that "our internal world is formed by, or grows out of, the external world"; and that the activities of the external world are truly reflected in the internal world. Like Chernyshevskii and Dobroliubov, he emphasized the primacy of physiology over psychology; and he too considered physiology the only source of valid models for studying social organization. By solving the riddles of life, he felt, physiology could help solve the fundamental mysteries of human existence.*

Antonovich believed in the unity of "thought" and "existence," content and form. He firmly rejected the idea of *a priori* categories (or forms) of thought, such as Kantian space and time. Our cognition, according to him, reflects the external world in all particulars; hence man's thought does not impose its laws on nature. He rejected the Kantian idea of the unknowability of the thing-in-itself, and expressed profound faith in the power of science and the limitless widening of its horizons.

To Antonovich, science also embraced the study of culture, behavior, and history, but it was clearly set off from religion. "Religion and natural science," he stated, "are phenomena of two completely different orders, which have no meeting ground.... The essence of religion is belief, an unconditional trust in authority and a childish subordination to it.... The essence of

---

* Antonovich, "Sovremennaia fiziologiia i filosofiia," p. 227. The philosopher P. D. Iurkevich expressed a contradictory view, claiming that physiology could not provide models for a rigorous study of culture and society because it had no tools to penetrate the mysteries of psychic phenomena (Iurkevich, No. 4, pp. 930–34). According to Iurkevich, each science is limited by its own methods, which are useless to other sciences.

science, on the other hand, is skepticism and a critical attitude toward every authority."[53] However, he was willing to treat science and religion as complementing each other, since each satisfies a specific human endowment and need. Religion satisfies some of the primeval human needs; but science is an index of cultural progress and man's growing mastery over nature. Antonovich's philosophy is one of scientific optimism; yet he essentially accepted the idea of "two truths," which was first emphasized by Lomonosov in an obvious effort to convince the church authorities that science was not a foe of religion, that the two depended on different experiences and sources of wisdom.

Antonovich saw in the omnipotence of science a guide to a better way of life. His idea that all the sciences were parts of the same logical continuum led him to justify the application of natural scientific methods to the study of society, history, and the human mind. His philosophy was a thinly veiled attack on contemporary theological thought as the ideological arm of a social system based on autocracy, widespread illiteracy, and serfdom. Arguing that there are no absolute truths, and that there could be none, Antonovich examined the crumbling autocratic ideology to show that many cherished truths of the past had become illusions of the present.[54] The materialistic concept of the unity of science, the historical relativity of scientific laws, and the intellectual superiority of the scientific spirit were all parts of a new ideology, which undermined the autocratic system and speeded its downfall.

In one respect, Antonovich was unique among the philosophers of the sixties: his enthusiasm for science was strong enough to make him eager to become a professional scholar. His special interest was geology, and his knowledge of this discipline elevated him far above the fashionable dilettantism of his contemporaries. He is even credited with a scientific discovery: in 1871, he identified the first secondary segment of the Devonian formation to be observed in Russia, and published his findings in the *Mining Journal*.[55]

### POPULISM: A REALISTIC VIEW OF SCIENCE

By the end of the 1860's, the Nihilist exaltation of the omnipotence of science had begun to show signs of faltering, and the time had come for a more realistic reappraisal of the place of science in modern society in general and in Russian society in particular. N. K. Mikhailovskii and P. L. Lavrov were the architects of the Populist philosophy, the new orientation that

answered these needs. The two expressed different views in the realms of
political ideology and political strategy; but their views in social philosophy,
historical theory, and the philosophy of science, though not identical, were
remarkably similar. "Subjective sociology"—the most popular sociological
orientation in Russia during the last decades of the nineteenth century—was
formulated primarily by Mikhailovskii and Lavrov. Contemporary writers
added to the unity of the Populist social philosophy by overlooking multitudes of fine differences in the theoretical ideas of Mikhailovskii and
Lavrov.

During this period, Populism dominated most of the intellectual avenues that connected the urban centers of thought with the awakening humanity of the countryside. It grew out of diverse social thoughts and ideological bents, and its exact origins are lost in the dialectical whirlwind of
great hopes and bitter disappointments that came in the wake of the reforms
of the early 1860's. Populism was a synthesis of Slavophilism—which had
exalted the uniqueness of the Russian soul and emphasized the *obshchina*
as the guidepost of the Russian social order—and Westernism, with its exaltation of scientific knowledge, inclination toward utopian socialism, and
belief in the individual as the motive force of history.[56]

The Populism of the 1870's was a reaction to the Nihilism of the 1860's:
it was a search for social action based on a system of principles that were
regarded as closer to the pulse of Russian life than those advanced by the
Nihilists. The philosophy and sociology of Populism were blended into a
messianic cult that promised the Russian people a joyful voyage to a better
future, to a new society steeped in equality that was unattainable in the
West. Populism was a diffuse movement with no codified ideology or formal organization. It was dominated by a "repentant nobility"—an expression of Mikhailovskii's—eager to bridge the long-standing gulf between
the muzhiks and the seignorial intelligentsia.

A consistent and carefully formulated antimetaphysical orientation was
the basic characteristic of Populist philosophy. Mikhailovskii identified two
principal faults of metaphysics: an utter disregard for the concrete needs of
human life and a deep-seated contempt for positive knowledge.[57] Lavrov
went further, arguing that "the philosophy for modern life" must reject both
materialism and idealism. The weakness of materialism, he said, was that
it indiscriminately reduced all thought, scientific, religious, and metaphysical, to matter and motion. Idealism, on the other hand, could not be har-
monized with individual sciences because it attached metaphysical rather
than scientific meaning to such concepts as "idea," "reason," and "spirit."

Philosophy, according to Lavrov, must abandon metaphysics and concentrate on epistemology and on the history and sociology of knowledge. It must examine and synthesize "objective knowledge," as expressed by the spirit of the time. It must consider the growth of "rational thought" to be the index of cultural progress. According to Lavrov, the modern historical affirmation and expansion of "rational thought" signified the transformation of "instinctive technology" into scientific technology, religious sentiment into moral consciousness, and undisciplined intellectual curiosity into ordered, objective inquiry about nature and society. In Lavrov's view, the basic task of history is to study the effects of expanding human knowledge on personality and society.

Although Lavrov rejected materialism and idealism on the ontological level, he was more favorably disposed toward Kantian transcendental idealism on the epistemological level. In a public lecture in St. Petersburg in 1860, he said that both materialists and idealists talked about the essence of phenomena, and not about the phenomena themselves. "The entire external world gives us only phenomena, revealed by impressions. Every science deals only with phenomena.... Phenomena have an independent and *real* existence [for me] only on the basis of my own judgments."[58] In presenting the "Copernican significance" of Kant's epistemology to his countrymen, Lavrov emphasized that nature is created by man on the basis of his own impressions, and that there are no epistemological differences between scientific creativeness, "artistic models," and "moral ideals." He viewed man's internal world as "the source of nature, the source of history, and the source of individual consciousness." Phenomenological knowledge was to him not only the basis of science, but also the basis of art, morality, development of personality, cultural integration, and universal history.[59] Indeed, he extended the idea of the "subjective" nature of scientific knowledge to include culture as the total embodiment of human achievement. Philosophy, which gives "meaning and human significance to everything with which it deals," must abandon the futile question of ontological primacy—the essence of the thing-in-itself, whether it be material or spiritual—and must confine itself to exploring the nature and extent of scientific knowledge.

Despite these qualifications, the Populists and their allies recognized science as both an instrument and a measure of cultural progress. In introducing the complete positivist philosophy to Russia in 1868, Lavrov made it known that many French positivists were "medical men and graduates of the Ecole Polytechnique," and that M. Littré, one of Comte's leading heirs, was also a renowned French "scientist." But science could not do everything. Modern philosophy, according to Lavrov, must accomplish three tasks: it must unify the basic knowledge supplied by the sciences; it must separate scientific thought, as the most advanced level of knowledge, from unscientific speculation; and it must fully explain the interdependence of external reality, individual cognition, and the development of humanity.[60] The best philosophy, according to Lavrov, combines the antimetaphysical orientation of Comtean positivism with the subjectivism of Kantian epistemology.

The Populists differed from the Nihilists in two important respects: they rejected the notion that science is a panacea for social ills and the only criterion of enlightenment; they also stressed the logical, methodological, and epistemological differences between the exact and natural sciences on one hand and the social sciences and the humanities on the other. As critics of Nihilist scientism, they recognized the historical dimensions of many values and sources of wisdom not anchored in man's rational faculty. Lavrov argued that in order to perform its role more efficiently, science must rely not only on man's cognitive powers but also on intuition; in this way, the arts and the sciences could complement each other. Pisarev and Antonovich had proclaimed that the arts should be subservient to science, that their primary function must be to popularize scientific knowledge. To Lavrov and Mikhailovskii art and science were equal; combined, they were the most potent source of positive wisdom.

Both Mikhailovskii and Lavrov regarded all the sciences as interdependent disciplines. Just as a good historian must sometimes consult the natural sciences to understand the motive forces of history, so a good natural scientist must not disregard history if he wants to improve the methods and concepts of his discipline and recognize the growing social demand for specific types of knowledge. However, Mikhailovskii's and Lavrov's central theme is that the natural and social sciences are far from being identical, despite their logical kinship and functional interdependence.

When the Populists emphasized the unity of science, they were under the spell of French positivism. When they elaborated on the differences between the social and natural sciences, their ideas represented a synthesis of two Russian traditions: the idealism and intuitionism of the 1840's, and the scientific materialism of the 1860's.[61] The coalescence and refinement of these two traditions made it possible for the intellectuals of the 1870's to differentiate between the natural sciences, which were concerned with the search for factual truth, and the social sciences, which were concerned with both facts and ideals. The word *pravda*, says Mikhailovskii, denotes the subject matter of social science, for it means both "truth" (facts) and "justice" (ideals). But because the social sciences search for ideals, or guiding values, they cannot rely on "objective principles"; they must be essentially subjective. As the historian Ivanov-Razumnik commented, the sociological theory advocated by Mikhailovskii was objective in its construction and subjective in its application.[62] Because moral elements permeate social life, said Mikhailovskii in 1869, natural-scientific methods alone are inadequate tools for the study of social reality.[63] In sociology, ethics, and psychology, said Lavrov in his *Historical Letters* (1869), there is very little need for "the tools of the physicist, chemist, and physiologist." The social sciences depend primarily on the gradual improvement of "approximate truths" derived from history and biography.[64]

The "subjectivist sociology" of the Populist leaders regarded the human personality, a product and a creator of culture, as the central theme of its investigation and as the quintessence of the historical process. The Populists made impressive strides toward a theoretical codification of the basic Nihilist thoughts on the progressive affirmation of personality as the index of cultural progress. The "subjective" nature of the social sciences, according to Mikhailovskii and Lavrov, was complementary to the "objective" nature of the natural sciences. They viewed the social sciences as both "subjective" and "objective"—but mostly "subjective"—and agreed that these sciences do not, and cannot, formulate universal laws, but instead produce limited empirical generalizations. Because of this subjectivist orientation, the Populist leaders rejected Darwinian sociologies.

Mikhailovskii rejected the struggle for survival as a key principle for the understanding of social evolution because it considered only "external" conditions of change. He was also opposed to Spencer's and von Baer's idea of evolutionary social change from structural and functional homogeneity to heterogeneity. He fully accepted the principle that social evolution does not affect every part of culture equally—that technological progress, for example, may be accompanied by esthetic and moral decline.[65] Mikhailovskii's key argument was that evolution cannot be explained by any single principle. Social evolution, according to him, is marked by an increased division of labor and a decreased self-sufficiency of individual social groups. The evolution of personality, on the contrary, is characterized by an increasing completeness and internal unity of the individual. The complexity of history lies in the need to reconcile the growing heterogeneity of society with the growing homogeneity of the individual.

In his *Historical Letters*, Lavrov argued that the natural sciences have more theoretical precision and practical usefulness than the social sciences, but that the difference between the two sets of sciences is mostly one of method and logic, rather than one of epistemology.[66] The natural sciences, he claimed, cannot answer all the riddles of human existence, but they provide the first step in the right direction. Moreover: "Natural science is unquestionably the basis of all rational life. Without a full understanding of its criteria and basic laws, man remains blind and deaf to his most common needs and his highest ideals. Strictly speaking, a man to whom natural science is completely alien is a man without modern education."[67]

The leading Populists had a broader and more flexible definition of science than the Nihilists, and were thus in a better position to cope with the great intellectual fermentation then taking place in Western Europe. The Populists informed the Russian reading public of many Western developments: Spencer's efforts to achieve a logically coherent synthesis of scientific knowledge and to formulate a scientific sociology; the influence of Darwinism on social, economic, and political theory; economic materialism; and the beginnings of neopositivism and neo-Kantianism. The sweeping theories of social change advanced by Sir Edward Tylor in *Primitive Culture*, by H. T. Buckle in *History of Civilization in England*, and by Sir Henry Maine in *Ancient Law* were critically discussed and widely disseminated. The Populists themselves owed their biggest intellectual debt to Comtean positivism, which they imitated in rejecting metaphysics and *a priori* knowledge, identifying philosophy as a generic term for all sciences, and insisting that observation, experimentation, and verification were the guiding rules in the acquisition of positive wisdom.

The Populists absorbed the underlying rationalism of Comte's positivism, Darwin's evolutionism, and Marx's historicism. These combined influences led them to search for the general lines and historical particulars of social development, and made their world outlook historical and scientific, subjective and objective, at the same time. "There is no doubt," said Mikhailovskii, "that social change is governed by certain laws; but it is just as true that the *consciousness of free choice* guides man in his activities."[68] Mikhailovskii recognized both a positivistic and a humanistic approach to the study of social change. He also claimed that social conditions determine which of the two approaches will be emphasized in a given historical age. Alluding to Nihilist scientism, he claimed that the contemporary Russian interpreters of social change were overly concerned with establishing general laws of social dynamics, a useless endeavor.

Populism was both an ideology and a call to social action. It was guided by the idea of social progress, identified with the belief that the future would bring full social equality and justice to Russia and that the peasantry, not the bourgeoisie, would be the main agent of general progress.[69] The idea of progress, in turn, was neither a metaphysical assumption nor a poetic expression, but the unifying principle of a social theory. The Populists' contributions to actual social change may be subject to conflicting interpretations, but their contributions to the development of modern social sciences in Russia are unarguable. They gave the social sciences a place independent of both philosophy and the natural sciences.

The Populists were acquainted with the leading Western views on science as a cluster of values, a social institution, and a catalyst of change; however, they approached Western ideas with caution and sober criticism. Mikhailovskii, for example, subjected Buckle's assertion that the natural sciences are essentially democratic (an idea that Pisarev accepted dogmatically) to critical analysis, and concluded that Buckle's argument was inadequate. Buckle had noted the great interest in natural science in France on the eve of the French Revolution, and had assumed that the two were causally related—that scientific thought had stimulated the growth of revolutionary forces committed to democratic ideals. "The lectures of chemists, of geologists, of mineralogists, and of physiologists were attended by those who came to wonder, as well as those who came to learn.... In Paris, the scientific assemblages were crowded to overflowing."[70] According to Buckle, all social classes were attracted to science. "The hall of science is the temple of democracy. Those who come to learn confess their own ignorance, abrogate in some degree their own superiority, and begin to perceive that the greatness of men has no connection with the splendor of their titles ... but that it depends on the largeness of their minds, the powers of their intellect, and the fullness of their knowledge."[71]

Mikhailovskii remarked that the lectures of German philosophers, religious preachers, medieval scholastic thinkers, and ancient Greek philosophers had also attracted people from all social strata, eager to widen their intellectual horizons. He wondered how Buckle would have explained the fact that Professor N. A. Liubimov taught physics at the university (and thus allegedly helped the cause of democracy) and at the same time wrote reactionary articles in the *Russian Messenger* and *Moscow News*.[72] Mikhailovskii acknowledged some truth in Buckle's assertion that the intensified interest in natural science in France had stimulated the growth of democratic revolutionary forces. First, by undermining the authority of the Church, the sciences had undermined feudal institutions and thus indirectly helped the cause of liberty and equality. Second, the natural sciences had asserted that social inequality had no basis in nature, but was a historical phenomenon that could be changed by concerted human action. Third, by modernizing technology, science had brought about the rise of an industrial class, which fought for liberty and equality in order to abolish the social superiority of the landed aristocracy.[73]

He was quick to add, however, that the experience of France was in many respects unique. Whether the brilliant scientific discoveries and investigations of the nineteenth century could contribute to the strengthening of democratic principles depended on the structures of individual societies. In other words, natural science was likely to help the democratic process only in countries that already had strong democratic elements.[74] Mikhailovskii also warned that the same scientific ideas may strengthen democratic principles in some respects and weaken them in others. Darwinism, for example, was democratic in that it weakened the justification for feudalism, and antidemocratic in that it justified class struggle. Technology leads to man's increased control of nature, but it may also lead to chronic unemployment. The benefits that the common man receives from science may be offset by the ruthless techniques of economic exploitation employed by the bourgeoisie.

Since Buckle was not really very eager to turn the French experience into a universal sociological law, Mikhailovskii's criticism did not actually apply to him. It could have been far more justly applied to Pisarev, who, in his youthful enthusiasm and revolutionary zeal, saw the natural sciences not only as a panacea for social ills, but also as the infallible guideposts to democracy. The most important conclusion of Mikhailovskii's discussion of science and democracy is that although democracy creates favorable conditions for the growth of science, science by itself will not democratize a society.

Commenting on the contemporary Russian situation, Mikhailovskii said that even though there were no political parties in his country, it was easy to tell the liberals from the conservatives. "The program of the people labeled 'conservatives' includes, among other things, hatred for democratic ideas and fear of the harmful influence of the natural sciences." On the other hand, "The program of people labeled 'liberals' includes an admiration for both the natural sciences and democratic ideals."[75]

The guiding stars of the 1870's worked in an atmosphere that was more somber and more taxing than that of the 1860's. The "men of the sixties" were moved by youthful exuberance and passionate radicalism; the "men of the seventies" were more sober in their judgments, and less radical in their social and political thought. To Pisarev (and Turgenev's Bazarov), individualism recognized no established rules of morality; to Mikhailovskii individualism was morality *par excellence*. Pisarev emphasized the individual's conflict with society; Mikhailovskii emphasized the individual's search for identity with society. Pisarev had little knowledge of science but a wholesome belief in its power; the Populists were well versed in science but recognized its limitations. To Pisarev and Antonovich, science was above individual cultures; to the Populists it always carried a national imprint.

Steeped in the modern philosophical and scientific thought of Western Europe, the Nihilists sought to spread modern knowledge in the countryside; but they had neither the patience nor the inclination to learn from the people the prosaic problems of everyday life. The Populists and their numerous allies took a broader view: to them, the education of the countryside required the dedicated work of men who were as eager to learn as they were to impart knowledge.[76]

The Nihilists considered science and religion contradictory and viewed their championing of science as a direct assault on religion. The more moderate Populists, like Mikhailovskii, considered science and religion complementary forces, the former providing positive knowledge and the latter guiding social action.[77] When Mikhailovskii talked about the compatibility of religion and science, he made it clear that he was not thinking of religion as a repository of sanctified illusions and prejudices but as a source of moral principles.

The differences between the Nihilists and the Populists were broad and significant; but there were also substantial similarities. Mikhailovskii readily acknowledged this fact, and considered himself a follower not only of Chernyshevskii and Dobroliubov, but also of Pisarev. Both Nihilists and Populists believed in the intellectual and social power of science, even though the Populists were unwilling to treat it as a force dominating all other domains of culture. Both firmly maintained that a rational social theory was indispensable for sound social action on a large scale. More significantly, both schools put forth powerful arguments in favor of social, moral, and intellectual conditions that would encourage the growth of scientific thought. Both subscribed to the idea of progress, which they interpreted as a gradual perfection of morality and an increasing affirmation of man's rational powers. The essence of both philosophies was "critical individualism," an unceasing challenge to authority of all kinds. According to Lavrov, "The rational scientific ethic deems it a duty of every man to fight with all his power against everything that stands in the way of development [i.e., progress] and criticism."[78] Both generations of thinkers emphasized practical utility as a criterion for judging the worth of knowledge, and both stressed the incalculable advantage of science over metaphysics and theology. The Nihilist thinkers equated metaphysical thought with autocracy, and science with democracy. Mikhailovskii contended that science did not necessarily open the doors to a world of democracy; but he viewed science, in contrast to metaphysics, as an organization of thought governed by democratic principles.

Unlike the preceding decade, the 1870's must be measured by two yardsticks: one for the official world of autocratic government, and the other for the world of the intelligentsia as proponents of unofficial ideological currents. Government activities during the decade were marked by a flagrant retreat from the libertarian philosophy embodied in the great reforms of the 1860's. The renewed emphasis on grammatical classicism in education, the growing ruthlessness of censorship authorities, the savage uprooting of the last vestiges of liberal officialdom, and the heightened police terror everywhere all illustrated the revived intransigence of the government. Though acting as private individuals, M. N. Katkov and P. M. Leont'ev were subsidized by the government in order to carry on a journalistic campaign against the forces of enlightenment and social justice.* The unofficial world of the 1870's, best represented by the Populist intelligentsia, did not deny the libertarian tradition of the 1860's, but worked successfully to make it more realistic.[79] The Populists played a major role in making science a vital component of modern Russian thought.

### N. IA. DANILEVSKII: SCIENCE AND THE NATIONAL CHARACTER

As interpreters of the broader cultural attributes and roots of science, Mikhailovskii and Lavrov shared the limelight with N. Ia. Danilevskii, a trained biologist and a widely read philosopher of history. Danilevskii played two roles. His dream of a forthcoming dominance of Slavic culture and his implicit belief in the intrinsic unity of all Slavic cultures supplied a ready-made ideology for the reactionary forces of Panslavism, which opposed Populist liberalism. On the other hand, his cogent sociological thought, which included a brilliant sociology of science, supplemented the intellectual mainstream of Populism. It is the second role that we are concerned with.

---

* During the 1860's their work for the cause of conservatism had often been covered by a thin veneer of liberal verbiage, or had been done in governmental committees away from the eyes of critical journalists. During the 1870's they completely unmasked their conservatism, and conducted several campaigns against the active and potential critics of Dmitrii Tolstoi's educational policies. See Kornilov, *Obshchestvennoe dvizhenie*, p. 169; and Nevedenskii, pp. 420–82.

Danilevskii's *Russia and Europe*, published in 1869, is a forceful philosophical treatise on the successive emergence and decline of discrete "cultural-historical types." These types do not represent different levels of cultural progress, but different plans for the arrangement and integration of cultural material.[80] The contemporary world, Danilevskii thought, was dominated by two cultural-historical types: the German-Roman type, which was on its way out; and the Slavic type, which was still being formed, and which, when fully developed, would be marked by original religious, economic, social, and political institutions. The Slavic cultural-historical type, like any other, was unique in its dominant values, but it also contained solid blocks of borrowed cultural material. Science, for example, was viewed by Danilevskii as "the most majestic phenomenon" of the modern world, which was essentially a product of the German-Roman culture. Science was a highly functional but basically borrowed component of Russian culture. Danilevskii thus replaced the Slavophil concept of unique and uncomplementary cultures with a concept of unique yet complementary cultures. Danilevskii agreed with the Slavophils' views on the alleged decline and moral degeneracy of Western culture. However, he admitted that Russia must depend on the West for her knowledge of material tools and industrial techniques, which were vital to the realization of her cultural potential and her national genius.

Mikhailovskii endorsed Danilevskii's idea of cultural-historical types, but criticized his romantic portrayal of the Slavic character. Mikhailovskii remarked that Danilevskii was under the spell of Cuvier's nontransformist views; and that he was accordingly occupied more with the cyclic activities and discreteness of cultural-historical types than with the broad lines of cultural evolution.[81] Actually, both Mikhailovskii and Danilevskii endeavored to portray Russian culture as an individual historical phenomenon that was part of a higher civilization. Moreover, both agreed that the peoples of one cultural-historical type can and should become familiar with the achievements of other cultural types, and should adopt the products of science and technology even if these were intrinsically alien to the spirit of the receiving nation.

Danilevskii gives special attention to the intricate relationship of science with individual cultures. His discussion of this topic—actually a refined revival of the Slavophil concern with the "national" characteristics of science —makes up one of the most delightful and thought-provoking chapters of *Russia and Europe*. He offers three basic generalizations, each reinforcing his general philosophy of history.

First, since each cultural-historical type has its own unique attitudes, it is logical to expect that science is not everywhere and at all times associated with the same values. In some cultures it may be a central cultural force, whereas in others it may be purely peripheral. This generalization, warns Danilevskii, applies to creativeness in science, not to the utility of science. Russian culture is not characterized by a great interest and productivity in science, but this does not mean that science is not of vital importance in developing the country.

Second, whether scientific thought is original or borrowed, it is affected by the dominant values of the culture that uses it. The national bias—a purely subjective phenomenon—finds its way into every science. However, the more established and more exact a science is, the less it is colored by national character. As scientific truths become more firmly established, the national bias loses its power, which opens new horizons of scientific inquiry.[82]

Finally, each civilized nation may show a predilection for individual sciences. Danilevskii mentions Pascal, Descartes, Clairaut, D'Alembert, Monge, Laplace, Fourier, Legendre, Lagrange, Poisson, Cauchy, and Leverrier to show the great interest of the French nation in pure and applied mathematics.[83] He mentions an almost equally long list of German experts in linguistics and comparative philology. England, according to him, produced all the true pioneers of geology.

National predilections for science are manifested both in the primary contributions of individual peoples to different sciences and in the primary contributions of different peoples to the same science at various stages of its development. Danilevskii was particularly interested in the second situation, and discussed it at length. According to him, the historical growth of a science shows five distinct stages of development, best illustrated by the history of astronomy, in his opinion the most exact of all physical sciences.

The first, or primitive, period in the growth of astronomy was dominated by the collection of empirical data. The second period was ushered in by Hipparchus's formulation of an artificial system of astronomical knowledge —"artificial" because it did not depict the true structure of the universe, and "system" because it brought existing astronomical knowledge together in a logically coherent body. The third period was reached with Copernicus's formulation of a "natural system," which depicted the true state of the universe, but not the precise relations between its components. The fourth period was opened by Kepler's "limited empirical laws," derived from the general Copernican heliocentricism, which were an essential step toward a full explanation of the cosmic order. The fifth and crowning period was that of the "general rational law," which began when Newton formulated a universal law unifying all the particular astronomical laws into a comprehensive logical system.[84]

Danilevskii took pains to show that each new stage after the first in the growth of astronomy had been ushered in by a different national group: the stage of the artificial system by the ancient Greeks, the stage of the natural system by the Slavs, the stage of limited empirical laws by the Germans, and the stage of the general rational law by the English.[85] After tracing several other sciences through the same stages, Danilevskii discussed the contributions of individual peoples to the evolution of scientific thought in general. He observed that although the Germans had not brought a single science to the stage of a "natural system," they shared with the English "the glory of elevating science to the higher stages of development."[86] The English alone had contributed to the emergence of every kind of stage. The Germans were particularly strong in raising individual sciences to the level of limited empirical laws, and the French in producing natural systems.

Danilevskii concludes: "The fruits of science are of more value to all of mankind than the other products of civilization, which cannot be transmitted so completely from one people to another, particularly from one cultural-historical type to another. However, in one respect the sciences do not differ from the arts, the national spirit, and the national government: they too bear an imprint of the national character. But the differences in the subjective qualities—the psychological makeup—of the nations contributing to the development of science do not explain all the sources of national imprints on the development of science. In some sciences the subject of inquiry is essentially national. Such are all the social sciences."[87]

Danilevskii clearly appreciated the growing role of science in Russian culture. However, his contention that Russia was a borrower rather than a creator of scientific thought has been seriously challenged by most Russian thinkers. This negative idea is more the result of Danilevskii's lack of intimate familiarity with the original scientific research going on around him than the result of his Slavophil bias. For example, his perfunctory survey of the development of chemistry convinced him that this science had not yet reached the last stage of logical development, the stage of the general rational law. This statement was printed in the year that D. I. Mendeleev produced the most general chemical law formulated in the nineteenth century: the periodic law of chemical elements.

It may have been too late for Danilevskii to consider Mendeleev's great scientific feat, but it was not too late for him to examine many others. A. M. Butlerov was making substantial contributions to the founding of modern structural chemistry. At the same time, I. M. Sechenov was laying the groundwork for Pavlovian physiology, and the St. Petersburg school of mathematics, fathered by P. L. Chebyshev, was well on its way to giving modern probability theory some of its most fruitful concepts. This was also the period when the world of scholarship began to grasp the revolutionary magnitude of N. I. Lobachevskii's non-Euclidean geometry, and when A. O. Kovalevskii's and I. I. Mechnikov's pioneering work in comparative embryology was widely acclaimed. The great creative period of Russian science had already begun.

## CHAPTER TWO

# Science and Educational Reform

## NEW EDUCATION AND SCIENCE

The spirit of the Reform found its purest expression in the passionate debate on educational reform, which attracted many leading intellects of the time. The leitmotiv of the debate was best described in a note written by a group of eminent Moscow University professors in 1861: "In our time every Russian man senses a profound need for education as the only way out of the social evils that bear heavily on our people. . . . It is for this reason that young men are fully conscious of their great historical role. A student in Russia is not a person who studies but a person who teaches, and our society looks on him with pride and respect. In the eyes of many, the student represents the future hope of Russia."[1] The debate covered the full spectrum of problems affecting modern education: the sociological foundations of education, the relationship of psychological knowledge to teaching techniques, the challenges of growing economic specialization to the traditional curriculum, the role of education in blending the sacred values of the past with the exacting secular demands of the new era, and so on. Our discussion, however, will be limited to the aspects of this fateful and exciting controversy that were related, directly or indirectly, to science as a specific mode of inquiry and as a vocation.

The Crimean debacle was interpreted in many quarters as an unavoidable result of Russia's backwardness in science and technology, a backwardness produced by the official policies of Nicholas I, which had placed a disproportionate emphasis on classical education. After 1828 biology, physiology, chemistry, and geology were not taught in gymnasiums, and mathematical training was seriously limited. The teaching of natural sciences in the universities was handicapped by the inadequate preparatory training of students, by poorly equipped laboratories, and by the relatively low salaries of those engaged in scientific research as a vocation. When A. S. Norov,

Minister of National Education, stated in a speech at Kazan University in the fall of 1855, "We have always regarded science as an essential necessity, and now we regard it as our first need," he was mixing hypocrisy with a bold look toward the future. When he stated in the same speech, "If our enemies are superior to us, they owe their advantage solely to the power of their education," he publicly acknowledged the willingness of the government to modernize public instruction and to bring education into line with the new social, military, and economic demands.

In 1856, the famous surgeon, anatomist, and educator Nikolai Pirogov published a truly exciting and provocative essay, "The Questions of Life." Pirogov argued that the dilemma of modern education could not be resolved by simply switching from a classical to a scientific curriculum; rather, there should be a sound balance between the two. Recognizing that specialized education was a necessary response to the complicated demands of modern life, he argued that in order to be truly effective and socially beneficial, specialization must be preceded by a broad training in the *humaniora* —the knowledge "indispensable for every man."[2] He demanded that training in citizenship be accessible to all estates, and that it be dedicated to the preservation of Russian political institutions. Humanistic training, to Pirogov, was the same as moral education. It was an indispensable step in the gradual development of young people's intellectual awareness, giving them the capacity to absorb specialized knowledge and the skill to undertake independent work in many fields of scholarship.[3] Specialized training, by contrast, imparted practical scientific knowledge and was a preparation for scientific research.

Pirogov's educational ideas were not always clear, but his great reputation as a scientist gained him a large and influential following. Chernyshevskii and Dobroliubov both endorsed the idea of general education wholeheartedly. All the leading journals opened their pages to discussions on educational themes. The *Journal of the Ministry of National Education*, for example, devoted much space to discussing educational philosophies in the West. And K. D. Ushinskii, rightly called the founder of Russian pedagogy as a distinct discipline, wrote a special article analyzing and endorsing Pirogov's views. He said: "N. I. Pirogov was the first person in our country to study education from a philosophical point of view and to recognize that it goes far beyond school discipline, didactics, and the rules of physical education—that it is related to the deepest questions of the human spirit ... and, indeed, to the most profound questions of human existence."[4]

Pirogov's timely pronouncements provided only one of many stimuli for the flourishing educational literature. The Sunday School and Going to the People movements stimulated much talk about the principles and techniques of popular education. Lev Tolstoi was publishing his education journal *Iasnaia Poliana*; and F. M. Dostoevskii argued that modern learning should be made accessible to the Russian peasant, and that the "idea of civilization" should be organically linked with the cultural uniqueness of the Russian people. Tolstoi viewed the educational role of science from the standpoint of humanity, Dostoevskii from the standpoint of Russian culture. Tolstoi took pains to distinguish between *vospitanie* (moral education) and *obrazovanie* (intellectual education), defining *vospitanie* as a transmission of value judgments and *obrazovanie* as a transmission of knowledge. In Russia, he said, *vospitanie* was basically limited because it was a coercive process; and because *obrazovanie* was not fully separated from *vospitanie*, it also lacked the requisite element of freedom.

Tolstoi's pedagogical writings suffered from many paradoxical statements and muddy arguments, but they fully expressed the urgent need for complex reforms in the educational system. His arguments were essentially a plea for the free transmission of knowledge. *Vospitanie* as it then existed in Russia, he felt, transmitted only the values of privileged groups; even as institutions dedicated to *obrazovanie*, the universities did no more than train experts for government service. True education should not only perpetuate estate and class interests, but also develop the full moral and intellectual capabilities of individuals *qua* individuals. Russian universities were ill-equipped to do this because they were organized as bureaucratic components of the government apparatus, and because professors were primarily government officials. "Nobody has ever thought of establishing universities to satisfy the needs of the people. Our ignorance of these needs would have made such an undertaking impossible in the first place. The universities have been established to satisfy partly the needs of the government and partly the needs of high society.... The government needs public servants, medical personnel, jurists, and teachers, and universities have been founded to train them. At the present time, high society needs liberals of a special cast—and these, too, are trained by the universities.... It is frequently stated that the shortcomings of universities have their origin in the shortcomings of lower schools. I am of the opposite opinion: the shortcomings of public schools, particularly the *uezd* schools, have their origin in the false goals of the universities."[5]

Tolstoi did not prescribe a panacea for the ailments of the complex educational organism, nor were his diagnoses always correct—for example, his complaints against liberal government officials. He was preoccupied with the comparatively simple problems of the Iasnaia Poliana education venture, was too much swayed by a personal philosophy that denied the idea of cultural progress, and was generally guided by social pessimism. But he made two impressions of great consequence on his contemporaries: he pointed out that the intellectual and moral questions of modern educational philosophy were inseparably woven together, and he made it clear that the Russian educational system denied both instructors and students the basic freedom to express views critical of established institutions and values. Pirogov wanted a new educational system that would make Russia better able to cope with the problems of modern industrial civilization and at the same time preserve the religious and moral foundations of autocracy. Tolstoi wanted an educational system that would liberate the individual from social chains, but he failed to define the educational processes that would ensure a more efficient adjustment to the complex demands of the day.

Pisarev, too, was very much interested in education; to him it was a guidepost to a better future, a future essentially incompatible with autocracy and its sacred culture. Pisarev was also concerned with the nature of *vospitanie* and *obrazovanie*; but unlike Pirogov and Tolstoi, he argued that these should not be concurrent processes. *Vospitanie* should not extend beyond the preschool period, and *obrazovanie* should begin where *vospitanie* stops.[6] "While *vospitanie* places the teacher between the child and surrounding nature, *obrazovanie* places the child in direct contact with nature. . . . *Vospitanie* emphasizes obedience, but *obrazovanie* teaches the man of the future how to live and realize his potentialities."[7] Relying on Buckle, he asserted that mankind was moving forward with the assistance of accumulated knowledge and discoveries, and that moral precepts exercised no influence on "the speed and results of historical development." This view led him to conclude that "a child needs knowledge, and not moral studies."

Pisarev's educational discussion was neither straightforward nor explicit. As a critic of sacred culture, he was under careful surveillance by the censorship authorities and had to rely on circuitous writing, depending on the reader to draw ideological conclusions. However, it is safe to assume that Pisarev opposed *vospitanie* because it essentially stood for the perpetuation of the existing social and moral order, and that he championed *obrazovanie* so strongly because it was the most effective instrument for the creation of a "new man." Depending on its curricular emphasis, *obrazovanie* is either humanistic or scientific; Pisarev endorsed scientific *obrazovanie* as the only true pathway to modern existence. Humanistic education, he said, played an important role only while the natural sciences were still undeveloped; contemporary humanistic education was merely a dysfunctional vestige of the past that was "sentenced to death by science and common sense." In the Russia of his time, Pisarev said, humanistic education owed its existence "to the deep roots of our ignorance and the limitless range of our disinterest in the intellectual welfare of future generations." He added: "Thanks to ignorance and routine, the natural sciences have been so much standardized in our society that advice to build the foundations of our formal education on them would be regarded by many enlightened educators as a delinquent encroachment on the intellectual purity of our school youth.... Behind the natural sciences stands the specter of materialism, invented by the sorcerers and soothsayers of *Moscow News*."[8]

Dobroliubov, Chernyshevskii, Antonovich, Pisarev, and other "materialists" of the day were indeed the chief advocates of a natural-scientific basis of formal education, for they treated the natural sciences—and the intellectual climate that these require—as the basic means of undermining the theological and metaphysical foundations of autocratic ideology. The mark of the age, however, was that all influential writers recognized the exact sciences as a vital part of the modern curriculum; they differed only in their emphases. Most of these men did not generate the growing interest in natural science themselves, but merely recognized a new spontaneous educational trend that was sweeping the country. According to D. N. Ovsianiko-Kulikovskii: "A strong interest in natural science was manifest in Russia as early as the 1850's. By the end of the decade scientific interest was fully formed. Young men strove to enroll in physico-mathematical and medical faculties. Chemistry and physiology were particularly valued. The leading natural scientists, foreign and native, were held in high esteem, regardless of their political views. The widespread attacks on authorities of all kinds did not interfere with the general respect for the scientific contributions of such scholars as Liebig, von Baer, and Darwin. At times, these names and the scientific ideas associated with them preoccupied the minds of young men no less, if not more, than such intoxicating words as 'people,' 'freedom,' 'society,' 'brotherhood,' and 'justice.'... Study of the sciences and the diffusion of materialistic philosophy were considered the most important, if not the only, path to useful work and to a constructive role in the progressive and libertarian movement."[9]

The effort spearheaded by Pirogov, Tolstoi, and Pisarev was aimed chiefly at establishing a well-balanced curriculum for the elementary schools and gymnasiums, a curriculum in harmony with the material and spiritual needs of the country. But it also had philosophical overtones and ideological undertones. Some writers demanded curriculum reforms to keep pace with the needs of current liberal reforms, others fixed their eyes on a future society, and still others were swayed by nostalgia for the passing days of the autocratic-feudal system. The conservatives, led by M. N. Katkov, wanted a secondary education that would recognize the didactic and practical value of the natural sciences but would continue to emphasize the classics. Pisarev, representing the other extreme, considered mathematics and the natural sciences to be the only source of true education. Most writers wanted a blend of the two, and these were represented most eloquently by Pirogov. Chernyshevskii and Dobroliubov, even though they were fervent champions of a philosophy based on natural science, also favored a blend of classical and scientific education.

The 1864 gymnasium statute crowned the official effort to find a satisfactory compromise between the different views expressed in the Moscow and St. Petersburg journals. It introduced two kinds of gymnasiums: classical gymnasiums and "real" gymnasiums. Classical gymnasiums were designed to serve as college preparatory schools; real gymnasiums were intended to provide a general education for students to whom universities were not accessible, either for financial reasons or because their estate origin precluded them from holding high government positions. Although the real gymnasiums provided terminal education, their graduates, if able to pass stiff entrance examinations, were allowed to enroll in the higher professional schools, which operated outside the context of the universities. The critics of the new statute claimed that the double system of schools was instituted to satisfy the growing demand for secondary and higher education by the middle classes—particularly the burgeoning industrial and mercantile groups—and at the same time to preserve the privileged position of the nobility. In 1863, with the most liberal of the great reforms already effected, the children of the nobility still made up 73 per cent of the total gymnasium enrollment.[10] The new statute diversified and expanded the system of education, but it also preserved the preemptive right of the children of nobility and high government officials to the best education the country could offer.

The curricula of the two types of gymnasiums differed greatly. The classical gymnasiums held 48 class meetings in Greek and Latin per week, and the real gymnasiums held none. In the natural sciences, on the other hand, the real gymnasiums held 32 class meetings per week, and the classical gymnasiums 12. In mathematics and modern foreign languages, the differences between the two were not significant. With its heavy emphasis on a natural-science education, the real gymnasium had no precedent in Russian history. According to the 1828 gymnasium statute, in effect until 1864, the entire weekly teaching of the natural sciences consisted of six class meetings in physics; even the new classical gymnasium offered twice as many.

The 1864 statute was full of paradoxes, and was doomed to be short-lived. Although it nominally subscribed to the principle of universal education, it still favored the higher estates. It opened the universities primarily to young men with classical educations, who were not as prepared to study the natural sciences as were the graduates of real gymnasiums. Instead of settling the great educational debate, the 1864 statute gave impetus to a new and still more vigorous controversy. The controversy grew rapidly, and left much bitterness in its wake, but the gymnasiums moved along at an exceedingly slow pace. An educational expert stated subsequently: "The 1860's left little imprint on our gymnasium—on its character, organization, and curriculum."[11] By 1864 the Reform spirit was still alive but it was rapidly losing its libertarian orientation: the subsequent development of the gymnasiums bore a heavy imprint of increasing reaction.

Regardless of its immediate educational and social effects, the 1864 gymnasium statute symbolized the beginning of a new era in the history of secondary education in Russia. The enrollment of middle-class students grew at a slow but constant pace, although it was not until the next generation that the nobility ceased to provide most of the Russian intellectual elite. In 1862 the government had made a feeble effort to abolish aristocratic boarding gymnasiums as institutions incompatible with the spirit of the Reform, but it quickly retreated under the pressure of conservatism and the influence of those who favored gradual reform. Nevertheless, many boarding gymnasiums in the provinces were closed as a result of the growing impoverishment of large segments of the nobility, and some survived only because they began to admit young men of middle-class origin.[12]

In the era of Nicholas I the Russian educational system had been ruled by a unique blend of two guiding principles: the estate principle (*soslovnost'*) and the principle of specialization. By feudal law, people should be trained only for the vocations open to their estates. Since the universities were primarily training grounds for higher government officials, they were not meant to be accessible to the lower estates, though this rule was never strictly applied. According to an expert in Russian educational history: "By supporting estate differentiation in schools—the unique educational needs of each estate—the government safeguarded the old aristocratic Russia, with all its social divisions. This policy had no use for schools dedicated to general education and accessible indiscriminately to all estates. Each estate occupied a special position on the social-status ladder and had its own educational needs. Persons who received an education superior to the needs of their estates strove to rise above their hereditary social status. This practice challenged the established order and threatened to destroy the barriers that separated various groups. The persons who left their natural places in society spent their lives 'torturing themselves by constant dreams and diverting other people from the true path of tranquil existence.' "[13]

The emancipation of the serfs and other liberal reforms of the 1860's accelerated the downfall of the estate school and the specialized education identified with the estate system. The educational reforms did not institute equal education for all estates, but they did recognize its necessity; and, in principle, they were on the side of the historical trend toward educating all citizens, whatever their class. Moreover, the 1860's were also distinguished by the emergence of secondary schools for girls. In the true spirit of the epoch, private firms were allowed for the first time to publish gymnasium textbooks; this, in turn, offered local school authorities a wider choice in the selection of required reading material. The Ministry of National Education no longer published textbooks, but its Curriculum Committee was given the task of formulating the official views on the merits of privately published materials.[14]

### UNIVERSITY REFORM

Russian university reform, which reached its high point with the university statute of 1863, was more complex than gymnasium reform, and left a deeper imprint on its age. It had its antagonists as well as its champions; but it was essentially another important reform following the spirit of the Emancipation, and was executed in an atmosphere of revolutionary fervor and libertarian spirit. It was also influenced by a succession of student disorders, which reached alarming proportions and at times threatened to start a major social and political conflagration. The growing demand for professional personnel to staff modern industry, government bureaucracy, and the military establishment was also a powerful incentive: the government explained that it had to transform universities "to meet the pressing demands of the day."[15] The reform was also an official response to the growing public demand that the universities cease to be merely the training centers for future government officials and establish better ties with society at large.

Professors, young and old, who visited Western Europe in unprecedentedly large numbers, brought back to Russia a new enthusiasm—an intellectual vigor and scientific curiosity that swept the laboratories and classrooms of the great universities. Pirogov spoke in their behalf when he said that the universities were the pulse of modern social life, and could perform their social functions only if they became free centers of instruction and learning. Many enlightened contemporaries agreed with Pirogov's sober utterances in favor of pure science. More than ever before, leading Russian intellectuals stressed the need to free scientific inquiry from control by the official organs of the state. Science, in the popular image, became the critical study of both nature and society. There was a particularly strong movement in favor of infusing the spirit of science into the study of social and political reality. Boris Chicherin emphasized that political science *qua* science must avoid one-sided views, and must "explain all the elements in the life of the state, all its aspects in their infinite diversity."[16] A few years later, P. G. Redkin, professor of law at St. Petersburg University, told his students that true universities are the places where "every *authority* is pushed aside, so that the *truth* can begin to speak for itself." He added: "In its modern orientation, science is independent, just as truth is independent; it stands above all external interests, all biases and prejudices; it is fearless ... and self-purposeful.... It operates on the principle that truth, which includes everything rational, must be given practical application sooner or later. As our national proverb states, everything changes; only truth remains, and truth alone is practical."[17]

University reform proceeded slowly and with extreme caution. At first specific legal acts eliminated the more oppressive academic restrictions imposed under Nicholas I, particularly those dating from the panic of 1848. The students, for example, regained their traditional right to attend Western universities, and professors were again allowed to select the rectors and deans. The policing duties of university inspectors were drastically curtailed. The organization of government stipendiaries as a corporate body—established by Nicholas I to ensure that students who belonged to privileged families with proven loyalty would dominate university life—came to an abrupt end, and henceforth the stipends were issued on the basis of academic achievement.[18] The decree prohibiting the hiring of foreign university professors was voided, and the universities were allowed to purchase Western books without harassment by the censorship authorities.[19]

In 1858 the government authorized the professors of St. Petersburg University to draft a proposal for a new university statute. The intent was not to introduce minor corrections into the 1836 university statute, but to postulate clearly and forcefully the principles of a completely new statute. The professors concentrated on the basic educational and organizational needs of modern universities: academic autonomy, extensive ties with society at large, a modern curriculum, and the organized recruitment of new instructors. They demanded such liberal changes as increased authority for faculty councils, affirmation of the students' right to form their own organizations independent of university control, tuition waivers for poor students, and more liberal regulations for postgraduate studies. A draft of the new statute was submitted to a special committee of high government officials appointed by the Minister of National Education.

The statute proposed by the St. Petersburg professors was the subject of much discussion and controversy. The question of student organizations provoked the most heated public debate. The ultraconservative groups regarded proliferation of student organizations, all protected by university autonomy, as a flagrant and dangerous violation of the essential tenets of autocratic government, and were even willing to replace universities by special schools open only to persons with proven loyalty.[20] Some conservative officials felt that a substantial reduction of enrollment in all universities was the best method for curbing student unrest.[21] The historian N. I. Kostomarov, representing the other extreme, thought that there was only one way to do away with mushrooming student organizations: the state must open universities to all persons regardless of their social origin, and must give all institutions of higher education a free hand in performing their educational and scientific duties. The progressive group considered the Collège de France, with its broad curriculum and liberal admission policies, the model that Russian universities should try to emulate. The third and most influential group considered student organizations an indispensable educational and social component of university life. "To break the students into isolated grains of sand," Chicherin asserted, "would kill the university by submerging all its most noble features in a nondescript world of trivialities."[22]

The "university question" received its most thorough and sympathetic treatment in the writings of Pirogov, who was profoundly aware of the sociological significance of student organizations and their activities. "If a barometer forecasts turbulent weather, it should not be destroyed or hidden away, but should be studied carefully and treated as a guide to suitable action. The same applies to human society. Whenever the political life of a society moves as evenly as the mechanism of a clock . . . universities treat the pursuit of science as their primary function.... Science and social life each experience their own changes and upheavals; but all social transitions, upheavals, and catastrophes are reflected in science, and through it in the universities."[23]

Student organizations and movements, according to Pirogov, were a part of the universities' struggle to adapt themselves to the needs of modern life. The unsettled character of university life merely reflected the unsettled conditions in the country. The widespread demands for academic autonomy were part of a general search for independent activity (*samostoiatel'nost'*)—a search that inspired many enlightened men, regardless of their professional identification and social status. Prompted by the growing student unrest, Chicherin wrote to his brother in October 1861: "At the present time our first need is to give all social groups a significant degree of independence, without which life is meaningless. Without this freedom, we are doomed to remain forever in the same conditions that led to the miseries of the Crimean War. Moreover, independent action can no longer be denied. Our society has felt the joys of independence [from total government control], and will never again accept full subordination [to state authorities]."[24] Student organizations, as Vladimir Odoevskii pointed out, were only one part of an accelerated rebellion against the dark forces of expiring feudalism. Pirogov lamented the obvious absence of conditions favoring efficient, viable student organizations in Russia. He recognized, however, that only university autonomy could prevent these organizations from growing into a destructive social force. He was fully cognizant of the revolutionary proportions of student disorder, but was farsighted in realizing that the use of brute police force was neither a moral nor an effective path to academic peace.

Pirogov realized that under the conditions of Russian autocracy there was little hope of achieving full academic autonomy. However, he viewed autonomy as a basic condition of university freedom, and freedom as a basic condition for the growth of universities as educational institutions and research centers. By academic autonomy, Pirogov meant the management of university affairs by an elected council of professors. He argued that without a separation of university administration from government bureaucracy the universities could not operate in consonance with local needs and traditions; nor could they institute differential salaries based not on bureaucratic ranks and administrative positions but on the scientific achievements of individual professors, the best guarantee for the uninterrupted growth of scientific thought.[25] But even though Pirogov marshaled formidable arguments in favor of university autonomy, he did not give it a forthright endorsement. He favored it as a general principle, but doubted its compatibility with the prevailing conditions in Russia. He was convinced, however, that Russian universities would not become flourishing scientific centers unless the autocratic government surrendered some of its traditional prerogatives. He talked with authority and had many followers, both in and out of the government.

In 1861 the authorities became alarmed at the growing wave of student dissatisfaction, and took various measures to curb nonacademic activities in universities. E. V. Putiatin, a conservative admiral, replaced the liberal E. P. Kovalevskii as Minister of National Education, and was immediately given the task of restoring peace and order in the schools. A series of new regulations prohibited student assemblies and student negotiations with university administrators through elected representatives. The elected managing boards of numerous organizations were replaced by students appointed by university authorities. The students lost the right to disburse the funds of their credit unions without prior approval by university inspectors. In 1859, there had been 1,019 students enrolled in St. Petersburg University, and 650 of these did not have to pay tuition because they came from poor families.[26] Now, the government ordered that no more than two students from each province could be granted free tuition.

Gravely disturbed by the growing popular demand for university reforms, the government actually considered abrogating the last vestiges of academic autonomy. According to A. V. Nikitenko, Alexander II told the Minister of National Education in the spring of 1861 that he was inclined to abolish "several universities" if student disturbances did not come to an end.[27] However, no universities were abolished. Owing to the persistent and dedicated efforts of Pirogov and many "moderate liberals" (as they were called by Nikitenko) in high government positions, the struggle to obtain operative autonomy for Russian higher education was kept alive and brought to a fruitful conclusion. Because of the sobering influences from these quarters, the liberal A. V. Golovnin was appointed the new Minister of National Education at the very end of 1861.

By 1862 the government was convinced that punitive legislation could not restore the normal functioning of the universities. The inflammatory spirit generated by disaffected students was only one problem. Just as serious was the rapid deterioration of the universities as scientific centers and sources of government officials. Nikitenko noted in March of 1861: "Our universities are beginning to degenerate. University students are demoralized; professors have lost prestige and influence.... Many teaching positions are vacant, and many others are soon to be vacated because gifted young people steer clear of academic careers.... Never before ... have our universities been in such a critical state."[28] And in 1862 an official statement by the Ministry of National Education noted: "The scientific activity of our universities has obviously declined; many teaching positions are vacant, and many are filled by unqualified persons."[29] The inadequacies of university instruction led to an alarming shortage of both scholars and trained personnel for government service.

The new university statute, finally enacted in 1863, incorporated the ideas of a select group of leading intellectuals, who had demanded that the universities be given corporate rights and be considered special communities enjoying a wide area of independent action. The universities could now elect their own deans and rectors. Above all, the statute gave each school a university council made up of regular and associate professors.[30] The council had the last word on the organization of scientific research and teaching programs, and on the curricular adaptations of individual universities to local conditions. It also allocated stipends and played an important role in the preparation of university budgets. It assumed the major responsibility for the selection of promising students who would be sent to Western European universities for advanced study in preparation for university teaching. The council was in charge of all questions related to the appointment, retention, and promotion of the instructional staff, and had full control of university publications. Finally, each council elected a three-man university court to handle student grievances and disciplinary problems.

This newly won autonomy gave the universities a bright view of the future, but its range was limited. The government-appointed curators of school districts retained their traditional right to have the final word on such important matters as the appointment or dismissal of instructors and administrative personnel. They reviewed all actions involving the disbursement of funds. Essentially, the curators were the defenders of autocratic monarchism in the world of academic "republicanism." For example, during the student unrest of the early 1860's the curator of St. Petersburg University was a retired military man uninterested in the world of scholarship. The influential *Fatherland Notes* found it paradoxical that the new statute gave the universities autonomy and at the same time preserved the powerful office of curator. In Chicherin's opinion, the new statute left the curator's jurisdiction deliberately vague, so that he could assume decisive authority in times of crisis.[31] For the same reason, G. A. Dzhanshiev called the statute "the result of an insincere compromise," even though he recognized it as a "substantial step forward" in the history of Russian universities.[32] The journal *Contemporary* wrote: "The statute is only an external form, in no way guaranteeing the future growth of universities as scientific centers."[33]

Although the 1863 statute recognized the right of professors to form elective groups representing their personal and community interests, no similar right was granted to students. A writer stated subsequently that "the university charter of 1863 gave professors full autonomy and treated students as stepchildren."[34] However, the statute did improve the supervision of student activities. Before 1863, the official in charge of this supervision was an inspector—as a rule a nonacademic person—who exercised "special and direct control over the moral life of all university students." Independently or in consultation with the rector, the inspector could impose penalties on students who violated the prescribed rules of conduct. Much of the student dissatisfaction during the late 1850's and early 1860's was a reaction to the arrogance of inspectors. The 1863 statute entrusted the supervision of student affairs to two persons: the prorector (always a professor) and the inspector (always a university graduate). These two officials were guided by the rules set up by the council of professors; and student violators were handled by the university court, whose judgment was subject to review by the university council.

The restoration of academic peace by granting university autonomy was only one of the two basic concerns of the 1863 statute; the other was the upgrading of educational and scientific standards. First the university curriculum was substantially expanded: whereas the 1835 statute had called for 265 teaching positions in the country's five universities (not including Dorpat University), the 1863 statute called for 497 positions. Much of this expansion occurred in the physics and mathematics departments. The 1835 statute, for example, authorized only one teaching position in pure mathematics and one in applied mathematics, the latter primarily covering mechanics. In 1864, Moscow University was authorized to appoint two to three professors and as many docents in pure mathematics alone, and two separate professors for theoretical and practical mechanics.

The statute defined the fields that made up the university curriculum; but the professors were given a great deal of freedom to use their own judgment and experience in selecting classroom material and particular areas of emphasis. During the late 1860's, for example, the famed mathematician P. L. Chebyshev, teaching at St. Petersburg, offered separate courses in number theory, probability theory, the integration of equations, and the theory of definite integrals.[35] The statute also allowed universities to establish new clinics, laboratories, and museums, and to modernize existing ones. In most universities budgets for the maintenance of auxiliary scientific and instructional units were doubled, and at St. Petersburg they were quadrupled.[36] Ivan Sechenov stated two decades later that these new facilities were mainly responsible for the growing quality and magnitude of scientific research in Russia.[37]

The 1863 statute inaugurated an era of rapidly growing specialization in academic training. In every university, all the natural and exact sciences had formerly been offered by the Faculty of Physics and Mathematics, and students enrolled in this faculty were required to take its entire curriculum. The result was a general but very superficial education. The new statute authorized the universities to divide their faculties into departments. This measure, immediately adopted by all universities, was intended to give higher education more depth and more specialization. Students majoring in mathematics, for example, were no longer required to take courses in comparative anatomy, botany, and the other natural sciences.

Despite these progressive measures, the new statute did very little to facilitate the training of university instructors, whose numbers, in proportion to the growing needs, were rapidly shrinking. It simply authorized the universities to retain each year a number of new graduates with proven scientific ability who would work for higher degrees and prepare themselves for teaching on the highest level. In essence, instead of prescribing a rigid method for the procurement of new instructors, the government preferred to let individual universities resolve their dilemmas by relying on their own experience and needs. This decision amounted to passing the buck: the problem was acute, and there was no simple road to success. The 1863 statute called for 497 teaching positions in all universities, but at the time only 249 positions were filled.[38] And even these statistics do not present the full gravity of the situation, for they did not indicate the large number of positions occupied by incompetents. The shortage was particularly acute in the exact sciences.

In 1862 a special decree voided the existing rules against hiring foreign professors, and authorized the universities to search the Western academic market for new instructors. However, growing intellectual nationalism and an intense resentment of "German science" in Russia worked against a successful implementation of this measure. The search for foreign professors was also hampered by another major obstacle: German scholars, who had formerly held a good many of the teaching posts in Russian universities, were no longer interested in positions outside their own country. The lasting peace in Germany, the consolidation of the German empire, and the spectacular growth of German higher education were the main conditions contributing to this attitude. Gone were the days when Russia could attract such giants as the naturalist Peter S. Pallas, the embryologists Caspar Wolff and Karl von Baer, and the astronomer F. G. W. von Struve.

After 1860 the universities tried to fill vacant teaching positions by recruiting competent persons from the various branches of government and from private enterprises. Student unrest and unattractive salaries made this technique a dismal failure. The 1863 statute tried to remedy the situation by introducing the position of private docent, which made it possible for qualified men to engage in part-time teaching without giving up their nonacademic occupations. The salaries of professors were also substantially raised. However, the nervous atmosphere created by increased student disturbances continued to make university teaching unattractive to those outside the academic community. Moreover, private docents, pursuing two vocations, were too busy to engage in research and thus strengthen the universities as scientific centers.

The most effective method of acquiring new instructors was the careful selection of promising students, who could then work closely with individual professors and undertake advanced studies in leading Western European universities. From 1862 to 1865, over 100 students received government stipends for study abroad. The universities were given not only the right to select the students, but also the right to supervise their work.[39] Nikolai Pirogov, whose scientific work was famous in Western Europe, was for a time the chief supervisor of foreign training, and his advice, recommendations, and contacts opened the doors of many laboratories and research institutes to Russian students. Ivan Sechenov observed that in the early 1880's about one-half of the Russian professors engaged in teaching the natural sciences were men who had studied abroad during the late 1850's and early 1860's.[40]

On April 17, 1890, on the twenty-fifth anniversary of the founding of Odessa University, Professor V. I. Modestov told a gathering of instructors and officials: "Despite the hardships of ... our economic, social, and moral life, one thing is certain: during the last 25 years our science has made great strides forward. ... The intellectual development that gave birth to Russian science has its origins in two events, which together made the early 1860's the most memorable years in our cultural history: the sending of young men to foreign universities in 1862 and 1863 for advanced studies and preparation for teaching, and the promulgation of the university statute of June 18, 1863."[41] Modestov was apprehensive about conditions in Russia at the time of his speech; in science he saw the only ray of hope for the future of his country.

The 1863 statute, and the intellectual upsurge that inspired it, helped the universities become the foremost centers of scientific investigation in Russia, a position that had previously been occupied by the St. Petersburg Academy of Sciences. There was a growing interest in higher education. The total enrollment in the five national universities was 4,641 in 1865, 5,151 in 1875, and 9,344 in 1881.* The enrollment of middle-class students was on the upswing, but the gentry continued to be the dominant group for some time. In all the universities, 67.2 per cent of the students in 1864–65 were of noble origin or belonged to the families of high government officials. In 1880, this percentage was reduced to 46.7. At St. Petersburg University, where most of the country's highest aristocracy was educated, the nobility made up 80 per cent of the total enrollment in 1860–61, and 65 per cent in 1899. At Khar'kov University, which was more typical, the young noblemen made up 71.2 per cent of the total enrollment in 1864–65, 51 per cent in 1875, and 41 per cent in 1885.[42] At Moscow University, the figures were 68.1 per cent in 1861, and 51 per cent in 1902.

The changing social composition of the universities was most graphically illustrated by the increasing enrollment of indigent students. At Kazan, Kiev, and Odessa, for example, the number of students who required financial assistance rose from an average of 49 per cent in 1866 to 78 per cent in 1874.[43] There was a sharp decrease in stipendiaries during the 1880's, and one can only assume that the government was unwilling to allocate the necessary funds. Since the percentage of needy students increased more rapidly than that of young men from the middle and lower classes, it seems certain that many stipendiaries came from the impoverished nobility.

The growing army of poverty-stricken students strongly influenced the academic and social character of Russian universities during the closing decades of the nineteenth century. *Fatherland Notes* observed in 1879 that the material condition of students had been deteriorating continuously, and that most students could not find part-time employment to help finance their education.[44] The same journal noted that poorer students had finally begun to look for factory employment as a last resort in their search for financial security. The students began to form various organizations to help them alleviate their plight, most commonly credit unions, student restau-

---

* The five universities were those at Moscow, Khar'kov, Kazan, St. Petersburg, and Kiev. Dorpat University served primarily Baltic Germans. Odessa University admitted its first students in May 1865. One of its original aims was to provide higher education for Slavic students from the Balkans.

rants, and communal libraries for textbooks and other basic reading material. The establishment of these self-help associations was in direct conflict with the 1863 statute; moreover, the organizations were natural targets for government repression because they could so easily become political action groups.

It is difficult to determine whether student action or government overreaction added more to the growing social and intellectual unrest in Russia. In any case, the general turmoil interfered with the normal life of the university, particularly the actual process of education. On the crest of the revolutionary wave, however, came a renewed enthusiasm for free criticism of authority, whether in ideology or in science; and as a result, scientific thought advanced more rapidly than before. The damage done by the rising revolutionary tide was more than compensated for by the emergence of new values and new social and economic conditions that favored scientific investigation and rationalist thought in general.

The universities were legally open to all social classes. For economic reasons, however, they were virtually inaccessible to the lower urban classes and the peasantry. The number of students from peasant stock at St. Petersburg University was so small that they were listed in the category "other classes" in the tabulation of Brockhaus and Efron's *Encyclopedic Dictionary*. In Khar'kov University in 1865 there were only three students of peasant origin in the total enrollment of 545; even twenty years later young men of peasant stock made up only three per cent of the total enrollment.[45] By way of comparison, the peasants made up 81.5 per cent of the total population in 1870, and the nobility 1.2 per cent.[46]

Whereas peasants were kept out of the universities by economic measures, women were barred by law. In the early 1860's several girls were enrolled in St. Petersburg University and the Medical and Surgical Academy. In order to give this new "custom" a legal basis, the academic councils of St. Petersburg, Kazan, and Khar'kov universities recommended to the commission entrusted with the preparation of the new statute that young women be formally granted equal access to university education. The commission incorporated this proposal in an early draft of the statute, but eliminated it from the final version.

The advocates of higher education for women were not silenced by the apparent antifeminist orientation of the 1863 university statute. Led by several influential ladies from Moscow and St. Petersburg high society, and backed by a solid contingent of university professors, they continued to demand equal education for both sexes. In 1869 they were given permission in St. Petersburg and Moscow to institute "systematic public lectures" open to both men and women. Among the lecturers were such leading scholars as D. I. Mendeleev and I. I. Mechnikov in St. Petersburg and F. A. Bredikhin and V. V. Markovnikov in Moscow.[47] Encouraged by this development, Professor V. I. Guerrier of Moscow University obtained permission to institute a program known as the Higher Courses for Women. The first students were admitted in 1872, and the curriculum emphasized mathematics and the natural sciences. In 1878 similar "courses" were opened in St. Petersburg on the initiative of Professor K. N. Bestuzhev-Riumin; with an initial enrollment of 759, these "courses" placed primary emphasis on the humanities.[48] At the very end of the 1870's similar "courses" were instituted in Kiev, Kazan, and Odessa. The Medical and Surgical Academy was the first institution of higher education to become coeducational. In 1872 it instituted special courses in various branches of medicine which were open to women. The coeducational orientation of the Academy was short-lived; however, it paved the way for special medical institutes for women.

The leading commentators on the philosophy of higher education had differing ideas on the most essential social functions of universities. There were those, like E. P. Kovalevskii, who thought that the universities could be "nurseries of scientific knowledge" only if they pursued purely intellectual interests and left character-building and moral edification to other institutions.[49] D. I. Pisarev had other reasons for demanding that universities dedicate themselves exclusively to scientific pursuits: he argued that whereas the function of moral education was to preserve the old values and worn-out feudal institutions, the function of scientific education was to pave the way for a new Russia that could be an active part of Western civilization. The ultra-conservative forces, by contrast, claimed that the basic task of the university should be moral education, and that all scientific disciplines and ideas incompatible with the sacred values of the established social order should be eliminated from the curriculum. The largest and most influential group was made up of men who advocated a balanced synthesis of moral and intellectual education. This group's most influential spokesman was Pirogov, who, speaking of formal education in general, stated that sound scientific education was the *sine qua non* of moral education, and that "to science, and only to science, the school owes its powerful influence on society." This idea was the cornerstone of the 1863 university statute, which, despite its serious shortcomings, was a step in the right direction.

According to Ivanov-Razumnik, the "era of the 1860's" extended from 1856 to 1866–68.[50] It was in large part a reaction to Russia's dismal showing in the Crimean War, and began with the first favorable responses of the government to the mounting popular demand for extensive reforms in social and economic relations. The era ended with the attempt on Alexander II's life by D. V. Karakozov, a student at Moscow University; the oppressive government reaction to this incident began in 1866 and lasted for the rest of the century.

The transition from the age of liberal reforms to the age of reaction was not sudden. Some writers consider 1861 the year that divided the "1860's" into two periods: 1856–61, when the intelligentsia had faith in "the good intentions" of the reform-oriented government; and 1861–66, when a growing conflict between the government and the intelligentsia became apparent. During the second period a revolutionary element appeared in the thinking of the powerful wing of the intelligentsia influenced by Chernyshevskii and the Nihilists. These people viewed the emancipation of the serfs not as an isolated reform, but as the groundwork for a complete revamping of Russian society. They knew, however, that the government would not go this far—that complete reform required revolutionary measures. The Emancipation was followed by intensified student disorders, an ideological articulation of mounting discontent in the countryside, the Polish Uprising, a rise in the militancy and influence of the journals *Contemporary* and *Russian Word*, and a general feeling among the intelligentsia that persons more progressive than A. I. Herzen should guide the revolutionary movement.

The government did not respond to the growing discontent and violence by abandoning its liberal policies: the university statute of 1863, the gymnasium and *zemstvo* statutes of 1864, and the censorship law of 1865 were essentially liberal documents, and all remained in force. But each of these measures represented the maximum of official liberalism; as soon as each was officially enacted, it became a target of crippling legislation, which eroded many of the government's liberal commitments and opened the gates to the forces of frightened reaction. In fact, the grand reforms of the 1860's were carried out in an atmosphere of continual contradiction. The 1865 censorship law, for example, eliminated all "preliminary" censorship—i.e., the official surveillance of written material before its publication—but imposed several other limitations on the freedom of the press. In the summer of 1862 the government temporarily banned the publication of *Contemporary*, a month or two after the French journal *Revue des deux mondes* had labeled it a socialist publication and at the time of a vitriolic campaign against it in the more conservative St. Petersburg journals. Chernyshevskii, the editor, was exiled to Siberia.

An episode that occurred during the protracted preparation of the 1865 censorship law was a typical example of the confusion and mixed sentiment that characterized the government's approach to liberal reforms. In 1863 A. V. Golovnin, the Minister of National Education, inaugurated the work on the censorship law by stating that the first matter to be decided was whether the censorship agencies should be subordinated to the Ministry of National Education or the Ministry of Internal Affairs. He favored the latter ministry, and presented the following argument.

"It is the duty of the Ministry of National Education to protect literature and to help it grow and prosper. This ministry is much closer to literature than any other government office; and because it is obligated to protect literature, it naturally cannot judge literature impartially. Concerned with all aspects of literary activity, the Ministry of National Education tries not only to erase the errors committed by literature but also to improve the services that literature renders to society. This attitude produces lenience in the performance of censorial duties.

"Moreover, the Ministry of National Education is obligated to ensure the progress of all branches of science that require free investigation. Truth cannot triumph without free discussion and conflicting opinion. . . . By protecting only those ideas that are considered truths at a given moment, censorship authorities limit the freedom of thought. The Ministry of National Education, in charge of censorship, would try slowly and carefully to remove these limits, and to give literature more latitude, restraining and suppressing only the extremes. In determining the extremes, there is plenty of room for the arbitrary judgment of each individual censor; but each censor, if he worked within the framework of the Ministry of National Education, would always tend to be more lenient, and to allow a broader latitude of printed opinion.

"The position of the Ministry of Internal Affairs in regard to censorship is completely different. This ministry is not obligated to protect literature, to help it, or to find ways of developing it. Since the ministry's only obligation is to see that the law is not violated, it is in a better position than the Ministry of National Education to judge the significance of individual violations by examining them in conjunction with other undesirable developments in the country. The role of the Ministry of Internal Affairs in censorship is clearer, more definite, and easier, and is therefore more practical."[51]

Golovnin wanted to have his cake and eat it too. He wanted the Ministry of National Education to safeguard and expand the freedom of thought in science and literature; at the same time, he wanted the Ministry of Internal Affairs to strengthen censorship by coordinating it with the activities of ideological or political police. He wanted to have both freedom of thought and the police machinery for suppressing it.

The statute of 1865 placed the censorship machinery under the Ministry of Internal Affairs, headed at the time by P. A. Valuev, who at first supported the liberal reforms but turned very conservative when he became a minister. The new statute ostensibly liberalized government surveillance of the printed word. Valuev saw to it, however, that the interpretation of the statute was as conservative and repressive as circumstances allowed. A. V. Nikitenko, a direct participant in many government decisions relevant to censorship, noted that Valuev was imbued with the traditional official contempt for "every intellectual movement" and was convinced that "each administrative ruling is superior to and more powerful than any idea."[52]

Both the university and gymnasium statutes of the 1860's were full of similar inconsistencies. Both, for example, dichotomized moral education (*vospitanie*) and intellectual education (*obrazovanie*), associating each with a distinct curriculum. Both statutes recognized the teaching of religion as the safest path to a sound moral education. The 1863 university statute expanded the religious curriculum by adding a special course on the history of the Russian Church—a course that was neither moral nor intellectual training, but sheer antiquarianism. The lawmakers ignored Pirogov's advice that the teaching of science is the best, most lasting, and most challenging source of moral education. They had heard the same opinion expressed by Lev Tolstoi, who at that time claimed that whereas the content of science is the best source of intellectual education, the contagious enthusiasm with which scientific knowledge is transmitted to students is the best source of moral education. Both statutes were committed to a philosophy that treated science as a good source of useful knowledge but a bad approach to moral education. In official terms, of course, moral education meant preserving the moral code of the autocratic regime.

The emphasis on religious education was part of the government's covert effort to ensure the stability of the regime by relying on the rigid conservatism of the Orthodox Church to slow down the forces of rationalism, science, and social change. As the chief pillar of autocratic ideology, the

Church itself was much in need of a strong defense against the radical ideas of science, which challenged some of its major teachings. The translation of Darwin's *Origin of Species* into Russian was soon followed by the translations of Sir Charles Lyell's *Principles of Geology* and *Antiquity of Man*. G. H. Lewes's *Physiology of Common Life* was widely interpreted as a source of proof that psychology was a natural science, dependent on physiology in the same way that physiology is dependent on chemistry. Russians could now read translations of selected works by Thomas Huxley and John Stuart Mill, who not only described the great achievements of modern natural science but also expressed firm views on such vital questions as the relationship of science to freedom and democratic institutions, the beneficial role of science in moral education, and the foundations of a scientific study of ethical systems. "At the time of the emancipation of the serfs," noted N. V. Shelgunov, "our science sought to explain the causes of the poverty and wealth of nations, and the conditions underlying the vigor, power, and prosperity of states.... We translated Adam Smith, Ricardo, Stein, Louis Blanc, and even Thomas More and Étienne Cabet."[53]

The government and the commission for drafting a new university statute accepted the idea that science and religion performed complementary social roles; but they also realized that the boundaries separating the two were not clearly drawn, and that religious thought would gradually lose the upper hand in certain branches of knowledge. In the debate that preceded the reintroduction of philosophy teaching in 1860, many officials were strongly in favor of treating psychology as a branch of physiology and therefore as a discipline fully independent of theology, an idea that was temporarily endorsed by ecclesiastical authorities.[54] The government heeded Metropolitan Filaret's warning that the advance of modern science would strengthen materialism, which would in turn undermine sacred culture. But it was equally attentive to the unequivocal pronouncement of I. E. Andreevich, a professor at St. Petersburg University: any action against scientific thought in Russia would inevitably lead to the destruction of the nation and the triumph of unmitigated passion and anarchy.[55] In the end, the expansion of the religious curriculum was overshadowed and effectively neutralized by an even greater expansion of the science curriculum.

The return of educational conservatism became official in 1866 with the appointment of Count Dmitrii Andreevich Tolstoi as Minister of National Education, a position that he held until 1880. Tolstoi abandoned the *glasnost'*—the encouragement and consideration of public views—in educational matters, and relied solely on the trusted bureaucrats with whom he surrounded himself. In the words of one of his critics, he behaved as if he were the Minister of Internal Affairs—the chief of gendarmes—rather than the Minister of National Education.[56] Before his appointment, Tolstoi spent a year as Attorney General of the Holy Synod, and acquired intimate knowledge of the Church's reaction to the liberal educational reforms. Like Sergei Uvarov, Nicholas I's Minister of National Education, he tried to change the spirit and institutional makeup of public education in order to make it a stronghold of the autocratic ideology.

D. A. Tolstoi was an established historian of Russian educational institutions. His lengthy surveys of education in eighteenth-century Russia showed a thorough study of archival material, careful analysis, and measured judgment. But Tolstoi, though dispassionate in his analysis of cultural developments in the distant past, was an unflinching supporter of contemporary autocratic ideology. As a scholar of eighteenth-century history he was calm and thorough; as a champion of the conservatism of his age he acted from fear, and with nostalgia for feudal institutions. He was firmly convinced that the vitality of Russian culture and the unity of the Russian polity depended on the aristocratic and estate principles of social stratification. Tolstoi's educational philosophy was dominated by two interdependent goals: preserving the supremacy of the aristocracy as a social and cultural force, and reviving the autocratic principle as the supreme means of politically integrating the Russian state and society. Together with M. N. Katkov and K. N. Leont'ev, he belonged to the group of intellectuals who claimed that the reforms of the 1860's had hurt the soul of Russia, its autocracy and aristocracy; and that it was almost too late to put the country back on the path of "natural" development.

Tolstoi felt that the emancipation of the serfs had not only eliminated the economic source of the aristocracy's social power but also made it possible for the nonaristocratic urban classes (*raznochintsy*), including the new bourgeoisie, to reach positions of influence in the intellectual world. The widely circulated term "realism" stood essentially for the *raznochintsy* ideology, which apotheosized individualism, rationalism, and achieved status— all in sharp contrast to the autocratic ideals. The *raznochintsy* viewed science as the center of human culture, and in doing so undercut the broad cultural base of religion. In their youthful enthusiasm, they became determined foes of the tradition-bound culture. But the reverse was true as well: most persons who openly tried to preserve the social preeminence of the aristocracy were severe critics of science as a source of true enlightenment and moral education.

The defenders of the aristocracy during the 1860's were of two basic kinds. The first consisted of men like Chicherin, who regarded the aristocracy's fall from its traditional position of authority and influence as a major hindrance to any extensive modernization of Russia. Chicherin thought it paradoxical that in the age of a generally acclaimed "Europeanization" of Russia the aristocracy was under constant attack, even though it was the only group bringing Western education to Russia and was incomparably more "Europeanized" than any other estate or class.[57] The second group, headed by D. A. Tolstoi, thought that overthrowing the aristocracy was inadvisable on moral grounds, since this action would undermine the value system of Russian society. Chicherin was actually pleading for a painless exodus by the aristocracy; but Tolstoi wanted to enhance and perpetuate the political power of the aristocracy by making appropriate changes in educational institutions. For example, he revived the aristocratic boarding schools, which were designed to give young noblemen a secondary education based on estate exclusiveness.

The revised gymnasium statute of 1871 abolished the "real" gymnasium and retained only the classical gymnasium. The real gymnasium was replaced by the "real school," which was specifically defined as an institution "oriented toward practical needs and toward the acquisition of technical knowledge"—in other words, a trade school.[58] Tolstoi and his close aides tried to bolster the power of the nobility by relying on the persistence of estate psychology: they thought that students from the middle and lower urban classes would naturally gravitate toward the real schools and thereby leave the classical gymnasiums—the only direct way to university education —with a predominantly aristocratic enrollment. If this happened, the nobility would have a virtual monopoly of the decision-making positions in the government. To further these aims, Tolstoi erected numerous barriers— such as increased tuition fees, reduced scholarships, and stiff entrance examinations—to keep young men from the middle and lower classes out of the universities. These barriers, however, were intended not only to aid the nobility, but also to keep overall university enrollment down and thereby minimize the role of the universities as centers of radical activity.

Tolstoi's strategy was unsuccessful, primarily because the sociology of secondary and higher education was considerably more complex than he was able or willing to see. The universities, for example, were not at all arenas of irreconcilable conflict between the nobility and *raznochintsy*, but instead centers of cooperation between the pauperized, "repentant" noblemen and various urban middle classes. The poor student, noble or not, was the typical student, and his numbers grew steadily. For example, during the early 1870's, close to 80 per cent of Odessa University students, 72 per cent of Kazan University students, and 60 to 70 per cent of Kiev University students needed financial assistance.[59] By the late 1870's Tolstoi realized that the traditional supremacy of the nobility in university enrollment was on its way out; and that most noblemen then attending the universities were a new breed, who sought higher education as a substitute for their hereditary elite status rather than a reinforcement of it. At this time he began to emphasize high standards of quality in academic work as a means of limiting enrollment.

Tolstoi was concerned with advancing the cause of the aristocracy as the bulwark of the autocratic system; but he was just as concerned with the survival of autocracy itself. His major methods for maintaining autocracy were the institution of gymnasium classicism and the abolition of the autonomy granted to universities by the 1863 statute.

Tolstoi gave a forthright explanation of his stand in favor of gymnasium classicism: "Some subjects [taught in the gymnasium] influence the development of all sides of the human mind, ennobling it and making it more sublime. The study of classical languages and literature belongs to this category. Other subjects lead only to a one-sided development of young people. Since these subjects exercise no influence on moral and aesthetic education, they attract the exclusive and premature attention of young people either to political and social problems, as in the case of jurisprudence, or to the material world, as in the case of the natural sciences. In the study of ancient languages—and sometimes in the study of mathematics—all the knowledge imparted to the students is under constant and nearly errorless control, which discourages the formation of independent opinions. In all other subjects, particularly in the natural sciences, the student's interpretation of acquired knowledge is beyond the teacher's control. For this reason, these subjects may engender personal opinions and differing views."[60]

The 1871 gymnasium statute eliminated the natural sciences almost completely from the curriculum.[61] Classical subjects made up 41 per cent of the total curriculum, mathematics 14 per cent, the Russian and Church-Slavic languages 12 per cent, and modern foreign languages 10 per cent.[62] So far as was possible the knowledge imparted was devoid of ideological connotations. Tolstoi's classicism was rightly identified as "grammatical classicism"; it emphasized the learning of classical languages as ends in themselves rather than as tools for the direct study of ancient Greek and Roman literature, history, philosophy, and political thought. After the 1871 gymnasium statute was enacted the demand for Greek and Latin teachers was so great that many positions were filled by men trained in other fields; in this way many graduates of the theological academies received teaching positions. A search was also made for teachers from other Slavic countries. By a special agreement with Tolstoi's ministry, Leipzig University opened a new institute of classical philology to fill the vacuum in Russia.[63]

V. I. Modestov, himself a professor of classics, was the most outspoken critic of Tolstoi's classicism: "In our country there is no fertile ground for a philological education because the genius of our people has had a truly realistic orientation and because the greatest fruits of our intellectual work ... have been produced not in the philological disciplines but in mathematics and the natural sciences." Commenting on Modestov's observation, Shelgunov stated that although mathematics and the natural sciences were far from flourishing in Russia, classical philology was in full decline, and was "dominated by foreign professors."[64]

As we have seen, Tolstoi was interested not only in purging the gymnasium curriculum of ideological elements but also in making gymnasium studies arduous in order to keep the enrollment down. But whatever its motives and expectations might have been, the new curriculum did not severely damage the preparation of students for university studies. It did not offer a modern, balanced education; but because of its emphasis on mathematics and the grammatical complexities of classical languages, it cultivated intellectual discipline, logical precision, and scholarly perseverance. Gymnasium graduates were weak in substantive knowledge and modern scientific ideas, but strong in disciplined study habits.

#### D. A. TOLSTOI'S ATTACK ON UNIVERSITY AUTONOMY

Ever since the establishment of Moscow University in 1755, on the model of contemporary German universities, the idea of academic autonomy had had many enemies in Russia. To its foes, who were particularly numerous at times of crisis, university autonomy was an artificial and injurious grafting of democratic republicanism onto the body of autocratic monarchism.

The 1863 statute gave the universities partial autonomy in hopes of bringing student unrest to an end. By the time Tolstoi was appointed Minister of National Education, however, it had become clear that student dissatisfaction and general restlessness were still gathering momentum, and that the cure should be sought elsewhere. From 1863 to 1884, the students fought to enjoy the legally guaranteed university autonomy, the professors tried to hang on to their gains, and Tolstoi proceeded to apply restrictive measures designed to enforce direct government control over every phase of university life. In this struggle, Tolstoi, relying on the coercive mechanisms of the state, had the upper hand. The situation was forcefully described by the comparative pathologist I. I. Mechnikov: "Even while the 1863 statute was still in effect ... many decisions of the university councils were annulled by higher authorities. The position of professors, who had nothing to do with anti-government activities, became literally unbearable. Persons like myself, who were dedicated only to science and detested politics, found themselves in an extremely difficult position and began to think of resigning to save their health and nerves."[65]

During the 1870's most professors fought to extend the rights of academic autonomy to the students. At a time when the government regarded the students as the real source of political turmoil and revolutionary activities, the leading professors argued that the legal recognition of students as a corporate component of the universities was the best way to restore academic tranquillity. Associative autonomy, they contended, would give students a vehicle for expressing their collective views and improving their financial status. Professors also felt that the autonomy guaranteed them by the 1863 statute could not be consolidated into a vital force as long as it was not backed up by a similar autonomy for students.

In 1875 Tolstoi appointed a special commission to plan the steps toward a more direct government administration of universities. In response, the councils of Moscow and St. Petersburg universities reaffirmed their belief in academic autonomy, and the gulf separating the professors from the Ministry of National Education began to widen. The professors of St. Petersburg University stuck firmly by their council's decisions not to communicate with any member of the commission and not to abandon the spirit of the 1863 statute. The first victim of Tolstoi's campaign was the eminent historian Sergei Solov'ev, who was forced to resign as rector of Moscow University. When Tolstoi himself resigned in 1880—to become Minister of Internal Affairs, a position for which he was better suited—he appointed a group of his trusted aides to a commission charged with drafting a new university statute that would embody autocratic ideology.

Although the educational policies of the 1870's negated the liberal policies of the early 1860's, the spirit of the academic community continued in the same tradition. Tolstoi's reactionary measures did not kill the free spirit of the university, the enthusiasm of the teaching staff, or the intellectual quest of the students. When Maksim Kovalevskii began to teach comparative law at Moscow University in 1877, he could see the signs of Tolstoi's war against academic autonomy; but he was also impressed with the sense of freedom and social duty that pervaded the university atmosphere. He wrote: "The university was the center of all our interests. For the groups outside its walls, it was a fountain of all leading currents of social thought. It benefited from the dedication of these currents to freedom. Most leaders of the university community were dedicated to the love of knowledge, the freedom of scientific thought, and the search for independent public activity. Most professors wanted to see the completion of the reforms that had started in February 1861, and had only contempt for each new reactionary development."[66]

A large majority of Moscow University professors publicly condemned the pronouncements of their colleague N. A. Liubimov, professor of physics, in favor of a new university statute.[67] Vladimir Solov'ev, who later became a widely read religious philosopher, endorsed Liubimov's conservative ideas, but was so much scorned by his colleagues and students that he found it necessary to resign as docent at Moscow University.[68] Similar episodes occurred in other universities, but very few professors actually resigned in response to Tolstoi's declared war on academic autonomy.

Professors everywhere helped preserve the institutional integrity of universities by providing a near-unanimous resistance to the implementation of Tolstoi's reactionary policies. The momentum generated by the great scientific achievements of the 1860's continued to inspire promising young scientists. Most Russian scientists who acquired international reputation during the 1860's were still active members of university communities, and these men helped maintain a continuity in the development of scientific thought. However, almost all the leading scientists of the 1870's and early 1880's acquired their scholarly reputations during the 1860's.

During the 1870's the quality of university students improved perceptibly, in part because of Tolstoi's decision to make studies more rigorous and demanding. In 1869 Tolstoi recommended that university councils study practical ways of engaging the students in serious research under the guidance of instructors, "since passive listening to lectures cannot be considered conducive to adequate education."[69] His aim was to keep students so preoccupied with their studies that they would have little time for illegal extracurricular activities. The negative effects of oppressive laws were somewhat offset by the positive effects of increased government donations for the establishment and maintenance of university laboratories and research facilities. The government policy requiring professors to use the laboratories exclusively for teaching purposes was largely ignored, since the professors depended on them for their own research.

During the 1870's there was a substantial increase in the number of qualified persons applying for teaching positions in Russian schools. Since the late 1850's Russian students and scholars had streamed to the leading universities and laboratories of Western Europe in search of advanced scientific knowledge and modern research methods. Most Russians went to Germany and France, but there were also solid contingents in England, Sweden, Italy, and Switzerland. In Russia itself, the universities of the 1870's produced a wider range of modern scientists. This was a natural result of the expanded curriculum and the modern departmentalization of faculties, which substituted specialization in depth for the earlier encyclopedism. The growth of specialized studies had two advantageous results: it produced a new generation of students highly qualified for postgraduate training in Western Europe; and it stimulated the growth of learned societies, which helped the graduates maintain active contact with professors and professional colleagues.

In the 1870's, somewhat less than in the 1860's, the universities benefited from the intense social consciousness of professors, who were eager not only to advance the frontiers of knowledge but also to produce direct solutions to the many practical problems facing the country. A. M. Butlerov, who formulated a widely recognized theory of structural orientation in chemistry, took time to read practical papers in apiculture at the Free Economic Society. D. I. Mendeleev's study of the country's industrial potential was of great practical importance, as were V. V. Markovnikov's studies of the Caucasian naphtha deposits and V. V. Dokuchaev's pioneering studies of the Russian *chernozem*. Social scientists also tried to bring direct benefits to society. When M. M. Kovalevskii joined the Law Faculty of Moscow University in 1877 he was very much impressed with the practical work that his colleagues made a part of their general scholarly activities. A. I. Chuprov made notable contributions to the development of *zemstvo* statistics, I. I. Ianzhul advanced cogent arguments for the abolition of certain forms of indirect taxes, and Sergei Muromtsev wrote on the role of law in creating social equality.[70] All these scholars made the university a vital social institution. They made scholarship a part of social living and a guide to improved social welfare. For most scholars, a concern with practical problems was not a substitute for scientific theory and pure academic work: it was a vital, though unofficial, part of their academic commitment.

In brief, the 1870's saw the universities continue to be a battleground of contending ideologies even as they continued to improve the quality of academic training and widen the horizons of scientific scholarship. Because political unrest in the universities was much more visible than scientific and educational activity, men close to the government began to complain about a general decline in higher education. To correct this erroneous but widespread opinion, the famed physiologist Ivan Sechenov published an article in the *Messenger of Europe* in 1883. Describing the diverse scientific activities in Russian universities, Sechenov said that the growth of science between the 1860's and early 1880's had begun the final phase in the Westernization of Russia—a process started by statesmen, continued by literary men, and brought to new heights by the chemists, physiologists, and mathematicians who above all others had enabled Russia to join "the family of enlightened nations."[71] He explained that Russian university science appeared to be declining only because the press did not give adequate publicity to the variety and the magnitude of research conducted in university laboratories. He proudly cited the recent statement of an English scholar that Russia had turned out more independent studies in chemistry than England.[72] Sechenov was impressed with the fact that for the first time symposia in histology and physiology published in Germany contained chapters by Russian scholars. He had to admit, however, that the scientific work of the 1870's, despite its notable achievements, did not emulate either the pioneering zeal or the theoretical depth of that produced during the 1860's.

## CHAPTER THREE

# Scientific Institutions

## THE ST. PETERSBURG ACADEMY OF SCIENCES

In 1865 the St. Petersburg Academy of Sciences, Russia's oldest and most eminent scholarly institution, marked the 140th anniversary of its founding. The preceding four decades had been particularly productive. The astronomer F. G. W. von Struve, the chemist Hermann Hess, the embryologist and anthropologist Karl von Baer, the mathematicians M. V. Ostrogradskii and P. L. Chebyshev, the naturalist A. Th. Middendorff, and several others carried the Academy to new heights of international fame. The Academy more than compensated for the meager development of scientific thought in the universities, which had suffered under the oppressive legislation of Sergei Uvarov, Nicholas I's Minister of National Education. In these years Alexander von Humboldt and Roderick Murchison launched their survey expeditions in various parts of the Russian empire, beginning a series of geographical and geological researches sponsored by the Academy. The Pulkovo Observatory, a subsidiary of the Academy, was founded in 1839, and rapidly grew into one of the leading astronomical centers in the world, opening a new era of international cooperation in the study of the heavens.

Despite its illustrious scientific achievements and prominent position in Russian culture, the Academy was resented by large segments of the intelligentsia. Since the middle of Nicholas I's reign, it had been common to refer to the Academy as a "German institution," a label that was in circulation as late as 1918. The most common charge against the Academy was that it neglected the intellectual and practical needs of Russia, and discouraged the development of native Russian scientists. This resentment reached a new peak in the 1840's, when foreign scholars founded the Russian Geographical Society and the Russian Archaeological Society, reserving the top administrative positions for themselves. The internal strife in these two societies led to open attacks on foreign scholars, and in the early 1850's native Russian scholars were given positions of authority and prestige. In the Academy, however, foreigners maintained their preeminence not by holding high administrative posts but by occupying a majority of the academic positions. In 1841, the St. Petersburg Academy of Sciences absorbed the Russian Academy—founded by Catherine II in 1783 to work on a Russian dictionary and to conduct literary studies—which was made up almost exclusively of Russians; this greatly increased the numerical strength of native Academicians. However, in the Department of Mathematical and Physical Sciences (which also covered the biological sciences) and the Department of History and Philology most positions were still occupied by foreign scholars.

After the Crimean War much thought was given to modernizing the Academy of Sciences. As it then existed, the Academy could not cope with the current revolutionary strides in the natural sciences, the growing technical complexity of the country's economic problems, and the widespread popular enthusiasm for scientific knowledge. In general, it was out of place in the new cultural climate, which was strongly influenced by a combination of realistic nationalism (in contrast to the romantic nationalism of the 1840's), positivism, and libertarianism. But it was easier to perceive the Academy's problems than to remedy them.

In 1857, the Academy was commissioned to work on a new statute that was expected to liberalize its internal administration and its relations with the government. At the same time the question of institutional autonomy was raised by the universities. Chronic student unrest compelled the government to concentrate on the universities, and the projected Academy statute was dropped before it reached higher government committees. In 1863, immediately after the passage of the new and more liberal university statute, the Academy was again authorized to draft a new statute. The Academicians were requested to confer with university professors in order to define a broader base of cooperation between the Academy and the institutions of higher education. A part of the press also participated in heated discussions of the projected statute and the role of the Academy in national life. The new proposal reached the State Council in 1865, but for unknown reasons it was never signed into law. Instead, the 1836 statute, a basically conservative document, was slightly amended, primarily to give more independence to the Astronomical Observatory at Pulkovo and the Main Physical Observatory at St. Petersburg. Nothing was done about the Academy's demands for increased authority vested in academic councils.

Although the government was not favorably disposed toward basic changes in the internal organization of the Academy, it did help with the Academic budget. The Academicians received substantial salary increases and were given a higher civil-service standing. Additional funds were granted for laboratories, museums, and libraries. A modern scientific workshop was built on the ruins of the old chemical laboratory, ravaged by a fire in 1859. The anatomical and ethnographic museums were reorganized and expanded. Private donations increased substantially, allowing the establishment of several annual prizes for outstanding work in specified scientific fields.[1]

After 1860 much was done to make the Academy a truly national institution. Only three of the 23 Academicians elected from 1860 to 1880 were born outside the Russian empire. Although most of the Russians were no match for von Baer, von Struve, Helmersen, and other illustrious foreigners of the past, they were carefully selected men of considerable promise. Several would have been welcomed at any academy in Europe, notably F. V. Ovsiannikov in comparative anatomy and physiology, A. M. Butlerov in chemistry, A. V. Gadolin in crystallography, E. I. Zolotarev in mathematics, and A. S. Famintsyn in botany. Equally illustrious were the historian S. M. Solov'ev, the Russian intellectual historians P. P. Pekarskii and M. I. Sukhomlinov, and the comparative Slavic philologist F. I. Buslaev. Among the leading Academicians elected before 1860 but still actively engaged in scholarship were the mathematicians P. L. Chebyshev and V. Ia. Buniakovskii, the chemist N. N. Zinin, and the crystallographer N. I. Koksharov. During the 1860's, however, the Academy lost many of the great men, mostly foreigners, who had made its reputation. By 1865, Wilhelm von Struve, the founder of the Pulkovo Observatory, and Heinrich Lenz, the pioneer of electromagnetic theory, were dead, as were the mathematician Ostrogradskii and the mineralogist A. T. Kupffer. Von Baer had retired to Dorpat, and Middendorff had left the Academy because of poor health.

In 1861 the Academy began publishing the *Journal of the Imperial Academy of Sciences*. The *Journal* was the first lasting scientific periodical in the Russian language, and was published continuously until 1895, when it was replaced by another publication in Russian. The *Journal* carried Russian translations of articles published in the Academy's other journals, as well as original material of its own. It was intended for members of the scientific elite who were eager to keep up with modern developments in all the major natural sciences. Unfortunately, the contributions of the *Journal*, perhaps because they were too technical, did not reach such popular and fervent champions of the scientific attitude as Chernyshevskii, Pisarev, and Antonovich.

During the 1860's the Academy began to publish papers written by Russian scholars who were not formally associated with it. This practice strengthened the contact of the Academy with the new scientific forces in universities and other schools of higher education. Thanks to the watchful eye of F. V. Ovsiannikov, for example, the Academy's *Bulletin* published important papers by I. M. Sechenov, I. I. Mechnikov, and A. O. Kovalevskii, the Russian pioneers in modern physiology and comparative embryology. A. S. Famintsyn began to publish papers in the *Bulletin* ten years before he was elected to the Academy.[2] The ties of individual members of the Academy with various government agencies, learned societies, and institutions of higher education became closer and more extensive than ever before. Many Academicians offered courses at St. Petersburg University and several professional schools situated in the capital. Thanks to the teaching activities of scholars like Chebyshev, O. I. Somov, Butlerov, and Famintsyn, students kept abreast of modern developments in individual sciences.

The activities of Chebyshev, the Academy's leading mathematician, are typical of the many ties that connected the Academy with society at large. Chebyshev was enormously productive as a scholar, publishing 84 studies in his lifetime; he also taught mathematics at the University. He was an active member of the Curriculum Committee of the Ministry of Education, which had the important job of selecting gymnasium textbook manuscripts. He required that each adopted textbook be didactically sound and up-to-date. Chebyshev was also an advisory member of the Technical Committee of the Main Administration of Artillery.

Every important learned society in St. Petersburg benefited from the dedicated work of individual Academicians, even though the societies were by this time in a position to rely mostly on their own large memberships. The Russian Geographical Society provided future Academicians with indispensable field experience, and gave established members the opportunity to undertake scientific trips in search of new empirical knowledge or solutions to acute practical problems.

In 1865 the Academy commemorated the centennial of the death of Mikhail Lomonosov, "the father of Russian science." For the first time, the collective effort of the speakers produced a complete picture of Lomonosov as a poet, grammarian, historian, and scientist. In the past Lomonosov had been praised as a poet, *or* as a historian, *or* as a scientist, with the result that the full range of his genius was not appreciated. Although some of the speakers at the 1865 ceremony doubted the modern value of many of Lomonosov's physical and chemical theories, they succeeded in giving their listeners an unforgettable picture of his genius in many fields of scientific theory and the philosophy of science. Lomonosov was presented as a man who had fought with courage and determination to make the Academy a national institution, dedicated to Russian science. His scholarly legacy was presented as a major source of the modern Russian rationalist tradition; and this new image of him gave added support to modern claims that reason and science were the true beacons of the Russian intellectual tradition.

The massive reexamination of Lomonosov's work was only part of the Academy's interest in the history of Russian science and scientific institutions. Even before the centennial, in 1862, Petr Pekarskii had published the two-volume *Science and Literature in the Age of Peter the Great*; in the words of a contemporary, this work was "an entire library of factual information on the beginnings of our intellectual development."[3] The two volumes dealt with the coalescence of various intellectual traditions—including Kievan learning and secular contacts with Western thought during the seventeenth century—that had made it possible for Peter I to undertake drastic programs on behalf of science and secular education.

At the end of the 1860's Pekarskii was commissioned to write a history of the Academy, which he completed in 1873. Biographical in approach, the work described the painful growth of the Academy from its shaky beginnings in the late 1720's to the celebration of its fiftieth anniversary. No previous work had shown the historical growth of the Russian scientific tradition in such detail. Written critically and placed into a broad cultural context, Pekarskii's study is still one of the richest sources of information on the most vital phase in the early history of Russian science. It was reviewed very favorably by most leading journals, who saw in it a valuable historical document and a monumental expression of contemporary concern with the intellectual power of science. Some reviewers commented on the gradual growth of the ranks of native Russian scientists, and urged concentrated efforts to make the Academy a truly national institution. A writer in the *Messenger of Europe* noted that the Academy had at first been a foreign institution on Russian soil (and even a part of Germany's *Drang nach Osten*), and that there was still a wall separating it from Russian society.[4]

In 1871, the St. Petersburg Academy's *Journal* began publishing in installments *A History of the Russian Academy* by the Academician Mikhail Sukhomlinov. Totaling over 4,000 pages, this study is a veritable encyclopedia of Russian intellectual history from 1783, the year the Russian Academy was founded, to 1841, the year it was transformed into the Second Department of the St. Petersburg Academy of Sciences. Since the two academies had many joint members, this book is to a large extent a history of both institutions. It is particularly valuable because it begins where Pekarskii's study stops. Because of its biographical orientation, it is a mine of information about all the Russian members of the Academy of Sciences during the closing decades of the eighteenth century and the beginning of the nineteenth century. The scientific achievements of Russian pioneers in natural history, mathematics, mineralogy, chemistry, and astronomy are fully portrayed, as are the attitudes of these early scholars toward the general scientific and philosophical currents in the West and the relations of Russian scientists with their Western peers. Sukhomlinov was particularly successful in placing Russian scientists and their work into the broader context of Russian intellectual culture. He described the formative years in the growth of two great Russian scientific traditions, natural history and mathematics, but he also offered valuable documentary source material on the social and cultural forces that impelled the growth of science. In particular, the emergence of intellectual segments in the Church, among the enlightened aristocrats, and throughout the middle classes is richly documented.

Pekarskii's and Sukhomlinov's histories did not reach a wide audience. They were written in the cold style of historians staying close to the documentary material, were lacking in the finer points of organizational logic, and were too bulky. They did much, however, to alleviate the bitter and largely unwarranted attacks on the Academy as a foreign institution, and to create a picture of Russian science as an intellectual process with historical continuity and firm roots. Above all, these studies offset the opinion, prevalent in some influential circles of the intelligentsia, that scientific thought was not an essential component of Russian culture; this notion often decorated the pages of the *Russian Messenger*, and was built into Danilevskii's philosophy of history.

Sensitive to the nationalist and libertarian forces unleashed by the Reform, the Academy strove to find for itself a vital, and at the same time unique, place in the general scheme of scientific institutions. K. S. Veselovskii, permanent secretary of the Academy, spoke on behalf of his colleagues when he stated repeatedly that the Academy should dedicate itself primarily to theoretical work, to pure science. He was defending the intellectual supremacy of the Academy in the growing network of scientific institutions, but he was also trying to offset the overemphasis that the Nihilists placed on the pragmatic and technological functions of science. He mentioned no antagonists, but he addressed himself to the "realists"—the "men of action" typified by Pisarev—who were prone to measure the value of scientific knowledge by its immediate practical usefulness to Russian society. In his annual report for 1865 Veselovskii stated: "It is unfortunate that the conditions under which we live exercise an unfavorable influence on the Academy and its institutions.... We may find consolation in our dedication to pure science and in our love for Russia. Our service to science is a service to Russia. Science is one and indivisible for the entire enlightened world; and since our country is an inseparable part of the enlightened world, we do not separate science from Russia. A person who enriches the most abstract branches of mathematics makes no less a contribution to Russia than a person who explains a page of our national history or throws new light on the natural riches of our country. We reject the idea that some sciences are more useful and others less useful, or even useless, to Russia.... To safeguard the interests of pure knowledge is the duty of the Academy."[5]

By placing the emphasis on "pure science," Veselovskii wanted to pinpoint the most useful place for the Academy in Russian society at a time when the institutional basis of scientific inquiry was expanding in every direction, with the accent on institutional specialization. He and his colleagues knew that the once towering position of the Academy in the total scheme of institutionalized scientific inquiry was shrinking rapidly and irretrievably. They heeded the candid warning of one critic of the projected new Academy statute: "The natural sciences and technology are being attended to by specialized institutions and learned societies on a wider basis and with more success.... The mathematicians working in universities are in no way inferior to their colleagues in the Academy."[6] By the 1860's the Academy was no longer "the primary scientific institution of Russia," a title given it by the 1836 statute. There were whole fields of scientific inquiry—embryology, anatomy, and physiology, for example—whose most productive work was done in other institutions. Especially in chemistry and mathematics, valuable work was done in the leading universities.

The Academy was no longer the only clearinghouse for scientific ideas, nor was it the only channel for the influx of scientific ideas from the West. However, it continued to serve as the central agency for maintaining regular contact between Russian and foreign institutions of learning. Much to its credit, it added such contemporary Western European giants of science as Lyell, Darwin, Virchow, Huxley, and Helmholtz to its corresponding membership. Moreover, the Academy took the lead in encouraging the

general growth of science. Its funds were greatly increased by private donations, and it instituted many new prizes, including the Lomonosov and Karl
von Baer awards, for original contributions to individual disciplines. Mendeleev and Sechenov were among the first Russian scholars to receive these
highly coveted awards. Finally, the Academy expanded its list of scientific
journals, and thus made more space available for the publication of original
papers by Russian scholars not associated with the Academy.

The Academy's own scientific output increased considerably; its position
in the total picture of Russian scientific investigation declined primarily because the output of the universities and specialized learned societies increased even more. But in the versatility and quality of its scientific work,
the Academy was not surpassed by any other single Russian scientific institution. A committee of Moscow University professors, appointed to evaluate
the proposal for a new statute for the Academy, made a prophetic statement
when it demanded that the Academy, in its relations with other Russian scientific institutions, should strive to be "a star among stars, and, if possible, to
shine as a star of the first rank."[7]

### THE UNIVERSITY AS A SCIENTIFIC CENTER

Not until the end of the 1860's did the government begin to help the
universities expand their research facilities, an obligation to which it was
committed by the 1863 statute. The instruments, working space, and technical staffs of university laboratories were no match for the great scientific
workshops in the leading Western universities. The systematic expansion
of individual laboratories was seriously hampered by budgetary uncertain-
ties: sometimes the annual budgets contained no funds for laboratories, not
even for repairs or the purchase of material necessary for the most elementary experiments. During the 1860's, contemporary scholars especially noted
the shabby condition of Mendeleev's chemical laboratory at St. Petersburg University and the overall deficiencies of the facilities at Kazan and
Khar'kov. In many cases, the gross inadequacy of material equipment was
partially compensated for by the youthful enthusiasm of the professors, who
belonged to the new generation and were dedicated to both teaching and
scientific inquiry.

Eventually, however, the government began to act on its promises. During the 1870's the existing laboratories expanded gradually, and many new
ones came into being; progress was modest, but the improving quality of
instructors and the much greater amount of practical research expected from

most students made the laboratories the centers of university science. The higher technical schools also benefited. N. N. Zinin's chemistry laboratories in the Medical and Surgical Academy, L. N. Shishkov's in the Artillery School, and F. F. Beilstein's in the Technological Institute were scientific workshops of the modern type.[8] The new laboratories allowed professors to intensify their personal research and helped students acquire basic experience in independent research. With expanded research facilities, most universities could now train their own future professors and scholars in many scientific fields. Small wonder, then, that Sechenov called the research provisions of the 1863 university statute "a gigantic contribution to Russian natural science."[9] Russian laboratories were still meager by Western standards, and were built almost exclusively for educational purposes; however, some of them showed signs of becoming adequate research workshops.

The expanding facilities of laboratories and other research workshops stimulated the formation of specialized fields within the larger research areas. At St. Petersburg University, for example, the botany department was now split into two distinct specialties, plant morphology and plant physiology, each headed by an established scholar. Interest and increasing specialization in the study of living nature was aided by the foundation of new biological field stations equipped with modern laboratories. The first such station was established in Solovetsk on the initiative of N. P. Vagner, a professor at St. Petersburg University. At Moscow University, mineralogy and geology were split into separate chairs, and soon paleontology was added as an independent subject.[10] Physiology was no longer a subject taught only in medical schools, and it ceased to be fully identified with histology; in St. Petersburg, I. M. Sechenov made it not only a distinct academic subject but also an area of great emphasis.

A typical university professor of the new generation differed tangibly from his predecessors, particularly those in the era of Nicholas I. He was usually guided by Claude Bernard's laconic pronouncement that "a theory is merely a scientific idea controlled by experiment,"[11] and by the principle that a scientist must not generalize until he has considered the actual data in detail. He was concerned with the rigor of the modern experimental method and with the great theoretical ideas that gave this epoch a prominent place in the annals of scientific thought. As a writer, the new professor stuck closely to experimental results and the general ideas that gave them coherence and larger meaning. As a teacher and public lecturer, he showed familiarity with the great philosophical ideas of the time, particularly those related to science or to the genesis of knowledge in general. John Stuart

Mill's studies in logic, Thomas Huxley's efforts to give a broad philosophical basis to the theory of biological evolution, and Comte's treatment of science as the most trustworthy index of cultural progress all reached wide audiences and became popular topics of discussion. Even the old-fashioned encyclopedists, typified by A. N. Beketov, differed from their predecessors in that they were not empirical naturalists but general popularizers of the great scientific ideas of the time.

The typical new university professor received some of his predoctoral education in Western universities, but he also went there periodically to further his postdoctoral studies. Karl Ludwig's laboratories in Vienna and Leipzig, for example, provided research facilities for most of the leading Russian physiologists of the last four decades of the nineteenth century, most of whom also worked in the laboratories of Emil du Bois-Reymond, Hermann Helmholtz, Claude Bernard, and other scholars in the field. The Russian chemists, interested primarily in organic chemistry, streamed through the laboratories of C. Wurtz, F. A. Kekulé, H. Kolbe, R. Bunsen, and E. Erlenmeyer, absorbing up-to-date knowledge and widening their Western intellectual contacts. The two young biologists A. O. Kovalevskii and I. I. Mechnikov, destined to become giants of Russian science, worked in the laboratories of Western universities; but they also undertook completely independent embryological studies of the rare microfauna of the Mediterranean and Adriatic seas. The publication of scientific papers written by young Russian scholars in the leading Western scientific journals was now a common occurrence, and Russian geographers and ethnographers carried their research far beyond the boundaries of the Russian empire.

In St. Petersburg, university professors were much closer to the pulse of Russian social and intellectual life than the relatively insulated members of the Academy. Many Academicians were engaged in an active and purblind defense of vested interests in the world of scholarship, which hampered the free diffusion of up-to-date theories and hypotheses. It was on behalf of academic conservatism that Karl von Baer opposed Darwinism, even though the embryological research of his younger days was an important part of the mainstream of evolutionism. For the same reason, Academician V. Ia. Buniakovskii continued to write scorching essays against non-Euclidean geometry for years after Lobachevskii's ideas began to receive recognition by Western mathematicians, and F. V. Ovsiannikov kept physiology close to the interests of histology (and practical medicine). University professors were more in tune with the great changes of the sixties and seventies; to them, the search for knowledge and the active diffusion of modern ideas were vital tasks of immediate social importance. It was the university professor rather than the Academician who introduced Darwinism to Russian audiences, made the names of Liebig, Bunsen, Helmholtz, and Ludwig as respected in Russia as they were in Germany, and made young Russians aware of Claude Bernard's trenchant attack on biological vitalism. It was the professor, not the Academician, who helped science reach the larger community as both a body of knowledge and a powerful ideological weapon.

The universities had their quota of professors with vested interests in eroded scientific theories and views, but these men were rare, and were powerless in academic councils. Conservative professors were overshadowed by the new breed of scholars, who were more interested in bringing to Russia new developments and new branches of science—such as agrochemistry, evolutionary paleontology, experimental physiology, microscopic anatomy, and spectral analysis—than in upholding ideas that belonged to the past. The university professors of the 1860's reflected the spirit of the time by cultivating a skeptical and critical attitude toward every authority, in the realm of ideas as much as in everyday life.

When the chemist N. N. Sokolov took time in his chemistry lectures to acquaint his students with the positivist philosophy of Auguste Comte, he acted as a dedicated exponent of scientific optimism, which permeated the main currents of thought in the 1860's. Sokolov was particularly taken by Comte's interpretation of social change in terms of cultural progress, which Comte equated with the development of science. This was the same Sokolov who in 1859–60, together with A. N. Engelhardt, had published the first Russian chemical journal, contributing much to the popularization of structural chemistry in Russia. Impatient with the research facilities at St. Petersburg University, Sokolov also founded what proved to be the first private chemistry laboratory in Russia, though it was short-lived.

The growing popular interest in scientific thought in Russia was responsible for the proliferation of learned societies founded within the framework of individual universities, and for the more frequent congresses of scientists, who gathered to share their research experiences, institute new publication facilities, and take a collective look at the problems, challenges, and promises of Russian science. In both these activities the Russian scholars followed well-established German models.

The 1863 statute authorized the universities to establish general or specialized scientific societies with the right to organize laboratories and museums, send research teams to various provinces of the empire, seek private donations for scientific inquiry, and publish scholarly studies. These societies strengthened scientific ties among the Russian institutions of higher education, and also maintained steady contacts with foreign learned societies, primarily by the exchange of publications and the election of honorary members from abroad. Their primary task was to spread new scientific knowledge among those who could not obtain higher education and those who, after completing higher education, were eager to keep up with modern developments in their specialties, in the neighboring disciplines, or in science in general. The learned societies helped promising young scholars acquire research experience, and gave them an opportunity to present their papers before established scholars. They also tapped the scientific talents of men who were not connected with educational institutions.

One of the most successful of these new societies was the Society of Admirers of Natural Science, Anthropology, and Ethnography, founded in 1864 at Moscow University. The geologist G. E. Shchurovskii and several other influential members of the new society felt that the Society of Naturalists, a part of the University since 1805, did not meet the intellectual challenges and the cultural needs of the day. According to the popular geographer D. N. Anuchin, the old Society's publications, all printed in foreign languages, "were of greater service to Western European science than to Russian science; they could just as well have been published in the West."[12] Anuchin also noted that the secretary of the Society preferred to speak in French or German at meetings, and that the minutes of all meetings were recorded in French. Moreover, the Society of Naturalists was an exclusive club that allowed very few younger scholars to join its ranks, particularly if they were not proficient in German and French. It made no effort to maintain intellectual contacts outside its own comparatively small ranks.

The Society of Admirers of Natural Science, Anthropology, and Ethnography at first faced formidable opposition from the older professors associated with the Society of Naturalists, and was also handicapped by financial difficulties. But it was immediately successful in launching a modest series of publications, selecting only those contributions written in the Russian language. Eventually the Admirers also organized several scientific exhibits. The ethnographic (1867), polytechnical (1872), and anthropological (1879) exhibitions drew surprisingly large numbers of visitors, and were noted cultural events of the time. The ethnographic specimens displayed at the exhibition of 1867 became the nucleus of the university's ethnographic museum. The polytechnical exhibition of 1872 led to the establishment of the Polytechnical Museum, which soon became a forum for popular lectures on scientific themes of current interest. The new museum attracted streams of visitors, including many from outside Moscow—testimony to the growing popular interest in modern science. The founding of the museum coincided with the emergence of a new type of Russian self-taught inventor: the talented man who combined basic scientific knowledge with natural dexterity and a flair for mechanical innovation.

The new Moscow society was a prototype of the lively associations founded in most universities by the end of the 1860's. It was also the first of the specialized societies. Of the fourteen specialized societies founded during the remainder of the century, the best-known was the Moscow Mathematical Society, officially chartered in 1867 but actually existing from 1864.[13] Chebyshev, commenting on the situation in his capacity as a member of the Curriculum Committee of the Ministry of National Education, recommended not only that the new association be officially chartered but also that it be granted government subsidies and free mailing privileges. Chebyshev stated: "In addition to the great importance of mathematics in general education and technology, this science is of particular interest to us. In the opinion of foreign scholars, confirmed by the history of education in our own country, this is the science for which we show a special talent and in which we can to some degree compete with the West."[14]

The Moscow Mathematical Society began as a small circle of mathematicians who met in the homes of older colleagues to report on new books, read papers on mathematical topics, and keep abreast of current developments in Russia and abroad. In 1864 the Society began to organize public discussions on selected topics in mathematics and related sciences, particularly physics. However, from the beginning it was concerned primarily with the fundamental problems of modern mathematics. In 1865 the members decided to publish the *Mathematical Symposium* in two volumes annually, and within a few years the first issue was distributed. This was the first Russian journal devoted exclusively to mathematics, and also one of the first Russian scientific periodicals to publish its papers in the Russian language. At first its growth was slow, but at the end of the century it expanded rapidly. The *Symposium* today, published jointly with the Soviet Academy of Sciences, is one of the leading mathematical journals of its kind in the world.

A. Iu. Davidov, one of the founders of the Mathematical Society, spelled out its basic philosophy when he stated in 1869 that the basic task of mathematics is to study "the laws of nature" unobstructed by a one-sided search for practical knowledge. Many students of the history of Russian mathematics believe that this early emphasis was an important factor in the gradual growth and consolidation of a specific mathematical tradition at Moscow

University, which culminated in intensive work concentrated on the most detached and abstract branches of mathematics. The Society also performed an important service in bringing together the many tributaries of Russian mathematical thought. The very nature of its content made mathematics a comparatively secluded academic occupation; as a rule, mathematicians had very little to do with the growing *haute vulgarisation* of scientific thought and with the various public exhibitions. However, the *Mathematical Symposium* reached not only practicing mathematicians but also high school teachers and other graduates in the exact sciences, keeping them abreast of new developments.

The mushrooming of scientific societies led to the first Russian scientific congresses, another innovation born in the intellectual climate of the 1860's. Here again, Germany provided a model and a tested pattern of action. In 1860, K. F. Kessler and F. V. Ovsiannikov visited the German Congress of Naturalists and Physicians held in Königsberg, and reported their impressions to Russians in the most glowing terms. In 1861 and 1862 Kessler succeeded in organizing two local meetings of Kiev naturalists and natural science teachers. Kessler's unwavering determination, the growing popular demand for more intensive personal contacts between scholars, and D. A. Tolstoi's favorable recommendations all helped national gatherings of Russian scientists become a reality.[15]

The First Congress of Russian Naturalists and Physicians met in St. Petersburg in 1867. The organizing committee, selected from the members of St. Petersburg University's Faculty of Physical and Mathematical Sciences, included the chemists Dmitrii Mendeleev and B. N. Menshutkin, the astronomer A. N. Savich, the physiologist F. V. Ovsiannikov, and the botanist A. N. Beketov. The Congress was attended by 600 natural scientists, including 200 from outside St. Petersburg. The venerable Karl von Baer was asked to preside over the Congress, but his advanced age and the difficulties of transportation between the capital and Dorpat, where he had retired, made it impossible for him to accept the invitation. Kessler, now at St. Petersburg, was the logical person to fill the honorary position declined by von Baer; he was elected unanimously in appreciation of his dedicated work toward making this first national congress of Russian scientists a reality.

Reporting on the first meeting of the Congress, a St. Petersburg journal stated: "The gathering was extraordinarily diverse and enthusiastic. Most of our leading scholars were there, and there were all kinds of specialists from the physical and mathematical faculties, teachers of secondary schools, persons in military uniforms, old and young men eager to meet each other, and old friends with joyous greetings. The entire assembly looked like a single family gathering together after prolonged separation; all faces expressed great and true joy."[16] The same journal observed that the meetings were also attended by many private citizens, including a solid contingent of St. Petersburg ladies. All 2,500 seats in the university auditorium were filled at the plenary meetings.[17]

The plenary sessions of the Congress concentrated on the general problems of scientific theory and the broader cultural role of scientific thought. Individual speakers presented their ideas about the relation of the natural sciences to education, jurisprudence, and agriculture; several papers dealt with more general topics related to the popularization of science.[18] All the papers read at the plenary sessions had one common theme: the role of science as the only avenue to improved social well-being in modern Russia. The papers read at the special sections of the Congress showed the wide variety of scientific problems that had attracted the attention of scholars, and demonstrated the modernity of Russian research techniques and theoretical interests.

The general impact of the St. Petersburg Congress transcended all the expectations of its organizers. It established a new and more personal channel of cooperation in the pursuit of science, intensified the exchange of ideas, and helped lay the foundations for a number of Russian scientific traditions. The Congress was not a spurious expression of scientific enthusiasm, but the beginning of a complex network of complementary developments, all contributing to the mainstream of Russian science. The decision of the Congress to hold similar meetings in the future was immediately acted on: the Second Congress was held in Moscow in 1869, the Third in Kiev in 1871, the Fourth in Kazan in 1873, the Fifth in Warsaw in 1876, the Sixth in St. Petersburg in 1879, and the Seventh in Odessa in 1883. The Thirteenth Congress, the last in the series, convened in Tiflis in 1913. The Second Congress established the Sevastopol Biological Station, which was supported by both government and private funds and was planned to encourage intensive study of the flora and fauna of the Black Sea. The station was closely associated with the Society of Naturalists at Odessa University.[19] At the Seventh Congress Ilya Mechnikov read a paper presenting the first formulation of his theory of phagocytosis, a fundamental concept of comparative pathology.

The national congresses of naturalists were the first institutional mechanism that gave Russian scientists the opportunity to publicly state their collective views on the social roles of science, educational policies, government research, and professional problems.[20] During the 1880's the government tried to limit the work of congresses to the presentation of scientific papers and the organization of exhibits of scientific instruments. The congresses continued to make public statements on national issues, but, relying on self-imposed restraints, they made no effort to enter the arena of organized political action. For example, the Second Congress recommended the establishment of a permanent national association of persons engaged in scholarly work; but the government discouraged the idea, and the leaders of the Congress made no effort to translate the general recommendations into a detailed plan.

The First Congress had formally recommended that all universities establish learned societies on the model of the Society of Admirers of Natural Science, Anthropology, and Ethnography at Moscow University. The response of the academic community was very favorable: during the next three years such societies were organized at St. Petersburg, Kazan, Kiev, Khar'kov, and Odessa; and in 1882 one appeared at Warsaw.[21] All these learned bodies were bent on establishing closer ties between science and society, and on providing the scholar with an effective outlet for presenting the fruits of his research. In field work, however, each society limited itself to a specified region; this practice made it possible for each society to use its financial resources in the most rational and effective manner, and to sponsor specialized projects that required intensive research by a number of different disciplines. Regional specialization and close cooperation between scholars from neighboring disciplines produced a new genre of naturalist studies combining modern scientific theory and regional research. However, the basic preoccupation of these societies was still descriptive work; they contributed more to the diffusion of scientific ideas and the gathering of raw data than they did to scientific theory and scientific synthesis.

Realizing that Russia, besides needing general naturalist societies, also needed specialized scientific societies founded on the model of the Moscow Mathematical Society, the First Congress endorsed a proposal made by the young chemist N. A. Menshutkin, who asked that he and his colleagues (including Mendeleev) be allowed to form a chemical society. The government responded favorably to this recommendation of the Congress; on October 26, 1868, the Russian Chemical Society became a reality, and immediately undertook to publish a journal. N. N. Zinin, who first reduced aniline from nitrobenzene and who founded the first Russian school of chemistry, was appropriately elected chairman of the new society. It was at a meeting of this society held on March 18, 1869, that Mendeleev made public his discovery of the periodic law of elements.

The Chemical Society was in effect a national organization, and its journal, open to all Russian chemists, met the acute need for a publication of chemical studies in the Russian language. Instead of scattering their papers in various German and French journals, Russian chemists were now able to make their individual studies integral parts of a larger national effort. The journal also aided the emergence of a new scientific community of Russian chemists. For the first time, the pages of a specialized journal were open to chemists who were competent in their science but could not write in French and German—and since many new scholars came from the middle classes and lower nobility, the number of those who learned foreign languages through private tutoring was declining drastically. During its first ten years, the membership of the Chemical Society increased from 48 to 119.[22]

The activities of the Society provided a positive answer to the complaint of leading educators that Russian students were notorious for quickly forgetting everything they had learned in universities. Referring to the situation in the 1850's, the historian S. M. Solov'ev noted that the nation suffered immeasurable intellectual losses because of inadequate communication of scientific knowledge, which prevented university graduates from keeping abreast of new developments in their respective fields. The chemist A. M. Butlerov related a conversation with Liebig in which the great German chemist stated that in his laboratory at Giessen University he had observed the very competent work of many talented young Russians but was surprised that most of them did not pursue chemical studies after returning to Russia.[23] Like the naturalist associations, the Russian Chemical Society helped ensure a constant and organized flow of scientific information through the printed word, through periodic gatherings of people with common intellectual interests, and through personal contact between persons of different academic status, accomplishment, and age. It met the growing need for postgraduate scientific work, which was so necessary to professional men employed outside the academic research centers, and also provided extracurricular research opportunities for promising and dedicated undergraduates.

In 1872, on the initiative of several professors at St. Petersburg University, the Russian Physical Society was founded. In 1878 it merged with the Russian Chemical Society to form the Russian Physical and Chemical Society, whose official journal was published in two parts, one for physics and one for chemistry. Kazan University was the home of a local Society of Naturalists; and at Khar'kov University the most active associations were the Society of Experimental Sciences (founded in 1872) and the Mathematical Society (founded in 1879).

In 1884, in a paper read at a special gathering of the members of Moscow University's Society of Admirers of Natural Science, Anthropology, and Ethnography, K. A. Timiriazev endeavored to define the social functions of learned societies. He thought that their major contribution was in helping to establish a better balance between various components of the scientific process—particularly between "pure" and "applied" science. In learned societies he saw a convenient instrument for neutralizing the potential dangers of overspecialization and enriching the empirical substratum of science. He urged these societies to defend the interests of "pure" science, dedicated to the search for truth regardless of its immediate utility and ideological correlates. Their job was, above everything else, to make critical thought an organic ingredient of modern life. Although he acknowledged the important role of learned societies in the popularization of scientific knowledge, Timiriazev argued that this function should be performed primarily by men who combined an active participation in scientific work with a full appreciation of the broader cultural significance of scientific thought. An effective popularizer of science, he thought, was one who instilled in society at large a more profound appreciation of the beneficial role of scientific theory and helped weaken the influence of those who judged science only by its contributions to the solution of current technical problems.[24]

### INDEPENDENT LEARNED SOCIETIES

The adjective "independent" is used here to designate the learned societies that operated outside the framework of the universities and the Academy, though relying at least partially on government subsidies. Of 26 learned societies under the jurisdiction of the Ministry of National Education in 1865, only seven received continuous financial help from the government;[25] but all of them benefited from the close cooperation of Academicians, university professors, independent researchers, and government officials interested in science avocationally.

In 1865 the Free Economic Society, Russia's oldest learned society, celebrated its hundredth anniversary. It had been named "free" in its original statute because it was not directly subordinated to any department of the government, even though it subsequently worked under the supervision of, and was subsidized by, the Ministry of State Properties. At first the Society was dedicated to the improvement of agricultural technology and the dissemination of practical knowledge, but its work gradually widened to include agricultural economics and soil science. Thanks to direct assistance from the country's leading scientists, its activity was diversified and productive, if not glamorous or widely publicized.

Spurred by what Timiriazev called "the general awakening of the entire country," the Free Economic Society responded to the national "rejuvenation" of the 1860's by infusing new life and determination into every branch of its activity. It was already engaged in several major programs to popularize science, and its publications continued to carry popular articles on specific problems in agricultural technology, rural architecture, and sanitation. To fight the staggering proportion of illiteracy among the rural population, the Society established in 1861 a special committee to undertake a broad and detailed study of education in various provinces; it was this committee that made the first recommendations for universal elementary education and for extension courses. The Society also sponsored periodic agricultural exhibits to inform the farming population about modern agricultural tools and equipment. It continued its long-established sponsorship of popular lectures. In 1860 the Society's lectures in physics, chemistry, and forestry were so popular that on many occasions its spacious lecture hall could not accommodate all those who attended.[26]

The Society's sponsorship of scientific experiments and other research activities benefited greatly from the growing efforts of scientists who joined the general movement—led most energetically by the Nihilists in the 1860's and by the Populists in the 1870's—to eliminate the traditional barriers between the intelligentsia and the common man. Scientists of the highest caliber and reputation were eager to handle specific research projects with very practical objectives. At the height of his intensive theoretical work in structural chemistry, for example, A. M. Butlerov also chose to join the Free Economic Society, and contributed several articles on agriculture. The Society published his book, *The Bees: Their Life and the Basic Rules of Rational Apiculture*, which went through eleven editions. It also delegated Butlerov to organize the agricultural section at the All-Russian Fair held in Moscow in 1882. A Moscow newspaper reported that Butlerov's exhibit provided not only a physical model of modern beekeeping techniques, but also "an auditorium under the open skies," where "excellent popular lectures were read on the life of bees and on the fundamental principles of rational beekeeping."[27]

During the 1860's the Society placed special emphasis on the agricultural use of chemical fertilizers, a problem that necessitated a systematic study of the types of soil in various regions of the country. The Society sponsored several experimental farms to study the effects of chemical fertilizers on both the crops and soil. In 1865 D. I. Mendeleev submitted detailed recommendations in favor of these experiments. The research conducted on these farms laid the groundwork for a comprehensive and systematic study of Russian soils and for the emergence of soil science as a distinct discipline. Continuing Mendeleev's work under the sponsorship of the Free Economic Society, V. V. Dokuchaev organized two expeditions for the study of *chernozem* in 1878–79. The findings of these expeditions were incorporated in Dokuchaev's classic *Russian Chernozem* (1883), a systematic study of the types and distribution of the black soil of Russia. Although Dokuchaev is considered the founder of Russian soil science—and justifiably so—he was initially inspired by the Academician Franz Ruprecht, who in 1866 published his *Geobotanical Studies of Chernozem*, which dealt with the origin and composition of black soil.

The basic weaknesses of the Free Economic Society were that it often undertook more research projects than it could finance and carry to a conclusion, and that it was too strongly influenced by dilettantes with antiquated scientific ideas. Nonetheless, its contributions to Russian science and society were great. Perhaps the most impressive work done under the Society's sponsorship was in agricultural economics, in the most general meaning of the term. The Society's Department of Auxiliary Sciences (founded in 1859) examined statistical and theoretical problems in economics and demography. This department's Political and Economic Committee concentrated on three sets of problems: the theoretical analysis of the interrelationship of land, capital, and labor as the basic economic categories; the social and economic organization of production; and the commercial problems of agriculture, such as transportation, marketing, taxation, and banking.[28] The Society was quick to devote its research activities to the sociological and economic problems created by the emancipation of the serfs, the expansion of hired labor in agriculture, and the organization of multi-crop farming. In 1867–68 it joined the Russian Geographical Society in sending expeditionary teams to eight districts to study the production and commercial distribution of grains; the findings of these teams were published in numerous monographs between 1870 and 1876.[29]

In 1864 the government decreed the formation of district and provincial *zemstva*, a new type of local community that was to enjoy limited autonomy in the management of basic local cultural and economic affairs. Immediately after establishing the *zemstva* the government began to interfere with them by creating special safeguards to protect its own interests in the countryside and by imposing many restrictions on local transportation, education, health, and insurance. Even so, the *zemstvo* program produced great changes in rural life. The Free Economic Society was one of the very few institutions that made concerted efforts to gather valuable data related to this unique social experiment and to supply contemporary economists of several specialties with empirical information.

The Russian Geographical Society had been founded in 1846, and entered the Reform era as an active institution with a large membership, many departments and regional branches, rich financial endowments, and several specialized journals. It, too, was a group in which Academicians, university professors, independent scholars, and avocational scientists met and worked on a common ground. It benefited from the work of established scholars like von Baer and von Struve, but also from the work of newcomers like P. P. Semenov, N. M. Przheval'skii, and A. I. Voeikov. Working closely with the Geographical Society were many of its provincial branches, including the Caucasian Section in Tiflis, the Southwestern Section in Kiev, the East Siberian Section in Irkutsk, and the West Siberian Section in Omsk. The Geographical Society was the first Russian learned association to count women among the contributors to its publications, and in 1877 two women were elected "cooperating members" of the Society. O. A. Fedchenko is remembered for her expeditionary work in Turkestan, and A. Ia. Efimenko for her pioneering study of the folkways, mores, and "juridical customs" of the Lapps, Karelians, and Samoeds.

As in the past, the sponsorship of geographic expeditions both within the empire and abroad was the Society's most important job. Because the Ussuriisk area, recently annexed by Russia, was a geographic and ethnographic *terra incognita*, it attracted the attention of many enterprising geographers; and because the government felt that the area was of great military value, research there was assured of more than adequate financial support. Turbulent Central Asia also required careful and thorough geographical and ethnographic scrutiny. Both these territories were gateways to China, Manchuria, and Tibet, all vast lands with many districts virtually unknown to outsiders.

The expeditionary work in the Ussuriisk area, Russian Central Asia, and the neighboring Chinese and Mongolian territories, which took place between the late 1850's and the middle 1870's, produced a new breed of geographer-explorers, whose academic interests included many disciplines from orthography to ethnography and who had a flair for reporting interesting daily observations without trying to place them into scientifically rigorous categories. N. M. Przheval'skii, the most enterprising of these men, described the plan of his work in these words: "Emphasis should first be placed on purely geographical investigations, and then on natural-historical and ethnographic investigations."[30] Przheval'skii and his peers closed an era of geographical exploration, the era of natural-historical breadth, scientific encyclopedism, and geographical narrative. They did not solicit the help of specialists, but their explorations laid the groundwork for the specialists of the next generation. They also enriched the literature of exploration, which was a readable and attractive vehicle for satisfying the popular interest in descriptive science. Przheval'skii identified his own work as "scientific reconnaissance."[31]

Much of the material collected by these explorers was never processed and published, but the quantity of raw information collected was enormous. For example, in 1886 a committee of the Geographical Society estimated that Przheval'skii's data on the flora of Tangut and Mongolia, if published, would require 1,600 printed pages and 200 sets of drawings; and that his data on mammals would take 710 pages and 60 sets of drawings. It was also estimated that the processing of his more specialized materials would produce large monographs on reptiles and fishes, as well as on geological, astronomical, and hypsometric observations.[32]

Przheval'skii represented one type of naturalist associated with the Geographical Society. Another type, in the minority, was represented by N. A. Severtsov, who, even though some of his writings had encyclopedic breadth, was a specialist with solid theoretical grounding. Though concentrating on the collection of raw data, he did pioneering work in zoological and ornithological systematics, and had a flair for theoretical questions of larger magnitude. In addition to descriptive accounts of his travels in Turkestan, he published interesting papers on the ecology of the fauna in Voronezh Province, "zoological ethnography," the zoological regions of the Arctic areas of Russia, and the relationship of mountain formations in highland Asia to the distribution of animals.

Most members of the Geographical Society were guided by an acute awareness of the need for a fuller and more rational understanding of the natural and human resources of their country. But most of them also belonged to the St. Petersburg elite and were loyal servants of the autocratic government. They were conservative in their appreciation of scientific theory, and avoided all discussions of the broader ideological and philosophical attributes of science. However, one member of the Society, P. A. Kropotkin, was in a category by himself. He was dedicated simultaneously to an impartial study of the natural resources of his country and to a very partial revolutionary struggle against the autocratic government. He was a first-rate scholar and explorer, pioneered the study of glaciation, and introduced new ideas and interpretations into the study of Siberia's topography. In 1874, as a reward for this work, he was offered the chairmanship of the Society's Section of Physical Geography.[38] The reward, however, went undelivered, for the secret police arrested him the next day. He was charged with illegal and conspiratorial activities inspired by the First International, and was sentenced to two years in the Peter and Paul Fortress. While in prison, he wrote a two-volume study on the glacial epoch. His friends in the Geographical Society made it possible for him to have access to the resources of the library of the Academy of Sciences.

In 1876 Kropotkin left Russia for Western Europe, where he lived, mostly in London, until 1917. In the West he became a moving force in the Anarchist movement, but he did not completely abandon his interest in geology and geography. In 1898, for example, in a paper read before the British Association for the Advancement of Science, he advanced the hypothesis that all North Asian plateaus over 900 meters in altitude had been covered with ice during the glacial epoch, and that the glaciers had descended as low as 300 meters. On the basis of his personal geological observations in the Baikal area, he formulated a theory of Quaternary ice covers in North Asia, which was subsequently upheld and elaborated by the geologist V. A. Obruchev. In his study of the Baikal region, Kropotkin also established the existence of plateaus as a special type of mountain relief. "Plateau," of course, was a known geographical label before Kropotkin: what he did was to define it as a basic and independent type of the earth's relief. He showed that plateaus have as wide a distribution as mountain ranges, and described their distinctive normal characteristics in detail.

In the 1860's and 1870's the Geographical Society began to expand its activities in many directions, but it continued to emphasize the collection and publication of practical knowledge. One of its new concerns was systematic climatology, which was most thoroughly investigated by A. I. Voeikov. Voeikov's major work, *The Climates of the Earth,* was based on data collected by many scholars working in all parts of Russia and over a long period of time. The book was much more than a survey and synthesis of empirical data; it was an articulate study of the physical processes involved in climatic variability, and a bold effort at comparative climatology. Voeikov's work attracted the attention of Western scholars not as a mere repository of raw data but as a source of challenging hypotheses, ingenious theoretical insights, and important general conclusions.

The work of the Geographical Society in ethnography, sociology, and demography was also extensive and diversified. In 1864, the ambitious statistical work done by a special department of the Society prompted the government to establish the Central Statistical Committee, made up exclusively of Society members. During the first 33 years of its existence, the Committee was headed by the geographer P. P. Semenov-Tian-Shanskii, a champion of statistical studies of Russia's human and cultural resources. At its founding, the Committee immediately embarked on a systematic collection of specialized statistical data; eventually, it administered a census of the St. Petersburg population in 1869, the first such undertaking in Russia. The number of people engaged in gathering statistical data grew rapidly, and in 1870 the first All-Russian Statistical Congress was held, to discuss mutual problems and to consider the feasibility of a national census. Two years later, St. Petersburg hosted the eighth session of the International Statistical Congress.

The Geographical Society, having less money and a more limited access to official information than the Central Statistical Committee, conducted its statistical research on a more modest scale. Nevertheless, its collected data soon became voluminous, and served as a basis for research on many aspects of the nation's economy and social life. As its major effort, the Society published the *Geographical-Statistical Dictionary of the Russian Empire* in five volumes (1863–85), a source that could not be ignored by any student of contemporary Russia. The Society also helped district *zemstva* collect local statistical data, a novel but challenging task whose chief agents were the local priest, teacher, physician, and "repentant aristocrat." The "statistical methods" of this project, however, lacked mathematical refinement and occasionally produced generalizations of doubtful validity.

The moving force behind all these new statistical studies—which were as noble in their aspirations as they were primitive in their scientific safeguards and methods—was P. P. Semenov-Tian-Shanskii.[34] As one modern geographer noted, from 1849, when Semenov joined the Geographical Society, to 1914, the year of his death, the history of the Society was essentially the history of the scholarly activity of this ambitious, brilliant, and tireless man. Semenov translated long sections dealing with the geography of Asia from Karl Ritter's *Die Erdkunde*, and enriched them with many comments and supplementary information.[35] The publication of the first volume of this translation in 1856 marked the beginning of modern geography in Russia, for it inaugurated a systematic search for regularities and laws governing geographical configurations. Semenov also popularized Alexander von Humboldt's views on interdisciplinary and conceptually integrated studies of specific geographical regions. However, he acquired his reputation primarily as a descriptive geographer who wrote graphically and lucidly and who searched for unique specimens of flora and fauna to enrich museum and university collections. He pioneered a new geography in Russia without abandoning the charms of the old one. In championing statistical studies of human geography, Semenov was more an advocate of scientific precision than a contributor to a more rigorous methodology. This, however, does not reduce his historical importance as a pioneer in the use of statistical techniques for marshaling data of sociological, demographic, and economic relevance. For example, his "statistical-geographical" survey of a township in Riazan province was the first Russian community study to focus on the dynamics of social stratification.

Semenov belonged to a small group of Geographical Society members who were concerned with the social functions of science and whose work contributed greatly to the spirit of the Reform era. In order to inaugurate a more effective statistical study of acute social and economic problems, Semenov divided the country into fourteen economic districts, delineated on the basis of carefully chosen physical and economic features. "In our realistic century," he said, "science has no room for hazy scholastic distractions: it is concerned with the study of natural resources and their subordination to human control." He added that the duty of every scholar who "does not want to be a cosmopolitan but desires to share the life of his countrymen" is to make a concrete contribution to the advancement of scientific knowledge and to endeavor to make science a part of national life.[36] Semenov did more than talk about social conscience. He was appointed a member of the government commission for drafting the legal measures for the emancipation of the serfs, and was given ample opportunity to place his scholarly erudition at the service of a great social cause.[37]

The Geographical Society was the most ambitious, the most versatile, and in some respects the most amateurish learned association operating outside the universities and the St. Petersburg Academy of Sciences. Other societies, both old and new, were less general and more limited in financial and intellectual resources. Of the older associations, one of the more active was the Mineralogical Society, which after fifty years of very modest work entered a flourishing era in 1866, when a government grant allowed it to undertake an intensive geological study of the country. Headed by the crystallographer N. I. Koksharov, a member of the Academy of Sciences, the

Society began to publish two serials, the *Journal* and *Materials on the Geology of Russia*.[38] These publications were preceded by *The Mining Journal*, which had been published by the Mining Institute since the 1820's and carried many valuable articles on the geological study of Russia and the development of modern geological theory. In addition, the St. Petersburg Society of Naturalists had a special department for geology and mineralogy that published its own journal.

During the 1860's many new learned associations came into being. They pursued different specialties, but most were dedicated to the concrete application of modern scientific knowledge. The Russian Technical Society, founded in St. Petersburg in 1866, and the Moscow Society for the Dissemination of Technical Knowledge, founded in 1869, both worked ambitiously to bring science and industry into closer contact. The Society of Russian Physicians, founded in Moscow in 1861, published the *Medical Gazette*, a popular bimonthly, which was replaced in 1879 by the more serious and professional *Transactions*, published annually in two volumes. The chief functions of the Society were to disseminate the latest medical knowledge among its members, either through the printed word or through formal meetings, to grant scholarships to selected medical students, and to sponsor free clinics. The success of this organization led to the formation of two similar associations in Moscow during the 1870's, the Moscow Medical Society and the Moscow Surgical Society; both of these published periodic symposia and sponsored free medical service. The names of the Russian Entomological Society (founded by Karl von Baer in St. Petersburg), the Moscow Archaeological Society, the Ural Society of Naturalists, the Society for the Study of Western Siberia, and the Moscow Society for the Acclimatization of Cereals show the wide area of scientific problems that generated sufficient popular interest to warrant the formation of independent learned societies.

The founding of the Juridical Society in Moscow in 1863 was part of a growing interest in the scientific study of social phenomena. During the reign of Nicholas I, under the ideology of official nationalism, law was taught in the universities on a purely descriptive level: the duty of professors was to survey the principal categories of law, and students were expected to memorize the main substantive and procedural norms of the Russian legal code. Legal theory and legal philosophy had no place in the university curriculum. Although the publication of the *Complete Collection of the Laws of the Russian Empire* in 1830 provided a solid basis for work in legal theory, the government saw to it that the teaching of law did not exceed the level of description. During the next three decades only two "theoretical" studies of law appeared in Russia: one outlined the unique features of the Russian legal tradition, and the second summarized the basic trends in the history of the Russian legal code. Finally, in the Reform era, the enactment of a series of fundamental laws affecting the very structure of the Russian polity stimulated widespread interest in the social effects of the legal code and its component parts. Under the influence of Comtean positivism, John Stuart Mill's social philosophy, and the German school of historical jurisprudence, Russians developed a strong interest in the sociology of law. However, it was not until the 1880's that outstanding contributions were made in this field.

The growth of the Juridical Society was slow, but from the very beginning it was dedicated to the study of law as a social force open to scientific generalization. In 1867 it began to publish the *Juridical Messenger*, which gradually became a serious journal that solicited contributions from representatives of the leading schools in jurisprudence. The Society also sponsored the cataloging of legal customs or mores and the gathering of material on the everyday routine of the new rural courts. As part of this effort, it helped the *zemstva* work out procedures for collecting statistical data covering the full scope of changing conditions in the rural community. But in all this the Society was guided by the belief that the collection of empirical data was essentially unsatisfactory unless it could provide the basis for a comparative study of law aimed at discovering the uniformities and regularities in social and legal life.

The learned societies established during the 1860's and 1870's were more an expression of the popular endorsement of science as a major cultural force than an effective source of modern scientific thought. It was not until the 1880's that the learned societies became flourishing centers of scientific inquiry; at that time specialized societies, dominated by professional scientists, established their superiority over the traditional "naturalist" societies, in which the dilettante had often played the central role. The old-fashioned societies continued to serve as a bridge between scientists and society at large by popularizing science as a system of knowledge and a vocation, by instilling the spirit of science into all phases of social life, and by collecting funds earmarked for scientific research.

THE SCIENTIFIC COMMUNITY

The Age of Emancipation produced great men of science and buoyant scientific traditions; but more important, it also produced the first scientific community in Russia. The rise of new scholarly collectivities—learned societies, scientific *kruzhoky*, collective research projects, naturalists' congresses, and scientific and technological expositions—provided the social and psychological ties that held the scientific community together, and invested that community with energy and purposefulness.

The scientific community was a network of diverse institutions with varying degrees of dedication, size, and durability. Some institutions were national and others were purely local; but all had formal organizations, duly elected members, and established financial resources. A striking feature of Russian institutions was the comparatively great overlapping of membership. The chemist A. M. Butlerov, to give a typical example, was a member of the St. Petersburg Academy of Sciences, a professor at St. Petersburg University, and an active member of both the Russian Physical and Chemical Society and the Free Economic Society; moreover, his scientific activity was closely and concretely associated with all these affiliations. This overlapping of membership made intimate personal contact an institutional component of Russian scientific scholarship.

In Russia, scientific institutions of all types commonly cooperated with each other, particularly in complex research undertakings requiring talent and material resources beyond the capacity of individual organizations. The Russian Physical and Chemical Society, for example, combined its resources on several occasions with the Academy of Sciences and St. Petersburg University to handle various large research problems. The proliferating regional studies brought together the members of various naturalist societies, the Geographical Society, the Mineralogical Society, and the Free Economic Society. Most of the successive congresses of naturalists and physicians were made possible by the dedicated efforts of national and provincial organizations. In advocating the first national congresses, K. F. Kessler had emphasized that these meetings, generally acclaimed in Germany, would be even more fruitful in Russia, where the enormous geographical distances "made the personal acquaintance of scholars with each other exceedingly difficult." "In our country," he wrote, "it is not unusual for ten or more years to elapse before a zoologist or a botanist meets another zoologist or botanist." He added that this isolation greatly restricted the intensity and compass of scientific work, and that it precluded investigations requiring the collaboration of many persons.[39]

Overlapping personnel and unified action were two sources of the growing community feeling in Russian science. An equally vital stimulus came from the numerous informal organizations. Their work, spontaneous and unchartered, helped bring the scientific establishment closer to the mainstream of Russian intellectual culture. To the literary *kruzhoky* of Nicholas I's era were now added scientific *kruzhoky*, which engaged in heated debates on current topics drawn from the growing discoveries in evolutionary biology, structural chemistry, electromagnetism, neurophysiology, chemical crystallography, and many other fields. More significantly, the scientific *kruzhoky* injected the vital elements of personal temperament, intellectual bent, spontaneous cooperation, and human warmth into scientific work. They were effective equalizers, bringing established savants and aspiring newcomers into a direct relationship unobstructed by the rigidity of formal organizations.

The friendly gatherings of old and young scientists in the homes of P. L. Chebyshev and A. N. Korkin were an important factor in the emergence of the "St. Petersburg school" of mathematics. The young men who gathered around A. G. Stoletov in the new physical laboratory at Moscow University benefited more from personal contact with their teacher and each other than from the underequipped workshop where they conducted scientific experiments. The group produced no "school in physics," but its stimulating interaction helped a long list of young scholars rise to scientific eminence. The famous Kazan school in chemistry owed its existence primarily to personal contact between teachers and promising students, which extended far beyond the premises of the university. The mathematical *kruzhok* that met in the modest home of Professor N. D. Brashman of Moscow University was the first step toward the establishment of the Moscow Mathematical Society. The First Congress of Russian Naturalists and Physicians, one of the most memorable events in the intellectual history of nineteenth-century Russia, was initiated not by an institution but by a group of professors from St. Petersburg University—including Mendeleev and Menshutkin—who spent long hours discussing ways and means of giving new impetus to scientific pursuits. Often the *kruzhoky* extended beyond the scientific community, and scholars mixed with men engaged in other professional and intellectual endeavors. For example, I. M. Sechenov's ties with the unwieldy world of Nihilism were noted by his contemporaries.

The scientific community did not escape the rising nationalist sentiment of the 1860's, which it usually expressed in pronouncements favoring an emancipation of "Russian science" from foreign tutelage. The struggle for "Russian science," sometimes reduced to mere declarations without concrete plans for action, was given a straightforward formulation by G. E. Shchurovskii in his address before a huge gathering at the Second Congress of Russian Naturalists and Physicians in 1869: "The Russian natural-history congresses are an extraordinary phenomenon, for they have opened a new era in the history of Russian natural science. The traditional absence of concentrated scientific work in Russia once drove our scholars to Western European centers where science was highly developed; but the congresses have helped us mobilize our forces for a scientific study of Russia herself. The Western centers should not lose all significance for us; however, they should serve only to supplement Russian science.... From now on, the scientific achievements of the West should be transplanted to Russia not as naked truths without any practical value for the Russian people but as ideas that can be absorbed by our culture. If we continued to concentrate on cosmopolitanism and the abstract ideas of mankind, we would not be able to defend the honor of our nation and our position in Europe, for we would not have our own national, Russian science."[40]

Shchurovskii's speech was an example of the more extreme defense of the national character of science. More typical were the opinions of such influential scholars as Veselovskii, Mendeleev, and Semenov-Tian-Shanskii, who regarded science as a part of Russian culture that was international in its content and national in its usefulness for the solution of the pressing needs of the country. Most Russian scientists demanded a drastic increase in Russian scientific manpower and in scientific writing in the Russian language. They believed that the nation's needs in industry, agriculture, transportation, defense, and health should be the main factor in determining priorities in scientific research.

Nationalism in science was also identified with the struggle against foreign scientific strongholds in Russia, and against the excessive dependence of Russian scientists on Western universities, laboratories, libraries, and intellectual innovations. At the Fifth Congress of Russian Naturalists and Physicians, held in Warsaw in 1876, a speaker stated that Russia was much in need of native professors trained in national institutions and engaged in an independent search for scientific knowledge. He did not believe that Russian science should be isolated from universal scientific trends, but he was firmly convinced that Russia would be "a satellite of other nations, not only in a scientific but also in a moral sense," as long as she did not rely on her own scientific endeavor.[41] The scientific community became particularly intolerant of the dominant position occupied by foreigners in the leading Russian scientific institutions. It was widely believed that this dominance slowed down the development of a national science, and that foreign scientists tended to synchronize the scientific work in Russia with the Western scientific endeavor rather than with national needs.

The Seventh Congress of Naturalists, held in Odessa in 1883, joined the Russian Geographical Society in criticizing the extravagant government subsidies given to the Main Physical Observatory, which was staffed almost completely by foreigners. The Physical Observatory did most of its work in meteorology, a theoretically underdeveloped branch of physics, and was supported by a network of poorly equipped local meteorological stations; A. G. Stoletov complained that it spent ten times more money annually than the physics laboratories of all the Russian universities put together.[42] Mendeleev used the work of scholars identified with the Physical Observatory as an example of primitive science, detached from theory and the search for scientific laws. The government was mostly interested in the practical utility of organized weather forecasting and was ready to import foreign scholars to do the job with existing techniques. Stoletov spoke on behalf of the scattered Russian scientists who were concerned with the theoretical and practical possibilities opened up by modern developments in electromagnetism and thermodynamics. Like the Pulkovo Astronomical Observatory, the Main Physical Observatory maintained very tenuous ties with the mainstream of Russian science. The widespread criticism from the Russian scientific community was not in vain, for within a generation both these organizations became truly Russian institutions. In the meantime, the bitter criticism of "foreign institutions" added new strength and purposefulness to the aspirations and ideology of the scientific community.

In 1880 a group of Russian Academicians, led by Chebyshev and Butlerov, nominated Mendeleev for the chair of chemistry and technology in the St. Petersburg Academy of Sciences that had recently been vacated by the death of Zinin. A majority of Academicians voted against Mendeleev, just as they had voted against his appointment as an "adjunct" six years earlier. The occasion provided the Russian scientific community with a powerful incentive to reaffirm its unity and intensify its struggle against foreign domination of the leading scientific institutions. Individuals, learned societies, and faculties, all acting spontaneously, sent emotional letters and telegrams expressing bitter disapproval of the Academy's vote. A petition signed by fourteen members of the Physical and Mathematical Faculty of Moscow University stated: "The history of many academic elections has clearly shown that the voice of the men of science in the Academy has been suppressed by negative influences, which have consistently opposed opening the doors of the institution to Russian talent.... In the name of science, in the name of national pride, and in the name of justice, we consider it our duty to condemn these actions, which are incompatible with the dignity of a learned body and injurious to Russian society."[43] Another petition, signed by representatives from all Russian institutions of higher learning, stated that its primary aim was to alert the public to the Academy's discrimination against Russian scientists.

The leading newspapers and journals demanded a reexamination of the Academy's organization and philosophy, and a closer integration of Academy activities with national life. According to Professor V. I. Modestov, writing in the *Voice*, the Mendeleev affair was clear proof that the "interests of science" were not yet synchronized with the "interests of society."[44] M. A. Antonovich declared that the mere attack on "the German scholars" did not pinpoint the main dilemma of Russian science. In reality, he wrote, the cultural exclusiveness of the Academy, most graphically expressed in the exclusion of Mendeleev, was part of a planned isolation of the press and the entire system of national education from the central issues of national life.*

During the two months following the announcement that the Academy had voted against admitting Mendeleev to full membership, the great chemist was elected an honorary member by close to twenty Russian universities and learned societies.[45] The reaction reached a climax in 1882, when the journal *Rus'* published a long article by Butlerov that flatly accused the Academy of stubbornly continuing to discriminate against Russian scholars.[46] Butlerov added more fuel to the fire by making public the decision of his Academy colleagues to support Oscar Backlund, who did not speak Russian, for a position of "adjunct" in astronomy, thus bypassing the Russian astronomer F. A. Bredikhin, who had already made noted contributions to science.

Apparently moved by the first massive manifestation of a scientific community in Russia, Mendeleev wrote a memorandum presenting his own recommendations for a reorganization of the Academy. His primary aim was to make the Academy more responsive to the needs of the country and the emergence of new scientific disciplines. He wanted the Academy to sponsor various kinds of collective research, to publish all studies in Russian, to help scholars outside its organization to find publication outlets for their

---

* In 1882 the government responded to the general demand for a firmer integration of the Academy into the national system of scientific institutions by appointing D. A. Tolstoi as President of the Academy. Tolstoi's most important job was to restore peace in the Academy by curbing the nonscientific activities of such liberal Academicians as Butlerov and Famintsyn. As Minister of National Education, Tolstoi concentrated on abolishing the comparatively liberal organization of the universities and restoring the old autocratic principles; as President of the Academy his main assignment was to preserve the essentially conservative charter of 1836. An old and tired man, he merely succeeded in slowing down the Academy's adjustment to the demands of modernization.

scientific contributions, and to be alert to the acute needs of a changing economy. He thought that not only the Academy but also the universities and the leading learned societies should be granted the right to participate in the election of future Academicians; this method "would ensure the best representation of all the Russian scientific forces in the Academy."[47] For unknown reasons, Mendeleev chose not to publish this memorandum.

Actually, Mendeleev had lost the election by one vote. He would have been elected if all the Russian Academicians had voted in his favor; but K. S. Veselovskii, Permanent Secretary of the Academy, had voted against him not on scholarly grounds but from the fear that Mendeleev would have supported Butlerov's growing criticism of the Academy. It was popular, however, to think that Mendeleev was the victim of a foreign conspiracy alone. Whatever the details of the Mendeleev affair, it became an event of national significance and gave the Russian scientific community added unity and dedication. The resulting nationalist outburst of Russian scholarship hastened the nationalization of the Academy of Sciences. Eventually the national bias of the Academy lost ground in turn, as a new social and ideological bias began to assert itself. The new generation became less concerned with the national composition of the Academy, and instead labored to make membership in it open to all Russian scholars of acknowledged accomplishment, regardless of their ideological positions and social background. The nationalism of the Russian scientific community was not nurtured by blind demands for a Russian science isolated from the broader world of science, but by a profound desire for more extensive Russian participation in the world of scholarship, which could best be achieved through a more rational and effective mobilization of native talent.

The popular pressure on scholars to write in the Russian language opened the gates of scientific scholarship to many young men from the middle and lower classes. However, the same pressure tended to reduce the value of science as a source of international prestige, since very few foreign scholars could read Russian. This was a serious problem, for Russian scientists were as eager to reach the world of scholarship outside Russia as they were to ensure a wide circulation for their ideas at home. At the Fifth Congress of Russian Naturalists and Physicians, Mendeleev stated that since most foreign scholars did not speak Slavic languages, "much of our work is lost to science"; he urged that summaries of the current work of Russian scientists be published in foreign languages.[48] The Congress had no financial resources to carry out Mendeleev's recommendation, but the growing productivity of Russian scientists could not but make a favorable impression in the West. In 1883 Sechenov wrote that summaries of the papers presented at meetings of the Russian Physical and Chemical Society were regularly dispatched by English, French, German, and Italian correspondents to their respective chemical societies.[49] The first systematic publication of summaries of Russian scientific works in any Western language was inaugurated in France in 1886, a tangible acknowledgment of the growing Western interest in Russian scientific scholarship.[50]

Competition between nations for priority in scientific discoveries is as old as modern science. However, it did not become a part of Russian culture until the 1860's, when the national consciousness of Russian scientists was rising and when more and more of them were undertaking pioneering research of broader theoretical significance. The problem of priorities took many forms and shapes. A. P. Borodin—best known as a composer—did not like F. A. Kekulé's claim that the theoretical insight behind Borodin's experimental study of valeraldehydes had been derived from Kekulé's own work. But Borodin, more reticent than most scholars, expressed his unhappiness only in a few personal letters to his wife. Butlerov's attempts to ascertain the priority of his theory of chemical structure led his disciples, particularly Markovnikov, into an emotionally charged campaign against Kekulé, whose pioneering work had helped lay the foundations of structural chemistry. Mendeleev's struggle to disprove claims that Lothar Meyer and/or J. A. Newlands were the real discoverers of the periodic law of elements assumed even wider proportions. In defending the priority of their discoveries, Borodin, Butlerov, and Mendeleev fought for "Russian science" as much as they fought for personal honors. They very seldom allowed themselves to transgress the boundaries of academic propriety, and fought their individual battles by carefully reconstructing the genesis and inner logic of their novel ideas and identifying the place of these ideas in the relevant currents of scientific thought.

I. I. Mechnikov's relentless attack on Karl Rudolf Leuckart, the eminent German parasitologist, was quite a different instance of rivalry. As a student at Giessen University, Mechnikov conducted an intensive and successful study of the phenomenon of alternating free-living and parasitic generations in roundworms (Nematoda); he worked very closely with Leuckart, who was interested in the same problem. In 1866 Mechnikov publicly accused Leuckhart of having published Mechnikov's findings as his own. Supposedly, Mechnikov went so far as to publish a pamphlet putting the label of thief on his teacher.[51] Nobody will ever know the exact degree of veracity in these accusations. Only one thing is certain: Mechnikov was lucky in having the opportunity to work with such a scientific giant as Leuckart, who helped him realize his own talents. The incident did not detract from the grandeur of Leuckart's scientific work, nor did it stand in the way of Mechnikov's rise to enviable heights of scientific achievement.

The priority squabbles were for the most part relatively mild, and did not prevent Mechnikov, Butlerov, and Mendeleev from recognizing the debt Russia owed to Western scientists. These men particularly praised the German scholars, who had opened their laboratories to Russians and contributed so much to the growth of modern scientific thought in Russia.

The social homogeneity of Russian scientists contributed tangibly to the internal unity of the scientific community. More than 80 per cent of the leading scientists came from the nobility, from affluent commercial families, or from the families of well-placed bureaucrats. In a sense, the 1860's and 1870's were the period of "repentant noblemen" in science as much as in literature and other expressions of intellectual endeavor. For all practical purposes, the world of the scholar was an independent enclave in the dwindling orbit of aristocratic Russia; but owing to the temper of the time, these scientist-aristocrats were dedicated more to the democratic spirit of science than to the exclusive rights of noble estates. The fact that most of them came from the lower rungs of the higher estates brought them into close and sympathetic contact with the new "men of action"—the fermenting and uncrystallized "class" of *raznochintsy*. University students showed a similar pattern: during the middle 1860's two-thirds of the students came from high-status families, but they "betrayed" the cause of the nobility by spearheading a widespread libertarian movement.

The absence of feuding philosophical schools in scientific scholarship also aided the inner unity of the Russian scientific community, whose basic orientation was a quiet, unelaborated, and unarticulated philosophical materialism. The more contentious defenders of philosophical realism operated outside the realm of science. In Russia, as in Western Europe, this was a time of change: vitalism ceased to be considered a part of positive knowledge; the theory of evolution removed teleology from the province of science; psychology was linked with physiology, and physiology with chemistry. The echoes of Maxwell's effort to formulate a complete picture of the mechanical unity of the world reached Russia, as did the news of Claude Bernard's endeavors to subordinate the data of physiology to the universal laws of matter and the calculable precision of the experimental method. At the same time, Darwin's biological theory brought forth a new "creative thought": in the words of Helmholtz, widely disseminated in Russia, Darwin showed "how the adaptability of structure in organisms can result from a blind rule of a law of nature, without any intervention of intelligence."[52] Immediately afterward, Thomas Huxley propounded "the relations of man to the lower animals." Materialism was written deeply into every science, and there was little need to make it a subject of explicit discussion. Materialism was a source of unlimited scientific optimism: it nurtured a belief in the potential omniscience of science, in man's limitless ability to accumulate understanding of the laws of matter and relate them to the laws of the universe.

In 1872 Emil du Bois-Reymond, one of the greatest physiologists of his age, delivered the famous lecture "On the Limits of the Knowledge of Nature" before a gathering of German naturalists and physicians in Leipzig. He proclaimed that in approaching "the enigma of the material world" the scientist had long been accustomed to saying "we do not know [*ignoramus*], but hope to learn"; on the other hand, in approaching the enigma of what matter and force actually are, the scientist had confessed "we will never know [*ignorabimus*]."[53] The speech was of epochal significance: it introduced phenomenological relativism into science, and challenged the limitless potentialities of a science based on the cumulative study of matter and force. It began a war on scientific materialism and mechanism—a war declared not by a professional philosopher but by a great and influential scientist.

The words of Du Bois-Reymond reverberated throughout the scientific world of the West. The speech was immediately published in a French translation by the *Revue scientifique de la France et de l'étranger*, and in an English translation by the American *Popular Science Monthly*. The Russian scientists themselves were not sufficiently impressed with Du Bois-Reymond's pronouncements to comment on them and translate them into Russian. However, the essay did not go unnoticed in Russia. True to the spirit of the time, a Russian translation was published by the religious journal *Orthodox Review*. Whatever the motives of the *Review* editors might have been, the publication of Du Bois-Reymond's paper foreshadowed the beginning of an intensified struggle between the scientific and nonscientific orientations.[54] However, for the time being it brought no harm to the blissful tranquillity that ruled supreme in the Russian scientific community. The struggle between the "idealists" and "materialists" in the house of science was not avoided, but it was postponed.

In Russia, the scientific community was in nearly unanimous agreement on what constituted the essential characteristics of modern science. The strength of science, said Mendeleev, is in hypotheses and "doctrines," not in the mere accumulation of empirical data. He spoke for his colleagues when he said that the more theoretically advanced a science is, the more useful it is as a source of practical knowledge. According to V. O. Kovalevskii, science that is limited to purely descriptive knowledge "should not be called science, for this term presupposes laws and their theoretical elaborations."[55] Indeed, Mendeleev and Kovalevskii echoed Louis Pasteur's cogent pronouncements: that "without theory, practice is no more than the routine given by habit"; that "theory alone can bring forth and develop the spirit of invention"; and that there are no such categories as theoretical science and applied science, but only "science and the application of science."[56] A. Iu. Davidov, a founder of the Moscow Mathematical Society, stated in 1869: "Even though practical application is the ultimate aim of all scientific knowledge, the sciences must not be bound by this goal. Scholars who are guided by the idea of practical utility seldom see their toils crowned by success. The only true aim of science is the search for the laws of nature."[57] In its vision of what Pasteur called the culture of science, the Russian scientific community was one with its Western European counterparts.

The real strength of the Russian scientific community was in its many ties with society at large, as testified by the swelling private donations to the Academy of Sciences, universities, and learned societies, the increased circulation of scientific journals, the incipient interest of industrial entrepreneurs in financing selected research projects, and the overflowing assemblages of curious citizens who gathered to listen to lectures on scientific themes and to view scientific exhibits. In 1869 the *St. Petersburg News* made the following comment on Professor E. V. Pelikan's public lectures on various physiological themes: "Not long ago the teaching activity of professors was limited to small circles of students, and the ideas developed by professors could not reach society at large. Now we are witnessing the beginning of an epoch of strong desire for scientific knowledge in a wide cross section of the population. Bright thoughts illuminate our social life, free words are coming from universities, and the professors face an audience made up not of selected groups but of all contemporary society."[58]

Unswayed by rosy journalistic accounts, Markovnikov noted in 1879 that Russia still needed much effort to ensure a sound link between science and society.[59] He did not intend to minimize either the growing cultural depth of Russian science or the profound importance of pure theory but to note the lack of more fruitful and mutually beneficial ties between a particular science (chemistry) and a particular branch of industry. Though reminding his countrymen that the ultimate value of science is judged in terms of its practical usefulness and tangible contributions to national strength and well-being, he noted that in order to be socially useful science must aim simultaneously at theoretical enrichment and practical application. He made it eminently clear that the new industrial entrepreneur did no more than apply the mounting knowledge acquired in scientific laboratories. Mendeleev, writing on the same theme, stated that the "mechanical" industry, based on changing the shape of various substances, was being supplemented by the "chemical" industry—the industry of the future—based on the transformation of substances themselves. The "mechanical" industry had its historical roots in artisanship, whereas the "chemical" industry depended completely on modern science.

In 1884, K. A. Timiriazev stated candidly that despite the great upsurge of scientific interest in Russia since the end of the Crimean War, the ties between science and society were not yet firm enough. In Russia, he said, one could not as yet encounter "a member of Parliament who today speaks at a public meeting in favor of a reform and tomorrow is ready to present a paper on the habits of bees and ants to the members of a learned society."[60]

## CHAPTER FOUR

# The Life Sciences

Darwin's theory of evolution, introduced to Russia in 1861, was enthusiastically received by a wide assortment of intellectuals, ranging from biological laboratory investigators to the most dedicated Nihilists. The reasons for this immediate success are not difficult to pinpoint. In the first place, Russia in the 1860's did not have as strong an antitransformist tradition as did the Western European countries, particularly France, the homeland of Cuvier.[1] Even the Russian theologians produced no strong, organized opposition to Darwinism until the middle 1870's. A famous embryologist noted in 1883: "In Western Europe Darwin's theory was opposed by firmly established traditions, but in Russia it was received with great sympathy. This theory arrived in Russia during a time of social upheaval and was quick to acquire full citizenship rights. It is still highly regarded."[2]

Russia was ideologically ready to absorb the full impact of Darwinian thought. Because Russia was in the throes of intense social ferment, and because a solid core of high officials were dedicated to change, Darwin's ideas of evolution were compatible with the spirit of the Reform era. The Nihilists and their ideological allies immediately gave evolutionism a prominent place in their attacks—mostly indirect and implicit—on the official ideology, which regarded the key autocratic institutions and values as timeless. M. A. Antonovich noted many years later that the "men of the sixties," dominated by "an unselfish search for knowledge" and a keen appreciation of the natural sciences, were particularly attracted to Darwinism because it had "a broad philosophical base," it explained a general biological phenomenon simply and naturally, it was sustained "by a mass of facts from all the natural sciences," and it was supported by many leaders of contemporary science.[3]

Pre-Darwinian transformism had been expressed in the works of several leading Russian naturalists, mostly in Lamarckian terms. K. F. Rouillier in general biology, G. E. Shchurovskii in geology, L. S. Tsenkovskii in microbiology, and N. A. Severtsov in ecology were all favorably impressed with the concept of evolution. In 1860, before Darwin's ideas reached Russia, the *Russian Messenger* printed an article by the youthful A. N. Beketov entitled "Harmony in Nature." Writing in the Lamarckian spirit, Beketov argued that the law of a double adaptation of species—the functional adaptation of an organism's parts to the organism as an indivisible whole and the further adaptation of the whole to the surrounding environment—is the law that governs the gradual transformation of the living world and determines the survival of individual species.[4] The essence of his argument was that nature is subject to constant, universal change; and that this change is not whimsical but takes place according to regular laws of nature. Beketov's article, the crowning point of the pre-Darwinian evolutionary tradition in Russia, showed that Russia was intellectually ready for evolutionary biology.

The first Russian comment on the ideas presented by *The Origin of Species* was printed in 1860 in the *Journal of the Ministry of National Education*, a publication read primarily by gymnasium teachers and traditionally dedicated to safeguarding official ideology from the possible corrupting influences of modern scientific theories. The unsigned comment consisted primarily of a Russian translation of a paper by Sir Charles Lyell on the artifacts found in post-Pliocene deposits. Although Lyell read his paper before the appearance of *The Origin of Species*, he referred to the forthcoming publication of Darwin's work, and to the scientific revolution that he expected to come in its wake. The Russian commentator appended a short criticism of the "metaphysical" views of H. G. Bronn, a famous German zoologist and paleontologist, on the general laws governing the development of the organic world.[5]

The *Library for Reading*, a relatively conservative journal, published the first Russian popular summary of Darwin's ideas in 1861. The anonymous writer disagreed with some philosophical implications of the theory of biological evolution, but gave a detailed, careful, and generally favorable survey of the main arguments set forth in *The Origin of Species*. He thought that Darwin had successfully transformed "teleology" from an obscure metaphysical presupposition to a useful scientific concept. He also noted that Darwin's "brave search for a grand understanding of the universe" could not but increase man's power to "remake" nature, particularly in the organic world.

S. A. Rachinskii, a professor of plant physiology at Moscow University, was the first member of the scientific community to help disseminate Darwin's ideas in Russia. In addition to having written a score of articles on natural-history themes for the *Messenger of the Natural Sciences*, a popular journal edited by Professor K. F. Rouillier, Rachinskii had translated into Russian *The Plant and Its Life* by M. J. Schleiden, *The Physiology of Common Life* by G. H. Lewes, and *The Glaciers of the Alps* by John Tyndall. A personal interest in evolutionary thought attracted him to Darwin's theory. He was the first Russian translator of *The Origin of Species* (1864), and the first Russian scholar to publish a detailed essay on Darwin's contributions to modern biology. He presented Darwin's evolutionary idea as the crowning point in the development of modern science; and it was certainly true that the Russian publication of Darwin's work marked the beginning of modern biological thought in Russia.[6]

In the 1860's and 1870's three groups of interpreters of Darwin's theory tried to reach a wider audience. The first was made up of Nihilists like D. I. Pisarev and M. A. Antonovich, who approved of Darwinism as a scientific theory fastened to a materialist philosophy. It also included young scientists like K. A. Timiriazev and I. I. Mechnikov, who wrote popular essays on the Darwinian theory and its relations to philosophical thought. The second group, which also included scholars, defended the scientific soundness of Darwin's ideas but sought to prove that Darwinism did not necessarily support philosophical materialism. A. P. Bogdanov was a typical representative of this orientation. The third group consisted of intellectuals who condemned Darwinism for its alleged scientific shortcomings, atheistic bent, and ethical relativism. M. N. Katkov, a stubborn defender of the aristocratic ideology, gathered some of the adherents of this school around the *Russian Messenger*, a conservative journal that he edited.

N. D. Nozhin belonged to the large group of young Russians who were inspired by the scientific value of Darwin's work and were convinced that all the cardinal problems treated by biology had a direct bearing on the workings of society.[7] According to Nozhin, only a social science anchored in biology could resolve "the conflict in human society between those who work and those who live from the work of others," and could serve as a guidepost for the solution of other equally complex problems.[8] As a practical effort, he produced a Russian translation of Fritz Müller's *Für Darwin*, which stimulated the first evolutionary studies of invertebrates and the emergence of evolutionary embryology. Inspired by Müller's work, Nozhin spent some time in Naples, where he studied the evolutionary growth of coelenterates (primarily medusas), summing up his findings in a scholarly paper published by the St. Petersburg Academy of Sciences. Although he accepted Darwinism as a great step forward in biology, Nozhin denied that the struggle for existence was the supreme law of organic evolution. To him, the cooperation of "similar individuals" was the main source of both biological and social evolution, whereas the conflict between "dissimilar species" was a "pathological" phenomenon. With his emphasis on the progressive affirmation of individual "wholeness" and the growing complexity of cooperation, Nozhin foreshadowed the Populist sociology later advanced by N. K. Mikhailovskii and P. L. Lavrov.[9]

Dmitrii Pisarev was not interested in conducting empirical research in evolutionary biology, nor in translating Darwinism into the precepts of a socialist ideology. He simply wanted his countrymen, regardless of their scientific sophistication, to grasp the full breadth of the intellectual revolution wrought by Darwin's ideas. The Darwinian theory, according to him, helped modern man understand a whole new world of universal causal relationships between natural phenomena. "In nearly all branches of natural science Darwin's ideas have brought about a complete revolution: botany, zoology, anthropology, paleontology, comparative anatomy and physiology, and even experimental psychology have found in his discoveries the guiding principle that will integrate the numerous observations already made and put investigators on the way to new fruitful discoveries."[10] Pisarev was interested in Darwinism primarily as a new triumph of rationalism, a new philosophical orientation antagonistic to every kind of metaphysics.

Darwin's *Descent of Man* was published in 1871; in the same year three Russian translations of this work appeared almost simultaneously. This event stirred up M. P. Pogodin, a relic from the era of official nationalism, to write an article against Darwinism in 1873 and to attempt the consolidation of Russian anti-Darwinists. Pogodin was 73 years old when he began his crusade. He was modern enough to recognize the scientific merit of the evolutionary theory, but he felt that this was more than outweighed by its negative influence on religion. The anti-Darwinist crusade did not reach high intensity until the 1880's, and culminated in the work of N. Ia. Danilevskii and N. N. Strakhov. The foes of Darwinism, when they finally appeared in strength, operated on three fronts: some attacked it on religious grounds, others on moral grounds; and still others tried to show the intrinsic weaknesses in its scientific method and theoretical generalizations. Theologians dominated the first group, journalists the second, and conservative scientists the third. All these controversies, however, were puny when compared with the general attitude of the times. In the Russia of the 1860's Darwinism was widely accepted as an idea giving unity to all the sciences of life, a new philosophical orientation, and a call to social action. Among scientists, it was viewed primarily as a theoretical challenge and a pathway to new empirical knowledge. For its empirical proofs, the evolutionary idea depended primarily on three highly specialized sciences that count Russian scholars among their most prominent researchers: embryology, paleontology, and comparative anatomy.

### THE BROTHERS KOVALEVSKII AND I. I. MECHNIKOV

Aleksandr Onufrievich Kovalevskii dedicated his life to verifying evolution as a law of nature and a source of new scientific knowledge.[11] He began his higher education by enrolling in the Institute of Communications, an aristocratic school that placed virtually no emphasis on liberal education; dissatisfied with its curriculum limitations and general regimentation, he soon transferred to St. Petersburg University and enrolled in the Faculty of the Physical and Mathematical Sciences (which also embraced all the biological sciences). His training was general and interdisciplinary, as was customary at the time. In 1862 Kovalevskii graduated with distinction, having added two years of foreign study at the universities of Tübingen and Heidelberg to his education in Russia. His contemporaries remembered both his dedication to scholarship and his identification with the great movement toward a social and intellectual emancipation of Russia. He was very much aware of the ideological and sociological implications of Darwinism, and was personally acquainted with Bakunin and Nozhin, who were inclined to see in the theory of biological evolution a model for a future socialist society. But his temperament and scholarly dedication made him inactive in the world outside academic life; he was an academic man of as pure a cast as his times would allow. The spirit of reform dominated the intellectual climate in which he worked, but it did not dictate the scientific standards of his research. It is primarily for his enthusiastic dedication to science that the mathematician Sof'ia Kovalevskii labeled him a "towering Nihilist."[12]

Several intellectual influences shaped Kovalevskii's interest in the field of embryology. Russia has a long tradition of thought in this area, and such men as Caspar Wolff, Christian Pander, and Karl von Baer, all members of the St. Petersburg Academy, are almost synonymous with the history of pre-evolutionary embryology. Kovalevskii admired the grandeur of this pioneering work, especially that of von Baer. However, L. S. Tsenkovskii's inspiring lectures in microzoology and a thorough drilling in microscopy, both encountered at the University, probably exerted a more direct influence. In Germany, Kovalevskii had the good fortune to work with H. G. Bronn, the German translator of *The Origin of Species*, from whom he learned that the concept of biological evolution, if it were not to become a stultifying dogma, must be treated as a hypothesis requiring vigorous scientific verification. In 1864, he read Fritz Müller's *Für Darwin*, which deals with the growth of the Crustacea and is cast in evolutionary terms. This book almost certainly helped Kovalevskii decide to make evolutionary embryology his true vocation.[18] Finally, in selecting the lancelet (*Amphioxus*) as the first object of his research, Kovalevskii was undoubtedly influenced by his German teachers H. A. Pagenstecher and K. R. Leuckart, who had conducted a joint study of the morphology and development of this marine species. To these multiple influences, Kovalevskii added his personal qualities: a proclivity for thoroughness in research, a sense for methodical work, and enormous patience and perseverance. His embryological work started in Naples in 1863 and lasted until the late 1880's, when his attention turned to functional-morphological studies of invertebrates.

Kovalevskii arrived in Naples well aware that embryology, one of the most important divisions of natural history, had not yet adduced sufficient and satisfactory information to support evolution as a general natural law. At that time, the Darwinists were turning to embryology in search of a common pattern in the embryonic development of all animal species. If such a pattern existed, it would provide incontrovertible proof for the basic idea of evolutionism: the common origin of the earth's entire fauna. Von Baer's studies had implied a common plan in the embryonic development of all vertebrates. The basic question facing the evolutionists was whether there was a universal developmental plan covering both vertebrates and invertebrates.

Kovalevskii made lancelets the first object of his embryological study because they were believed by scholars to occupy a place in the taxonomic twilight between the vertebrates and invertebrates; at the time, *Amphioxus* was generally considered a fish-like vertebrate. In his magister's dissertation, defended at St. Petersburg University in 1865, Kovalevskii presented the findings of his embryological study of lancelets, crowned by his conclusion that these organisms actually belonged to a subtype of Cephalocordata, the taxonomic group nearest to the vertebrates. He opened a new gate for the development of embryology by showing that the embryos of lancelets follow the pattern common to the invertebrates in the earlier phases of their development, but that they resemble the vertebrates during the later phases. Kovalevskii's defense of his dissertation was widely noted by Russian scholars, and it also found an echo in public opinion. Karl von Baer, then 73 years of age, hastened to congratulate Kovalevskii for his "first-class study," even though he thought that the evolutionary ideas of the young scholar were strictly hypothetical. Kovalevskii did not choose to answer von Baer, but he knew—even though he did not state it explicitly—that his dissertation was actually an effort to expand von Baer's embryological theory so that it would account for the developmental unity of the animal kingdom in a manner consistent with Darwinian evolution.

Kovalevskii's research in Naples was not limited to lancelets; his investigation of ascidians provided the information for his doctoral dissertation, which he defended in 1867. He showed that ascidians, at that time usually included in the Mollusca, were actually a group closely related to the vertebrates. Relying mostly on a comparative study of the embryonic growth of lancelets and ascidians, he concluded that such basic processes of embryonic growth as germ-layer formation and gastrulation are common to all animals. Darwin himself later acknowledged Kovalevskii's study: "If we may rely on embryology, ever the safest guide in classification, it seems that we at last gained a clue to the source whence the Vertebrata were derived.... We should then be justified in believing that at an extremely remote period a group of animals existed resembling in many respects the larvae of our present ascidians, which diverged into two great branches—the one retrograding in development and producing the present class of ascidians, the other rising to the crown and summit of the animal kingdom by giving birth to the Vertebrata."[14]

Kovalevskii returned to the study of lancelets and ascidians several times; each time he further improved his research techniques and gave additional support to his conclusions. His embryological studies covered many other animal forms, always selected on theoretical grounds. He studied ctenophores—the most complex of the animals that develop only the first two germ layers—with the idea of discovering the rudimentary characteristics of triploblastic animals.[15] He studied worms and arthropods to find out whether their embryonic growth could be explained in terms of the theory of germ layers. Specific embryological and anatomic problems likewise led him to painstaking studies of *Balanoglossus*, the Brachiopoda, and the Coelenterata. The general ideas of biological evolution and the common origin of all animal species were firmly embedded in Kovalevskii's thinking; but much of his investigation was concerned with specific problems related to the patterns of embryonic growth in individual animal species, and he often shed new light on the related problems of taxonomy, anatomy, and morphology. In the words of one of his eminent disciples and colleagues, "the theory of evolution was the main impulse of his entire activity." To Kovalevskii, Darwin's evolutionism was not only a great idea in need of substantive verification but also a path to new sources of biological knowledge.

As a professor, Kovalevskii was successively affiliated with the universities of Kazan, Kiev, Odessa, and St. Petersburg. In every community he found secondary academic interests: helping to establish and maintain a naturalist society, searching for unique local invertebrates, and conducting entomological surveys. As a teacher at Kiev University, he did much to modernize the zoological museum and the comparative anatomy laboratory. He participated in the Third Congress of Russian Naturalists and Physicians held in Kiev in 1871, and for a time served as chairman of the Kiev Society of Naturalists. All these activities, however, were incidental distractions from his main interests in comparative embryology.

Although quiet and retiring, Kovalevskii had many contacts with the Western world of scholarship. He traveled extensively in search of new, challenging subjects for embryological inquiry; he corresponded with Darwin and other leaders of modern evolutionary biology; he adduced new material calling for a revision of some of the more important ideas of C. Kupfer, an eminent German scholar; and he cooperated with the French embryologist A. F. Marion on a study of "the embryogenetic history" of coral polyps.

As a founder of modern comparative embryology, Kovalevskii shared honors with I. I. Mechnikov. The two embryologists, each in his early twenties, met in Naples in 1865, both attracted by an interest in the embryology of Mediterranean fauna. In 1888, on the occasion of a jubilee conference in his honor, Kovalevskii stated: "In all my studies I went hand in hand with my comrade and working associate I. I. Mechnikov. We constantly exchanged thoughts; and at the present gathering, at which you have praised my work, I would appreciate it if you would remember him too."[16] In temperament the two were opposites: Kovalevskii was a shy, retiring man who felt at ease only in the isolation of his research; Mechnikov was a man of fiery temperament, constantly on the lookout for academic skirmishes. But in fame, enthusiasm for science, and scholarly achievement they were very similar, though they adopted very different approaches to their subject.

Kovalevskii paid such close attention to the precise, logical presentation of details that he had little time to formulate generalizations and to take a broader view of his discipline. He was led to important conclusions, but these were stated with the maximum economy in words and were mostly implicit. E. Ray Lankester, an eminent British scientist, said of Kovalevskii: "His writings are singularly free from generalizing theory.... His delight and his power lay in the making and recording of exact observations destined to build up our understanding of animal structure on a sound basis."[17] It was Kovalevskii who recommended that Kazan University's Society of Naturalists adopt the motto *In specialibus generalia quaerimus*. Mechnikov, by contrast, combined a meticulous regard for details with a flair for generalization and a lively writing style. In 1866 he produced a lengthy critical essay on the origin of species, the philosophical implications of the idea of evolution, and the types of current evolutionary research. He stressed the need for a more precise definition of such concepts as the struggle for existence, natural selection, and transformation.[18] Though accepting Darwinian evolutionism, he was reluctant to accept the struggle for existence as a motive force in the development of both the organic world and human society.[19]

Kovalevskii wrote chiefly to record the findings of his research. Mechnikov often clarified his ideas by turning his verbal guns on the leading embryologists (and biologists in general) with whose ideas he happened to disagree. Such luminaries of the time as A. Kölliker, F. M. Balfour, E. Haeckel, and E. R. Lankester were among his main targets. Kovalevskii believed that science and politics do not, and cannot, exist in absolute isolation from each other; but he never elaborated on this idea in either a formal speech or a published paper, although he briefly acknowledged the "political" fact that the rational orientation of science was the best source of social optimism and the only path that could lead Russia into the family of civilized nations.[20] Mechnikov shared Kovalevskii's faith in rationalism, but he was a vociferous advocate of the full separation of science and politics. He also had initial doubts about several details of Kovalevskii's claim that the embryonic development of vertebrates and invertebrates was identical; in 1865 he attacked Kovalevskii's magister's thesis and went on to publish an article enumerating its unsubstantiated scientific claims. Nevertheless, the two men became great friends, and the area of their disagreement gradually became of minor importance. Many factual details in the work of the two scientists do not pass the rigorous test of modern embryological research, but their contributions to the scientific recognition of evolution as a universal process must go unchallenged.

At first Mechnikov concentrated his own research on the embryonic growth of such marine invertebrates as cephalopod mollusks, starfish, sea urchins, sponges, coelenterates, and crustaceans; later he also examined a variety of insect life. His initial studies were of uneven quality: some were hastily prepared, but others showed the marks of accomplished scholarship and great imagination. His classical work on the embryology of the Echinodermata contained detailed information on the embryonic growth of several different species, and he was able to make cogent suggestions for taxonomy.[21] Even while continuing comparative-embryological studies of germ layers, Mechnikov shifted his main interest to the more complex theoretical questions related to the genealogy of animal organisms. This led him to study the earliest phases in the embryonic growth of sponges, the lowest division of multi-celled animals, in hopes of determining the origin of the higher Metazoa. Mechnikov's first major work in comparative embryology, *Embryological Studies of the Medusae*, was greeted by Kovalevskii as a capital work in the field, excelling not only in its presentation of rich new scientific material but also in its critical elucidation of previously accumulated knowledge.[22] This study gave a vivid and heavily documented expression to Kovalevskii's and Mechnikov's claim for the universality and homology of germ layers.

In the early 1880's Mechnikov's scientific work underwent a radical change. The switch came as a logical result of the growing depth of his embryological work, together with his increasing realization that comparative embryology alone could not provide a full understanding of the biological unity of the animal kingdom. In 1883, in a study of intracellular digestion in the invertebrates, he concluded that a number of essential problems of metazoan genealogy could be understood only by studying the "physiological history" of organs.[23] Much of embryology, he said, dealt with organs either in an atrophied state or in the process of formation and ignored their normal functioning. He established that intracellular digestion is characteristic of a great number of invertebrates; and that the digestive functions are performed by phagocytes, the most important of which are mesodermal cells, derived from the mesoderm in the process of embryonic development. But, Mechnikov claimed, the function of the phagocytes is not limited to the digestion of food alone: they also envelop and digest certain parts of the larvae that have ceased to be functional. After a number of intricate experiments, he came forth with the thesis that phagocytes are capable of engulfing and digesting all extraneous matter; and that they ultimately perform a "prophylactic function" by destroying not only atrophied organs but also any injurious matter coming from outside, such as infectious germs.[24] With his explanation of phagocytosis Mechnikov formulated a cellular theory of immunity whose contributions to modern medicine are widely acclaimed. For the remainder of his long life he worked in comparative pathology, always building on the phagocytosis theory.

A few years after turning to the field of comparative pathology Mechnikov left Russia to join the Pasteur Institute in Paris. The reasons for his decision to leave Russia reveal the unfavorable conditions that hampered the scientific work of professors during the 1870's and 1880's, particularly in provincial universities. Although the work of both Mechnikov and Kovalevskii was widely noted in the West, both were overlooked by Moscow and St. Petersburg universities, and were forced to accept positions in the provinces.* Their scientific ideas were considered stylish and untested; and even their discipline, comparative embryology, was treated as secondary to histology, which provided a bond between physiology and anatomy. The Academy of Sciences, a leading force in scientific conservatism, preferred the well-established paths of scientific thought to the radical new approaches stimulated by Darwinism. Naturally enough, the research facilities provided in Moscow and St. Petersburg were unmatched by provincial institutions, which also had smaller libraries, fewer noted scholars, and an overabundance of petty academic intrigues. Kovalevskii's personal correspondence recorded the anguish and emptiness of life in Kazan and Kiev, and Mechnikov wrote a special article depicting the paralyzing effects of the unhealthy intellectual atmosphere in Odessa.[25]

Mechnikov was greatly disturbed by the growing efforts of the government to eliminate the concessions to academic community made by the 1863 statute. But he was even more disturbed by the constant student unrest that plagued the universities in the late seventies and early eighties. At this time some conservative intellectuals believed that the period of accelerated development in Russian scientific thought had given way to a period of apathy and general stagnation. Mechnikov did not belong to this group; however, he did not mix politics with science, and in view of the growing political upheaval in scientific centers he felt that he had no alternative but to leave the country. He noted subsequently: "My intimate acquaintance with Herzen's circle in Geneva and Bakunin's in Naples helped strengthen my determination to work in the field of science and my conviction that science would produce more good things for man than the game of politics."[26]

---

* Mechnikov's bid in 1869 for a position at the Medical and Surgical Academy in St. Petersburg did not materialize; he was a professor at Odessa University from 1870 to 1882; Kovalevskii taught at Kazan in 1868–69, at Kiev from 1869 to 1874, and at Odessa from 1874 to 1882.

Kovalevskii and Mechnikov both found life unpleasant in the oppressive climate of the provincial academic communities. However, they did not succumb to the harshness of this uninspiring environment, and during the seventies both published in profusion. They made many scientific trips to the Mediterranean and other places, and they continued to maintain productive contacts with Western European embryologists. In his *Treatise on Comparative Embryology*, published in London in 1880–81, Francis M. Balfour described the full scope of their rich work and integrated it with current Western scholarship.[27] By these activities, Kovalevskii and Mechnikov did much to transform their provincial universities into lively academic places with constantly climbing standards in both teaching and scientific inquiry. The two men overcame the limitations around them because to them, to use a phrase of Lankester's, science was a cult for which no sacrifice was too great and no difficulty too repellent.[28]

It was no accident that when Mechnikov resigned from his teaching position at Odessa in 1882, his place, on Kovalevskii's recommendation, was occupied by V. V. Zalenskii (known to Western scholars as W. Salensky), who had an impressive list of publications in comparative embryology and was widely known in the West. Zalenskii, too, was a dedicated evolutionist, and was interested in the study of homologies. His monographic studies, some of huge proportions, dealt with the embryonic growth of coelenterates, nemerteans, annelids, and mollusks.[29] He was especially noted by contemporaries for his original interpretation of the differentiation of the mesoderm. But Kovalevskii, Mechnikov, and Zalenskii between them covered essentially every branch of invertebrate embryology. For his distinguished contributions to comparative embryology, Zalenskii was elected a member of the St. Petersburg Academy of Sciences in 1897, seven years after a similar honor was paid to his friend Kovalevskii. Zalenskii was a strong link between early comparative embryology and its modern representatives; he was also among the last Russian embryologists to write scientific papers almost exclusively in German and French.

In *The Origin of Species,* Darwin stated that the final victory of the evolutionary theory was contingent on substantive support from paleontology, but not until this science accepted evolution as a working hypothesis. Soon after *The Origin of Species* was published, evolutionary paleontology became a flourishing discipline, which claimed among its pioneers T. H. Huxley in England, E. D. Cope and O. C. Marsh in the United States, and Albert Gaudry in France. In Russia, the chief researcher in this field was Aleksandr Kovalevskii's younger brother Vladimir.[30] Vladimir Kovalevskii was both a noble product and a tragic victim of his time. He championed the ideology of the Emancipation, which he distilled and purified by the philosophy of rationalism and modern scientific thought. In contrast to Mechnikov and Aleksandr Kovalevskii, he was as unsettled as the time in which he lived. When he committed suicide in 1883 at the age of 45, V. O. Kovalevskii had devoted only five years of his life to original scientific work; but what he produced during these short years was enough to place him among the founders of evolutionary paleontology.

At the age of twelve Vladimir entered a school of law, a six-year institution designed to train carefully selected children of noble origin for government service. In the eyes of his family, faced with rapidly dwindling economic resources, this school was the shortest and safest path to security for their younger son. But he did not like law, and showed an early interest in natural science, mostly under the influence of his older brother. During the late 1850's he was part of a group of young men—including N. V. Shelgunov, the poet M. L. Mikhailov, and the brothers A. N. and N. N. Beketov—who combined intellectual accomplishment with enthusiasm for the libertarian ideals of the Reform era. In the early 1860's he traveled in Western Europe, though as a tourist rather than as a student in search of formal education. He spent no time in Western libraries, but he met Russian émigrés. Under the influence of A. I. Herzen, he decided to go to Poland to stir up Polish opposition to Russian autocracy. This interest was short-lived, and Vladimir soon returned to Western Europe, where sustained work in libraries introduced him to the rapidly expanding world of modern natural science.

In 1863 Kovalevskii returned to St. Petersburg and plunged with the utmost enthusiasm into an ambitious program of publication. The books he offered were all translations, many of them his own, and their subjects ranged from physics, chemistry, and astronomy on one hand to sociology and history on the other. He favored works that heralded turning points in modern natural science and the philosophy of science. The translated works published by Kovalevskii were so broad and diversified that they could satisfy the curriculum of a liberal arts college. Russians could now read in their own language the works of Darwin, Huxley, Brehm, Lyell, Agassiz, Virchow, Kölliker, Vogt, Leuckart, Moleschott, and Mill.[31]

In the middle of this work, Kovalevskii took time out to go to Italy and join Garibaldi's staff as a correspondent of the *St. Petersburg News*. This interest was not a mere whim of Kovalevskii's mercurial personality, but part of a strong personal philosophy that combined the ideology of modern science with the search for emancipation from the evils of the past. He stated in 1866: "Science in general, and the natural sciences in particular, are dedicated to improving and raising the level of human and social life ... and, if they are not so oriented, they are not aware of their rational goals."[32]

In 1868 Kovalevskii married S. V. Korvin-Krukovskii—the famous Sof'ia Kovalevskii—and in 1869 the young couple left for Western Europe, where they remained, with short intermittent visits to Russia, until 1874. It was during this period that V. O. Kovalevskii wrote all his original scientific studies. His basic works, a series of monographs on the fossils of horses, were written in 1872–73.

After intensive and systematic preparatory work, Kovalevskii decided to study the evolution of horses from the late Eocene to the present time. Before he settled on this field, he had studied crystallography, mineralogy, geology, the embryology and paleontology of invertebrates, and the paleontology of vertebrates.[33] In 1871 he wrote to his brother: "I still do not know what independent research to undertake and when to start it; everything seems to indicate that at first I should engage in an intensive and detailed study of zoology, comparative anatomy, and ontogeny in order to acquire broader and more general views."[34] He felt that a modern study of fossils should aim at providing the accurate knowledge of animal forms and their transitions that was needed to explain the progressive evolution of living nature. He was determined to examine evolution as a universal law of nature; and he selected horses for study because of their wide geographical distribution, their present-day existence, their relatively long traceable history, and the abundance of their fossils. Although he was led into paleontology by the grand appeal of the evolutionary theory, Kovalevskii did not skimp on the tedious museum research that provided a broad empirical base from which to operate. By studying individual fossils deposited in various museums, he often gained new information leading to more precise paleontological interpretations.

In interpreting the data that finally enabled him to arrange fossil horses into a single line of development, Kovalevskii was guided by the principle that the form of each organ was determined by the function it performed, and that each change in function was caused by a change in the organic and inorganic environment. Kovalevskii considered the progressive reduction of the foot to be an important index of the evolution of horses, and made a clear distinction between inadaptive and adaptive reduction. In inadaptive reduction "inheritance is stronger than modification," whereas in adaptive reduction "modification keeps pace with inheritance."[35] Inadaptive reduction, he felt, had caused the extinction of entire genera.

Modern paleontologists claim that the present-day horse is not a lineal descendant of the fossil indicated by Kovalevskii, but they agree that he gave an essentially correct interpretation of the evolution of the horse's foot and dentition.[36] The American paleontologist George Gaylord Simpson calls Kovalevskii's study of the history of horses and other ungulates "one of the first and greatest triumphs of evolutionary paleontology." Noting that most of the phylogenetic details of Kovalevskii's studies were later found to be erroneous, Simpson nevertheless acknowledges that the Russian paleontologist "deciphered all the essentials of the structural development of the modern horse."[37] The greatest tribute paid to Kovalevskii's work came from another American scientist, H. F. Osborn. Referring to Kovalevskii's study on the classification of fossil ungulates, Osborn stated: "This work is a model union of the detailed study of form and function with theory and the working hypothesis. It regards the fossil not as a petrified skeleton, but as having belonged to a moving and feeding animal; every joint and facet has a meaning, each cusp a certain significance. Rising to the philosophy of the matter, it brings the mechanical perfection and adaptiveness of different types into relation with the environment, with changes of herbage, with the introduction of grass. In this survey of competition it speculates upon the causes of the rise, spread, and extinction of each animal group. In other words, the fossil quadrupeds are treated biologically—so far as it is possible in the obscurity of the past."[38]

Kovalevskii viewed the struggle for existence as the motive force of biological evolution; but unlike most Darwinists of his time, he rejected the notion of evolution as a unilinear process. Instead, he felt that the structural changes in the organic world represented an extraordinarily complex multilinear evolution, for only this fact could accurately explain the immense variety in the adaptive potentialities of the organic world.[39]

The popularity of Darwinism in Russia during the 1860's and 1870's was noted by many contemporaries. Darwin himself excitedly wrote to Sir Charles Lyell in 1867 that "a Russian who is translating my new book [*The Variation of Animals and Plants Under Domestication*] into Russian" had paid him a visit. From this man, Darwin learned that *The Antiquity of Man* had gone through several Russian printings; and that in Russia Buckle's *A History of English Civilization* had been republished six times and *The Origin of Species* four times.[40] The Russian referred to by Darwin was Vladimir Kovalevskii. Darwin presented him with a set of galley proofs of *Variation*, and by a quirk of technical circumstances the publication of the first volume of this work in Russian preceded the publication of the English original by some seven months.[41] Darwin's publishers in England waited for technicians to complete the engravings of illustrative material, but Kovalevskii "borrowed" illustrations from the Russian translation of A. E. Brehm's *The Life of Animals*, published one year earlier.

Though recognized and appreciated abroad, Kovalevskii was neglected by his own country. His translations during the 1860's, which spread the idea of evolution throughout Russia, made him suspect in the eyes of the authorities. Moreover, his connections with Herzen and other rebellious émigrés did not win him friends in official circles. He had no sponsors in the universities because he was not a product of the regular undergraduate training in Russia. He had not gone through tightly constructed programs under the viligant eyes of academic supervisors; he had not been selected by a university for postgraduate studies leading to a teaching appointment; and he had not received a government stipend to study in Western European universities. Neither the Academy of Sciences nor any of the universities offered him a permanent position. Eventually, he began to engage in business ventures that took him away from the world of science without giving him financial security.

In his last letter to his brother, Vladimir Kovalevskii wrote that a broader acquaintance with philosophy and ethics might have made his suffering less painful, for it would have given him a better understanding of the pitfalls of academic life. Implicitly, however, he recognized that most of his troubles stemmed from the deadening formalities adhered to by the Russian universities in the selection and training of future professors. His intellectual wandering had led him to bypass all these formalities, and no one can deny that he did so with success.

### IVAN SECHENOV

No Russian scholar has been regarded as a purer symbol of the spirit of the 1860's than Ivan Mikhailovich Sechenov, the great physiologist. He was a creator of his age as much as he was a product of it. He tied science to philosophy, and both to the realities of social life. Mechnikov observed that Sechenov's thought and action "came from the very depths of his soul"; and that although Sechenov's great perspicacity was the most impressive feature of his personality, he was also a man of tender heart and profound feeling.[42] It was precisely because of this combination of powerful intellect and altruistic sentiment that Sechenov became a towering figure in those areas of human activity where the most effective ties between science and society were sought. Sechenov's contributions to Russian science go far beyond his published work: he excelled as a teacher, a public lecturer, an ambassador of goodwill in the universities outside Russia, a spokesman for the younger generation of prominent Russian scientists, and a champion of equal education for both sexes and all estates.

Sechenov differed from Mechnikov, Zalenskii, and the Kovalevskii brothers in that he was more directly identified with the philosophy of scientific materialism and its social and ideological correlates; but, unlike Pisarev and Antonovich, he was not given to flowery prose, verbal pugnacity, or passionate condemnations of traditional values. His carefully weighted statements and dispassionate writing often confused the official censors, who learned to appreciate his use of circumspection and tightly woven logical arguments bolstered by experimental data. In 1866, for example, the censorship authorities called for court action against Sechenov on the ground that his "Reflexes of the Brain" was "an attempt to explain the psychical functions of the brain by reducing these functions to muscular movements produced in response to external material stimuli"; and that he was therefore treating "all human acts, without exception, as purely mechanical processes." Sechenov's "materialistic theory," said the censors, reduced "even the most human of all human endowments to the level of a machine devoid of consciousness and free will," which was un-Christian.[48] A year later, the court ruled that no action could be taken against Sechenov because his book did not transgress any law. An expression of materialistic ideas was not punishable by law if it was not accompanied by a direct attack on Christian beliefs and morality. Implicit in the court's ruling was an essentially correct appraisal of Sechenov as a scholar who had not succumbed to the lures of an antireligious philosophy and a revolutionary ideology, but had instead presented his physiological studies as undiluted science. Despite his many extracurricular diversions and obvious philosophical commitments, Sechenov was a scientist *par excellence*, and experimental skill was the backbone of his strength as a scientist.

Sechenov's life reflected and influenced the temper of the Reform era. More than any other life of his time, it gave the aspirations, achievements, and dilemmas of his generation a profound personal expression. It epitomized Russia's painful search for the intellectual tools of modern civilization, and vividly illustrated the work of a scientist in a society whose dominant values were torn by a widening conflict. In sum, Sechenov's life offers an important glimpse of Russia's intellectual resources at the beginning of the modern age.

Sechenov was born in 1829 in the village of Teplyi Stan, which was located in what was then Simbirsk province and is now the Gorky region. His father was a retired army officer of aristocratic origin, and his mother a peasant woman with an admixture of Kalmuk blood. Teplyi Stan was one of the rare Russian villages that produced a rich assortment of men of knowledge, and the *Reminiscences* of Academician A. N. Krylov portray life there in great detail. The western half of the village was inhabited by the Filatov family, which produced a score of leading humanistic scholars and writers; the eastern part belonged to the Sechenovs. Krylov was related to both families, and as a boy spent many summers in Teplyi Stan. Other relatives of the Sechenovs were Aleksandr, Sergei, and Boris Liapunov, who also spent summers in the village before they became men of prominence—Aleksandr as a mathematician, Sergei as a composer, and Boris as a linguist. Krylov's description of Teplyi Stan centers on the early 1870's, when Sechenov was widely known as a physiologist and exercised an electrifying influence on the young men who came in personal contact with him. Sechenov, on summer visits to his birthplace, would lecture his friends and neighbors on physiological topics. Young Krylov was particularly impressed with the lectures that Sechenov illustrated by dissecting frogs; he himself learned "about every organ of the frog," and was able, in turn, to lecture younger children on the subject.[44]

In 1843 Sechenov entered the Main Engineering School in St. Petersburg, a six-year military institution designed to give young men of noble birth a specialized education in an atmosphere "uncontaminated" by daily contact with lower social classes. In 1848 he was posted to an engineer battalion in Kiev with the rank of second lieutenant. He resigned after a year and a half of military service, and in 1851 enrolled in the Medical Faculty of Moscow University.* He liked the close ties of the university with the community, and was particularly impressed with T. N. Granovskii's public lectures on historical themes, which were designed to show the deeper meaning of history when viewed as a process rather than a chronicle of events. Sechenov

---

*In his autobiography, Sechenov noted that the daughter of his commanding officer had first made him aware of the intellectual challenges of Moscow University, and had influenced him to resign from the military and enter medicine. "I went to her house as a youth who had so far been swimming apathetically down the channel into which fate had thrown me, without a clear idea of where it might lead me. But I left her house with my life's plan prepared, knowing where to go and what to do. Who, if not she, rescued me from a situation that could have become a noose for me, showing me the possibility of leaving? To what, if not to her influence, was I obliged for going to the University to do that which she considered foremost—to study medicine and to help my fellow man?" Sechenov, *Avtobiograficheskie zapiski*, p. 37; see also Iaroshevskii, p. 21.

had kind words for the professors of the natural sciences, but was generally unimpressed with their research output and teaching skills. Many years later, he wrote that until 1860 Russian universities valued professors who were good orators much more than professors actively engaged in scientific research; and that a student could graduate in chemistry from Moscow University without ever having seen a chemical laboratory.[45]

Sechenov arrived at Moscow University at a time when Nicholas I, frightened by the revolutionary currents in Western Europe in 1848, was desperately trying to insulate Russia from all Western ideologies. Both students and professors were forbidden any advanced studies at Western universities. Strict censorship drastically reduced the influx of philosophical literature, and also suppressed entire branches of the natural and social sciences. The many anachronistic features of autocratic monarchism were constantly in evidence, and left an indelible impression on the students. The Crimean debacle and the death of Nicholas I gave rise to widespread popular demands for basic social changes and transformed the universities into centers of ideological and intellectual ferment. It was in this atmosphere that Sechenov graduated from Moscow University in 1856. For both scientific and ideological reasons, he decided to study physiology in the leading Western European centers of experimental science.

At that time the Russian intelligentsia were attracted to the works of Karl Vogt, Ludwig Büchner, and Jacob Moleschott, which, even though they were of doubtful scientific quality, provided the ideas necessary to challenge official ideology, orthodox religious thought, and idealistic metaphysics. When Hermann Helmholtz, Karl Ludwig, Emil du Bois-Reymond, and Ernst von Brücke produced theories that reduced physiology to applied physics and chemistry—a direct attack on vitalism—the Ministry of National Education became eager to entrust the teaching of physiology to men who fully endorsed the doctrine of a completely separate "matter" and "spirit," and who opposed all efforts to tie psychology to physiology. Philosophical dualism became the cornerstone of the official ideology, which viewed the spiritual life as a direct emanation from divine power, unobstructed by the laws of nature and history. However, by the time Sechenov had graduated, social critics like Dobroliubov and Chernyshevskii had opened a relentless journalistic campaign against this attitude—proposing, instead, to seek chemical interpretations of physiological phenomena and physiological explanations of psychological phenomena.

The difference between Dobroliubov and Chernyshevskii on the one hand and Sechenov on the other should be noted. All three were products of the social and intellectual conditions that gave momentum to the popular pressure for extensive social reform. But in the field of science the first two were amateurs who were more eager to build a materialistic ontology than to do justice to modern experimental science; and neither of them had much knowledge or appreciation of the meticulous and far-reaching experimental researches of Johannes Müller, Du Bois-Reymond, Helmholtz, and Ludwig, the scholars that Sechenov chose to study under in the West. In physiological knowledge and interests, Sechenov was a generation ahead of Dobroliubov and Chernyshevskii; he did share their philosophical views, but his strength was in experimental science.

Sechenov began his Western studies at the University of Berlin, where he attended the lectures of Johannes Müller in comparative anatomy, Emil du Bois-Reymond in animal electricity, Gustav Magnus in physics, and Heinrich Rose in chemistry. In addition, the physiologist Felix Hoppe-Seyler allowed Sechenov to use his laboratory to study the physiological effects of alcoholic intoxication, a grave national problem in Russia. This study led to Sechenov's first scientific paper, published in Rudolf Virchow's *Archiv für die pathologische Anatomie und Physiologie,* and later attracted him to Karl Ludwig's laboratory at Vienna for new investigations of the same general problem. In 1859 Sechenov found himself in Heidelberg, working under Hermann Helmholtz in physiology and R. W. Bunsen in chemistry. After short visits to several other leading laboratories, he returned to Russia in 1860. In a very short time he successfully defended his doctoral dissertation, again dealing with the physiology of alcoholic intoxication, at the Medical and Surgical Academy in St. Petersburg; he was immediately appointed an instructor at that school.

Sechenov recommended himself by his scholarly publications, but his fame had other sources of equal importance. The favorable publicity given to Lewes's *Physiology of Common Life,* published in a Russian translation in the early 1860's, played no small part in attracting Russian intellectuals to modern physiology and its experimental and philosophical orientations. In the general intellectual atmosphere, which greatly favored physiological thought, Sechenov stood out as an accomplished speaker and a master at conducting scientific experiments in the classroom. His audiences were impressed both by the ideological undertones of his lectures and by his skill in handling modern electrical apparatus while demonstrating the workings of the nervous and muscular systems.

In 1861, the Academician N. N. Zinin, impressed with Sechenov's work, offered to recommend him for the position of adjunct in the St. Petersburg Academy of Sciences. Sechenov declined, saying that he had not yet earned such a distinct honor. Instead, he chose to go to Paris and work in the laboratory of Claude Bernard, where he was able, for the first time, to conduct completely independent research with the most modern equipment. Here, on the basis of a series of experiments involving the correlation of nervous and muscular activities in frogs, Sechenov formulated his famous theory of central inhibition—that is, of the existence of special mechanisms in the central nervous system that when stimulated produce a suppression of spinal reflexes. This theory opened new avenues in physiological research, particularly in studying the coordination of reflex movements, and continued to attract the attention of experimental physiologists and physiological psychologists for many decades. It is the very cornerstone of the Pavlovian tradition in neurophysiology.[46] Sechenov wrote his study of reflex inhibition in German and dedicated it to Karl Ludwig, his friend and teacher. He concluded the paper with the statement that he did not intend his generalizations to include any animals other than frogs.[47]

Immediately after returning to St. Petersburg, Sechenov undertook to place his experimental findings in a broader setting. The first result was a lengthy semipopular essay entitled "An Attempt to Establish the Physiological Basis of Psychical Processes." The editors of *Contemporary*, to whom he first offered his manuscript, liked the paper, but the censors objected to it vehemently. However, because of Sechenov's unobtrusive style and matter-of-fact tone, the censors finally allowed the essay's publication, on the condition that it be placed in a scholarly journal and given a different title; it eventually appeared in the *Medical Messenger* in 1863, under the title "Reflexes of the Brain." Sechenov had received ample warning that his ideas would bring him into conflict with the censorial authorities and other protectors of official ideology. In 1860–61 the conservative *Russian Messenger* had published a series of articles on the incompatibility of experimental physiology with the precepts of Christian morality. In addition, Sechenov presumably knew that official harassment had forced his teacher Karl Ludwig to leave the University of Zurich and accept a position with the Medical and Surgical Academy in Vienna.[48]

"Reflexes of the Brain" extended the doctrine of central inhibitory mechanisms to cover all animals, including man. In this and several subsequent studies Sechenov was concerned primarily with establishing a physiological theory of psychical processes. The German physiologists of the time favored the reduction of physiology to applied physics and chemistry; Sechenov extended this idea by reducing psychology to applied physiology. He insisted that any scientific definition of an organism must also define the environment that influenced it, since the organism could not exist independently. The central idea of Sechenov's experiments was that the external stimulation of specific sensory elements accounted for the origin of all psychical phenomena. He asserted categorically that "the real cause of every human activity lies outside man."[49] In essence, he tried to give physiological proof of John Locke's empiricist dictum: *nihil est in intellectu quod non antea fuerit in sensu.* All of man's psychical activities, according to Sechenov, could be explained as reflexes, which could be explained, in turn, only by the physiology of the central nervous system. He claimed: "The time will come when men will be able to analyze the external manifestations of the functioning of the brain as easily as the physicist now analyzes a musical chord or the behavior of a freely falling body."[50]

Sechenov's basic contributions to science were in the physiology of nerve centers, and he continued to try new approaches and experimental techniques in search of a more precise explanation of the inhibitory functions of the brain. But his research covered a much wider area, and he produced papers like "The Pneumatics of the Blood," "The Fluorescence of Crystalline Lenses," and "An Essay on the Working Movements of Man." He was among the first neurophysiologists to recognize the ability of the nervous system to summarize subthreshold stimulations. His study of galvanic phenomena in the nervous activity of the frog helped inaugurate an intensive study of bioelectrical phenomena in the central nervous system. During the 1860's Sechenov made his contributions in the area where psychology meets physiology, for which he is mostly remembered today. The second phase of his research activity centered on the area where physiology meets chemistry. He formulated a theory of pulmonary air, and his research on the absorption of gases by salt solutions helped introduce more precise techniques in the study of cellular respiration. His concern with psychology during this period was of a more general and popular nature, but in *The Elements of Thought* (1878) he foreshadowed Pavlov's study of the role of sensory input in the formation of abstract notions of the external world. Sechenov published several textbooks, among which *Physiology of the Nervous System* (1866) was particularly well received; he also translated several Western textbooks into Russian.

Sechenov's lectures at the Medical and Surgical Academy were models of logical coherence and were always rich in content. More than a mere disseminator of knowledge, he placed his primary emphasis on the training of future scholars. Soon, most university chairs in physiology were filled by his disciples: V. V. Pashutin, I. R. Tarkhanov, P. A. Spiro, V. K. Voroshilov, B. F. Verigo, A. F. Samoilov, N. E. Vvedenskii, and several others.[51]

To the Nihilists and other foes of official ideology, Sechenov epitomized the growing movement for intellectual emancipation. It was not an accident that Bazarov, the hero of Turgenev's *Fathers and Sons*, was a medical student who studied physiology and was skilled in dissecting frogs. Gossip in St. Petersburg and Moscow had it that Kirsanov, the forward-looking hero of Chernyshevskii's *What Is to Be Done?*, was modeled on Sechenov.[52] Sechenov received much of the credit for opening the Medical and Surgical Academy to women, and for sending the first Russian women to study in Western European universities. V. O. Kovalevskii's Russian translation of Darwin's *Variation of Animals and Plants* came out under Sechenov's general editorship, as did an 1871 translation of *Descent of Man*.

Sechenov's popular lectures and writings brought him enemies as well as admirers. Censors, conservative professors, and reactionary journalists were constantly attacking him. Some, typified by Boris Chicherin, dismissed Sechenov as too perverse to see that "morality can never be derived from physiology."[53] Others merely tried to show that his writings, despite their scientific spirit and comparatively complex logic, represented an indirect but uncompromising attack on society and its sacred values. In 1871 the historian K. D. Kavelin published a book entitled *The Tasks of Psychology* with the primary purpose of bringing together and endorsing the negative criticisms of Sechenov's theory. He emphasized introspection as the only valid source of psychological knowledge, and attacked the deterministic nature of Sechenov's philosophy. The occasion, of course, only gave Sechenov a further opportunity to sharpen his arguments and clarify his thoughts. Mendeleev was among those who defended the scientific foundations of Sechenov's theory against attacks of this kind, claiming that modern neurophysiology "does not work against moral precepts but against superstitions."[54]

The successive decades saw the two camps irreconcilably split. At the beginning of the twentieth century, the growing ranks of neovitalists, theological anti-Darwinists, and all kinds of spiritualists viewed Sechenov's work as the mainstay of materialism and a source of inspiration for social rebels. The admirers and followers of Sechenov found their chief spokesman in I. P. Pavlov. In 1915, Pavlov could not attend a meeting of the Moscow

Scientific Institute commemorating the tenth anniversary of Sechenov's death, but he sent the following telegram: "Unable to be present personally, I will at least take part in the commemorative meeting by cable. Sechenov's teaching of the reflexes of the brain is, in my opinion, a sublime achievement of Russian science. The application of the reflex principle to explain the activity of the higher nervous centers is proof that causality can be applied to the highest forms of organic nature. For this reason, the name of Sechenov will forever remain dear to the Russian scientific world."[55] A decade earlier, Pavlov, then at the peak of his scientific achievement and influence, had announced that in his opinion Sechenov deserved the title "father of Russian physiology."*

Sechenov himself, writing in his autobiography, had also named a "father of Russian physiology": Karl Ludwig. Most leading Russian physiologists of the last quarter of the nineteenth century had worked in Ludwig's laboratories and under his supervision, and Sechenov felt that Russia owed a tremendous debt to this great German scholar, who seemed to have a special soft spot in his heart for Russian students. Ludwig was known internationally as an inspiring teacher of scientific research; and by the time he was an old man, one could point out as many as 300 active physiologists from every civilized nation who had been helped by him. He was "the teacher of teachers for the whole physiological world."[56] His special interest in Russian students may well have resulted from his close friendship with Sechenov, his first disciple from Eastern Europe, with whose scientific work, experimental dexterity, and theoretical daring he was very much impressed. The two men corresponded for many years, Ludwig usually reporting sentimentally on the achievements of young Russians working in his laboratory.

Sechenov patterned much of his life after Ludwig: both men avoided academic ceremonialism and showed a great distaste for administrative

* Pavlov made similar statements on several occasions, always with the greatest enthusiasm. In 1913, speaking before the members of the Society for the Moscow Scientific Institute, he reminded his audience that exactly fifty years had elapsed since the publication of "Reflexes of the Brain," which had set forth principles that later grew into "an immense force for directing the contemporary investigation of the brain." He then described its author as "the pride of Russian thought and the father of Russian physiology." (I. P. Pavlov, *Lectures*, p. 222.) Pavlov amplified these statements in 1923: "The most important motive for my decision [to undertake a study of conditioned reflexes], even though an unconscious one, arose out of the impression made upon me during my youth by the monograph of I. M. Sechenov, the father of Russian physiology.... The influence of thoughts which are strong by virtue of their novelty and truth, especially when they act during youth, remains deep and permanent even though concealed. In this book, a brilliant attempt was made, altogether extraordinary for that time ... to represent our subjective world from the standpoint of pure physiology." (*Ibid.*, p. 39.)

work; the intellectual horizons of both reached far beyond physiology; and both were accomplished craftsmen in the laboratory. Sechenov learned from Ludwig to treat his students as future scholars—as active apprentices in the field of scholarship rather than as passive receivers of diluted knowledge. Both Ludwig and Sechenov made it a point to keep their students abreast not only of contemporary developments in physiology but also of physiological problems that were still awaiting scientific treatment. Like all of Ludwig's students, Sechenov brought to Russia the most modern ideas in physiology and the habit of rigorous discipline in every phase of research; he never abandoned or modified the idea that modern physiology was in essence applied physics and chemistry, carefully worked out in the laboratory.

The mainstream of Russian physiological thought, reaching its apogee in the contributions of Ivan Pavlov, has four basic characteristics. It emphasizes the area of research where neurophysiology and psychology meet. It is dominated by the idea that the cerebral cortex controls the entire mechanism of nervous integration. It incorporates the principle that the relationship between the individual and his external environment explains most of the activity of the central nervous system; in this area physiology meets sociology. Finally, Sechenov, and Pavlov after him, placed both the nervous system and the external environment in a biological and social evolutionary framework, although this area did not form a significant part of their research. The combination of Sechenov's theory of reflexes as the basic elements of man's psychical life and Darwin's general biological theory opened a new avenue in the study of man: the study of human behavior in evolutionary terms, which sought common denominators in human and animal psychology.

In looking for the nervous sources of human behavior, Sechenov pioneered the modern study of reflex action; but in defining psychology as a science of the origins of psychical phenomena, he failed to anticipate the growth of many branches of psychology that operate outside the realm of physiological reductionism. In Russia, he helped develop psychology as a scientific discipline by fighting the intellectuals who made psychology part of idealistic philosophy. However, the idea that psychology, even divorced from metaphysics, must still go far beyond neurophysiology in order to cover all the scientifically significant problems of human behavior escaped him completely. His main contribution to the development of modern science must be sought not in his physiological reductionism but in his championship of an empirical psychology, free of metaphysical controls and de-

pendent solely on rigorous scientific methods. The critics of Sechenov's theoretical orientation, in fact, were usually the leading adversaries of scientific psychology in general.[57]

Sechenov was not only a pioneer in several branches of physiology but
also a champion of science as an attitude and a world view. N. E. Vvedenskii stated in 1906 that "Reflexes of the Brain," particularly its opening statements, showed that Sechenov was influenced by the emotionally charged
conflict between the proponents of materialistic, idealistic, and dualistic ontologies that dominated the intellectual climate of the early 1860's; but that
his "profound respect for science and incorruptible love for truth soon
freed him from the fetters of this one-sided concern."[58] Sechenov did not
sacrifice scientific criticism to ideological dogmatism, even though his scientific thought inevitably exercised some ideological influence. The fact that
an overwhelming majority of the Russian intelligentsia of the 1860's had
read "Reflexes of the Brain" or were familiar with its contents is a testimony
to both the scope of Sechenov's influence and the intelligentsia's growing
search for a link between ideology and the natural sciences.

## K. A. TIMIRIAZEV

Like most of the leading Russian scientists of the 1860's, Kliment Timiriazev, Russia's pioneer in modern plant physiology, came from a noble
family of rapidly declining fortunes; and like others, he decided to study the
natural sciences only after he had sampled the humanistic areas of academic
endeavor. He enrolled in St. Petersburg University in 1860, at the age of
seventeen, and before he graduated in 1866 he had written on topics ranging
from "The Hunger in Lancashire" and "Garibaldi in Caprera" to Darwin.
During 1867 he worked as an assistant to Mendeleev on an experimental
farm in Simbirsk province, subsidized by the Free Economic Society. Mendeleev was studying the influence of mineral fertilizers and various types
of farming techniques on grain production, but Timiriazev also designed
his own research project, which was concerned with the absorption of solar
energy by plants.[59] At the First Congress of Russian Naturalists and Physicians, held that year, he presented a paper describing the instrument he
had contrived to apply artificial light in order to obtain a more effective
spectral analysis of light absorption.[60]

Timiriazev then spent a year in Paris, where he studied under J. B. Boussingault, a pioneer in agricultural chemistry, and also under the thermo-
chemist Marcellin Berthelot and the physiologist Claude Bernard. He gained

valuable and original material for several scholarly papers (one of them published in the German *Botanische Zeitung*), which provided the ground-work for his master's thesis, *The Spectral Analysis of Chlorophyll* (1871). In this work, he examined a double process in plant nutrition, the absorption of carbonic acid from the air and the absorption of light energy from solar rays; these were the two complementary processes subsequently named photosynthesis. Gradually, Timiriazev expanded his studies in plant physi-ology to include the problems of mineral nutrition, the multiple functions of water, and the processes of growth and respiration.

Although some of Timiriazev's ideas did not pass the test of later labora-tory research, his work in photosynthesis was of great pioneering value, par-ticularly in studying the effects of color on photosynthesis. The basic ques-tion that troubled many scholars of his age was which color region of the solar spectrum was most effective in stimulating the breakdown of carbonic acid by plants. As early as 1844 the American John Draper had reported that the strongest effect was achieved by a yellow-green light—a surprising claim, since we now know that this wavelength is only weakly absorbed by chlorophyll. Several of Timiriazev's contemporaries tried to explain Dra-per's findings. Pfeffer asserted in 1871 that light energy had no connection with photosynthesis. Other authors injected an anthropomorphic element by attributing special significance to the fact that yellow not only liberates a maximum of oxygen in plants but is also the spectral area with maximum effect on the human retina.

Timiriazev criticized all these orientations. He insisted that the energy of absorbed light was the source of photosynthesis, and that light was ab-sorbed by a photosensitive pigment, chlorophyll.[61] Draper, he said, had identified the yellow-green wavelengths as the source of maximum oxygen liberation because of his primitive experimental equipment, which could not produce spectrally pure light. By using a special monochromatic illu-minator, Timiriazev proved that red was the color with maximum ab-sorption by chlorophyll and maximum photosynthetic efficiency. His ex-perimental findings were confirmed by several contemporaries; but his interpretation triggered a lively discussion concerning the relationship of the maximum rate of photosynthesis to the maximum absorption of solar energy, a problem that has not yet been fully resolved.

Timiriazev combined scientific experimentation with a definite theo-retical orientation; but, according to his critics, some of his theoretical con-clusions ran ahead of his experiments. He was determined to give experi-mental support to three leading scientific beliefs of his time: the universality of the law of the conservation of energy, the reducibility of the processes of life to the laws of chemistry and physics, and the general validity of the Darwinian evolutionary law. He viewed photosynthesis as a most graphic example of the transformation and conservation of energy, the physico-chemical process in the life of plants, and the role of the struggle for existence in organic evolution.[62] If Timiriazev did not actually formulate a generally accepted theory of photosynthesis, the reason lay in the complexity of the problem that he tackled and the paucity of helpful hints accumulated by preceding generations of scholars. Even today, "We know relatively little about the photosynthesis of plants under natural conditions in the field and the seas."[63]

Timiriazev left most of the questions of photosynthesis unanswered, but in the process of formulating and presenting his ideas he did much to introduce the spirit of modern science to Russia. He placed all his major ideas within the broader context of modern scientific currents and used them to show specific links between various natural sciences. Timiriazev, an accomplished historian, used examples from the history of science to point out the deeper significance of new ideas and to provide a broad background to the diffusion of scientific knowledge and the study of scientific thought as an integral part of contemporary intellectual history. His more popular papers contain a wealth of quotations from Goethe, Lamarck, Comte, Helmholtz, Darwin, Huxley, Du Bois-Reymond, Boltzmann, Bernard, and many other great scholars of the nineteenth century, all carefully chosen to show the place of science in modern culture and to express a philosophy of scientific optimism. He wrote many articles on the history of the biological sciences, skillfully analyzing the lives of individual scientists, the historical and logical framework of their scientific ideas, and the sociological significance of their major theories.

Timiriazev was the most effective popularizer of Darwinism in the Russia of his time. His public lectures were written in lucid prose and delivered with great oratorical skill. He aimed at stylistic precision, and succeeded in conveying the most complex and logically involved concepts to the general public. Darwinism, to him, was the crowning point of a long intellectual tradition in which Lamarck had played an important role. He took special pains to acquaint his audiences with the philosophical significance of Darwinism, particularly its undermining effects on idealistic metaphysics and teleological orientations, and he attacked the pseudoscientific ideas advanced by vitalistic biology. He opposed all those who claimed that Darwinism contradicts the fundamental principles of moral life and who used their attacks on Darwinism in particular to minimize the cultural import of modern science.[64]

Timiriazev, like the Nihilists, saw science as the noblest index of man's intellectual accomplishments and the safest road to a better life and a richer culture. However, he warned his countrymen that science could flourish only in societies that guaranteed freedom of inquiry and exempted scholars from many of the utilitarian demands of society. In 1875, introducing his popular lectures on "The Life of the Plant" to a huge and enthusiastic audience gathered in the principal lecture hall of the Moscow Polytechnical Museum, he stated: "The development of science can be determined only by the logical sequence of its achievements, never by the external pressure of necessity. Scientific thought, like every form of mental activity, can work only under conditions of absolute liberty. Oppressed by the weight of utilitarian demands, science can produce only pitiable, artificial work, after the same kind as any meager and mechanical work of art fashioned under similar circumstances. We may ransack the archives of any science and yet find scarcely one daring idea, one brilliant generalization which owed its origin to its application; and, *vice versa*, history is full of examples of discoveries, which, though unassociated with any practical purpose, have become the source of innumerable practical issues."[65]

Many scholars, of various philosophical and ideological leanings, would not accept Timiriazev's idea that the discovery of the greatest ideas in science was not stimulated by the practical needs of society. However, though he may have exaggerated the case for "pure science," he did so with a definite purpose: he wanted to impress on his audience the idea that Russia could not hope to emulate the intellectual achievements of the Western nations unless she allowed her scientists the freedom of individual self-assertion. He did not advocate a total separation of science and society; he merely tried to define the best conditions that a society could provide to ensure itself the benefits of modern science. In his own time, he said, Russian society had begun to realize the value of modern experimental plant physiology to agriculture; through agriculture, society and plant physiology had acquired a "community of interests." He quickly added, however, that this community of interests did not authorize society "to dictate to science its modes of action or methods of development." Science, on its part, had no right "to retire, as it were, into a sanctuary, concealing itself from the public gaze and expecting its utility to be taken on trust."[66]

During the 1860's and 1870's many leading physiologists of the next generation produced their first scholarly works. V. Ia. Danilevskii embarked on a long and successful research career with his galvanometric studies of the electrical activities of the cortex and the psychomotor centers. During the late 1870's and early 1880's, N. E. Vvedenskii, Russia's greatest physiologist next to Pavlov and Sechenov, completed the first phase of his studies of the rhythmic behavior of stimulated nerves and the intimate structure of inhibitory mechanisms. And Ivan Pavlov had embarked on the first phase of his long scientific work: an experimental study of the centrifugal nerves of the heart and the neural mechanisms regulating blood pressure.

## CHAPTER FIVE

# The Sciences of the Physical and Chemical Universe

## CHEMISTRY IN TRANSITION

Most Russian scholars of the 1860's looked upon chemistry as the earliest and the most firmly established natural science in their country; and the chemists of the 1860's were products of a Russian heritage as much as they were the disciples of great Western scholars. The Russian tradition in chemistry was born in Kazan University during the 1840's, mostly through the efforts of two young men: N. N. Zinin, who first reduced aniline from nitrobenzene; and Carl Claus, who experimented with platinum and discovered ruthenium. The Kazan chemical "school" brought to Russia the techniques of modern laboratory research and an awareness of the vital importance of theory; and A. M. Butlerov, the first and most eminent product of this "school," rose to fame because he successfully brought complex theoretical questions into practical laboratory work.

Although the Russian chemical tradition was born in Kazan, it reached full development in St. Petersburg during the 1850's. In 1848 Zinin was transferred to the Medical and Surgical Academy in St. Petersburg, and in 1855 he was elected an adjunct of the St. Petersburg Academy of Sciences. He arrived from Kazan with modern laboratory skills but somewhat outdated theoretical concepts; however, through the Academy's extensive communications with the West, he was soon exposed to the theories of Charles Gerhardt, Auguste Laurent, Hermann Kolbe, J. B. A. Dumas, and a whole array of other eminent scholars who were then seeking universally applicable explanations of compounds, radicals, valency, and the mechanisms of reactions. And all of St. Petersburg's ideas did not come from the West. When Zinin arrived in St. Petersburg, two eminent chemists were already working there: Carl Julius Fritzsche, a member of the Academy of Sciences, and Aleksandr Voskresenskii, a professor at St. Petersburg University.

C. J. Fritzsche was primarily a laboratory chemist interested in various aromatic hydrocarbons (he himself discovered retene and chrysene). In 1840 he obtained aniline from indigo heated with alkali, two years before Zinin showed conclusively that aniline can be reduced from nitrobenzene. He also discovered the carbazole in coal tar, and produced pure anthracite for experimental purposes. Fritzsche's professional advice was sought by the government, which appointed him to several committees dealing with practical applications of chemistry—e.g., analyzing the mineral waters of the Caucasus, and producing an alcohol and turpentine mixture that would provide effective but cheap lighting for the streets of St. Petersburg.[1] Fritzsche was primarily a practical chemist, and his work was not influenced by the heated theoretical controversy that gave birth to modern structural chemistry.

A. A. Voskresenskii's interests were mostly in the realm of theory. He kept abreast of the newest developments in chemistry and was a skilled lecturer, but he had little taste for research and made few original contributions to theory. His lectures at the Main Pedagogical Institute, however, were among the most important influences on D. I. Mendeleev's decision to study chemistry. Writing about Voskresenskii for a well-known biographical dictionary, Mendeleev pointed out Voskresenskii's real contributions to Russian chemistry: "Firmly convinced that one-sided views cannot lead to true knowledge, he urged us, the beginners, to compare the views of Berzelius and Liebig with the theories of Dumas, Laurent, and Gerhardt, which at the time were just beginning to receive recognition, though they were still far from reaching a position of prominence. Moreover, he clearly saw the superiority of the French school, and predicted the downfall of the dualist views that reigned in the 1840's."[2] Teaching simultaneously in several schools in St. Petersburg, Voskresenskii had a share in training most of the leading Russian chemists of the second half of the nineteenth century. Besides Mendeleev, his students included such important names in Russian science as N. N. Sokolov and N. A. Menshutkin.

Zinin, Fritzsche, and Voskresenskii helped make St. Petersburg the center of Russian chemical research. Several contemporaries noted the existence of a lively *kruzhok* of St. Petersburg chemists as early as 1854. By 1859 two young scholars, N. N. Sokolov and A. N. Engelhardt, had enough support from the younger generation of St. Petersburg chemists to begin the *Chemical Journal*, a private venture that lasted two years.[3] The first issue carried a long essay by Sokolov on contemporary theoretical orientations in chemistry. The appearance of this journal marked a turning point in the history of Russian chemistry: after 1859 the leading Russian chemists were interested not merely in echoing the new theoretical developments in chemistry, but in adding to them. They emphasized both laboratory experiments and the intellectual search for a logical, philosophical and structural unity in their discipline.

Many factors contributed to the widespread Russian interest in chemistry during the 1850's. Though meagerly equipped by Western standards, chemical laboratories were still the best scientific workshops in Russian universities. Moreover, chemistry effectively combined a search for knowledge of immediate practical value with the most abstract and challenging theoretical explorations. It covered a wide area of specialized knowledge; and it appealed to the intelligentsia, who saw it as the one science that could by itself provide a sound basis for a fuller and more objective understanding of life in all its manifestations. To Russian biologists, as to Vogt and Büchner in the West, chemistry was a bridge between the study of life and the study of inorganic matter; many influential scholars treated it as the basis of physiology, which they considered, in turn, the only valid basis of psychology. Of the scientific ideas coming to Russia from the West, none were more steeped in theoretical controversy, philosophical subtlety, and academic challenges than those of chemistry. A remarkably high proportion of the Russian students who flooded Western universities after the Crimean War managed to take courses in chemistry, even when their major interests were in other disciplines. It was virtually impossible to find a Russian chemist of the time who had not taken a course from Justus von Liebig at Giessen, Heinrich Rose at Berlin, R. W. Bunsen at Heidelberg, or Marcellin Berthelot at the Collège de France.

To most Russians prior to 1850, chemistry was only another name for a pharmaceutical art monopolized by the Germans. Zinin's laboratory at Kazan, and his lectures to large and diversified audiences, helped dispel this myth and make chemistry a special challenge to the nation's young natural scientists. However, the rapidly growing interest in chemistry far outstripped the increase in competent chemists. Voskresenskii, at times, taught classes in six different St. Petersburg schools simultaneously; and the University of Moscow in the 1850's was still looking for a chemistry professor who was proficient in both experimental and theoretical work.

As another innovation, Sokolov and Engelhardt, the editors of the *Chemical Journal*, established the first private chemical laboratory in Russia. Both the journal and the laboratory were experimental ventures; and both came to an early end because of prohibitive expenses and the government's generally negative attitude toward private scientific ventures, but not because of any lack of genuine public interest in chemistry. After 1863 the government's appropriations for university laboratories were much increased, and the need for a private effort became less pressing. According to Timiriazev's later recollections: "With the arrival of Butlerov from Kazan and the appearance of N. A. Menshutkin the picture changed: new scientific [chemical] laboratories were established and scientific activity [in St. Petersburg University] became as intensive as in any Western university. Other schools of higher education also began to build laboratories of the modern type . . . such as, for example, Zinin's laboratory in the Medical and Surgical Academy and Shishkov's in the Artillery School. Beilstein . . . who had previously taught at Göttingen University, built the laboratory of the Technological Institute, which in some respects surpassed the university laboratories."[4]

Nevertheless, the seeds of private chemical experimentation were firmly planted, and it was not uncommon to find amateur experimenters setting up small laboratories in their homes or places of business. One glassware store in St. Petersburg even opened a new department selling retorts and other chemical apparatus.[5] Upon his return from the Paris Exposition in 1867, Mendeleev wrote a popular volume on the exhibits of modern products of the chemical industry; to his great surprise the book was sold out within a year.[6] But laboratories grew in number more than in quality, and it was not until the end of the century that the scientific workshops in Russian universities could match their German models. The increase in chemists actively engaged in the advancement of their science was correspondingly slow. When the Russian Chemical Society was founded in 1868, it had 35 members, mostly from St. Petersburg; 30 years later the membership stood at 293. From the very beginning, however, the dilettantes greatly outnumbered the professional chemists.

The rapid growth of chemistry produced many new disciplines, most of which had strong representatives in Russian institutions of higher education. A. I. Khodnev, who lectured at Khar'kov University, wrote a comprehensive survey of "physiological chemistry"; he was succeeded at Khar'kov by N. N. Beketov, who in 1865 launched the first Russian course in physical chemistry. At Kazan University, A. M. Butlerov lectured on inorganic and organic chemistry, but reached a wider audience through his popular course in "technical chemistry." Mendeleev lectured on organic chemistry and wrote the first original Russian book on the subject. V. V. Markovnikov began his academic career in the early 1860's by teaching inorganic chemistry and analytical chemistry; but he also taught and wrote about new theoretical developments in organic chemistry. N. A. Menshutkin wrote a textbook on analytical chemistry that was translated into German and English. In the lecture halls and the steadily proliferating journals, such expressions as thermochemistry, electrochemistry, agricultural chemistry, physical chemistry, and theoretical chemistry were no longer mere labels but well-defined topics of specialized study.

During this great upsurge in chemical thought, Aleksandr Butlerov and Dmitrii Mendeleev stood out among their contemporaries, and their contributions marked the first great triumph of modern Russian science. Their scientific ideas, duly noted by contemporary Western chemists, had a special significance in Russia: for these ideas proved clearly that the Russian nation had become an active contributor to one of the most advanced branches of modern science.

### THE BIRTH OF STRUCTURAL CHEMISTRY: A. M. BUTLEROV

Like most of the leading Russian scholars who produced their major scientific work in the 1860's and 1870's, A. M. Butlerov came from the gentry. He completed most of his secondary education in a boarding school designed to shelter children of noble origin from early contact with lower social groups and to drill them in conversational French and German. (Years later, when Butlerov made his first tour of Western Europe, his impeccable French and German opened many doors for him that might otherwise have remained closed.) At this time the public gymnasiums emphasized classical and philological education, and chemistry was completely ignored; but in the boarding school an enterprising instructor began teaching Butlerov chemistry with the help of elementary experiments.

Butlerov enrolled in Kazan University in 1844, and began to study inorganic chemistry under Carl Claus and organic chemistry under N. N. Zinin, the only courses available. Claus, however, divided his interest between chemistry and botany; and Zinin left Kazan University in 1847, before Butlerov had learned enough to appreciate the full scope of chemical theory and experimental techniques. Later in life, Butlerov was to build on the chemical legacy of Claus and Zinin, but it would be inaccurate to call him their disciple.[7] He majored in entomology and botany, but selected chemistry as the area of emphasis in both his magister's and doctoral dissertations. In 1850 he was appointed an instructor at Kazan, where he remained for the next seventeen years. By 1852 Claus was no longer at Kazan, and Butlerov took over as director of the university's entire chemistry program.

At this time, many new and controversial developments in chemistry were beginning to filter into Russia (e.g., the first volume of Gerhardt's *Traité de chimie organique* in 1853, and Laurent's *Méthode de chimie* in 1854). But Butlerov, busy with teaching assignments and laboratory experiments, found it difficult to absorb the new ideas, and continued to travel the safe, well-beaten paths of traditional chemistry. When his doctoral dissertation was rejected by a committee at Kazan University, Butlerov chose to defend it at Moscow University, known at the time for its low standards in chemical teaching and research. His dissertation showed an intimate knowledge of the experimental literature on various branches of organic chemistry, but also displayed a pronounced lack of critical judgment and theoretical integration. He was well aware of this weakness, and wisely decided not to publish the dissertation. However, he did publish nearly two dozen routine articles on various aspects of horticulture and fruit-growing in the journal of the Kazan Economic Society and other periodicals. It was not until 1857 that he made chemistry his sole scientific interest.

Prior to 1857 Butlerov, with aristocratic aloofness, made no firm commitment to any branch of science; he selected research topics according to his whim of the moment. His great gifts as a public speaker made teaching attractive to him, and he spoke with eloquence and competence to students and gatherings of Kazan citizens. According to one of Butlerov's colleagues, the social ferment and general awakening that paved the way for the great reforms of the 1860's finally led Butlerov to abandon his aristocratic detachment and absorb the spirit of the new time; and the unprecedented challenges of the Reform era itself made him aware of the true grandeur of science as an instrument of social progress.[8] To him, as to so many of his contemporaries, science was no longer simply a noble pastime, but had become a powerful weapon for rejuvenating Russian society.

Butlerov was closely associated with the so-called Kazan school in chemistry, and he had received a doctorate in a Russian university without studying in the West. For these reasons he was lauded by his compatriots as the purest example of Russian scientific training.[9] Markovnikov remarked that Butlerov did not visit the West as a student, but as "a fully formed scholar."[10] To G. G. Gustavson, he was a Russian scholar "in the broadest sense of the term."[11]

Butlerov, for his part, was firmly convinced that his first visit to Western Europe, in 1857–58, was the real begining of his transformation from a drifting student into a dedicated scholar. At the time he was a full professor, and his Western tour was designed to combine relaxation with visits to the leading centers of chemical research. With meticulous care and refinement, he recorded his impressions of various European countries and cities and discussed the lessons that he thought Russia could learn from the more technically advanced societies. He extolled the social dedication of men of knowledge, but wondered whether the ideas of liberty, equality, and fraternity could be successfully transplanted to Russia.[12] He doubted the sincerity of those Russian aristocrats who were the chief spokesmen for libertarian ideas.

Very few Russian scholars of the time saw and learned more during a Western visit than Butlerov. His linguistic proficiency, personal charm, and combination of intellectual curiosity with academic maturity opened many doors for him.[13] He attended lectures at various universities, visited and carefully examined a dozen major laboratories and several chemical industrial plants, compared notes with the young Russian scientists he met in various universities, and exchanged ideas with many leading chemists, from the veteran Justus von Liebig to the youthful F. A. Kekulé. In Paris he had a chance to converse with and attend the lectures of such scientists as Charles Wurtz, J. B. Boussingault, E. M. Peligot, Henri Deville, and A. J. Balard in chemistry, and Victor Regnault and A. H. Becquerel in physics.[14] Laurent and Gerhardt were now dead, and both had been ostracized before their deaths because of their daring attacks on the established theories of chemistry. But by this time the old school had lost its monopoly, and wherever Butlerov went he heard about the new vistas opened by Laurent and Gerhardt. Thus Butlerov came face to face with the most challenging and acute theoretical problems of organic chemistry in an informal, painless way. His genuine dedication to scientific thought made him welcome at the meetings of the newly founded Paris Chemical Society, organized mostly by rebellious young men to discuss the current problems in chemistry in an atmosphere unrestricted by formal organization. Butlerov himself presented several reports on a wide variety of topics.

In Charles Wurtz's laboratory at the School of Medicine in Paris Butlerov was given the opportunity to conduct original experiments. In two months, he had completed his first investigation of methylene iodide, which opened a series of experiments that was continued in Kazan. For the next twenty years Butlerov was engaged in continuous experimental work, which produced a number of new compounds and reactions.[15] Working with methylene iodide in 1859, he obtained the polymer of formaldehyde, which he named dioxymethylene. In 1860 he produced hexamethylene tetramine; and in 1861 he synthesized a sugar-like substance by treating "dioxymethylene" with milk of lime, providing "the first example of the synthesis of a carbohydrate from relatively simple substances."[16]

In his lectures to Kazan University students, Butlerov concentrated on the theoretical complexities and dilemmas of modern chemistry. He emphasized the increasing efforts of leading chemists to give their discipline more conceptual consistency and logical unity and to raise it to a higher level of abstraction. Jean Dumas's "old theory of types," Gerhardt's "new theory of types" (or "formal types"), and Hermann Kolbe's theory of "real types" were among many current efforts to organize chemistry logically. Each theory contributed to the advance of chemical theory and the emergence of a unified system of chemical formulas. But all these theories were concerned with the mechanical rather than the chemical structure of molecules: that is, they were concerned with the typologies of chemical reactions and the similarities of formulas produced by substitution, rather than with the arrangement of atoms in the molecules of chemical compounds. Gerhardt had spoken for the champions of these theories when he expressed open doubt of man's ability to ever penetrate the inner structure of atoms.

The growing emphasis on the study of atomicity, affinity units, chemical bonds, and atomic weights proved to be a necessary logical step toward a structural or chemical study of molecules. The first major step was made in 1858 by A. S. Couper and F. A. Kekulé, who established the quadrivalency of carbon and explained the linking of carbon atoms with one another. They offered the first full explanation of the atomicity of carbon and its compounds. Kekulé next defined organic chemistry as the science of carbon compounds. The Chemical Congress at Karlsruhe in 1860 settled some of the problems of atomic weights. These developments made it possible to establish molecular formulas and to present them graphically. Some of the most troubling problems of the past—such as the relations of homologous series of organic compounds to each other—could now be viewed in a clearer perspective.

In 1861 Butlerov, now an established scholar, made his second journey to the West, ostensibly to observe the chemical laboratories in Germany, Belgium, and France. But his mind was preoccupied with chemical theory and the vistas opened by the latest contributions of Kolbe, Kekulé, and Couper. In September he read his famous paper "The Chemical Structure of Substances" before the Thirty-Sixth Congress of German Naturalists and Physicians in Speyer. Noting that the accumulation of chemical facts was running far ahead of chemical theory, he hinted that the basic weakness of Gerhardt's theory of types, and of all other "mechanical" theories, lay in their dependence on a physical rather than a chemical analysis. Butlerov emphasized the need for a study of the linking of atoms into molecules, and introduced the concept of "chemical structure" to denote the distribution of the affinity links of the atoms in all compounds. His main point was that the molecules of chemical compounds could be understood only in terms of the arrangement of their constituent atoms.[17] Viewing the theoretical openings made by Couper and Kekulé as the key to a higher level of chemical abstraction, he argued that a study of consistent patterns in the combining of atoms would be the most promising means of developing a unified theory of organic chemistry. Finally, Butlerov made the prophetic announcement, which at the time made no impression on his listeners, that a consistent application of the structural theory would provide a single formula for every chemical compound.[18] Butlerov's paper was an effort to bring together the various uneven strands of a developing structural theory in chemistry, and to speculate on its future development; he summed up the lines of thought leading to the structural theory at the earliest phase of its development. In 1906, the Finnish chemist E. Hjelt stated: "Butlerov understood the concept of constitution or structure as synonymous with the relative arrangement of atoms in molecules, and their relations with and independence of each other.... His observations created a firmer and clearer basis for the elucidation and critical examination of chemical isomerism."[19]

Returning to Russia, Butlerov concentrated all his energy on the defense and elaboration of his new theoretical ideas. He translated his paper on the structure of chemical substances into Russian and published it in the *Journal of Kazan University* in 1862; he also wrote several additional articles on the subject in German and Russian. In order to bolster his theory with factual data, he went back to the laboratory and conducted experiments aimed at synthesizing acetic acid. These experiments led him to the discovery of tertiary alcohols, and eventually to the synthesis of new types of tertiary spirits—a factual clarification and extension of the concept of isomerism. An equally impressive support for Butlerov's structural theory was provided by the experimental studies that enabled him to explain tautomerism in 1876.*

---

* "Isomerism" is the term used to describe two chemical compounds that contain the same kinds and proportions of atoms but differ in the structural arrangement of these atoms. Tautomerism is a state in which two isomers change into one another very readily and usually exist in a state of equilibrium. Both ideas are fundamental to the structural theory of chemistry.

In 1862-63 Butlerov reorganized his university course in organic chemistry along the lines of the new theory. And in 1864-66 he published his *Introduction to the Complete Study of Organic Chemistry* in three small volumes. His basic intent was to apply the idea of chemical structure to the most important classes of organic compounds; but he also indicated the possibility and advantages of uniform chemical formulas. Butlerov published the *Introduction* in Russian because it grew out of his lectures. However, the book's emphasis was more on a systematic application of the idea of chemical structure to the major chemical compounds than on the substantive material presented. It was not meant to be a textbook; and even if it had been so intended, it could not have competed successsfully with Mendeleev's *Organic Chemistry* (1861), an unadorned synthesis of accumulated facts with minimum theoretical involvement. To give his ideas wider circulation, Butlerov published a German translation of his book in 1867. However, by that time Kekulé had published his famous study of aromatic compounds, which incorporated the new structural principles. Butlerov, obviously wishing to establish his priority in the articulation of the new theory, insisted that the title page of the German edition of his book indicate that the work had originally been published in Russian.

Butlerov was decidedly unhappy about the refusal of the leading German chemists to acknowledge his major contribution to the theory of chemical structure, but he registered no direct complaints. His student V. V. Markovnikov, however, took it upon himself to uphold the honor of Russian science. In his magister's dissertation (1865), Markovnikov accused Kekulé of devious efforts to present himself as the founder of the new theory.[20] The German chemist Lothar Meyer, speaking on behalf of Kekulé, asserted that the new theory was a direct outgrowth of Kekulé's discovery of the quadrivalency of carbon; and that Butlerov's main contribution consisted of giving a name to the atom-chain theory that grew out of this discovery.[21]

The belligerency of both parties to the controversy was a thoughtless violation of the ethos of science, which regards the advancement of scientific knowledge as a continual integration of contributions by many men and schools of thought. Markovnikov's accusation was particularly unfortunate in that it was directed against German scholarship, to which Russian science was so much indebted. Butlerov, Markovnikov, and every other contemporary Russian chemist of consequence had improved their professional skills at German universities and had benefited from direct contact with men like Liebig, Eilhard Mitscherlich, Bunsen, Kolbe, Kekulé, and Emil Erlenmeyer. By his description of the great cordiality and respect accorded him by Kolbe, Markovnikov himself attests to the high academic regard that the leading German chemists had for their Russian visitors. But the unnecessary attack on Kekulé was part of the growing pains of Russian science, and stemmed from the popular desire for intellectual emancipation from both internal autocracy and Western tutelage. It was not a malicious campaign by ungrateful men, but rather a poorly timed action by ambitious scholars seeking greater honor for their country in the history of modern science.

At home, Butlerov faced another kind of opposition: some of the leading Russian chemists refused to accept the structural theory, which they considered one-sided and overly speculative. For the first time in Russia, a modern scientific orientation became a subject of academic controversy and the source of a productive and stimulating debate. In the 1877 edition of his famous *Principles of Chemistry*, Mendeleev said that "the ideas of the structuralists cannot be regarded as true"; and in a paper read before the Russian Physical and Chemical Society in 1878, N. A. Menshutkin claimed that isomerism was still an unexplained mystery, even though the structuralists claimed to have given it a consistent and thorough scientific explanation. Butlerov defended his theory before scientific forums with dignity and growing dedication. He became a spokesman for "chemical realism," and viewed Menshutkin's skepticism as "chemical nihilism." Aided by opinions from abroad, Butlerov's views won out: in the 1880's Mendeleev stopped his attacks on the structural theory, and in the 1890's Menshutkin became one of its staunchest supporters.

While the academic battle went on, Butlerov became the leader of a flourishing and influential school of Russian chemists.[22] His first disciple was Markovnikov, who distinguished himself by his pioneering work in the study of the organic compounds of petroleum and established the first effective ties between academic chemistry and Russia's young chemical industry.[23] A. M. Zaitsev, another disciple, became well known for his studies of the transformation of alcohols and for his experimental elaboration of the theory of chemical structure with reference to the isomerism of butyl alcohols. Zaitsev trained more active research chemists than any other scholar of pre-Soviet Russia. A. E. Favorskii, who was born at the time when Butlerov was formulating his theory of chemical structure, made the study of isomeric phenomena his lifework, and played a leading role in the advancement of stereochemistry. His scientific work spanned three generations, and was a strong link between Butlerov and the Soviet chemists.

The academic community held Butlerov in high esteem, and regarded his scientific contributions as major proof of the maturity of the Russian scientific mind. As soon as the German translation of Butlerov's *Introduction* was published, he was transferred to St. Petersburg University and was elected a regular member of the Academy of Sciences. In St. Petersburg his work grew in volume and diversity, culminating in his studies of tautomerism. As a noted senior professor, Butlerov could afford to teach highly specialized courses without running the risk of empty classrooms. He offered special courses on nitrogen compounds (1871), acids (1872), hydrocarbons and metalo-organic compounds (1873), and the history of chemistry (1879–80).[24] He was an active member of the Russian Chemical Society and attended several congresses of Russian naturalists and physicians. As was customary for all scholars interested in linking pure and applied science, Butlerov joined the Free Economic Society, under whose auspices he wrote extensively on the scientific foundations of beekeeping. It was on his initiative that the Moscow Society for the Acclimatization of Animals and Plants established a beekeeping section, making him its honorary president.

A. M. Butlerov made his mark in many fields outside chemistry. But outside that field, he was most identified with the nineteenth-century fad of spiritualism—an interest that may seem anomalous to the modern reader. During the 1870's spiritualistic seances, imported from the West, were fashionable in St. Petersburg; and as in the West, they attracted educated men from widely differing professions, including leading scientists. The whole idea was taken quite seriously. In 1876, for example, Alfred Russel Wallace, who had published a paper setting forth the ideas of biological evolution one year before the appearance of Darwin's epoch-making study, published *On Miracles and Modern Spiritualism*, allying himself with champions of mediumistic experiences. No one really knows what attracted Butlerov to this modern mysticism; but it is a fact that during the 1870's and 1880's he was one of the most dedicated spiritualists in St. Petersburg and wrote extensively in defense of spiritualist philosophy.

During this period, Butlerov the scientist was completely separated from Butlerov the spiritualist. Butlerov the scientist was a model of perfect adjustment to the great advances in the codification of scientific theory; Butlerov the spiritualist was influenced by the upper classes of St. Petersburg, who searched for a world unaffected by the challenges of "materialistic" knowledge and the failings of a disintegrating value system. He saw no sharp lines separating the scientific and mediumistic paths to knowledge, but made no serious effort to reconcile the two logically and philosophically. His spiritualistic writings were loose translations of fragments from the works of such Western writers as J. K. F. Zöllner, a well-known astrophysicist from Leipzig who combined mathematical and epistemological erudition with spiritualistic revelations in an attempt to establish a concept of four-dimensional space.[25]

In his purely scientific debates with N. A. Menshutkin, Butlerov implicitly recognized the limitless potentialities of scientific knowledge; his spiritualism, on the other hand, was a pseudoscience intended to overcome the shortcomings of true science. He deviated from his philosophy of scientific optimism only once; in a paper entitled "The Basic Concepts of Chemistry," published posthumously, he stated: "A belief in that which lies beyond the province of scientific knowledge may exist together with a full recognition of scientific truths. But a blind belief in the infallibility of scientific theories always leads to an unscientific, unfounded skepticism, and keeps one from discovering new, real truths that lie beyond the province of favorite theories."[26]

Butlerov apparently viewed spiritualism as a new religion, based not on the collected sayings of the Church Fathers but on objective, verified facts acquired by direct observation and experiment; spiritualism was thus the only religion compatible with science. Perhaps, in his old age, Butlerov became alarmed at the incompatibility of materialistic thought—to which he had added tangibly—with a belief in human immortality. Whatever his reasons, Butlerov's active participation in the mediumistic movement caused a great deal of consternation among his St. Petersburg colleagues. In 1875 the Russian Physical Society appointed a special commission to investigate the claims of spiritualists; among the members were Butlerov, as a spokesman for spiritualism, and Mendeleev, as its principal adversary. The commission eventually issued a report condemning spiritualism as a phenomenon inimical to the normal growth of scientific thought. Butlerov withdrew from the commission after several unsuccessful seances, but he refused to sever his relations with the spiritualist movement. Indeed, he attracted several scientists, particularly younger chemists, to the cause of spiritualism, though most of these joined to please their eminent patron rather than from inner conviction.

Butlerov's spiritualistic influence suffered an irreparable setback in 1876, when Mendeleev published a collection of essays interpreting spiritualism and its intellectual dogmatism as a negation of science and the true scientific spirit. Mendeleev was genuinely—and justifiably—concerned about the extraordinarily wide publicity given to spiritualism in Russia, mostly because it was supported by such influential scholars as Butlerov and the biologist N. P. Vagner. Moreover, the *Messenger of Europe* and the *Russian Messenger* presented spiritualism as a serious intellectual movement, supported by Western scholars like Wallace, Sir William Crookes, and J. K. F. Zöllner, all scholars of great repute.

Butlerov the spiritualist did not survive his age, and is of interest only as an index of the troubled culture of the high society of St. Petersburg. Butlerov the scientist, however, has been remembered by succeeding generations for his many contributions to the development of a vital branch of modern science. He belonged to the eminent group of chemists who purged their science of the metaphysical claim that the inner structure of matter could be explained only by the presence of a living force immune to laboratory experiments and irreducible to chemical formulas. This antivitalist view, however, was not explicit either in Butlerov's theory of chemical structure or in his philosophy.

### DMITRII IVANOVICH MENDELEEV

Much of the research in inorganic chemistry during the first six decades of the nineteenth century was concerned with the study of natural substances and their reduction to basic elements. In 1814 Berzelius used 34 symbols to represent the elements known at that time; by 1852 Leopold Gmelin's handbook of chemistry listed 52 elements. As the midpoint of the century approached, the leading chemists began to wonder whether the discrete elements that form natural compounds could be arranged in a natural system characterized by measurable regularities. Without such a system chemistry could never emulate physics as a science of universal laws of nature. The improved laboratory techniques of the mid-nineteenth century, from gravimetry to spectrum analysis, helped researchers discover new elements; but the formulation of general principles binding these elements into an ordered, natural system was a far more difficult task. There was an acute need for men who could combine technical proficiency with a philosophical overview of chemistry in all its major ramifications, a profound theoretical interest, and a great deal of intellectual daring.

In 1869 Dmitrii Ivanovich Mendeleev presented the world with the periodic law of chemical elements, which established that the 64 elements known at the time were demonstrably the components of an integrated natural system. To the traditional notion of the diversity of nature, Mendeleev added the hard and fast fact of the unity of nature. Elements are individual and unique because their atomic weights are associated with definite and discrete chemical qualities; but they also form an undivided whole, an integrated series arranged in the order of increasing atomic weights and encompassing all the elementary forms of natural substances. The recognition of this complementary unity and individuality of elements is the essence of the periodic law. Moreover, there is a definite, periodic pattern in the recurrence of elements with similar physical characteristics. In Mendeleev's words, "If all the elements be arranged in the order of their atomic weights a periodic repetition of properties is obtained." The periodic law states: "The properties of the elements, as well as the forms and properties of their compounds, are in periodic dependence or, expressing ourselves algebraically, form a periodic function of the atomic weights of the elements."[27]

As it was presented in 1869, Mendeleev's law required substantial refinement and verification: his initial periodic table of elements had blank spaces to be filled by elements as yet undiscovered; it misplaced some elements because their atomic weights had been incorrectly determined; and it did not express many essential relationships between elements.[28] As he gradually shortened and regrouped the table, Mendeleev realized that the verification of the periodic law depended primarily on two conditions: the verification of the accuracy of the atomic weights of elements as demanded by the table (in some cases these weights differed from those established empirically), and the discovery of new elements to fill in the gaps in the table. Less than two decades after the publication of his first paper on the natural sequences of elements, Mendeleev was able to announce that research done by several scholars had satisfied these conditions. What happened is best described by Mendeleev himself:

"The laws of nature admit no exceptions, and in this they clearly differ from such rules and maxims as are found in grammar, etc. The confirmation of a law is only possible by means of the deduction of the consequences proceeding from it, which would without it be impossible and unforeseen, and by verifying these consequences by experiment and further proof. Therefore, when I saw the periodic law, I deduced such logical consequences from it as could show whether it were true or not. Among them was the prediction of the properties of undiscovered elements and the correction of the atomic weights of many, and at that time little known, elements. Thus uranium, for example, was considered as trivalent, $U=120$; but as such it did not correspond with the periodic law. I therefore proposed to double its atomic weight, $U=240$; and the researches of Roscow, Zimmermann, and others justified this alteration. It was the same with cerium. . . . It was necessary to do one or the other—either to consider the periodic law as completely true, and as forming a new instrument in chemical research, or to refute it. Acknowledging the method of experiment to be the only true one, I myself verified what I could, and gave every one the possibility of proving or confirming the law, and did not think, like Meyer . . . that 'it would be rash to change the accepted atomic weights on the basis of so uncertain a starting point.' In my opinion, the basis offered by the periodic law had to be verified or refuted, and experiment in every case verified it."[29]

Mendeleev's view of the complementary diversity and unity of chemical elements did not stand the test of the modern revolution in physics. His principle of diversity was a reaffirmation of Daltonian atomism, the theory held by most leading scientists during the first nine decades of the nineteenth century. It was based on the assumption that atoms were both indivisible and immutable. During the 1890's both of these suppositions were irrevocably refuted. At the very end of the century Ernest Rutherford introduced the concept of "the electronic constitution of the atom," and the subsequent work of J. J. Thomson and Niels Bohr extended this idea to matter in general. The atom was no longer regarded as a formless, unstructured particle, but as a specific, structured aggregate of protons and electrons. At the same time, studies of radioactivity produced the discovery that certain elements, such as uranium and radium, emitted bursts of radioactive energy, a process subsequently related to the natural transmutation of elements. This discovery, in turn, raised the possibility of man-made elements. The ninth such transuranium element discovered, produced in a laboratory of the University of California at Berkeley and having the atomic number 101, was named Mendelevium.

Although Mendeleev's ideas of the immutability of chemical elements and the unstructured nature of atoms collapsed in the twentieth century, his idea of the unity of chemical elements, as manifested in the periodic recurrence of similar physical properties, has received additional verification. Modern atomic physics added new strength to the periodic law by introducing the *atomic number* (the number of protons in a nucleus) as a serial number for each element. In addition, H. G. J. Moseley established that the X-ray spectrum of every element was directly related to its position in the periodic system. His experiments also cleared up a number of questionable points in Mendeleev's table, and sustained it as a law of nature. Every new improvement added to the stature of the great chemist and to the comprehensiveness of his law.

Mendeleev brought the classical period of atomistic chemistry to completion, and he was very much aware of the fact. His theory also connected classical atomistic chemistry with the modern theory of atomic structure based on radioactivity and the discovery of the electron. Mendeleev himself was unaware of this contribution, for he was overcommitted to Newtonian physics, which he considered a model for raising chemistry to the level of an abstract and conceptually unified science. He ignored altogether the great breakthroughs of modern atomic physics. To be sure, his preoccupation with a wide variety of practical problems made it impossible for him to keep track of all the theoretical and experimental developments in physics. It must also be noted that Mendeleev died before the new ideas were revealed in significant detail—six years before Moseley proved conclusively that the periodic law was fully sustained by atomic physics.

The periodic law was the culmination of Mendeleev's scientific labors.[30] But to fully understand the place of this great man in the Russian scientific tradition and in the intellectual culture of his time it is necessary to examine not only the academic experiences, scientific pursuits, and personal interests that led him to discover this law, but also the broader area of all his diverse scholarly activities.

The great Russian chemists of the later nineteenth century used a variety of approaches in their research. Aleksandr Butlerov stuck consistently to the scientific dictum that chemistry must rely exclusively on chemical—as distinct from physical—analysis in its search for a logically autonomous system of knowledge; to him, chemistry was a distinct science in both its subject of inquiry and its methodology. N. N. Beketov, another distinguished chemist of the time, used chemical methods to study physical phenomena: for example, he endeavored to establish the chemical qualities of electrical current, thermal energy, and spectral analysis.[31]

Mendeleev, by contrast, concentrated on the physical and mechanical analysis of chemical phenomena. In the words of a modern physicist: "Although a chemist by training and a student of chemical substances, Mendeleev always approached his subject with the broad view of a physicist, and regarded chemical processes and states as the still-unsolved problems of physics."[32]

Unlike Butlerov, who was convinced that chemistry could achieve the universality and precision of physics only by relying on its own resources, Mendeleev contended that chemistry had to become a specialized extension of physics. In a lecture delivered at the Royal Institution in London in 1889, he advocated a harmonization of the guiding propositions of contemporary chemistry with "the immortal principles of Newtonian natural philosophy"; this process would bring about "the advent of true chemical mechanics."[33] Twenty years after formulating the periodic law, Mendeleev wrote that his main concern was with the application of the law of gravitation to the chemical world; he went so far as to differentiate between universal gravitation, which was equally applicable to all bodies, and chemical gravitation, which was unequally applicable to all bodies and operated only at very small distances.

Although Mendeleev was most productive in the challenging area where physics and chemistry meet, it would be an error to label him a chemical physicist or a physical chemist, for some of his studies were strictly physical and some strictly chemical. Moreover, his research gradually extended far beyond the boundaries of chemistry and physics: he wrote with great dedication about the problems of modern industrial technology, Russian natural resources, and the role of education in general enlightenment and the training of future scientists.[34] All his writings exhibited personal involvement, disciplined thought, and didactic intent. To his colleagues and students, he was known not only as a man of gigantic intellectual stature, but also as a diligent worker with inexhaustible energy. It took him only three months in 1861 to complete his *Organic Chemistry*, a tome of 500 printed pages.

Mendeleev was born in 1834 in Tobol'sk, Siberia. His father, the son of a village priest, was a respected teacher of philosophy and the fine arts, and served as director of the provincial gymnasium and public schools. His mother came from a pioneer commercial family that had built the first factories in Tobol'sk but later suffered a decline in fortunes. In the year Mendeleev was born, his father became temporarily blind, and was forced to retire on a relatively small pension. In order to boost the family income, Mendeleev's mother reopened and managed a small glass factory, which had been given to her by her brothers and which produced mostly pharmaceutical instruments. Both parents combined a respect for intellectual and artistic pursuits with an enterprising spirit and a high moral commitment to work. In dedicating his *Study of Aqueous Solutions by Means of Specific Gravity* to his mother, Mendeleev noted that her last testament to him had been to persist in work that acknowledged science as the most potent weapon in man's continual struggle against "prejudices, injustices, and mistakes."

In 1849 Mendeleev graduated from Tobol'sk gymnasium, and a year later he enrolled in the Main Pedagogical Institute in St. Petersburg, the country's chief center for the training of gymnasium teachers. The Institute was run as a garrison: the life of the students was thoroughly regi-mented, and the least deviation from the prescribed rules of behavior called for such punishments as flogging or solitary confinement. The Institute's primary task was to train teachers who would be blindly dedicated to the preservation of the autocratic system; N. A. Dobroliubov, one of its alum-ni, noted that only a handful of graduates had achieved recognition in literature and the sciences. Despite its anachronistic educational philosophy and its preoccupation with servile patriotism, the Institute offered solid courses in several natural sciences, which were taught by individual pro-fessors from St. Petersburg University and by members of the Academy of Sciences. The Institute's Faculty of Physical and Mathematical Sciences included such luminaries of Russian science as the mathematician M. V. Ostrogradskii, the physicist Heinrich Lenz, the zoologist J. F. Brandt, and the chemist A. A. Voskresenskii. Retiring, studious, and sickly, young Mendeleev did not suffer from the strict discipline for which the Institute had acquired an unenviable reputation. By this time both his parents were dead, and he had no relatives to whom he could turn in emergencies; but the Institute, as a "closed institution," had sufficient dormitory facilities to accommodate all its students, and could offer him the personal security of a second home. Mendeleev appreciated the solid teaching, the daily con-tact with professors, and the closeness of students to each other. It was to the credit of his teachers, however, that they recognized his talents and made it possible for him to advance professionally.

In 1857, after two years of chemistry teaching at gymnasiums in Sim-feropol and Kiev, during which he gained his magister's degree from St. Petersburg University, Mendeleev was appointed a private docent at that in-stitution; and in 1859 he was sent to Western Europe to study modern techniques of chemical research. After two years in the West, mostly at Heidelberg University, he was reluctant to return to Russia, and applied for an extension of his Western studies. In a letter written in December 1860 and addressed to the curator of the St. Petersburg school district, he lamented the poor research conditions in Russia, which kept the output of scientific work at a comparatively low level. In order to live reasonably, he said, Rus-sian scholars were compelled to take on various "extraneous occupations" in addition to their pursuit of science. Therefore, at a time when experi-mental work in the exact sciences demanded undivided attention on the part of experts, an overwhelming majority of Russian scholars were at best part-time scientists. In Russia, he added, there was also a serious shortage of facilities for experimental work. Russian scientists were forced to spend considerable time keeping laboratories in satisfactory working order, a job that in the West was entrusted to mechanics. Also, in Russia there were neither public nor private laboratories operating outside the universities or independently of educational commitments. Finally, in Russian university laboratories there were no assistants who could relieve professors in teaching the students elementary research techniques.[35] Thus Mendeleev joined the chorus of young scientists whose ideas found a concrete expression in the 1863 university statute, which provided the legal groundwork for a rapid expansion of university laboratories. However, his plea for an extended stay in Western universities fell on deaf ears, and in 1861 he was back in St. Petersburg teaching chemistry at the Engineering School and at St. Petersburg University.

In 1865 Mendeleev successfully defended his doctoral dissertation (dealing with the mixture of alcohol and water) at St. Petersburg University, and was appointed a full professor of technical chemistry at that institution. Although his courses covered the entire spectrum of chemistry, and his publication list grew at a rapid pace, he devoted much time to practical work. In 1863 a petroleum firm sent him to Baku to investigate the unique chemical features of Caucasian naphtha. In 1867 the government appointed him to help in organizing the Russian pavilion at the Paris Exposition. At the same time he conducted research on the effectiveness of chemical fertilizers under the sponsorship of the Free Economic Society, and helped organize the Russian Chemical Society and the First Congress of Russian Naturalists and Physicians. At other times, he studied the chemistry of Russian soils, and looked into the feasibility and practical advantages of irrigating land on the lower Don, Volga, and Dnieper.

Mendeleev's scientific works are generally of three kinds. Some are primarily theoretical and belong to the general category of basic research. Others, designated as textbooks, reveal Mendeleev as a masterly synthesizer of modern chemical knowledge. The third category consists of works in applied science, and includes not only a rich assortment of physical and chemical studies but also extensive research into the economics of Russian industry and agriculture.

A keen interest in theory stayed with Mendeleev from his college years to the end of his life. He wrote and published his first papers while studying at the Pedagogical Institute. After a brief descriptive paper on the chemical analysis of the orthites and pyroxenes (published by the Russian Mineralogical Society in 1854 in the German language) he completed a large study on isomorphism and its relationship to specific volumes. This purely theoretical work showed Mendeleev's intimate familiarity with the chemical literature of the time and his interest in expressing the regularities of nature in scientific laws. With this book he committed himself to a search for "chemical relations," which eventually led him—though not by preconceived plan—to the discovery of the periodic law. Mendeleev's magister's dissertation, defended at St. Petersburg University in 1856, also dealt with specific volumes and isomorphism. Here again, his theoretical bent led him to classify natural phenomena in terms of an underlying regularity.[36] He said years later that whereas isomorphism was a typical property of the elements of the same chemical group, specific volume—"one of the most striking examples of periodicity"—illustrated the recurrence of similar chemical qualities in simple bodies arranged in order of their atomic weights.

Both isomorphism and specific volumes are manifestations of a limited "periodicity" of natural phenomena, for both are related to isolated groups of substances and do not reveal the more universal similarities and classificatory principles. However, they do suggest the regularities that exist on a higher and more comprehensive level. This is not to say that Mendeleev chose to study isomorphism and specific volumes as preliminary steps in a planned search for a universal periodic law. It is true, however, that these studies figured in the development of his major theoretical interests, which eventually led to the discovery of the periodic law. The same may be said for his experimental studies of the expansion of gases and liquids, conducted at Heidelberg in 1859–60; and of his doctoral investigation of water-alcohol compounds, in which he sought to unravel the quantitative regularities in the relationships of internal cohesive forces to chemical composition in different substances.

In all these undertakings Mendeleev was a theoretician *par excellence.* He was an alert and active participant in the search for broader theoretical foundations in chemistry, which occupied many of the leading European chemists of the time. It should not be assumed, however, that all the theoretical studies Mendeleev undertook during this period added fresh new bricks to the rising edifice crowned by the periodic law. He admitted, for example, that his experimental studies of capillarity, conducted in Heidelberg and intended "to provide the key for understanding many physicochemical questions," did not throw any new light on the cohesive forces operating in liquids.

In his theoretical grounding, Mendeleev was not a product of the Russian chemical tradition in the same sense in which Butlerov and Markovnikov were. The laboratory facilities at the Pedagogical Institute were negligible, and the young Mendeleev spent most of his time in library research. From the very beginning he was an independent scholar, and he sought out his own scientific problems with no outside guidance in the selection of reading material. His teachers recognized his great talents at an early stage, and encouraged him to undertake graduate studies. When he took the matriculation examinations in chemistry, several leading Russian chemists, including the Academician C. J. Fritzsche, were invited to be present. By the time Mendeleev went to Heidelberg at the age of 25, he was already a recognized scholar with an enviable reputation. Sechenov noted that Mendeleev was the unofficial leader of the *kruzhok* of Russian students in Heidelberg because, despite his age (he was five years younger than Sechenov), "he was an established chemist, whereas we were students."[37] Most of this early reputation rested on the wide horizons of his knowledge and the depth of his theoretical concerns.

A thorough familiarity with the burning theoretical questions of contemporary chemistry enabled Mendeleev to take an active part in the first International Congress of Chemists, held in Karlsruhe in September 1860.[38] The purpose of this gathering of 127 illustrious chemists was to iron out some of the existing conceptual and terminological inconsistencies in the field, which prevented effective communication among chemists and hampered the growth of chemical theory. The participants concentrated on a precise determination of the concepts of atom, molecule, equivalence, and atomicity. The congress's first concern was to establish a "rational terminology," a uniform system for the determination and expression of chemical formulas. Mendeleev was especially impressed with the famous speech of the Italian chemist Stanislao Cannizzaro, which pleaded for exact measurements of molecular weights on the basis of the criteria established by Gerhardt, following Amadeo Avogadro's gas hypothesis. Mendeleev himself was a member of the committee that drafted the policy resolution of the congress, and he was quick to sense the scientific fruitfulness of substituting exact measurements of atomic weights for the empirical norms of the past. Without the Karlsruhe Congress, it is likely that discovery of the periodic law would have been delayed for some years.

Mendeleev's major theoretical interest, next to the natural classification of elements, was in the chemical nature of solutions. According to his "chemical" or "hydrate" theory, solutions are not mechanical mixtures but chemical combinations; moreover, they are "ordinary examples of chemical reactions," chemical interactions of solvent and soluble. Solutions are associations of hydrated molecules in a state of dynamic equilibrium and uneven dissociation. Mendeleev admitted that his "chemical" theory was only one of many possible hypotheses.[39] In commenting on J. H. van't Hoff's "physical" theory (1885), which was based on the study of osmotic pressure in gases and solutions, Mendeleev claimed that the "chemical" and "physical" explanations of solution were not mutually exclusive: the "chemical" theory, he thought, applied to dilute solutions, and the "physical" to concentrated solutions. However, Mendeleev rejected Svanté Arrhenius's theory of ionic dissociation on the ground that it represented a return to electrochemical explanations. In so doing, Mendeleev isolated himself from one of the most exciting and fruitful developments in modern physical chemistry. Modern chemists interpret the process of dissolving as both a chemical and a physical process.

Mendeleev's intensive concern with chemical theory was only one source of the ideas that built up to the periodic law; the second was his concern with the writing of chemical textbooks for university students. In 1861, immediately after his return from Germany, he wrote *Organic Chemistry*, the first systematic and thorough textbook in this field written by a Russian scholar. It was received favorably, and earned him the Academy of Sciences' Demidov Prize of 1,000 rubles. Mendeleev's reputation, previously great only among professional chemists, now began to reach the intellectual world beyond chemistry, the government bureaus, the industrial entrepreneurs, and the general public.

*Organic Chemistry* was essentially a compilation, with little theoretical articulation and depth. Its main value was that it introduced Russian students to the entire spectrum of substantive knowledge of organic chemistry. At the same time, the process of writing it gave Mendeleev a bird's-eye view of the empirical facts of organic chemistry and an added perspective in his search for regularities and classificatory principles in the world of chemistry in general. The book defined chemistry as a science "concerned not only with the study and comparison of forms and qualities of chemical substances ... but also with the discovery of laws of chemical change."[40] Mendeleev advised his readers not to bury themselves in empirical data and lose sight of theoretical integration and abstraction, but to grasp the full meaning of the great new ideas of Ampère, Gerhardt, and Cannizzaro, which made modern chemistry a single system of categorized knowledge. His pertinent theoretical observations, however, did not receive elaborate treatment, and *Organic Chemistry* became known primarily as an encyclopedia of organic substances.

In 1867 Mendeleev was appointed professor of general chemistry at St. Petersburg University. He immediately offered a course in inorganic chemistry; and since there was no modern textbook available in the Russian language, he undertook to write one. He was eminently qualified to meet this challenge, for during the preceding six years, in addition to having published *Organic Chemistry*, he had written a series of articles on "technical chemistry" for an encyclopedia, conducted successful research in the compounds of water and alcohol, campaigned for the organization of analytical chemistry as part of the university curriculum, and translated Gerhardt and Chancel's *Analytical Chemistry* into Russian.

In 1868–69, Mendeleev published the first two parts of his *Principles of Chemistry*, which were mostly on an introductory level. It was while writing the third part in 1869 that he discovered the periodicity of elements, which he then used as a classificatory principle in selecting and arranging the groups of elements that became the main subject of his analysis. In 1870 the fourth and last part of the textbook was published; at the same time, the periodic law became widely known through a series of articles that Mendeleev published in Russian and German.

*Principles of Chemistry* was an immediate success, for it was a lucid, comprehensive, and ingenious synthesis of up-to-date knowledge in inorganic chemistry. However, it was not immediately recognized as the first "popular" presentation of the periodic principle as a law of nature and a classificatory criterion. Lord Rutherford remarked many years later: "The ideas of Mendeléef at first attracted little attention, for the chemist of his day was more occupied in adding to the chemical facts than in speculating on the relation between them."[41] At the time of its publication, Mendeleev's work was decidedly superior to all the existing textbooks in inorganic chemistry, and it was soon translated into English, French, and German. As the new editions came out, Mendeleev added selected, up-to-date accounts of new developments in theory and notable additions to substantive knowledge. The footnotes grew longer and more interesting; many are tiny essays on Mendeleev's views of the philosophy and logic of science in general and chemistry in particular. T. E. Thorpe wrote in *Nature* in 1888 that the *Principles* "is one of the classics of chemistry"; and that "its place in the history of science is as well-assured as the ever-memorable work of Dalton."[42]

The *Principles* was well received in Russia. It was an inexhaustible source of inspiration for Russian scholars, and it led scores of them to important work in theoretical and applied chemistry. Mendeleev did not found a distinct school of chemistry; yet in a sense all modern Russian chemists are his disciples, for all have been inspired by the magnificent scope of his work and the depth of his wisdom. More than any other work, *Principles of Chemistry* encouraged Mendeleev's compatriots to write in their native tongue, for it showed clearly that Western scholars could no longer ignore the increasing volume of scientific works written in the Russian language.

Approximately one-quarter of Mendeleev's published works belong to the general category of applied science. In this field Mendeleev traveled a long and winding road, and his achievements were of an uneven quality. For the most part his applied studies were not directly related to his specialties in theoretical chemistry. Here, he was guided less by the theoretical needs of modern chemistry than by the practical needs of a society involved in the process of modernization. At the beginning of his scientific career his work was primarily theoretical; and during the initial phase of his teaching career he combined basic research with the writing of chemistry textbooks. As he grew older, however, his interests covered a constantly expanding area of scientific problems, and he began to place a great deal of emphasis on the practical application of modern scientific knowledge. Much of this interest was connected with his earlier field studies of soil, petroleum, and chemical fertilizers.

At an industrial congress held in Moscow in 1882 Mendeleev delivered a long speech entitled "Thoughts on the Conditions for the Development of Factory Production in Russia." During the rest of his life he continued to speak and write extensively about the problems of industrialization, industrial organization, and industrial economy in Russia. His writings on these topics are a mixture of common sense, perceptive comments on the relationship of science to industrialization, simple statements on the nature and social role of science, and extensive demographic, economic, and sociological surveys. To Mendeleev, industrialization was first a problem of applied science and then one of economics and sociology. He took every opportunity to stress the need for a truly scientific approach to the burgeoning of Russian industry, and to remind his colleagues that "the forests of facts and oceans of ideas" pertaining to the technological, economic, and social organization of industry would remain dormant as long as they were not organized by scientific doctrines and hypotheses.

At a time when agrarian socialism, in one form or another, was supported by a large segment of the Russian intelligentsia, Mendeleev advocated industrialization as the only sound path to a more prosperous and civilized future for his country. An increasing complexity and efficiency in industrial technology was to him the best proof of cultural progress. Men-

deleev's championship of Russian industrialization is firmly linked with his
ardent advocacy of closer ties between science and industry. He said: "The
advancement of experimentally verified knowledge and the development of
education in physics and chemistry represent the first essential condition for
the growth of our industry."[43] He prodded the natural scientists to supply
the necessary knowledge for the industrial progress of the country; at the
same time, he criticized the official educational policies, which favored a classical education and were dedicated more to the preservation of the autocratic social order than to the economic advancement of the country.

The emergence of independent research in chemistry by Russian scholars, according to Mendeleev, coincided with the emancipation of the serfs
in the 1860's. At that time several dozen Russian chemists were engaged in
basic research, and the recruitment of German chemists to serve as Academicians or professors had been almost completely discontinued. The swift
"nationalization" and increasing popularity of chemistry led to the formation of the Russian Chemical Society at the end of the 1860's. The Society,
however, emphasized "the search for chemical truths for their own sake
and their abstract significance," that is, "the philosophical conquest of nature." Mendeleev observed unhappily that in the 1880's Russia still lacked
a bridge between the world of theoretical science and the world of industry. He insisted that industrial technology was not only the most modern
form of applied science but also the most effective testing ground for the
claims of scientific theory.

Despite their many astute statements, Mendeleev's economic studies are
easily the weakest part of his scholarly output. He often mixed several
genres of writing, from simple statistical compilations and autobiographical sketches to editorializing of epic proportions, intricate discussions of
industrial technology, and subtle discourses on the nature of science. These
studies do not have the modern theoretical grounding and logical unity
displayed so consistently in Mendeleev's purely scientific writings. Even
so, Lev Tolstoi was rather hasty and unfair when he depicted Mendeleev's
*Toward an Understanding of Russia* as a book rich in information but poor
in judgment.[44]

Mendeleev's rich life was a fortunate coalescence of theoretical and applied research, educational activities, popularization of scientific knowledge, and defense of the scientific attitude. Overlying this spectrum of dedicated labor was a carefully thought out philosophical viewpoint.[45] The
overriding importance of science is easily the dominant thought in this
philosophy. Mendeleev contended that a command of knowledge drawn

from physics and chemistry was the yardstick by which the general education of modern man should be measured, just as versatility in the classicist tradition had marked a well-bred man a century or so earlier. Commenting on Lomonosov's famous pronouncement that the time was approaching when Russia would produce its own Platos and Newtons, he stated that Russia would do much better if it forgot all about the Platos and doubled its search for Newtons.[46]

Mendeleev thought that the word "atomism" best described his conviction that the relationship between the chemical qualities of elements and their atomic weights provided the key for understanding the chemistry of the inorganic universe and elevating it to the heights of Newtonian physics. Mendeleev was a "materialist" in a nonphilosophical sense: his "materialism" did not transcend a purely scientific interest in atomism, and had no metaphysical leanings. Indeed, Mendeleev rejected philosophical materialism with the same determination that he rejected idealism. He criticized the materialistic legacy of Büchner, Vogt, and Moleschott, which (embellished with scientific terminology) had made a strong impression on Chernyshevskii and the Nihilists. In his later years he also rejected materialism as an ideology and as a philosophy of history.[47]

Mendeleev called his own philosophy "realism," and was very eager to keep it free of any admixture of both idealism and materialism. Realism, as a philosophical vantage point, meant several things to Mendeleev. Above everything else, it recognized a strict dividing line between science and metaphysics. For this reason, Mendeleev was unequivocally opposed to spiritualism when it flared up in the 1870's and claimed a number of leading Russian scientists among its most active converts. To him, the only sound philosophy was one anchored in the facts of science. "In our time," he stated, "the contribution of the natural sciences to emergent philosophical views has been firmly established."[48] Such a philosophy could become an effective instrument for alerting society to the latest contributions of science, and could help scientists themselves clear their thoughts of ideological intrusions that stood in the way of an effective and rational application of positive knowledge. The guiding principle of science, and of realism, was a disciplined skepticism: "Do not take anything for granted; be constantly alert to the need for verification. . . . Science knows no final truths."[49]

Mendeleev sought a middle ground between the philosophical extremes; yet his realism was not a simple reconciliation. He viewed matter, force, and spirit as the basic ontological categories, but he did not elaborate a philosophy in which each of these was treated as an absolutely independent category. Instead, he identified "matter," "spirit," "will," and "force" as "categorical concepts"—as the ontological keys for understanding the world in its totality.[50] In one of his last writings he noted that the general problem of the distinct origins and unique characteristics of matter, force, and spirit transcended the legitimate boundaries of science.[51] Mendeleev resented the tendency of D. A. Tolstoi and his followers to interpret the exclusive concern of modern natural scientists with matter and force as a denial of "spirit," and thus by implication a denial of the spiritual foundations of Russian culture. However, his writings gave "matter" a preeminence in two ways: it was the only ontological category to which he paid real attention, and it was closely related to his atomistic philosophy.

Mendeleev consistently rejected the sweeping demands and uncritical presuppositions of philosophical materialism; but he also criticized conservative writers who saw a threat to the moral code in scientific efforts to explain psychological phenomena in physiological terms. His argument was that modern physiologists followed the path of science and therefore depended on the most stringent moral and logical criteria in formulating their conclusions.[52] Mendeleev also avoided the crude exaggerations and the pitfalls of Nihilism as propounded by Pisarev and Antonovich. To him, science was not a panacea for all human ills; nor was it the only source of enlightenment, though he once asserted that "science marks the power and the glory of our time and is the basis of all accomplishments of universal value."[53] He did not regard religion and science as incompatible, but was inclined to equate the divine truths of religion with the objective truths of science. Science, according to Mendeleev, was not limited to "subjective" or "human" paths, but aspired to unravel the "divine" or "objective" truths.[54] However, in his writings this essential compatibility of science and religion received hardly more than a passing endorsement.

Mendeleev did not accept the Nihilist demand that the arts be dedicated primarily to the popularization of science and play a role subservient to scientific work. To him, science and the arts sprang from different human endowments and performed different cultural functions. As two distinct approaches to the study and appreciation of nature, science and the arts were the gateway to the higher development of culture; it was through both the scientific and the artistic interpretation of nature that man could best learn to appreciate "the infinite, the supreme, the rational, the divine, and the inspirational" in the world that surrounded him.[55] Because of his great appreciation of art, Mendeleev was elected a member of the Academy of Arts in St. Petersburg.

The Nihilists looked at science as a powerful intellectual weapon for breaking down the existing society and building a new one, which they never depicted in precise terms. To them, science was a tool of social revolution. To Mendeleev, on the other hand, science was an instrument of social evolution. He was not a defender of the social status quo; but neither was he interested in destroying the existing society and replacing it with any socialist schemes. Instead, he felt that society should be modernized by careful, systematic, and gradual industrialization. Mendeleev saw in science an accumulative process of intellectual evolution. He noted that the Karlsruhe Congress of Chemists had marked the successful inauguration of modern chemistry because it combined "freedom of scientific inquiry . . . without which science could not advance but would become petrified, as in the Middle Ages" and "scientific conservatism . . . without which the roots of past studies could not bear new fruit."[56] In a combination of unrestrained search for new theories and profound acquaintance with the knowledge inherited from earlier generations of scholars, Mendeleev saw the soundest means of scientific advancement. And as a product of the gradual intertwining of old and new knowledge, science provided a reliable model for gradual social change.

Mendeleev championed "the gradual emergence of an industrial civilization as the most natural environment of [modern] man's social life";[57] and he thought that "gradualism" was the best term to describe his views on social change. He considered capitalism a social system ideally equipped to reap the fullest benefits from modern industrial technology, and was critical of the liberal Populists who were convinced that Russia's unique historical and cultural tradition would allow her to skip capitalism as a phase of social development. In these views Mendeleev was unmistakably the product of his family upbringing; he combined the intellectualism of his father with the entrepreneurial spirit of his mother.

Before 1870, Mendeleev was too preoccupied with research and teaching to give systematic thought to the general problem of science's relationship to society. But as his fame grew and his research expanded to cover many areas of technology and applied science, he began to pay more attention to the unique cultural characteristics of science. He pleaded for a more realistic and versatile role for science in Russian society; but he realized that this was unlikely to come about unless there were changes in the official attitudes toward scientific inquiry and science as a social institution. Above all, the government—and other social agencies interested in harnessing scientific knowledge for the benefit of the state and the community at large—had to abandon the erroneous notion that the more abstract and theoretical a science is, the less practical value it has. Appealing for extensive government financial assistance to basic research, Mendeleev said that the credit for modern technological progress belonged to men who were steeped in scientific doctrines and hypotheses; and that ideas of this sort did not widen the gap between science and society, but narrowed it. He spoke for the leading Russian scientists of his age when he said: "Only when truths are sought for their own sake and for their absolute purity are they applicable in real life";[58] i.e., the more comprehensive a scientific theory, the greater its practical utility. The essence of his appeal was: Do not dilute science to make it more acceptable socially, but teach the responsible representatives of society to appreciate theory as the true source of scientific power.

The strength of theory, according to Mendeleev, lay not only in the formulation of general concepts and the discovery of the laws of nature, but also in the blending of objective knowledge with a specific world view. Science was to him both a system of facts and concepts and an open-ended field of hypotheses and philosophical thought. His Introduction to the fourth edition of *Principles of Chemistry* (1881) contains a forthright statement of his views on science as a cultural force:

"Like every other science, chemistry is at once an instrument and a goal. It is an instrument in the service of practical ends. With its help, substances of every description are brought under human control. It opens the way to the exploitation of natural resources and the creation of new substances. . . . In this sense, chemistry does not differ from simple descriptions of things seen and perceived, and indeed differs only slightly from the practical arts. . . . [But] in chemistry, as in every advanced science, there are higher aspirations, unrestricted by specific temporal goals . . . which express a world view related to the subjects of chemical inquiry. This world view transcends mere familiarity with the fundamental scientific facts and the generally accepted exact conclusions; it also includes hypotheses that explain, express, and evoke relations and phenomena that are not yet fully established. Since the scientific world view changes drastically, not only from one period to another but also from one person to another, it is an expression of creativity; it draws on all human intellectual resources, and it is the highest and most important form of scientific development. Each scientist endeavors to translate the world view of the school he belongs to into an indisputable principle of science."[59]

Just as society must understand the true nature of science, so science must be alert to social needs. In a speech delivered at the Sixth Congress of Russian Naturalists and Physicians in 1879, Mendeleev warned his colleagues never to forget their sacred duty not only to extend the realm of "universal science" but also to devise applications of scientific knowledge that would benefit their country.[60] Whereas K. A. Timiriazev stressed the popularizing of scientific knowledge as a prerequisite for a rational and enlightened society, Mendeleev advocated achieving the same goal by a broader technological application of modern science.

As one major step toward achieving all these goals, Mendeleev urged a more rational distribution of research and teaching duties among university professors. He knew that many of the most promising Russian scientists of his generation were achieving much less than they might have because they were forced to take on excessive teaching loads in order to supplement their incomes. By tradition, particularly strong in St. Petersburg, popular professors were encouraged to teach in as many as half a dozen institutions at the same time. Mendeleev knew, for example, that his teacher A. A. Voskresenskii, whose promise had been heralded by Liebig, had made no important scientific contributions primarily because most of his time was taken up with heavy teaching chores at St. Petersburg University, the Main Pedagogical Institute, the Communications Institute, the Central Engineering School, and two military schools.[61] Voskresenskii's predicament was by no means unique to him. A similar warning came from Chebyshev, who noted that simultaneous teaching assignments in several institutions had prevented the mathematician Mikhail Ostrogradskii from making full use of his great talents.

Mendeleev realized that the edifice of science is built with material supplied by many scholars belonging to different generations and countries; and that scientists who make profound theoretical discoveries are greatly indebted to the many investigators who have accumulated the data on which these discoveries are based.[62] He said that to achieve greatness, a scientist must not only make a discovery but also convince his peers of the validity of his claims. Lavoisier had been a great scientist because he was successful on both counts: he announced great scientific ideas and verified them experimentally. Mendeleev did not put himself in this category. He was rightfully proud that he had made a great scientific discovery and recognized its significance, but he scrupulously acknowledged that his periodic law of elements had been experimentally verified by other scientists. He was unduly modest, however, in asserting: "For my part, I consider Roscow, De Boisbaudran, Nillson, Winkler, Brauner, Cornelley, Thorpe, and the others who verified the adaptability of the periodic law to chemical reality as the true founders of the periodic law, the further development of which still awaits fresh workers."[63]

Throughout this argument, Mendeleev's view of the international foundations of scientific thought is clear and forceful. He strove to convince his countrymen that the international nature of science was in no way incompatible with Russian thought and social values; and that Russian realism had more in common with modern scientific thought than with the multitudinous varieties of philosophical irrationalism. Nevertheless, he found it important to emphasize that the idea of "national science" should not be taken lightly. Scientific orientations did indeed vary from one country to another, and it was often easy to identify the country of a chemist solely on the basis of his theoretical bent.[64]

As for Mendeleev's place among the great men of science, we can do no better than repeat Lord Rutherford's statement that the periodic law is a "remarkable generalization" covering all the elements known to science; and that Mendeleev was the logical man to make the discovery, for he had a "philosophic mind," a rare gift among the chemists of his time.[65]

### P. L. CHEBYSHEV AND THE ST. PETERSBURG SCHOOL OF MATHEMATICS

Mathematics has a long tradition in Russia. By the 1860's it had developed such solid roots in Russian culture that P. L. Chebyshev could proudly call it a national science. In 1869, K. S. Veselovskii noted the central position and historical continuity of mathematics in the St. Petersburg Academy of Sciences, and observed that during the 1860's the Academicians were engaged in a great diversity of mathematical studies, particularly in "higher algebra, higher geometry, integral calculus, number theory, theoretical mathematics, and anthropological statistics."[66]

In 1863 the mathematical curriculum of the universities was expanded to allow for four to six instructors in mathematics at each university and for a long overdue separation of mechanics from mathematics.[67] The community of mathematicians grew perceptibly, and it was no surprise when the Moscow Mathematical Society appeared and soon became a going concern. The Society intensified personal contact between the older, tested scholars and the most promising representatives of the new generation, and helped to keep Russian scholars informed of the most up-to-date mathematical thinking in the West. At first, it concentrated on reports of new developments in mathematics; but it gradually made original mathematical investigation its prime objective.[68] By special government authorization, the Society's *Mathematical Symposium* reached every gymnasium.

The idea of mathematics as a Russian "national science" was largely a response to the growing Western recognition of Russian contributions to the field. For several decades Western scholars had been reading articles written by Russian mathematicians and published in such erudite journals as Crelle's *Journal für reine und angewandte Mathematik* and Liouville's *Journal des mathématiques pures et appliquées,* and by the 1860's they had begun to express their admiration. In 1860 the Paris Académie des Sciences honored Chebyshev for his many outstanding contributions in various branches of mathematics by electing him a corresponding member.[69] The first volume of Joseph Bertrand's *Traité de calcul différentiel et de calcul intégral* (1864) summarized and enthusiastically commended two of Chebyshev's papers.[70] Several letters written by Karl Gauss, made public after his death, showed clearly that that great mathematician was interested in Lobachevskii's non-Euclidean geometry. And a symposium on the calculus of variations published in 1861 in England contained contributions from the Russian mathematicians M. V. Ostrogradskii and N. D. Brashman.[71]

Because mathematics was cold, logically involved, and ideologically neutral, it was not especially attractive to the growing ranks of science enthusiasts in Russia.* The Nihilists of the 1860's and the Populists of the 1870's found in mathematics neither support nor inspiration for their social and ideological designs. Contact between mathematicians and natural scientists, except those interested in some branches of physics and astronomy, was nonexistent. In educational circles mathematics was considered the best tool for sharpening cognitive processes and logical precision without exposing the students to ideological values. Even the curriculum of theological acade-

---

* The academic aloofness of mathematics, which detached it from the vagaries of practical existence, was not complete. For example, N. E. Zernov, a Moscow professor, and the Academician V. Ia. Buniakovskii used calculations derived from abstract probability theory in an effort to determine "economically sound and morally justified" insurance premiums. They also sought, on a small scale, to determine suitable methods of prediction in "the vital areas of national economy and demography, for which little, if any, adequate official statistical data were available." However, both Zernov and Buniakovskii were more interested in the practical applications of probability theory than in adding more mathematical and logical precision to it. Contemporary Western scholars, for the most part, also ignored the theoretical aspects of probability; true to the spirit of the Gaussian tradition, they tended to concentrate on the branches of mathematics that emphasized absolute rigor in operation and proof.

mies included algebra, analytical geometry, mechanics, and integral and differential calculus; however, during the 1860's these schools rapidly cut back their mathematical courses.[72]

The greatest Russian mathematician of the 1860's and 1870's was Pafnutii Chebyshev, a model scientist, a major link in the Russian mathematical tradition, and a fountain of ideas and challenges for scholars in several branches of mathematics. Chebyshev's dedication to mathematics was strongly influenced by his own personality and personal history. As a boy, he suffered a slight leg injury that prevented him from playing with neighborhood children and forced him to devise solitary "games" requiring a minimum of locomotion. At first he carved simple toys with a penknife, and then gradually began to construct working mechanisms of various kinds. A model of a wheelchair constructed by Chebyshev was displayed at the Chicago World's Fair in 1893, and an adding machine constructed by him is deposited in the Conservatoire des Arts et Métiers in Paris.[73] Over the course of his long life he constructed 40 prototypes and 80 modifications of mechanisms; some of these resulted from the playfulness of his imagination, and some were "illustrations," or models built to test various transformations of motion. Not surprisingly, Chebyshev was one of the founders of the modern theory of mechanisms. During his frequent visits in Western Europe he divided his time between academic conversations with eminent mathematicians and visits to local factories to study "practical mechanics."[74]

Chebyshev had a keen interest in James Watt's parallel linkage, which led him to search for a more reliable means of calculating the transformation of rectilinear into circular motion and produced a lasting preoccupation with the construction of mechanisms producing specific trajectories of motion. Motivated by these interests, Chebyshev elaborated a new branch of mathematics, which dealt with the approximate representation of functions. He introduced the notion of "the best uniform approximation," one of the fundamental concepts in the modern theory of approximation. Chebyshev and his disciples also introduced several basic methods for obtaining the best approximations to arbitrary individual functions by using polynomials, all of which are widely used today.*

A series of papers on number theory, the first published in 1852, showed that Chebyshev's interest was not always motivated by practical needs. The theory of numbers is a "mathematician's mathematics"—a branch of math-

---

* It must be noted, however, that the German mathematician Karl Weierstrass provided the first rigorous general proof for the theoretical possibility of approximating continuous functions by algebraic polynomials, thus providing the theoretical foundation for Chebyshev's techniques (A. D. Aleksandrov *et al.,* II, 267–68).

ematics important more because of its contributions to the refinement of mathematical conceptualization than because of its direct application in various sciences. Chebyshev identified number theory as "transcendental arithmetic," a special science that borrows the concept of number from arithmetic and the concept of equations from algebra and transcendental analysis, but is essentially different from both arithmetic and algebra. By looking at both numbers and equations from a special point of view, the theory of numbers "encompasses completely new results for arithmetic and the theory of determinate equations."[75] Chebyshev's interest in this field began when, as a young man, he helped in the preparation of the St. Petersburg Academy's edition of the works of Euler, the founder of the modern theory of numbers.

One of the most difficult problems in number theory, the distribution of prime numbers in natural sequences, has attracted the attention of mathematicians since the time of Euclid. Euclid himself was the first to prove the theorem that there were an infinite number of primes, and Euler provided a new proof for the same theorem. In 1808 Adrien Legendre arrived at an empirical formula for the approximate determination of primes within prescribed numerical sequences. Chebyshev, however, was the first to establish the distribution and frequency of primes in given series of whole numbers. In this and other projects, he showed extraordinary skill in applying simple algebraic operations to very complex mathematical problems and a profound familiarity with both historical and current work in the theory of numbers. In return, his memoirs received appreciative and serious consideration by eminent workers in that field (notably Joseph Serret, Charles Hermite, H. Minkowski, and A. Ia. Khinchin). In particular, Chebyshev tried to improve on the work of Joseph Bertrand; and Chebyshev's contribution, in turn, was later refined by J. Hadamard. Chebyshev's study of the quadratic forms of positive determinants, which also grew from his interest in number theory, was followed up by several of his more distinguished disciples.

Today, Chebyshev is known mostly for his contributions to probability theory, and his name is particularly associated with the law of large numbers and the central limit theorem. The law of large numbers allows one to calculate the connections between probabilities and particular frequencies of random variables; the central limit theorem makes possible a theoretical explanation of the so-called normal dispersion of probabilities in many natural phenomena.[76] For a time Chebyshev's work was ignored in the West—mostly because of a rapidly decreasing interest in probability calculation—but the continuity of its influence was sustained by his followers among the younger generation of Russian mathematicians. When Western mathematicians "rediscovered" probability theory, today a basic instrument in several branches of physics, Chebyshev's contributions received wide recognition, not so much in their original form as in the elaborations and refinements of A. M. Liapunov and A. A. Markov, his leading disciples. Liapunov's own central limit theorem and Markov's "chains" are essential tools for modern probability theory. Guido Castelnuovo rightly regards the work of these and other Russian mathematicians as the most important contribution to probability theory since the time of Laplace.[77]

In 1859, at the age of 38, Chebyshev was elected to full membership in the St. Petersburg Academy of Sciences, and was simultaneously appointed a professor at St. Petersburg University. Through frequent visits to Western Europe he maintained personal contact with leading mathematicians in France, Germany, and England; and in 1874 the Paris Academy elected him an *associé étranger*, the first such honor to be granted a native Russian since Peter the Great. The recognition of his contributions in the West, his strategic academic position at home, the acknowledged brilliance of his mind, the remarkable lucidity of his ideas, and his efficiency in teaching combined to make Chebyshev the progenitor of a distinct St. Petersburg school in mathematics. His influence began to be felt in the 1860's, coinciding with the rapid rise in the number of Russian mathematicians and the general upsurge in scientific endeavor.

Chebyshev was a complete mathematician, and his interest in mathematics dominated all his activities. He was a member of the Curriculum Committee of the Ministry of National Education, the Technical Committee of the Main Administration of Artillery, the Council of the St. Petersburg School District, and the Moscow Mathematical Society; but in all these offices he acted strictly as a professional mathematician. In scientific circles, he took an active part in several sessions of the French Association for the Advancement of Science and in several congresses of Russian naturalists—reading papers, participating in discussions, or exhibiting his mechanical models.

Chebyshev's mathematical legacy consisted to a large extent of brilliant but open-ended ideas, essentially incomplete and much in need of further elaboration and refinement. According to one of his students, the fact that Chebyshev published the results of many of his investigations without proofs played an important role in the formation of a unique Russian school of mathematicians. Attracted to the legacy of their master, Chebyshev's disciples often came up with original discoveries.[78]

Chebyshev's first disciples were A. N. Korkin (1837–1908) and E. I. Zolotarev (1847–78), neither of whom came even close to emulating the productivity, originality, and mathematical erudition of his teacher. Korkin, after brilliant investigations at the beginning of his academic career, soon became overcommitted to his teaching duties at St. Petersburg University and the Naval Academy and gave up serious mathematical work. Zolotarev met an accidental death in the same year that he was elected an adjunct of the Academy of Sciences in recognition of his published work and great promise. Nevertheless, the two were true disciples of Chebyshev, and as such helped to found the St. Petersburg school in mathematics. Both believed, like their teacher, that true mathematicians should apply their skills and talents to the search for algorithms leading to the solution of practical problems. The practical function of mathematics was not to serve the growing needs of modern technology, but to help empirical sciences resolve their methodological difficulties and sharpen their theories. This outward orientation prevented the members of the St. Petersburg school from recognizing and appreciating the resourcefulness of various Western European inward orientations, which were dedicated to pure abstractions and could not be reduced to empirically identifiable algorithms.

The first important contribution of the Chebyshevian school was a joint effort by Korkin and Zolotarev on the theory of quadratic forms, which attracted comment even in the West. Charles Hermite remarked that the project had produced "profound results"; others agreed, and the reputation of the St. Petersburg mathematicians was firmly established. Chebyshev's school subscribed to no philosophy and had no ideological overtones; it stood apart from the intense social and intellectual ferment that pervaded Russia after the 1850's. However, at the time when the Ministry of National Education favored the teaching of mathematics in gymnasiums as a source of exacting logical exercises with a minimum content of undesirable substantive knowledge and ideological influence, Chebyshev's school acquired its distinctiveness and reputation by its unswerving dedication to close ties between mathematics and substantive inquiries.

The advent of the St. Petersburg school coincided with an increased interest among Russian scholars in the mathematicization of the physical sciences, and with the first extensions of mathematical research techniques beyond physics and astronomy, which had been their traditional fields of

application. Chemists, crystallographers, physical geographers, social stat-
isticians, demographers, and economists now looked to mathematics, at
first cautiously, for more accurate and reliable methods of inquiry. The
next generation produced an impressive number of physical scientists (typified by N. E. Zhukovskii, E. S. Fedorov, and A. N. Krylov) who made
tangible contributions not only to their respective disciplines but also to
mathematics.

### THE TRIUMPH OF NON-EUCLIDEAN GEOMETRY

At a meeting of the teaching staff of Kazan University held on February 23, 1826, N. I. Lobachevskii had presented the basic outline of his non-
Euclidean geometry. Subsequently, splitting his working time between
scholarship and administrative duties, he wrote a series of essays in Russian,
French, and German in an effort to attract the attention of the academic
community to the possibility of constructing a logically integrated and consistent geometric system without accepting the universal validity of Euclid's fifth postulate (the so-called parallel postulate). Lobachevskii died in
1856, so far largely unrecognized by the world of scholarship. Only Karl
Gauss, generally considered the greatest mathematician of the nineteenth
century, openly commended Lobachevskii's scholarship: it was on Gauss's
recommendation that the Göttingen Learned Society elected Lobachevskii
a corresponding member.[79]

It is not difficult to see why most of the scientific community at first rejected non-Euclidean geometry. In the first place, by challenging the Euclidean legacy, Lobachevskii had challenged a science built on assumptions
that were generally considered as obvious as they were universal. In the
validity of its axioms and postulates and in the inner consistency of its logic,
Euclid's geometry was the model of a perfect science. Moreover, scholars
were reluctant to even consider the possibility that one man could by himself establish a complete science, particularly when his creation did not have
an experimental basis. Finally the new geometry appeared so contrary to
nature as seen by man that it was considered useless from a practical standpoint.

The greatest single triumph of Russian mathematics during the 1860's
was the eventual recognition of the revolutionary sweep of Lobachevskii's
non-Euclidean geometry by the international community of scientists. In
1866, the French mathematician Guillaume Jules Hoüel published a French
translation of Lobachevskii's *Geometrische Untersuchungen*, to which he

appended several extracts from Karl Gauss's letters to H. C. Schumacher, written in 1831 and published in 1860, four years after Lobachevskii's death.[80] The letters revealed Gauss's interest in the basic principles of Lobachevskii's geometry and a particular concern with its effect on the Euclidean theorem referring to the sum of angles in a triangle. In 1867 Hoüel himself published an original work on the fundamental principles of geometry, making use of Lobachevskii's ideas.[81] Interest in Lobachevskii's non-Euclidean geometry began to grow rapidly. In the same year came the posthumous publication of G. F. B. Riemann's famous lectures on the foundations of geometry (delivered in 1854), in which the German mathematician proposed a new geometry built on the notions of geodetic lines and curved surfaces in spaces with any number of dimensions.

In 1868 the Italian mathematician E. Beltrami published a volume on non-Euclidean geometry showing the logical feasibility of three geometries: the Euclidean, in which the sum of angles in a triangle is equal to two right angles; Lobachevskii's system, in which the sum is less than two right angles; and a third geometry in which the sum exceeds two right angles.[82] In a popular lecture delivered in 1870, Hermann Helmholtz relied on Lobachevskii, Riemann, and Beltrami in challenging the Kantian notion of space as an "*a priori* mode of external perception" and arguing in favor of geometry as an empirical science.[83] By 1871, Felix Klein was able to undertake a synthesis of non-Euclidean ideas, and defined the separate systems of "hyperbolic geometry," "elliptic geometry," and "parabolic geometry."

In a lecture delivered at the Royal Institution in 1873, the English mathematician William Kingdon Clifford went so far as to compare Lobachevskii with Copernicus in his effect on mankind's conception of the cosmos.[84] According to Clifford, Lobachevskii's criticism of the foundations of geometry coalesced with the related ideas of Gauss—and later those of Riemann and Helmholtz—to form a concept of space much broader than the one on which ancient geometry was built. In the words of J. R. Newman: "The assumptions which were very properly made by the ancient geometers are practically exact . . . for such finite things as we have to deal with, and such portions of space as we can reach; yet the truth of them for much larger things, or very much smaller things . . . is a matter to be decided by experiment, when its powers are considerably increased."[85] By challenging the universality of Euclid's axioms and postulates, Lobachevskii helped to ally geometry with the experimental sciences.

According to the French mathematician Henri Poincaré, Lobachevskii's thought was eventually built into fundamental developments that forced mathematics to abandon intellectual absolutism but gave it, in return, powerful tools and wide new areas for theoretical investigation and practical application. When Einstein's general theory of relativity was formulated in 1915, several branches of mathematics—thanks to non-Euclidean geometries—were already "relativized" and prepared to pursue the new possibilities that it raised in the modern physical and chemical sciences. Poincaré talked with authority when he proclaimed that Lobachevskii's geometry had ceased to be an idle exercise in logic and had proved its applicability to practical matters, as demonstrated by the help it gave to Felix Klein and himself in the integration of linear differential equations.[86] Poincaré based his "law of relativity" on the claim that "no experience will ever be in contradiction to Euclid's [parallel] postulate; nor, on the other hand, will any experience ever contradict the [parallel] postulate of Lobachevskii."[87] In the apparent conflict between "geometrical empiricism" and "rationalism" generated by the non-Euclidean systems, Poincaré saw a fruitful area of mathematical investigation. Even the earliest non-Euclideans, observed Bertrand Russell, realized that geometry had become, at least in part, an empirical science and not a branch of pure mathematics; and that "the geometry which is required by the engineer or the astronomer is not a branch of pure mathematics, but a branch of physics."[88]

Although scientific appreciation of Lobachevskii's work was gathering momentum in the West in the 1860's and 1870's, Russian mathematicians were silent until close to the end of the century.[89] The only exception was Viktor Buniakovskii, who, in defense of the vested interests of the Academy mathematicians and their St. Petersburg and Moscow followers, took it upon himself to attack all digressions from the sacrosanct axioms and postulates of Euclid's geometry. Butlerov, too, though meaning no harm, hampered Lobachevskii's cause by making non-Euclidean geometry part of his defense of the compatibility of science and spiritualistic theories.[90] In 1868, prompted by the publication of Hoüel's translation and essay, Kazan University held a commemorative meeting in honor of Lobachevskii, at which the main speaker thanked Hoüel for his efforts in bringing Lobachevskii's ideas to the attention of the international scientific community.[91] But even this speech dealt mostly with Lobachevskii as a man and a teacher, and made no effort to attract the attention of Russian mathematicians to the new vistas opened by the non-Euclidean geometries.[92]

The challenge of the non-Euclidean geometries bypassed Chebyshev altogether. Not only was he preoccupied with his own investigations, but he was also hampered by his feeling that nineteenth-century mathematicians should seek their topics of investigation in the legacy of pre-nineteenth-century mathematicians. It was by staying close to the established paths of mathematical science that the St. Petersburg school of mathematics made its appeal and achieved its successes. Despite its initial conservatism, however, it rapidly caught up with the spirit of the changing mathematical culture, and soon became an important servant of modern empirical science.

The work of both Chebyshev and Lobachevskii, in different ways, helped remove mathematics from Olympus and bring it down to earth. Essentially, Chebyshev spoke on behalf of Lobachevskii when he said: "Mathematics has passed through two periods. In the first, its duties were defined by the gods . . . and in the second by the demigods. Now we have entered the third period, in which its duties are defined by man and his needs." The mathematical ideas of Chebyshev and Lobachevskii are among the greatest contributions to twentieth-century physical science and technology.

### ASTRONOMY, CRYSTALLOGRAPHY, AND PHYSICS

The extensive mathematization of astronomy since the time of Copernicus had prompted Auguste Comte to proclaim it the most exact and perfect of sciences. But for various reasons, the development of a strong mathematical tradition in Russia was far ahead of any noteworthy astronomical tradition. Astronomy in Russia was dominated by foreigners for a longer period than any other science. In the 1860's, thanks to the talents and industry of F. A. Bredikhin, Russian astronomy at last began to make important contributions to the mainstream of astronomical thought. Bredikhin worked in several fields of astronomy. In his earliest studies, concerned with comets' tails, he substituted rigorous analytical procedures for Bessel's approximative calculations of the effect of the sun's repulsive forces on the formation of the "heavenly wanderers." He also applied mathematical analysis to the study of meteors, a branch of astronomy that at the time was generally considered the least susceptible to mathematical treatment. The first true Russian astrophysicist, he made spectroscopic observations of the sun, comets, and nebulas.

Bredikhin's spectral studies of comets, in particular, were truly pioneering, and helped lay the foundations for the modern mechanical theory of comet formation and the modern electrical theory of comet illumination. In 1876 he suggested that there was a mathematically calculable relationship between the initial speed of cometary particles and the repulsive force of the sun; and that all comets, on the basis of this relationship, could be classified into three basic types. In his work before 1877, Bredikhin concentrated on this unified system of cometary forms; but in his subsequent work he devoted a great deal of attention to "anomalous" comets, the rare examples that deviated from the general typology.[93] This digression from the established pattern necessitated the intensive spectral observations that helped Bredikhin formulate his mechanical theory of comets. Just as Mendeleev sought to unveil a unity in the diversity of chemical elements, and Butlerov to establish the regularities in chemical bonds, Bredikhin tried, on the whole successfully, to bring scientific order into the most unpredictable of cosmic phenomena.

It was Bredikhin's long work on the types of comets, based on a mathematically rigorous interpretation of all the relevant data accumulated by the world's leading experts, that brought him the most enthusiastic praise from his Western peers.[94] R. S. Ball, Astronomer-Royal for Ireland, stated in 1884 that there were three highly important developments in the modern study of comets: "the determination of the connection between the comets and shooting stars ... the spectroscopic researches of comets ... [and] the investigation of the tails of comets. . . . The first of these subjects must be forever associated with the name of Professor Schiaparelli, the second with the name of Huggins, and the third with the name of Professor Bredikhin."[95] As astronomers everywhere began to verify and refine Bredikhin's claims, many learned societies paid him homage by electing him an honorary or corresponding member; among these were the St. Petersburg Academy of Sciences, the Leopoldean-Carolinean German Academy of Natural Sciences, the Royal Astronomical Society in London, and the Italian Spectroscopic Society.

Axel Gadolin, a crystallographer born in Finland and educated in Russia, also relied on mathematics to elevate his field to a higher plane of abstraction. Gadolin's scientific ambition paralleled that of Butlerov, Mendeleev, and Bredikhin. The individual ventures of these men were not attended by equal success and academic glamor, but all were recognized as truly pioneering scientific contributions.

Depending on what he labeled "the law of rationalities in distribution of parameters," and on mathematical deduction, Gadolin established 32 basic crystal symmetries, a very ingenious device for the crystallographic classification of minerals. In 1867 he published *An Introduction to All Crys-*

*tallographic Systems and Their Derivation from a Single General Principle,*
which waited two decades to receive the attention it deserved. In the 1890's
it was finally recognized as a scientific landmark, and was republished as
a volume in Ostwald's *Klassiker der exakten Wissenschaften.*[96] There
were several reasons for the slow acceptance of Gadolin's typology. He
had drifted from one scientific interest to another, and before the publication of the *Introduction* he was virtually unknown to most crystallographers, particularly those abroad. In addition, crystallographers everywhere
were skeptical about any universal law of crystal forms; most mineralogists found "mathematical" crystallography unpalatable and stayed away
from it. Finally, Gadolin's ideas were not wholly original; they were to
some extent a revival and refinement of the ideas contained in a stimulating study written by the German crystallographer J. F. C. Hessel, which
had been published in 1820 and completely overlooked by Hessel's contemporaries because of its exacting mathematical demands. Gadolin's
major contribution was in introducing several new classificatory categories
into the system of symmetries.

Although Gadolin's work was neglected by specialists in his own field,
the St. Petersburg Academy of Sciences, with a long tradition in crystallographic studies, was quick to award him the Lomonosov Prize in recognition of his contributions. In 1873 he was elected a corresponding member of the Academy, and in 1890 a full member. The First Congress of
Russian Naturalists was given a full report on Gadolin's achievements.[97]
These honors were well deserved. Gadolin's work was a significant index
of the growing mathematicization of natural science in Russia. It was also
a vital link in the evolution of crystallography in nineteenth-century Russia, which began when V. M. Severgin popularized the systematic collection and arrangement of minerals by applying René Haüy's pioneering
theories of crystal structure and culminated in the splendid work of E. S.
Fedorov, who produced the first algebraic equations depicting the symmetries of crystals.

Russia had only a few crystallographers in the nineteenth century, but
an inordinately high percentage of them were brilliant. The first of these
was A. T. Kupffer, a Baltic German who had studied crystallography
under the guidance of Haüy and received private mathematical training
from Gauss. His classic study on the precise measurement of the edges of
crystals earned him a coveted prize from the Berlin Academy of Sciences
some forty years before Gadolin enunciated his general crystallographic
law. Equally important was Kupffer's *Handbuch der rechnende Krystal-*

*lonomie* (1831), a work dedicated to the methodology of crystallographic calculation. Although he did not publish any crystallographic works in Russian, Kupffer was a vital link in the development of the Russian crystallographic tradition. As a teacher and researcher, he had a solid following among Russian mineralogists, whom he inspired to elevate their work above mere descriptions of minerals, seeking out general structural principles.[98] He popularized "crystallonomy" not only as a study of geometrical regularities in the formation of crystals, but also as a study of the chemical and physical properties of crystals. His contribution to the mathematicization of crystallographic studies was, however, limited primarily to the detection of errors produced by the use of various types of goniometers in measuring crystals; he relied on methods that had been used by Legendre and Gauss to correct astronomical observations, and paid special attention to Laplace's probability theory.[99] Kupffer died in 1865, two years before Gadolin published his *Introduction*.

In 1863 N. I. Koksharov published the first Russian textbook in crystallography, which summed up the results and methods of the discipline and speculated on the main lines of its future development. A disciple of the famous German crystallographers C. S. Weiss and C. F. Naumann, Koksharov was one of the most thorough and systematic students of mineralogy in Russia. He did not advance crystallographic methodology, nor did he go beyond natural crystals; but no minerals available in Russia escaped his measurements. Even in the 1860's, Koksharov still depended on the methods of measurement devised at the beginning of the century, but this did not prevent him from achieving surprising precision.[100] Gadolin, and later Fedorov, were able to open new paths in the development of crystallography in part because Koksharov's voluminous studies had given them a full initiation into the scientific challenges of the field. In the words of a modern Russian scholar: "The works of Koksharov laid the solid foundation for a geometrical study of the structure of natural bodies. . . . The works of Gadolin achieved the highest level of generalization derived from observed facts."[101]

The St. Petersburg Academy of Sciences made perhaps the greatest contribution of all to the development of Russian crystallography, for it rarely failed to recognize and honor the true pioneers in this discipline, and always elected them to its membership.

As the nineteenth century passed its midpoint, the great upsurge in physics in Western Europe led first to new discoveries and theoretical consolidations in electrodynamics and thermodynamics and then, toward the end of the century, to the blending of electrodynamics and optics. New laboratories sprang up everywhere, and a constantly increasing mathematicization of physics became the order of the day. In 1873 J. C. Maxwell relied on mathematical equations to express the unity of electricity, magnetism, and light, bringing classical physics to a close and heralding the advent of new theories of matter and radiation.

During the 1860's and 1870's Russia kept up with the new developments in physics; but it did not produce any great physicists comparable to Mendeleev in chemistry, Sechenov in physiology, Chebyshev in mathematics, and Bredikhin in astronomy. Although mathematics had reached a high development in Russia, laboratory facilities were primitive and sparse. The Academy, for a long time the center of physical research, entered the 1860's impoverished in competent manpower as well. The Academicians Moritz Jacobi and Heinrich Lenz were by then old and not actively engaged in research. Jacobi did not have any Russian disciples, and Lenz had only a few. New members of the Academy followed not the mainstream of physics, but its various tributaries, such as geophysics, crystallography, and astrophysics. Outside the Academy, things looked somewhat more promising—particularly after the founding of the Russian Physical Society in 1872, the establishment of small but modern physical laboratories at Moscow and Kiev universities in the 1870's, and the increasing concern of the Moscow Society of the Admirers of Natural Science, Anthropology, and Ethnography with physics after 1881.[102]

Although the 1860's and the 1870's did not produce great Russian innovations in physics, they did witness widespread efforts to ensure the flow of modern physical ideas into Russia. No single Russian scientist was strong enough to search for a unity in fragmentized scholarly effort, to challenge the views embedded in tradition, or to seek for broad new scientific paths. In the science of electromagnetism the ideas of Oersted, Faraday, Kirchhoff, Franz Neumann, Wilhelm Weber, and William Thomson (Lord Kelvin) were still filtering into Russia. However, during the 1870's the most enterprising Russian scientists, still very few in number, were gradually introduced to the avalanche of new ideas stemming from the genius of J. C. Maxwell (who was quick to acknowledge his own debt to Russia's mathematicians). Again, it was great German physical laboratories—particularly Kirchhoff's and Helmholtz's—that introduced young Russian scholars to modern ideas. The work of the leading Russian physicists of the time was marked by bold efforts to improve laboratory techniques, and by its connection with the various problems of electrodynamics raised by Maxwell's studies. Whether they studied the behavior of thermoelectric metals (M. P. Avenarius), the techniques for measuring electrical oscillations (R. A. Kolli), the electromagnetic qualities of dielectrics (N. N. Shiller, P. A. Zilov), the magnetic qualities of metals and magnetized fluids (A. G. Stoletov), or one of many other problems in electrodynamics and thermodynamics, these Russian physicists were no more than modest innovators.

In Russia, it was not the depth but the magnitude of physical studies that stood as the distinguishing feature of the age. This was a period of lively but unsystematic concern with geothermic measurements, meteorological observations, thermodynamic experiments, scattered problems in molecular physics, and terrestrial magnetism. Most of this work was devoid of theoretical analysis, and there was hardly any effort to synchronize empirical induction with mathematical deduction. Russian scientists distinguished themselves more in contributing to the theoretical integration of chemistry than to that of physics. When mathematics was used in physics, it was used to formulate "empirical laws of limited magnitude." This was a period of catching up with the Western achievements of the past, exploring new areas of research, and encouraging projects for the future development of physics in Russia.

PART II

SCIENCE IN THE AGE OF CRISIS
1884–1917

## CHAPTER SIX

# Universities, Politics, and Science

## THE UNIVERSITY STATUTE OF 1884

The Russian university statute of 1884 was a document of momentous political and ideological significance. It uncompromisingly denied academic autonomy to the institutions of higher education and scientific research, completely negating the academic libertarianism that had been generated by the ideological ferment of the Reform era and built into the 1863 university statute. The new statute reaffirmed the government's intent to dedicate the universities primarily to the preservation of monarchical absolutism. At no other time in modern Russian history did the universities more clearly reflect social pressure than during the reigns of the last two tsars; and at no other time was the government so determined to destroy the true spirit of university life. In inaugurating the 1884 statute, the government worried about its own survival, not the university's.

The government regarded the universities as centers of social rebellion and felt compelled to tame them. It could not act straightforwardly, however, for it knew very well that the universities had never before been so important to the nation's welfare. The need for trained professionals with higher education was constantly growing. Industrialization, railroad construction, and mining had begun to move at a faster pace. The growing complexity of international relations and the increasing role of power politics forced the Russian government to harness modern mechanics, chemistry, and metallurgical technology in order to modernize the country's armed forces. In handling the universities, the government was caught in a dilemma: on one hand, the universities played a vital part in modernizing the national economy; on the other hand, they were an equally vital link in the growing resistance to the autocratic system.

To talk about the modern university is to talk about the intellectual core of institutions engaged in the advancement and diffusion of scientific knowledge. It became increasingly clear during the last decades of the nineteenth century that science is a very complex component of modern culture. Its most direct and practical aim is the advancement of material culture, and it therefore reflects the advancement of *civilization*, as defined by Alfred Weber. Science's most important by-product is the introduction of intellectual values, especially values critical of sacred institutions; as a source of these values, science is a part of nonmaterial *culture*. The Russian government—and the guardians of the official ideology—accepted science as a part of Russian civilization but had grave doubts about its worth as a part of Russian culture.

By the 1880's the Russian universities had become bastions of a political rebellion that threatened to undermine the most cherished values and institutions of autocracy. University students championed both the critical spirit of science and a higher and nobler spirit of citizenship; and student unrest during the waning decades of tsarist autocracy was both a portentous reflection and an important source of the increasing weaknesses in the Russian polity. The government distrusted the students on political grounds, but it also distrusted the spirit of science—the spirit of free inquiry, cultivated skepticism, and a critical attitude toward every authority. The 1884 university statute committed the government to an educational policy directly opposed to academic autonomy and freedom of scientific inquiry. It was the most important part of a broad official reaffirmation of the autocratic system, during which the arch-conservatives attempted to combine the tenets of autocratic ideology into a coherent, unified system of moral precepts and institutional commitments.

The enactment of the 1884 statute came as no surprise to professors and students, for a succession of decrees and administrative decisions had already reduced the 1863 statute to a meaningless document, particularly in matters relating to academic autonomy. In 1867 the government ordered the university authorities to share their supervision of student activities with the police; in 1877 the police were given the right to enter the universities at will in order to disperse illegal student meetings; and in 1879 the supervision of student activities was placed directly in the hands of special inspection boards acting independently of academic councils. University courts, which had been appointed by faculty councils, were abolished. During the 1870's D. A. Tolstoi, the Minister of National Education, openly attacked the libertarian features of the 1863 statute and appointed a special committee to bring it into line with the rising official conservatism.

The 1863 university statute had not really caused the great scientific upsurge of the Reform era; rather, both were expressions of the spirit of change that permeated all of Russian life in the years following the Crimean War. Although the statute was never given a chance to be really effective, it gave the academic community hope, as well as a certain *esprit de corps*. It also became a symbol of national triumphs in science, although it was often given credit for achievements that had resulted just as much from other favorable reforms. In a report on "The State of the University," delivered on January 14, 1884, the rector of Khar'kov University expressed what may be rightfully considered the academic community's assessment of the achievements stemming from the positive influence of the statute:

"University activities increased rapidly after the enactment of the 1863 statute. Although it is true that the rapid growth of higher education coincided with a general rise in the intellectual life of Russian society, a closer study shows that many new developments in the universities, particularly in teaching and research, were directly influenced by the statute. I refer not only to the increase in the ranks of scientists and to the development of university research, but also to the introduction of rational methods of instruction. An immediate result of the new statute was the increased recognition of Russian scholarship in the West. In many fields of scientific endeavor Russian names began to appear alongside those of Western scientists. Russian scientific studies have grown in number and have manifested increasing independence of Western guidance. Students have also benefited from the statute, particularly from the introduction of a rational system of practical [laboratory] activities and a wider use of demonstrations in teaching. The number of students engaged in scientific work has increased. More students now participate in the work of learned societies organized at universities than ever before, and many of them strive for more independence in scientific work. The present conditions of university life enable students to view the sciences not only as examination subjects but also as real sources of higher knowledge and higher intellectual development.... [The universities have ceased to be] random aggregates of specialized schools and faculties that train one-sided, narrow specialists in medicine, philology, law, and other fields. The university has become a universal school of higher education ... cultivating both intellectual and moral qualities in its students."[1]

The rector went on to say that the university had ceased to be no more than a provider of theoretical education for young people, and that it had established many active ties with the society at large. He noted the active part played by universities in the organization of *zemstva*, the reorganization of judicial institutions, public health, and local education, the fight against illiteracy, and the improvement of agricultural production. And he spoke for a majority of the academic community when he identified the 1863 statute as the force that had made these achievements possible. Most university professors were well aware of the weaknesses in the 1863 statute—for example, its failure to grant students the right to form independent associations—but in general they treated it as an embodiment of principles indispensable for the prosperity of higher education.

The most essential difference between the university statutes of 1863 and 1884 was in their provisions for the handling of student unrest. The 1863 statute relied on freely elected university councils to maintain peace and order in the academic community. By 1884, the government saw no advantages in the continued existence of academic councils, and it either reduced their jurisdiction or bypassed them altogether by instituting new supervisory agencies. The 1863 statute essentially relied on persuasion to appease restive students; the 1884 statute relied on various coercive mechanisms, including the brute power of the police. The real tragedy of the 1884 statute was that it did not extinguish rebellion in the universities, as had been intended; on the contrary, it added new fuel to an already existing conflagration. Some experts think, not without justification, that student unrest before 1884 was not political in nature—that the students merely sought to improve their living conditions and professional status and were not, at least not consciously, part of a broader revolutionary movement.

With the growing enrollment of the *raznochintsy* and impoverished gentry in the universities, the economic plight of the students had become a major problem in university life. During the 1870's, for example, 70 to 80 per cent of all students needed financial assistance, and as the turn of the century approached the percentage became even higher. To ease their financial predicament, the students began to organize all sorts of mutual-aid societies, as well as cooperative dormitories, restaurants, study clubs, and libraries. The government considered all these organizations illegal, and every independent group action by students was met by open hostility on the part of responsible officials. Stipends were reduced, and their distribution was made contingent on the police record of individual students. To keep the students preoccupied with curricular activities, the universities were ordered to institute various "quiz sessions," library research projects, and laboratory exercises as requirements for graduation. Abused and desperate, the students turned more and more often to demonstrations, strikes, and riots.[2]

By 1878 there was unrest in every Russian university. The government proclaimed the disorders the work of political agitators and issued the Rules of Inspection (1879), which removed all supervisory and disciplinary functions from the university court (appointed by elected university authorities) and vested them in a bureaucratic inspection board. As early as 1874 a government commission had stated that the autonomy of faculty councils deprived government officials of "any direct influence on the general conduct of affairs" in the universities, and that the most influential professors made no effort to bring student disorders to an end.[3] The 1879 rules were the spark that finally transformed student organizations into revolutionary bodies. The resignation of D. A. Tolstoi in 1880 and the government's hasty annulment of the repressive measures instituted since 1866 were too late to stem the tide of rising student discontent. The assassination of Alexander II in 1881 provoked a quick return to official attacks on academic autonomy and student organizations, and soon the last signs of the spirit of the 1860's disappeared.

A government manifesto of 1881 made it clear that the preservation and consolidation of the autocracy were once again the chief concerns of the state. The Ministry of National Education rededicated itself to a full implementation of the two principal educational policies of Sergei Uvarov and Dmitrii Tolstoi: classicism and estatism.

Classicism, i.e., a disproportionate emphasis on ancient philology in the gymnasiums, was expected to free instruction from undesirable ideological influences. (It should be noted that since the late 1870's sizable contingents of gymnasium students had taken part in most protests initiated by university students.) The "impracticality" of classical education was also expected to keep poor students out of the gymnasiums, and hence out of the universities.

Estatism (*soslovnost'*) implied a reorganization of the educational system in such a way as to help the nobility solidify and advance their position as the elite of Russian society and the bulwark of the Russian state. Many conservatives (led by M. N. Katkov, K. N. Leont'ev, and N. A. Liubimov) and some liberals (represented by Boris Chicherin) felt that the reforms of the 1860's had weakened the cohesion of Russian society by undermining the estate system, which was dominated by several grades of nobility. The ideologists of conservatism agreed that the future of Russia lay neither in socialist designs nor in the democratic spirit of the 1860's, but in an unqualified revitalization of autocracy and aristocracy. It was in this spirit that I. D. Demianov, Minister of National Education from 1882 to 1897, issued the famous "Cook's Letter," which decreed that "the sons of coachmen, servants, cooks, laundresses, small shopkeepers, and such people" should not be allowed to enroll in public schools.[4]

In 1887 the government issued the first in a succession of rulings setting quotas on the admission of Jews to universities, in hopes of controlling one important source of middle-class students. The raised registration fees at universities were also intended to maintain an aristocratic majority. But actually, the heart of the problem was not in the numerical balance of the nobility and lower estates. The real challenge was in the growing dominance of the *raznochintsy* mentality among all students, both noble and middle-class. The *raznochintsy* psychology was the expression of a new, reformist ideology, which saw the ideal future of Russia as a progressive affirmation of social equality and political freedom. According to the historian P. V. Miliukov, the bulk of the students of the 1870's were socialistically oriented, even though more than half of them came from the families of nobility and government officials. Conservatives were particularly incensed by the liberal leanings of the comparatively affluent gentry, as evidenced particularly by a loyal participation in *zemstvo* activities. The willingness of many university professors, mostly of noble origin, to defend the cause of the students and the ideals of the Reform era was also a source of annoyance in high government circles.

The conservative writers of the 1880's condemned the reforms of the 1860's for unleashing the social and economic forces that had deprived the nobility of its preeminence in political affairs. According to one writer, the reforms had replaced the "organic" principle that linked the monarchy with the people through clearly defined estates with "mechanical" principles that treated individuals as individuals.[5] The intelligentsia, in particular, was singled out as a symbol of the rootlessness of the new social relations, and as the prime mover in the erosion of the estate principle and the alienation of the people from the old values.[6] Among other things, the influence of the intelligentsia was responsible for the popular view of science as an intellectual force behind progressive politics and social radicalism; because of this influence, Russians had not developed "a metaphysically and religiously neutral science" but a "science irreconcilable with both religion and metaphysics."[7] The 1884 university statute was designed to neutralize the influence of the intelligentsia by setting up barriers that would prevent the universities from supplying recruits for the rapidly growing ranks of the intelligentsia.[8]

The statute of 1884 made the subordination of the universities to the Minister of National Education direct and absolute.[9] The university rector was no longer an official elected by the university faculty, but a government bureaucrat appointed by the Minister of National Education and directly subordinated to the curator of his school district. The Minister was autho-

rized to determine the staffing policies for each university, to institute various procedures for the control of classroom activities, and to appoint, promote, and dismiss professors. In carrying out these functions, the Minister
relied less on the rectors than on the curators of school districts, highly
placed bureaucrats who often had little or no knowledge of academic life.
Elected academic councils still existed, but their work was reduced to routine curricular matters.[10] A commentator stated subsequently that "the elimination of the elective principle undermined the dignity and the authority of
professors." The professors particularly resented the exclusive right of the
Minister to fill teaching vacancies.

Whereas the 1863 statute had expressed the government's distrust of
students and trust of professors, the 1884 statute was distrustful of both professors and students. In addition, police supervision of student activities was
now given statutory endorsement.[11] The statute defined only the general
policies affecting university students. The Rules for Students, issued in 1885
to implement the statute, recognized the students as individuals with no
"corporate rights"—i.e., no right to form independent associations—and
stipulated the fines to be imposed on students who disobeyed the many new
regulations.

No measure was more resented by both professors and students, and
none did more damage to the development of the university as an educational and scientific center, than the establishment of special state commissions to conduct examinations in the major university courses.[12] By controlling the examinations, the government controlled the material presented
in professors' lectures. To coordinate the content of lectures with the examination questions formulated by the state commissions, each professor
was required to submit his written lectures to the Ministry of National
Education for approval. For all practical purposes, the examination questions for many courses were written before the lectures were given, and
the lectures were tailored to fit the examinations.

Since the question lists prepared by the government were handed out
to the students at the beginning of each academic year, there was little reason to attend most lectures. However, to keep students busy and out of mis-
chief instructors were required to double the number of examinations, to
hold discussion meetings, and to give assignments requiring heavy library
or laboratory work. For some courses, no state examinations were required;
on this basis the government divided courses into primary and secondary,
using its own standards to evaluate each course.[13] Worst of all, by introducing uniform plans for courses, the new system left no room for professors

to stress their own theoretical views and research experiences. It made instruction an impersonal process, closed the doors to new scientific ideas, and placed the primary emphasis on the most elementary knowledge. As the historian S. M. Solov'ev had forewarned in the 1870's, it took the spirit of science out of the universities.

Most professors, students, and journalists interpreted the new statute as a tragic defeat for the universities. Even K. P. Pobedonostsev, a staunch exponent of modern Russian conservatism, expressed disapproval of its uncompromising attack on the cherished tenets of academic autonomy.[14] In an article published in the *Lomonosov Symposium* in 1901, the chemist V. V. Markovnikov expressed the sentiment of the university community by stating that the statute of 1884 had erased all the great institutional advances made by Russian universities during the preceding fifty years. He also expressed serious concern with the disruptive effects of the constant changes of government policy toward higher education. "Our universities are constituted on the model of German universities. All of the latter have preserved their original statutes and treated them as sacred documents; but our universities have had four different statutes during the last eighty years. Each change of the statute disrupted the normal growth of university science; on occasion, the shocks were staggering. The disruptive nature of the changes was further aggravated by the fact that new statutes represented no improvement on the ones they displaced, and stood in the way of the normal growth of scientific research and instruction.... The changes often expressed the mood of politicians and the police, and had nothing in common with science. All of this led to an artificial infusion of politics into university life, although this was exactly what the authorities had intended to avoid."[15]

The immediate effects of the new statute were devastating. Some professors sought employment in nonacademic professions, and Russia began to produce its first academic emigrants. With the exception of Moscow University, the enrollment in all the major schools of higher education began to dwindle, and did not begin to increase until 1890. To weaken the universities further, the government began to establish tightly controlled pedagogical, technical, and medical institutes. In 1887 tuition fees increased, and no student was allowed to register until he submitted an affidavit showing that he did not belong to organizations disapproved of by the government.

At first it looked as if the new statute and the successive restrictive rulings had accomplished their goal: the universities became places of deadly

silence. The traditional contacts between professors and students were drastically curtailed, and a new kind of student—sometimes called a "careerist"
—appeared on the scene. Most student organizations, however, had not
disappeared, but had merely gone underground. The *zemliachestva* (organizations that united students from the same regions) worked quietly and
steadily to resolve the financial, educational, and political plight of their
members. The growing revolutionary movement in St. Petersburg and Moscow—in which various shades of socialists, including the first Russian
Marxists, became spokesmen for the growing urban proletariat—gradually
reached the universities.

In 1887 the students of Kazan and Moscow universities issued declarations condemning the government's attacks on the university community.
In 1890 a group of students from St. Petersburg University asked Mendeleev to transmit a petition in favor of academic autonomy to the Minister
of National Education.[16] The famous chemist was rebuked by the Minister
and resigned in protest, adding more fuel to the smoldering conflict. Two
years later the plant physiologist Kliment Timiriazev and 42 other professors were reprimanded by the Minister of National Education for their
public statements on behalf of a group of arrested students.

During the 1890's the battle for university autonomy became an open
political struggle, a battle against tsarist oppression. By the middle of the
decade the *zemliachestva* had begun to form "united councils" in order to
coordinate the activities of their separate groups. The gravity of the situation in 1897 was best depicted by the philosopher S. N. Trubetskoi: "During the thirteen years of the new statute the university has begun to look
like a sick man who can maintain a rather unsteady order in his work
only by external pressure. The university has also produced a group of
Young Turks in the form of centralized student organizations. These
Young Turks have in effect organized their own university, with its own
leadership, activities, and science—a free and reckless university with a peculiar but solid organization that follows completely antiacademic principles."[17]

Student organizations of many descriptions formed the "invisible university" to which Trubetskoi alluded. They fell into three general groups.
The *zemliachestva* were the major representatives of the first group, acting
as a force that tied together the other student organizations. Students'
hostels and various mutual-aid societies were representative of the second
type. The third type was represented by the "circles of self-education," a
counterpart of the officially instituted "science *kruzhoky.*" The official *kru-*

*zhoky* were led by instructors and were usually engaged in work relating to classroom activities; but the students' own organizations were illegal discussion groups. In light of the state examinations and the diminishing number of elective courses, the students tried to make up for the university's failure to offer a balanced, flexible curriculum.

Toward the end of the 1890's the united councils of student organizations began to hold national congresses, and conflict with the police became a daily experience. In 1896 a congress of *zemliachestvo* representatives adopted a resolution urging the students to join the ranks of the Workers' Union, and political action in favor of "constitutional government and democracy" became the preeminent concern of the university community. It was commonly felt that academic autonomy, a basic condition for the modernization of the universities, could not be restored without revolutionary changes in the country's government. Mob disobedience, utter disregard for authority, and the utopian dream of a future academic community organized on democratic principles were the forces behind the rising tide of student violence.

As the universities became the scene of violent disorders, the government panicked, and as usual could turn only to repression and threats. The Provisional Regulations of June 29, 1899, threatened to induct all students participating in antigovernment demonstrations into military service. Newly formed committees, made up of representatives from the Ministry of the Armed Forces, the Ministry of Internal Affairs, and the Ministry of Justice and headed by the school district curators, were authorized to apply drastic disciplinary pressures to restore order. For all practical purposes, the universities were under martial law. During the next three years, more than a thousand students were expelled.

The Provisional Regulations did not tame the student movement. In 1900, representatives of student organizations from most of the universities met in Odessa and charted a common plan of action. In 1901, the government ordered that 183 students from Kiev University be inducted into the army as a punishment for participation in antigovernment demonstrations. This provoked serious disturbances in most universities, and brought protests from various organizations engaged in clandestine political work. The chemist N. A. Menshutkin made it clear that the professors were unable to persuade the students to follow a more peaceful course of action for the simple reason that the university councils had been divested of any real authority. In 1900, for example, the University Council of St. Petersburg had met only once, and had dealt only with the presentation of awards for student papers and similar routine matters.[18] Angered by the new wave of disorders, the government retaliated. To localize dissent, it ordered that in the future no young man could register in a university outside his school district. A decree of 1902 established special disciplinary courts of professors, which were expected to investigate charges of disorder against individual students, and to expel undesirable elements from the universities.

In 1905 the universities were in the forefront of the revolutionary insurrection that threatened to topple the tsarist regime. St. Petersburg University, a scene of constant outbreaks since 1899, was closed from October 1905 to October 1906. Frightened by the spread of revolutionary action, the government voided the 1884 statute and replaced it with the Provisional Regulations of August 27, 1905, which reestablished academic autonomy and for the first time recognized the students' right to organize independent associations. A concerted effort by professors, expressed in many petitions demanding an unqualified restoration of democratic faculty councils, contributed greatly to the students' success. However, petitions or no, the decision to issue the Provisional Regulations was not initiated by the Minister of National Education but by the head of the police, General D. F. Trepov.[19] In reality the various reforms enacted were scarcely more than temporary measures aimed at restoring order in the universities; and because the student rebellion rapidly spilled over to become a general political uprising against autocracy, the government was reluctant to make good its promises.

The academic community, of course, received the 1905 Provisional Regulations with great enthusiasm. Kliment Timiriazev interpreted the various changes as an official recognition of the full citizenship of students and the inseparability of science from society.[20] S. N. Trubetskoi, now the rector of Moscow University, stated: "The victory of academic autonomy, for which we have waited so long, means not only a moral victory for the university, but also a triumph for Russian society."[21] However, Russian society at large, caught up in a virtual revolution, scarcely noticed the university reforms. And conservative circles close to the government argued that the new autonomy of university life could not survive for long because the Russian academic world, both professors and students, was not yet mature enough to use its freedom responsibly.

By 1907 peace and order were restored in the country, and the reformed universities were soon under attack by the ultraconservative political organizations. The Moscow branch of the Union of the Russian People, the major reactionary group in the country, issued a statement deploring the new developments in higher education; it demanded that the universities be rededicated to training government officials loyal to the autocratic system, and that strong penalties be imposed on students taking part in political demonstrations. A. A. Tikhomirov, the leader of the ultraconservative professors and the most ardent supporter of government policies, wrote that the 1884 statute had freed professors from the burden of "emotional involvement" in university elections and allowed them to pursue their scholarly work in tranquillity; he thought that the deteriorating atmosphere in universities was caused not by the rigidity of the 1884 charter but by laxness in the implementation of many of its provisions.[22]

These and other complaints from conservative groups had a strong influence on the Ministry of National Education, which soon began a gradual retreat from its liberal commitments to the universities. The change was hastened by the Ministry's alarm at increased political activities in the universities, although most of these were peaceful and orderly. The official retreat began on June 11, 1907, when the government issued a set of Rules for Student Organizations and Meetings, which forbade the existence of student organizations "incompatible with the law and the spirit of the Russian state." The Rules gave university councils the authority to approve the charters of science *kruzhoky* and various types of mutual-aid societies organized by students; but they explicitly prohibited the formation of any organizations that aspired to unify and speak on behalf of all students.[23] On November 27, 1908, the Senate, acting in the capacity of supreme court of the empire, announced that the autonomy granted to the institutions of higher education should not be equated with full independence from the Ministry of National Education, but should be interpreted only as a freedom granted to university councils in selecting rectors and prorectors and as a right of faculty members to participate in regulating the curriculum and instructional plans.[24]

In its new role as an ideological and political center, the university also came under criticism from various quarters other than the government and reactionary political groups. The ex-Marxists N. A. Berdiaev and P. B. Struve resented the transformation of the universities into a narrow domain of the intelligentsia alone. Lenin praised the universities for making themselves a part of the organized "workers' resistance" to the autocratic system, but many conservatives and liberals criticized them for exactly the same things. According to one commentator, the universities had substituted an ephemeral search for political and social improvements for their traditional dedication to the search for scientific truth; that is, they had transferred their activity from the realm of culture to the realm of politics.

Outsiders tended to regard the university as an arena for two major contending forces: the "autonomists," who treated the university as an integral part of the struggle against the existing political system, and the "academicists," who wanted complete detachment from activities not traditionally defined as part of the intellectual life of the university. Both groups professed an unqualified dedication to the role of the university in the advancement of scientific knowledge; and both acknowledged the pivotal importance of science in modern society, although they differed over the proper place of science in a specifically Russian culture. The autonomists were convinced that the advancement of science in Russia required a change in the entire structure of Russian society. The academicists felt that the university could not operate as a true scientific center unless it renounced all active social and political roles and reestablished the proper limits of academic isolation. The cause of the academicists was enhanced by a concurrent proliferation of study groups involved in purely intellectual debates. Moscow University, for example, had "the circle of Christian students," "the circle of students engaged in the study of empirio-criticism," and many others of a similar nature.[25]

A closer look into the life of university students, however, shows that the supposed split between autonomists and academicists was only a blurred approximation of the existing situation. Actually, the students were split into many factions, which varied politically from the most belligerent Marxists to equally belligerent archconservatives; between the extremes were various shades of social democrats, social revolutionaries, liberals, and moderate conservatives. The general unrest in the country, the sharpening of ideological conflicts in many intellectual pursuits, and the growing repression of the academic community tipped the scales somewhat in favor of the extreme autonomists.

In general, the period 1906–10 was one of relative tranquillity in the universities, particularly in comparison with the stormy developments before 1905.[26] The ideological conflict was manifested more in stimulating debates in student *kruzhoky* than in shouted slogans and mob action. The students took more seriously to their books, and the professors felt relieved of protracted tension and violent disruptions in the normal flow of university life. The university quickly began to assert itself as the true center of Russian scholarship. Despite the apparent calm, however, the fire was not completely extinguished. On the contrary, it gradually built up new strength; and in 1910 it burst out again, enveloping Moscow University in a conflagration of revolutionary proportions.

The troubles of 1910 were precipitated by V. M. Purishkevich, a leader of the reactionary Black Hundreds. On March 10, 1910, Purishkevich delivered a scorching harangue in the Third Duma against so-called revolutionary students, and demanded that the Minister of National Education take measures to purge the universities of all undesirable elements. The Moscow students called a protest meeting, and during the spring and summer many of them went to prison; by autumn the situation was grave. The first real violence took place on November 8, after a student meeting that convened to commemorate the death of the novelist Lev Tolstoi but ended in a bitter attack on state educational policies. Other meetings followed in rapid succession, each displaying increased antagonism toward the authorities. More students were arrested, and the university administration became utterly confused and demoralized. On December 10, the government ordered the helpless university authorities to expel all organizers of meetings and instigators of violence. On January 11, 1911, it prohibited student meetings on the university premises, authorized the police to enter the university to disperse even the smallest gatherings of students, and demanded that students charged with disorderly conduct be immediately dismissed. The police, but not the university administration, were authorized to bring in the armed forces to disperse student gatherings. The rector and university councils were transformed into an auxiliary arm of the police. The promises of the Provisional Regulations of 1905 suddenly collapsed, and another period of hope and excitement in Russian academic scholarship came to an end.

These student disorders and government retaliations resulted in what contemporaries referred to as "the destruction of Moscow University," the country's oldest institution of higher education. The rector of the university and his two chief assistants chose to resign rather than serve as tools of the police. The government retaliated by ordering a dismissal of all professors who were members of the university council. Within a month 130 professors and instructors—almost one-third of the entire faculty—had either resigned or been dismissed. Among these were P. N. Lebedev, K. A. Timiriazev, V. I. Vernadskii, N. D. Zelenskii, N. A. Umov, V. K. Tseraskii, and S. A. Chaplygin, the core of the Russian scientific elite, who now found themselves not only without employment but also without access to laboratories.[27]

Mikhail Lomonosov, in helping to found the first Russian national university at Moscow, had expected to speed the emancipation of Russian scholarship from Western tutelage and to counterbalance the domination of the St. Petersburg Academy of Sciences by foreign scientists. The function of the Academy was to bring science to Russia; the function of Moscow University was to make science a part of Russian culture by creating native scientists. The catastrophe of 1911 showed that Moscow University, and its sister institutions in other cities, had not yet found a stable, unchallengeable place in Russian culture.

When peace was restored in the ravaged university, L. A. Kasso, the Minister of National Education—whose impatience with both the restless students and the confused professors had started the outburst in the first place—stated that it would take a long time for Moscow University to heal its wounds and again become a fountain of scientific knowledge. The remedy, he said arrogantly, did not lie in a new, more liberal statute, but in a gradual attempt to eliminate the "chronic illnesses" of Russian universities. Indeed, Moscow University now faced one of these illnesses—resulting, as usual, from bureaucratic interference. There were over a hundred vacant teaching positions, and the university would have to completely rebuild its depleted staff.

Kasso acted on the fears of the government rather than the weakness of the universities when he prepared a preposterous plan for establishing special "seminars" at the universities of Berlin, Heidelberg, and Paris in order to train future Russian professors. His plan was designed to remove carefully screened young men from the rebellious atmosphere of the national universities and to make government control over their training more direct and comprehensive. The young men sent abroad would learn the techniques of modern scientific work, "and would acquire first-hand knowledge of the organization of universities abroad," which would enable them to "revamp the Russian schools and restore a healthy academic atmosphere."[28] While working out the details of these foreign "seminars," Kasso extended his harassment to every university. He made extensive use of his official prerogatives to appoint, transfer, dismiss, and harass professors, to review the selections of instructors made by university councils, to punish those who dared to criticize educational and national affairs, and in general to destroy the last residues of academic autonomy.[29]

In 1912 and 1913 there was increased, though not violent, unrest among the students, and educational and scientific work slowed down. Prominent scholars publicized the plight of the universities. The historian D. I. Bagalei disclosed the financial difficulties of higher education.[30] The mineralogist V. I. Vernadskii criticized the official policy of shifting the emphasis in higher education from universities to specialized professional schools, and charged that unwarranted interference by the Ministry of National Education with the internal life of universities was the main source of the general confusion in academic circles and the deterioration of educational and scientific activities.[31] Vernadskii also resented the meetings of "rightist professors," which were treated by the Ministry as official councils of the academic community, even though they represented a small, atypical fringe group. Another noted professor, K. A. Timiriazev, started a public campaign to find an appropriate refuge for the scholars who had been dispossessed of laboratory facilities, and pleaded for the establishment of independent research institutes.[32]

Kasso died in 1914, several months after the beginning of Russia's involvement in World War I. He was replaced by P. N. Ignat'ev, a moderate liberal and a man of great energy and perseverance. As had happened so many times in the past, the change of ministers produced a general change in the official view of education and its role in the political community. Ignat'ev discarded most of Kasso's reactionary plans, including the foreign training of future professors, and immediately undertook to revise the university statute and make it acceptable to both professors and students. The revision was completed on May 14, 1915, but the new statute did not reach the appropriate legislative forums and was never ratified.[33]

Russia's involvement in World War I opened a new phase in the history of her national institutions of higher education. The immediate result was a wave of intense patriotism, which drew together many different political orientations and world views. The conservative professors interpreted the war as a sickness of Western European culture, which, as they saw it, had overemphasized utilitarian considerations and mistakenly ignored spiritual values. Their protestations, steeped in patriotism and veiled in philosophical verbiage, also restated the conservative opposition to scientific culture, the secularization of wisdom, and the very concept of the modern university. An emotional emphasis on the spiritual uniqueness and moral depth of Russian culture gave these pronouncements an air of revised Slavophil romanticism.

Most professors were eager to transform the technical and research facilities of the universities into a component of the war effort. University laboratories undertook military research, and soon began to produce goods varying from explosives, airplane parts, and poison gas to surgical instruments and drugs.[34] Every university, technical institute, laboratory, and observatory made some contribution to the war effort. Never before had Russian scientific centers and Russian industry been in such close contact. However, a dearth of modern laboratory equipment and inadequate supplies of raw materials and instruments imposed drastic limitations on the contributions of universities to the war effort. Deficiencies of this kind were especially severe in certain highly specialized areas, such as the production of optical equipment—one tragic result of the uneven development of Russian science. Many persons blamed the crippling government decrees of the past for this problem. Now, too late, the state attempted to remedy the situation. Minister Ignat'ev quite sincerely demanded that ten new universities be opened immediately; and in an unprecedented wave of enthusiasm, several cities offered free sites and large financial donations to attract future universities.[35]

In spite of this enthusiasm, the war was a disruptive force in the growth of Russian universities. Increasing numbers of students divided their time between studies and patriotic activities, working in hospitals, relief organizations, public transportation, and several other vital areas depleted of manpower by military mobilization. All the universities and many of the scientific institutions in the western regions of Russia were moved to the interior of the country, and were reduced to a primitive existence. A critical shortage of fuel contributed to dwindling class attendance at all universities; and in Moscow and Petrograd the shortage of housing became so acute that many students were sent to their homes in the provinces. A further decrease in university enrollment occurred after February 1916, following the enactment of a law allowing the general conscription of students into military service.

Military setbacks and the growing economic deterioration of the country created continuous government crises, as well as grumblings from the left wing among the students. In the autumn of 1916 Minister Ignat'ev was replaced by Professor N. K. Kulchitskii, who promptly repudiated the educational philosophy of his predecessor. Kulchitskii did not carrry out any reforms, but his negative attitude toward academic autonomy helped revive discontent among both the professors and the remaining students. Although no serious disturbances took place, the leftist students began to proclaim more and more openly their conviction that the future of Russia depended more on an internal revolution than on the outcome of the war.

THE GROWTH OF UNIVERSITY SCIENCE

Science is both a mode of inquiry and a world view. As a mode of inquiry, it is strictly a part of secular culture; but as a world view it profoundly affects sacred culture. In post-Reform Russia, science made tangible contributions to secular culture in the fields of general education, industrial technology, agricultural production, public health, and military technology.

It also provided a mounting challenge to sacred culture, whose values, intolerant of change, sustained the autocratic system, the Church, and the aristocracy. The ideologists and supporters of the monarchical system habitually regarded the values of autocracy and the values of science as incompatible. The most eloquent spokesman of conservatism, Nikolai Berdiaev, stated: "We have always equated the scientific spirit with progressive politics and social radicalism."[36]

Indeed, the authorities were afraid not of science but of the scientific spirit—the searching, critical, and always skeptical pursuit of truth. Most Ministers of National Education from D. A. Tolstoi to the Revolution made constant efforts to purge science of the scientific spirit, but only damaged both in the process. This ideological warfare, reinforced by reactionary legislation, did not challenge the very existence of scientific thought; but it seriously slowed scientific development. On a more concrete level, the government was usually remiss in its obligations to meet the universities' growing financial needs. In 1914, D. I. Bagalei wrote in the *Messenger of Europe*: "The funds assigned to the universities by the government in accordance with the staffing formulas promulgated in 1884 . . . have increased very slowly and unevenly, and have not kept pace with the natural growth of these institutions, the extraordinarily large increase in the number of students during recent years, or price increases."[37]

These ideological and financial difficulties did not prevent the universities from making noticeable progress between 1884 and 1914. By the end of the nineteenth century the Russian university was not only a modern educational institution but also the indisputable center of Russian science. Even the most severe critics of the official attitudes and policies toward education were ready to acknowledge that scientific thought in Russia had made appreciable progress. The microbiologist V. L. Omelianskii was thinking chiefly of Russian universities when he made the following statement:

"Did the development of the natural sciences in Russia in the nineteenth century justify the characterization of that epoch as the golden age of the natural sciences? Our answer can justly be an affirmative one. . . . The path that Russian natural science traveled in the nineteenth century was truly amazing! Russian naturalists contributed to every branch of positive science, and left a rich legacy to the new century. Many extraordinary ideas, and often entire branches of natural science, developed from the labors of Russian naturalists, a fact that was generally acknowledged. As leading scholars in their respective fields, eminent Russian scientists were invited to contribute chapters to various foreign symposia dealing with special branches of natural science."[38]

Other commentators were also impressed with the growing respect of Western scholars for the contributions of the leading Russian scientists. The classical philologist V. I. Modestov noted the rapid disappearance of foreign professors from Russian universities. Timiriazev, in an address entitled "The Holiday of Russian Science," noted the fulfillment of Lomonosov's hope that Russia would produce its own Platos and Newtons; and he claimed that in some areas Russian scientists had not only caught up with the work of their Western European peers but surpassed it.[39] He added that science, along with *belles lettres*, had achieved more maturity and creative power in Russia than any other form of intellectual expression. All these commentators had an almost romantic faith in science as a vital index of Russia's cultural advancement, and all were very much aware of the growing role of universities as centers of scientific investigation.

The forces that helped the universities survive the oppressive measures of the government took many forms. Some came from the impetus generated by the growth of industry, and others from the intellectual needs of a society caught in the irreversible process of modernization. There was a great deal of private financial support for scholarship, and the government made more funds available for laboratories and institutes. The growing membership of learned societies, the stimulating effect of new scientific developments in the West, and the spontaneous response of universities to the accelerated growth of modern science all combined to assure the university and university science of tangible progress.

What the government took away by oppressive legislation it gave back by its readiness to help the universities expand their facilities for experimental work. As part of the plan to keep students too involved in their studies to take an active part in political activities, the government helped develop a wide variety of auxiliary educational and research institutions in the universities. The official policy of strengthening the universities' power to supervise students did not reduce the constant threat of mass disorders, but it did provide more opportunity for training in research techniques. After 1906 the emphasis in the universities shifted from broad lecture courses to specialized studies in which the lectures were supplemented by practical exercises of various types. Modern laboratories sprang up in all universities. The preceding generation had witnessed an accelerated transformation of permanent science exhibits into working laboratories; now the more advanced laboratories became complex research institutes. For example, Moscow University's Physical Institute, founded at the end of the century, consisted of four distinct laboratories, including the one in which P. N. Lebedev made his famous measurements of the pressure of light.[40]

The growth of laboratory facilities—though these were still meager by Western standards—had many beneficial results. Established scholars could now embark on more complex and challenging research projects, and the younger scientists received a sounder training. The laboratories became centers in which the formal academic atmosphere was blended with the informal spirit of science *kruzhoky* (perhaps the most influential of these was I. P. Pavlov's physiological laboratory in the Institute of Experimental Medicine). In the laboratories, dedicated scholars found a refuge in times of political crisis; and it was in the laboratories that young professors and students learned to appreciate the limitless scope and practical value of science.

During and after the 1890's the government made a determined effort, using German models, to develop a system of specialized professional and technical schools as a supplement to the university system. It was eager to keep as many students as possible away from the universities but not away from higher education in general. By 1914 Russia had 98 schools of higher education, with a total of 121,700 students. This included the country's ten universities, which had little more than a quarter of the total enrollment.[41]

There were three categories of higher schools outside the universities. A typical institution of the first type had no research facilities and was engaged exclusively in training practical specialists in a given field. This group included all "courses for women" and all of the sixteen women's institutes, as well as many pedagogical, agricultural, commercial, and technical institutes. The second category included the older specialized institutions that placed primary emphasis on teaching but also had limited research facilities; it was represented by the Moscow Institute of Agriculture, the Military Medical Academy, the Naval Academy, the Institute of Mining, and the Institute of Communication Engineering. Most of these institutions were active contributors to the general advancement of scientific knowledge. The Institute of Mining published one of the country's oldest scientific journals. At the end of the nineteenth century the Naval Academy began to publish its *Proceedings*, whose first number was completely taken up by A. N. Krylov's noted essay on determining the orbits of comets and planets from only a few observations. Subsequently, this journal also carried Krylov's translation of Newton's *Principia Mathematica*. The Moscow Institute of Agriculture was given a new statute in 1913, making it the leading national center of agricultural research; this school operated several experimental stations and a meteorological observatory.

The third category was made up of new institutes that placed equal emphasis on high-quality professional education and research in specialized fields. Typical of this group were the Electrotechnical Institute and the Polytechnical Institute, both founded in St. Petersburg in the late 1890's, as well as the polytechnical and technological institutes founded in Kiev, Warsaw, and Tomsk at approximately the same time. The most elaborate of these, the St. Petersburg Polytechnical Institute, contained economic, metallurgical, electromechanical, and shipbuilding departments. All these schools brought science closer to the growing industrial needs of the country, expedited the flow of technical knowledge from abroad, and applied modern research facilities to highly specialized problems; however, none of them emerged as great scientific centers. Their most important contributions were in widening the base of the science curriculum, in providing supplementary research facilities and new periodical publications, and in making it possible for the universities to concentrate on theoretical research.

Surprisingly, the establishment of polytechnical institutes did not cause a decrease in the number of university students studying natural science. On the contrary, between 1880 and 1912 the percentage of natural science students in all universities grew from 20 to 27 per cent of the total enrollment. During the same period, however, the enrollment in the medical faculties of the national universities decreased: in 1880 medical students made up 46 per cent of the total enrollment; in 1899 they made up only 22.9 per cent, and it was not until World War I that enrollment increased again.[42] The complicated nature of medical instruction and the relatively limited space available contributed to these figures. Also, in its eagerness to establish higher professional schools outside the universities, the government founded several separate medical schools. Among these, the women's medical institutes played a particularly important role; the St. Petersburg Medical Institute for Women, for example, had 1,330 students in 1912. With these numerous institutes handling much of the teaching, the medical faculties at universities were able to place a greater emphasis on research.

The medical faculties of the national universities were the first scientific centers in Russia to set up complex, specialized institutes. In 1917, the Medical Faculty of Moscow University had twelve institutes—notably the Institute of Physiology and the Institute of Comparative Anatomy—and thirteen clinics. In 1884 the Moscow City Duma gave the university approximately 10 hectares of land as a site for new medical training facilities. A special committee studied the clinical facilities of many Western European universities; and, thanks to liberal donations by several industrialists, the university was able to set up an entire cluster of medical clinics, which became a vital research and teaching component of the Medical Faculty. This happy combination of efforts by professors, city authorities, and private citizens more than compensated for the government's hesitancy to make large capital investments in medical research facilities. The government's major contribution at this time was in establishing medical training centers, which had minimum research facilities.

The growing popular appeal of the Russian universities was manifested most clearly in rapidly increasing enrollments. University education appealed equally to "careerists" who sought a better station in life for themselves and idealists who sought a better way of life for Russian society. Soon after the enactment of the 1884 statute, the enrollment in the eight universities fell slightly (from 12,939 in 1885 to 12,495 in 1890); but it then climbed steadily until 1909, when it reached 38,600. On the eve of World War I 35,700 students were enrolled in Russian universities. During this period, new universities were established at Tomsk (1888) and Saratov (1908). The biggest increases came in the enrollment of students from the middle and lower classes. In the middle of the 1860's nearly 70 per cent of the students had belonged to noble or bureaucratic families; but by 1885 the figure was only 50 per cent, and by 1915 it was 35 per cent.[43]

## UNIVERSITY-AFFILIATED LEARNED SOCIETIES

During the turbulent decades of ideological strife and political repression, the growth of Russian universities as scientific centers owed much to the learned societies that were affiliated with institutions of higher education. Most of these societies depended more on the enterprising spirit of professors and on private donations than on government sponsorship. For this reason, most of them were useful in connecting the universities with society at large. These societies were of three general types: undifferentiated general societies, differentiated general societies, and specialized societies.

The first category included the societies that dealt with all natural sciences and did not have specialized departments. These were the old-fash-

ioned naturalist societies, whose catholic interest in science was matched
by their commitment to "empirical science." The most famous and durable
of these groups was the Moscow Society of Naturalists, founded in 1805,
which operated as an institutional component of Moscow University. The
Society at first concentrated on descriptions of Russian fauna and flora,
but in the late 1880's it began to study Russian geology. When the physicist N. A. Umov became president of the Society in 1897 its activities
branched off in many directions, and it was not unusual for its *Bulletin* to
contain articles on general theoretical questions in physics, crystallography,
and chemistry, as well as meteorological observations and descriptions of
Russian natural resources. Through the regular exchange of publications
with foreign learned associations, the Society collected one of the major
Russian libraries in the natural sciences. Until the end of the tsarist era it
published most of its papers in foreign languages, which made it easier for
foreign scholars to keep abreast of scientific developments in Russia but
also made the Society unpopular with the younger Russian scholars, who
preferred to write in their native language.

The regular meetings of the Moscow Society of Naturalists allowed specialists from many fields to keep track of general theoretical currents and
interests in science, exchange ideas with experts in other disciplines, and
listen to firsthand reports on current developments in foreign universities
and laboratories. In 1911, for example, the members heard speeches on the
conflict between old and new theories in physics, the theoretical contributions of J. H. van't Hoff, the International Congress of Radiology and Electricity at Brussels, and the new developments in ecological research.

The Moscow Society was not a research center, but a science club where
scholars could meet in an atmosphere unburdened by formalities. It sponsored research by giving financial aid to scholars doing fieldwork in botany,
zoology, or geology, and also provided them with a journal through which
they could publicize the results of their labor. It had no laboratories, stations, or observatories; however, its modern and efficiently organized libraries provided scholars with quick access to valuable journals published
by learned societies in Russia and many foreign countries. The Society's
long history, honored place in Russian scholarship, and enviable international prestige influenced the government to support it with comparatively
large financial donations.

The second category of learned societies included the differentiated general associations, which were divided into specialized departments, each
with its own membership, tradition, and interests. These associations were

usually modeled after the Moscow Society of Admirers of Natural Science, Anthropology, and Ethnography, and they were attached to every university. The original purpose of the Moscow prototype (founded in 1863) was to prepare popular descriptions of museum specimens and to publish manuals for the systematic gathering of scientific materials, but it soon developed other aims.[44] Besides carrying out an extensive publication program and organizing scientific exhibits, the Society sponsored scientific fieldwork and research. For example, F. A. Bredikhin received a grant to help him in astronomical observations, A . T. Babukhin was sent to Egypt to study bioelectricity in fish, and A. O. Kovalevskii was given money to finance his embryological research in Western Europe.[45] Among other recipients of financial aid were university students and hundreds of amateur scientists. In 1887 a private donation enabled the Society to establish a series of annual awards for outstanding publications in science.

At the beginning of the twentieth century the Moscow Society had six departments and three sections, each with specialized pursuits and publications. In the 1890's the unusually slow development of Russian geological studies received wide notice, and several naturalist societies began to pay more attention to the earth sciences. The Society's geological section, the last to be established, was soon the most active, sponsoring a collective effort in paleontology and other earth sciences. In this undertaking, the Society was fortunate to have had A. P. Pavlov, a pioneer in modern Russian geology, among its active members. The anthropological and ethnographic sections of the Society, and the zoological and botanical departments, limited their work primarily to surveys and empirical description of natural and cultural details. The physiological department existed mostly on paper. The chemistry department dealt mostly with cataloging the mechanisms of various chemical reactions and the characteristics of individual compounds. The physical science department counted among its active members such distinguished theoreticians as Iu. V. Vul'f, a noted crystallographer, and N. E. Zhukovskii, a founder of modern aerodynamics. The geographical department was engaged in highly diversified work, combining surveys of various regions with theoretical and methodological studies of the changing role of geography in the family of modern natural sciences.

Other university societies of the differentiated type were engaged in similar activities—combining individual efforts with broader collective action, soliciting private donations, sponsoring national meetings of scientists, and providing a useful base for the extension of university education and graduate studies. They joined the practical interests of the government and the society at large with the specialized theoretical interests of universities. They satisfied amateurs enthused by the spirit of science as much as they appealed to professionals troubled by the current philosophical problems of science or the gigantic breakthroughs in modern physics. For young beginners in science, a society like this was "a school, a laboratory, and a lecture auditorium"; for seasoned scholars, it was "a field for planting seeds and reaping the harvest."[46] In addition, each society had certain unique characteristics developed in response to local needs and conditions. The Odessa University Society of Naturalists, for example, had a special mathematical section that published many papers written by local teachers and university students; this was a great help to the comparatively small scholarly community in Odessa.[47]

The St. Petersburg Society of Naturalists, founded in 1868, worked under especially favorable conditions, and was one of the most advanced and active learned associations in Russia during the last quarter of the nineteenth century. Its most active and productive associates were members of the St. Petersburg Academy of Sciences. The Society of Naturalists cooperated with many national learned societies whose headquarters were in St. Petersburg—notably the Russian Geographical Society, the Russian Mineralogical Society, and the Free Economic Society. Some of the most important papers of the mineralogist V. I. Vernadskii, the crystallographer E. S. Fedorov, the physiologists I. M. Sechenov and I. P. Pavlov, the botanist I. P. Borodin, and the microbiologist D. I. Ivanovskii were published in the Society's *Proceedings*. In general, the Society concentrated on the biological sciences, leaving physics and chemistry to the more specialized Russian Physical and Chemical Society, a sister institution affiliated with the University. The Society of Naturalists played a leading role in the organization of several scientific expeditions to various parts of Russia. It was also the prime mover in the establishment of the Solovetsk Biological Station on the White Sea, which engaged in the study of marine life and trained graduate students and young scientists in the anatomy, embryology, and taxonomy of marine fauna.[48]

No other learned association outdid the St. Petersburg Society of Naturalists in popularizing science. The Society sent its publications free of charge to many city libraries, museums, and schools, and organized many natural-history excursions led by experts in botany, physical geography, geology, soil science, agriculture, and forestry and open to all interested citizens. It also invited private citizens interested in science to participate in the work of some of its specialized committees (e.g., the Crimean Committee), whose success depended on a blend of scientific research and civic spirit. In the early 1880's the Society sent a special circular to *zemstvo* authorities, local schools, and provincial government officials appealing for more popular participation in the study of Russian flora, and suggested that regional groups might prepare herbariums of local plants for the botanical collection of St. Petersburg University.[49] The results of the circular were most rewarding; and from 1885 on, the Society conducted a general campaign to establish local scientific museums in the various *zemstva*. Together with all this, the Society participated extensively in the periodic congresses of Russian natural scientists.

The third category of learned associations operating within the institutional framework of universities were specialized societies; these were typified by the Moscow Mathematical Society and the Russian Physical and Chemical Society, the former affiliated with Moscow University and the latter with St. Petersburg University.[50] Both societies were truly national, and both represented the highest theoretical and methodological achievements of the exact sciences in Russia. These specialized societies did not try to stimulate popular interest in their disciplines, but instead sought to advance scientific knowledge by providing professional scholars with encouragement, criticism, intellectual contacts, and an outlet for publication.

The *Mathematical Symposium*, published by the Moscow Mathematical Society, carried papers by most of the leading mathematicians in the country, and was a vital source of new information for young scholars and university graduates. From the very beginning the *Symposium* printed all its papers in Russian, which undoubtedly accelerated the development of mathematical thought in Russia and the emergence of particular national interests in mathematics. True, this practice made it more difficult for foreign scholars to keep informed of the contributions of Russian mathematicians; but the isolation was only partial. The St. Petersburg Academy of Sciences continued to publish many papers in foreign languages, and most of the leading Russian mathematicians contributed to Western mathematical journals. Thanks to the scholarly output and widespread appeal of the Moscow Mathematical Society, Moscow University became the main source of mathematics professors for Russian schools.

The record of the Russian Physical and Chemical Society was equally impressive, and every important chemist or physicist in Russia contributed to its *Journal*. Between 1869 and 1913, the Society's membership grew from 35 to 514; the 1869 volume of the *Journal* had 264 pages, the 1913 volume 2,078.[51] Although printed in Russian, the *Journal* was as international in its appeal and influence as were the most reputable foreign-language publications of the St. Petersburg Academy. The *Journal* reported on all important experiments carried out in the physical and chemical laboratories at St. Petersburg University and other institutions of higher education; it also published both theoretical and historical papers. One feature unique to this periodical was a regular survey of the investigations reported in foreign publications. This cosmopolitan orientation was so strong that many leading scholars, both Russian and foreign, published their more important studies simultaneously in the *Journal* and in the major Western periodicals. Moreover, the chemical societies of Berlin and Paris had special correspondents in St. Petersburg to report on the Society's activities and publications.

The Physical and Chemical Society sponsored only two national meetings—the well-known Mendeleev Congresses in 1907 and 1911—but its members were the main participants in the sessions in physics and chemistry that were held at the Congresses of Russian Natural Scientists and Physicians. The Society was also interested in educational problems, and in 1913 it joined other groups in sponsoring the first All-Russian Congress of Instructors in Physics, Chemistry, and Cosmography.[52]

Medical societies of every description were a part of the intellectual life in all Russian universities. In 1912, Moscow University alone had seven such societies, most of them founded during the last decade of the nineteenth century.* Through these societies, professors of medicine met not only with their colleagues and students, but also with the more progressive local physicians. Most medical societies published annual volumes of selected papers in their respective fields. The newest scientific ideas reached the medical community with remarkable speed; at the same time, the feedback of practical experience presented new challenges to university experts, clinics, and laboratories. None of these societies produced startling scientific ideas, and none attracted the attention of Western scholars; but as a group they played a key role in the growth and diffusion of modern scientific knowledge in Russia.

PRIVATE ENDOWMENTS

During the reign of Nicholas II the universities received tangible help from private endowments. These donations helped maintain a relatively high ratio of financial grants to students, which offset the concurrent reduction of government aid. For example, 161 of the 1,231 students at Khar'-

---

* Affiliated with the Faculty of Medicine at Moscow were the Society of Neuropathologists and Psychiatrists, the Physical and Medical Society, the Moscow Therapeutic Society, the Surgical Society, the Society of Pediatricians, the Moscow Society for Venereal Diseases and Dermatology, and the Society of Obstetricians and Gynecologists. (*O–MU*, 1911, pp. 168–86.)

kov University in 1900 received stipends, but only 58 had government stipends; the others depended on private sources.[53] Bequests of private libraries
to the universities were a common phenomenon.[54] Nor were students the
only ones to benefit: in 1911 the budget of the St. Petersburg Public Library
was sufficient to purchase only 40 new Russian volumes and 1,202 foreign
volumes; outside sources, mostly private, were responsible for the additional
acquisition of 1,671 Russian and 5,211 foreign books. Most learned societies
affiliated with the universities received government financial assistance;
but most, particularly the naturalist associations, also depended on private
donations. Many of the awards given by learned societies for outstanding
scientific studies were provided by private citizens. Laboratories were often
supported in the same way. Moscow University's modern clinics at Devich'e
Pole owed their existence to combined financial aid from the government,
the municipal authorities, and private donors.[55]

In 1909 a completely new kind of learned association appeared on the
Russian academic scene: a society sustained entirely by a private donor. Its
name was the Kh. S. Ledentsov Society for the Advancement of the Exact
Sciences and Their Practical Applications, and its bases were Moscow University and the Moscow Higher Technical School. In 1903 Ledentsov, a
wealthy entrepreneur, had asked S. A. Fedorov, director of the Technical
School, and N. A. Umov, a professor of physics at the University, to help
him prepare a workable plan for the formation of a learned society dedicated to the advancement of scientific theory and technology.[56] At first, the
Ministry of National Education was skeptical of the very idea of a private
scientific institution, and was especially perplexed about its proposed affiliation with the two Moscow schools. The Ministry did not have an established
means of supervising a private association whose administration was divided
between two public institutions of higher learning.

In 1909 the new society finally received a government-approved statute,
and immediately began an active career. Unlike other learned groups, the
Ledentsov Society was a complex enterprise whose cultural functions were
specified by the founder and were faithfully executed because of his careful
financial provisions.[57] The Society awarded research grants to deserving
scholars, maintained a regular exchange of scientific periodicals with Western institutions, set up numerous "commissions of experts" to search out
worthy scientific projects, and began an intensive program of research in the
areas of common interest to science and industry. Most traditional learned
societies sponsored scientific work in which professionals met dedicated
amateurs and in which "science" covered an area of inquiry ranging from

the mere cataloging of observed natural phenomena to the most modern theoretical involvement. The Ledentsov Society, however, had no room for amateurs or for descriptive science, and concerned itself only with the newest theoretical and practical branches of science.

To traditional learned societies, the pursuit of science was as much a hobby as it was a professional and essentially practical undertaking; the Ledentsov Society existed to support the professional scholar who had proved his talent and whose project was judged by his peers to be sound both theoretically and practically. In 1911, the Society helped Ivan Pavlov to expand his neurophysiological laboratory in the Institute of Experimental Medicine. P. N. Lebedev received funds to modernize the physics laboratory of Moscow University, in which he and twenty assistants studied the physical properties of electromagnetic waves. With the Society's help, N. E. Zhukovskii was able to conduct special experiments in the aerodynamic laboratory of the Moscow Technical School, and V. I. Vernadskii undertook laboratory studies in the spectroscopic analysis of minerals as part of a larger project for studying the radioactive elements found in Russia.[58] Many less illustrious members of the scientific community also benefited; and on one occasion, the *Journal of the Russian Physical and Chemical Society* was published on time only because of an emergency allocation by the Society. A special biological station on the Kara-Dag volcanic massif in the Crimea was also on the Society's budget.

When Moscow University was temporarily closed down in 1911, the Ledentsov Society acted quickly and resolutely to help those professors who, by resigning from their university posts, had lost access to laboratory facilities. Some of these men resolved their difficulties by joining the faculties of private schools, and some left for St. Petersburg in search of more favorable working conditions. A few scientists were left entirely to their own devices. Among these were P. N. Lebedev, the country's leading physicist, and M. A. Menzbir, an eminent biologist and a former deputy rector of Moscow University. The Ledentsov Society immediately granted a special fund to the Moscow Society of Naturalists to provide adequate working space and research facilities for Menzbir. And Lebedev actually became a rallying point for those who wanted a healthier institutional structure in Russian science. He declined an invitation from Svanté Arrhenius to join the research staff of the Nobel Institute in Stockholm, and another from several of his colleagues who asked him to move to St. Petersburg and work in the Central Bureau of Standards and Weights (which had also offered a position to Mendeleev after his resignation from St. Petersburg University in 1897).

Instead, Lebedev received help from three private institutions: Shaniav-skii University, the Moscow Society for a Scientific Institute, and the Ledentsov Society. Shaniavskii University provided space for a temporary laboratory, the Moscow Society assumed the task of soliciting private support for a new research center, and the Ledentsov Society advanced sufficient funds to build a modern institute of physics.

Lebedev died in 1912, and the search for a suitable scientific workshop for him was transformed into a broad effort to extend the organizational base of Russian science beyond the rigidly defined framework of government institutions. Many leading scientists were now convinced that Russia needed a private sector in higher education—not to replace the government sector, but to complement it. They felt that in private schools, free of administrative regulations, the rate and intensity of student disorders would be drastically reduced. They also argued that the demand for higher education was growing so fast that it could not be satisfactorily met by government resources alone. Professor N. P. Zagoskin, in his *History of Kazan University*, lamented the absolute monopoly that "government science" had enjoyed in Russia since the time of Peter the Great, and undoubtedly felt that private initiative would produce a more versatile development of science.[59] A group of the nation's most eminent scientists, led by Lebedev, Umov, Timiriazev, and Vernadskii, wrote articles and delivered public speeches in favor of the establishment of research institutes independent of the universities. The success of Shaniavskii University in Moscow, founded by a private donor, proved conclusively that there was a great popular demand for private forms of higher education. This school, also known as Moscow City University, provided a model for many communities that were eager to establish thier own institutions of higher education. A similar but smaller institution, founded in the Siberian city of Tomsk, was greeted by the prestigious *Messenger of Europe* as "a nursery of science with a democratic complexion."[60]

The great difficulty that Moscow professors experienced when looking for new research facilities in 1911 showed that Russia was very much in need of a central organization that could coordinate the national endeavor in science. In 1911, the organizers of the Moscow Society for a Scientific Institute announced that they were interested in creating a private academy of sciences, a central forum of the "national research institutes." The government's negative attitude toward private control of education and science, the organizational and economic difficulties engendered by World War I, and an unrealistic assessment of the existing institutional strength of Russian science combined to prevent the establishment of such an academy. However, the Society for a Scientific Institute did gather sufficient funds to establish the Physical Institute in Moscow, an elaborate system of laboratories and libraries in which a surprisingly large number of young physicists began their careers in research.[61] In 1918 the Soviet authorities nationalized the Physical Institute and used it as a model in establishing modern scientific workshops in many fields.

The seeds of science planted in the 1860's produced bountiful harvests by the turn of the century. Laboratories grew in number and improved in quality. Numerous scientific schools gathered around the notable scholars in a dozen specialized institutions of higher education. In times of political crisis, university scholars drew inspiration and courage from the inner momentum of their disciplines and the great scientific strides being made in the West. The universities became the true center of the national effort in science; and in learned societies, government science bureaus, and the Academy of Sciences the most prominent members were always professors. Without I. P. Pavlov's physiological laboratory at the Institute of Experimental Medicine, N. E. Vvedenskii's physiological laboratory at St. Petersburg University, P. N. Lebedev's physical laboratory in Moscow University, and a score of similar workshops the Academy of Sciences would not have achieved and maintained its high standards. The Academy, in fact, became primarily an exhibit of the major achievements of university scholarship.

The universities more than weathered the tumultuous political storms in this age of crisis. They were beacons throwing a steady light on the mysteries of nature and transforming some of them into measurable facts of science. It was primarily through the scientific workshops and forums of the universities that J. J. Thomson's discovery of the electron, Marie and Pierre Curie's research in radiation, Einstein's theory of relativity, and many other revolutionary scientific ideas first reached Russian scholarship.

## CHAPTER SEVEN

# The Academy and the Learned Societies

## THE ACADEMY OF SCIENCES

In judging the Academy of Sciences as a representative institution of Russian science, two peculiar features must be noted. In the first place, the Academy favored the humanities and social sciences over the exact and natural sciences: of the 70 scholars elected to full membership in the Academy from 1890 to 1917, only 28 were in the sciences. In the second place, it was essentially a conservative institution, better known for the past achievements of its members than for its commitment to the development of new approaches and ideas. Pioneering work—e.g., that of N. E. Zhukovskii in aerodynamics, D. I. Ivanovskii in microbiology, E. S. Fedorov in crystallography, and P. N. Lebedev in the study of electromagnetic waves—gained little recognition from the Academy. Meanwhile, the rich ideas of modern physics and biology found their way to Russia mostly through the universities and polytechnical institutes.

The basic institutional weakness of the Academy was that it continued to elect new Academicians and adjuncts to fill vacated positions rather than responding to the changing needs of science by opening new Academy chairs. The libertarian spirit of the Reform era did nothing to change this. In the late 1850's and early 1860's the government, responding to strong demands from representative segments of the scientific community, promised to replace the Academy's anachronistic statute of 1836 with a new and more liberal charter; but in 1865, without explanation, the government rejected the draft statute prepared by a special committee appointed by the Minister of National Education, and nothing more was heard of the matter.

In 1882 D. A. Tolstoi, the most energetic and unbending champion of autocratic ideology, was simultaneously appointed Minister of Internal Affairs, Chief of the Gendarmerie, and President of the Academy of Sciences. In the same year he helped draft the provisional rules that eliminated the last vestiges of freedom of the press. When Tolstoi died in 1889, Prince K.

K. Romanov was appointed President of the Academy; his presence eliminated the last traces of autonomy. The government was determined to prevent the general restlessness in universities from disrupting the tranquillity of the Academy. It strove to create an "academic science," a science untouched by the contaminating influences of ideological conflict and social unrest. Until 1893 the Academy received inadequate funds from the government, and could not undertake any complex research projects.

In spite of governmental restrictions, as well as innate conservatism, the Academy underwent three important changes in the years 1884–1917. First, it ceased to be dominated by foreign scholars and at long last became a national institution in both human composition and cultural orientation. Second, the Academy's institutional apparatus was appreciably enlarged, and its ties with the universities and other centers of scientific research were multiplied and strengthened. Finally, the Academy's concern with practical problems of national significance assumed wider proportions and was more precisely articulated. Each of these developments is worthy of closer examination.

The spontaneous protest in 1880 against the Academy's refusal to admit D. I. Mendeleev to full membership was the real beginning of efforts to make the Academy a truly national institution. All the Academicians elected from 1890 to 1917 were born in the Russian empire, and only one was of German ethnic origin. In 1899, the Academy came even closer to the intellectual pulse of national life by establishing a Section of Fine Arts, which gave honorary membership to such literary giants as Lev Tolstoi, Vladimir Solov'ev, and Anton Chekhov. The Academy was now beginning to receive many more private donations, which came mostly from industrial and commercial entrepreneurs.

The Academy's judgment in selecting new members was closely watched by the university community, which often found the selections capricious by its own standards. The Academicians, for example, turned down the nomination of the physicist A. G. Stoletov for full membership in the Academy, and instead elected Prince B. B. Golitsyn, an untested aspirant, to the rank of adjunct. Although Stoletov was not an exceptionally strong scientist, he enjoyed an enviable reputation among university professors as a teacher and as a spokesman for the scientific community; the Academy, however, favored scholars who were not deeply involved with political affairs. The Academy made another grave error in electing E. S. Fedorov as an adjunct rather than a regular member. Fedorov was a leading crystallographer of his time, and was 43 years old at the time of election; traditionally, the position of adjunct was filled by young scholars, promising but un-tested.

For the first time, membership in the Academy was not universally cov-eted by university professors. In 1896 D. N. Anuchin, a professor of geogra-phy and ethnography, was elected a full member of the Academy; but in 1898 he gave up this honor in order to continue his association with Moscow University, both as a professor and as president of the Society of Admirers of Natural Science, Anthropology, and Ethnography.[1] In 1906 the Academy elected V. I. Vernadskii an adjunct, and in 1909 he was made an extraordi-nary member. He accepted both positions only because the Academy al-lowed him to continue his affiliation with Moscow University, which was better equipped to support his research interests.[2] Vernadskii finally moved to St. Petersburg in 1911, after resigning from his teaching duties to protest L. A. Kasso's oppressive educational policies.

The differences between the new Academicians and their predecessors were extensive. Before the 1890's most Academicians had engaged in teach-ing primarily to boost their income, and their association with the univer-sities had been very limited. Their identification, both sentimental and pro-fessional, was primarily with the Academy. Most Academicians elected in the 1890's, however, regarded themselves as representatives of the univer-sities and technical schools, and had close ties with these institutions. Of the more notable Academicians, Ivan Pavlov maintained close relations with the Military Medical Academy and the Institute of Experimental Medicine, and A. A. Markov carried a full teaching load in mathematics at St. Peters-burg University. N. S. Kurnakov not only taught at the St. Petersburg Poly-technical Institute and the Electrotechnical Institute but also helped these schools establish chemical research laboratories. In the past, most Academi-cians had taught elementary courses that had little to do with their prin-cipal research interests. The new Academicians, often with the help of modern experimental techniques, taught specialized courses related to their own research. Because these new Academicians were closely identified with the university community, they enjoyed much more prestige than their predecessors; they eradicated the traditional barriers that had split the Academy and the universities into isolated and somewhat antagonistic com-munities.

The Academicians of the old school had been isolated from political life. Even during the great social and ideological ferment of the 1860's, most of them had retreated into their ivory towers. But by the end of the century, most Academicians, as citizens and professors, could not remain isolated from the new social ideas. None of the Academicians joined a revolutionary movement; but most advocated a system of educational and scientific centers that would enjoy true institutional autonomy and free intellectual communication, and most criticized the unhealthy academic conditions created by the university statute of 1884. In January 1905 sixteen Academicians joined 342 university professors and instructors in signing a "Note on Educational Needs in Russia," which condemned the extensive police control of national education and demanded more liberal government policies.[3] In the same year the Academy registered a complaint with the government against the use of Academy buildings to house troops engaged in suppressing the revolution that had broken out in the streets. A special committee of the Academy urged the government to grant Ukrainians the right to speak and write in their native language—a point of great dispute at the time.[4] The general assembly of the Academy also endorsed freedom of the press.[5]

The Academicians of the preceding generation had remained aloof from the philosophical controversies of the time, no matter how closely these were related to specific scientific disciplines. The new Academicians did not shirk philosophical involvement; however, the philosophical crisis in the West during the 1890's was too vast and too complex to find full expression in the Academy. For example, the contemporary criticism of the epistemological foundations of Newtonian mechanics (inaugurated by Ernst Mach) and Euclidean geometry (Henri Poincaré) caused no excitement in the Academy. But various neo-Kantian, neopositivistic, and neovitalistic schools of thought counted Academicians among their leading supporters. This involvement did not produce any spectacular developments in philosophy, but it generated lively discussions centered on the nature and psychological limitations of knowledge and on the relationship of science to morality. For the first time, it was not uncommon to read philosophical articles written by Academicians and published in journals that reached a broad group of educated readers.[6]

The second great change in the Academy between 1884 and 1917 was a gradual transformation of its structure and orientation. In 1893 the government finally approved a new table of organization for the Academy, and also granted larger subsidies for research. By the turn of the century, the Academy was a permanent showcase of Russian scholarship at it best. Its laboratories were now open to selected young scholars of great promise, and its publications included valuable contributions from scholars outside the Academy.

Instead of being a self-contained oasis of scholarship, the Academy was now the chief clearinghouse for the nation. Through its numerous publications the best products of Russian science were made available to foreign scholars, and it coordinated the participation of Russian scholars in the international scientific congresses that had occurred with increasing frequency since the middle 1880's.[7] It was also the prime organizer of international congresses held in Russia. The Academy was especially active in the International Union of Academies, which included eighteen learned associations from a number of European countries. It took an active part in preparing an international bibliography in the exact and natural sciences, which was published by the Royal Society in London. This effort was of great help in the preparation of the Academy's own *Russian Bibliography in Mathematics and the Natural Sciences,* which it published in nine volumes (1904–16).[8]

The expansion and modernization of the Academy were slow but continuous. In 1894 the Special Zoological Laboratory was founded as an adjunct of the Zoological Museum, each having its own publications. The Physiological Laboratory, founded in 1889, did not blossom until 1907, when Ivan Pavlov became its director.[9] The Botanical Museum started the publication of special monographs in 1905, and helped establish the Laboratory of Plant Anatomy and Physiology, which played a leading role in forming a strong Russian tradition in morphological studies. In 1912, V. I. Vernadskii founded a small laboratory, housed in private quarters, to facilitate his study of the radioactive elements found in Russia; this and similar laboratories became important training centers for younger scholars, and were equally important as gathering places for experts in the same fields. The Academy was particularly successful in expanding its publication activities and its professional contacts with the universities and learned societies.

The expanding research apparatus of the Academy produced new methods of scientific inquiry. The Academy's annual progress report for 1906 stated that the traditional isolation of Academicians in scientific research was now giving way to collective efforts that often involved several dozen scientists in the same project. These undertakings required intricate techniques of experimentation and an integrated theoretical framework. The Zoological Museum, the pioneer of this collective research, soon emerged as an independent research center working within the Academy, and was followed by the Geological Museum, the Mineralogical Museum, and the Museum of Anthropology and Ethnography.[10]

The famous astronomical observatory at Pulkovo was an autonomous research center formally affiliated with the Academy. Founded by F. G. W. von Struve in 1839, this observatory had grown into one of the leading institutions of its kind in the world. Its international reputation rested on the high quality and modernity of its equipment, as well as the superb scholarship of its associates. In 1886 it acquired a large astrophysical laboratory and began extensive research in the application of spectroscopic and photographic techniques to astronomical studies. In addition, the observatory workshop built many of the smaller astronomical instruments, some of excellent quality. The Pulkovo Observatory was the last stronghold of foreign scholarship in Russia. Under the reign of Struve and his disciples, which lasted until the 1880's, the only Russians working there on a permanent basis were mechanics and custodians. In 1890 F. A. Bredikhin became the first Russian director of the observatory; and in his annual report for 1890 he noted that his most pressing task was to make Pulkovo accessible to promising Russian astronomers.[11]

The Main Physical Observatory, which managed a network of meteorological observatories throughout the country, was also affiliated with the Academy. It was primarily concerned with weather forecasting and seismological reports, and most of its work was on the level of empirical science. Because of this practical orientation, it was favored by the government; and because it was the Academy's chief physics department, the Academy contributed little to the theoretical and experimental development of modern physics.

The third great change in the Academy was the appearance of an interest in applied science. The Academy had always been ready to supply the government with expert advice on many practical questions that required scientific research; but it had always felt that its main concerns were in "pure" science. After 1860, individual leaders of the intelligentsia—and some scientists—began to complain that the Academy was dedicated more to enriching the theory of "Western science" in general than to resolving the concrete problems of Russia's own economy, health, and culture. They thought that an emphasis on applied science would help the Academy become a true national institution. The revolutionary upheavals in 1905 produced new critics, who claimed that the Academy had not made the institutional changes necessary to meet the needs of modern times and to become an organic part of Russian society.

As in the past, the Academy's representatives dismissed these criticisms by insisting that science, to function effectively, must not be forced to concentrate on the solution of current practical problems—that science must be guided first by the logic of its internal development and then by external social and cultural needs. S. F. Ol'denburg, permanent secretary of the Academy, stated that the primary function of science was to advance its own body of knowledge, regardless of practical considerations. "The most valuable discoveries in physics and chemistry," he emphasized, "do not necessarily help solve current technical problems." He added that when science is forced "to subordinate its immutable laws to constantly changing conditions of social life," it runs the risk of losing its most precious attributes, independence and objectivity.[12]

Nevertheless, after 1905 the Academy expanded its practical work in many directions, gaining a firmer foothold in Russian society. Most Academicians, on their own initiative, took part in many scientific activities that directly answered current national needs. After the famine of 1907, for example, A. S. Famintsyn helped organize a special Academy commission to conduct an interdisciplinary study of the effects of wet smut (the wheat disease *Tilletia tritici*) on human and animal organisms and to search for wheat varieties of higher quality. As an expert in probability theory, A. A. Markov helped the Pension Fund of the Ministry of Justice establish a mathematical basis for the determination of retirement funds. V. I. Vernadskii was noted for his enthusiastic participation in *zemstvo* activities; F. N. Chernyshev helped a special government commission to prepare plans for a long railroad tunnel in the Caucasus; and from 1897 to 1904 I. P. Borodin was a member of the Scientific Committee of the Ministry of Agriculture and the head of its Bureau of Applied Botany.[13]

Russia's involvement in World War I brought a tremendous need for practical research that would solve the acute problems of national defense. In the spring of 1915 the general assembly of the Academy unanimously decided to set up the Commission for the Study of the Natural Productive Forces of Russia—the KEPS.[14] For the first time in its history, the Academy had a centralized scientific agency that directed and coordinated the practical research of its members. The task of the KEPS was not only "to heal the wounds inflicted by the current war" but also to help the country "reach the level of development and power to which it is entitled by the richness of its resources."[15]

The initial efforts of the KEPS were mostly aimed at providing expedient technological aid for industries connected with the war effort, such as aviation, military electrical instruments, and the production of explosives, poison gases, radio equipment, and medical supplies. The wartime disruption of foreign trade revealed Russia's almost complete dependence on Western industry for most types of technical equipment. The chemical laboratories, for example, were crippled by a shortage of the imported acids and reagents that were needed for experimental purposes.[16] Working against insurmountable odds and always short of funds, the research groups set up by the KEPS did not produce startling results. Poor laboratory conditions forced a disproportionately large number of scholars to engage in empirical descriptive work. Several Academicians were kept busy surveying the mineral deposits in various parts of the country, without helping science, industry, or the war effort.[17]

Despite its immediate failures, which were mostly the result of unfavorable conditions, the KEPS contributed a great deal to the Academy and to Russian science in general. Above all, it demonstrated the vital importance of coordinated research and the pressing need for closer relations between science and industry. In one major effort during the fall of 1915, the KEPS undertook a massive interdisciplinary study of the rich geological and hydrological resources of Kara-Bugaz, a bay on the Caspian Sea. The study brought together scholars interested in many different areas: the physical and chemical qualities of natural heat-resistant materials; the salinity of Russian saltwater lakes; the industrial potential of platinum; and the distribution and chemical characteristics of tungsten, antimony, lithium, zinc, fluorine, iron pyrites, lead, iodine, sodium sulfate, and many other minerals of growing industrial importance. Interdisciplinary research under the sponsorship of the KEPS also laid the foundations for Russia's modern optical industry.

The main contribution of the KEPS to the development and modernization of Russian scientific thought was threefold. First, it demonstrated the usefulness of investigating one scientific problem from the vantage points of different disciplines. Second, it unified scientific manpower that had been scattered throughout the country by breaking down the Academy's barriers of aristocratic detachment, by involving many scholars in vital projects, and by extending help to previously neglected scientists on the fringes of organized scholarship. Third, and perhaps most important, it helped to modernize the institutional base of research in Russia's natural resources.[18] Vernadskii was firmly convinced that the complex system of research projects initiated by the KEPS had clearly demonstrated the advantages of a national network of research institutes: the time had come for the universities to become "powerful centers oriented toward research," and special research institutes with a variety of orientations were also needed. Vernadskii saw the proliferation of research groups during World War I as the main trend in the development of modern Russian science, and he anticipated that the complex research units established by the KEPS would soon become modern institutes. He lauded the Ministry of Agriculture for setting up a number of research agencies, and was impressed with the plan to establish a physical institute in Moscow with the help of the Ledentsov Society.

There was good reason for Vernadskii's enthusiasm. An experimental chemical plant in St. Petersburg, set up by the Russian Physical and Chemical Society to provide a link between research laboratories and Russia's growing chemical industry, was the first in Russia to produce hydrocyanic acid, cyanogen chloride, sodium, and arsenic.[19] During the war years, the Academy of Sciences worked on plans for the establishment of the Lomonosov Institute, a proposed complex of laboratories and other facilities for coordinated research in physics, chemistry, and mineralogy.[20] A similar institute for the biological sciences was also under consideration. In 1917 the KEPS approved the formation of the Institute for the Study of Platinum and the Institute of Physical and Chemical Analysis.

The Academy entered the fateful year of 1917 with many dreams, plans, and unfinished undertakings. The war produced great progress in organized scientific research, having removed many of the barriers that had traditionally isolated the Academy from the larger scientific community. But it had also drastically reduced the Academy's relations with scientific scholarship outside Russia, made the procurement of certain types of laboratory material exceedingly difficult, and shifted the emphasis in research from broad theoretical studies to concrete projects for national defense.[21]

After the February Revolution, the "republicanism" of the Academy was for the first time fully compatible with the political philosophy of the government. Two Academicians, S. F. Ol'denburg and A. S. Lappo-Danilevskii, were given high positions in the Provisional Government, and the Academy itself enjoyed an unprecedented degree of autonomy. The high point was reached on May 15, 1917, when the Academicians were allowed to elect a president from their own ranks, instead of accepting a state appointee. The honor went to Aleksandr Karpinskii, the "Father of Russian Geology," who had been a member of the Academy since 1896 and had received the Cuvier Prize from the Paris Academy of Sciences for his phylogenetic studies based on paleontological data. For the first time in its history, the Academy was headed by a scientist.

### THE CHANGING PROFILE OF INDEPENDENT LEARNED SOCIETIES

Although most of the learned societies that were not affiliated with institutions of higher education received government subsidies, they were supported primarily by private donations, membership fees, and income from their publications. During the first half of the nineteenth century the unspecialized natural history societies were the most popular; but after the 1860's the naturalist societies, which were divided into sections covering the major disciplines, received the most attention. During the 1890's and the first two decades of the twentieth century many specialized societies were founded. The emphasis was no longer on encyclopedism and empiricism but on specialized scientific theorizing.

Until 1888 Russia had no astronomical learned society, even though the Pulkovo Observatory was one of the leading institutions of its kind in the world, and even though most universities had some astronomical instruments. It was not until the end of the nineteenth century that Russian astronomers made any efforts to communicate with the public, and they were among the last scientists to adopt Russian as the language of scientific communication. In 1888 a high school teacher in Nizhnii Novgorod founded the Circle of Admirers of Physics and Astronomy, which soon started to publish an annual astronomical calendar. In 1890 the Russian Astronomical Society was founded in St. Petersburg, and it immediately began to publish extensively. It was followed by the Moscow Society of Admirers of Astronomy (1908) and then by the Russian Society of Admirers of Cosmology (1910). As a group, these associations appealed to an unusually wide audience, ranging from the dilettantes of the *kruzhok* at Nizhnii Novgorod to professionals occupying the key positions in the Russian Astronomical Society (initially led by F. A. Bredikhin, the director of the Pulkovo Observatory).

While the new learned societies were still searching for the most effective organizational principles and communication techniques, the older associations were busy keeping up with the needs of modern Russian society and the advances in the different sciences. The Russian Geographical Society, founded in 1845, was typical of this group. Previously the Society had been interested primarily in collecting geographical data with some practical (i.e., economic or military) use; now it gradually began to conduct research that aimed at advancing the methodological and theoretical horizons of science.

"Geographical travels" to unexplored lands in and out of Russia continued to be the most glamorous activities of the Society; but systematic studies of problems related to various branches of physical and human geography began to receive increasing emphasis.[22] The government, for its part, viewed the Society as an instrument of Russian territorial expansion and a means of collecting administrative information in Asia. It was through the Geographical Society that the government gathered economic, ethnographic, and demographic information in the Chinese, Tibetan, and Mongolian areas far beyond the boundaries of the empire.

To a host of eminent Russian scientists who came into their own during the early twentieth century, the Geographical Society was actually a school of postgraduate study—an initiation into the art of research. Such leading scientists of the twentieth century as the geologists V. A. Obruchev and N. I. Andrusov, the geographer L. S. Berg, and the botanist V. L. Komarov, all members of the Academy of Sciences, were much indebted to the Society, which provided them with opportunities for field experience and was always ready to publish their research papers.

No other scientific institution made a deeper penetration into the provinces than the Geographical Society, which had branches in Tiflis, Kiev, Irkutsk, Vladivostok, Khabarovsk, and Omsk. These branches, though formally a part of the Geographical Society, initiated and conducted their own regional studies, and many published their own transactions. Teachers, priests, engineers, and army officers were the most active members of the local branches, which also attracted private donors and affluent dilettantes.

The Siberian branches of the Society enrolled many political exiles, and some of these made contributions of lasting value. I. D. Cherskii, who had been exiled for his participation in the Polish uprising in 1863, collected valuable fossils and conducted local surveys of the extant fauna. Two other members, the ethnographers V. G. Bogoraz and V. I. Iokhelson, became accomplished students of tribal cultures and languages during their enforced exile.[23] When they were free to leave Siberia, both joined the research staff of the Jesup North Pacific Commission (directed by the American anthropologist Franz Boas), which was then conducting a study of the historical and cultural ties between the prehistoric Siberians and the American Indians. Bogoraz's studies of the Chukchee and Iokhelson's monographs on the Koryak and Yukaghir are among the classics of Siberian ethnography.[24] Several Siberian natives—Buryats and Central Asians—also became actively involved in the Society's projects in their homeland; and many eminent members of the Society began to realize the plight of the downtrodden, non-Russian races of the empire, and were willing to speak on their behalf before the St. Petersburg authorities.

In 1884 geography was added to the curriculum of the national universities. The Geographical Society greeted the event with enthusiasm, and its journals began a broad discussion of the various didactic problems related to geography.[25] At first the subject was under the Faculty of History and Philology, and was viewed as an auxiliary of history. D. N. Anuchin, who introduced the teaching of geography at Moscow University, made it clear that geography, as "an essential supplement to history," gave more precision to historical perspective and "contributed to a better understanding of the development of human culture."[26] Although the establishment of geography in the universities coincided with a great expansion of expeditionary research in Russia, the number of students majoring in geography was surprisingly low.[27] It attracted students like the poet Andrei Belyi, who wanted an education in the natural sciences but had no interest in a firmly defined specialty.

In 1887 the Ministry of National Education authorized the transfer of geography from the Faculty of History and Philology to the Faculty of the Physical and Mathematical Sciences; and in 1888 a special committee recommended that the cluster of sciences closely related to geography be organized into a special department within that Faculty. The government's rejection of this ambitious plan was supported by many scholars, who believed that geography was rapidly being superseded by specialized disciplines equipped with modern research tools and working on important theoretical problems.

In the late nineteenth century Russia had a comparatively large number of active geographers; but only a few of these worked on the integration of existing empirical knowledge, the advancement of theory, and the improvement of research techniques. The models of modern geographical studies continued to come from the West. The preceding generation of Russian geographers had been inspired by the monumental works of Karl Ritter and Alexander von Humboldt; the geographers of the 1880's and the 1890's found additional guidance in the studies of G. K. C. Gerland, F. P. W. Richthofen, Alfred Kirchhoff, Friedrich Ratzel, and several other scholars who integrated geography with geology, physical anthropology, astronomy, botany, zoology, and demography.

The outstanding characteristic of Russian geography at this time was a rapid growth of specialized disciplines within the field. Soil science, a distinctively Russian pursuit, emerged from a combination of geographical, geological, and biological research. Russian geology, which had a relatively late start, relied mostly on the information collected by geographers. The new fields of zoogeography and phytogeography produced new supports and challenges for Darwin's theory of evolution and reinforced the traditionally strong ecological orientation of Russian naturalists. Thanks to the work of Karl von Baer, Russia had been one of the first countries to develop physical anthropology as a distinct discipline; and anthropogeography was pursued by entire sections of various learned societies, particularly in Siberia, Central Asia, and the Caucasus, the regions inhabited by heterogeneous racial and ethnic groups. L. S. Berg, influenced by a three-volume study of Lake Geneva by the Swiss scholar F. A. Forel, conducted an extensive study of the Aral Sea, founding Russian limnology. And V. I. Vernadskii's mineralogical study of the distribution of elements and chemical investigations of the soil and the earth's crust opened more new vistas for geographical research.[28]

L. S. Berg, one of the most prominent members of the Geographical Society, was a rare scholar among his contemporaries, for he was both a geographer *par excellence* and a natural scientist of great accomplishment and influence. His papers on climatology, limnology, soil science, geology, glaciology, and phytogeography were as solid as his widely discussed studies in ethnography, institutional history, the history of geography, and the theory of education. As an encyclopedist, Berg closed one era in the history of geography; as an accomplished expert in specialized "geographical" disciplines, particularly ichthyology and limnology, he opened a new era by helping to free these disciplines from geographical tutelage and encouraging their independent development. Berg ended his career working as a limnologist, an ichthyologist, and a codifier of geographical habitat types. Throughout his life, however, he considered himself to be no more than a self-taught geographer, and his conclusions seldom went beyond empirical generalizations based on data visible to the naked eye. Berg's greatest work as a systematizer of geographical knowledge—particularly his delineation of geographical zones and climates—was accomplished after 1920.[29]

In the nineteenth century the Geographical Society accumulated a vast amount of social, economic, and ethnic data; and at the beginning of the twentieth century, several members of the Society made serious efforts to use these data as an empirical base for broader sociological studies. Perhaps the most illustrious product of this expanded effort was V. Semenov-Tian-Shanskii's *City and Village in European Russia* (1910), a skillful synthesis of geographical, ethnographic, demographic, and historical data on the morphology and the dynamics of local communities. The author's main contribution was his careful analysis of the external conditions responsible for the emergence of different types of rural and urban communities.[30] Though a geographer, Semenov-Tian-Shanskii was not a geographical determinist; according to him, the unique typology of Russian communities was a result of the combined influences of natural habitat and historical vicissitudes.

The Geographical Society and its numerous branches were not the only institutions dedicated to geographical research. For example, D. N. Anuchin, the most productive and influential Russian geographer before L. S. Berg, was associated with Moscow University and the Moscow Society of Admirers of Natural Science, Anthropology, and Ethnography, which supported an outstanding geography section. A typical representative of the old school, Anuchin defined geography as a comprehensive science of the earth—"a science that is identified with physical geography, biogeography, and anthropogeography on one hand, and with descriptions of individual regions on the other."[31] Geography, he wrote in 1892, comprised seven distinct sciences: (1) astronomical or mathematical geography, based on astronomy and geodetics and related to cartography; (2) geophysics, connected with physics, astronomy, and geology; (3) physical geography, subdivided into orography, oceanography, and climatology; (4) biological geography, subdivided into zoogeography and phytogeography; (5) anthropogeography, concerned with the racial and ethnic distribution of mankind; (6) regional geography; and (7) the history of geography.[32] Anuchin was known primarily for his numerous topographical studies of Russia, but he also wrote extensively on physical anthropology and paleoethnography, emphasizing the peoples of Siberia.[33]

Of all the sciences, geography did the most to reach people in every corner of Russia. It strengthened the rationalist trend of the Russian intellectual tradition by widely disseminating scientific explanations for the workings of the universe and the nature of earth and man. More clearly than any other science, it showed that scientific thought was essentially democratic, originating not in the revelations of unchallengeable sacred authorities but in man's secular and challengeable search for objective wisdom.

The most active learned association at the turn of the century was the Russian Technical Society, which had been founded in 1866 for the purpose of imparting scientific knowledge to industry and raising the level of technological literacy among Russian workers.[34] In 1897 the Society had close to 2,000 members enrolled in 23 branches throughout the country. Many local branches published their own journals, usually following a strict line of specialization: for example, the Kiev branch concentrated on sugar beet cultivation, the Baku branch on the chemistry of petroleum and the technology of its production. All these journals were financially secure, thanks to both private endowments and government subsidies, and they were the only periodicals dedicated exclusively to the technology and economics of modern industry. There had been other efforts to start industrial journals, but all were abortive. The *Messenger of Industry, Technical Review, Technical Symposium,* and *Technician,* among others, did not survive because there was little demand for the type of knowledge that they provided. According to a contemporary, these journals were read only by self-taught technicians and inventors, and were largely ignored by the engineers and managers who ran the modern industrial enterprises.[35] The Technical Society alone had adjusted itself to the very tenuous interaction between the theoretically sophisticated scientists and the practically oriented industrial technicians, and had tried to create a general awareness of the vital link between science and industry.

From its very beginnings the Technical Society attracted a broad range of members, from internationally prominent research scientists like Mendeleev to lowly "inventors" living in the dim isolation of remote provinces. It occasionally aided scientific research of practical significance: for example, it financed Mendeleev's study of the elasticity of gases and N. E. Zhukovskii's research in aerodynamics; and at various times it appointed special commissions to study such diverse problems as acetylene lighting, chemical fire extinguishing, and the chemical composition of naphtha.[36]

The Technical Society's most beneficial activity was its support of the various technical schools that had been set up to raise the technological competence of Russian industrial workers. The Society sponsored public exhibits of the latest technological developments and organized Russian displays at various international fairs. In 1880 it helped organize an elaborate electrical engineering exhibit in St. Petersburg in which P. N. Iablochkov's technique of making electric lamps was the most notable attraction; and in 1896, for the Sixteenth Industrial and Artisan Fair in Nizhnii Novgorod, it set up a demonstration exhibit of several modern inventions, including X-ray equipment.[37] Since the Society was interested in developing harmonious relations between industry and society, it often became involved with labor politics. It supported the demands of entrepreneurs for protective tariffs, but it also echoed the growing demand for more favorable working conditions in industry.[38]

During the late 1880's and the 1890's new medical societies were founded in over fifty Russian cities, joining the many similar groups that already existed. Most medical associations were expected to advance the collective interests of their members, but they also sponsored periodic meetings to discuss modern medical developments. The transactions of these meetings provided a unique and refreshing synthesis of "theoretical" medicine and the accumulated wisdom of practicing physicians.[39] Many of the specialized medical societies in St. Petersburg, Moscow, and Kiev published periodic symposia in their respective fields.

The N. I. Pirogov Society of Russian Physicians, founded in 1883, was the most notable of the new medical associations. At first the Society drew its members almost exclusively from St. Petersburg and Moscow, but in 1892 it secured government permission to operate on a national basis. The most important of the Society's operations were the "Pirogovian congresses," held every second or third year. Like other medical meetings, Pirogovian congresses established a working cooperation between practicing physicians and medical researchers. But in contrast to other congresses, which concentrated on specialized branches of medicine and on purely scientific problems, the Pirogovian congresses dealt with preventive medicine, placing particular emphasis on social problems of medical significance; this interest transformed them into instruments of public opinion on vital social problems. The Pirogovian congresses were able to harness resources for the fight against recurrent cholera and other epidemics, and were the champions of preventive medical service in the countryside. Under their influence, country physicians conducted social, economic, and demographic surveys, gathering important medical statistics.[40]

During the 1890's, the Pirogov Society was the major intellectual, ideological, and political force behind the fast growing *zemstvo* medical corps —physicians with a social consciousness.[41] In 1865, only 48 physicians practiced outside the larger towns; by 1904 the number had risen to 1,608. The *zemstvo* medical service was organized to ensure both a steady flow of modern medical knowledge to the village and a feedback of valuable field information from practicing physicians. Every *zemstvo* physician felt that he must perform two functions: provide direct medical service, both therapeutic and prophylactic, and collect statistical data to reveal local peculiarities in the distribution and social causes of various diseases.

*Zemstvo* medicine produced a new physician, best described in *Russian Zemstvo Medicine*, a symposium prepared for the Twelfth International Congress of Medicine: "The *zemstvo* physician can achieve beneficial results only if he is acquainted with everything relating to the life of the people: he must fully understand the local conditions of his district and the sanitary habits, resources, needs, customs, prejudices, and cultural standards of the inhabitants. Without a full knowledge of the life of the local populace, a physician could not hope to identify the causes of many diseases that occur in various regions, to acquire the needed confidence in the struggle against prejudices and for sound hygienic practices, and to avoid ephemeral medical techniques and rely on the only true medicine—hygiene."[42]

The *zemstvo* physicians respected modern bacteriology primarily as an auxiliary of hygiene; while Pasteur and Koch were learning to fight disease germs, the *zemstvo* physicians were fighting the conditions that bred them.[43] To the scientific means of fighting epidemics, they added the sociopolitical means; they did not resolve the grave problem of public health in rural Russia, but they added a new dimension to the professional attack on it. The *zemstvo* medical facilities were pitifully underequipped, and the physicians' real strength lay in teaching peasants the virtues and techniques of sanitation.

The government was in favor of the *zemstvo* physician's therapeutic work, in which he acted as a skilled technician; but it looked with great suspicion on his work in the sanitation field, which was motivated by social ideals and a desire for sweeping reforms in the rural community. After the 1905 revolution many *zemstva*, succumbing to violent government pressure, abolished their sanitation departments; and by 1913, only 150 *zemstvo* physicians were engaged exclusively in hygienic work. Nevertheless, the journals of the Pirogov Society continued to publish and assess the empirical findings of *zemstvo* physicians, and to suggest appropriate social remedies for the problems that came to light.

At the beginning of the 1890's Russia was struck by recurrent famines and epidemics over huge areas of the country. The inability of the established authorities to handle these grave national problems produced many new *zemstvo* activists, who worked in the fields of public health and sanitation. Congresses of *zemstvo* doctors discussed the problems of decentralized medical administration, permanent physicians' councils, clinics and observational units in the countryside, the modernization of medical facilities, and the gathering of medically relevant information.[44] Under the influence of the *zemstvo* doctors, the Pirogov Society also began to advocate fundamental political reforms, from improvements in public health to an eight-hour working day and universal education.

In 1904, after the government had rejected the eightieth in a series of recommendations for the amelioration of the adverse conditions affecting the health and the welfare of the nation, the Society decided to rely on its own resources. But in 1905 the government rejected the Society's petition to hold an extraordinary congress to plan medical action against the current cholera epidemics in southern Russia. The delegates met anyway, and issued a bellicose appeal to all physicians to join the struggle of the working people against "autocratic bureaucracy." The assembled physicians demanded universal suffrage, a secret ballot, political and religious freedom, and the transfer of the police force from state to local control. "Only when these preliminary conditions are met," said the resolution of the congress, "will it be possible to organize a realistic, planned struggle against national calamities and epidemics; only then will our country be able to conquer plague, cholera, and other epidemics."[45]

The Pirogov Society's great concern with social medicine did not prevent it from facing the general problems of medicine as both a profession and a science. It was the Society that led campaigns for uniform medical nomenclature in Russia, for special institutions devoted to the "advanced training" of doctors with practical experience, for the institutionalized cooperation of university clinics with rural medical institutions, and for research centers on the local level.[46] After the 1905 revolution the Pirogov Society concentrated on protecting the professional interests of Russian physicians. This change of heart resulted primarily from increasing government action against the programs of social medicine organized by freethinking groups. However, the libertarian fire of the Society was not completely extinguished until the Soviet authorities, interested more in state medicine than in social medicine, put a stop to the Society's activities.

The Pirogov Society earned an honorable place in the annals of Russian science primarily by its consistent use of modern science as a source of ideas and actions directed against the anachronism of combined autocratic despotism and rural superstition. A Pirogovian physician followed a simple and straightforward philosophy: to him, national health and welfare depended on science, and science flourished only in a free society. He believed that democracy, science, and social welfare were closely interrelated necessities of modern existence. In his humanitarianism and dedication, he was the noblest of all modern Russian champions of science; he added little to the mainstream of scientific thought, but did much to make science an important part of Russian culture.

The Free Economic Society, the oldest independent learned society in Russia, was also concerned with rural welfare. To some extent, this concern was reflected in the Society's sponsorship of scientific research on subjects related to agriculture. More than any other learned association, it cherished the words of the great French chemist and statesman Marcellin Berthelot: "Scientific agriculture is rapidly replacing traditional agriculture, and is helping to expand the riches of nations beyond all expectations."[47] V. V. Dokuchaev, the founder of soil science, conducted his initial fieldwork under the auspices of the Society. But the Free Economic Society's real interest was in agricultural economics and rural sociology. Its efforts to collect the empirical information indispensable for a scientific study of natural resources and economic development were not emulated by any other learned society. In 1914 it appointed a special commission to study "theoretical problems," in hope of discovering broader meanings in the existing empirical data and modernizing the techniques of economic research. The Society approached the chronic problems of Russian agriculture in a spirit of scientific analysis, offering concrete proposals for their solution.

The Free Economic Society's "literacy committees" collected information on the attitudes of the rural populace toward the goals and practices of modern education, and took a leading part in the dissemination of scientific knowledge. The Society advocated universal education, and these committees were the chief components of its concerted struggle against widespread rural superstition and the deeply rooted cultural isolation engendered by estate stratification. The Society also recognized the urgent need for a systematic collection of information on the activities and problems of the *zemstva*: its *Zemstvo Yearbook* was one of the most valuable sources of rural economic and sociological information published in Russia. The *Yearbook*'s statistical surveys, a fertile source of information indicating the need for social and economic reform, were particularly welcomed by the activists who advocated the full emancipation of the rural community.

During the 1890's most active members of the Free Economic Society agreed that the main source of the chronic ills of Russian agriculture lay not so much in technological underdevelopment as in the political backwardness of the country. The Society's *Transactions* featured numerous articles that advocated sweeping political reforms. Many of the Society's members came from the new entrepreneurial class, who were increasingly critical of the widespread and deeply rooted vestiges of aristocratic power in the agricultural economy. The Society's criticism was backed up by penetrating scholarship, which aided both the growing demands for basic social reforms and the objective study of Russian social and economic realities.

In 1899, alarmed at this growing criticism of national agricultural policies, the government decided to revoke the Society's charter and ordered that its future activities be limited to research in agricultural technology. In spite of many recommendations from special commissions, the government refused to approve a new charter; but meanwhile, the Society continued its traditional activities unofficially, and intensified its concern with the mounting political crisis. In 1905 it went on record in support of the proposal for an elected constitutional assembly, which would take over all political authority and would hasten the introduction of democratic political institutions.

However, the Free Economic Society was more liberal in its pronouncements in favor of political reforms than in its demands for basic institutional changes in the national economy. The Soviet government considered the Society overcommitted to private agriculture and made no effort to help it resume its activities after World War I.

## CHAPTER EIGHT

# The Philosophical Challenge

### IDEALISTIC METAPHYSICS AND SCIENCE

As we have seen, Russian philosophy in the 1860's was dominated by Nihilism, which identified the premises of philosophy with the facts of science and viewed science as the most reliable index of cultural progress. The Nihilists campaigned successfully against metaphysics and philosophical idealism, greatly aided by the temper of the time, which placed a premium on liberal reforms and secular wisdom. The cleric P. D. Iurkevich, an eloquent critic of Nihilism and allied philosophies, advanced cogent arguments and showed remarkable erudition and depth; but he was ignored by his friends and scornfully dismissed by his foes. A philosophical historian of the following generation noted that the one-sided sympathies of the public and the polemical talent of his adversaries worked against Iurkevich.[1] The idealist N. N. Strakhov had to admit that during the 1860's philosophical idealism was "sick."[2]

The Populist philosophy of the late 1860's and the 1870's agreed in two important respects with Nihilism: it opposed metaphysics and it extolled scientific knowledge as the most trustworthy source of philosophy. Like the Nihilists, the Populists accepted Comtean positivism; but unlike the Nihilists, they rejected the materialism of Büchner, Vogt, and Moleschott. In their treatment of scientific knowledge as essentially subjective, P. L. Lavrov and the other early Populists foreshadowed a strong revival of philosophical idealism in Russia.

During the 1870's idealistic metaphysics gradually grew into a major philosophical orientation that opposed both Nihilist "materialism" and Populist "positivism." It soon splintered into several currents, but remained united in its unqualified adherence to idealist ontology. The main architects of the new idealism were Boris Chicherin, a Hegelian with original ideas, and Vladimir Solov'ev, a modern champion of Slavophil mysticism. Both came from the academic community: Chicherin taught constitutional law at Moscow from 1861 to 1868, and Solov'ev lectured in modern philosophy at St. Petersburg in 1875–77 and 1880–82.

In *Science and Religion* (1879) Chicherin presented his philosophical "system" and offered an assortment of views on science as a unique mode of inquiry and a specific set of cultural values. He rejected the positivist idea that religion, metaphysics, and science represent successive phases in the progress of intellectual culture, and was inclined to view science as the least important of the three. According to Chicherin, each of the three orientations depends on two types of experience: external and internal. The internal experience, on which science depends the least and religion the most, more clearly reveals absolute reason—the truth and logic that are independent of any experience. Chicherin's "absolute reason" is not the Kantian *Ding an sich* but an ontological entity, a direct link between man and God. Indeed, "The absolute, as the objective principle of existence, is called God in every language."[3] The absolute injects meaning and order into external experience and gradually raises it to the level of absolute knowledge.

In Chicherin's view, scientific knowledge is shallow, since it is "limited to the explanation of purely mechanical relations."[4] Science is only a first step toward the absolute; philosophy, by contrast, can achieve a full understanding of the absolute, and religion is "living communication with the absolute."[5] For this reason, science achieves its best results when it is associated with rationalist metaphysics. The Nihilists used science to justify socialism as a political program; but for Chicherin, scientific principles can sustain socialism only when they are associated with ontological materialism, "the lowest view to which the human mind can descend."[6] If unchecked by religion and idealistic metaphysics, an overemphasis on natural science could reduce man to an animal, and his community to a regimented socialist camp. This notion, as expressed in *Science and Religion*, became a standard argument of most Russian idealistic philosophers during the 1890's and the early twentieth century.

Chicherin attacked all philosophical systems that treated science as the purest and most reliable index of the intellectual achievements of modern man. Nevertheless, he consistently defended the notion that scientific knowledge is an essential component of advanced culture.[7] As a Hegelian, Chicherin treated science as one of the major sources of the raw data from which the grand principles of rationalist metaphysics could be deduced: in *Positive Philosophy* (1892), he dissected the philosophical foundations of the principal sciences to verify his idea that metaphysics alone could penetrate the innermost depths of natural and social reality.[8] True wisdom, he felt, could be arrived at by combining "experience," categorized and purified by science, with "speculation," the method of metaphysics.[9] As a Hegelian, Chicherin regarded logic as the only bridge between science and metaphysics. As a "rationalist," however, he recognized only one kind of metaphysics—a metaphysics anchored in science.

Chicherin's philosophy helped create an intellectual atmosphere favoring the revival of metaphysics; but it did not become a part of the mainstream of idealistic philosophy in Russia, probably because of its Hegelian orientation. As a philosopher, Chicherin belonged to the German rather than the Russian metaphysical tradition.

Vladimir Solov'ev, unlike Chicherin, combined metaphysics with irrationalism and mysticism; in essence, he readapted the Slavophil philosophy of the 1840's and 1850's, creating the most powerful and widespread idealistic philosophy of modern Russia.[10] Solov'ev's *Crisis of Western Philosophy* (1874) provided a sweeping criticism of Western philosophical thought, from the "vulgar empiricism" of Bacon and Locke and the "skepticism" of Hume to Kant's transcendental idealism, Comte's positivism, and Hegel's absolute rationalism.[11]

According to Solov'ev, traditional epistemology, whether rationalist or empiricist, viewed the human rational faculties as the only source of trustworthy knowledge. However, he argued, belief, imagination, and creation can also produce knowledge; and mystical experience, which is often superior to reason, is the most human and most powerful inspiration of all. Convinced that the separation of science from religion in Western philosophy had destroyed the internal unity of knowledge, Solov'ev proposed a new epistemology, based on mysticism. For him, man's true power lay not in the experimental facts of science but in a metaphysical synthesis of science, philosophy (particularly epistemology and ethics), and religion.[12] In Schopenhauer's "blind will" and Hartmann's "superconsciousness," both of which he interpreted as efforts to break the stranglehold of absolute rationalism, Solov'ev saw some hope for the future development of Western philosophy. In essence, Solov'ev was proposing a metaphysical system that recognized an absolute principle—a "concrete and all-unifying spirit"—as the source of universal meaning. Spiritualistic metaphysics, in turn, was the starting point for the grand system of religious philosophy that was Solov'ev's most important philosophical achievement.

Solov'ev's metaphysical constructions, epistemological criticisms, and ethical evaluations contain only the most sketchy outlines of a philosophy of science. Science, in his opinion, has three basic limitations—epistemological, ontological, and ethical. Epistemologically, it is limited by its dependence on man's rational faculties, and is deprived of spiritual and mystical knowledge. Ontologically, science adheres too closely to the mechanical laws of nature, projecting them into the biological, psychological, and cultural worlds. It is also handicapped by its separation from religion, which provides the safest path for man's progressive emulation of the absolute spirit. Ethically, science is powerless to handle the growth of moral precepts, which originate in the absolute spirit and not in human societies or the physical world. Solov'ev strongly denounced the social scientists and philosophers who treated morality as a social phenomenon subject to scientific analysis.

In addition to these views on the intellectual limitations of science in general, Solov'ev had definite ideas about the unique shortcomings of Russian science. Science in Russia, he said, did not reflect the national character; it was, by implication, a Western importation with no roots in Russian culture. The Russians were "competent in science," but their contributions had been fragmentary. As if he had never heard of Lobachevskii and Mendeleev, Solov'ev argued that no Russian had produced ideas contributing directly to breakthroughs in individual sciences. Writing at the end of the 1880's, he stated that the best Russian contributions in both the natural and the social sciences were a matter of the past, and that Russian science had passed its zenith and had begun an irreversible decline.[13]

In a rhetorical effort to convince his countrymen that their pride need not be hurt by the "low development" and hopeless future of science in Russia, Solov'ev emphasized that science was only an auxiliary sphere of intellectual activity: it provided little opportunity for truly creative work and was not really an accurate expression of the Russian spirit.[14] Science was useful as a basis for technological progress, but otherwise it was only "diffuse material" that could not be built into a firm intellectual edifice without the help of philosophy. Only by adopting the philosophical world view could the Russians achieve personal freedom and give full expression to their unique national character.

The strength of Solov'ev's philosophy was its brilliantly logical exposition and integration of complex ideas; because of the remarkable logical unity of his work, he is generally considered the first systematic Russian philosopher.[15] According to Evgenii Trubetskoi, Solov'ev's philosophy is the converging point of two extremes: a belief that there is a mystical element in the acquisition of even the most elementary knowledge and a belief that even the most abstruse theosophic idea can be expressed with the rigor and precision of a geometrical axiom.[16] All this should not obscure the fact that Solov'ev attached little value to science as a source of wisdom. The Slavophils condemned the sciences outright; Solov'ev condemned them by placing them in an intellectual and cultural setting only slightly related to the inner orientation of Russian thought. He magnified the philosophically weak points of science—particularly the overreaching aspirations of the mechanistic orientation in the natural sciences and the organismic orientation in the social sciences—and overlooked the effect of contemporary philosophical criticism, which was even then helping to free science from the crippling rule of mechanism.

Solov'ev's uncompromising war on empirical sociology, nonteleological historicism in the studies of nature and society, physiological psychology, and sociohistorical theories of morality gave comfort only to the champions of the official ideology, who placed the autocratic system above all vicissitudes of earthly fortune and historical causation. Indeed, his eschatological dream of a state-society based on the full affirmation of "God-Manhood" was a theocratic idealization of Russian autocracy. By the end of the century, however, when the autocracy had begun to depend for its survival primarily on the police force, Solov'ev was no longer willing to base his divine society on the autocratic model. Abandoning his earlier ideas, he became sure that no existing state could offer a model of the divine abode.

Solov'ev quickly acquired a reputation as a writer gifted with artistic talent, intellectual erudition, and polemical forcefulness; but at first few Russians paid any serious attention to his philosophical system. One reason for this was his glorification of the autocratic attributes of a future theocratic polity at a time when the academic community was engaged in a critical struggle against the growing encroachments of the government. In fact, Solov'ev was closely associated with Professor N. A. Liubimov, the most vociferous advocate of rigid government control over scholarship.[17] Also, Solov'ev abandoned philosophy during most of the 1880's, which greatly reduced his intellectual influence.

In general, the 1880's were unexciting years for Russian philosophy. The old Populists were no longer interested in philosophical discussion. Chernyshevskii's "The Character of Human Knowledge" (1885) marked the end of the non-Marxian tradition in Russian materialistic philosophy with a bitter outcry against the mounting "idealistic" tendencies of some of the leading modern scientists, notably Rudolf Virchow and Emil du Bois-Reymond. Before the ink of Chernyshevskii's essay was dry, A. I. Vvedenskii published his first essays criticizing the prevalent mechanistic orientation of the physical sciences. The Marxists, led by Plekhanov, were too busy with social, economic, and political discussions to pay much attention to the philosophy of science. They were concerned more with changing the world than with understanding the intricacies of its dynamics; their work, however, gave rise to a considerable new interest and sophistication in philosophy during the 1890's.

Metaphysical idealism, an orientation that gathered momentum during the 1890's and the first decade of the new century, had two main currents.[18] The first originated in Slavophilism, the basic writings of P. D. Iurkevich, and the ontology of Vladimir Solov'ev; it placed mysticism above rationalism, metaphysics above physics, and revelation above the experimental method of science. The most influential and respected member of this group was Sergei Trubetskoi, a professor of philosophy at Moscow University during the turbulent years before the conflagration of 1905. The second current was represented by nonacademic philosophers who combined Solov'ev's irrationalism and mysticism with the Nietzschean distaste for humanism and the Marxian denigration of bourgeois values. The most eloquent spokesman for this group was Nikolai Berdiaev, who began his philosophical odyssey as a Marxist, later combined Marxism and Kantianism, and ended by defining mysticism, eschatological metaphysics, messianism, and *sobornost'* as the quintessence of the Russian national character.[19]

For many years Sergei Trubetskoi edited *Questions of Philosophy and Psychology*, which began publication in 1889 and soon became Russia's leading philosophical journal. In this position, he played a decisive role in the consolidation of various idealistic currents into a major school of philosophy—a hybrid of Boehme's and Baader's mysticism, Schelling's irrationalism, and Hegel's objective idealism, all tempered by Slavophil messianism and antirationalism. Trubetskoi built most of his theories on Solov'ev's ideas; and like Solov'ev, he believed in many sources of knowledge, emphasizing sensual experience (science), pure intellect (philosophy), and belief (religion). But he gave religious mystical experience the main credit for revealing to man the "pan-unity" of knowledge—i.e., the "essential," the "absolute principle," the "world soul," or the Christian God, whom Trubetskoi presented as an ontological principle that unifies man's ultimate intellectual, aesthetic, and moral experience.

Like Solov'ev, Trubetskoi regarded divine authority as the ultimate source of all human knowledge. Solov'ev, however, was interested primarily in the nature and inner logic of this divine authority or "unconditional principle"; Trubetskoi dealt mostly with the diversity of knowledge that flowed to and from the world soul. Solov'ev clarified and elaborated the ontological foundations of idealism and built an ethical system on them; Trubetskoi used the same idealistic ontology as the basis for an elaborate epistemological theory. Solov'ev had a flair for broad philosophical statements in which journalistic expediency was blended with the logical rigor of scholarship; Trubetskoi was a journalist in articles dealing with the burning problems of academic autonomy, but a consistent scholar in his philosophical and historical studies. V. I. Vernadskii later said that Trubetskoi, rather than Solov'ev, was the first Russian to free philosophy from journalistic embroidery and make it a systematic part of Russian scholarship. In this sense, he was one of the first "pure and original" philosophers raised in Russia.[20]

In his early writings, Solov'ev had presented Russian autocracy as an embryonic model of the divine state on earth, and had woven it into a complex metaphysical system. Trubetskoi, by contrast, operated on two levels: as a metaphysicist he steered away from political identifications, but as a "journalist" he recognized autocracy as the ideal form of government for Russia. Though a devoted monarchist, he advocated broad relaxation of the curbs on political freedom. Whereas Solov'ev had spelled out the inferiority of science to idealistic metaphysics and religious mysticism in straightforward terms, Trubetskoi's downgrading of science was more implicit and less dramatic.

Solov'ev, in his emphasis on religious experience, greatly resembled the Slavophil idealists of the 1840's in that he prophesied a decline of Western European philosophy and a glorious triumph of Russian religious metaphysics. Trubetskoi, too, followed the Russian idealistic tradition and sought a metaphysical explanation for the Slavophil *sobornost'*; but he placed his philosophical ideas in the context of the general European intellectual tradition. According to him, "Greek enlightenment and Christianity are the foundations for all of European civilization," and he undertook to throw new light on the "internal relationship" of these two traditions.[21] Solov'ev sought to demonstrate science's incompatibility with the innermost depths of Russian culture; Trubetskoi felt that science had no connection with the spiritual essence of Western civilization in general. Solov'ev's stand was chiefly a reaction to the excesses of Nihilist scientism, and Trubetskoi's was a similar response to the scientific aspirations of Marxian socialism and neopositivism. Both men were also affected by the new philosophical orientations in Western Europe that were generated by the radical new developments in physics and biology. Sociologically, Solov'ev and Trubetskoi wavered between an outright endorsement of Russian theocracy and an escape into the foggy skies of metaphysical unreality.

The second major line in the development of Russian metaphysical idealism differed from the first in two respects: it did not produce or attract any thinkers to compare with Solov'ev and Trubetskoi; and all of its advocates had at one time been identified with Marxian philosophy. Although professing to be admirers and followers of Vladimir Solov'ev, these philosophers were still preoccupied with the intrinsic weaknesses of Marxian thought. Solov'ev and Trubetskoi concentrated on building and codifying an idealistic ontology. The idealistic ex-Marxists, however, devoted most of their efforts to fighting Marx's materialist ontology. Nevertheless, they remained true to some of the most important tenets of Marxian ideology: they were, for example, consistently hostile toward the bourgeoisie and its social and moral values. They did not show any particular sympathy for Russian autocracy, but they rarely published any criticism of tsarist political institutions.* Indeed, they helped the established order by their bitter and continuous attacks on the many secular factions that were then drawing the attention of the masses to the staggering social and political problems of the country.

Nikolai Berdiaev, the leader of this current of mystical philosophy, felt that a gigantic "spiritual conflict" between secular and religious world views dominated Russian thought in the early 1900's. Siding with the religious philosophy of the Slavophil and Solov'ev traditions, he announced: "In my essays I campaign for the union of man with God, for the embodiment of the spirit in social life, and for the mystical union of love and freedom.... I have abandoned Marxian pseudo-*sobornost'* and decadent, romantic individualism for the *sobornost'* of mystical neo-Christianity."[22] Berdiaev was enthusiastic about the growing number of Russian philosophers who, he thought, understood the shortcomings of scientism and were bringing about a resurrection of the Platonic tradition and a widespread recognition of "the eternal rights of metaphysical creativeness."[23] One sign of these new trends, he felt, was the growing reaction against naturalism in the arts, exemplified by the emergence of Russian Symbolism. "Symbolism is supported by theoretical aesthetics, which can under no conditions consider the arts to be a

* On one of these rare occasions N. A. Berdiaev asserted: "In the autocratic police state all nonmaterial culture is contraband." Even the spiritual forces that do exist, he said, serve material ends. For example, Lev Tolstoi's expulsion from the Russian Orthodox Church had been motivated not by the religious interests of the Church but by the political interests of the Holy Synod, which acted on behalf of the government. Berdiaev, *Sub specie aeternitatis*, pp. 139, 143.

reflection of reality. The idealistic world view recognizes the independent significance of beauty and of artistic creativeness in the life of man."[24]

Berdiaev thought that metaphysical idealism in philosophy, art, and ethics could build a nobler future for men everywhere. His opinions in these areas were dominated by his conviction that man's essential intellectual, moral, and aesthetic endowment did not derive from human society but from a suprasocial, spiritual force, which Berdiaev identified with the Christian God. The Populists and Marxists had claimed that man must rely on his own resources rather than on divine assistance to bring about a better life on earth. But human society, according to Berdiaev, does not generate progress; it is only a workshop in which the divine plans are translated into reality.

Berdiaev identified his metaphysics as spiritualistic rather than idealistic, and preferred the ontological "spirit" to the epistemological "idea." He had very little use for epistemology as developed by the various neopositivist and neo-Kantian schools, for it was built on the notion that all human knowledge was relative and was derived from man's senses and rational faculties. He wanted to build a new epistemology that would recognize religion as a source of primary, absolute knowledge and science as a source of secondary, phenomenal knowledge. "The facts of science," he argued, "are phenomenal facts, whereas the facts of religion are essential facts."[25] Moreover, essential facts underlie all phenomenal facts. Berdiaev insisted uncompromisingly on the superiority of religion to science as a mode of inquiry: religious contemplation, not scientific experiment, was the source of absolute wisdom. Science slides over the surface of Kantian *phenomena*, but religion takes man into the depths of Kantian *noumena*. S. N. Bulgakov, another ex-Marxist, summed up this relationship in the following passage: "Metaphysics has a higher degree of competence than science, not only because it can resolve problems that are above the reach of knowledge acquired by experience but also because it relies on speculation, which answers questions that experimental science has no power to resolve."[26]

Berdiaev's metaphysics, in a way, is an elaboration of Solov'ev's "concrete idealism," which is, in turn, a reworking of Slavophil philosophy. It is "idealism" because spiritual monism is its basic principle; and it is "concrete" because the universal "spirit" is viewed not as an abstract principle but as an objective reality. Concrete idealism is a categorical negation of two traditional idealisms, both closely associated with the development of scientific thought and the rationalist tradition; Berdiaev identified them as "epistemological idealism" and "abstract idealism."[27] Epistemological idealism, which is derived from Kant's *Critique of Pure Reason*, reduces philosophy to a comprehensive study of the nature and logic of scientific knowledge and purports to show the intellectual sterility of metaphysics; throughout, it stays within the limits of man's rational capacities. "Abstract idealism," derived from Hegelian philosophy, recognizes the ontological core of the universe only as an abstract principle from which the laws of the world may be deduced by logical exercises; it is "panlogical" and totally rationalistic.

Berdiaev attacked these two idealistic traditions primarily because of their close association with the development of science. He attacked neo-Kantianism and Empiriocriticism as antimetaphysical and pro-scientific philosophies, and condemned Marxism, a branch of Hegelianism, for its completely "rationalistic" and "scientific" interpretation of the evolution of man and his culture and society. Neo-Kantianism and allied philosophical schools, according to Berdiaev, sanctioned the historical relativism of cultural values and moral precepts. Idealistic metaphysics had no room for relativism: through religious and mystical experience, it sought absolute knowledge applicable to both history and ethics.

In an essay on the philosophy of A. S. Khomiakov, Berdiaev gave his version of the major trends in Russian philosophy at the beginning of the twentieth century: "At the present time, Russian philosophers are at the crossroads and know the paths that have already been traveled and have led to a wasteland. Such paths are rationalism and Kantianism, which have inevitably led to Hegelianism, an empty and transparent philosophy. For us there is only one path: the path leading to the knowledge of the essential; the path of spiritualism unburdened by the sins of rationalism and abstractionism." "The final wisdom and real power," he said in another essay, "are given only in the religious gnosis."[28]

Berdiaev's scorching attacks on what he identified as science—he was unaware that many great scientists of his age were also critics of rationalistic extremism in science—helped him marshal philosophical and logical arguments to defend his idealistic ontology. But they were also a belated denigration of the accelerated growth of secular culture—that is, the intellectual modernization of Russia. He resented the application of the evolutionary theory to "scientific" ethics, the interpretation of human history by means of "rationalistic" categories, and the study of the development of human personality in environmental and physiological—i.e., scientific—terms. In effect, Berdiaev summarily condemned all ideologies that rejected the official interpretation of autocratic institutions as "superhistorical," "suprasocial," and timeless. His occasional criticism of the police system on which the government relied was more than offset by his attacks on the rising forces that opposed autocracy.

Berdiaev was very much impressed with the religious revivals that were then taking place in several parts of the country, and he interpreted them as a reaffirmation of the true spirit of Russia. He praised the religious thinker and novelist D. S. Merezhkovskii for organizing "religious-philosophical meetings" at which church and lay dignitaries exchanged religious views on the important questions of modern life. He also commended Lev Tolstoi for "placing the questions of religious consciousness at the center of attention."[29] The great achievements of Russian scientists between 1890 and 1910 went unnoticed by Berdiaev, who viewed the Russian Symbolists' detachment from social reality and retreat into literary abstractionism as a truer expression of Russian culture than the scientific contributions of Pavlov and Mechnikov, Russia's first Nobel Prize winners.

On occasion, Berdiaev did recognize science as an important component of modern culture: "I respect science as much as my critics do, I recognize our need for it, and I am aware of its strong potentialities."[30] However, he was too busy damning the vices of modern science to dispassionately analyze the critical spirit and utilitarian value of scientific thought. Without going into the epistemological depths and dilemmas of modern science, he opposed it because to his mind it was incompatible with the religious-metaphysical system to which he subscribed. On one occasion he admitted that science and "mystical religion" had entirely separate intellectual orbits, so that conflict between them was unnecessary.[31] But he was the last man to stick to this dictum. The intellectual sterility and moral decadence of science and the rationalist tradition were the central themes of his philosophy.

Berdiaev claimed that he attacked science only when it moved into the areas of thought that rightfully belonged to religion and philosophy, or when its spokesmen claimed that it was the paramount source of modern enlightenment. "Science supplies true knowledge about the laws of nature, but it errs when it teaches the impossibility of miracles and other sources of wisdom."[32] The "religious gnosis," he contended, transformed the partial truths of science into "full truths," which were the most meaningful guides for human action. To Berdiaev, there was no such thing as a trustworthy scientific study of biological evolution, social development, morality, or human personality; and these areas should forever remain the domain of religious metaphysics. Science, he implied in many passages, had no legitimate authority to generalize about human history, society, and culture.

Berdiaev displayed his greatest zeal in attacking the notion that science was the key to modern enlightenment. He summarized his feelings as follows:

"What role do we give science in the development of culture and the history of mankind? We must state outright that science performs a secondary, ancillary function, and that the viewpoint of rationalistic enlightenment is profoundly alien and completely unacceptable to us. We have declared an irreconcilable war on rationalistic culture, which distorts the spiritual nature of man.... Perceptive and thoughtful critics could find in this answer a solid and fundamental ground for an attack on us; yet the belief that we deny science and represent a reaction against it is an elementary misunderstanding that does not deserve a serious rejoinder. In actuality, we are not against science but against rationalism—against encroachments of positivism on the unity and totality of human nature.

"It cannot be sufficiently reiterated that science cannot be a creator of values or a guidepost of life; that beyond the scientific-rationalistic knowledge accessible to our inadequate reason looms infinity, which the positivists and all rationalists in general do not acknowledge and cannot fathom; and that in the final analysis science itself would benefit if its applicability were clearly delimited.... The more scientific and positive science becomes, the more philosophical and metaphysical philosophy becomes, and the more religious religion becomes.... All this can be stated briefly: We respect science no less than our critics ... but we are the enemies of rationalistic enlightenment and side with the human spirit, which is outside the control of science and impervious to a purely logical examination."[33]

The crux of Berdiaev's crusade against the cultural and intellectual claims of science is expressed in the statement: Science cannot reach the secrets of human creativeness because it cannot enter the kingdom of freedom.[34] By "freedom" Berdiaev does not mean freedom of speech, assembly, or conscience, but rather strict conformity to a moral code unbound by natural or social causation and independent of historical tides. Man's rational capacities can decipher the "pluralistic" aspects of nature and natural determinacy, but they cannot grasp either the "unitary" principle of the world or the basic indeterminacy—i.e., "freedom"—of man's spiritual and social life. In other words, rationality helps in collecting raw empirical data but not in understanding the unity of nature and the timelessness of the ethical code. Evolutionism, a culminating point of modern rationalism, commits a great sin: "the worship of the god of indispensability instead of the god of freedom."[35]

With equal consistency, Berdiaev belittled the role of the utilitarian principle in appraising knowledge. The natural sciences, of course, were valuable only so far as they were practical, although this very fact placed them low in the hierarchy of cultural values. The utilitarianism of the social sciences, by contrast, made them completely valueless: to Berdiaev, the scientific approach to the study of moral norms and the evaluation of the ethical code was a cowardly retreat from the world of superscientific freedom into the world of social and historical causation. On the same ground, he attacked every popular sociological theory of his time.

A culture that recognizes individuality in the assessment of values, social norms, and intellectual authorities provides particularly favorable stimuli for scientific thought, since individuality of this kind goes hand in hand with skepticism—with consistent, culturally organized questioning of ethical norms and ideas. An emphasis on individuality and skepticism, in turn, favors relativistic views on the laws of both nature and society. In most of his philosophical writings Berdiaev paid a great deal of attention to individualism, and his most eloquent passages are odes to individual freedom. The human personality, according to him, consists of two egos, "the empirical I" and "the ideal I." The empirical I is the part of the personality molded by the conditions of social life; it is transient, ephemeral, and of little consequence. The ideal I is a human expression of the absolute moral code, which is free of mundane influence. The empirical I is unfree, for it reflects the dominance of society over the individual. The ideal I is the true source of human freedom because it is not determined by "the approval or scrutiny of other men, by social usefulness, or in general, by the external world."[36] For Berdiaev, then, freedom and individuality were expressions of man's uncritical attitude toward the sacred values of his culture, and were not related to the questioning mind, which supports the development of scientific thought.

Berdiaev's criticism was aimed not so much at the substance of science as at the values that make up the scientific attitude. He must be given credit for recognizing the intrinsic evils in the cultural imperialism of science. But his feelings were so strong that he invariably overstated his case, and often ended by condemning all aspects of science. To him, the most essential aspects of Russia's religion and culture were seriously threatened by the growing enthusiasm for scientific thought. In his crusade against this enthusiasm, he relied on Dostoevskii's pronouncement that science was no part of Russian enlightenment, as well as Tolstoi's statement that science could not answer the basic needs of humanity because it was thinly spread over far too vast a field of inquiry.

Berdiaev did not take the trouble to analyze the ideas of some of the leading Russian scientists of his time, who viewed science and religion as complementary cultural forces, each satisfying a basic human and social need. Vladimir Vernadskii, a leading Russian geochemist, was one of those who emphasized the compatibility of scientific, philosophical, and religious scholarship. And in a public lecture in 1903, the noted chemist Nikolai Beketov argued: "The moral foundations of religion are strengthened by scientific investigations." For example, he said, "physiology, relying on physics, chemistry, and anatomy, has precisely determined the conditions of man's moral life...and has thus laid the foundations for a better existence."[37]

Russian philosophical thought, unlike that of the West, has consistently regarded idealism as a philosophy of social and political conservatism. The conservative philosopher M. M. Rubinshtein stated in 1907: "In our country, idealism belongs to the systems of thought labeled as reactionary, which makes it unpopular with the enlightened reading public."[38] "To this day," wrote P. Kudriavtsev, another conservative philosopher, "there is a tradition in our country that philosophical idealism is closely tied to political conservatism."[39] Both Rubinshtein and Kudriavtsev referred to idealistic metaphysics, as represented by Berdiaev.

Berdiaev's campaign against rationalism and science was only part of a calculated attack on democracy as a political philosophy and mode of social organization. He detested science in part because the scientific world view is democratic in its origin, claims, and aspirations: it is supported not by authority but by empirical proof, which, in principle, is available to all men. Berdiaev's religious viewpoint, by contrast, is aristocratic: the divine wisdom, the "essential knowledge," is created only by the select few who can successfully enter the world of mystical experience.

To Berdiaev, democracy combined many undesirable characteristics: "a skeptical social epistemology"; "a degradation of the qualitative, value-immersed aspects of life"; and "an unhealthy kind of social existence." It signified "the despair of a society's dying will."[40] Worst of all, democratic ideology was the extreme of rationalism; and it advocated a totally rational organization of human life, which would treat all men as "arithmetical units" of equal value. Moreover, it claimed that this could be done by human ingenuity alone, with no divine intervention; indeed, democracy denied the very existence of any irrational principles of social organization. According to Berdiaev, "Christian brotherhood is not democratic equality."[41] And he never retreated from his conviction that science, as a secular knowledge of quantity, was the basic instrument of democracy. To the great Lomonosov, who followed the Baconian tradition, the pursuit of science had been a religious duty of every pious man; for Berdiaev, an unrelenting war on science and democracy occupied the same position.

In 1904, Berdiaev wrote that "the growth of idealistic speculation and idealistic currents in philosophy, literature, and social thought may be considered the most important development in Russian culture during recent years."[42] He was quick to add, however, that the idealistic revival had not followed a uniform line of development. The proponents of idealism were united by their opposition to materialistic philosophy, but were otherwise divided into two major groups: the "ontological idealists," Berdiaev's group, concerned themselves with spiritualistic metaphysics and "transcendental religion"; the "epistemological idealists," on the other hand, followed the antimetaphysical teachings of Hume, Kant, and Comte. The ontological idealists, in extravagant terms, glorified the concept of a suprasocial sacred culture and defended the purity of the Russian soul. The epistemological idealists kept in touch with modern developments in secular learning, wrote in a reserved and erudite philosophical idiom, and were unconcerned with the Russian soul.

"Epistemological idealism" was a label applied to various neopositivists and neo-Kantians not by their champions, who were mostly of liberal political orientation, but by their adversaries on both the Right and the Left. The followers of Avenarius and Mach, who were the leading neopositivists, held that their own views transcended both materialism and idealism. However, the Marxist eclectic A. V. Lunacharskii introduced and endorsed Avenarius's epistemology as "positive idealism." Though coming from several traditions and differing in their approaches and aims, the epistemological idealists had one thing in common: all of them stressed the essentially subjective nature of human knowledge. Berdiaev and other ontological idealists were determined to show the superiority of spiritualistic metaphysics to science. The epistemological idealists were equally eager to demonstrate the growing interdependence of science and epistemology. Some of them flirted with spiritualistic metaphysics and were lured into the world of mysticism; but most consistently opposed every kind of metaphysics. Ontological idealism was essentially the philosophy of religion, whereas epistemological idealism was the philosophy of science.

Aleksandr Vvedenskii, at the beginning of his academic career, was the first Russian scholar to make the philosophy of science a major concern. A staunch neo-Kantian, he became profoundly interested in the philosophical foundations of the natural sciences, and subjected the basic postulates of classical physics to an elaborate epistemological analysis.[43] Science, according to him, cannot penetrate the essential nature of the universe and its components, but deals only with the dynamic aspects of nature: chemistry and physics, for example, explain the "how" but not the "why" of natural phenomena.[44] Concerned primarily with the intellectual limitations of science, Vvedenskii maintained that true wisdom depended not only on the "authenticated" knowledge of science but also on the "unauthenticated" judgments of "conscious religion."[45] The "thing in itself" is inaccessible to human reason, and hence to empirical science; but it is accessible to "intuitive judgment" or "intellectual intuition" and to metaphysics.[46]

Vvedenskii was particularly critical of the mechanistic paradigm that had dominated the physical sciences since the time of Democritus. According to him, this theory was guided by atomism, which arbitrarily assumed that all of nature was built up from indivisible and immutable particles. He did not deny the obviously great achievements of mechanistically oriented science, particularly since the time of Galileo, Descartes, and Newton; but he was quick to add that despite all these successes the existence of a "qualitatively and quantitatively immutable universal matter" had remained unproved and would continue to be unprovable.[47] Following Kant, he claimed that atomism had given scientists unlimited freedom to replace "a real knowledge of nature" with "a play of imagination."[48] A science based on the primacy of soul (dusha), he felt, would have been no less valid than a science based on the primacy of matter, since neither could "prove" its basic premise.[49] In these arguments, Vvedenskii was not trying to formulate a new science paradigm, but was implicitly defending the superiority of "critical philosophy" to "mechanistic science."

Vvedenskii made no great contributions to critical, or neo-Kantian, philosophy; nor did he point out any new possibilities in physical theory. His epistemological exercises suffered from his dogmatic acceptance of introspectionist psychology as the only sound science of human behavior; and he dismissed every experimental or physiological approach to psychology as unscientific.[50] Vvedenskii's "critical" philosophy was mostly a logical exercise that ignored the philosophical thought of the more modern neo-Kantian and neopositivist schools. His contribution lay primarily in bringing to Russia a philosophical orientation that gave scientific learning an important place in the theory of knowledge. He was among the first Russian philosophers to recognize the profound epistemological implications of Lobachevskii's non-Euclidean geometry, Mendeleev's periodic law, and Butlerov's structural theory of chemistry.[51]

Vvedenskii's close association with the Moscow Psychological Society, which was dominated by V. S. Solov'ev's philosophical legacy, eventually led him to abandon the philosophy of science and turn to metaphysical speculation about such timeless problems as freedom of the will and the meaning of life. He joined the "metaphysical idealists," who dealt at length with the limitations of science and the limitless potentialities of philosophy. Berdiaev spoke for this group when he declared that a true philosopher not only searches for knowledge inaccessible to science but also expresses "the general orientation" of his time, "engendered in his soul by the universal social process."[52] The differences in the thought of these metaphysical idealists were overshadowed by their common belief in the intellectual superiority of idealistic philosophy to experimental science. This orientation was most forcefully expressed by R. Iakovenko in a long article published in the Russian edition of the international journal *Logos*.[53]

According to Iakovenko, philosophy and science can be compared in four different ways, each comparison showing the decided superiority of philosophy. The *psychological* comparison shows that philosophical thought is "psychically immanent," direct, and continuous; science, on the other hand, is essentially sensory, circuitous, and discontinuous. The *epistemological* comparison shows that science is dominated by limited, rational thought derived solely from sensory data, whereas philosophy gains its knowledge from "philosophical intuition," the only source of pure and independent wisdom. The *methodological* comparison shows that although both science and philosophy demonstrate critical thought, scientific knowledge is conditional, approximative, relative, and heavily dependent on arbitrary hypotheses, whereas philosophical knowledge is unconditional, definitive, absolute, and free of hypotheses. The *ontological* comparison reveals that science deals with reality in fragments, but that philosophy draws a unitary picture of the universe—a picture that is "complete, simple, and free of contradictions." Science deals with the ephemeral, philosophy with the essential.

Iakovenko codified the thought of idealistic philosophy from A. I. Vvedenskii and L. M. Lopatin to N. O. Losskii and S. Frank. All these men dealt extensively with the fundamental problems of the theory of knowledge; and all, in the final analysis, supported their epistemological claims by relying on the sacred authority of idealistic absolutes. In their view, the basic weakness of science was its inability to answer certain fundamental questions about the universe: it could not reveal the essence of life, the internal nature of man, the true makeup of chemical elements, the ultimate conditions of cosmic and social evolution, or the purposiveness of natural processes.[54] All these idealistic philosophers spent far more time in pointing out the intrinsic limitations of science than they did in actually building a philosophy that might reveal the ultimate nature of the universe and its components. Their philosophy was essentially conservative, and was dedicated to preserving the sacred values of autocratic ideology, which preferred the metaphysician's mysticism and spiritualism to the criticism and materialism of the scientist. Their criticism of classical physics, in fact, was a thinly veiled attack on science in general. Failing to sense the gigantic intellectual impact of the crisis in physics at the end of the nineteenth century, most of these philosophers did not notice the rapid ascent of a new science—a science that was unhampered by the old materialistic and mechanistic ontology.

But there was another new and powerful current of epistemological idealism that was usually referred to as "scientific philosophy." The members of this school believed that science and philosophy were essentially inseparable, and that they complemented each other. The background for scientific philosophy in Russia came from the German philosophers Carl Göring, E. Laas, Joseph Petzoldt, and Alois Riehl, who had endeavored to cleanse the Kantian critical philosophy of its implicit metaphysical and "agnostic" elements and had accepted the label "positivism" for their basic views. According to a Russian observer, this acceptance of the term positivism was indeed a sign of the times: "It expressed a growing alliance of empiricism with a critical philosophy freed from the limitations of the Kantian tradition, and it showed that the time was fast approaching when a new philosophy, the scientific philosophy, would triumph."[55]

The new combination of "empiricism" and "criticism" found its most eloquent spokesman in Richard Avenarius, a professor at Zurich University and the founder of the *Quarterly for Scientific Philosophy*. The scientific philosophy of Avenarius not only combined the great intellectual traditions inaugurated by Kant and Comte but also reflected the growing concern of many leading scientists with basic epistemological questions. During the middle decades of the nineteenth century philosophy and science had been separated: while philosophy turned to metaphysical problems, the sciences underwent a rapid process of fission to produce new experimental disciplines such as psychophysiology, psychophysics, and physical chemistry. Unhappy with the presumptuous intellectual claims of metaphysics and feeling an acute need to evaluate the basic propositions and logical principles of individual sciences, many scientists now entered the arena of epistemological debate. The new philosophical movement that they generated reached Russia primarily through the work of Avenarius, whose influence in Western Europe never matched his popularity in Russia.*

To Avenarius, no sort of philosophy is independent of science, and all knowledge, whether empirical, scientific, or philosophical, is built on the same epistemological foundations. His *Critique of Pure Experience* and other works represent a remarkably complete effort to depict the inner logic of thought sequences, from simple sense perceptions to the complex sequences articulated not by individuals but by societies. In his view, science, religion, and the arts all follow different manifestations of the same basic sequence in the growth of human wisdom; and the development of each begins with experience, which is never free of affective overtones. Scientific knowledge is both subjective and objective: it is subjective because its only sources are the experiences of individual persons; and it is objective because it becomes "pure" and meaningful when society has developed far enough to purge it of elements that reflect the idiosyncrasies of individuals.

Avenarius, like Mach, elevated the epistemological concept of knowledge above the traditional struggle over the ontological preeminence of matter or idea: to him, both matter and idea were derivations of experience. His emphasis on the psychological foundations of experience, the sociological nature of "pure experience," and the principle of economy in the thinking processes led some of his contemporaries to call him a materialist and a relativist; but his views on the essentially subjective origin of human knowledge and his phenomenalistic orientation led many materialists to label him an idealist and an agnostic.

The essence of Avenarius's philosophy is expressed in four basic propositions. First, "philosophy of science" is a redundancy, for there is no more basic philosophy than the one built on science. In the existence of nonscientific or antiscientific philosophy in his day, Avenarius only saw evidence of the continuing infancy of certain branches of philosophical thought. Second, empirical knowledge, the basis of all human wisdom, is not a mere reflection of the outside, objective world, but a result of man's interaction

---

* By contrast, Ernst Mach, the philosopher-physicist who codified a scientific philosophy essentially similar to Avenarius's (and who also introduced Einstein to the epistemological tradition that favored a relativistic interpretation of human knowledge), was not as popular in Russia as he was in the West.

with the environment in which the "psychic" and the "physical" cannot be separated. There is no essential difference in the subject matter of the natural sciences and psychology. Third, scientific concepts expressing the regularities of natural phenomena are only hypothetical constructions that the human mind distills from the chaos of experience data; the power of science lies more in the descriptive data of experiment and experience than in highly artificial and tenuous theories. Fourth, diversified individual experiences are combined in ordered empirical generalizations and logical concepts owing to man's basic social, or "interindividual," unity; this operates most effectively through language, which superimposes discrete verbal labels on a jumble of sense impressions. Avenarius's philosophy appealed to the many Russian intellectuals who saw in science the highest achievement of modern civilization, had no sympathy for metaphysics, and were seeking a middle position in the traditional struggle between materialism and idealism.

In the early 1900's philosophy teaching in the universities, once the exclusive domain of the clergy, was a monopoly of philosophers who were secular in general orientation but were not particularly opposed to spiritualistic metaphysics and mysticism. The most important Russian champions of Empiriocriticism and similar philosophies, however, worked outside the academic community and were actively identified with various ideological movements opposed to autocracy. V. V. Lesevich, the original sponsor of the new "scientific philosophy" in Russia, was a Populist, and had written a series of essays on the modern philosophical implications of Populist principles. Viktor Chernov was a Neopopulist who endeavored to provide a modern philosophical backing for Mikhailovskii's "subjective method in sociology." A. A. Bogdanov plunged into the waters of Empiriocriticism in hopes of enriching Marxian philosophy. All three treated philosophy as an ideological weapon and advocated broad changes in the Russian political and social system.

V. V. Lesevich's philosophy of science was part of a larger ideology that demanded extensive social and political changes in Russia. Lesevich chose to work for a democratic polity by attacking the ideological and philosophical pillars of autocracy. "Moral truths," he argued, could no longer be accepted in their orthodox (i.e., religious and metaphysical) form, but must face the rigorous demands of scientific measurement and verification. The supernatural and mystical view had lost all meaning and usefulness because of the great advances in science; only "reason, science, and freedom" could guarantee a better future for human society.[56] Positivism, according to Lesevich, was the modern philosophy of life, for it had introduced modern ideas of personality and society, elevated human thought to new heights of precision and clarity, and substituted the clearheaded thoughts of science for the dreams of mystical metaphysics.

In a lengthy article entitled "What Is Scientific Philosophy?" (1888–89), Lesevich advised his readers that the unique intellectual event of the modern age was not the rediscovery of philosophy by scientists; rather, it was the "transformation of philosophy in the spirit of positive knowledge...the emergence of a new philosophy that does not precede the sciences...but completes their work." He argued that there was no conflict between true science and philosophy; and that the two must cooperate closely, philosophy providing science with a general orientation and science supplying philosophy with substantive knowledge. He fully endorsed Avenarius's view that philosophy could not expect to present a coherent and fully integrated world view without relying on the hard facts of natural science. The true functions of philosophy, he said, were to establish the maximum acceptable range of scientific abstractions, to record scientific generalizations, and to indicate the interrelations between individual scientific facts and general scientific laws.[57]

Lesevich did not stand dogmatically on the ideology of Populism. Instead, he tried to clarify the subtler aspects of the Populist world view by relying on the epistemological theories of Riehl, Laas, and Avenarius, which he considered the greatest philosophical legacy of the past.[58] By defending "scientific philosophy," he actually defended science as a world view. To him the victory of science in his age was a victory of intellect over the dark forces of ignorance and anachronistic ideological maxims: it would liberate ethics from theology, psychology from metaphysics, political science from formal jurisprudence, and sociology from the philosophy of history. Every part of culture could now be reevaluated by minds freed from the intellectual straitjackets of the past.

Lesevich undertook a minute analysis of the "scientific philosophy" of Riehl and Avenarius in order to reaffirm the Populist claim that the future progress of Russia lay in critical thought, secular wisdom, and recognition of the individual as the true functioning unit of the polity and the intellectual community. He also wanted to strengthen the Populist claim that the future of philosophy was not in the struggle between materialism and idealism (or objectivism and subjectivism) but in the recognition of a firmer, more basic, and yet empirically verifiable source of knowledge. While

N. K. Mikhailovskii endeavored to formulate "a scientific explanation of Russian reality," Lesevich marshaled modern philosophical support for Mikhailovskii's scientific attitude.

Viktor Chernov, another supporter of scientific philosophy, was among the architects of Neopopulism, which differed from the original Populism in recognizing the paramount historical and social role of the industrial proletariat (though still regarding the peasantry as the core of the Russian polity), and in identifying social equality, rather than communalism, as the cornerstone on which the *obshchina* was built. Neopopulism developed from attempts to blend the ideology of Mikhailovskii and Lavrov with the inescapable development of industrial technology in Russia. The process of modernizing the legacy of the early Populists drew the Neopopulists into the arena of modern philosophy.

Chernov fully accepted the sociology of Mikhailovskii and Lavrov, feeling that it blended the individual and social, real and ideal, objective and subjective, and theoretical and practical worlds into a "total philosophical view." Moreover, it had "exercised a powerful influence over the minds and the hearts of the most active generations of the Russian intelligentsia."[59] Chernov devoted a lengthy essay to an epistemological discussion of the fundamental agreement of Populist sociology's "subjective method" with Avenarius's "scientific philosophy." In Georg Simmel's pronouncement that "being and truth are only relational concepts" (that is, the conventions of society are based on the experiences of individuals rather than on objective reflections of reality), Chernov saw a link between Populist philosophy and Empiriocriticism.[60] "The reader who is familiar with so-called Empiriocriticism—a philosophy connected particularly with the name of Avenarius—will readily recognize the degree to which this philosophy, as a 'world view based on the principle of minimum expenditure of energy,' corresponds to the needs set forth by N. K. Mikhailovskii in the name of the common man."[61]

Chernov waged a particularly bitter battle against the Russian neo-Kantians, who made a rigid distinction between "things as we see them" and "things in themselves"—between the knowable and the unknowable—and thus imposed artificial limits on the development of science. He rejected the idea that the boundary between science and religion is permanently fixed, and implied that the intellectual orbit of religion was gradually shrinking as science advanced. Science, to him, was not only experiment and investigation, which guide human reason, but also a moral orientation that guided human conscience.[62] Science and scientific philosophy, both rooted in man's practical needs, were the culminating achievements of the human intellect.

Chernov argued that knowledge is neither "objective" in a Marxian sense nor "subjective" in a neo-Kantian sense; instead, it results from a complex interaction between the ego and its environment. Personal experience, the product of this interaction, is impure and chaotic; only through the acceptance of "social truths" is it purified and transformed into the intellectual material from which the logical structure of human wisdom is built. Social truths, in turn, are determined by the practical needs of society. Positive knowledge, therefore, is individual in origin, social in its criteria of systematization, and utilitarian in its standards of legitimation. Chernov rejected Marxism for three reasons: it contained much "prephilosophical" or "pseudophilosophical" materialism; it made unsound use of Hegelian "contradictions" in the historical, social, and intellectual processes; and, by giving priority to "objective reality" as a source of knowledge, it minimized the value of subjective knowledge.

Chernov also rejected the Nihilist and Marxian view of the social sciences as straightforward methodological extensions of the natural sciences. In the natural sciences, he argued, there is a qualitative difference between pure science and applied science; pure science tries to determine the general laws governing certain sets of phenomena; applied science combines these laws with empirical knowledge to resolve the practical problems of society. Practical needs are never a guiding force in the theoretical sciences. In the social sciences, however, practical needs are "not only the criteria for channeling theoretical truths into applied science but also the *facts* of theoretical investigation."[63] This, according to Chernov, was the view embodied in the "subjective sociology" of Mikhailovskii and Lavrov. Chernov was especially pleased that S. N. Iuzhakov, otherwise a critic of subjective sociology, had endorsed the same view when he stated: "Our entire social terminology has a subjective, teleological coloration, which Mikhailovskii has identified as a utilitarian dimension."[64]

The social scientists, according to Chernov, had to recognize that both their "theories" and their "practical orientations" were essentially value judgments. He noted that the natural and social sciences, though similar epistemologically, were quite different sociologically and methodologically. Chernov rejected Spencer's claim that social theory should be free of any practical purposiveness. His long, involved, and articulate essay in the philosophy of science had one unmistakable objective: to show that science was the only sound world outlook for a Russian society oppressed by the lingering feudal institutions and everywhere groping toward a modern existence.

Mystics like Solov'ev and Berdiaev sought to escape the painful existence of a society in crisis by ascending to the ideal polity of the divine powers, and Marxists were preoccupied with laying out a totally new society on earth; Chernov, by contrast, faced the Russian realities of his day. He thought that science was deeply embedded in Russian culture, and was a sure indication of his country's essential willingness to advance itself. To him, science embodied the three basic principles of modernity: the historical relativity (and secularity) of knowledge, rationality in the accumulation and systematization of wisdom, and utilitarianism in the social valuation of knowledge.

During the 1890's and the early years of the twentieth century Russian Marxists did not present a united front on either philosophical or programmatic questions. At times it seemed that every leading champion of Marxism had his own interpretation of dialectical materialism. Bulgakov and Berdiaev represented the growing group of Marxist intellectuals who drifted into idealistic and mystical metaphysics. Lenin was the leader of a group that stayed close to Marxian doctrine and devoted a great deal of energy to organizing an activist political movement. Plekhanov was typical of those who allowed themselves a broad interpretation of various Marxian propositions without abandoning their fundamental commitment to Marxism. An even less orthodox group sought to make Marxism a twentieth-century philosophy and introduced sweeping theoretical and ideological changes that gradually brought them into direct conflict with some of the central doctrines of historical and dialectical materialism. This group had no leader, but its most productive and influential member was A. A. Malinovskii, better known by his pseudonym of A. A. Bogdanov.

Bogdanov's intellectual career was long and eventful. In the 1890's he was a champion of what he labeled "scientific philosophy"; in reality, this was a diffuse but searching combination of the mechanistic materialism of the 1850's and the neopositivism of the 1880's. Bogdanov's materialistic orientation brought him into Marxian circles, and his neopositivist leanings made him an enthusiastic spokesman for modern science as an advanced world view and as the only sound basis of philosophy. A passing phase of enthusiasm for Wilhelm Ostwald's "energeticism" (which gave energy an "ontological primacy" over "matter") led him deeper into the newest neo-positivist writings, and eventually he became a great admirer of Mach and Avenarius.*

The influence of Bogdanov's extensive writings led many Russians to extend the term "Empiriocriticism," coined by Avenarius, to include the philosophy of Mach. The creed of this new Russian orientation had been expressed by Mach himself, who believed that the prevailing physical conception of matter as the basis of all reality was "merely a perversion." On the contrary, said Mach, reality was built up entirely from what he called elements, "which, when standing to one another in a certain known relation, are called sensations."[65] Ascertaining the interrelationships of these "elements" or "sensations," according to Mach, was the real problem of every science. Bogdanov defined Empiriocriticism as "the contemporary form of positivism, which combines the most modern methods of natural science and the newest achievements in philosophical criticism."[66]

Gradually, Bogdanov's attention focused on Marxism, and he tried to modernize Marxist philosophy by combining it with the ideas of Mach and Avenarius. His deep involvement in Empiriocriticism, however, did not weaken his dedication to revolutionary work. In 1903 he became an editor of *Pravda*, after having served three years of enforced exile for political activities. When the Russian Social Democratic Party split into two factions later in 1903, he sided with the Bolsheviks. He finally became a "Communist" after having abandoned many of his earlier leanings toward materialist philosophy.

Bogdanov thought that Marxism provided a sound social theory but an antiquated general philosophy: he was in favor of economic determinism and recognized class struggle as the motive force of history; but he felt that dialectical materialism as a philosophy of nature needed a major overhaul. He found both the Hegelian "law of contradictions" and the uncompromising monism of mechanical materialism incompatible with the achievements of modern science. He also rejected the subjectivism of Locke's and Hume's empiricism and the objectivism of Marxian epistemology—though he was ready to admit that compared with idealism, "materialism was always incomparably closer to the progressive currents in science."[67] Empiriocriticism, Bogdanov felt, was not a denial of materialism and empiricism but a "continuation" and "improvement" of those philosophies.[68]

By combining Empiriocriticism with Marxism, Bogdanov produced

---

* For a discussion of Bogdanov's sociological views, see pp. 446–54.

a philosophical hybrid that he termed Empiriomonism.[69] He agreed with Chernov that all knowledge was at first subjective, originating in the experiences of individuals. Criticism in terms of social norms or conventions, however, could isolate all individual idiosyncrasies from experience, discover regularities in nature and society, and create objective knowledge. And since knowledge was the basis of social communication, societies were essentially psychological entities. Empiriomonism blended this social empiricism with a technological determinism derived from Marxism. Bogdanov felt that the natural sciences were particularly effective in producing objective knowledge because they dealt simultaneously with technological needs, social standards, and individual experiences.

In his writings, Bogdanov selected the ideas that suited his philosophy from the reservoir of contemporary Marxian and neopositivist thought and made them parts of an integrated world view. He seldom searched for philosophical and ideological adversaries; nevertheless, he was persecuted by the police and ignored by the academic philosophers, most of whom were committed to idealistic metaphysics. Bogdanov was also a prime target of Lenin's campaign to purge Bolshevism of philosophical revisionism. His identification of scientific laws and propositions as social conventions and his thoughts on the epistemological relativity of scientific knowledge were a direct challenge to two basic tenets of Marxian philosophy: the doctrine that sensory data were wholly objective and the idea that the laws of nature and society were absolutes.

Although Bogdanov was aware of the growing crisis in the natural sciences of his time, his enthusiasm was mostly for the new "scientific philosophy." His world view was dominated by the principle that "only continuous, active ties with science as a whole could help philosophy make progress and avoid aimless wandering through commonplace and indefinite ideas."[70] According to Bogdanov, a sound philosophy had to be based not on a mechanical and uncritical identification with traditional science but on a profound acquaintance with the newest developments in scientific thought. For example, any philosopher who superimposed an existing system of philosophical thought on Mendeleev's notion of the immutability of chemical elements had lost all ties with the irresistible growth of science: he was a poor philosopher because he was a laggard scientist. Worst of all, the philosophers who were unfamiliar with the newest developments in science were also ignorant of the ideological significance of the technological revolution. In one respect, Bogdanov remained a true Marxist: to him, philosophy was "the highest organizing form of class ideology."[71]

The Russian Machians and Empiriocritics strove for originality and sought broader sociological implications for their theories of knowledge, and their efforts produced such labels as Empiriomonism, Empirical Realism, and Empiriosymbolism.[72] Underneath their differences in detail and modes of presentation, however, all these schools agreed that science, as the most advanced mode of human inquiry, must rise above the confusion that had so far characterized the ontological dualism of "matter" and "spirit," and must also avoid the sterility of extreme materialism or idealism. All attributed cognitive primacy to experience, in which the object and the idea—i.e., matter and spirit—are so "correlated" that they become sterile concepts when treated as separate ontological entities.

In echoing Mach's pronouncement that "matter" was a useless concept of "old" science, the Empiriocritics attacked the implicit materialism of the natural scientists; and they must be counted among the philosophical pioneers of the twentieth-century scientific revolution. They firmly believed in the epistemological unity of all the sciences, from physics and chemistry to psychology and sociology.[73] By fighting ontological materialism in science, they sought to rid scientific thought of the last vestiges of metaphysical obscurantism. However, their favorable treatment of Ostwald's energeticism was the best proof that they had not fully allied themselves with modern "scientific philosophy," which strove to elevate itself above the traditional conflict between materialistic and idealistic metaphysics. Apparently, the Empiriocritics had not fully grasped the antimetaphysical orientation of the scientific revolution at the turn of the century.[74]

MARXIAN EPISTEMOLOGY

Friedrich Engels died in 1895. His passing coincided with an upsurge in revisionist currents that threatened to uproot the very foundations of Marxian philosophy. Most revisionists had read and were influenced to varying degrees by Friedrich Albert Lange's *History of Materialism*, a masterly study written some thirty years earlier. Lange presented a new philosophical outlook based on a subtle reconciliation of Kantianism with philosophical materialism.

Combining Kant's transcendental idealism with Hermann Helmholtz's physiological theory, Lange criticized the basic assumption of "natural-science materialism": that man, relying on the methods of the exact sciences, could eventually penetrate the innermost secrets of the "thing in itself." Unlike the orthodox materialists, Lange recognized science as only one of several vital modes of inquiry, each having a particular strength and advantage. Although he favored socialism, he opposed the narrow identification of socialism with scientism—the view that science was the only safe guidepost to an ideal society. Ethics, he said, could not be reduced to science, and religion could elevate the human mind to planes of wisdom closed to the scientific mind. Materialism separated the "true" from the "good" and the "beautiful," and made "empirical truths" the only basis of human creativity; it thus prevented science from rising above the "limitations of the senses" and establishing a complementary relationship with religion. Lange sought to construct an "animistic" materialism that would interpret moral life by metaphysical "free will" rather than scientific determinism.

Hermann Cohen, a stalwart of the Marburg school of neo-Kantianism, expressed similar views but brought them within the fold of philosophical idealism; many contemporaries saw in his ethical philosophy an endorsement of socialism. According to Cohen, Kant's ethical views made him "the true and actual founder of German socialism."[75] Both Lange and Cohen had a great affinity for the natural sciences; and both understood and appreciated the great revolution in science during the second half of the nineteenth century. Cohen, for example, was an eloquent advocate of the increasing mathematicization of the sciences. But both men regarded the dogmatic adherence of most contemporary scientists to ontological materialism as "a general enfeeblement of philosophical effort" and "a retrogression of ideas."[76]

During the 1890's and the early 1900's, the strongest influence on Marxian revisionists came from Eduard Bernstein, a prolific writer whose lucid analyses of the political, economic, moral, and philosophical foundations of socialism reached an international audience. In 1879 Bernstein became an ardent supporter of the Marxian gospel; but even then he voiced serious reservations about some of the cardinal ideas advanced by Marx and Engels.[77] At the end of the 1890's, he caused great consternation among Marxist-oriented Social Democrats in Germany by calling for a sweeping reexamination of the basic propositions of dialectical materialism. He preferred the motto "Back to Lange" to "Back to Kant," but said: "Just as the philosophers and investigators who stand by [the latter] motto are not concerned with going back to the letter of what the Königsberg philosopher wrote, but are only concerned with the fundamental principles of his criticism, so Social Democracy would just as little think of going back to all the social-political views of Friedrich Albert Lange."[78] Bernstein was particularly impressed with Lange's campaigns for the emancipation of the working people and for scientific freedom, without which the accumulated errors of the past could not be rectified. Social Democracy, Bernstein argued, needed the critical spirit of science to ward off the paralyzing effects of ideological dogmatism.

Even though Bernstein became a staunch revisionist, he did not attack Marxian ideology or economic determinism; however, he did question the sociological range and the epistemological foundations of Marxian "science." The philosophical side of his revisionism included three basic propositions. First, he attached only a secondary significance to the dialectical method, which he considered totally inadequate for the analysis of historical problems with multiple variables. He argued that the Hegelian "negation of negation" overemphasized the role of conflict as a source of change in nature and society.[79] The dialectical process, after all, was only one aspect of the general evolution of both nature and society. Second, Bernstein rejected Marx and Engels's claim that their version of socialism was fully compatible with science. Socialism, he said, was an "ism," not a science; socialism might find extensive use for science, but was not a science in itself. Finally, Bernstein, following Lange and Cohen, accepted the Kantian view that ethics transcended science. He concluded that science did not use a dialectical method; that the socialist movement, to be fully understood, could not be described in scientific terms alone; and that the scope of science did not include the complexities of moral life.

Bernstein fully endorsed Lange's view that German Social Democracy, in order to survive, must constantly reassess its ideology and philosophy and abandon its dogmatic adherence to scientism. "The socialist movement," he said, "does not depend on any theory." A theory could explain socialism and point out its future course; but any theory had to work with existing social relations and possibilities.[80] Socialism, Bernstein implied, demanded the creation of new human relations, whereas the power of science was limited to elucidating the existing ones.

Plekhanov fought Bernstein's revisionism and steadfastly reaffirmed his faith in the scientific attributes of dialectical materialism as codified by Marx and Engels; but most Russian Marxists of the 1890's found it necessary to modify the basic teachings of the masters. From the beginning, Russian Marxism attracted men with many different sympathies and attitudes: "determinists and indeterminists, champions of 'consciousness' and persons ready to be swept by 'spontaneity,' future revisionists like Peter Struve and Tugan-Baranovskii as well as future Bolsheviks like L. B. Krasin, D. B. Goldenbakh-Ryazanov, and Yu. M. Steklov."[81] Thus the seeds of discord were planted before the movement was fully organized, and Russian Marxism was slow in becoming ideologically unified and politically effective.

Russian revisionism had many sources. In order to pass the vigilant censors and avoid dangerous underground work, many "Legal Marxists" found it necessary to curb their revolutionary zeal and trim their writings of the more radical Marxist teachings. Others changed their ideas under the influence of the dominant themes of contemporary thought. In the 1890's, for example, Russia was still going through an intensive revival of idealism, and all the philosophy chairs in the universities were held by idealist philosophers. It was not surprising that many staunch Marxists gradually expanded their ideology to accommodate idealism. Another group of revisionists felt that the ideas of the masters had to be changed to fit Russian conditions. The "economists," for example, gradually drifted away from the Marxian theory of revolution and began to argue in favor of evolutionary changes through economic reforms. Most Russian revisionists rejected Marxian determinism and sought to magnify the historical role of "spontaneous" social forces that could not be reduced to scientific laws. The ideas of the German philosophers Heinrich Rickert and Wilhelm Windelband, who recognized epistemological and methodological differences between the natural and the social sciences, appealed to the more moderate Russian Marxists.

Lange's *History of Materialism* was translated into Russian by the conservative philosopher N. N. Strakhov, and was published in 1883–84. It became the most widely read philosophical treatise in Russia during the early 1890's, and instilled in many Russian Marxists a profound appreciation of the challenging thoughts emanating from various neo-Kantian schools. Many Russian Marxists became passionate followers of "ethical socialism," particularly after they realized that it was philosophically feasible to inject socialist content into Kant's "categorical imperative."

Russian Marxists were not burdened by extensive organizational duties and political activities during the 1890's, and they had ample time to consider general theoretical questions. However, censorial vigilance and growing political persecution greatly restricted the publication of Marxian studies. The more Marxism was truncated, the easier it was for its spokesmen to avail themselves of the public press. The Marxists of the 1890's necessarily concentrated much more on the theoretical intricacies of economic determinism than on revolutionary politics and broader ideological and philosophical problems.[82]

With so much time for theorizing, it is not surprising that Russians made the earliest and most extensive efforts to blend Marxism with Empiriocriticism and Machism. Although Ernst Mach admitted that Kant's *Prolegomena to Any Future Metaphysic* had initially inspired him to search for a scientific philosophy elevated above all metaphysics, his philosophy eventually differed from neo-Kantianism in several important respects.[83] Unlike the neo-Kantians, Mach claimed that the domain of philosophy began and ended with science; that the theory of knowledge, particularly scientific knowledge, was the crucial area of philosophy; and that scientific epistemology, as developed by him, was on a plane above idealism and materialism. The Marxian neo-Kantians tried to curb the excesses of Marxian rationalism and scientism, and strove to inject a moral philosophy into historical materialism. The Marxian followers of Mach and Avenarius, who were particularly numerous in Russia, tried to modernize dialectical and historical materialism by placing due emphasis on the "subjective" dimension of knowledge, which Marx and Engels had been unwilling to acknowledge; but they also believed that modern science needed the help of Marxian socialism, without which it would stagnate.

A. V. Lunacharskii, an eloquent spokesman of the Machian group, noted: "Present-day scientific philosophy, cultivated primarily by the natural scientists, has remained at a certain level of development and cannot make further progress solely because it operates outside the grand framework of scientific socialism. But scientific socialism is now reexamining the ideas of Kirchhoff, Maxwell, Hertz, Ostwald, and a whole array of other great naturalists, whose contributions have been summed up by Mach with remarkable clarity and by Avenarius with equally impressive versatility. Marxism is accepting these ideas because they are akin to it; in making them part of its thinking, it will strengthen and expand the majestic temple of proletarian philosophy."[84] To spread the new philosophy, Lunacharskii later published a popular survey of the basic ideas contained in Avenarius's *Critique of Pure Experience*.[85]

A typical Marxist follower of Mach and Avenarius in Russia did not abandon his Marxian identification even when he found himself drifting farther and farther away from the very core of Marxian thought. When the Social Democrats split into the Bolsheviks and the Mensheviks in 1903, the Machians were represented in both camps. In reality, their basic approach was squarely between Marxism and Machism. They tried to inject social content into Machian epistemology and at the same time to rejuvenate Marxism by making its champions aware of human psychology in the interpretation of social causes, functions, and processes. They also tried to modernize dialectic as a method of science by bringing it into accord with Machian epistemological subjectivism. The Machians themselves held many different opinions on philosophical details, conceptualization, and methods of systematization; but they all agreed that Marxian epistemology, which interpreted sense perceptions as mere reflections of outside reality, was a vestige of metaphysical materialism hampering a full appreciation of the revolutionary developments in the sciences, particularly in physics. The usual practice of Machian Marxists was not to make direct attacks on orthodox views, but merely to ignore them. In their own minds, they were not fighting Marxism, but were dedicated to building a modern system of Marxian thought. Nevertheless, their cumulative reforms threatened to obliterate the philosophical and ideological unity of orthodox Marxism.

All of these revisionist currents were highly disturbing to V. I. Lenin, who could not but associate the philosophical splintering of the Bolsheviks with the concurrent growth of political factionalism—a growth manifested most typically in the rise of *Otzovizm*, a movement led by a group of Social Democrats who demanded the immediate recall of all Marxists holding elective positions in the government. Looking about him, Lenin saw many other alarming signs. International leaders of Social Democracy like Karl Kautsky asserted that the Mensheviks were the true champions of Marxism in Russia, and that the Bolsheviks had completely succumbed to the bourgeois lures of Machian philosophy. Most Western Europeans, in fact, tended to recognize Plekhanov, a Menshevik, as the most authoritative spokesman for Russian Marxists. In Russia, Bogdanov was attempting to identify the Bolshevik ideology with his philosophy of Empiriomonism, a hybrid of Machian subjectivism and Marxian objectivism. Even worse was the appearance of Lunacharskii's book *Religion and Socialism*, which urged Marxists to lend their support to a "social religion" trimmed of all supernaturalism, which would help build a bridge between the "advanced" intelligentsia and the working masses.[86] Lenin was convinced that this philosophical and ideological factionalism weakened Bolshevism's resistance to the mounting attacks of academic philosophers and their allies, who espoused idealistic and mystical metaphysics.

In 1909, to counter the revisionist writings, Lenin published *Materialism and Empiriocriticism*, whose aggressive style violated every "professorial nicety." It is a rambling, bitter essay, full of journalistic epithets, verbal scolding, and outright cynicism. Nevertheless, it is one of the basic documents in the history of Marxian thought; though narrow in its content, it is broad in its implications. Rising above the particular interests of the Bolshevik organization and addressing himself to all those who identified themselves as Marxists, Lenin insisted vehemently that the dialectical materialism of Marx and Engels could tolerate no philosophical compromises but must be accepted or rejected in its entirety. Dialectical materialism, he argued, was flexible enough to meet the challenges of new intellectual currents, such as the contemporary crisis in physics, and it did not need to borrow from other philosophical orientations. Eclecticism had no place in Marxian philosophy.

Addressing himself to the Russian Machian Marxists and relying on the authority of Engels, Lenin emphasized that there were only two basic and totally incompatible philosophical orientations: materialism and idealism. The numerous modern philosophies—Machism and Empiriocriticism, Pragmatism and neo-Kantianism, Vitalism and Immanentism, Empiriomonism and Critical Realism—were only variations of the same idealistic ontology and epistemology. They were also variations on the same sociology, and expressed a profound crisis in capitalist society and a desperate effort to reconcile the warped values of a decadent social system with modern intellectual advances, particularly in science. The intellectual legacy of Marx and Engels was a sacred component of proletarian culture, and none of its propositions could be challenged by true Marxists. Lenin admitted the need for momentary secular adaptations or readjustments of dialectical materialism, and he himself was not adverse to giving a new emphasis to selected Marxian propositions. But to him, the basic ontological and epistemological axioms of the Marxian legacy were unchallengeable.

Despite its broad philosophical and political significance, *Materialism and Empiriocriticism* is essentially an essay in epistemology, and its basic concern is with the origin, the compass, and the validity of human knowledge. Like Engels's *Ludwig Feuerbach* and *Anti-Dühring*, it pays particular attention to scientific knowledge, and it may be considered the chief Marxian work in the philosophy of science. Lenin completely rejected the Machian notion that philosophy and science were inseparable; philosophy, he felt, was independent of scientific thought, although it had a kind of symbiotic relationship with science. The function of science was to explain particular components of objective reality, whereas the tasks of philosophy were to guide scientists in interpreting their results and to integrate scientific thought with ideology.

It is not difficult to see why Lenin chose to attack Machism and Empiriocriticism rather than the advocates of mystical and revivalistic metaphysics, even though the latter were sworn enemies of Marxism. Operating on the assumption that the "external" enemies and their philosophical position were clearly defined, he concentrated his attacks on the men who professed to be political Marxists and philosophical non-Marxists. In essence, he wanted to give philosophical unity to Russian Marxism. In this he imitated Engels, who had criticized the work of a materialist philosopher (Eugen Dühring) in an effort to elucidate the finer points of the Marxian theory of knowledge. While gathering research material, Lenin hit upon the idea of modernizing Engels's theory of science by reworking it to encompass the broader meanings of the revolutionary discoveries in contemporary physics.

The origin of knowledge and the relation of thought to being are the central themes of *Materialism and Empiriocriticism*. Most of the ideas presented in this book are derived from one proposition: "Matter is a philosophical category designating the objective reality that is presented to man by his sensations; it is copied, photographed, and reflected by our sensations while existing independently of them."[87] In other words, matter is an epistemological and an ontological category: epistemologically it exists independently of the human mind, and ontologically it precedes it. Truth is a reflection of the outside world, and not a product of the "organizing power" of the human mind. Lenin argued that the least deviation from this materialist view would inevitably lead to mysticism and fideism. He had no use for Helmholtz's "symbols" and "hieroglyphs," Avenarius's "pure experience," or Mach's "elements," for all these men agreed that human knowledge was not a mechanical, or "true," reflection of the outside world but a mental construction; in this view, matter was a subjective category dependent on human cognitive power.

Lenin was concerned primarily with establishing the nature of scientific truth and proving that science and dialectical materialism were in complete harmony. However, he concentrated on pointing out and attacking the weaker points of "idealistic" theories of knowledge rather than on marshaling scientific support for his own contentions. He conceded that dialectical materialism was still ignored by almost all scientists, and could not identify a single Russian scientist as a Marxist. However, he said, scientists were "instinctive materialists," implicitly opposed to Machism and other "idealistic" theories of scientific knowledge.

In formulating his theory of scientific knowledge, Lenin took pains to avoid the pitfalls of classical materialism. He viewed the efforts of the classical materialists to define matter in terms of a specific substance or of such qualities as inertia, weight, or impenetrability as empty exercises in scholastic philosophy. The ontological primacy of matter, said Lenin, did not allow a scientist to reduce biological, psychological, and social phenomena to the same set of material laws. Each one of these fields is a separate reality, subject to its own processes and demanding specific techniques of scientific inquiry, but all have one thing in common: all exist independently of the human mind. The laws governing social development are as independent of man as are the laws governing nature.

According to Lenin, scientific truth—that is, objective truth—is relative and absolute at the same time. It is relative not in an epistemological but in a historical sense: the scientific knowledge of each historical period is limited by certain socioeconomic conditions, or by inadequate techniques of inquiry; scientific truth may be objective, but man's idea of it is constantly growing and changing. However, scientific truth is also absolute, since it gives a picture, though only a partial one, of the objectively existing reality. As a reality existing outside the human mind, matter is absolute, for it is universal and timeless; but every human definition of matter in terms of its inner structure is historically relative and therefore limited. To Lenin, the "idealists" who interpreted the discoveries of radiation and electrons as a proof of the "dematerialization of matter" were not challenging the universal definition of matter but were simply indicating man's current understanding of the structure of matter. The classical materialists, on the other hand, were philosophically unprepared to account for the revolutionary discoveries of modern physics: they were shackled by their own interpretation of the Newtonian mechanistic paradigm as an absolute description of matter rather than a historically relative explanation of material structure.

Modern discoveries in physics, Lenin assumed, had completely unhinged classical, or mechanistic, materialism; but they had also stimulated a wide revival of "idealistic" orientations in the theory of knowledge, which Lenin attacked violently. He simplified his attack by placing the label of "idealism" on every philosophical trend that was not explicitly materialistic. The Immanentists, who had only scorn for science, and the neopositivists, who regarded science as the quintessence of philosophy, were lumped into the same category. The endeavors of many contemporary philosophers and scientists to rise above the ontological limitations of both materialism and idealism made no serious impression on Lenin.

Lenin knew that he had very few philosophical friends. Undaunted by this isolation, he sought allies in the world of scientific scholarship, feeling that most contemporary scientists were materialists of an "unconscious" or "instinctive" variety.[88] They were essentially on the right track, but they lost a great deal of scientific and philosophical perspective because of their general ignorance of dialectic as a process of logic and history. Dialectical materialism, Lenin argued, was fully upheld by the discoveries of modern physics. "The destructibility and the inexhaustibility of the atom and the mutability of all forms of matter and its motions have always been strongly emphasized in dialectical materialism."[89] Dialectical materialism had insisted on "the approximate and relative character of every scientific proposition on the structure of matter ... on the absence of absolute boundaries in nature, and on the transformation of moving matter from one state into another."[90]

Lenin's efforts were made difficult by the great popularity of the "idealistic" philosophies among the leading physicists; but he found some solace in the fact that the antithetical relationship of the positive contributions of modern physics and the negative (i.e., decadent) idealistic conclusions deduced from them was another graphic illustration of the workings of dialectic.

The crisis in physics caused by the "dematerialization of matter" and the separation of motion from matter generated a great deal of philosophical confusion among the physicists; but, according to Lenin, it did not undermine the materialistic foundations and empirical products of the experimental method. Most "physical idealists" were idealistic only in their epistemological views, and remained materialistic in their scientific work. This applied even to such ardent idealists as Mach, Poincaré, Ostwald, and P. Duhem. Lenin noted optimistically that physical idealism was an aberration in the growth of modern science, and that the final victory of dialectical materialism as the philosophy of physics was inevitable. "The 'physical' idealism of today, like the 'physiological' idealism of yesterday, merely means that one school of scientists in one particular branch of natural science has slipped into a reactionary philosophy, being unable to rise directly from metaphysical materialism to dialectical materialism. Modern physics is in the process of making this step. But it is approaching the only true method and the only true philosophy of natural science not directly but by zigzags; not consciously but instinctively; not clearly perceiving the 'final goal' but drawing closer to it gropingly, hesitatingly, and sometimes even blindly. Modern physics is in travail; it is giving birth to dialectical materialism."[91]

In dissecting the causes of the "crisis" in physics, Lenin paid special attention to the growing mathematicization of physics and the increasing use of relativism in the interpretation of physical laws. With regard to the mathematicization of the sciences, he said: "The great successes achieved by science, especially a closer understanding of the homogeneous and simple elements of matter whose laws of motion can be treated mathematically, have actually encouraged the mathematicians to overlook matter. 'Matter disappears,' and only equations remain.... Hermann Cohen, who ... rejoices over the idealistic spirit of the new physics, goes so far as to advocate the introduction of higher mathematics in the gymnasiums ... in order to imbue high-school students with the spirit of idealism."[92] Relativism was viewed by Lenin as an outgrowth of the development of science by its own internal momentum: "All the old truths of physics, including those regarded as firmly established and incontestable, have proved to be relative truths; hence there can be no objective truth independent of mankind. Such is the argument not only of the Machians but of the 'physical' idealists in general."[93] According to Lenin, the physical idealists were not wrong in recognizing an element of relativity in scientific truth; their error was in not seeing that "every scientific truth, notwithstanding its relative nature, contains an element of absolute truth," that is, a true reflection of the objective world.

Unlike the Russian scientists of his age (notably the chemist D. I. Mendeleev and the physicist P. N. Lebedev), Lenin did not challenge the scientific veracity of the theories that arose from the discoveries of the 1890's. Welcoming the experimental verification of the divisibility of atoms, he prophesied the future discovery of new nuclear particles. In accommodating dialectical materialism to the triumphs of modern physics, he pushed matter as an ontological category into the background and focused his attention on matter as an epistemological phenomenon: he treated matter as a source of knowledge, not as the stuff of which the world was made.

*Materialism and Empiriocriticism* did not produce an intellectual storm in Russia. It was reviewed here and there, but most journals with a national circulation ignored it. Moreover, the Russian translations of Wilhelm Ostwald's *Natural Philosophy*, Gustave le Bon's *Evolution of Matter*, and Pierre Duhem's *The Aim and Structure of Physical Theory*—all echoing epistemological subjectivism and all published in 1910—helped strengthen the antimaterialist orientation of the Russian Machians and their allies. History, however, was on the side of Lenin's book. Less than a decade after its publication it became the cornerstone of the official Soviet epistemology and philosophy of science.

The most important legacy of Lenin's remarkable work was the dictum —not always strictly adhered to in the Soviet Union—that dialectical materialism must make constant adjustments to the new triumphs of science.

Lenin adduced several examples of the "dialectical" nature of modern science, but he was forced to admit that the pioneers of modern physics were in no way indebted to dialectical materialism. He made dialectical materialism, in its relationship to science, a passive, adaptive philosophy that consolidated the gains of the past but did not offer any guide to future scientific investigation. He strove to rejuvenate and enrich the Marxian philosophy of science and to identify the true interests of modern science with the Marxian doctrine. However, his primary interests were much more practical. His work gave the Bolsheviks new strength in their ideological struggle with the Mensheviks, and for the first time since 1903 established them as the Russian heirs of Marx and Engels.

After 1903, G. V. Plekhanov also tried to generate an interest in Marxian epistemology among Russian readers. His introduction to the second Russian edition of Engels's *Ludwig Feuerbach* spelled out the Marxian notions of the epistemological exteriority and ontological primacy of matter and the relative, dialectical nature of formal logic.[94] In 1908 he addressed two open letters to A. A. Bogdanov restating the Marxian theory of knowledge and criticizing the basic principles of Machism. These letters (subsequently included in Plekhanov's *Materialismus Militants*) paved the way for a wider appreciation of Lenin's philosophical work in Russia.[95] They were the major Menshevik contribution to the Marxian theory of knowledge.

*Materialism and Empiriocriticism* made the philosophy of science a Marxian clearinghouse of ideas connecting science with ideology. The neopositivists felt that modern philosophy was completely subsumed in science. Lenin, however, placed philosophy on a pedestal and trusted philosophers to perform two not always harmonious functions: defending the interests of ideology in the house of science and working out minute ideological adjustments to the great ideas of modern science. Underlying these two tasks was a romantic belief in the absolute knowability of the world—a categorical rejection of phenomenalism in all its aspects. Lenin insisted that scientific optimism was a pivotal value of societies built on the Marxian blueprint, and demanded that natural scientists be active contributors to the philosophy of science.[96]

Until the October Revolution, no Russian physicist of consequence incorporated the epistemology of Engels and Lenin into his thinking. Most natural scientists agreed with the Marxists that the reign of mechanistic philosophy had run its course; but none accepted Lenin's views of the epistemological exteriority of matter, the nonqualitative difference between absolute and relative truths, and the total knowability of the world as parts of an indivisible philosophical package. We have dealt with Lenin's philosophy of science at length not because it left a strong imprint on its age, but because it helped create a new society, to which it contributed a fully formed theory of knowledge.

## CHAPTER NINE

# Biological Evolution: Facts and Controversies

## COLLECTORS AND SYSTEMIZERS

The two dominant features of the Russian biological sciences during the last four decades of the tsarist era were the modernization of the methodological apparatus for empirical studies and the widespread application of Darwinian evolution as a universal law of organic nature and as a heuristic principle in the coordination and interpretation of data. The "new" Russian naturalist looked at organic nature as an endless but ordered field of diverse phenomena. In addition to adducing empirical support for the general law of evolution, he searched for particular laws expressing morphological, ecological, and other uniformities in the natural world.

Biological studies after 1880 acquired a number of new characteristics. First, many new areas of the vast Russian empire were subjected to systematic biological surveys. Some notable results of this effort were S. I. Korzhinskii's model studies of Turkestan, N. P. Vagner's *Invertebrates of the White Sea*, A. N. Beketov's studies of the flora of the Arkhangelsk region, and the first solid descriptions of the Arctic by Russian naturalists. Second, the advancement of research techniques, particularly microscopy, opened new areas of the animal and plant worlds to systematic study. Algology and mycology became firmly entrenched branches of botany, and helminthology emerged as an important part of zoology. Finally, very few zoologists and botanists were still satisfied with simple geographical surveys or searches for new species of plants and animals. Instead, they adopted more rigorous methodological tools and a far greater degree of theoretical refinement and abstraction. Most students of flora and fauna became systematizers: some operated within the established phylogenetic systems; others emphasized geographical distribution, and still others ecological dynamics. The study of the Russian flora and fauna became much more than the study of a vital part of the nation's natural resources; now, it was also an area for testing, elaborating, and revising the basic ideas of biological theory.

The first serious comprehensive study of Russian flora and fauna had been undertaken by the Second Kamchatka Expedition in 1733–43. A century and a half later, Russian scholars possessed vast stores of raw information on the living nature of their country, and were in a position to undertake comprehensive taxonomic studies that opened new vistas for more penetrating studies of nature. For the first time, the entire flora of the empire was presented in all its varieties and regional gradations. S. I. Korzhinskii, for example, lectured on the systematics and distribution of plants, drew up a botanical map of the historical-geographical regions in the eastern part of European Russia, and prepared a comprehensive review of the plants of Russia for the *Encyclopedic Dictionary* of Brockhaus and Efron. Many botanical studies were concerned with the demarcation of vegetation zones and with regularities in the distribution of individual plants and the evolution of local flora.[1] Work on the systematics of the Russian fauna was even more advanced. For the first time, comprehensive studies of individual species or other taxonomic groups began to appear: M. A. Menzbir's *Birds of Russia*; L. P. Sabaneev's *Fishes of Russia*; L. S. Berg's detailed studies of fishes in Lake Baikal, the Amur basin, and Turkestan; and K. A. Satunin's *Mammals of the Caucasian Territory*. These studies often combined the comparative methods of modern embryology and anatomy with a cultivated search for ecological undercurrents and evolutionary processes.

Many of these local field studies provided promising Russian biologists with the indispensable apprenticeship that led them to the forefront of modern biological research. Korzhinskii later became one of the pioneers of mutation theory, and I. P. Borodin soon adopted Western European neovitalism, which challenged the "materialistic" bias of Darwin's evolutionism. A typical Russian naturalist adhered to the Darwinian theory but was inclined to ignore or disclaim its Malthusian "bias." By the beginning of the twentieth century the encyclopedic naturalist had fulfilled his historical role in Russia, giving way to specialists in the many new branches of modern biology. But it was primarily the stores of knowledge accumulated by the old-fashioned naturalists that enabled the Academy of Sciences to embark in 1911 on the publication of the monumental *Fauna of Russia and Neighboring Areas*.

Despite their somewhat excessive concern with the systematics of plants and animals, Russian scholars, for the most part, were content to apply the classificatory procedures and principles established by Western scholars. In 1914 N. I. Kuznetsov became the first Russian to formulate a consistent taxonomy of plants; but the influence of such German taxonomists as A. Engler and R. Wettstein was so powerful that Kuznetsov's efforts went virtually unnoticed.[2] A few Russian scientists were as eager as their Western peers to search for more comprehensive and reliable criteria of classification. In 1889, E. A. Shatskii claimed to have established that certain alkaloids obtained from plants had identical qualities in plants of the same family, providing a chemical indicator of genetic proximity. Shatskii's results were not too reliable, but they opened a new field for Russian taxonomists—that of comparative plant biochemistry.

If there was one dominant feature in the work of Russian naturalists, it was an emphasis on plant and animal ecology. Very few naturalists deviated from the basic theories of environmentalism: the living world and its physical environment were viewed as interacting and constantly changing variables. In particular, the view that present-day animal forms should be explained in terms of past geographical conditions generated a lively interest in geology and paleontology; and paleogeography became an established discipline. This interest in paleozoology and paleobotany was one aspect of a sustained concern with the morphological changes caused by environmental influences. Comparative anatomy helped to trace morphological differences between the animals of various ecological zones. The best naturalistic studies of the Russian flora and fauna were at the same time the best descriptions of the different habitats in Russia.

## EVOLUTIONISM AND NEOVITALISM

Even though Darwinism entered Russia in the overwhelmingly favorable climate of the Reform era, it did not go unchallenged for long. Most of the early critics were conservative publicists and idealistic philosophers, who were worried less about the scientific veracity of Darwin's basic ideas than they were about the adverse effect of those ideas on official ideology. The opinions of these critics, however, were feeble and inarticulate, and were not widely publicized.

The scientific community's chief critic of Darwinism was the venerable Karl Ernst von Baer, the greatest embryologist of the pre-Darwinian era. In 1876, the year of his death, von Baer summed up his objections in a lengthy essay, and maintained that Darwin's principal claims had no valid scientific basis.[3] As a champion of the teleological principle of evolution, he was particularly annoyed by Darwin's commitment to the role of external causation in evolutionary change. But despite his many objections, he was willing to admit that Darwin was a genius of the first rank. Von Baer's essay was not taken seriously by most contemporary biologists, probably because its arguments were full of unclear allusions and self-contradictions.

In 1885 N. Ia. Danilevskii published a monumental work entitled *Darwinism: A Critical Study*, which totally condemned Darwinian evolution both as a science and as an ideology. Danilevskii charged that Darwinism supported a materialistic world view and was based on a dubious elimination of every teleology. He also charged that Darwin's theory was based on untested propositions and faulty logic; it was not a set of scientific propositions but a "philosophical view."[4] Darwin erred in assuming that changes in nature were accidental. To Danilevskii, the universal law of nature was not Darwin's "chaotic" natural causation but the gradual unfolding of a supreme "intellectual principle."

Darwin attributed the origin of new variations of plants and animals to chance, and he defined "chance" as a large number of unknown causes. He was careful to emphasize that he recognized only natural causes and rejected any notion of possible interference by supernatural or mystical forces. Danilevskii's work is in essence a synthesis of the objections to this view expressed by two intellectual sources: isolated scientists who were unhappy with Darwin's use of unpredictable chance rather than predictable, uniform, and universal causation; and the religious thinkers and metaphysicians who disliked Darwin's elimination of supreme intelligence and teleology from the history of living nature. Danilevskii gave credit to a long list of scholars who added to the mounting criticism of Darwin's theory: Karl von Baer; the paleontologists Louis Agassiz, A. Milne-Edwards, H. G. Bronn, and J. Barrande; the comparative anatomist Richard Owen; the histologist Albert Kölliker; the physiologist P. Flourens; the zoologist Carl Burmeister; and many others. He thought, however, that these criticisms were cries in the desert, and took it upon himself to coordinate them and show their full meaning.

Danilevskii himself assuredly had the academic qualifications to undertake a critical assessment of Darwinism. He had graduated from St. Petersburg University with a major in the natural sciences, and had produced several studies in descriptive ichthyology. In 1869 he surprised the reading public by publishing *Russia and Europe*, a philosophical work depicting the Russian national character as a unique historical structure that was essentially alien to the "materialism" and rationalism of modern natural science. In a sense, *Russia and Europe* was "a view of universal history from the vantage point of Russian nationality" as conceived by Danilevskii.[5] The forcefulness of Danilevskii's argument and the philosophical bent of his prose attracted many readers, but only a few of these were finally converted to the conservative cause of Panslavism, which Danilevskii was trying to advance.

Danilevskii contended that Darwin's analogies between the variations of domestic and wild animals were not founded on empirically defensible facts. The wide variations among domestic animals, he said, did not lead to the emergence of new species, and Darwin exaggerated the evolutionary importance of artificial selection among domestic plants and animals. The struggle for existence, according to Danilevskii, was found in nature only as an ephemeral phenomenon. He also contended that Darwin had overlooked the continual emergence of useless, and sometimes harmful, features in plants and animals. Disregarding the contributions of V. O. Kovalevskii, he denied that there was any paleontological support for Darwin's theory.[6] In attacking Darwinism as a scientific theory, Danilevskii did acknowledge that evolution was a law of nature; but he himself spearheaded the rise of Russian "neo-evolutionism," a growing movement dedicated to broadening the concept of evolution far beyond "natural selection." His achievement was novel: he contributed to a wider acceptance of biological evolution, but at the same time he spurred the enemies of "natural selection" to further attacks on Darwinian transformism.

Following the old Slavophil argument that science, rationalism, Protestantism, and humanism reduced the noblest intellectual endeavors to the comprehension level of the masses, Danilevskii charged that the great popularity of Darwin's theory was a result of its simplicity and appeal to uncultivated minds. At this time, the most extreme reaction dominated the social and educational policies of the St. Petersburg government, the universities were temporarily silenced, and the children of "coachmen, servants, cooks, laundresses," and other such people were officially proclaimed unfit for education. Danilevskii found it opportune to interpret Darwin's evolutionism as a conspiratorial endorsement of class struggle.

N. N. Strakhov, who some 25 years earlier had been among the first to inform the Russian public about the grand new ideas presented in *The Origin of Species*, assumed the task of spelling out the scientific, philosophical, and ideological implications of Danilevskii's work. In a lengthy review published in the conservative *Russian Messenger*, Strakhov labeled Danilevskii's book "a true triumph of the Russian mind and sentiment" and a masterpiece of world literature.[7] He credited Danilevskii with having offered incontrovertible arguments against natural selection as a motive force in biological evolution.[8] But even this passionate endorsement of Danilevskii's ideas failed to spur the Russian anti-Darwinists to united action against the "materialism" of evolutionary biology; and until the very end of the 1880's most Russian biologists had "a negative attitude" toward Danilevskii's ideas.[9] In spite of Strakhov's praise, the St. Petersburg Academy of Sciences refused to award any prize to Danilevskii's book. The Academicians detected major flaws in Danilevskii's geological arguments, and appraised the book as a mere compilation of existing anti-Darwinian arguments.[10] The philosopher Vladimir Solov'ev, the dean of the metaphysical revival, claimed that Danilevskii concentrated so exclusively on debunking Darwin's theory that he failed to provide an alternative scientific explanation of the origin of species.[11]

By far the most active Russian champion of Darwinism was Kliment Timiriazev, a pioneer in the study of photosynthesis. By the time Danilevskii's book and Strakhov's review appeared, Timiriazev's *Brief Essay on the Theory of Evolution* had gone through two editions and was one of the most widely read scientific popularizations in Russia. In April 1887, Timiriazev, in a long lecture at Moscow's Polytechnical Museum, dissected and attacked the philosophical and biological arguments of Danilevskii. This lecture was an important event in the history of Russian biological thought, for it marked the beginning of an organized war between the Darwinists and anti-Darwinists. Ten years earlier the Darwinists had concentrated on explaining Darwin's ideas to huge and appreciative audiences; now they were forced to defend these ideas against a wide variety of attacks.[12]

Timiriazev rejected Danilevskii's claim that Darwin's law of natural selection was equivalent to a law of universal chaos. He also rejected Danilevskii's notion of the purposiveness and predetermination of biological change. Neither the Empedoclean absolute of random change nor the Aristotelian teleological principles were built into Darwinian theory, he felt. Darwinism substituted the *causa efficiens* for the *causa finalis* as an organizing principle of nature—a principle that contrasted with the sterility of the "law" of chance and the "law" of predetermination.[13]

Danilevskii had died while his book was in press, and Strakhov took it upon himself to answer Timiriazev's criticism. At the end of 1887, Strakhov published a long essay in defense of his friend. He recapitulated Danilevskii's main arguments against Darwinism, which were based on long citations from Kölliker, Karl Nägeli, and a score of other biologists, and summed them up in the verdict that Darwin's theory consisted of "indefinite premises" and "incorrect generalizations."[14] He challenged Timiriazev's efforts to make Darwinism an integral part of the mechanistic model of the universe by extending "the iron law of external causation" to the living world; nor was he impressed with Timiriazev's attempts to combine Darwin's theory of evolution with the law of the conservation of energy. Most of all, he resented Timiriazev's—and Darwin's—failure to see any connection between the harmony of nature and the work of a "supreme intelligence."

Strakhov criticized Timiriazev for attacking not only the scientific ideas but also the philosophical implications of Danilevskii's book. Strakhov himself tried to give his readers the impression that Danilevskii's *Darwinism* was a strictly scientific study containing no philosophical preconceptions or organizing principles. By avoiding philosophy, he said, Danilevskii had avoided the metaphysical pitfalls that marred the scholarship of such great scientists as Hermann Helmholtz, Emil du Bois-Reymond, and Karl Nägeli.[15] However, Strakhov was willing to accept Danilevskii's views on the intrinsic harmony and aesthetic quality of nature and the purposiveness of evolution not as metaphysical assumptions but as unchallengeable scientific data.

Timiriazev countered by asserting that neither Danilevskii nor Strakhov had really kept "philosophy" out of their attacks on Darwinism. In fact, they had condemned it not on scientific grounds but because they saw in it a challenge to their world view. Strakhov's essays were in part a thinly veiled attack on the "materialism" of natural science and an insinuation that science had entered an era of irretrievable decline. Most of all, Timiriazev criticized Strakhov's claim that the wholesale acceptance of Darwin's theory in Russia was just another example of the basic weakness of the Russian scientific community, which blindly accepted all Western scientific ideas instead of carrying on independent, creative scholarship. Hidden in Strakhov's verbiage was the contention that science, in essence, offered no opportunity for the Russian genius to truly express itself. Both Danilevskii and Strakhov believed in a "science" that had no room for universal causes independent of a guiding supreme intellect.[16] To them, said Timiriazev, science was a mere appendage of theology. Whatever their primary interests may have been, it was obvious that they were interested more in protecting Russian sacred culture from the erosive influences of scientific "materialism" than in advancing the cause of modern science.

Timiriazev eventually attempted to defend classic Darwinism against all critics of the evolutionary idea, both inside and outside the scientific community. In a series of public lectures on the "historical method" in biology (1889–1900), he traced the gradual expansion of modern biology from the development of the comparative method in morphology and experimental techniques in physiology to the widespread use of historical evidence in many fields.[17] Although the historical method was particularly useful in embryology and paleontology, it enriched every other branch of biology as well, and formed a link between biology and sociology. According to Timiriazev, Darwin had not invented the evolutionary idea, but had merely produced a grand synthesis of empirical data collected by many generations of biologists. Thus an enormous amount of proof for the validity of biological evolution had been open to public inspection all along. In applying a "historical view" to the study of nature, Darwin had done for biology what Laplace had done for astronomy, Lyell for geology, Comte for sociology, and Marx for economics.[18]

Strakhov was basically correct when he called Timiriazev a "pure" Darwinist who adopted every argument, supposition, and theoretical inference set forth by the great English naturalist.* However, he overlooked Timiriazev's broader theoretical orientation, which transcended the mere exposition of Darwin's ideas. Timiriazev's own evolutionism combined three ideas: Darwin's concept of natural selection; the Newtonian mechanistic idea of the universality of causality and continuity in the work of nature; and Comte's extension of the idea of progress from the world of organic life to the world of human society and culture. To Timiriazev, Darwinian evolutionism was not only a great idea of modern biology but also a triumph of the scientific world view in general. Darwinism, he claimed, was one of the primary reasons that the nineteenth century was the "century of science."[19]

Until the late 1880's, the leading Russian biologists stuck closely to the major principles of "natural-scientific materialism," which extended the laws of Newtonian mechanics to living nature and reduced all phenomena

---

* In a lengthy review of Timiriazev's essays M. Filippov, a trained mathematician who wrote popular articles on the leading theories of modern science, criticized Timiriazev for his tendency to consider the Darwinian legacy a closed system with no need of further elaboration and improvement. Timiriazev's dogmatic acceptance and passionate defense of Darwin's ideas, according to Filippov, were responsible for a delayed diffusion of modern biological ideas in Russia. He noted that while the West was engaged in an all-out battle between neo-Darwinists and neo-Lamarckians, Russia was still preoccupied with a struggle between the proponents and the adversaries of classical Darwinism. Filippov also opposed Timiriazev's contention that every rejection of the struggle for existence as a key to evolution was a dangerous flirting with vitalism. M. Filippov, "Darvinizm," No. 32, p. 994.

to physics and chemistry. In the 1890's the old "materialists" were still very much in the saddle, but they were no longer immune to criticism from biologists who challenged the absolute reign of the mechanistic-deterministic orientation in many branches of their science. The antimechanistic view, in part, grew out of a favorable response of a segment of the academic community to the growing philosophical and theological criticism of Darwinism.[20] It was also influenced by a revival of vitalism, known as neovitalism in Western Europe, which sought a nonmechanistic explanation of living forms and offered a teleological interpretation of the history of living nature.

At the opening of Tomsk University in 1888, S. I. Korzhinskii covered many of the key points of neovitalism in a lecture entitled "What Is Life?" He felt that "mechanistic" theories were far too widely applied to the study of the living world. "Metabolism and the transformation of energy are problems that the mechanistic orientation has treated with success. But these phenomena are only ancillary processes or external attributes of life. The essence of life cannot be unveiled by mechanical investigations."[21] This essence, according to Korzhinskii, is a special quality of protoplasm— a "living energy" that cannot be related to chemical and physical qualities for the simple reason that "its creations have nothing analogous in the inorganic world." Unable to provide an ontological explanation of neovitalism, Korzhinskii looked for epistemological support: "It would seem that by accepting the existence of . . . a special living principle we go back to vitalism and reject the mechanistic theory as incorrect. However, such a conclusion would not be completely justified. Every day, scholars observe that no opinions are entirely incorrect, just as no opinions are absolutely correct. Every view contains a share of truth, and every conclusion represents only a partial answer to a question."[22]

Neovitalism became popular in Russia at the very time when men like Timiriazev and Strakhov were battling over the nature and validity of Darwinism; and Darwinism, in fact, was its chief reason for existence. The competent scholars who originally popularized the movement, like Korzhinskii, were willing to accept many of the basic Darwinian ideas, and really sought nothing more than an expansion of the narrowly mechanistic theory of evolution. But Timiriazev, and others like him, could accept no departures from the mechanistic framework. This intransigence tended to push the neovitalists into a more extreme position, and the disputes over Darwinism rapidly became fiercer than ever.

In 1889, the Academician A. S. Famintsyn published an essay on Danilevskii's *Darwinism*, trying to take a more moderate position than those of Strakhov and Timiriazev.[23] Famintsyn gave Danilevskii credit for "detailed explanations" of the basic issues involved in the controversy over Darwinism. However, he charged that throughout Danilevskii's book the scientific principles of Darwin's theory were interpreted incorrectly.[24] There was no basis for Danilevskii's view that Darwin's conception of evolution denied the existence of a supreme deity: even such leading anti-Darwinists as Albert Wigand and Karl von Baer acknowledged explicitly that Darwin had made a deliberate effort to avoid attacks on particular religious convictions and on the nature of religion in general.[25] Famintsyn's essay was a measured, thoughtful plea for an objective assessment of the Darwinian scientific legacy. It recognized the revolutionary sweep of Darwin's thought, but also emphasized that Darwinism needed constant revision and empirical testing. In conclusion, Famintsyn tried to make his countrymen aware that the notion of biological change involved more than just the Darwinian concept of evolution.

Famintsyn's plea elicited the first serious statement on Darwinism from I. P. Borodin, a noted plant physiologist and later a member of the St. Petersburg Academy of Sciences. In 1894 Borodin published an article entitled "Protoplasm and Vitalism," which attacked the mechanistic "dogma" of contemporary life scientists and asserted that the progress of modern biology depended on the categorical recognition of the existence of a "living force" outside the laws of physics and chemistry.[26] Noting that vitalism had appeared as a philosophical orientation in several sciences, Borodin greeted it as a powerful challenge to the "materialism of the 1860's." He did admit that the mechanistic view had a place in natural science; but he was convinced that the absolute truth was not accessible to man in the first place, and that mechanistic and vitalistic orientations should complement each other in the search for relative truths. "The evidence for or against each of these views may appear convincing to some persons and less so to others, depending on personal orientations and on the mood of the time." Borodin also repeated the familiar charge that the mechanistic approach in biology could not answer the question of the origin and meaning of life—the essential problem of biology.

Timiriazev, of course, immediately attacked Borodin's ideas, both in print and in popular lectures. A consistent defender of an integrated Newtonian-mechanistic and Darwinian-historical philosophy of nature, Timiriazev was a sworn enemy of any doctrine that could be classed as idealistic metaphysics. He considered himself a product of, and a spokesman for, "the materialism of the 1860's." He felt that physiology was a link between organic and inorganic nature, and asserted: "Everything that has been achieved in physiology is a product of the application of physical and chemical methods [and laws] to the study of living phenomena."[27] Timiriazev attacked Borodin for questioning the universal validity of mechanistic determinism and for asserting that the views of the mechanicists and the vitalists were "only the statements of belief of these two scientific camps."[28] He was quick to equate Borodin's relativism with a belief in the severely limited compass of scientific inquiry. To Timiriazev, the challenges generated by the crisis in modern physics demanded a bold look toward the future rather than a passive retreat into the metaphysics of the past. Borodin chose not to defend himself against this attack and not to elaborate on his criticism of mechanistic biology.

In 1898, A. S. Famintsyn wrote a long essay intended as a detailed answer to the mechanistic orientation in biology. The work was not particularly original, but it presented a well-balanced array of details drawn from the contemporary neovitalist literature. Like Korzhinskii and Borodin, Famintsyn was well able to list the shortcomings of mechanistic biology but had serious difficulties in articulating a meaningful vitalistic alternative. The mechanistic claim that life was no more than "a play of physicochemical forces in the protoplasm," he said, was "not a strict conclusion from exact knowledge, but only a modern scientific dogma."[29] He endorsed the neovitalist idea of a "living principle"—not a "living substance" or a "living force"—as the distinguishing characteristic of the organic world, and also praised Richard Avenarius's theory of knowledge as a guidepost for the future development of biology.

According to Famintsyn, the mechanistic theory, of which Darwinism was a classic example, was only a limited source of biological knowledge, for it did not explain the very essence of life. Famintsyn explained the non-mechanistic aspect of biology, which contrasted with the totally mechanistic nature of physics and chemistry, on simple epistemological grounds: the phenomena of life are accessible to our study on both their external and their internal sides, whereas inorganic phenomena are only accessible from their external side. Thus biological phenomena have a physicochemical (or mechanistic) dimension and a psychological (or vitalistic) dimension, and both must be taken into account. Famintsyn attacked any approach that neglected either aspect; for this reason, he criticized modern psychologists, who had been exceedingly slow to undertake an evolutionary study of psychic life and to regard sense organs as sources of knowledge and instruments of adaptation to external conditions.[30] Similarly, by criticizing the one-sided mechanistic orientation of Darwinism, Famintsyn wanted to expand Darwin's evolutionary ideas beyond the traditional limits of biology.

The Russian neovitalists did not disassociate themselves completely from the established antivitalistic tradition in biology. As scientists, they continued to support the traditional views; but as philosophers, they acknowledged the grave shortcomings of their own research methods. They followed the established paths of science, but at the same time they challenged the narrow horizons of materialism, scientific or otherwise. They accepted the law of the conservation of energy, even though it contradicted the basic ontology of vitalism. They criticized the Darwinian legacy only to the extent that *The Origin of Species* was considered the mainspring of mechanistic biology. The neovitalists' main contribution was in pointing out that life and its development could not be fully understood in terms of mechanical models, but only by studying the total configurations of organisms. To the mechanicists, the egg always came before the chicken; to the vitalists, the chicken before the egg. The Russian neovitalists tried to encompass both views.

Because the philosophical standpoint of the neovitalists was so close to metaphysics, they were not taken seriously by most contemporary scientists. As scientists, however, many neovitalists were among the leaders of their generation. Unlike Danilevskii and Strakhov, they were not motivated by the official ideology in their efforts to reconcile Darwinism with modern developments in biology. Famintsyn, for example, supported academic autonomy, the right of students to organize protective associations, and the general democratization of the Russian government; his criticism of materialist philosophy and the mechanistic view in biology was in no way a defense of autocratic ideology.

### NEO-DARWINISM AND THE EMERGENCE OF GENETICS

The Russian neovitalists were few in number, and none developed a complete, consistent biological theory. However, they did point out the pressing need for a major overhaul of mechanistic biology and a broader view of Darwinism. In doing so, they paved the way for the emergence of neo-Darwinism, an aggregate of views that rapidly gained prominence during the 1890's.

Neo-Darwinism meant several things to Russian scientists. The zoologist M. A. Menzbir, for example, did not need the term at all: to him, "modern Darwinism" was a term broad enough to include most evolutionary theories. Timiriazev, by contrast, could only regard neo-Darwinist ideas, like those of the metaphysical anti-Darwinists and neovitalists, as a total negation of the classic Darwinian formulation. In actuality, neo-Darwinism was no more than an attempt to modernize Darwinism by replacing some of its untenable propositions with new ideas more in accord with the results of experimental research. As it happened, the most significant and controversial of these new findings came from the recently established field of genetics.

During the 1880's the German biologist August Weismann was led by his experimental studies to conclude that reproductive cells were not affected by environment, and that acquired characteristics were not genetically transmitted. All changes in organisms between generations, he felt, were produced by new combinations—rather than internal modifications—of the "germ lines" that gave rise to the "sex cells." This idea conflicted not only with the Lamarckian tradition but also with Darwin's idea of "pangenesis," which held that the cells responsible for heredity were developed anew in every organism. Weismann's ideas received a generally unfavorable treatment in Russia, where the environmentalist tradition was unusually strong. One of the first critics was the Academician V. V. Zalenskii. Drawing on his own embryological studies of sea urchins, lancelets, and coral polyps, Zalenskii was able to show that some morphological changes resulted from adaptations to specific modifications in the environment; but he did not describe the actual processes involved in the transmission of acquired characteristics. He also argued against Weismann's narrow localization of the cellular agents of heredity.[31]

One of the most articulate of Weismann's Russian critics, M. A. Menzbir, acknowledged Weismann's adherence to Darwinism and his bold efforts to enrich the theory of evolution; but in Weismann's theory of heredity he also saw an example of the reflection of the "national character" in science. According to him, Weismann's "ids," "idants," "biophors," "determinants," and other biogenetic links "satisfied the need of the German mind for philosophy and classification, and strongly gravitated toward the moribund *Naturphilosophie*."[32] Like most other Russian critics, Menzbir overlooked Weismann's hard-headed reliance on the empirical results of modern cytological research. Weismann's idea of the inviolability of the "germinal plasm" is still a fundamental point of modern genetics, even though much of his cumbersome terminology has fallen by the wayside.

Menzbir could disagree with some of Weismann's theories and still regard him essentially as a modern Darwinist. Timiriazev, on the other hand, regarded Weismann as a typical anti-Darwinist. He particularly criticized the "metaphysical" nature of Weismann's two major ideas: the existence of a mortal "corporeal plasm" and an immortal "germinal plasm"; and the notion of "preformism," an apparent residue of *Naturphilosophie*. He charged that Weismann, searching for a "visual representation" of the material carriers of heredity, had invented a swarm of fictitious organic particles. Finally, in a fit of oratorical exuberance, Timiriazev claimed that narrow nationalism, in the form of "an abhorrence of everything English" and "an exaltation of everything German," had led Weismann and other German biologists to take an overly critical attitude toward Darwinism.[33]

Darwin himself had been convinced that the ultimate support for all the significant details of his theory would come from comparative anatomy, embryology, and paleontology. Weismann, however, was the first of a large group of neo-Darwinists who treated heredity as the key problem of evolution and who anticipated the emergence of genetics as a separate science. The early investigators of heredity were faced with two problems: identifying the mechanisms that transmitted hereditary traits and determining the speed with which new biological types are produced by cumulative changes in the hereditary base. Weismann tried to answer the first question, and in the process he turned against the Lamarckian tradition in biology.

The first scientist to approach the second problem was the Dutch botanist Hugo De Vries. Taking a clue from Lord Kelvin, De Vries attempted to resolve the apparent conflict between the physical theory of the development of life on earth, according to which life had existed no longer than 20–40 million years, and the theory of "the evolutionists of the gradual line," who supposed that billions of years must have elapsed before the appearance of mankind.[34] Working from his own intensive study of the evening primrose (*Oenthera lamarckiana*), De Vries postulated the theory of mutations to account for the sudden emergence of new species and morphological variations. The new concept became a major factor in modern biology, particularly after Eric von Tschermak "rediscovered" Mendel's genetic studies in 1900. Mutations, as envisaged by De Vries, are "spontaneous," and are therefore unrelated to changes in the environment. Moreover, the process of biological evolution is saltatory: it contains prolonged periods of morphological constancy and relatively short periods of drastic qualitative change. In 1901 and 1903, De Vries published the two volumes of *Die Mutationslehre,* in which he brought together the biological ideas he had developed during the preceding decade.

A few Russians had also been intrigued by the problem of saltatory change. Several years before De Vries published his book, the botanist S. I. Korzhinskii had published "Heterogenesis and Evolution," a lengthy essay presenting hundreds of examples of saltatory changes in the living world. Korzhinskii made a sharp distinction between individual, nonhereditary variations and "heterogenetic" changes produced by internal processes in the generative cells. By "heterogenesis" (a term borrowed from Kölliker) he meant the emergence of new species not by gradual processes but by occasional "leaps"; and he contended that these leaps were caused not by changes in the external environment, but exclusively by internal processes in an organism.[35] Thus Korzhinskii combined Weismann's idea of the independence of heredity from environmental conditions with the theory of saltatory changes. He had intended to construct his own theory from the data he had collected, but died before he could do so. Later researchers, however, were greatly aided by the numerous examples of saltatory change that he set forth. Moreover, his work tended to remind biologists that such important matters as heredity, variation, and the emergence of new species were still awaiting a satisfactory scientific explanation. Many Western biologists took serious note of Korzhinskii's efforts, whether or not they agreed with the tentative conclusions he offered.

One of the greatest influences on neo-Darwinism eventually came from the genetic theories of Gregor Mendel. I. F. Shmal'gauzen, a professor of botany at St. Petersburg University who did his major research on hybrids in the flora of St. Petersburg province, was the first Russian scientist to point out the great potentialities of Mendel's mathematical approach in studying the variations in animal and plant forms that resulted from hybridization.[36] However, Shmal'gauzen did not follow up the possibilities opened by Mendel's theory. And most other Russian scientists, like their Western peers, adopted the Mendelian theory as a research guide only after its "rediscovery" at the very beginning of the twentieth century.

As one might expect, Timiriazev was the principal opponent of Mendelism when it finally reached Russia. Timiriazev sensed the great potential value of Mendelian genetic laws, but was held back by a deeply seated commitment to Lamarckian environmentalism, which he never overcame. In his opinion, Mendelism allied mathematics with "anti-Darwinism," and also relegated the chemical and physical explanations of life processes to a position of secondary importance. Because of these drawbacks, he felt, Mendelism could do great harm to Darwinian evolutionism, for it would encourage scientists to abandon Darwin's reliance on external physical facts and open the way for a resurgence of metaphysical and idealistic thinking.

For all these reasons, Timiriazev detested the introduction of Mendelism into Russia. However, the wide support given to the theory by the leading Western European scholars led him to abstain from excessive criticism, and even to search for compromises. Somewhat belatedly, he admitted that Mendelism did not run counter to Darwinian evolution, but was one "episode" in the grand upsurge of scientific thought issuing from the theoretical principles formulated and elaborated by Darwin and the other English naturalists.[37] He endorsed the claim of Alfred Wallace that the current acceptance of Mendel's experimental theory as a radically new step in biological research only showed how little attention modern biologists had paid to Darwin's *Variation of Animals and Plants Under Domestication*, which illustrated Darwin's full appreciation of the problems subsequently studied by Mendel.[38]

In 1909 Timiriazev and the pathologist I. I. Mechnikov represented the Russian scientific community at a convocation held at Cambridge University to commemorate the centenary of Darwin's birth and the fiftieth anniversary of the publication of *The Origin of Species*. Timiriazev was immensely impressed with the festive spirit of the proceedings, and was proud to be among the recipients of honorary doctorates from Cambridge. But other details of the convocation brought him less pleasure, and even some disappointing afterthoughts. Some of the most ebullient praises of Darwin's scientific contributions came from August Weismann, William Bateson, and Hugo De Vries—whom Timiriazev had consistently accused of having injected the eighteenth-century metaphysical doctrines of "preformism and *emboîtement*" into modern scientific theories of biological change.[39] At the Cambridge gathering, Timiriazev undoubtedly learned that Darwinism had become a much broader biological theory than he had anticipated; and he could not help but notice that the papers read there mentioned the name of Korzhinskii more often than that of any other Russian biologist.

Also in 1909, a group of Russian scientists noted the centenary of Darwin's birth by publishing *In Memory of Darwin*, a symposium edited by the physicist N. A. Umov. In this volume, Timiriazev informed Russian readers of the Cambridge festivities, and used the opportunity to reaffirm his skepticism of the theories of Mendel, Bateson, De Vries, and Korzhinskii. Quoting Ray Lankester, he stated that the theory of natural selection and the struggle for existence was still "complete, inviolable, and fully convincing, regardless of all the efforts to refute it."[40] Searching for a broader application of Darwin's scientific legacy, Timiriazev also examined a paper by the astronomer George Darwin, Charles's son. Before introducing his thoughts on applying the mathematics of rotating fluid to the study of the evolution of cosmos, George Darwin noted that the evolution of states or governments was analogous to changes in certain types of motion in that it varied between full stability and total chaos; and that at times of crisis social stability was reestablished and the continuity of political history restored, but only by a change in the type of government.[41] At this time of chronic political crisis in Russia, Timiriazev relied on the authority of Darwinian science to create an impression that the time had come for a change in the type of Russian government, since this was the only realistic—and scientific—way to preserve the continuity of Russia's political history.

By fighting the ideas of Mendel, Bateson, and De Vries, Timiriazev actually helped to publicize them and make them a lively topic of academic debate. The Marxist G. V. Plekhanov was quick to recognize in the theory of saltatory changes in the organic world a new proof for the law of dialectics as the supreme law of natural development. He endorsed De Vries's notion that the gradualist theory of the origin of species hindered an experimental study of the basic problems of modern biology.[42] After 1910 there was continual friction between the traditional Darwinists and the neo-Darwinists. Each group produced both scholars interested primarily in experimental research and popularizers interested in spreading Darwinian views among the informed public.

Among the Russian students of biological transformation, I. V. Michurin and N. I .Vavilov should especially be noted—not because they were widely acclaimed at this time, but because they played a great part in carrying the war between the adherents and the critics of Lamarckian theory into the Soviet era, perpetuating a bitter conflict in which ideology eventually penetrated the innermost depths of modern biology. Both scholars achieved a full codification of their theories after the October Revolution; but both built the foundations of these theories before 1917.

I. V. Michurin was a man without formal higher education, and was little known to the academic community until he was raised to high prominence by the Soviet authorities. A successful horticulturalist, he belonged to the legion of self-taught "scientists" and inventors who combined native ingenuity with a strong desire to add something new to man's eternal effort to tame nature. In his experimental orchards, Michurin studied the adaptation of various plants (usually fruit trees) to carefully manipulated conditions of external environment. He worked out several basic principles for the hybridization and acclimatization of plants and developed unique grafting techniques to apply these principles.

Michurin reported the results of his experiments in the *Messenger of Horticulture*, in *Fruit Growing and Truck Farming*, and in other journals not likely to be read by academic biologists. He did in practice what Timiriazev advocated in theory; yet Timiriazev seems to have ignored his work. Both men held that nature is open to infinite modifications, and that man could effect changes in species and varieties by altering their physical environment. However, as a practical horticulturalist rather than a theoretical biologist, Michurin dealt primarily with the transformation of individual organisms. It was T. D. Lysenko, a self-professed follower of Michurin, who used Michurin's experiments as a springboard for his ambitious and unsubstantiated claims of phylogenetic transformation (that is, the genetic transformation of entire species). In his pre-1917 writings, Michurin considered Mendel's genetic laws a "metaphysical myth"; during most of the 1920's he took a more conciliatory attitude toward the ideas of modern genetics, but still avoided using them in his research.[43]

In 1908, when the *Messenger of Horticulture* noted the completion of Michurin's twentieth year of continuous experimental work, N. I. Vavilov was a second-year student at the Agricultural Academy in Moscow, the best school of its kind in Russia. Besides receiving a modern education in biology, young Vavilov learned to appreciate the profound significance of the growing conflict within the Darwinian tradition over the problem of heredity. Because of his outstanding abilities, the Academy retained him for postgraduate studies in artificial selection. In 1909 he read a paper on Darwinism and experimental morphology, and in 1912 he published one on the usefulness of genetics in agronomy. A government grant made it possible for Vavilov to work in several leading Western European laboratories. In England he made the acquaintance of William Bateson, who left a strong impression on him and reinforced his inclination to look for ways in which genetics could contribute to the taxonomy and evolutionary morphology of plants. In an ingenious study of the genetic basis for the immunity of certain cereals to fungous diseases, published in the British *Journal of Genetics* in 1914, Vavilov utilized a wide range of modern genetic knowledge.[44]

In 1916 Vavilov undertook fieldwork in Tadzhikistan and Persia—the first of many expeditions to various areas in search of a full classification of domestic grains and their wild cousins. The specimens collected on these expeditions, compared with information from the botanical literature, helped him develop a comprehensive theory of the origin and concentration of cultivated plants. In 1917 he published a small monograph on the origin of cultivated rye, one of the most widely distributed cereals. Carefully tracing the various stages in the biological history of rye from wild forms to the most recent cultivated varieties, he provided valuable techniques for studying the history of other Old World cereals, and established that Southeastern Asia was the original habitat of rye and wheat. In this study, he showed the usefulness of comparative linguistics in tracing the evolution and distribution of domestic plants. Vavilov's experimental work led him to formulate his law of homologous series. According to this law, related species or genera go through similar series of hereditary variations, and familiarity with the development of one species or genus makes it possible to predict the forms that will develop in related groups.[45]

Vavilov belonged to a growing group of Russian biologists who studied the transformation and variability of plant and animal species in terms of both external and internal influences. These men acknowledged the role of habitat in morphological and physiological changes, but they thought that the concept of natural selection was scientifically inadequate because it allowed for an infinite and unpredictable variability in living forms by making change dependent on random variations. They claimed that both the deeper regularities in biological evolution and the actual role of external influences could be meaningfully detected only by recognizing the importance of inherent, or "automatic," determinants of change. Vavilov, and others like him, implicitly rejected Timiriazev's charge that Mendelism and similar orientations sprang from a revived ideology of ultraconservatism, which was determined to stop the wheels of history and, in the case of Russia, to perpetuate antiquated political institutions. Vavilov's generation of scholars was unencumbered by the Nihilist philosophy of science that was so important to Timiriazev. Vavilov himself did not tamely follow any of the great masters of biology, but endeavored to develop new techniques for gathering empirical data and conducting experiments. He was convinced that the future of transformation studies was neither in the theory of the inheritance of acquired characteristics nor in Weismann's idea of the immortality of the "germ line," but in a balanced and advanced combination of the two views.

Although a full analysis of Vavilov's scientific work falls outside the scope of this book, it should not go unnoticed that he died a martyr—a victim of Stalin's and Lysenko's reliance on brute power to wipe out the scientific ideas that he advocated. Today, with Stalin dead and Lysenko dethroned, the Soviet Academy of Sciences has "rehabilitated" Vavilov and unhesitatingly named him "the pride of our nation."[46]

## MAJOR ORIENTATIONS

After Darwin, evolution became the most fundamental and comprehensive law of biology, for it unified paleontology, embryology, anatomy, cytology, and genetics. In Russia, as in the West, a few biologists sought to discredit Darwinism; but the vast majority tried to refine it and to find new applications for it as a conceptual tool of scientific inquiry. During the first two decades of the twentieth century, the Russian biologists concerned with various aspects of the Darwinian legacy fell into five broad categories.

The first group was represented chiefly by Timiriazev and Menzbir, who wrote extensively in defense of Darwinism as a scientific and philosophical idea but did little, if any, empirical research directly related to the law of evolution. They were essentially codifiers, and did not face the need for additional conceptual refinement and methodological precision in evolutionary studies. To them, Darwinism signified the triumph of the mechanistic view in biology. "The biology of the nineteenth century," said Menzbir, "accepted the idea that the phenomena of life could be fully explained in mechanistic terms and felt that the future progress of biology would only reinforce this conviction."[47] The advantage of the mechanistic approach, as seen by Menzbir, was in the proven effectiveness of its methodology and the simplicity and generality of its concepts. He stated: "We know the difference between motion in the inorganic world and motion in the organic world. But we also know that ever-present motion, from molecular motion to the motion of cosmic bodies, bestows structural unity upon the infinite diversity of natural phenomena."[48]

The second category was represented by a small group of biologists who dedicated their lives to an uncompromising attack on the theory of evolution. The unofficial leader of this orientation was A. A. Tikhomirov, a professor of zoology at Moscow University who had done creditable work in artificial parthenogenesis and its practical application in breeding silkworms. Echoing the views of N. Ia. Danilevskii, Tikhomirov claimed that Darwinism was not a scientific theory but a "pseudoscience," an ideological dogma that had succeeded primarily because of its sociological implications. In his lectures in general zoology, he concentrated on showing his students that Darwinism had no basis in facts;[49] and that it encouraged atheism and thus "blocked the paths leading to the truth."[50] At the end of the 1890's, when the Russian universities lost the last vestiges of autonomy, Tikhomirov was appointed rector of Moscow University; he held this post until 1904, when he was given a high position in the Ministry of National Education. He was so honored by the government not for his scientific achievements or academic reputation, but for his persistent campaigns against the scientific ideas most incompatible with autocratic ideology.

A few trained biologists joined Tikhomirov in his anti-Darwinian crusade; but most of his support did not come from biologists at all, but from a small number of theology professors who sought to deal with scientific themes. Their essays appeared in religious journals with a very limited circulation, and were generally ignored by the scientific community; nevertheless, these writers, unlike most of the earlier theological anti-Darwinists, purported to base their arguments on science itself. I. A. Chemen's *Darwinism: A Scientific Study of Darwin's Theory of the Origin of Man* (1892) was the first product of this approach. In this huge volume, reminiscent of Danilevskii's earlier study, the author presented a collection of excerpts from current writings on anthropology, anatomy, physiology, embryology, psychology, and even mathematics, all carefully selected to "prove" that many facts of the exact sciences directly contradicted Darwin's theory.[51] Later theological critics of Darwinism popularized various modern biological ideas that seemed to demand major revisions in Darwin's original theories. Some writers endorsed neo-Lamarckism, in which they saw a refutation of absolute causality (i.e., external determinism) in organic nature and an implicit recognition of universal teleology.[52] Others popularized Mendelian genetics, which they saw as a denial of the Darwinian view of man as a product of organic evolution.[53] But all of these theological writers, although they helped bring the ideas of such leading biologists as Kölliker, Nägeli, Weismann, De Vries, and Mendel to Russia, were generally careless with scientific information and were prone to rely heavily on sheer sophistry.

A third and very large group of Russian biologists did not concern themselves with the universal principles of Darwinian evolutionism, but worked on detailed ramifications of the evolutionary process as related to the specific problems of their own research. They wrote no general treatises or essays related to Darwinism, for their primary aim was to add new types of depth studies to the field of evolution. They made no general pronouncements about the theory of evolution; but they helped widen its empirical base, refine its methodology, and bring it into harmony with modern genetics.

The fourth category included those biologists who were concerned with both the general theory of evolution and concrete research. The most eminent representative of this group was A. N. Severtsov (a son of the Academician N. A. Severtsov, a nineteenth-century ecologist and naturalist-traveler). Severtsov lived well into the Soviet period, and was elected a member of the Soviet Academy of Sciences in 1920; but his reputation as a leading Russian evolutionist was established before 1917. His important empirical work, which eventually led him to reexamine the general principles of the theory of biological evolution, was in the morphological study of lower vertebrates. His studies of the evolution of the extremities of lower reptiles, the head of the Cyclostomata, and the nerve structure of fish gills convinced him that a study of the phylogenesis of individual organs was the safest path to understanding the phylogenesis of organisms, which would allow a fuller comprehension of evolution.

Severtsov showed that the phylogenesis of organisms was not a mechanical summation of the phylogeneses of specific organs, but a higher and more complicated level of integration. For example, in the evolution of any animal some organs change relatively rapidly and progressively, some change slowly, some change regressively and become atrophied, and some remain static.[54] All differential changes must be taken into consideration in a phylogenetic study of any existing species. Severtsov's research also extended to paleontology, evolutionary embryology, and genetics. In an effort to refine Ernst Haeckel's biogenetic law, he showed that all the descendants of a single being do not preserve the ancestral characteristics equally. Haeckel had assumed that new characteristics emerged only in grown organisms; but Severtsov hypothesized that new characteristics could in fact emerge at any stage of ontogenesis, thus bringing evolution closer to genetics.[55] In all of this Severtsov combined empirically supported generalizations with logically derived hypotheses.

Severtsov was, in a sense, the most complete evolutionist of the immediate pre-Soviet generation of Russian biologists. His work touched on most of the leading biological disciplines, and he carefully followed new theoretical and methodological developments in all the sciences concerned with evolution. Owing to the diversity of his interests, he reached many types of audiences. His popular speeches appealed to audiences who were theoretically unsophisticated but were eager to learn more of the Darwinian legacy. In general papers read before mixed groups of natural scientists, he concentrated on the complex intertwining of processes and conditions that explain the evolution of living nature. His detailed morphological studies, written with the utmost technical competence and scientific involvement, reached only a small group of specialists in evolutionary morphology.

The plant physiologist Vladimir Palladin was another Russian who combined the general and the specific in his studies of evolution. He cast his meticulous research in plant respiration in Darwinian terms, but he also acknowledged that Darwinism required more elaboration and a wider theoretical base. To Darwin's theory that the origin of species is linked with the structure of various organs he added the notion that the chemical composition of cells and the products of metabolism must also be considered. Palladin admitted that environmental conditions, particularly the struggle for existence, could change both the structure of organisms and the chemistry of their cells, but he added that many physiological phenomena (for example those related to "growth and enlargement") were determined not only by external conditions but also by heredity.[56]

In addition to Severtsov and Palladin, this fourth group of Russian evolutionists included many younger biologists, who were especially interested in reconciling the Darwinian theory of evolution with modern genetics. A large group of these men, including N. I. Vavilov, were associated with the Bureau of Applied Botany, a subsidiary of the Scientific Committee of the Central Administration of Land Tenure and Agriculture. Though founded in 1894, the Bureau only began to pursue organized research in 1908, when R. E. Regel' was appointed its director. In 1910, an entire issue of the Bureau's *Proceedings* was devoted to a Russian translation of Mendel's *Experiments in Plant Hybridization*.

Speaking for his group, Regel' emphasized that the struggle for existence is only a secondary factor in the emergence of new species and varieties, heterogenesis being the primary factor. Evolution does not consist of gradual modifications caused by the adaptations of organisms to external influences, but of sudden changes caused by new combinations of the internal carriers of heredity. The struggle for existence is actually a conservative force in nature, for it preserves the most adaptable forms of life, which are produced by advantageous combinations of "immutable hereditary factors." Another writer thought that whereas Darwin had explained how new species could emerge, Mendel had shown how they actually did emerge.[57] As geneticists, Regel' and his associates thought that they could not change the actual "hereditary factors" of cereal varieties; however, they organized their practical research in accord with the notion that they could produce better varieties of cereals by effecting superior combinations of these factors.[58]

The fifth and last category of evolutionists included the many biologists who did not engage in a direct study of evolution on either an empirical or a philosophical level, but who placed their investigations within an evolutionary framework. Although these scholars seldom mentioned Darwin and evolution, their scientific contributions can be fully appreciated only in the context of the Darwinian tradition. The most eminent representative of this group was I. P. Pavlov, whose empirical studies tacitly recognized evolution as the basic law of living forms and backed this idea with new evidence. Pavlov's physiological studies, from his study of the mechanisms regulating blood vessels to his analysis of the adaptive importance of conditioned reflexes, acquire a much greater meaning when viewed as a part of the Darwinian tradition. Pavlov made it clear that in his opinion, "Charles Darwin must justly be considered the founder of the modern comparative method in the study of the higher [nervous] activities of animals."[59]

Despite its strong environmentalist bent, Russian Darwinism was very sensitive to developments in the West, and rapidly accepted new theoretical ideas, research procedures, and areas of inquiry. Moreover, it produced many original scholars who contributed new data and ideas of their own. Russian biologists were remarkably consistent in viewing biological evolution as a two-pronged process—a process in time and a process in space. The evolutionary idea was firmly anchored in a strong national interest in ecology, zoogeography, and phytogeography. The impact of Mendelism in Russia was to modify, rather than uproot, this tradition. Directly or indirectly, every major Russian research biologist during the first two decades of the twentieth century sought to find a workable compromise between Mendelism and Lamarckism. N. I. Vavilov spoke for most Russian geneticists when he endorsed T. H. Morgan's view that although "natural selection does not play the role of a creative principle in evolution," Darwin's theory performed "an immense service in pointing out where to look for the materials on which a scientific theory of evolution must depend."[60]

The leaders of various libertarian ideologies were hesitant to accept Darwin's "struggle for survival" as a prime mover of biological evolution. N. K. Mikhailovskii, the progenitor and chief architect of Populism, saw cooperation rather than competition as the most universal source of change. Similarly, Petr Kropotkin regarded "mutual aid," not the struggle for survival, as the fundamental principle of history. Chernyshevskii bitterly resented all efforts to transform the negative inferences drawn from the Malthusian law into a positive law of progressive evolution.[61] M. A. Antonovich claimed that the imputation of a Malthusian bias to Darwin's theory was totally unwarranted. According to him, the theory of Malthus and the theory of Darwin were two completely different things, and any connections between the two were purely external: Malthus's theory dealt with certain artificial conditions of human society, whereas Darwin's theory dealt with the natural conditions of the entire living world. "Economic statistics" could refute Malthus's theory, but not Darwin's.[62] The Russian Marxists, in particular, viewed the struggle for survival as a law of both biological and social development. In the words of Plekhanov: "The investigation of Marx begins precisely where the investigation of Darwin ends.... Marxism is Darwinism in its application to the social sciences."[63]

## CHAPTER TEN

# The Triumphs of Experimental Biology

### IVAN PETROVICH PAVLOV AND NEUROPHYSIOLOGY

Among the leading Russian scientists of the nineteenth century, three men —the mathematician Nikolai Lobachevskii, the chemist Dmitrii Mendeleev, and the physiologist Ivan Pavlov—stand out by the particular greatness of their accomplishments and the broad scope of their influence. Of the three, Pavlov is by far the best known in the West, partly because of the broader scope of his scientific contributions and partly because of the wider popular appeal of his ideas. Lobachevskii's masterly logic was employed in a field so abstract as to be for a long time ignored by experts, let alone educated laymen. Mendeleev's periodic law of elements was easier to grasp and appreciate, but its intricacies appealed to very few people outside the world of scientific scholarship. Pavlov, however, dealt with the processes of life itself, and his work was always very close to the eternal questions that puzzle the scientifically uninitiated as much as they challenge the professional.

Lobachevskii, Pavlov, and Mendeleev also differed in their intellectual approaches to science. Lobachevskii's thinking had no empirical base, and his non-Euclidean geometry was a grand, abstract deduction. Mendeleev carefully sifted all the empirical evidence of contemporary chemistry to find a general pattern in the distribution of chemical elements; his periodic law, however, was partly an empirical generalization and partly a grand hypothesis that waited ten years for experimental verification. Pavlov's approach was quite different. All of his generalizations and theories were directly tied to evidence that he himself had obtained; and his two greatest abilities as a scientist were designing experiments and recognizing the general patterns in the data that resulted.

The simplicity of Pavlov's generalizations, the clarity and skillfulness of his experiments, and the universal appeal of the scientific problems with which he wrestled all made his name familiar to educated people all over the world. His papers were feature attractions at the international meetings of physiologists; and for the first time Western scholars began to visit Russia in search of new scientific ideas and methodological devices in the life sciences. Pavlov's enemies actually helped carry his name even further, for no psychological school, whatever its bias, could afford to ignore his ideas. To some, Pavlov's theories provided the base for a sound study of the human mind; to others they were a crippling obstruction derived from crude materialism. Idealistic philosophers, who were building new metaphysical systems based on the primacy of ideas, saw in Pavlov a foe who must not go unchallenged. And as social psychology gradually passed from a biological (or instinctual) to a sociological orientation, Pavlov provided a barrier that had to be overcome.*

In spite of his worldwide influence, Pavlov's scientific concerns were by no means enormous in scope. His chosen field was physiology, and he preferred intensive research in a relatively small number of fields within this discipline to extensive research in a large number of unrelated fields. However, the laboratory techniques and basic theories that he worked out from his limited areas of research were applicable to an enormous range of physiological and biological studies. During his long academic career, Pavlov concentrated all his efforts on three areas of physiological research: the cardiovascular system, the digestive system, and the central nervous system. Westerners are most familiar with his work on the last of these; and indeed, he is often thought of as a psychologist. However, his Nobel Prize did not come from his study of conditioned reflexes, but from his work on the digestive system.

Ivan Pavlov lived in three eras.[1] He was born in feudal Russia in 1849, at the time when Nicholas I had enacted a series of oppressive measures to neutralize the social and intellectual forces that threatened autocracy, aristocratic rule, and the institution of serfdom. He was educated and reached the peak of scholarly achievement in a post-Emancipation Russia dominated by reformist ideologies, a painful groping for technological modernization, and a mounting political turmoil. And he ended his unusually long scholarly career nineteen years after the October Revolution. When Pavlov was born, physiology had not yet made its way into the curriculum of Russian universities. By the mid-1860's, when he enrolled in Riazan theological school, physiology was a respectable academic disci-

---

* The sociologist Max Scheler solved the problem by regarding conditioned reflexes as the highest level of animal behavior, but not as the raw material out of which human behavior was built. Hence he interpreted them as a dividing line between man and beast.

pline, thanks mostly to Sechenov's influential studies. It was also a source of vital topics for public discussion; and the Nihilists, led by Pisarev and Antonovich, made it a cornerstone of their philosophy.

The libertarian spirit of the Reform era made deep inroads into theological schools, and Riazan was no exception. Feeling the staggering inadequacies of the official curriculum in light of the pressing intellectual needs of modern Russia, the theology students turned to secular writings that were dominated by a mixture of positivism and materialism. All these writings emphasized the modern scientific world view, but Pavlov and his friends were not impressed so much with the "scientific facts" presented as they were with the social and cultural possibilities of science. Physiology, especially as it related to psychology, was especially popular, and G. H. Lewes's *Physiology of Common Life* found more appreciative readers and exercised a more profound influence in Russia than in any Western European country. For a long time Pavlov could repeat long sections from this unusual book verbatim. It was most probably from Lewes that he learned that no physiological work can be successful without a study of the organism in as undisturbed a state as possible.[2]

In 1870 Pavlov entered St. Petersburg University, and in his third year he selected physiology as his major academic field. He graduated in 1875; in the same year, together with a colleague, he published his first physiological study, a report on the nervous conditioning of pancreatic functions. This work was routine, but it showed promise, and Pavlov's professors encouraged him to continue in scientific work. He immediately enrolled in the St. Petersburg Medical and Surgical Academy, determined to acquire a doctorate and a university position. For some time, his specialty and status were not clearly defined, and he was tossed from one adviser to another.

From 1876 to 1878, Pavlov worked as an assistant in the Academy's Veterinary Institute, where he was allowed to conduct some research of his own. It was here that he began to study the physiology of blood circulation. A summer spent in the laboratory of R. Heidenhain at Breslau University attracted his attention to the complex experimental problems of studying the physiology of digestion, but until 1888 his research was centered on cardiovascular problems. Throughout most of this period, Pavlov still had no clearly defined professional status, and most of the time he worked on research projects assigned to him by superiors.

In 1878, S. P. Botkin, an eminent professor at the Medical Academy, asked Pavlov to head a special laboratory set up to study the effects of various medicines on the heart. The laboratory was poorly equipped, but it gave Pavlov an opportunity to develop his outstanding organizational skills. Here he learned to organize collective research, to guide the students in their laboratory preparations for higher degrees, and to develop close working relations with others in his field. In particular, Pavlov learned a great deal from his superior Botkin, who was one of the pioneers of modern medicine in Russia. Botkin was firmly convinced that hospitals, clinics, and research laboratories were inseparable parts in an institutional structure that linked the modern life sciences with practical medicine. Pavlov adopted this view wholeheartedly, and all of his later research was directly concerned with the practical problems of medicine. He never aspired to be a physician, but dedicated his life to strengthening medicine's scientific foundations.

Pavlov identified science with scientific methodology, and scientific methodology with experiment. He gave very little thought to the ontological and epistemological foundations of modern physiology, which had been emphasized by such leading spokesmen of modern science as Hermann Helmholtz and Claude Bernard. The crux of Pavlov's scientific philosophy lay in one of his own remarks: "The more complex a phenomenon is—and what is more complex than life?—the more indispensable is an experiment." His special interest in physiology was the study of the nerve links that produce functional unity in organisms. Most of his contemporaries, interested in the chemistry of individual organs, relied on vivisection as a research technique; but Pavlov, investigating the dependence of individual organs on the nervous system, needed more complex methods. For the "analytical method" of the vivisectionists, he substituted the "synthetic method." His own explanation of the problem is dramatic and lucid:

"It has become abundantly clear that the usual simple cutting of an animal, the so-called acute test, is a source of many errors. The crude damage done to the organism creates many inhibitory influences that hamper the functioning of various organs. By its own nature, the organism as a whole— as an enormous system of component parts linked together in a delicate and purposive fashion—cannot remain indifferent to forces that threaten to destroy it. In its own interest, the organism must strengthen some functions and restrain others, temporarily abandoning some activities to concentrate on others that can yet be salvaged. This circumstance was formerly, and still is, a serious hindrance to the efforts of analytical physiology; but it creates an insurmountable obstacle to the development of synthetic physiology, which requires a precise determination of physiological processes in whole, normal organisms. Operative techniques, as methods of physiological research, have not yet been fully exploited; indeed, they have only now begun their development."[3]

Since there were no surgical techniques for synthetic physiology, Pavlov set out to develop them, and did so with great success. He combined a pair of steady hands with initiative, foresight, a fertile imagination, and unmatched perseverance. He was a leading pioneer in the application of antiseptic and aseptic surgical methods in physiology—techniques that enabled scientists to study the internal organs of animals without radically disturbing their normal functioning. His successes in making permanent artificial fistulae in the pancreas, in "sham feeding" dogs to obtain pure gastric juice, and in creating an artificial "small stomach" in dogs by surgery are all experimental feats that paved the way for modern laboratory research in physiology. This interest in experimental methods stayed with Pavlov for the rest of his life, and it is perhaps his most distinctive characteristic as a scientist.

During the 1880's Pavlov's work moved slowly. His salary was negligible and his position in the Medical and Surgical Academy (renamed the Military Medical Academy in 1881) was very insecure. He continued to spend much time on the routine laboratory tests demanded by his superiors. In 1883, however, he completed his doctoral dissertation, which dealt with the centrifugal nerves of the heart. Pavlov divided these nerves into four functionally differentiated categories, depending on whether they inhibited, weakened, accelerated, or augmented the contractions of the heart. His major contribution was the discovery of the accelerator nerve, which subsequently became the focus of a neurophysiological subdiscipline concerned with trophic innervation. The completion of the dissertation did not bring Pavlov what he wanted most of all: access to a laboratory in which he could freely conduct his own experimental work. However, he was immediately appointed a private docent and was given a stipend that allowed him to spend two years (1884–86) in two leading Western laboratories: the laboratory of R. Heidenhain in Breslau, where complex experimental work in the physiology of secretory processes was under way; and the laboratory of Karl Ludwig in Leipzig, known at the time for its work in heart innervation.

Pavlov chose to make a long sojourn in the West not only to avail himself of modern laboratory facilities, but also to demonstrate his experimental skills and achievements to Western physiologists. When he finally returned to Russia, he resumed his experimental work in the physiology of digestive processes at an intensive pace. In 1888, he charted the secretory nerves of the pancreas, and a year later he published the results of his experiments with "sham feeding" in dogs.* Besides opening new possibilities in physiological research techniques, these experiments reinforced Pavlov's conviction that the functioning of the digestive glands was regulated by a reflex mechanism.

In 1889–90 Pavlov applied for both the vacant chair in physiology at St. Petersburg University and the vacant chair in pharmacology at Tomsk University; but both institutions bypassed him, even though his successful experiments with sham feeding had made a great impression on the Russian scientific community. St. Petersburg selected N. E. Vvedenskii, an established physiologist with modern ideas. Tomsk University, owing to last-minute interference by the Ministry of National Education, selected V. N. Velikii, whose scholarly achievements were no match for Pavlov's but who had less radical ideas about the relation of physiology to psychology. The official ideologues, who had some support from scientists, favored the scholars who tied physiology to chemistry over those who tried to link it with psychology. To the state, the burgeoning neovitalism in physiology was far preferable to I. M. Sechenov's reflex theory, which was deeply ingrained in Pavlov's thought. At this time, the controversy did not receive a public hearing, for the views of the antagonists were not yet crystallized. The radical journal *Physician*, however, condemned the injustice done to Pavlov, and gave the first public notice of the rising appreciation of Pavlov's scientific achievements among his professional peers.

Fortunately, Pavlov's setbacks on the academic market were only temporary. Before the fateful year of 1890 was over, he received three offers: to teach physiology at Warsaw University, to head pharmacological studies at the Military Medical Academy, and to organize and head the physiological laboratory of the newly founded Institute of Experimental Medicine in St. Petersburg. He chose to accept the two positions in the capital, and occupied them for the remaining 46 years of his life.

The Institute of Experimental Medicine was founded by Prince A. P. Ol'denburgskii to give Russia "an advanced scientific-medical institution of an academic type."[4] Its primary purpose was to study the "most direct

---

* Sham feeding, as described by B. P. Babkin (p. 131), was performed on dogs who had undergone esophagotomy (surgical removal of part of the gullet) and had also been given an artificial gastric fistula. "The dogs were fed raw minced meat, which, because of the esophagotomy, fell out of the upper end of the gullet into a dish. The animal bent its head, took the same meat in its mouth and swallowed, and again the meat fell into the dish. . . . By this method of 'sham feeding' a large quantity of gastric juice could be collected from an empty stomach, and the juice so obtained was uncontaminated with saliva or food."

causes" of common contagious diseases of men and animals and to search for scientific means of combating them; in particular, it was expected to help in the growing fight against cholera, plague, and the other epidemic diseases that periodically afflicted the country. The Institute maintained its own staff of experts in physiology, pathological anatomy, epizootic diseases, and syphilology, and also opened its doors to visiting scholars who needed its extensive laboratories to pursue specific problems.[5]

As the head of the Institute's physiological section, Pavlov was finally able to choose his own research topics and associates. During the next ten years, he devoted the modern facilities of the new laboratory to a single purpose: the study of the nervous mechanisms controlling the digestive glands. The partial results of this work provided the substance for Pavlov's *Lectures on the Work of Digestive Glands* (1897), which was quickly translated into German, French, and English. The book was a magnificent summary of Pavlov's experimental techniques, and it emphasized his belief that the preservation of normal and complete functioning in organisms under study must be the guiding principle in physiological experiments. The *Lectures* contributed greatly to Pavlov's reputation, and in 1904 it won him a Nobel Prize. His laboratory now attracted many Western scientists, who appreciated the great challenge of the new neurophysiological ideas and the efficacy of the new experimental techniques.

The *Lectures* well deserved all this attention. Before Pavlov's work, the study of digestion had been one of the weakest branches of physiology. Only a few scholars had studied it, and they had two major failings: their approach was usually too abstract and deductive; and their experimental methods, usually vivisection, were inaccurate and unreliable. Pavlov, however, firmly believed that the advance of physiology depended most heavily on inductive methods, which should be applied to phenomena in their normal, or near-normal, state.[6] Philosophically and operationally, he felt, the method of inquiry was the essence of science. In studying the physiology of digestion, it had been necessary to build a new experimental methodology that would satisfy Pavlov's ambitious goals.

*Lectures on the Work of Digestive Glands* presented the details of numerous surgical methods devised in the Institute of Experimental Medicine, including the formation of pancreatic fistulae, gastric fistulae, and miniature stomachs. Each experiment concentrated on a specific problem; but all of them together unveiled what Pavlov considered the basic regularities in the functions of digestive glands. The book also discussed the sequences of digestive processes, the nature of fermentation processes, and the distinct roles of nervous and chemical factors in digestion. According to one of Pavlov's students: "After 1898, when the German translation of Pavlov's book appeared, every physiologist and medical man based his study of the normal and abnormal physiology of the alimentary canal on Pavlov's *Lectures*."[7]

At the Institute of Experimental Medicine Pavlov was engaged exclusively in research. At the Military Medical Academy, however, he lectured in pharmacology and helped selected graduate students with their doctoral dissertations. His students were mostly practical military physicians, who had little interest in studying the relationship of physiology to modern medicine. Pavlov himself had developed a profound appreciation of the scientific foundations of medicine, and he attempted to awaken a similar awareness in his students. He viewed pharmacology as part of experimental physiology, and foresaw a great future for it as a bridge between the practical work of the physician and the theoretical inquiry of the physiologist. As an example, he pointed out the usefulness of a pharmacological study of the role of chemical substances in animal organisms. Pavlov made these efforts to raise the scientific level of medicine at the time when Russian physicians, gathered in the Pirogov Society, were working with unprecedented devotion to raise medicine's social standards and obligations.

In 1893 Pavlov was elected vice-president of the St. Petersburg Society of Russian Physicians, and soon afterwards he became its president. The Society had long been the most influential of the many Russian medical associations, and its meetings and publications played an important role in spreading Pavlov's ideas. During the 21 years of his association with the Society, Pavlov read 35 papers and his students read 120; many of these were printed in the Society's journals.[8]

Because of his boundless energy and his deep sense of balance, consistency, and precise organization, Pavlov encountered no difficulty in coordinating his simultaneous association with a research institute, a school of higher education, and a learned society. By his own successes, he showed the advantages of a close relationship between the different types of institutions directly involved in the advancement and diffusion of scientific knowledge. Moreover, this triple affiliation not only enriched Pavlov's social life but also kept it closely tied to the scientific community.

Pavlov's experimental study of the nervous mechanism of digestion gradually led him to a new area of basic research: the nervous mechanisms of animal behavior and the apparatus of conditioned reflexes. Pavlov and his associates observed that laboratory dogs produced saliva at the mere sight of food; apparently their salivary glands responded to "psychical" excitation as well as physiological excitation. And if there was such "psychical" excitation, it was necessary to explain the relationship of the dog's secretion of saliva to his experience. After 1900, the question of acquired (or conditioned) reflexes gradually came to dominate Pavlov's research.

In Pavlov's opinion, the differences between innate and conditioned reflexes are not fundamental: both are initiated by stimulations of the peripheral nerve endings; both involve the central nervous system; and both produce physiological effects. However, conditioned reflexes are distinguished from innate reflexes by their extreme instability and temporary existence. Also, the nerve impulses of conditioned reflexes, unlike those of innate reflexes, pass through the cerebral cortex.[9]

In studying psychology, Pavlov long debated which way to turn: should he accept the dualism of the physiological and the psychical, a view prevalent in academic psychology, or accept a monistic view and regard physiology as paramount? The strong Russian tradition in neurophysiology and "reflexology," together with his own research experience and philosophical inclinations, finally led him to choose the second approach. He undertook to find a single basic psychical phenomenon that could also be studied as a purely physiological phenomenon. By objectively studying the development of this one phenomenon, he felt, one could build up a physiological description of the higher nervous activities of animals. Conditioned reflexes were the basic phenomenon that Pavlov finally selected. Speaking at the International Medical Congress in Madrid in 1903, he made his position clear:

"Objective investigation alone will gradually bring us to a complete analysis of the infinite adaptability that constitutes life on earth. Are not the movements of plants toward light and the seeking of truth through mathematical analysis essentially phenomena of one and the same order? Are they not the last links of an almost endless chain of adaptation taking place throughout the living world?

"We can analyze adaptation in its most elementary forms on the basis of objective facts. Is there any reason to change this method in studying adaptability in its higher forms? ... Guided by the similarity or identity of external manifestations, science will sooner or later apply the objective facts to our subjective world, and will thereby shed a bright light on our mysterious nature. ... The vital phenomena that men term 'psychical,'—

even though they can be objectively observed in animals—are only distinguished from purely physiological phenomena by degree of complexity."[10]

Pavlov steadfastly denied that the psychology of his time was based on objective methods, and dismissed it summarily as a system of subjective, introspective knowledge. "In thirteen years of research," he stated in 1914, "I have never had any success with psychological concepts. The [study] of the animal brain must not for a single moment leave the ground of natural science, which every day proves its absolute solidity and extreme usefulness. We can rest assured that in following the strictly physiological interpretation of the animal brain, astonishing discoveries await science, together with extraordinary power over the higher nervous system—discoveries and power not a whit inferior to other achievements of natural science."[11]

In rejecting psychology Pavlov was undoubtedly influenced by his negative attitude toward the metaphysical and idealistic leanings that dominated Russian academic psychology during the last two decades of the tsarist era. Some academics preached "psychology without metaphysics," as did A. I. Vvedenskii at St. Petersburg University; and others, notably G. I. Chelpanov at Moscow University, used "experimental introspection." Most academic psychologists used their discipline to support the official ideological crusade against the underlying materialism of modern experimental psychology, which was regarded as one more form of attack on the most sacred values of the established political order.

Although Pavlov's ontological views were radically different from those of his contemporary Sigmund Freud, the two men had the same attitude toward studying the human mind. Both believed that animal and human behavior could be reduced to basic regularities expressing a constant pull toward a dynamic balancing and coordination of the internal and external conditions of life. Both endeavored to eliminate the capricious and the undetermined from the basic structure of behavior. Both viewed behavior as a structured whole, and contributed to the downfall of associationist psychology and the mechanistic orientation in the life sciences.

For the last 33 years of his life, Pavlov worked to create an experimental basis for his theory of conditioned reflexes and to formulate physiological laws of animal and human behavior. Few scientists of his time would say that he had found satisfactory answers to many of his basic questions, but few would deny that he had raised multitudes of delicate questions whose answers required close cooperation between neurophysiology and the experimental psychology of learning. Together with E. L. Thorndike, he made a major contribution to the separation of psychology from philosophy and to the turning of several vital branches of psychology in the direction of experimental methodology.

As Pavlov's laboratory facilities expanded and the number of his research associates increased, he was able to explore more and more aspects of conditioned reflexes. His laboratories studied regularities in the formation and ontogenetic development of conditioned reflexes, the pharmacological aspects of chemicals that stimulated these reflexes, and the role of various areas in the cerebral cortex in forming conditioned reflexes and regulating external and internal inhibition. In all these experiments, Pavlov saw a hope of solving the eternal problems of the epistemological nature of "time" and the ethical nature of "freedom" by a solidly scientific approach. The expansion of research went hand in hand with the refinement of methodology and scientific nomenclature. In a deliberate effort to avoid psychological terminology, Pavlov applied original labels to the concepts that he developed to organize the data obtained from his research. Such concepts as "analyzers," the "concentration" and "irradiation" of inhibition or excitation, "internal" and "external" inhibition, and many categorizations of conditioned reflexes helped unify his research on both the empirical and the theoretical level.

Pavlov had become an established scholar at the time when the life sciences were the main battlefield in the war between neovitalism, which expounded a teleological point of view going back to Aristotle, and the mechanistic view, which divided nature into intertwined systems of causal relationships. Neo-Darwinism and anti-Darwinism flourished. From 1895 to 1910, both popular and scientific journals printed scores of articles dealing with the philosophical aspects of genetics, the mutation theory, neo-Lamarckism, Bergson's "creative evolution," and many other challenging ideas. Pavlov was alert to these influences, and found it necessary to develop or adopt a number of basic ideas that could guide his scientific work and define his philosophy of science. From the various conflicting orientations, he selected the ideas most closely expressing his own philosophy of science. This philosophy did not deal with either the ethical relevance of science or the place of science in a broader cultural context; it was concerned primarily with the general patterns of scientific explanation and the comprehensive organization of scientific knowledge.

Science, according to Pavlov, is systematized knowledge of the external world—an objective method of human thought and a practical technique with which man subdues nature and exploits its resources. Pavlov had great faith in the power of science; but he was well aware of its limitations, and did not deny the value of nonscientific modes of inquiry. To him, for example, science and religion were not mutually exclusive, and the expanding horizons of science did not encroach on the domain of religion. He often attended church services to enjoy the pageantry of the Orthodox liturgy and to revive the pleasant experiences of his youth.

Pavlov viewed philosophy and science as complementary: the goal of philosophy is to unveil the essence of natural phenomena; the goal of science is to understand the functioning of the mechanisms through which nature works. In examining the human brain, for example, science is not concerned with the ontological essence of the "psychical" and the "physiological," but with the functions of the cerebral cortex that are related to specific phases of consciousness. The scientist does not ask how the "matter" of the brain produces various states of consciousness, but how the brain actually functions in different situations of conscious life.[12] Pavlov made no effort to reduce all psychical phenomena to physiological actions, even though his interest centered on establishing the physiological processes underlying given psychological phenomena.

Scientific knowledge, as seen by Pavlov, is relative—that is, limited in its compass—but it is absolute in its reflection of external reality. "Natural science is the work of the human intellect as it investigates nature without leaning on interpretations and ideas derived from any sources other than external nature."[13] The scientist does not add to or subtract from nature; his job is to see nature in its absolute reality. Pavlov did not entirely rid his scientific thinking of a deeply seated mechanistic bias, and he had no use for the subjectivistic theories of scientific knowledge that were in full bloom at the time he began to study the physiology of the cerebral cortex.

Pavlov was always quick to criticize "animism," "subjectivism," and other forms of "idealism," but he never proclaimed himself a materialist. However, he did stay within the framework of classical materialism in two respects: he was convinced that mental activities were essentially adaptations of organisms to the external world, and that scientific knowledge was a direct reflection of this same external world. This "materialism" did not stem from an articulated philosophical view, but from Pavlov's professional concentration on the material bases of animal behavior.

Pavlov was convinced that a physiological investigation of the cerebral cortex was the only truly scientific way to study human and animal behavior; as a result, he was unable to realize that many of the nonphysiological branches of psychology were quite capable of being developed on a scientific basis. This oversight has given Pavlov the reputation of being a much more thoroughgoing materialist than he really was. He may have operated from the vantage point of a materialistic ontology, but he abandoned two cardinal principles of the mechanistic orientation in natural science: he rejected atomism in favor of a distinctly holistic view of nature, and he went beyond causal determinism to recognize the role of purposiveness in nature.

Pavlov's holistic orientation was embedded in the idea of "nervism," which he had inherited from S. P. Botkin. Whereas the "physicochemical" approach in physiology, dominant from 1850 to 1900, concentrated on the physics and chemistry of individual organs and was essentially analytical, the "nervistic" approach concentrated on the nervous integration of an entire organism and was essentially synthetic. The great German pathologist Rudolf Virchow had contended that a certain "sovereignty" existed not only in individual organs, but even in individual cells. Pavlov thought otherwise: "We must understand not only the function of every organ, but also the mechanisms through which the totality of all organs acts as a single harmoniously functioning unit."[14] He also agreed with Claude Bernard, who had identified an "organic harmony" that gave unity to all living beings and went far beyond rigorously determined physicochemical conditions. Pavlov called the field of his scientific endeavor "organ physiology"—in contrast to "cell physiology"—and expressed the hope that future investigations would fully reveal the interrelations among the component parts of individual systems of organs (such as the digestive system), and between these systems and external nature.[15]

Pavlov first advanced the holistic idea of neurophysiological research in his doctoral dissertation on the centrifugal nerves of the heart, and he continued to follow it in his later investigations of the digestive glands and the cerebral cortex. He emphasized repeatedly that his studies dealt with "whole" dogs, that is, healthy dogs uninfected by either disease or narcotics. Antiseptic and aseptic surgery was the major research technique used to meet the standard imposed by the holistic philosophy.

Perhaps because of his holistic views, Pavlov acknowledged that he looked at neurophysiological processes not only in terms of direct causes but also in the light of a general purposiveness existing in nature (*causa finalis*). He was careful, however, to make it clear that this idea of purposiveness was only a heuristic concept, and that it had nothing in common with teleological metaphysics. As such, it bore the same meaning as "gestalt" in psychology, "structure" in modern chemistry and biology, and "configuration" or "pattern" in cultural anthropology. The idea of purposiveness gave Pavlov new scientific insights and suggested research possibilities that might have been totally overlooked within the confines of specialized experimentation in the laboratory.

The complex, antivitalistic nature of Pavlov's views on the purposiveness of natural systems is best explained by himself:

"The functioning of a digestive gland, or of any other organ, falls into two distinct categories: continuous and normal functioning, and functioning under irregular and artificial conditions. The study of the latter conditions ... produces information that may help in the future search for the general characteristics of living substances. But knowledge of functioning under normal conditions explains the relations of the given organism with the external world, or the bonds between the component parts of the organism, i.e., it helps us to study questions related to the internal and external equilibrium of the organism. This, in essence, is the most pressing and fundamental task in the study of ... higher living organisms. It is clear that an equilibrium in the interaction of component organs and in relations with the external world is the basic condition for the survival of the complex forms of life.... This is the most general law pertaining to organisms. The constant striving for the preservation of this equilibrium can be viewed either as an adaptation, if it is regarded from the vantage point of the Darwinian theory, or as purposiveness, if we look at the organism in general from a subjective, anthropomorphic point of view. We should not object to these labels, which are only provisional, until we can arrive at more objective terms.

"The idea of adaptation or purposiveness, in the context just stated, serves as an inexhaustible source of scientific propositions ... and provides a powerful stimulus for a further study of the essential questions of life. But if the same idea is placed in a purely theoretical context, it quickly enters the domain of groundless fantasy. The exaggerations of the *Naturphilosophie*, and of some philosophically oriented contemporary biologists who apply purposiveness literally to physiology, have turned the scientific community against the idea of purposiveness—a prejudice that has recently been losing ground. However, the objectivists are still prone to regard the concept of purposiveness as an indication of teleological thinking, even when it designates pragmatically established relations. Also, since the idea of an organism as a whole system is inadequately rooted in physiology, such labels as 'adaptation' and 'purposiveness' bear a subjectivist taint, and all newly discovered cases of adaptation are often viewed as something unexpected and irregular, even though they may actually be nothing else but an essential property of the complex apparatus of the organism."[16]

Actually, Pavlov used the principle of purposiveness to break experimental research into two phases. The first phase consisted of a rigidly empirical experimental analysis; the second phase, guided by the notion of purposiveness, consisted of a detailed experimental demonstration of the ways in which the established functioning of a specific organ added to the equilibrium of the total organism. In both phases, said Pavlov, the scientist should work strictly in the laboratory. However, in the second phase he would be searching for an integrated picture of life—for a fuller understanding of the structure of life. Most important, this knowledge of the structure of life was used not to back up an ontological commitment, but as a methodological device to open important new paths for experimental research. Pavlov sought this new methodology of biological synthesis at a time when most physiologists were either confining their ideas to a physicochemical analysis of the phenomena of life or responding to the lures of revived vitalism.

In 1932, toward the end of his career, Pavlov refined his ideas on the complex nature of scientific inquiry. "The theory of reflex activity finds its support in three fundamental principles of exact scientific investigation: in the first place, the principle of *determinism*, i.e., an impulse, appropriate conditions, or a cause for every given action or effect; secondly, the principle of *analysis and synthesis*, i.e., the initial decomposition of the whole into its parts or units, and then the gradual reconstruction of the whole from these units or elements; finally, in the third place, the principle of *structure*, i.e., the distribution of the activity of force in space, the adaptation of function to structure."[17]

More by his deeds than by his utterances, Pavlov rejected the notion of the intellectual supremacy of science, as championed by Kliment Timiriazev; like Vladimir Vernadskii, Dmitrii Mendeleev, and most other leading Russian scientists, he worked to develop his own scientific discipline without slipping into the narrow confines of scientism, which denigrated all nonscientific sources of human wisdom. Although science, according to Pavlov, does not answer all the questions of nature and human existence, it is a powerful intellectual challenge and requires one's continued labor and undivided attention. Pavlov attracted many promising young scholars who were ready to abandon the Nihilist fusion of science with ideology and to limit science to the rigorous procedures of laboratory research techniques.

Pavlov's genius asserted itself both in the realm of ideas and in the concrete techniques of laboratory work. At the time of a profound crisis in physics, which deeply affected every natural science, he followed a course of moderation, combining mechanistic and structuralist views. In the words of one of his eminent contemporaries, Pavlov managed to join a strictly mechanistic, or Cartesian, view of "spatial ties" in natural phenomena with a decidedly historical view of "temporal ties."[18] All of these things made his views attractive to younger scholars searching for a philosophical vantage point that would not stand in the way of experimental research and would not disrupt the steady growth of biological thought.

The beginning of Pavlov's study of conditioned reflexes was also the beginning of the Pavlovian school in neurophysiology. In addition to his other abilities, Pavlov was an excellent teacher, always ready to illustrate his lectures with intricate experiments. Moreover, his laboratory in the Institute of Experimental Medicine was one of the most modern in Russia. For these reasons, the brightest and most promising students of physiology were eager to work under his supervision. He devoted much attention to graduate students, and spared no time in helping them set up the minutest details of their experiments. The relationship was one of intellectual symbiosis—a continuous exchange of ideas in search of new knowledge and new research techniques. In arguments with individual students who had proved their ability, Pavlov tended to cling tenaciously to his own ideas; but he often ended by reconsidering all the details of the dispute in private and, if necessary, retrenching or revising his views. His students produced a stream of criticism that helped him refine his theoretical and experimental ideas, and they also helped to open new avenues of research and to meet the challenges coming from physiologists of other orientations.

The power of Pavlov's profound personal influence on his students is depicted by L. A. Orbeli, one of his most eminent disciples: "Ivan Petrovich literally lived in the laboratory, and all his intellectual activity took place before the eyes of associates. Overt thinking was the most unique feature of his work. He did not hide his thoughts until they were ready for publication, but shared them as they occurred, giving his associates a chance to follow up all the ramifications of his ideas immediately.... This was the source of his greatest personal charm and a main factor in his influence on his co-workers."[19]

Pavlov's receipt of a Nobel Prize and the immediate worldwide recognition of his research on the cerebral cortex made him a national hero and further swelled the ranks of his followers. In 1905 the Military Medical Academy built a second and more modern physiological laboratory and placed it under his supervision. With two separate laboratories, he could train still more graduate students and pursue more problems. In 1908 he was elected a full member of the St. Petersburg Academy of Sciences, and immediately became the head of its physiological laboratory without abandoning his earlier affiliations. Earlier, the research conducted in the Academy's laboratory had depended solely on the passing interests of its affiliated scholars; now all research was based on Pavlovian ideas.

Pavlov's research empire reached a new peak in 1911, when the Ledentsov Society donated 50,000 rubles for the expansion of the physiological research facilities at the Institute of Experimental Medicine. The most visible result of this gift was the "Tower of Silence," a wing with soundproof chambers for the experimental study of reflexes and their behavioral superstructures. The need for this elaborate structure arose chiefly from Pavlov's new interest in the role of internal inhibition: in his new series of experiments, external stimuli, especially noise, had to be carefully controlled.

The research in the three laboratories under Pavlov's supervision had two areas of concentration: digestive processes and the mechanism of the cerebral cortex. After 1900, Pavlov limited his own investigations to the second category. However, he was the first major Russian scientist to introduce the idea of co-authorship of scientific studies based on cooperative research, and his name appeared on many of the papers produced in his laboratories. The study that introduced the conditioned reflex as a topic of neurophysiological research, for example, was conducted jointly by Pavlov and I. F. Tolochinov.

Pavlov was the first major Russian scholar to open scientific laboratories to women. These women were graduates of various medical institutes, and all combined a fair grounding in sciences related to medicine with clinical experience and research interest. Pavlov also helped to open research careers to Jewish scientists, even though anti-Semitism was an official policy of the government. It took a relentless determination on his part to persuade the Society of Russian Physicians in St. Petersburg to accept qualified Jews into its membership. One of Pavlov's graduate students was the first Jew to be elected a member of this society.[20]

The Pavlovian scientific legacy was part of a dominant trend in the Russian tradition in physiology; and the founders of this tradition were Pavlov's former teachers. From I. F. Tsion, his professor at St. Petersburg University and at the Medical and Surgical Academy, Pavlov learned to value the role of experiments in physiological research, especially the great potentialities of surgical experiments. From S. P. Botkin, he adopted the theories of "nervism" and structuralism. Perhaps the most powerful influence came from Ivan Sechenov, whom Pavlov called "the father of Russian physiology"; it was Sechenov who made the study of reflexes the central problem of the physiological study of the cerebral cortex. Pavlov unified and expanded the views that he inherited, and his implicit philosophy completely separated ideology from physiology. Neither Pavlov nor any of his major disciples showed any interest in the ideological battle that raged during the last two decades of the tsarist reign. Pavlov categorically rejected the Nihilist view of physiology as a source of models for a new society that would display the rhythmic regularities of life and conform to the laws of natural evolution.

Pavlov's students and followers fall into several categories.[21] During the 1880's Pavlov guided many doctoral candidates in their work on dissertations, and his task consisted primarily of giving technical advice on the organization and execution of experiments. During the 1890's he worked with military surgeons who were interested mostly in refresher courses in pathological physiology. At the beginning of the twentieth century, however, his laboratories began to attract established physicians with a flair for experimental research, and the Pavlovian school came into existence. Most of Pavlov's original disciples had worked solely within his laboratories and under his direct guidance or supervision. But gradually a new type of disciple emerged: the scholar who opened new lines of research and integrated them into the Pavlovian theoretical and experimental tradition. L. A. Orbeli, K. M. Bykov, and A. D. Speranskii, the chief men in this category, continued to follow Pavlov's guidelines under the Soviets.

One major reason for the rapid growth of the Pavlovian school was a general interest in physiology throughout Russia. The dominant physiological orientations, most claiming to have received their initial impetus from Sechenov's theories, agreed on various points, but each was unique in its overall theory, philosophical orientation, methodology, and aspirations. Three men besides Pavlov were particularly noted for the uniqueness of their interests and the impressive scope of their achievements: A. F. Samoilov, N. E. Vvedenskii, and V. M. Bekhterev. Each of these eminent physiologists passed through a phase of association with Pavlov, but each emerged as a completely independent scholar. These men made their most important contributions in research areas outside the bounds of the Pavlovian legacy; they also directly challenged some of the basic propositions of this legacy.

A. F. Samoilov, with a doctorate in medicine from Dorpat University, joined the Institute of Experimental Medicine in 1892 as a research associate in Pavlov's laboratory. He spent two years in the laboratory during Pavlov's intensive studies in the physiology of digestion. He mastered the Pavlovian techniques of surgical experiments; but Pavlov's physiological orientation did not appeal to him, and he moved to Moscow University to work in Sechenov's laboratory. Some forty years later Pavlov attempted to pinpoint the reasons behind Samoilov's decision to leave the country's most elaborate and exciting laboratory. His explanation sheds light not only on his own physiological orientation, but also on the bifurcation of physiological research in Russia at the turn of the century:

"I had counted very much on a long collaboration with Aleksandr Filippovich Samoilov, but to my regret he soon moved to Moscow to work in Sechenov's laboratory.... Each of us strives toward something that appeals to his own intellect.... I was and still am a pure physiologist, i.e., an investigator exploring the functions of individual organs, the conditions of activity of these organs, and the synthesis of the functions of separate organs into a common functioning of some section or other of the organism or of the whole organism. I have little interest in the fundamental bases of the functions of an organ and of its tissues, for which a chemical or physical analysis is imperative. Hence the division of physiologists into pure physiologists, physiological chemists, and physiological physicists. I depended primarily, and at times exclusively, on vivisection and physiological surgery, whereas Sechenov nearly always worked with chemical methods and physical instrumentation. Apparently Samoilov was attracted to instrumental or physical physiology; indeed, having attained a professorship, he subsequently concentrated his efforts on electrophysiology, and accomplished much in this area."[22]

Samoilov noted in 1904 that the "classical" period in physiology, created by the work of Helmholtz and others, had run its course; and that there was an urgent need for new orientations and methods of research. At the turn of the century, he thought, physiology was dominated by what he identified as the biological orientation, which studied the interaction of various organs under normal or near-normal conditions. Pavlov's surgical methods were the mainstay of this orientation. Although Pavlov and his followers conceded that the results of physiological research might one day be precise enough to be presented mathematically, they were convinced that the methods of obtaining data should continue to be uniquely biological. However, Samoilov advocated another approach to physiology, dominated by the idea that "a physiological phenomenon becomes perfectly clear to us only when we are in a position to explain it as a physicochemical process."[23] Indeed, "by applying the viewpoints of physics and chemistry to the study of biological processes in living organisms, we follow the only correct scientific path."[24]

Samoilov made his major contributions by applying the methods of physics to the study of physiological phenomena. At Kazan University, he established the country's major laboratory for electrophysiology and electrocardiography. These new techniques (developed under the influence of Willem Einthoven, a Dutch pioneer in electrocardiography) facilitated the systematic experimental study of the pathology of the heart, the innervation of the glands of internal secretion, and the work of the sense organs. Samoilov's most outstanding work was his study of two processes: the transmission of excitation from motor nerves to muscles, and the mechanisms underlying the flexibility of muscles.[25] In the process, he moved electrophysiological techniques, traditionally limited to purely academic problems, into the clinics and laboratories, where they could obtain results that were both theoretically challenging and medically useful.[26]

N. E. Vvedenskii was only a step below Pavlov and Sechenov among the great Russian physiologists.[27] His work was, in a way, a creative synthesis of Sechenov's physicochemical orientation and Pavlov's "pure physiology." In 1879, as a student of Sechenov, Vvedenskii published his first scientific paper, which dealt with the effects of light on the epidermal nerves of the frog. In 1884 he published the results of his telephonic studies of electrical phenomena in muscular and nervous systems, which established him as a pioneer in the use of complex electrical devices for neurophysiological research. He discovered measurable rhythms in the excitation and contraction of muscles, and was the first to establish that the excitation of a nerve produces a nervous tone very similar to a muscular tone. By a series of very intricate experiments, he was eventually able to prove that excitation and inhibition were only two different manifestations of the same physiological process. Vvedenskii must be credited with discovering the process of inhibition in the neuromuscular centers, just as Pavlov had described that process in the cerebral cortex.

As his research techniques improved and his theoretical insights expanded, Vvedenskii formulated a series of general propositions that indicated the great value of his approach to physiology. His theories dealt with the upper and lower limits of the power and frequency of excitation; with "functional mobility or lability" (i.e., the importance of the time factor in excitation); and with stationary excitation or "parabiosis" (his term for the unifying role of the nervous protoplasm in the excitation-inhibition process). All these ideas were based on his assumption that all forms of inhibition and excitation involved a single fundamental process, and on his experimental proof of the rhythmic nature of excitation. His explanations of the last two of these attracted the attention of the Pavlovian school, and were integrated into its general theory of the neurophysiological processes of the cerebral cortex.[28]

The gradual refinement and increasing generality of Vvedenskii's theories led him to bolder and more comprehensive views on the nature of physiology and its philosophical and methodological foundations. Toward the end of his rich scientific career, his views on physiology as a distinct natural science were very much like those of Pavlov. In opening the First Congress of Russian Physiologists in 1917, he defined his position with a near-paraphrase of Pavlov's statements of 1907:

"Even now we encounter physiologists who regard our science as physics and chemistry applied to the study of living organisms. However, after the 1880's this one-sided view met opposition from the so-called neovitalists. True, neovitalism did not open any new research avenues; but its general views were solidly founded. Even such simple processes as ... secretion and excretion could not be fully explained by physicochemical laws. It was necessary to recognize the selective and purposive activity of the living cells of the organism.... The more intense the physiological research, the more imperative it became to take two facts into account: the adaptability of an organism to the conditions of its existence, and the purposiveness of functions maintaining the life of the individual and the species. At the same time, the concept of the gradual evolution of animals and plants became more firmly established in the other biological sciences; this allowed for a treatment of adaptability and purposiveness not as metaphysical ideas but as qualities acquired by living organisms in a long struggle for existence and transmitted by heredity....

"The initial physicochemical scheme of life proved to be too narrow; when strictly applied, it could place physiology on a Procrustean bed. It is true that the physical matter of a living organism is subordinated to the laws governing inanimate matter; but it is equally true that the same organism presents complexities, variations, and changes that cannot be comprehended by the tools of physics and chemistry in their present state."[29]

Vvedenskii regarded the study of the physiology of the central nervous system as the most challenging theoretical and experimental problem of modern biology, as a potential source of practical answers to essential neuromedical questions, and as an arena in which many key propositions of modern scientific philosophy could be tested. But he also saw it as a guide or model for the study of culture. Intellectual culture, he felt, could achieve a high level of development only in societies that actively encouraged systematic and balanced intellectual work—that is, work regulated by the same principles that govern the nature and pattern of physiological processes. He boldly asserted that the cause of the relatively low Russian intellectual output lay in the absence of historically rooted stimuli for methodical work: "In our society, there is a deeply rooted habit of working sporadically, with long intervals of idleness.... This predilection to work in periodic energetic spurts is, perhaps, an outcome of our historical experience. For centuries Russians engaged mostly in agriculture, which required unusually intense working energy during the relatively short summer season and produced enforced idleness during the long, harsh winter months. But although we may excuse our unmethodical work in the past, it is still true today that ... we tire rapidly ... because our work is poorly executed and unsystematic."[30]

Vvedenskii noted that the work of Russian scientists as a group was particularly unmethodical. Like many of his eminent contemporaries, he claimed that two distinct conditions were responsible for the comparatively slow development of the Russian scientific tradition: the lack of continuity in the institutional support for science and scientific organizations, and the very limited cultural encouragement of personal initiative in intellectual work. Obviously reacting to continuous student unrest and the political conditions that fostered it, Vvedenskii pleaded for a stable and efficient educational system that would ensure the systematic and uninterrupted transmission of knowledge from one generation to another and would fully realize the intellectual resources of each individual. It would be much easier to adduce historical proofs for his identification of the negative influences on the growth of Russian science than to substantiate his notion of parallelism in the dynamics of physiological processes and intellectual creativeness.

Pavlov's third great contemporary was Vladimir Mikhailovitch Bekhterev. No Russian neurophysiologist covered a wider research area; and none made a more systematic, comprehensive, and perceptive survey of applied neurophysiology. Bekhterev wrote close to 600 scientific studies, including several multivolume works, which varied from unadorned experimental reports to general statements of a philosophical or sociological nature. He contributed enormously to the general knowledge of Russian physiology; but in addition, he boldly outlined the intrinsic limitations of Pavlovian neurophysiology and its intellectual claims, particularly in the rapidly expanding realm of psychology.

Many years of broadly based work in neuromorphology and the anatomy of the nervous system, culminating in a score of major discoveries, earned Bekhterev enviable fame both at home and abroad. His *Nervous Paths in the Spinal Cord and Brain* (1884) was a grand synthesis of modern neuromorphological knowledge about the structure of the cerebral cortex and the complex ties between its major components. In this work he developed the proposition that any individual section of the cerebral cortex, through its various ties with the periphery of the body, could perform several functions at the same time.

Bekhterev's achievements in neurophysiology were even greater, and he brought them together in his monumental *Basic Theories of the Functions of the Brain* (1903–7). Among many other topics, he reported on the discovery by himself and his associates of specific cortical areas that controlled various internal organs. This added new support to the claims of Sechenov and Botkin regarding the means of nervous regulation of life processes in animals.[31] Bekhterev's original contributions to neurophysiology consisted more of minute discoveries, particularly in the localization of cortical centers and in research techniques, than of broader theoretical formulations.

Neuromorphological research had led Bekhterev to neurophysiological investigation; and the latter, in turn, led him to "psychoneurology" or "neuropsychology," an area in which he acquired international fame. Bekhterev's first step in this direction was marked by his theory of "association reflexes" (essentially the same as Pavlov's "conditioned" reflexes), which he considered the foundation of all human behavior. Unlike Pavlov, he considered not only the role of motor actions in the formation of acquired reflexes, but also the role of verbal symbolization, which can help man to transcend the physical limitations of his environment. He devoted special attention to the development of highly specialized association reflexes from an initial generalized behavior pattern.

Bekhterev identified the psychology that he built upon the reflex theory first as "objective psychology" and then as "reflexology." With inexhaustible energy, he began to clarify and apply the general principles of his new psychology, writing on "collective reflexology" (focusing on the role of social interaction in the development of personality), "pedagogical reflexology," and "pathological reflexology." Bekhterev emphasized that he was interested in man as a "biological" being. His reflexology, as a natural science, was concerned primarily with the external and measurable manifestations of human behavior: for example, he studied facial expressions and speech as a unified system of symbolic communication. Although he acknowledged the vital role of "internal" determinants in human behavior, he confined his study to externals in order to remain objective. Unhappy with the associationist psychology that viewed such human endowments as cognition, memory, will, and emotions as discrete categories, he constructed a monolithic psychology built on reflexes. Unhappy with the introspectionist bent of associationist psychology, he stuck to topics susceptible to laboratory treatment and mathematical measurement.

Bekhterev differed from Pavlov in one important respect. Pavlov regarded "introspective" psychology as a branch of metaphysics, and treated the physiology of the central nervous system as the only source of scientifically reliable psychological information. Bekhterev, however, considered introspective psychology useful, although he was skeptical of its "scientific" value. Although the powerful influence of Pavlov's scientific stature tipped the scale heavily in favor of physiological psychology, Bekhterev's relatively moderate position did encourage a versatile development of psychology. His own statement of opinion is clear: "Reflexology in no way excludes subjective psychology.... It only limits the area of inquiry, based primarily on full self-analysis, as practiced in recent years by the so-called Würzburg school." In one of his last major works he noted: "The objective biosocial or reflexological study of personality and the study of the psychic phenomena through direct self-observation should not clash with each other. Indeed, the study of subjective processes in oneself should supplement the study of the objective manifestations of personality, so that the interrelation between both may be elucidated."[32] This reconciliation with "idealistic" psychology dealt a mortal blow to Bekhterev's theories in the Soviet era. At present, no scientist claims to follow in his footsteps, although his empirical contributions and his public activities are interpreted in laudatory terms.[33]

If Bekhterev's scientific career had any unifying thought, it was a consistent interest in neuropathology and psychiatry. As a young instructor at Kazan University during the late 1880's and early 1890's, Bekhterev made psychiatry a part of the curriculum. During the same period, he founded a psychophysiological laboratory, organized the Kazan Society of Neuropathologists and Psychiatrists, and began publishing the *Neurological Messenger* (1893), the first Russian journal of its kind. In 1893 he was transferred to the Military Medical Academy in St. Petersburg to head the department of psychiatry and neuropathology. Here, too, he organized several scientific societies, and also founded two journals: *Review of Psychiatry, Neurology, and Psychology* (1895), and *Psychology of Criminal Anthropology and Hypnotism* (1904).

Bekhterev's greatest organizational achievement was his founding of the Psychoneurological Institute in 1907 in St. Petersburg. The Institute, supported primarily by private endowments, was dedicated to "harmonious education" and to a systematic search for scientific explanations of nervous disorders. The educational assignment was entrusted to the medical, pedagogical, and juridical faculties, which were expected to educate their students in all the reflexological interpretations of man as a "biosocial" being. The entire program was centered on neurophysiology, which was pictured as both the key to a scientific understanding of human personality and the model of a perfectly functioning social system. "Harmonious personality," the highest goal of the Institute's educational program, was essentially a label for balanced, effective citizenship.

The Institute admitted all gymnasium graduates regardless of grades; and it encouraged all its students to participate in social movements and political action, even if these were inimical to the established order. Because it emphasized informal discussion, seminar work, and laboratory experiments, the Institute was particularly attractive to young people in search of a higher education that could meet the needs and ideals of a rapidly changing society; and nearly 10,000 students were admitted during the period 1907–17.

In spite of their popularity, the Institute's educational programs had little effect on Russian society—perhaps because reflexology, with its exorbitant "scientific" claims and its overly narrow views of social causation in the development of personality, was too limited and imperfect. In its social aspects, the Institute was only one more response to the turbulent ideologies of the time, and was very far from being a catalyst of social and cultural reorientation.

The Psychoneurological Institute's second major task was research, and here it was more successful. Soon after its inception, it acquired many scientific workshops for the advancement of neuropathological knowledge, among them an antialcoholic institute, a psychiatric hospital, an institute for epileptics, and a neurosurgical hospital.[34] Bekhterev also had a hand in founding many research centers outside the Psychoneurological Institute, including several that dealt with the behavioral development and mental health of children.

How do the work and achievements of Bekhterev compare with those of Pavlov? The two followed essentially the same neurophysiological orientation, and both rightfully claimed to have been disciples of Ivan Sechenov. Both combined a mechanistic search for the ultimate laws of human behavior with an explicit, though primarily heuristic, recognition of the role of purposiveness in nature. Both recognized the Darwinian law of evolution as the supreme law of modern biology and the best description of the dynamic adjustment of organisms to the external environment. Finally, Pavlov's conditioned reflex and Bekhterev's association reflex were one and the same thing. But there were some basic differences. Bekhterev's use of Ostwaldian energeticism as one of the ontological pillars of reflexology was completely alien to Pavlov, whose mechanistic orientation was little affected by the anti-Newtonian ideas of modern physics. Bekhterev covered an immeasurably larger academic field than Pavlov, but his work showed less depth and proved less challenging to future scientists in both its concrete discoveries and its theoretical propositions.

The lively arguments between the followers of the two great physiologists at meetings of the Russian Medical Society infused new life and excitement into the scientific community, and often led to the experimental verification of contested claims. Disagreements were constant, and no physiological school attained an unchallengeable authority. In 1911 Pavlov could not marshal enough votes to be reelected as president of the Russian Medical Society—not because his contributions were not widely recognized in his native country, but because there was great opposition to the possibility of a Pavlovian hegemony in physiology and medicine.

Bekhterev's greatest contribution to Russian science may well have been his opposition to Pavlov. Pavlov's defeat at the academic polls made not the slightest scratch on his scholarly eminence, but it added new strength and versatility to Russian physiology. As a Soviet interpreter of Pavlov's and Bekhterev's scientific legacies noted in 1965, the fact that no single theory was in a position to suppress contradictory views made Russian physiology a sound, comprehensive discipline.

## ILYA MECHNIKOV AND COMPARATIVE PATHOLOGY

Ilya Mechnikov left Russia for political reasons in 1888; and until his death in 1916 he was a leading member of the Pasteur Institute in Paris.* Nevertheless, he continued to maintain close relations with the scientific community in Russia, and published many articles in popular Russian journals. His writings on gerontology, the "philosophy of optimism," and the history of the rationalistic world view were widely read in his native land, although his strong materialist leanings were sharply criticized by conservative thinkers. He attracted a good number of promising Russian scientists to his laboratory at the Pasteur Institute, and thus became the progenitor of a noteworthy Russian school in microbiology, which included A. M. Bezredka, N. F. Gamaleia, and V. L. Omelianskii.[35]

One of Mechnikov's most important contributions to comparative medicine was his convincing proof that the study of the simplest living forms could aid researchers in understanding the most complicated pathological problems in human beings. He applied himself primarily to the task of answering the following questions:

"Do the factors...that evoke the series of phenomena known as inflammation in man and the higher animals produce any analogous conditions in the lower vertebrata...or in the invertebrata? Is the existence of a circulatory system essential for the setting up of inflammation, or does this also occur in animals that possess no blood vessels, and in this case how does the nervous system act? For inflammation to take place, is it necessary that the animal should possess a certain number of differentiated organs, or may it consist merely of an agglomeration of non-differentiated cells? Do we find anything analogous to inflammation in plants? Are there any instances of inflammatory action in unicellular organisms?"[36]

In his classic *Lectures on the Comparative Pathology of Inflammation* (1892), Mechnikov gave systematic answers to each of these questions. His starting point was his own discovery that the mesodermal cells, or phagocytes, in starfish not only perform the digestive functions but also envelop and digest parasites, foreign matter, and residual organs. On this theory, he formulated three basic propositions of comparative pathology.

First, inflammation is not a manifestation of disease, but part of the self-defense of an organism. It is an integral component, not an aberration, of the normal physiological processes.

* For information on Mechnikov's career before 1888, see pp. 111–15.

Second, inflammation is a biological phenomenon shared by the entire animal kingdom. "It is quite clear," said Mechnikov, "that inflammation in vertebrates, in which phagocytes leave the vascular system and rush to the invader, differs only quantitatively from similar phenomena in invertebrates."[37] He admitted, however, that since the vascular system plays a very important role in inflammation, the process is more characteristic of the higher vertebrates.

Third, inflammation is part of the adaptation of organisms to their environment, and is subject to phylogenetic changes. The most primitive forms of inflammation are combined with the digestive processes, and are the first attempts of organisms to defend themselves against harmful intruders. As species evolve, these self-defense functions are gradually transferred to the vascular systems. Mechnikov concluded that "disease and pathological processes are evolved in the same way as man and the higher animals themselves."[38] Since inflammation occurs in all animals, the comparative study of its dominant forms is a very important source of information on human pathology.

Mechnikov contended that his evolutionary phagocytic theory of inflammation strengthened the foundations of comparative pathology that had been laid in 1857–59 by Darwin's theory of natural selection, Pasteur's biological theory of fermentation, and Virchow's theory of cellular pathology. His own contributions made phagocytosis a stock term in modern microbiology, but his theory did not go unchallenged. The imputation of organic self-defense to mesodermal cells, for instance, was roundly attacked by the German bacteriologist Karl Fraenkel, who saw in it a return to vitalism, animism, and metaphysical teleology. In defending himself, Mechnikov extended the evolutionary view of pathology—and biology in general—to include psychology: "The accusation of vitalism and animism, which is unjustly cast at the phagocyte theory, might really be more appropriately applied to my opponents, who maintain that the psychical acts of the higher animals are fundamentally different in their nature from the more simple phenomena peculiar to the lower organisms."[39] He did not doubt that psychical phenomena were not *sui generis* but had evolved from "the simple actions that we observe in the lower organisms and in the cells of different animals." His theory, he argued, was not teleological, for it was based on the law of evolution, "according to which the properties that are useful to the organism survive while those that are harmful are eliminated by natural selection."[40]

The phagocytic theory of inflammation was the starting point for Mechnikov's cellular theory of immunity. In *Immunity in Infectious Diseases* (1901), he adduced many examples showing the existence of an inherited or naturally acquired immunity to infection, without which most plants and animals could not exist.[41] His main contention was simple: "Immunity to infectious diseases is part of the physiology of cells, and mainly a phenomenon of the resorption of microorganisms.... The latter is nothing else but an action of intracellular digestion." The study of immunity was thus a part of the study of digestion. The higher the development of phagocytosis, the less the danger of infection. Although some contemporary scientists, including Robert Koch, challenged the phagocytic theory of immunity, others viewed it as the most challenging and profound contribution to medicine since the famous lectures of Claude Bernard. It brought Mechnikov a Nobel Prize in 1908, which he shared with Paul Ehrlich.

With the exception of K. A. Timiriazev, Mechnikov was certainly Russia's most determined advocate of the superiority of science over other modes of inquiry. To him, science was built on an unlimited rationalism, a consistent "positivism," and a cultivated "agnosticism"; and the only acceptable moral code was one based on the rational ethics derived from and fully congruent with science. He had no use for William James's "religious" adherence to pragmatic relativism in appraising the social value of knowledge, Henri Poincaré's epistemological nominalism, and Henri Bergson's espousal of the superiority of intuition over reason.[42] In his opinion, all these orientations reduced science to a secondary mode of inquiry.

Mechnikov's scientific philosophy was seriously limited by his conviction that the basic problems of man and society resulted from "the disharmony of human nature"—that is, from certain physiological or anatomical imperfections peculiar to *Homo sapiens*, which could be explained exclusively in terms of the theory of natural selection and could be corrected with the help of natural science. Furthermore, he believed, science alone could help man eradicate social injustice. He concluded *The Nature of Man* (1903) with a laconic summary of his position: "If there can be formed an ideal able to unite men in a kind of religion of the future, this ideal must be founded on scientific principles. And if it be true, as has been asserted so often, that man can live by faith alone, the faith must be in the power of science."[43] In *The Prolongation of Life* (1908), Mechnikov combined a cross-cultural study of old age, a review of contemporary theories of senility, and an analysis of the "history of social animals" with extensive excursions into philosophy to describe the limitless possibilities of advantageous modifications of human nature in accordance with the facts of science.[44] As a philosopher, he unduly exaggerated the power of science; but as a scientist, he left science much richer than he found it.

## RUSSIAN MICROBIOLOGY: S. N. VINOGRADSKII AND D. I. IVANOVSKII

Mechnikov's influence in Russia was particularly strong among the many scientists interested in medicine and epidemiology. In Western Europe, the development of microbiology coincided with a drastic reduction in epidemics of cholera, plague, and several other deadly diseases; but in Russia the same development was induced by the sad fact that these diseases were still afflicting huge areas of the country. Both the government and private citizens were constantly alert to any new developments in public health. Among the *zemstvo* physicians, the prevalent opinion was that personal sanitation, social hygiene, and improved living conditions, rather than medical microbiology, were the proper way to fight epidemics. Without denying the advantages of these methods, dedicated scientists intensified their research into the biological causes of epidemics.[45]

Russian scientists who tackled the problem of epidemics needed a wide knowledge of medicine and biological theory, but they also needed a certain amount of personal courage. Many microbiologists died from diseases contracted while working in the epidemic-ridden areas; and many others died or were crippled while carrying out medical experiments on themselves to find cures for epidemic diseases. To scientists, however, the search for knowledge came first. The last letter written by a Dr. Deminskii, who had been investigating a plague epidemic among marmots in the Kirghiz steppe, speaks for itself: "I have contracted lung plague from the marmots. Come and take over the cultures that I have obtained. All my notes are in order; everything else will be revealed by the laboratory. Examine my body as a case of an experimental infection of a man by marmots."[46]

In spite of these dangers, microbiology attracted a great many young Russians, especially after 1890. The number of microbiologists grew so rapidly that in 1905 the Russian Microbiological Society was founded in St. Petersburg. This group immediately established itself as one of the most active learned associations in the country. Besides medical researchers, it included microbiologists who specialized in biochemistry, in aquatic microorganisms, in agriculture, and in morphology or cytology.

One of the greatest Russian microbiologists was S. N. Vinogradskii, who earned worldwide fame for his discoveries in the biochemistry of microbes.[47] Most of Vinogradskii's colleagues endeavored to perfect existing scientific knowledge and apply it to specific Russian problems; but he was most productive when he worked in areas previously untouched by science.

Vinogradskii was in some ways like Ilya Mechnikov. Both men were Russian expatriates who did their major scientific work abroad. Both were masters of modern experimental techniques. And both successfully pursued interests outside the realm of science, Mechnikov in philosophy and Vinogradskii in music, poetry, and graphic art. In temperament, however, the two were opposites. Mechnikov made friends easily, and was always ready for a friendly exchange of ideas or a fiery debate; Vinogradskii was an introvert who avoided strangers and had very few personal friends. Mechnikov enjoyed classroom theatrics and crowded laboratories; Vinogradskii felt uncomfortable even in small laboratories, and preferred total isolation.[48] In Ostwald's terminology, Mechnikov was a typical example of a "romantic" scientist, whereas Vinogradskii was a "classic" scientist.

Vinogradskii's earliest studies, dealing with the biochemistry of bacteria that consumed sulphur and iron, attracted scholarly attention because of their original research techniques. Particularly noted was the method of "selective cultures"—that is, the method of isolating particular microorganisms with the help of a planned use of specific chemical nutrients—which enabled Vinogradskii to answer several fundamental questions of microbiology. In these early studies, he showed that some bacteria obtained energy by oxidizing hydrogen sulfide to sulphuric acid, and others by oxidizing ferrous iron to ferric oxide.[49] In his later research, he grouped all the bacteria that obtain energy by oxidizing mineral compounds into one class, which he called "inorganic oxidants."

In a series of articles published in the *Annals* of the Pasteur Institute, Vinogradskii presented his findings on the nitrification of soil by chemosynthetic bacteria, which obtain energy from the oxidation of ammonia and use this energy to assimilate carbon dioxide. He proved that nitrifying bacteria could live and develop normally in a nutritional environment that contained no organic substances at all. He established that carbon dioxide could be transformed into organic carbon without the presence of chlorophyll.[50] Knowledge of the nitrification process proved to be of particular importance for agriculture: ammonia is easily lost by the soil; but nitrates are more stable, and can provide all the nitrogen required by plants. Vinogradskii was able to isolate pure cultures of each of the nitrifying bacteria, and his carefully controlled research showed that various stages of the nitrification process were carried out by different types of bacteria. This was a major breakthrough in the methodology of his field.

Vinogradskii's place in modern microbiology is best summed up by the eminent American bacteriologist Selman A. Waksman:

"He was a true pathfinder in the field.... Winogradsky's name is associated particularly with certain special branches of bacteriology which he not only discovered but also developed to a high stage of perfection. He carved out a special niche for himself in this science through his studies on the autotrophic bacteria, or those organisms which obtain their energy by the oxidation of inorganic elements and compounds. His other contributions to the knowledge of non-symbiotic nitrogen-fixing bacteria, his investigations on the oxidation of sulphur, on the bacteriology of cellulose decomposition, and on the methods of soil microbiology have further enhanced his position in the field of general bacteriology. His work established a basis for a better understanding of the nature and physiology of certain highly specialized and important groups of bacteria, whose significance soon became apparent in their application to the bacteriology of soil and water, to sewage purification, and to a variety of other natural processes."[51]

Vinogradskii's special concern with soil microbiology was inspired by the exceedingly strong interest of Russian scientists in the improvement of agricultural land. Since 1868, when the Free Economic Society appointed a special commission to study the biochemical composition of various types of agricultural land, Russian scientists had pioneered in the development of soil science as a separate discipline in the natural sciences. This gigantic undertaking provided established scholars with an attractive opportunity to engage in research of indisputable practical value; and it gave novices an ideal chance to sharpen their skills in modern research techniques and to join a major branch of Russian science.

Vinogradskii's education in Russia instilled in him a dedication to scientific work, but it was not until he had studied in the West that he gained any scholarly reputation. Ilya Mechnikov had moved to Paris as an established scholar, and the Pasteur Institute considered him one of its most illustrious members from the start. Vinogradskii's scientific career was quite different.

In 1873 Vinogradskii entered Kiev University and enrolled in the Faculty of Law. He soon transferred to biology; but after completing his first two years of university education, he left Kiev and enrolled in the St. Petersburg Conservatory to study piano under one of the great Russian masters of the time. Music, however, did not provide sufficient intellectual stimulus, and after a few years of inner struggle, Vinogradskii enrolled in the Department of Natural Sciences at St. Petersburg University. Influenced by A. S. Famintsyn's lectures in plant physiology, he finally found his true calling. After graduation, he was retained by the university to work for higher degrees, and immediately distinguished himself by an experimental study of the fungus *Mycoderma vini*. His findings were reported in a brief summary published in the *Proceedings* of the St. Petersburg Society of Naturalists.

In 1885, inadequate research facilities, as well as the intellectual crisis caused by the growing political reaction of the 1880's, prompted Vinogradskii to continue his studies in Western Europe.[52] At that time, microbiology was one of the least developed biological sciences in Russia: it was not part of the university curriculum, and until 1890 the country did not have a single microbiological laboratory that could meet Western standards.[53] With the founding of the Institute of Experimental Medicine in 1890, Russia acquired such a laboratory, and microbiology soon became a flourishing science.

From 1885 to 1888, Vinogradskii worked in the botanical laboratory of H. A. De Bary in Strasbourg University, and from 1888 to 1890 in the laboratories of Zurich University and the Zurich Polytechnicum. It was in Strasbourg and Zurich that he made his most important discoveries. Through participation in a current debate between the proponents of pleomorphism and monomorphism, he showed an acute awareness of the basic philosophical problems of modern microbiology. His use of "selective cultures" in the experimental study of bacteria enriched the research techniques of microbiology, and his intricate studies of nitrifying bacteria made soil microbiology a sound and promising discipline.

In 1890 Vinogradskii was offered academic positions at the Pasteur Institute, the Zurich Polytechnicum, and the newly founded Institute of Experimental Medicine in St. Petersburg. By this time, his thoughts, manners, and professional connections were more Western than Russian. Nevertheless, he decided to accept the St. Petersburg post, and returned to Russia as head of the microbiological department of the Institute of Experimental Medicine—attracted partly by a sense of obligation to his native land and partly by the promise of lavish experimental facilities. He was instrumental in founding the Institute's *Archives des sciences biologiques*, in which he published the last of his papers on the nitrification role of soil bacteria. But the goals of the Institute eventually led Vinogradskii into medical microbiology. He took an active part in the organization of medical campaigns against various epidemics, even making a trip to Paris to consult the epidemiologists of the Pasteur Institute. However, he managed to conduct some research on soil microbiology in 1893–95, and received wide acclaim for his work on the problems of nonsymbiotic nitrogen fixation—that is, fixation by organisms living outside any plants. After this discovery Vinogradskii's research began to lose momentum; but his organizational activities made him the most influential member of the Institute, and he became its director from 1902 to 1905.

Although he was a successful administrator, Vinogradskii preferred the isolation of personal laboratory work. In 1905 he took a leave of absence and moved to his estate in the Ukraine, and in 1912 he formally resigned from the Institute. His reasons were various: poor health, constant friction with government officials, and the gradual drifting of research in the Institute toward more practical medical problems. From 1905 to 1917 Vinogradskii lived in voluntary exile from the world of scientific scholarship. For reasons that are not clear, he left Russia again soon after the October Revolution. His interest in science was revived during a stay in Yugoslavia; and in 1922 the Pasteur Institute invited him to join its staff as the director of a new program in soil bacteriology, to be conducted on a special experimental farm at Brie-Comte-Robert, near Paris. This marked the beginning of a new phase in Vinogradskii's scientific career, and for the rest of his active life he concentrated on soil microbiology.

In 1925 the Soviet Academy of Sciences elected Vinogradskii an honorary member. The Royal Society of London and the Paris Académie des Sciences bestowed similar honors upon him. He died in 1953, at the age of 97. In the words of his biographer: "Thus passed from the stage a great bacteriologist, a man ... who contributed some of the most original approaches to our knowledge of the physiology of certain groups of bacteria and their role in soil processes.... Born and educated in Russia, he did almost all his scientific work outside his native land.... He was international in spirit, international in his work and in his outlook, international in his very life."[54]

Mechnikov's phagocytic theory and Vinogradskii's explanation of the role of bacteria in the nitrification of soil made microbiology a science of national emphasis in Russia. The next major victory for Russian microbiology, and microbiology in general, came from the experimental researches of D. I. Ivanovskii, the founder of virology. In 1887, while still an undergraduate student at St. Petersburg, Ivanovskii was sent by Professor A. S. Famintsyn to the Ukraine to gather information on a tobacco disease known locally as *raibukha*. His first publications, written jointly with V. V. Polovtsev, proved that this term covered two distinct diseases: *raibukha* proper and tobacco mosaic. In 1892 Ivanovskii published an independent paper on these two diseases, in which he remarked: "The sap of the leaves attacked by the mosaic disease retains its infectious qualities even after filtration through a Chamberland filter-candle."[55]

Ivanovskii's filtration experiments were the first step in the discovery of viruses—disease agents so small that they can pass through the finest filters. His findings were overlooked for several years; but in 1898 the Dutch botanist M. W. Beijerinck confirmed the results of Ivanovskii's experiments, identifying the filterable disease agent of tobacco mosaic first as a "contagious living fluid" and then as a "virus." A year earlier F. Loeffler and P. Frosch, working independently, had reported that the agent of foot-and-mouth disease in cattle also passed through bacterial filters. In 1901 Walter Reed and his associates established that yellow fever in man was also a virus disease.

The increase of data that these experiments provided led Ivanovskii to undertake a new study of the tobacco mosaic virus. He reported his findings in a lengthy essay published in 1902, which proved to be a major scientific document not only because of the ideas presented but also because of the novelty and intricacy of the experimental techniques described. Ivanovskii proved beyond doubt that the tobacco mosaic virus was the first of a new class of disease-carrying agents to be discovered by man. Ivanovskii's work with viruses, according to the American virologist W. M. Stanley, "should be viewed in much the same light as we view Pasteur's and Koch's relationship to bacteria." Stanley adds: "There is considerable justification for regarding Ivanovskii as the father of a new science of virology."[56]

In contrast to Mechnikov and Vinogradskii, Ivanovskii never worked in Western laboratories or associated with Western leaders in his field. Recognition of his discoveries was exceedingly slow, even in his own country. He was not a victim of either academic intrigues or bureaucratic inflexibility; the world was simply not ready during his lifetime to appreciate the tedious experimental work that he conducted away from the main currents of scientific thought. It was only when virology became an established discipline and began to examine its own history that his contributions received the recognition they deserved.

### M. S. TSVET AND PLANT PHYSIOLOGY

M. S. Tsvet's strongest contributions were not in the substantive facts of modern science but in methodology. He invented the method of chromatographic adsorption, which separates the components of a chemical mixture into spatially distinct segments. The German scientists L. Zechmeister and L. Cholnoky, in their classic work *Principles and Practice of Chromatography*, describe Tsvet's invention as follows:

"If a solution of several highly colored compounds is shaken with a suitable adsorbent, there takes place between the two phases a partition that is determined by mass-relationships and adsorption coefficients.... In his fundamental experiments, Tsvet extracted green leaves with light petroleum and poured the extract through a compressed column of finely powdered calcium carbonate contained in a vertical glass tube. He found that the apparently homogeneous pigmented contents of the slowly percolating solution underwent separation. In the upper part of the column a pale yellow ring appeared, immediately beneath it two green zones, and farther down three other yellow components.... Even more pleasing is the behavior of the chromatogram on treatment with adequate quantities of pure solvent."[57]

With chromatography, Tsvet demonstrated the composite nature of leaf pigment and made its individual components available in the purest natural forms for scientific study. Although Tsvet's own research was concerned primarily with cholorophyll, his method found many uses in organic chemistry, biochemistry, and physiology. The essential meaning of Tsvet's discovery is best expressed by himself: "Like the light radiations in a spectrum, a mixture of pigments is systematically separated on the calcium carbonate column into constituents that can be qualitatively and quantitatively determined." What spectography is to the isolation of basic colors in a spectrum, chromatography is to the isolation and measurement of basic components in many natural compounds. Essentially, it applies a physical method to the study of chemical problems.

The most outstanding feature of Tsvet's chromatographic adsorption method is its simplicity. The solution of a compound is poured into a glass tube filled with a substance that adsorbs the different components of the compound at different rates. The best adsorbing medium for chlorophyll, for example, is a powder of calcium carbonate. As the mixture sinks through the adsorbent, its components begin to separate into layers; the components most akin to the adsorbent are the first to separate and form the top layers. A repetition of the process purifies the components further. Paradoxically, it was the very simplicity of Tsvet's method that made contemporary scientists unwilling to use it. Tsvet described chromatography in 1910, but the method lay fallow until the 1930's. When it was rediscovered, it became the starting point for research on separating the components of various mixtures, determining the purity of these components, and establishing the differences between apparently identical components.*

Tsvet's biography reverses the usual story of the great Russian scientists, most of whom received their initial training in Russia before working in Western laboratories. Tsvet was the child of a Russian father and an Italian mother, and was born at Asti, Italy, in 1872. He received his higher education and early research training in Geneva. His main field was botany, and a special interest in cellular physiology led him to study the structure and functions of chlorophyll. After receiving his doctorate in 1896, he went to Russia, where he spent the rest of his life. At first Tsvet held low-paying positions with little promise for advancement. In the laboratory of A. S. Famintsyn he met D. I. Ivanovskii, and the two men, unable to find professional employment in St. Petersburg, joined the staff of Warsaw University. In 1908 Tsvet was appointed professor of botany and microbiology at Warsaw Polytechnical Institute. Displaced during World War I, he taught temporarily at Iur'ev University (formerly Dorpat, now Tartu); but when the Germans occupied the Baltic states he moved to Voronezh. He died in 1919, a decade before the chromatographic adsorption method was recognized as a major contribution to science.

Warsaw was a lively intellectual center with several institutions of higher education. Political activities were controlled more strictly than in Russian cities; but the scholarly community suffered less from vested academic interests, and could exercise more independence in investigating new approaches in science. Tsvet's intellectual interaction with Ivanovskii at Warsaw was casual, but it aided the research activities of both men.

During Tsvet's lifetime, Russian plant physiology more than kept pace with animal and human physiology. Animal physiology received its strongest impetus from the growing Russian concern with public health and from the powerful Russian tradition in neurophysiology. Plant physiology benefited from an equally strong national preoccupation with the chronic problems of Russian agriculture: the unpredictability of precipitation; the threat-

---

* In 1940, D. J. Campbell-Gamble suggested that science honor Tsvet's discovery in an unusual way: "It appears to have been overlooked that the surname of the Russian botanist who in an inspired moment discovered the principle of chromatographic analysis is identical with the Russian word for color. Tsvet himself, since he could not in modesty give, or appear to give, the process his own name, unveiled that unhappy hellenism 'chromatographic analysis.' The Russian language has now become a source of scientific terminology ... so there is no reason why chemistry should not acknowledge its great debt in this case by adopting for this beautiful method a name that at once designates the process and honors the discoverer. I suggest 'tsvetanalysis' or 'tsvetadsorbanalysis.' " (Campbell-Gamble, p. 598.)

ening depletion of marginal lands; and the precarious balance of organic and inorganic components in the soil of many areas. Russian animal physiology was dominated by the great prestige and influence of I. P. Pavlov, and by the discipline of neurophysiology, which placed a greater emphasis on "biological" rather than on "chemical" explanations of animal life processes. Plant physiology, on the other hand, was not dominated by any particular scientist or scientific orientation. It had no mainstream, but many independent currents. As a result, there was hardly a branch of plant physiology to which Russian scholars did not make important contributions.

Plant physiology was actually a generic term for a multitude of theoretical bents and experimental approaches. S. P. Kostychev and V. I. Palladin studied plant respiration. A. F. Lebedev continued Vinogradskii's studies of the chemosynthetic process in various types of bacteria. Vinogradskii and Lebedev studied the connection between respiration and photosynthesis, and A. S. Famintsyn the connections between the differentiation of cells and photosynthesis. Some scientists studied the differential chromatic adaptations of various plants, or the differential effects of varying intensities of light; others, led by M. V. Nentskii, tried to establish chemical and biological similarities between the green pigment of the leaves and human hemoglobin. D. N. Prianishnikov studied the physiological effects of various types of fertilizers, O. V. Baranetskii the rhythm of plant growth, and N. I. Vavilov the evolutionary role of plant immunity to diseases.[58]

Plant physiology was a meeting ground for scientists of many different specialties—botanists, biochemists, microbiologists, soil scientists, geneticists, agricultural biologists, and geographers. (After 1909, when higher agricultural education was opened to women, the field attracted an unusually large number of women, some of whom later became internationally known.)[59] Underlying this great diversity in views and specialties were two broad unifying orientations: the evolutionary and the ecological. Some scientists concentrated on the category of "time," and studied the physiological processes of plants to discern the mechanisms through which the universal law of biological evolution asserted itself. From the practical point of view, they tried to find ways of assessing the survival potential of plants important to human existence, and of aiding those with doubtful futures. Other scientists concentrated on the category of "space," and viewed plant life in terms of its ecological setting. This orientation did not deny evolution, but merely shifted the emphasis to the physiological correlates of interaction between plants and their physical habitat.

## CHAPTER ELEVEN

# Modern Mathematics

## PROBABILITY THEORY

One important task of mathematics is to provide effective research tools for other sciences. During the nineteenth century, however, the contributions of mathematics to science did not keep pace with the general progress of science. Darwinian biology, experimental physiology, structural chemistry, historical geology, comparative embryology, and many other great scientific developments owed very little, if anything, to mathematics. Alfred North Whitehead went so far as to say that the general influence of mathematics had actually declined in the nineteenth century. He did not mean to say that the productivity of mathematics had decreased; in fact, he boldly asserted that during that century mathematics had made "almost as much progress as during all the preceding centuries from Pythagoras onward." However, he said, many of the natural sciences had developed so rapidly that mathematics, despite its own titanic growth, could not supply them with suitable techniques of quantitative measurement and analysis when these were needed.[1]

Whitehead's remarks applied to Western Europe, but were even more true for Russia. By 1900, Russian science presented a paradoxical picture. Russian mathematics had climbed to unprecedented heights, and enjoyed international prestige in several major fields; yet the most outstanding Russian achievements in natural science were in the disciplines least influenced by mathematics. Comparative embryology, paleontology, structural chemistry, microbiology, and neurophysiology had advanced without any elaborate mathematical techniques; but mechanics and physics, the traditional province of mathematics, were among the weakest Russian sciences. This was true of physics until the very end of the tsarist regime; various branches of mechanics made marked progress, but not until the beginning of the twentieth century.

Despite its isolation, Russian mathematics, as it entered the twentieth century, was a flourishing and diversified science.[2] By far the most important branch of this science was probability theory. It has been said that even though mathematics is the most universal of all sciences, it still allows the expression of "national character"—that is, distinct national propensities and interests. Thus a French preoccupation with functions is as readily detectable as an English interest in applied mathematics, a German interest in basic mathematical operations, and an Italian interest in geometry.[3] Most Russian mathematicians agree that probability theory is the core of their country's mathematical legacy.

The history of probability theory is as old as the history of modern mathematics. It began in the seventeenth century; and such noted mathematicians as Huygens, Jacob Bernoulli, and Laplace gave a great deal of attention to it. By the middle of the nineteenth century, however, probability theory had been pushed into the background. The widespread attempt to formulate a complete mechanistic interpretation of nature demanded rigorous and precise methods of calculation, and most advocates of Newtonian science considered probability calculations essentially antithetical to the harmony and predictability of the mechanistic order of the world. The French mathematician Joseph Bertrand, for example, insisted that probabilistic calculations gave different answers to the same questions and were therefore useless in serious scientific research. Other leading scientists, notably James Clerk Maxwell, recognized the usefulness of probability theory; but only a very few, like the American physicist J. Willard Gibbs, recognized that probability theory was an indispensable methodological tool for the most advanced branches of modern science.

Curiously, the temporary eclipse of probability theory in the West coincided with its emergence as one of the central interests in Russian mathematical scholarship.[4] In 1846 V. Ia. Buniakovskii wrote a textbook on the subject, and a little later P. L. Chebyshev made probability theory the cornerstone of his St. Petersburg school in mathematics. Chebyshev rapidly became the chief advocate of a systematic search for absolute proofs of probabilistic theorems, and formulated the law of large numbers and the central limit theorem. He gave probability theory a dignified academic existence by introducing and methodically employing the concepts of "mathematical expectation" and "variance."[5]

Chebyshev stated his central limit theorem in 1887, in an effort to adduce proofs for the well-known probability theorem of Laplace and Poisson. However, he presented only a roughly sketched sequence of proofs, leaving the remainder to his disciples. In 1900 A. A. Markov derived very general and rather cumbersome proofs; but in 1901 A. M. Liapunov offered clear, simple, and conclusive proofs, making the central limit theorem a basic instrument of probability theory. The theorem asserts that if the causes of a large number of random effects are independent, and if individual influences are small in comparison with the total involved, then the distribution of the sums of these random variables can deviate only insignificantly from a normal distribution.[6] The value of this theorem is that it enables the scientist to study the aggregate effects of large numbers of independent random variables, avoiding cumbersome, uneconomical, and in some cases physically impossible studies of the effects of each individual variable.

While working on the application of probability theory to independent random variables, Markov became interested in a particular class of dependent variables, and eventually introduced the concept of "chained events"—the well-known Markov chains. A sequence of dependent random variables constitutes a Markov chain if it permits the probability of any event to depend exclusively on the outcome of the event directly preceding. Markov effectively shifted the attention of mathematicians to the distribution of variables in time. This was the basic step toward a general theory of stochastic processes: that is, a theory concerned with random variables that depend on one or several varying parameters. Today, Markov chains (and Markov processes in general) form an entire branch of mathematics whose potential has not yet been fully realized. Even so, modern research has created elaborate analytical instruments from them (stochastic differential and integral equations, infinitesimal and characteristic operators, additive functionals and superharmonic functions), and has produced new insights into the structure of large classes of Markov processes (diffusion processes, generalized Brownian motion, etc.).[7] Markov's ideas have been developed most extensively in the United States and the Soviet Union, although the contributions of German, French, English, and Japanese mathematicians have also been notable. Present-day scholarship has gone far beyond Markov's original theories, but some of his original formulations are still fundamental.

Chebyshev and his immediate successors (among whom Liapunov and Markov were the most original and productive) made major contributions to the study of random variables and the general theory of stochastic processes, but they did not construct a comprehensive, logically coherent system of probabilistic calculation. In fact, they did no more than apply isolated techniques of probability calculation to specific statistical problems, selected at random and mostly for purposes of demonstration. Markov's textbook, *The Calculus of Probabilities*, though rich in content and illustrations, was only a compilation of various methods of probabilistic calculation, with little internal unity. Moreover, all of these new developments were isolated from the intellectual revolution in modern physics, although physics drew tangible support from them once they were established. It was Henri Poincaré who first stated that all the sciences were "unconscious applications of the calculus of probabilities"; and that if probability theory were to be condemned, "then the whole of the sciences must also be condemned."[8]

In 1917, sensing the essential mathematical needs of the new physics, S. N. Bernshtein, another disciple of Chebyshev, made the first efforts to generalize and unify the various theorems of the theory of probability. However, his work took many years to complete, and was not altogether successful. In the 1920's, before his results were published, the contributions of Markov and Liapunov had been "rediscovered" and elaborated, and had become standard tools of mathematical physics.

In the great diversity of their mathematical interests, Markov and Liapunov were true followers of their teacher Chebyshev, who had almost singlehandedly founded the Russian school in analysis, the Russian school in number theory, and the Russian school in probability theory.[9] But they also went beyond the vistas opened by their teacher, and each cultivated his own interests, philosophy, and social views.

A. A. Markov was born in 1856 in Riazan, a prosperous commercial town southeast of Moscow that had also been the birthplace of Ivan Pavlov. His grandfather was a rural deacon, and his father a minor official. While still a gymnasium student, Markov wrote a paper presenting a "new" method for the integration of ordinary linear differential equations with constant coefficients and sent it to a number of leading mathematicians for critical appraisal. These men informed him that his method was not new; but, impressed by his obvious ability, they urged him to continue studying mathematics. In 1874 he entered St. Petersburg University, where he met Chebyshev and his disciples A. N. Korkin and E. I. Zolotarev (the last two noted for their work in quadratic equations). Markov became a loyal member of the mathematical *kruzhok* that met regularly in Korkin's home; and, by his own admission, it was at these friendly meetings that he was introduced to many of the ideas that suggested his independent research.

In 1877 Markov received a gold medal for a paper on the integration of differential equations with the help of continued fractions, and was invited to pursue his graduate studies at St. Petersburg. In 1880 he defended his magister's dissertation, which dealt with indefinite binary quadratic forms; and in 1881 he received a doctorate on the basis of a study dealing with various applications of continued fractions. As a professor at St. Petersburg University, he offered a variety of courses, but concentrated primarily on differential calculus, spherical trigonometry, and probability theory. In 1886 he was elected an adjunct by the St. Petersburg Academy of Sciences, and in 1896 he became a full member. Although Markov's fame rests primarily on his contribution to probability theory, he was a versatile mathematician. He published close to seventy studies on topics ranging from number theory and the theory of hypergeometric series to differential equations and probability theory. Most of his studies were either written in or translated into foreign languages.[10]

As a scientist, Markov strayed but little from pure mathematics. On one occasion, he did come out of his ivory tower to help the Ministry of Justice lay the mathematical groundwork for calculating its newly founded pension funds. It is doubtful, however, that he drew to any extent on his own probability theories in this project. As a citizen, Markov openly advocated institutional protection for freedom of thought and political action. He did not, however, ally himself with any organized political group, and all his public pronouncements were merely expressions of his personal convictions. The biographical data provided by his son (an eminent mathematician in his own right) show Markov as a courageous man with firm democratic convictions.[11]

Markov acted upon his convictions on several occasions. When the Holy Synod excommunicated Lev Tolstoi in 1901, Markov formally requested that he also be excommunicated. After all, he said, his *Calculus of Probabilities* challenged some of the basic biblical teachings. The Synod chose to ignore his petition, in an obvious effort to avoid aggravating the intellectual unrest in the country. In 1902 the Fine Arts Section of the St. Petersburg Academy of Sciences elected Maksim Gor'kii an honorary member; but after a few days the election was voided by a direct order of Nicholas II on the grounds that Gor'kii was under police surveillance. Markov regarded this request as a reckless attack on the institutional autonomy of the Academy and the intellectual integrity of the Academicians, and threatened to resign from the Academy. On June 3, 1907, the government disbanded the Second State Duma and promulgated a new law to govern the elections for the Third State Duma, thus violating the manifesto of October 17, 1905, in which it had promised not to enact new laws without consulting the Duma. Markov made it known that the new Duma, in his opinion, would not be a representative council but an "illegal mob," and requested that his name be taken off the register of voters. In 1908, the Ministry of National Education issued a circular aimed at checking student unrest by asking professors to perform various police functions. Markov protested again, refusing to act as a government agent in the university.

A. M. Liapunov shared with Markov a broad interest in mathematics, a special devotion to probability theory, and an illustrious academic career; but his family background, temperament, and way of life were quite different. He was born in 1857 in Iaroslavl, where his father was director of the Demidov Lyceum, a school of higher general education. Since the time his grandfather had occupied an administrative position at Kazan University in the 1820's, the Liapunovs had been known as a family of high culture, with close ties to the world of scholarship and the arts. One of Liapunov's brothers was the well-known composer Sergei Liapunov; another brother, Boris, was an eminent linguist. Among Liapunov's more distant relatives were the physiologist Ivan Sechenov and Aleksei Krylov, the Russian translator of Newton's *Principia Mathematica*.

After graduating from St. Petersburg University in 1880, Liapunov was retained to work for higher degrees in mechanics. In an autobiographical note, he acknowledged his debt to Chebyshev, who had aided his scientific career "first by lectures and then by counsel."[12] In 1885 Liapunov completed a study in the stability of ellipsoid forms of evenly rotating fluids, which earned him a magister's degree, recognition in Europe, and a teaching position at Khar'kov University. For several years he was the only man teaching mechanics at Khar'kov, a grueling task that forced him to concentrate most of his time on preparing lectures. However, he managed to publish two papers in the *Reports* of the Khar'kov Mathematical Society. When teaching pressure was finally relieved by the employment of additional instructors, Liapunov published more freely, first on the stability of motion in mechanical systems with limited degrees of freedom, and then on selected concepts of potential theory and probability theory.

In 1901 Liapunov was elected a regular member of the St. Petersburg Academy, filling the chair left vacant by the death of his teacher Chebyshev. His scientific work was now focused on the types of equilibrium found in evenly rotating fluids whose particles mutually attract each other according to Newton's law. In a series of papers, he proved the existence and stability of certain forms of equilibrium. This work was immediately noted in Western Europe, where there was a growing interest in the forms of equilibrium and their importance in cosmogony. Toward the end of his career, Liapunov studied various problems of the figures of equilibrium in heterogeneous fluids, and on the basis of these studies he sought to improve the theories of Legendre, Laplace, and Clairaut concerning the shapes of planets. Together with Henri Poincaré and George Darwin, Liapunov spearheaded the search for a mathematically acceptable explanation of the formation of various types of celestial bodies.

Liapunov's studies of equilibrium forms attracted very little attention in Russia, where mathematical physics of this specific kind had not yet taken root. It was mostly for this reason that at the beginning of the twentieth century he decided to write all his scientific papers in French. Unlike Markov, Liapunov had few ties with the Russian scholarly community, and he maintained a complete aloofness from the growing conflict between autocratic ideology and the scientific world view. He was among the few Academicians who did not undertake any teaching duties, and he avoided learned societies and congresses of scientists. He gathered no disciples around himself, with the lone exception of V. A. Steklov; his family and a very few academic friends satisfied his need for personal contact. An important feature of Liapunov's life was his correspondence with Henri Poincaré, George Darwin, Charles Emile Picard, and several other Western scientists concerned with the problems he was investigating. The Russian scientific community paid him the highest homage by electing him a member of the St. Petersburg Academy, but recognition also came from Western scientific institutions: he was elected a member of the Accademia dei Lincei in Rome and a corresponding member of the Paris Académie des Sciences, and was equally honored by several other scientific bodies.[18]

Markov and Liapunov, the most accomplished disciples of Chebyshev, were the backbone of the St. Petersburg school in mathematics. Although approximative calculation and probability theory were their chief interests, they made contributions in many other areas of mathematics, notably in differential calculus and number theory. Other disciples of Chebyshev focused their attention on other branches of mathematics. A. V. Vasil'ev, for example, was interested in general algebra, symmetric functions, and non-Euclidean geometry; and D. A. Grave studied the theory of groups.

The St. Petersburg school reached the peak of its development at the turn of the century, when it began to cultivate a more conciliatory attitude toward the "impractical" branches of mathematics. It was clear that Chebyshev's school was no longer characterized by its specific mathematical research interests, but by its general methodological and philosophical orientation. Chebyshev's followers, said Liapunov, all shared certain basic convictions: that mathematical investigation begins with particular, identifiable cases; that utility, both scientific and practical, is an important criterion in the selection of problems to be studied; that the problems finally selected for study will stand out by their theoretical complexity and will demand new methods of investigation; and that the particular problems investigated lead the way to a general theory.[14] The distinguishing feature of this school was not that it necessarily produced practical results but that it took practical needs into consideration before seeking out a general theory.

<h2>SOF'IA KOVALEVSKII: MATHEMATICS AND POETRY</h2>

Sof'ia Kovalevskii was unique among Russian mathematicians of the tsarist era. She was a talented mathematician, but mathematics was only a part of her varied intellectual life: she wrote poetry, a novel, popular articles on literary and scientific themes, and an autobiography; and she collaborated in writing a play. She turned to poetry writing when she was despondent, to popular journal articles when the struggle to earn a living allowed no time for scientific problems, and to mathematics when she had abundant time and leisure to indulge her intellectual inquisitiveness.

In no other creative activity did Sof'ia Kovalevskii achieve greater results or leave a more profound impression on her contemporaries than in mathematics. She was praised by the champions of female emancipation and by admirers of literary sentimentality; but the real and most sustained plaudits came from men of science, and especially from mathematicians. Henri Poincaré thought that her work made her a "model logician" among modern mathematicians.[15] The Swedish mathematician Gösta Mittag-Leffler hailed her as one who had removed the wall between mathematics and poetry and, by personal example, had shown that lucid, abstract thought was the common goal of both.[16] K. T. Weierstrass, a determined critic of the basic concepts of classical mathematical analysis, wrote that in his career he had had few students who equaled Madame Kovalevskii's "gift of comprehension, judgment, zeal, and enthusiasm for science."[17] The accolades came in a continuous stream: Charles Hermite, Joseph Bertrand, E. Picard, N. E. Zhukovskii, P. L. Chebyshev, A. G. Stoletov, and many others announced their admiration for the intellectual daring and achievements of the "princess of mathematics."

Sof'ia Kovalevskii was not a product of formal Russian mathematical scholarship: she did not receive formal mathematical education in her homeland, nor did she follow the Russian mathematical tradition. Her sex prevented her from entering a university, even though she was born into the nobility. However, her letters and autobiographical notes indicate that she was exposed to mathematics in early childhood, and that a few years before her departure for Western Europe she had received systematic tutoring in the more advanced branches of mathematical knowledge.

Sof'ia was born Sof'ia Korvin-Krukovskaia in Moscow in 1850. As a child on the family estate in Vitebsk province, she discovered her father's notes on Mikhail Ostrogradskii's lectures in differential and integral calculus and struggled for days to comprehend their inner logic. And from her favorite uncle, P. V. Korvin-Krukovskii, she learned to appreciate the philosophical depth of mathematical operations. She wrote: "From him I learned for the first time about the quadrature of the circle, about the asymptotes, approached but never reached by a curve, and about many similar things. Their meaning understandably escaped me; but they acted on my imagination and instilled in me a high respect for mathematics as a superior and mysterious science that opened a miraculous world to those interested in it but remained inaccessible to ordinary mortals."[18] In St. Petersburg, at the age of fifteen, Sof'ia took private lessons from a tutor who introduced her to the intricacies of analytical geometry and both differential and integral calculus.[19] Mathematics, however, was only one of her many interests at this time. She also attended Sechenov's public lectures on physiology, and was intrigued by Mechnikov's work in embryology.

As a woman, Sof'ia had no access to Russian universities, and at the age of nineteen she traveled to Western Europe to continue her education. Her motive for this action was primarily ideological, for she was one of the many young people who had adopted the philosophy of Nihilism. The Nihilists sought to uproot the established sacred culture and to build a new, revitalized Russia. One of the chief goals of this campaign was to raise the educational level of every citizen, especially in the area of concrete scientific knowledge. Sof'ia's biographer, Anna Carlotta Leffler, described her motivations as follows:

"To these young enthusiasts [i.e., Nihilists] personal happiness was a secondary consideration, the sacrifice of self for a common cause being the only great and noble motive. To study, to improve their minds, and to devote whatever power they possessed to the benefit of their beloved country, helping it in its hard struggle for freedom, in its progress from darkness and oppression to light and liberty—this was the idea which inspired the hearts of these young daughters of aristocratic families. Their parents, who had never dreamed of educating them for anything but their destination as ladies and married women, naturally took an uncompromising and hostile position at these signs of independence and rebellion, which now and then burst through the mysterious reticence usually observed by the young in the presence of their elders."[20]

To escape close parental control, it was not unusual for young Nihilist women to enter into fictitious marriages with young men of similar views. Sof'ia did this in 1868, and "married" Vladimir Kovalevskii, a young popularizer of Darwinian theory who was then preparing to go to Western Europe to study paleontology.* (In 1871 the marriage became legal.) In 1870 the Kovalevskiis left for Western Europe. Heidelberg University, a flourishing institution made famous by such stalwarts of modern science as Helmholtz, Bunsen, and Kirchhoff, was Sof'ia's first stop. She attended several courses, but the teaching of the mathematician Leo Koenigsberger, a disciple of Weierstrass, made the strongest impression on her; and at the end of 1870 she transferred to Berlin University to study mathematics under Weierstrass's personal guidance.

Karl Theodor Weierstrass was one of the greatest pure mathematicians of the nineteenth century. Attempting to make some of the main concepts of mathematical analysis more definitive and logical, he dedicated his life to elaborating the work of Niels Abel and Karl Jacobi on the theory of functions. He and his disciples awoke nineteenth-century mathematicians from their "dogmatic slumber" by pointing out the falsity of many accepted propositions. Although Weierstrass made no direct contributions to applied mathematics, he filled his lectures with practical illustrations and devoted a great deal of time to preparing specific suggestions for the improvement of "practical" mathematics. He was convinced, however, that the further refinement of abstract mathematical analysis was the only really effective way to improve applied mathematics. Weierstrass is usually listed with the great mathematicians who sought a complete formalization of mathematics, but he admitted that every great mathematician is also something of a poet, and uses both logic and intuition to achieve results.[21]

With short interruptions, Sof'ia Kovalevskii spent four years in Berlin. She benefited not only from close contact with Weierstrass, but also from her association with many outstanding mathematicians who were eager to find ways of applying Weierstrass's abstract theory to the mathematical needs of the modern physical sciences. In 1874, the University of Göttingen

* See pp. 115–19.

granted her a doctorate *in absentia* on the strength of three mathematical papers: an outstanding study of the theory of partial differential equations with analytical coefficients; an extension of Laplace's explanation of the form of Saturn's rings; and a study applying a class of Abelian integrals of the third order to elliptic integrals.[22] Weierstrass's recommendation had a great influence on the university's decision; and in making it, he emphasized that since this was the first time that a woman had applied for a higher degree in mathematics, the faculty should be particularly careful to uphold high standards in judging her contributions.[23] Sof'ia received her doctorate *summa cum laude*. It was not until 1895 that a German university granted a doctorate in mathematics to any female candidate on the basis of the customary examinations.[24]

In 1874 the Kovalevskiis returned to Russia with the academic reputation of both firmly established in the West. Sof'ia was well known to the many followers and admirers of Weierstrass; Vladimir was hailed as a founder of evolutionary paleontology, and Charles Darwin was profoundly impressed with his contributions. But in Russia there was no room for either: the country was not ready to support a separate academic position in evolutionary paleontology, and even less ready to employ a woman in any institution of higher learning. Sof'ia temporarily abandoned any sustained work in mathematics, although letters from Weierstrass kept her in touch with new developments in Western mathematics and expressed sorrow for her predicament. She would have had a difficult time in any case, for the St. Petersburg mathematicians, particularly Chebyshev and his school, were suspicious of Weierstrass and his pupils, whose emphasis on mathematical exactitude ran counter to the St. Petersburg propensity for probabilistic and approximative calculations. Chebyshev himself heard from Charles Hermite and other Western mathematicians about the high esteem in which they held Sof'ia's work, and he gradually came to acknowledge her ability; but there was not much he could do about finding her an academic position.[25]

In 1879 Sof'ia read a paper on Abelian integrals at the Sixth Congress of Russian Naturalists and Physicians, which met in St. Petersburg; and in 1883 she presented a paper on the dispersion of light in crystals to the Seventh Congress in Odessa. She kept relatively busy, but most of her energy was squandered on routine work, such as reviews and journalistic articles on popular themes. In the 1860's, she had been an enthusiastic Nihilist who placed great faith in the advancement of knowledge; in the 1870's she was an unemployed intellectual, a victim of anachronistic laws designed to defend the established political and religious order from the threat of secular culture and scientific rationalism.

In 1883, Sof'ia Kovalevskii was invited by Mittag-Leffler (at Weierstrass's suggestion) to teach mathematics at the newly founded University of Stockholm.[26] On her arrival in Stockholm, a local newspaper greeted her as a "princess of science." She was the first woman to hold a university teaching position in Sweden; and though first appointed as a private docent, she was soon promoted to the rank of full professor. Sof'ia's association with Stockholm University lasted until the end of her life (she died suddenly in 1891, at the age of 41). During this period she taught twelve different courses in mathematics, including the theory of partial differential equations, Weierstrass's interpretation of algebraic, Abelian, and elliptic functions, and Poincaré's application of differential equations to the study of curves.[27] She prepared several previously written papers for publication, wrote new ones, translated two of Chebyshev's essays for *Acta Mathematica*, and kept in close touch with Weierstrass and some of his other disciples. Now more than ever before her literary gifts also found a full expression. "Childhood Memories," "Nihilist Thoughts," "Reminiscences About George Eliot," and many other essays and stories made a favorable impression on her contemporaries. Most of her writings expressed a deep-seated nostalgia for Russia and a desire that her life story and scientific contributions be known to her compatriots.

In 1888, Sof'ia Kovalevskii's eminence as a mathematician rose to new heights: she received the Bordin Prize from the Paris Academy of Sciences for a paper on the rotation of a solid body about a fixed point, a topic that had challenged the imagination and mathematical skills of men like Euler, Poisson, and Lagrange.[28] Because of the particular importance of this study, the Academy decided to raise the monetary value of the prize from 2,000 to 5,000 francs. The paper's most impressive aspect was the "precision" and "elegance" of its mathematical apparatus, which was based on an analysis of infinite series, an integration of differential equations with the help of infinite series, and an extensive use of the hyperelliptic and Abelian integrals; in essence, it was a skillful application of a most abstract branch of pure mathematics to a practical problem of mechanics.

When word of Madame Kovalevskii's great success reached Russia, K. S. Veselovskii, the permanent secretary of the St. Petersburg Academy of Sciences, publicly lamented the crippling effects of Russian law, which made it impossible for a woman to occupy a university position even if she met the highest standards of modern scholarship. No Russian university, he noted sadly, could equal Stockholm in making academic accomplishment and teaching talent the sole criteria in selecting its scientific staff.[29] In 1889 the members of the St. Petersburg Academy of Sciences elected her a corresponding member, a purely honorific title; she was the first woman to receive this honor.

It is not really surprising that mathematics was the first Russian science to produce a great female scholar, for Russian mathematics had been blessed with great vitality, a rich tradition, and an impressive array of true pioneers. Sof'ia Kovalevskii was convinced that her total work was a synthesis of two Russian traits: a passionate attachment to the freedom of poetic experience and a profound regard for the rules of logic. Weierstrass had taught her to appreciate the logical intricacies of mathematics; but she had taught Weierstrass to recognize and appreciate the transcendental power of intuition and poetry.

### NEW ORIENTATIONS

One of Chebyshev's numerous gifted disciples was A. V. Vasil'ev, who helped make Kazan University an important center of mathematical research. Vasil'ev was as keenly aware of the philosophical problems of modern science in general as he was of the deeper meanings of the expanding frontiers of modern mathematics. From Chebyshev he learned to appreciate the great versatility of probability theory, but his main contributions were in areas untouched by his teacher. He produced noted works in higher algebra and the history of mathematics; and he was the first Russian scholar to resurrect the mathematical legacy of Nikolai Lobachevskii. During the 1880's, besides helping with the first modern Russian publication of Lobachevskii's collected works, he worked at organizing a centennial commemoration of Lobachevskii's birth. The centennial conclave was held at Kazan University in 1893, opening the modern era of intensive study of Lobachevskii's legacy by Russian mathematicians and philosophers.

In his keynote address at the centennial, Vasil'ev told his listeners that the English mathematicians J. J. Sylvester and W. K. Clifford had compared the impact of Lobachevskii's discoveries to the scientific revolution wrought by Copernicus's heliocentric system. He presented an astute analysis of the cultural milieu in which Lobachevskii had worked, and described the struggle of non-Euclidean geometries for recognition. He showed clearly that Lobachevskii had not worked in a cultural and intellectual vacuum, but had kept in touch, through several of his professors at Kazan, with the revolution in modern mathematics precipitated by the early work of Karl Gauss. The most interesting passages in the speech dealt with Lobachevskii's philosophical views: Vasil'ev thought that the great geometer had been a staunch adherent of Bacon's "sensualism," and, as a consequence, a determined foe of Kant's notions of space and time as "pure categories" independent of experience. He bolstered his argument by direct quotations from Lobachevskii's *New Elements of Geometry.*

It was also on Vasilev's initiative that Kazan University's Physical and Mathematical Society inaugurated an annual Lobachevskii Prize for outstanding achievements in mathematics. Henri Poincaré was among the original recipients of this honor, and his acceptance contributed greatly to the international prestige of Kazan University. In 1904 Poincaré contributed to the Society's journal a paper that spelled out the intricate mathematical and philosophical influence of non-Euclidean geometry on modern scientific thought (most notably, its effects on the geometrical representation of complex numbers, on the introduction of hypercomplex numbers into arithmetic, and on Georg Cantor's conceptualization of infinite quantities). The main contribution of non-Euclidean geometries, according to Poincaré, was in showing that many mathematical theories could and should be considered special cases of more general theories. Non-Euclidean geometries not only had legitimized the notion of spatial relativity, but had also set off a search for more general systems of mathematical thought. Above all, they showed that in addition to the mathematics of analysis there also existed a mathematics of intuition; and that the latter was the most vital modern source of mathematical wisdom.

Russian scientists had not waited for Poincaré to inform them of the full impact of Lobachevskii's contributions on modern mathematics. In 1897 Vasil'ev, at an annual convocation of professors and students, spoke briefly on the possible scientific validity of various geometries and on the philosophical significance of the relativization of geometric axioms and postulates. By this time, too, V. F. Kagan was publishing a series of detailed articles on a modern interpretation of Lobachevskii's contributions.[30] A. P. Kotel'nikov, another mathematics professor at Kazan, used W. K. Clifford's theory of biquaternions to construct a vector theory and a non-Euclidean mechanics of three-dimensional space.[31] There was no longer any need to legitimize non-Euclidean geometry; the time had come to show how this geometry was related to specific problems of modern research.

The immediate value of non-Euclidean geometries was not so much in the elaboration of their premises as it was in subduing the mathematical conservatism of the St. Petersburg school and opening the door to modern ideas and currents in mathematics. The belief common for several decades in Western Europe, that modern mathematics began where experimental inference stopped and intuition and logical inference took over, began to find Russian supporters for the first time since Lobachevskii. The new mathematics, as exemplified by Lobachevskii's non-Euclidean geometry, gave up the notion of the absolute validity of its axioms but acquired the freedom to investigate many topics previously closed to mathematical treatment. Classical mathematics did not collapse, nor did it lose its creative impetus; but from now on it shared the stage with new developments that were free of the narrow mechanistic view in science.

During the 1890's, N. Ia. Tsinger, a professor of mathematics at Moscow University, used non-Euclidean geometries to find philosophical arguments against "scientific materialism." He attacked "mathematical empiricism," which claimed that accumulated experience is the source of all mathematical wisdom, and instead defended the claim of "mathematical rationalism" that mathematical axioms and theorems were pure constructs of the human mind. Empiricism, said Tsinger, could lead to a dangerous materialism, which "degrades the dignity of man by negating his spiritual nature and by striving to make him a slave of matter." Both "moral sentiments" and strictly logical proofs should influence every objectively thinking man to reject empiricism. Tsinger began by stating: "Geometrical representations originate in the pure mind, and therefore command the ideal qualities of exactness and reliability." He concluded by defending the moral code and insisting that science was only one side of man's spiritual life. Truth could be approached in many other ways—for example, as "an ideal of beauty and harmony," or as "an ideal of goodness and honor, justice and humanity."[32] In the impressive conquests of science spearheaded by non-Euclidean geometries, Tsinger saw a reaffirmation of the idealistic foundations of scientific thought.

V. V. Bobynin, lecturer in the history of mathematics at Moscow University, did the most to popularize the philosophical and cultural analysis of mathematics. During the years 1880–1900, his writings made his countrymen aware of three comparatively new branches of mathematics: mathematical history, mathematical logic, and mathematical philosophy. Mathematical history, according to Bobynin, is a cultural study of the inner logic in the growth of mathematical thought: it traces the emergence and growth of integrated systems of mathematical ideas, and can provide the foundations for a philosophy of mathematics.[33] Bobynin himself was the first Russian scholar to offer a systematic historical survey of the Russian mathematical tradition.[34] Mathematical logic is the study of the basic processes of mathematical conceptualization, and was inaugurated in its modern version by George Boole's classic studies in the 1840's and 1850's. Mathematical logic reached Russia in the 1880's, thanks to Bobynin, but it failed to cause much excitement;[35] the same was true of Whitehead and Russell's *Principia Mathematica*, published much later. Finally, Bobynin defined mathematical philosophy as a combined study of the history, logic, and cultural significance of mathematical knowledge.

One of the most important concepts of modern mathematics is the theory of groups, which was initiated by the study of analogies between the properties of algebraic equations and the properties of various groups of natural phenomena. Group theory was first formulated in 1828-30 by the French mathematician Evariste Galois, as a by-product of his successful search for proofs that equations of orders higher than the fourth could not be solved.[36] The theory of groups could readily be applied to the study of many regularities in the physical world (for example, crystalline symmetries), and it yielded whole new methodologies for investigating the structural attributes of the groups of various natural phenomena. It has been called "an algebra without arithmetic," a "super algebra," and "the most general conception of mathematical tactics"; and it has led modern mathematics to previously unforeseen levels of abstraction.

Although group theory reached Russia during the 1860's, it was not until the end of the century that it attracted able and creative mathematicians. Even then, its chief proponents came from provincial universities unencumbered by strong commitments to traditional branches of mathematics. During the 1880's, A. V. Vasil'ev worked on the applications of finite groups of linear transformations in the study of rational automorphic functions. D. A. Grave, a professor of mathematics first at Khar'kov and then at Kiev, lectured his students on new developments in the theory of groups, and published the first Russian monograph on the subject in 1908.[37] He subjected Galois's theory to extensive modifications, and explored its relationship to the modern theories of invariants and quadratic forms. In 1914-15, O. Iu. Shmidt, a young private docent at Kiev University, published a series of articles under the general title *The Abstract Theory of Groups*, comprehensively explaining the theories of both finite and infinite groups. The primary value of Shmidt's work was in its rich anticipation of future developments in group theory.

Another new movement in mathematics was diametrically opposite to group theory: in essence it proposed a far more extensive arithmetization of mathematics. In the 1870's and 1880's the German mathematician Leopold Kronecker raised a considerable stir by his demands for a complete arithmetization of mathematics, which, he insisted, should be based on the real numbers alone. Kronecker did not have direct Russian supporters; but there were many Russians who advocated a much greater and more consistent emphasis on arithmetical calculation than was present in contemporary mathematics. Led by N. V. Bugaev and firmly identified with the Moscow Mathematical Society, the champions of this orientation argued that classical mathematics—and in particular differential and integral calculus—was dominated by a mechanistic view emphasizing universal causality and continuity and ignoring those phenomena of nature and society that are noncontinuous and "free."[38] By supporting this mechanistic orientation, according to Bugaev and his followers, classical mathematics gave unwarranted support to materialistic philosophy, the archenemy of the sacred culture surrounding the institutional complexes of autocracy. One follower of Bugaev made it very clear that he fought against the hegemony of algebraic calculations solely in order to preserve the Russian monarchy from the erosive influences of materialism and secularism.[39]

While defending "arithmology"—as he called his theory of discontinuous functions—Bugaev also contributed papers on freedom of the will and on "evolutionary monadology" to the journal of the Moscow Psychological Society, which was known for its interest in idealistic philosophy. "Evolutionary monadology" was Bugaev's label for a philosophical orientation combining the idea of progress as a universal principle of nature and society with a unique reinterpretation of Leibniz's "monads" (the psychical and physical nuclei of the universe). Eventually, a simplified monadology became the official philosophy of the arithmological school. Arithmology, as envisaged by Bugaev, drew its main support from number theory and probability theory. From number theory it borrowed the idea of the discrete—and therefore discontinuous—nature of numbers. From probability theory it accepted the notion of indeterminacy, or "freedom," as an important principle describing the behavior of many kinds of natural and cultural phenomena. In general, the Bugaev school was strong in emphasizing the shortcomings of abstract algebraic analysis, but it was weak in its efforts to produce a mathematical apparatus that would offset these shortcomings.

Calculus, according to Bugaev, made mathematics a science of absolute precision and predictability. But mathematics was much more than calculus—it also incorporated stochastic measurements, statistical calculations, and non-Euclidean geometries.

If Bugaev and his followers had not chosen to link "arithmology" with autocratic ideology, their arguments would have received more sympathetic attention from the academic community. But despite their bizarre super-patriotism, they had something positive to offer to their contemporaries. They deeply sensed that the development of modern science would depend increasingly on mathematical methodology, and they argued that mathematics, in order to meet its new tasks, must throw off outmoded traditions and develop more versatile theories and procedures. They underscored the great value of the increasing mathematicization of economics, demography, and other social sciences; and they also saw great merit in statistical studies of law and morality.[40] Their basic contribution, however, was in making their learned countrymen aware of the urgent need for thoroughly reexamining the basic foundations of mathematics.

Bugaev's philosophy of science is centered around two basic propositions. In the first place, all aspects of science must be associated with mathematical methodology. To mathematicize science is to apply all branches of mathematics to the study of the universe, and not just those that best account for natural continuities and causal sequences. In particular, mathematics must help science to study discontinuities and probabilities, which are not subject to key causes. In the second place, the analytical and arithmological approaches must be considered not as mutually exclusive but as complementing each other, for they help one understand different aspects of the same phenomena. According to Bugaev, "Causality and purposiveness, indispensability and random chance, self-assertion and self-denial—all these can and must operate in full harmony."[41]

The idealist physicist A. I. Bachinskii elaborated on Bugaev's scientific world view by providing examples from modern cell theory, Mendel's genetics, the theory of sound, and sociology, all illustrating the growing concern of modern scientists with discontinuous phenomena. The one-sided acceptance of the deterministic, or analytical, approach in science, said Bachinskii, had provided the groundwork for the emergence of modern materialism in general and economic materialism in particular, which explained the basic similarities between Darwinism and Marxism.[42] Integral and differential calculus supported a mechanistic world view that treated all natural phenomena as parts of one continuous process, expressed all natural processes in terms of uniform causal relationships, and dealt far too much with infinitesimally small phenomena.[43] Bachinskii went so far as to criticize Lev Tolstoi for his suggestion that human history could be regarded as a continuous process that could be deduced from the huge mass of historical incidents with the help of calculus.[44]

Bugaev's ideas were espoused and defended mostly by idealistic philosophers and theologians, who interpreted them as a mortal blow to the intellectual supremacy of science, and as a powerful, though indirect, defense of metaphysical and religious experience as a source of true wisdom.[45] The idealistic philosopher L. M. Lopatin saw in Bugaev's emphasis on discontinuous functions not only a negation of the exclusiveness of the deterministic view but also a recognition of "the mathematical indispensability of freedom."[46]

The first scholar to develop a method for assessing the magnitude of discontinuous infinite point sets was the German mathematician Hermann Hankel, who developed a "theory of measure." In 1901, using this theory and building on the work of Georg Cantor and Emile Borel, the brilliant young Frenchman Henri Lebesgue formulated the first general principles for computing the integrals of noncontinuous functions. Lebesgue did not follow in the path of the Bugaev school and its Western counterparts, which sought separate mathematical approaches to the problems of continuous and discontinuous functions; instead, he created a new and highly abstract theory that transcended, and therefore included, both continuous and discontinuous functions. His work acquired great importance with the advent of modern studies of the structure of matter and energy, which no longer assumed a continuity in the variation of many physical quantities. At the very beginning of the twentieth century Max Planck discovered that a black body radiates energy discontinuously—that is, in whole numbers, never in fractions, of energy packets (or "quanta"). It was not until the end of the 1920's, however, that the new physics and the theory of discontinous sets were combined. The man who made the first step in bringing the two together was A. N. Kolmogorov, a "second-generation" member of the Moscow school of mathematics.[47]

The Moscow school of mathematics, which included many outstanding contributors to the most modern branches of mathematics, gradually developed during the years immediately preceding the October Revolution. The roots of its major orientation were in the theory of functions of a real variable—a theory based on the theory of sets. The men who gradually built a distinct school of Russian mathematics on this theory were D. F. Egorov and his pupil N. N. Luzin.

During the first decade of the twentieth century, D. F. Egorov was the major professor of mathematics at Moscow University. He was noted for various contributions to geometry, but acquired particular fame as the organizer of a seminar on modern theories related to analysis. Around 1910 he became absorbed in the theory of sets and the theory of functions, and in 1911 contributed a paper entitled "A Series of Measurable Functions" to the *Comptes rendus* of the Paris Académie des Sciences. Egorov was the first Russian scientist to elaborate on the ideas of Borel and Lebesgue, introducing the theory of sets into Russian mathematical thinking.[48]

The most promising and active member of Egorov's seminar was N. N. Luzin, who graduated from Moscow University in 1906 and was given a government stipend to pursue graduate studies in mathematics. From 1910 to 1914, Luzin studied in Western Europe, mostly in Paris and Heidelberg. He spent more time in libraries than in classrooms, and wrote ten articles, each dealing with a specific problem related to the theory of functions; several of these papers were subsequently incorporated in his doctoral dissertation on the theory of integrals and trigonometric series. Luzin's work greatly elaborated the various properties of measurable functions as established by Lebesgue. He proved that every measurable function on an interval could be made continuous by changing its values on a set of arbitrarily small measure.[49] Discontinuous and various other forms of "bad" functions could be integrated not by bypassing analysis but by elevating it to a higher level of abstraction. In brief, the class of measurable functions became much larger than the class of continuous functions.

Luzin's rare mathematical gifts were matched by his resourceful teaching techniques. He made every lecture an ordered and logically intricate exercise in creative work for himself and his students alike. He managed to attract the most gifted students to his courses, involving them in informal collective research projects. These students formed a tightly woven *kruzhok* dedicated to the elaboration of Luzin's ideas and the constant search for new ones.[50] Their creative power was amply demonstrated in 1916–17, when the Paris Académie des Sciences published papers written by four undergraduates at Moscow.[51] These four studies marked the real beginning of the Moscow school. One of the four men, P. S. Aleksandrov, noted fifty years later: "All of us were in a constant state of exhilaration. Under all conditions and in every situation we talked about mathematics, and each of us knew what everyone else was doing. None showed the least inclination to abandon his work; and every achievement was greeted with great joy, no matter who was behind it."[52]

In one sense, Chebyshev's St. Petersburg school had been "practical" in its orientation, for its members had used concrete problems as the starting point for their mathematical studies. The Moscow school, on the other hand, received its initial impetus not from "practical" demands, but from a need to improve the formal tools of mathematical operations. It dwelt in the world of pure abstractions, and sought to generalize its theoretical formulations as far as possible by elucidating the inner logic of their mathematical expression.[53] During the late 1920's, when mathematics was called on to provide the methodological tools for studying discontinuities in physical nature, the Moscow school was at last ready to meet the challenge of new "external" and "practical" problems by providing a way to assess the magnitude of absolutely discontinuous infinite point sets. A. N. Kolmogorov did so by combining the new theory of point sets with probability theory, giving quantum physics one of its basic methodological tools.[54]

### APPLIED MATHEMATICS: N. E. ZHUKOVSKII AND A. N. KRYLOV

In 1900 the Moscow Mathematical Society celebrated the publication of the twentieth volume of its *Mathematical Symposium*. On this occasion, N. V. Bugaev, president of the Society, described the unique features of mathematics in the family of sciences and the peculiar position of mathematicians in the community of scientists. Mathematics, he said, performs three intellectual roles: it provides the most effective methodological tools for sciences dedicated to raising the level of human welfare; it "introduces harmony and order into the world view" by recognizing the love of truth as the highest criterion of intellectual existence; and it is the most effective medium for expressing the deductive powers of the human mind.[55] Mathematics provides the scholar with meager earthly rewards for two reasons: it draws its wisdom not from the external world, but only from the inner depths of the human intellect; and it has little connection with current events, social sentiments, and the arts, "which affect the imagination and emotions." Bugaev pointed out that mathematical knowledge, because of its inward orientation, cannot be effectively diffused beyond professional circles, which explains the relative isolation of mathematicians from society at large.

Compared to other scientists, mathematicians were in fact relatively isolated. However, Bugaev overlooked the existence of a new type of scholar who sought to establish a dynamic and mutually beneficial interrelationship between advanced mathematics and concrete technological problems. At the turn of the century, Russia began to produce first-rate scholars who concerned themselves with both theoretical and practical problems. This new breed of scientists was eminently represented by N. E. Zhukovskii and A. N. Krylov, who were among the best Russian scholars in both pure and applied mathematics but were also actively involved in engineering and organizational work in various branches of modern technology.

N. E. Zhukovskii was born in a small village near the ancient city of Vladimir. He graduated from Moscow University in 1868, and in 1872 began to teach mathematics at the Moscow Technical School; later, he also taught applied mathematics and analytical mechanics at Moscow University. As one might expect from his connection with both these institutions, Zhukovskii was constantly endeavoring to blend scientific and technical ideas, and to find simple practical applications for general theoretical propositions. His scientific work covered a wide area, including problems from general mechanics, hydrodynamics, the mechanics of solids, and astronomy. In all cases his search for general scientific propositions went hand in hand with his skillful refinement of experimental techniques and mathematical formulations. He never abandoned his unqualified loyalty to Newtonian mechanics, and never deviated from the belief that true science consists of mathematical expressions of experimental data. A complete scientist, according to Zhukovskii, must work to advance mathematical knowledge and adapt it to advances in the other sciences; but he must also utilize the potentialities of modern industry to widen the experimental base of science.

This dual ideal was best expressed in Zhukovskii's work in aerodynamics and aviation technology, to which he made universally recognized contributions. He was responsible for the first aeronautical laboratories in Russia, for the inclusion of aeronautics among the major fields covered at the Congresses of Russian Naturalists, and for the first Russian teaching courses in fields related to aviation. He was involved in the construction of several models of commercial and military aircraft, and in training Russian aviators during World War I. However, Zhukovskii will be remembered by future generations primarily as a pioneer in developing the mathematical foundations of aerodynamics and aeronautics. His most notable effort (though anticipated by the German physicist M. W. Kutta) was a theorem on the lifting force of an airplane wing, which he derived from the theory of functions of a complex variable. By 1900, Zhukovskii, although he did not teach mathematics, was generally considered the leading mathematician at Moscow University. That he did not work in isolation is best illustrated by the career of his younger colleague S. A. Chaplygin. Chaplygin is also considered a major pioneer in modern aerodynamics and aviation; and he too adapted both mechanics and mathematics to the needs of aerodynamics.[56]

What Zhukovskii did for aerodynamics, A. N. Krylov did for marine mechanics and engineering. He was rightfully called an encyclopedist of naval arts and sciences: he was a mathematician, a shipbuilding engineer and theoretician, an artillery expert, and a historian of science. In all these specialties, Krylov was first and foremost a practical seaman; however, one can also assert with some truth that in all his studies he wrote primarily as a mathematician. His major contributions were in the structural mechanics of ships, which he helped transform from an art into a mathematical discipline. According to a modern writer:

"For Krylov, mathematics and practical problems did not exist separately; the close unity of the two was evident everywhere in his work. He had no sympathy for purely theoretical schemes and abstract constructions, and stated many times that the overconcern of contemporary mathematics with rigor and precision of calculation ... deprives man of courage in his search for truth and makes him distrust intuition and common sense. Krylov had a profound understanding of the value of general mathematical methods as applied to concrete problems. Most of his works in mathematical physics were built upon a single method [related to differential equations with variable coefficients] whose extraordinary flexibility made it applicable to all the ramifications of the problem under consideration. The unity of mathematical method in all the many problems of the natural sciences was a popular theme in many works of Krylov."[57]

Krylov's approach was somewhat atypical of his time. After having made great progress between 1650 and 1825, mechanics entered a phase of relatively slow development. At the end of the nineteenth century, however, a critical reappraisal of the classical tradition was under way, thanks to the work of scientists like Henri Poincaré, who contended that Newton's mechanics was not the last word in this field, nor even the only possible system. Poincaré proclaimed: "Absolute space, absolute time, and even geometry are not conditions which are imposed on mechanics.... All these things no more existed before mechanics than the French language can be logically said to have existed before the truths which are expressed in French."[58]

Many of Krylov's contemporaries agreed with Poincaré and denigrated Newtonian mechanics. But Krylov was unaffected by the revolution in modern physics and mathematics; a keen and polished historian of science, he remained faithful to the tradition wrought by Newton, Euler, Lagrange, and Poisson, and employed only this tradition in studying his major scientific concern, the problem of the oscillation of ships in motion. In mathematical calculation—the real strength of his contributions to the structural mechanics of ships—Krylov relied almost entirely on differential equations with variable coefficients. He simplified these equations by the extensive use of two methods for obtaining the best approximation to arbitrary individual functions: algebraic polynomials, a method developed by Chebyshev; and trigonometric polynomials, which were based on an expansion of the functions in a Fourier series. Euler and Lagrange, he felt, were essentially correct in asserting that calculus produced accurate results not because of its intrinsic infallibility but because its errors tended to offset each other. Krylov assumed, contrary to popular notions, that all mathematical calculation was approximative. According to him, the methods of best approximations to selected individual functions developed since the time of Euler were fully adequate means of calculation; and, because of their relative simplicity, they were especially advantageous in all cases including large numbers of items. He argued that every calculation "must be arranged in such a manner that a final result of the required precision may be obtained by using the least number of figures and the least number of operations."[59]

Krylov had no use for the "inwardly oriented" branches of mathematics, which were more interested in adducing rigorous proofs for mathematical theories and formulas than in applying them; thus he rejected group theory, set theory, and non-Euclidean geometries. He preferred methods whose practical applicability could be readily tested and whose relative simplicity made them both economical and easily adaptable to new situations.

Krylov presented many of his mathematical ideas to international audiences, and contributed papers combining the "theory of ships" with his ingenious mathematical techniques to the *Bulletin* of the French Association Technique Maritime, the *Transactions* of the British Institution of Naval Architects, and the German *Enzyklopädie der mathematischen Wissenschaften* and *Mathematische Annalen*.[60] On many occasions, he read his papers before Western learned societies and participated in discussions on other papers relevant to the science of shipbuilding. It was under his influence that the Royal Naval College at Greenwich decided to instruct its students in the application of Chebyshev's quadrature rule to the structural mechanics of ships.[61] For his students at the Naval Academy in St. Petersburg, Krylov published a special volume bringing together many techniques for the approximative numerical integration of ordinary differential equations.

While the revolutionary trends in modern physics ushered in by quantum theory and the principle of relativity ended the undisputed domination of Newtonian mechanics in many areas of modern science, Krylov, like Zhukovskii, worked diligently to preserve and extend the valuable features of the Newtonian tradition. Krylov will be remembered not for his original contributions to mathematics but for the extraordinary fruitfulness of his endeavors to find modern applications for classical mathematics. In reading the great masters of mathematics, he paid equal attention to the logic of their arguments and the practicality and suggestiveness of their concrete examples.

Krylov's familiarity with the classic literature in mathematics and related fields helped him become one of the leading Russian translators of scientific literature. His rendering of Newton's *Principia* in Russian was one index of his great ability in this field, and was rightfully heralded as one of the greatest events in the history of modern Russian science. In over 200 comments on the translation, some of them several pages long, Krylov provided ample proof of his unmatched familiarity with the details of the Newtonian legacy.[62]

In 1916 Krylov was elected a member of the St. Petersburg Academy of Sciences in recognition of his contributions to mathematical physics and mechanics. During World War I, when the government, the scientific community, and society at large placed an increasing emphasis on the utilitarian value of science, Krylov was regarded as a model scientist, for he covered the full range of science, from its most abstract conceptions to its most useful applications. He was a prime mover in the Committee for the Study of Natural Productive Forces (KEPS), founded by the Academy in 1915 to coordinate the national defense effort in science.

Krylov was engaged in all the pursuits characteristic of the Russian scientists of his time: he was a theoretician, thoroughly at home with the legacy of classical mechanics and mathematics; he was a great experimenter, combining extraordinary intuitive power with sure hands and a sense for organization; and he was a successful teacher. When the revolution of 1905 forced the Imperial Naval Academy to discontinue its teaching activities temporarily, Krylov joined a group of mathematics professors who continued their teaching duties by meeting interested students in a local high school.[63] The lectures he delivered here formed the nucleus of his popular textbook in approximative calculation, published in 1911. Krylov was also a gifted administrator, and held many government posts during his career. For several years he headed the Naval Technical Committee (which had been entrusted with rebuilding the Russian navy after the disastrous war with Japan), holding the rank of lieutenant general. Finally he was an astute businessman; he greatly increased his earthly possessions by serving as a consultant to several private shipbuilding concerns and was a stockholder in at least one of them. Krylov survived the October Revolution easily; and at his death in 1945 he was one of the most honored Soviet scientists.[64]

Krylov may be compared with his prominent contemporary N. N. Luzin. Krylov, as we have seen, preferred to relate his mathematics, however abstract, directly to the physical world. For example, he applied the mathematical apparatus developed by Lagrange and Laplace for calculating the movements of celestial bodies to a scientific study of the rolling of ships on ocean waves. Luzin, on the other hand, built a highly abstract mathematical apparatus seemingly unrelated to the physical world. He worked in an intellectual climate dominated by the new freedom ushered in by non-Euclidean geometry, a freedom that allowed the mathematician to roam far beyond the visible physical realities, but also to meet the mounting challenge of the new physics unhampered by mechanistic determinism. In actuality, the lines of thought followed by Krylov and Luzin did not exclude each other; they were merely different and equally valuable aspects of modern Russian mathematics. Krylov, at least, recognized the existence of two mathematics: one concerned with the mysteries of the physical world, and the other with philosophical probing into the logic of mathematical thought. In 1929 Luzin was elected a regular member of the Soviet Academy of Sciences, filling a new position in philosophy, not mathematics. In recommending him for this position, Krylov wrote an impressive essay on the classical roots and eternal vitality of mathematical philosophy.[65]

## CHAPTER TWELVE

# Modern Physics and Chemistry

## THE CRISIS IN PHYSICS

Between 1880 and 1910 a series of remarkable discoveries challenged the basic axioms of classical physics. The notion of continuity in physical processes—the fundamental principle of the Newtonian legacy—was found to be inapplicable to the structure and dynamics of the microuniverse. At the same time, the notion of the indestructibility, immutability, and indivisibility of atoms was proved incorrect by the discoveries of Henri Becquerel, the Curies, and J. J. Thomson. Einstein's theory of relativity challenged the Newtonian interpretation of time, space, and mass as absolute categories independent of any reference points. Henri Poincaré found an appreciative and rapidly growing audience for his claim that a relativistic reorientation of mathematics was indispensable for the growth of modern mechanics and physics. Max Planck and many others made it clear that probability calculation would assume a dominant role in modern science. And mathematicians intensified their search for a suitable analytical approach to discontinuities and "irregularities" in the behavior of nature.

The new era of modern science was ushered in by men who were first and foremost experimenters, and most of the new ideas arose to explain the puzzling results of specific laboratory work. But the revolution in physics was not produced by experiments alone. Philosophical challenges, as well as the growing demand for a thorough reexamination of the theory of scientific knowledge, encouraged scholars to apply radically new interpretations to experimental data. Mach and a legion of neopositivists, building on the philosophical legacy of Bernard, Helmholtz, and Du Bois-Reymond, helped elevate the new science above the traditional battle between materialism and idealism. Contemporary epistemology emphasized the subjective element in the design, execution, and interpretation of scientific experiments in the laboratory.

The emergence of modern physics arose from the mounting criticism of the Newtonian mechanistic paradigm. Maxwell's theory had extended this paradigm to include electricity and magnetism, but had also exposed some of its fundamental internal inconsistencies and blind spots. At the end of the century, many physicists were busy tidying up Maxwell's formulation; some of them managed to stay within it and still make major contributions, while others abandoned it because of inconsistencies between its basic principles and the results of their own experiments. Thus the revolution in modern physics was a result of the inner logic of the development of science. The failure of the Newtonian mechanistic system and Maxwell's theory to account for some of the basic results arising from modern experimental techniques demanded a new theoretical approach.

The rise of modern physics was also related to developments in the other sciences. It should be remembered, for example, that Planck's discovery of discontinuities in radiation coincided with the rediscovery of Mendel's genetic laws and the publication of Hugo De Vries's studies of mutation, both supporting the idea of discontinuities in biological evolution. In social thought, the emphasis on continuity in the development of culture and society—as set forth in the works of Comte, Spencer, and Marx—came in for a critical reexamination. This effort led to a proliferation of historical orientations that emphasized the uniqueness and discontinuity of events rather than the generality and continuity of processes. The new physics and its supporting sciences connected natural phenomena that had previously been unconnected in the minds of scientists, and also opened previously untapped areas for scientific investigation. These new scientific developments did not abolish classical physics; they merely removed it from the areas where it did not belong and opened new domains that were beyond its reach.

A similar reorientation was spreading through all of modern culture. Formalism, epistemological relativism, and "indeterminism" were as characteristic of symbolism in poetry and cubism in painting as they were of quantum and relativistic physics. Modern physics and the modern arts refused to copy nature or to recognize and obey the absolute power of its objective laws; instead, they interpreted, changed, and "created" nature. By abandoning deterministic laws, they gave more freedom and more power to the intellect and intuition. The emphasis on precision in scientific and artistic expression was as strong as ever, if not stronger; but "precision" was redefined to mean the inner consistency and logical unity of a labyrinthine system of coordinated thought.

Mathematics, which united the sciences and the arts, was now engaged in a continuous process of creating new calculation procedures. In effect, mathematicians could now define for themselves the rules under which they would operate. This new freedom yielded many new prospects for the mathematical study of nature, and allowed the application of various mathematical procedures to the same substantive science. Modern wave mechanics and matrix mechanics, for example, are one and the same theoretical complex but are expressed through different mathematical apparatuses. Maxwell and other champions of the mechanistic orientation recognized the value of probability calculations as a preliminary and auxiliary procedure; but modern physicists made probability a fundamental concept and a prime methodological tool. Non-Euclidean geometry, philosophically and methodologically incompatible with classical physics, became one of the foundations of relativistic physics.

During the 1890's some of the leading Russian physicists sensed the growing crisis in their discipline, but none made an identifiable contribution to the victory of the new orientation. In Russia, physics was a slowly developing, unexciting, and diffuse science. Physics laboratories in the universities were poorly equipped, and served mostly as repositories of demonstration materials. In the St. Petersburg Academy of Sciences, interest was centered exclusively on meteorology, and the physical laboratory was more a museum than an active scientific workshop. Russia had no more than a dozen competent physicists, none brilliant enough to establish a distinct tradition or attract younger research scholars. The learned societies paid little attention to physics; they did not sponsor laboratory experimentation, and their publications ignored physical research. The physical section of the Russian Physical and Chemical Society was generally regarded as a weak partner retained out of courtesy.

The Mendeleevian tradition, which had so inspired Russian science earlier in the century, proved to be a conservative force working against the modern trend in physics. Mendeleev still viewed his periodic law of elements as a revelation that had raised chemistry to the level of Newtonian physics, and he stubbornly opposed the forces challenging the mechanistic orientation. Because of his influence, Russia developed a strong resistance to views espousing the divisibility and mutability of atoms. Mendeleev was convinced that the periodic law was incompatible with any notion of instability and compositeness in the atomic substance. Indeed, he was the last of the great nineteenth-century scientists who regarded the atomic theory as only a special ramification of Newtonian physics.

No serious Russian scientist of the late nineteenth century challenged the Mendeleevian tradition; and thus Russia played no part in developing the new physics. Mendeleev's ideas, however, were severely criticized outside the world of professional science. B. N. Chicherin, a jurist, a Hegelian, and a protector of religion and metaphysics from the encroachments of science, wrote a book and a series of essays combining sweeping philosophical statements and mathematical scholarship, in which he equated the structure of atoms with the structure of the solar system. Each atom, according to him, consists of a central mass with particles rotating around it, and the structure of each atom "indicates a possibility of its formation from simpler particles."[1] Although Chicherin wrote before radioactivity and the electron were discovered, his interpretation was a rough facsimile of the Rutherford-Bohr planetary model of atomic structure. But since his ideas were embedded in a maze of incomprehensible metaphysical verbiage and made no reference to the experimental contributions of modern physics, no serious scholar paid attention to them.

N. A. Morozov, an amateur scientist and a professional revolutionary, was imprisoned in 1881 for illegal political activities and was not released until 1905. He spent his years in prison examining the deeper philosophical aspects of Mendeleev's law, an interest developed in his youth. Cut off from any access to the new developments in experimental physics, but not from standard works on traditional chemistry, he built a completely abstract theory of elements and atoms. Morozov's theory, developed before 1901, contained two basic propositions: chemical elements are subject to evolutionary changes; and the evolution of elements is firmly linked with the transmutability and structural complexity of atoms.[2] All atoms, he claimed, are made up of three basic mass particles (structural hydrogen, "proto-helium," and "arkonii") and two electric particles (a positive and a negative). Morozov shared Faraday's belief that man would soon develop the necessary tools to transform the chemical elements at will.

After his release from prison in 1905, Morozov found that some of his claims were substantiated by the experimental work of Henri Becquerel, the Curies, and J. J. Thomson. Surprisingly, Mendeleev himself appreciated the seriousness of Morozov's theoretical interest, since Morozov was interested primarily in giving the periodic law of elements a broader, more modern interpretation. It was on Mendeleev's recommendation that St. Petersburg University awarded Morozov an honorary doctorate in chemistry. Morozov toured the country speaking on his pet topic: the coming of a new age of alchemy, which would actually achieve the transmutation of elements.[3] That his popular lectures found an appreciative audience is shown by the many honors awarded him. Within a short period, he was admitted to the Russian Physical and Chemical Society, the Russian Astronomical Society, and the

Society of Admirers of Natural Science, Anthropology, and Ethnography. In addition, he was elected president of the newly founded Cosmological Society.[4]

In 1874, J. C. Maxwell wrote to an American friend that he had been visited by the young Russian A. G. Stoletov, who, in search of a model for a laboratory to be built in Moscow, had come to England to study the organization and facilities of the Cavendish Laboratory at Cambridge.[5] Stoletov was the most determined and outspoken critic of the low standards of Russian research facilities, and worked diligently to make school administrators and government officials aware of the rapidly growing complexity of modern research instruments.

In spite of Stoletov and many others like him, no serious efforts were made to expand and improve Russian physics laboratories until the beginning of the twentieth century. The expansion of the physics laboratory at Moscow University in 1889 partly relieved the situation; and the newly founded polytechnical institutes provided additional laboratory facilities and trained a great many physicists. The major drawback of these particular laboratories was that they were overburdened with educational duties.[6] At the end of the century the one-room physics "laboratory" of the St. Petersburg Academy of Sciences, for many years almost completely deserted, was reactivated; but it took more than a decade to acquire even a few modern instruments, and was not officially designated a laboratory until 1917.[7] In 1907 the physics branch of the Russian Physical and Chemical Society began to publish a separate journal of respectable quality. Young Russian scientists now worked in the laboratories of Roentgen, Planck, and other leaders of modern physical thought. In 1912 the Society for the Establishment of a Scientific Institute was founded in Moscow, and, aided by the Ledentsov Society, it soon built the very modern Moscow Institute of Physics, which opened its doors in 1916.

At about this time the new physics began to reach Russia in the form of translated works. The publication of a series of symposia on modern physics, containing mostly translated articles by leading Western scientists, was begun in 1911 and was widely acclaimed. "The Structure of Matter," "The Principle of Relativity," "The Nature of Light," and "The New World Outlook in Physics" were among the titles in the new series. A parallel series dealing with modern ideas in mathematics offered a symposium on the challenges to mathematics resulting from the revolution in physics, and another on the epistemological and mathematical treatment of the concepts of time and space. In 1912 the Moscow teachers of physics founded the Moscow Society for the Study and Popularization of Physics. Through the journals *Physical Review* and *Electricity*, the ideas of the new physics reached active scientists, schoolteachers, factory engineers, and other interested professional groups.

During the last two decades before the October Revolution, physical thought in Russia was dominated by four distinct orientations, each claiming some of the leading physicists of the time among its adherents.

The first orientation was strictly Newtonian. Some of its leading champions were closely bound to the Maxwellian tradition; others carried the Newtonian mechanistic model into previously unexplored areas. Most of these men belonged to the older generation, who had received their education at the time when Maxwell was engaged in the enormous task of giving logical and mathematical unity to classical physics and of amalgamating electricity, magnetism, and optics into one science. They were excited by the discoveries and theoretical views of H. R. Hertz, Ludwig Boltzmann, and other leading physicists of the 1880's, and their own research was concentrated on such specific problems of the Maxwellian formulations as required clarification or experimental verification. Perhaps the foremost representative of this orientation was P. N. Lebedev.

Maxwell had been much concerned with establishing the pressure of light. He fully endorsed Faraday's notions of the existence of a lateral repulsion between lines of force, as well as tension along them, and formulated a theory of stress in material bodies. From this theory, he derived a mathematical expression for the pressure that would be exerted by a light wave on a metallic sheet capable of perfect reflection. For some time this theory was purely speculative, but in 1899 Lebedev produced incontrovertible experimental proof of the existence of light pressure.[8] Lebedev presented his findings first at a meeting of the Swiss Société Vaudoise des Sciences Naturelles and then as a report to the World Congress of Physicists held in Paris in 1900. His contribution made a profound impression on the international community of scientists and helped him procure funds at home for expanding and modernizing laboratory facilities at Moscow University. Lebedev's experimental work in this and other areas solved one of the basic riddles of the electromagnetic theory of light, and indicated an electromagnetic explanation of intermolecular forces;[9] it also helped introduce the notion of radiation pressure into astronomy. In his long study of the pressure of light on gaseous substances, Lebedev used twenty complex instruments, most of which he designed and constructed himself.[10]

Lebedev is remembered in Russia not only because he raised a vital field of physical research in his country to the highest Western standards, but also because he founded the first Russian school in physics. He attracted gifted students by his own scientific achievements, and molded them into a unified school by his profound sense for cooperation and organization. All the theses prepared in Lebedev's laboratory dealt with topics directly related to his own current research interests.[11] Immediately after Lebedev published his paper on the pressure of light on solid bodies, for example, two of his students began to work on the pressure of light on fluid and gaseous bodies. This work, in turn, provided preliminary hints for Lebedev's own studies.[12]

In spite of these close connections, Lebedev's supervision of the experiments conducted by his students was open and informal, the result being that most students had an intimate knowledge of all the projects conducted in the laboratory. Students' opinions were solicited in the construction of new experimental devices, whether these were directly related to their own projects or not. To the work in the laboratory was added a regular colloquium, an informal vehicle for exchanging news of the latest developments in physics and presenting the results of independent research carried out by Lebedev's students. This colloquium soon grew into the Moscow Physical Society.[13]

Lebedev's style of work provided his students with an ideal balance of three conditions indispensable for scientific work: the intuitive search for new aspects of the universal symmetry of nature; the opportunity for technical ingenuity in constructing experiments to examine the intricate problems of modern physics; and a thorough grounding in the mathematics needed to describe and organize modern scientific knowledge. According to one of his students, Lebedev looked at the "essential aspects" of nature with the inspiration of an artist and the quantitative precision of a rigorous mathematician: intuitive insights marked the first steps of his experimental work, and mathematical expressions were the end products.[14]

Lebedev's scientific work was not part of the mainstream of modern physics. He was too busy and too productive in elaborating and refining Maxwell's theories to meet all the challenges posed by the new discoveries that heralded the end of the mechanistic age. For this reason, his school began to splinter soon after it was formed. In modern Russia, however, no scientist equaled his contributions to the revitalization of physics and the advancement of experimental research. In 1912, six months before he died at the age of 46, Lebedev wrote to K. A. Timiriazev to propose a study of the relation of electromagnetic phenomena to gravitation. Perhaps, Timiriazev commented, this study would have provided a final synthesis of all physical phenomena.[15]

In addition to Lebedev, the stalwarts of the classical orientation in physics were N. E. Zhukovskii and A. N. Krylov: the first helped lay the foundations of modern aerodynamics; the second specialized in the structural mechanics of shipbuilding.* Their contributions were living testimony that the Newtonian mechanistic paradigm was still a rich source of scientific ideas. As late as 1918, Zhukovskii was convinced that the speed of light—the basic problem of electromagnetic theory—"will be resolved using the old mechanics of Galileo and Newton."[16]

The second orientation in Russian physical thought was represented by scientists who were loyal to the classical tradition but recognized the revolutionary sweep of the newer ideas and helped to disseminate them. In 1901, the scientists who attended the Ninth Congress of Russian Naturalists and Physicians heard of Planck's quantum hypothesis, one year after it was originally proposed.[17] The idea of experimentally verifying the composite nature of atoms, and the whole new world that this opened to scientific scrutiny, found enthusiastic supporters. The spread of new ideas was unusually rapid. X rays, discovered by Roentgen in 1895, were discussed by O. D. Khvol'son in a pamphlet published in 1896. Hermann Minkowski's famous mathematical treatment of a four-dimensional world (1909) was published in a Russian translation in 1911. In 1913, Niels Bohr gave a mathematical expression to Ernest Rutherford's planetary model of atoms; in the same year, two articles in the journal of the Russian Physical and Chemical Society gave detailed explanations of Bohr's achievement. By that time, too, Einstein's special theory of relativity had been interpreted in many published papers, some in semipopular journals. All these ideas reached Russia primarily through the writings or translations of scientists who were still basically loyal to classical physics.

The indisputable leader of this group was N. A. Umov, who was profoundly aware of the deeper philosophical implications of the mechanistic orientation. In his younger days, Umov's interest was primarily in abstract mathematical physics: vibrations in media of invariable elasticity; thermodynamic phenomena in elastic solids and fluids; the basic mechanisms of energy transmission; and the "hidden nature" of potential energy. Later,

* See pp. 356–61.

his attention was focused on experimental research; his studies of light dispersion with the aid of metallic screens and chromatic depolarization were particularly noted.[18] In his old age, he conducted a series of theoretical studies on the types of earth magnetism, ventured into several areas where physics met biology, and wrote extensively on the organization of physical research in specialized institutes and on the unique educational aspects of physics. Umov covered too many fields to do justice to any of them; but the breadth of his knowledge and his enviable gifts as an organizer and leader in learned societies, a physicist-philosopher, and a popularizer of science earned him great respect among scholars and made him a widely recognized leader of the scientific community.[19]

During the 1890's, Umov took an active part in the proceedings of the Society of Psychology and Philosophy, an organization affiliated with Moscow University and much concerned with the philosophical problems of science. This association may have stimulated his interest in the philosophical foundations of physics. Like the German physicist H. R. Hertz, he felt that the classical system of mechanics was unsatisfactory because it was incomplete, did not offer a clear definition of force, and contained superfluous hypotheses.[20] But he was also convinced that classical physics needed only an internal reassessment and clarification to retain its intellectual supremacy in the world of modern science. He therefore tried to modernize classical physics not by overthrowing its fundamental propositions, but by tightening its internal logic and methodological apparatus. At one time Umov thought that the future of physics depended on a switch from the Newtonian tradition, which emphasized experiment and experience, to the Cartesian tradition, which emphasized theory and mathematical deduction. He advocated the development and use of models that were deduced from mathematical propositions and did not necessarily meet the preliminary scrutiny of experience. He did not use modern terminology, but he came very close to advocating the complete substitution of mathematical models for mechanical models.

At the beginning of the twentieth century, Umov took serious note of the new developments in physics that could not be integrated into the Newtonian or Cartesian tradition. He was attracted primarily by the novelty and magnitude of the new discoveries, but he was also willing to look into their broader philosophical significance. Eventually he modified some of his mechanistic views, although he never abandoned his primary loyalty to classical physics. However, he was genuinely interested in the new developments, and his talent for analyzing and popularizing scientific ideas made him a most effective interpreter of the quantum and relativity theories.[21] Umov took special pains to rebuke the idealistic philosophers who continued to attack science as intellectually superficial. Science and poetry, he said, were the two most splendid expressions of human genius, and had been inseparable since the time of ancient Greece, when "the exemplars of achievements in the arts" had produced a mathematical treatment of harmony. Now, according to Umov, they were more firmly identified with each other than ever before, offering the safest path to a profound knowledge of truth.[22]

In *Scientific Word*, a journal dedicated to the popularization of new scientific achievements, Umov described the gradual development of an unorthodox orientation in science. Such discoveries as electric waves, X rays, and radioactivity, he said, could not be explained either in terms of classical physics or by crude empiricism.[23] "At the end of the century we thought that science had already penetrated the innermost depths of nature; but now we know that it had only worked on the thin surface of the physical universe."[24] The world unveiled by the physics and the chemistry of atoms had opened new paths to the comprehension of "a single reality lying far beyond our senses." But classical and modern physics did not exclude each other: the former dealt with the "external mechanics" that bound atoms into the recognizable components of nature; the latter was concerned with the "internal mechanics" of atoms.

Umov's two papers on the theory of relativity, the first in Russia on this topic, were original mathematical treatments of the four-dimensional nature of the universe.[25] In these studies, he used the invariant nature of the wave equation for the diffusion of light as the basis for a mathematical expression of the principle of relativity. N. E. Zhukovskii later called Umov's contribution "the best mathematical interpretation of the principle of relativity."[26] In his paper on quantum theory, published in 1913, Umov hinted that the new idea of the discontinuity of motion required a basic reorientation in the mathematical treatment of physical phenomena.

The third major orientation in Russian physics was dominated by men who had turned against the classical tradition primarily on philosophical and ideological grounds, attacking Newtonian physics as the mainstay of ontological materialism and revolutionary social thought. They treated the new physics as a rebuttal of both the narrow materialistic base of nineteenth-century science and the intellectual imperialism of the scientific mode of inquiry. They endorsed Henri Poincaré's contention that scientific knowledge could not be reduced to, or derived from, experience alone—that even the "self-evident" postulates of Euclidean geometry were mere conventions invented by the human mind. Newton's mechanical laws, they said, could not be proved or disproved by experience for they were logical constructions derived partly from sense data, partly from *a priori* categories of thought (in the Kantian sense), and partly from the heuristic conventions used to interpret empirical knowledge and scientific hypotheses. In fact, all scientific generalizations and concepts were "symbols" or "models" rather than mechanical reflections of the outside world. Whereas sensory data produced an ephemeral picture of the external world, the "models" and "symbols," which were constructions of man's logical mind, revealed the "essential" and "real" aspects of the universe.[27]

The chief spokesman for this orientation, which might be called "idealistic physics," was N. N. Shiller, a professor at Kiev University who was considered one of the leading Russian physicists of his generation. Shiller's research followed the established paths of classical physics, and he made his major scientific contributions in thermodynamics and electrodynamics. J. C. Maxwell took special note of Shiller's experimental determination of dielectric permeance.[28] Shiller thought that the mechanistic view of nature was unimpeachable as long as it was applied to a relatively limited area of investigation and did not stand in the way of new scientific and philosophical orientations.[29] Lobachevskii had shown that by changing a basic proposition it was possible to change the entire structure of geometry; and according to Shiller, physics and the other sciences could undergo similar changes if they ceased to regard traditional notions as unalterable axioms.

Shiller saw a particularly promising future for a physical science whose basic propositions would be independent of the concepts of magnitude, time, space, and matter. He believed that in the future science should depend less on ontological axioms than on a consistent and logical set of heuristic propositions; and that epistemological relativism and logical formalism should replace ontological absolutism and apriorism. Science would develop in two directions: some sciences would create new fundamental concepts by combining the existing ones; others would introduce totally new ideas unrelated to classical mechanics.[30] Above everything else, Shiller sensed the profound importance of mathematical models, which could enable a scientist to go far beyond the limitations of pure empiricism and mechanical models. Science, like the arts, was to him an interaction of subject and object: a description was scientific only when it integrated empirical data, reflecting the object, into general categories selected by the scholar.[31]

A. I. Bachinskii, a student of N. A. Umov, was another strong representative of idealistic physics. After graduating from Moscow University in 1899, Bachinskii was retained by his department to prepare himself for teaching and research duties. He was unusually skilled in experimental techniques, and made noteworthy contributions to molecular physics and thermodynamics; particularly important was his mathematical formulation of the relationship between the viscosity and specific gravity of fluids. Soon after graduating he began to consider the profound philosophical questions raised by the new discoveries in physics. He helped translate Henri Poincaré's *Science and Hypothesis* into Russian, and became the chief defender of Poincaré's ideas among the Russian physical scientists. Bachinskii argued that "matter" as the ontological base of physical phenomena was "an ephemeral and illusive idol," and that ideas, rather than concrete objects, were the real subject matter of physics and all other sciences. Many writers with metaphysical and theological leanings regarded Poincaré's attacks on the epistemological objectivism and ontological materialism of classical physics as a dangerous challenge to the authenticity and intellectual power of modern scientific wisdom. Bachinskii, however, saw in Poincaré's nominalism, subjectivism, and relativism an ideal means of formulating more effective scientific explanations of reality and opening new areas of scientific research. He was also convinced that the elevation of science above all ontological controversies would inevitably separate it from ideology and would ensure its neutrality in a world of clashing values and ideals.

O. D. Khvol'son, the author of a popular textbook in physics that was translated into German, French, and Spanish, attacked philosophical and scientific materialism on many grounds, concentrating primarily on its negative effects on religion and morality.[32] In presenting the rudiments of the special theory of relativity to the readers of the popular journal *Nature*, Khvol'son interpreted Einstein's contribution as the safest way out of the modern crisis in physics.[33] However, he was much quicker to adopt the philosophical views of modern physics than to revise his textbook to include theoretical explanations of the specific achievements of the new experimental techniques.

Although these idealistic physicists differed in philosophical detail and in the intensity of their opposition to materialism, they shared many ideas. The basic task of the scientist, according to all of them, is to describe the phenomena of nature in terms of "*a priori* schemes"—to order sense impressions into meaningful general knowledge by using preconceived abstract models.[34] "Materialists" of all descriptions acknowledged the *historical* relativity of knowledge, but the idealists also recognized the *epistemological* relativity of knowledge: to a materialist limited, relative truths would eventually lead science to complete, absolute truths; to an idealist there could be no scientific path to absolute truth. Whereas the materialists claimed that there was only one scientific truth, the idealists assumed the possibility of more than one truth. Bachinskii, for example, recognized in Maxwell's *Treatise on Electricity and Magnetism* a logical synthesis of at least four "different and contradictory theories." And as early as 1855 Maxwell had stated that it is always important for a scientist to have two views on the same subject and to accept the idea that different views are possible.[35]

The idealist physicists did not limit their philosophical pronouncements to purely academic matters. Bachinskii was convinced that materialism in physics was a by-product of economic materialism, the ideology of "scientific socialism." Khvol'son's philosophical path took him even further from the epistemological problems of physics. Among other things, he lectured on such popular topics as "knowledge and belief in physics," trying to show the intellectual limitations of science and the essential contributions of religious belief.[36] History was not kind to Bachinskii and Khvol'son: both lived to see the victory of the Soviet system, which, though paying homage to their scientific achievements, had neither sympathy nor patience for their extensive ventures into philosophical ideas antithetical to dialectical materialism.

The fourth major orientation in Russian physics was represented by young scientists who had received their formal education just as the foundations of the new physics were being laid and the paths of future research staked out. These men reached the peak of their creative work after the October Revolution, and helped to give physics a preeminent position in Russian science. In Russia, as in the West, the new ideas were taken more as guideposts for future research than as verified theories. In 1915, the chemist N. A. Shilov spoke for most of his colleagues when he made the following statement:

"With regard to the study of atoms, it can be asserted that the theory of Rutherford, like the theory of Thomson, only points out the future path of science. Only for Moseley's experimental data [which led to a confirmation of the periodic law of elements] is it possible to say that they will enter the realm of established ideas, even though their full nature cannot yet be specified. Bohr's views have been subjected to strong criticism by such an authority in the theory of internal atomic structure of atoms as Nicholson, and it is too early to know whether any of them will pass the test of future scientific scrutiny. However, the hypotheses of Rutherford and Bohr deserve serious attention, not only as the openings of a new phase in physical research but also for their intrinsic value. They are extraordinarily interesting as abstract ideas: by representing the atoms as complex worlds rotating around each other, they add support to the idea of unity in the structure of the universe, from its infinitely large to its infinitely small components."[37]

It was somewhat difficult to organize research based on the new ideas in physics, for none of the older Russian physicists were really able to assume the role of leadership and gather a circle of promising young scientists ready to undertake ordered and sustained experiments. There were, however, a few energetic younger physicists; and one of them, A. F. Ioffe, was particularly successful in inspiring a group of gifted students to follow the paths opened by modern physics. In 1916, Ioffe conducted a seminar on the main currents of new physical thought, and helped launch the brilliant academic careers of such leaders of Soviet science as P. L. Kapitsa, N. N. Semenov, P. I. Lukirskii, Ia. I. Frenkel', and Ia. G. Dorfman.[38]

Ioffe's concern with the new horizons in physics was molded by several influences. Most important, he was a Jew; and as such he came from an ethnic group that was prevented by discriminatory policies and attitudes from occupying tenured academic positions. Barred from the centers of scientific research, Russian Jews were in no position to identify themselves with the vested interests in science. In entering any field of scientific inquiry, they were not bound by loyalty to the reigning paradigms, theoretical systems, or ontologies; thus they tended to concentrate on the newest developments, which demanded a maximum of critical thought and a minimum identification with time-honored tradition.

Mathematics and physics were the sciences most affected by new ideas during the period 1890–1917, and it is not surprising that Russia's Jewish scholars were particularly drawn to them. V. F. Kagan was the first mathematician in Russia to make a creative effort to integrate Lobachevskii's non-Euclidean geometry with modern mathematical thought. S. N. Bernshtein extended the relatively limited ideas of the famous St. Petersburg school in mathematics by blending them with an original theory of functions, contributing to the modern theories of stochastic differential equations and axiomatic integration of probability calculations. Georg Cantor and Hermann Minkowski, each of whom helped create a new branch of mathematics, were born in Russia; but both were educated in Germany and employed in German universities. L. I. Mandel'shtam, who completed his training in physics at Strasbourg University, made a name for himself by his original studies of light dispersion. Although Strasbourg promoted him to the rank of full professor in 1913, he decided to return to Russia and accept the position of private docent at Odessa University. Several members of Ioffe's seminar in 1916 were Jews; and one of them had just completed a graduation thesis dealing with the challenges posed by the theories of Planck and Rutherford.[39]

The increasing role of Jewish scholars in the pioneering branches of modern Russian science was in part connected with the rapidly increasing number of Jewish students in the institutions of higher education. Since 1880, the access of Jews to those institutions had been limited by law: the quotas varied from 3 per cent of the total enrollment for St. Petersburg and Moscow schools to 10 per cent for Odessa schools. Five developments, however, worked in favor of an absolute expansion of Jewish enrollment:

First, the general enrollment in most schools more than doubled within a few decades. For example, in 1888 Moscow University could by law admit only 98 Jewish students; but in 1916 it could admit 336 because of increased enrollment.

Second, the rigid quotas were not always adhered to, and most school administrations tended to increase them. In 1899 Jewish students made up 18 per cent of the total enrollment at Kiev University, although the official quota was 10 per cent.[40] In 1916 there were 684 Jewish students at Moscow University rather than the 336 allowed by law.[41] In 1910, Jews made up 7.6 per cent of the total enrollment at St. Petersburg, where the quota was 3 per cent;[42] and in 1915 the de facto enrollment rose to 11 per cent.[43] The increase was not constant, and on occasion the government forced the school authorities to stick closely to the legal norms.

Third, many new institutions of higher education came into existence around the turn of the century; although they too had legal quotas, they absorbed many additional Jewish students. The new polytechnical and technological institutes showed a consistent tendency to exceed their quotas.

Fourth, several new private schools were founded during the first decade of the twentieth century. Typical of these were the Lesgaft Courses in St. Petersburg and Shaniavskii University in Moscow. These schools combined advanced teaching with popular courses in fields of current interest. Most important, they admitted students without regard to their ethnic, religious, or educational background. Among their professors were many leading scientists who supported the idea of private education. It was at the Lesgaft Courses that Ioffe offered the first systematic presentation of the theory of radiation to be given in a Russian school. Since the curricula of the private schools were not prescribed by the government, they could easily adapt to the needs of the rapidly developing physical sciences.

Fifth, after the early 1890's increasing numbers of Russian Jews applied to the leading Western European universities, where they came into direct contact with the leaders of modern science and absorbed the spirit of the current revolution in scientific thought. In 1912, according to V. I. Vernadskii, Jews made up the bulk of Russian students in Western Europe, who numbered "at least 7,000 to 8,000."[44] Some of them, like Hermann Minkowski, remained in Western Europe, but others returned to Russia, where they helped accelerate the growth of science, particularly after the October Revolution. Many of these students extended the spirit of scientific criticism into the realm of social and political action.

Like most Jews, Ioffe traveled a circuitous path before he became a tenured member of the academic community. Instead of attending a classical gymnasium—the indispensable step for enrollment in a Russian university— he graduated from a real (technical) school modeled on the German *Realschule*, and had to enroll in one of the higher technical schools. He selected the St. Petersburg Technological Institute, which had been founded in 1828 to prepare bright young men of middle-class origin for engineering and administrative positions in industry. This school had a competent teaching staff and modern laboratory facilities, and it gave Ioffe an excellent grounding in the physical sciences. After he graduated in 1902, his professors encouraged him to continue his education in the West, and he immediately enrolled in a practicum sponsored by Wilhelm Roentgen's laboratory at Munich University.[45] In Roentgen's laboratory, where he worked until 1906, Ioffe studied the electrical conductivity of various dielectric crystals, and earned a doctorate in physics for discovering an internal photoeffect in X-rayed crystalline quartz. However, the Russian academic authorities at this time recognized only the higher degrees received by those who had completed the Russian classical high schools, and Ioffe could do no better than accept an appointment as a laboratory assistant at the St. Petersburg Polytechnical Institute.

Despite his humble position, Ioffe found his association with the Polytechnical Institute most rewarding. He was promptly invited to join the teaching staff, and began giving a course in thermodynamics. The Institute, founded in 1902, did not have a strong tradition in classical physics, and Ioffe's superiors gave him plenty of freedom to explore new ideas. He continued his research on dielectric crystals, and began to study the nature of light, a topic that had attracted great physicists from Newton and Huygens to Maxwell and Einstein. In 1911, he published a paper on the photon theory of radiation in which he sought to find an accurate mathematical expression for entropy.[46]

At this time Ioffe wandered freely through the tangled jungle of modern physics. He concentrated on the physics of crystals and the theory of light, but he made frequent and occasionally prolonged excursions into many other research areas dealing with radiation. Two elaborate studies, one on the magnetic field of cathode rays and one on elementary photoelectrical effects, earned him a magister's degree from St. Petersburg University, a promotion to associate professor at the Polytechnical Institute, and an appointment as private docent at St. Petersburg University, where he offered a course in the theory of radiation. In 1915 a study of the mechanical and electrical qualities of quartz brought him a doctorate from the University and a promotion to the rank of full professor at the Institute.

None of Ioffe's Russian contemporaries did more to bring the spirit and the challenge of new physics to Russia: he lectured, conducted original research, delivered frequent reports at meetings of the Russian Physical and Chemical Society, and wrote reviews of current Western studies in physics and general articles for semipopular scientific journals. In 1920 he became the first Russian Jew to be elected a member of the Petrograd Academy of Sciences; and in 1921 he was among those who initiated the election of Albert Einstein to honorary membership.

Ioffe received both encouragement and powerful intellectual stimulus from Paul Ehrenfest, a young Austrian Jewish physicist who had earned his doctorate in Vienna studying under Ludwig Boltzmann. In 1905 Ehrenfest published an article on Planck's theory of irreversible phenomena in radiation, pointing out the need for a new, nonclassical treatment of quantum dynamics. During the next several years, he participated in discussions related to quantum mechanics and relativity theory, often focusing his attention on the major contradictions in classical physics. He distinguished himself particularly in the field of statistical mechanics. In 1907, Ehrenfest and his Russian wife Tatiana Afanas'ev (an accomplished mathematical physicist in her own right) moved to St. Petersburg, where they lived for five years. In 1912, the two wrote "The Conceptual Foundations of the Statistical Approach in Mechanics" for the German *Encyclopedia of Mathematical Sciences*. This study has continued to be one of the basic works on the fundamentals of statistical theory, and was translated into English in 1959. Ehrenfest's most important single contribution was probably his theory of adiabatic invariance, which played a vital role in codifying the methodology of quantum physics.

Although the pioneers of modern physics in the West considered Ehrenfest one of themselves, he could not even find employment in a Russian university: he was "an Austrian, a Jew, and an unbeliever"; and he could secure only a temporary, part-time job in a non-tenured position at St. Petersburg Polytechnic Institute. Undismayed and resourceful, he made an earnest effort to find a place for himself in the Russian community of scholars: he became an active member of the Russian Physical and Chemical Society; he read a paper at the Twelfth Congress of Russian Naturalists and Physicians, held in Moscow at the very end of 1909; and he participated in informal seminars in modern physics and in the *kruzhoky* of young scholars who were eager to raise the standards of higher education and to improve their professional status. Ehrenfest's seminar in the mathematical foundations of modern physics, open only to younger instructors and advanced graduate students, was a major catalyst in the growth of modern physical thought in Russia.[47]

During his entire stay in Russia, Ehrenfest was in close contact with Ioffe.[48] The two met regularly to discuss the newest developments in physics, and helped each other in setting up their respective research projects. They worked together in fighting the vested academic interests that thwarted an effective diffusion of new theoretical ideas, and were particularly critical of the physicists of St. Petersburg University, who spent most of their time repeating the experiments of the 1880's. Ehrenfest and Ioffe also took the lead in organizing young physicists to speak out on behalf of modern physical theory.[49] Acknowledging Russia's and his own debt to Ehrenfest, Ioffe noted: "By his talent for the critical analysis and precise formulation of physical problems, Paul Ehrenfest exercised a profound influence on the development of my scientific skills. He must be credited with the emergence of modern theoretical physics in St. Petersburg. With unequaled perseverance, he fought the formalism of university physics and its leaders."[50] Ehrenfest and Ioffe, and their younger followers, were among those who influenced the Russian Physical and Chemical Society to issue a public statement disapproving L. A. Kasso's oppressive measures against Moscow University in 1911.

In 1912, Ehrenfest left Russia. In Prague he met Albert Einstein, who wrote many years later: "[Ehrenfest] was looking for a sphere of work in Central or Western Europe. But we talked little about that, for it was the state of science at the time that took up almost all our interest. . . . His stature lay in his unusually well developed faculty to grasp the essence of a theoretical notion, to strip a theory of mathematical accouterments until the simple basic idea emerged with clarity."[51] Soon after this, Ehrenfest received momentous recognition of his scientific achievements and his great skills as a teacher. When H. A. Lorentz—"our master," as Einstein referred to him—decided to retire from regular teaching at Leyden University, he personally selected Ehrenfest as his replacement. Ehrenfest's seminars at Leyden became one of the primary centers of postgraduate training for young Russian physicists, particularly during the 1920's.

In Russia, as in the West, there was no clear boundary separating modern physics from the classical tradition. The theory of relativity was still a nebulous, though vast, formulation; and quantum physics had not yet achieved a satisfactory combination of theory and experiment. Many Russian physicists who were working in the new areas of physical research saw no reason to dissociate themselves from the classical electromagnetic theory. Their primary interest was in expanding the area of physical research, not in refining and codifying the new theories. Still, there was progress. Modern astrophysics became the main concern of the staid Pulkovo Observatory. D. S. Rozhdestvenskii became the first modern Russian physicist to work in optics; he eventually organized the first optical institute in Russia, which began to function in 1919. The interest in geophysics was strong enough to support a specialized journal. Thanks to developments in spectroscopy and the discovery of X rays, crystallography, which had a strong tradition in Russia, improved its methodology and widened its area of investigation.

The new physics inspired bold attacks on scientific traditions, vested academic interests, and the institutional conservatism of organized research. It called not only for new theoretical views and experimental procedures, but also for a drastic expansion of laboratories and the training of more professional physicists. Moreover, the opening of new frontiers in physics stimulated a lively philosophical controversy and made physicists the leaders in a debate that thoroughly sifted the epistemological and ontological foundations of modern science and eventually gave science a firmer foothold in Russian culture. The debate extended into all circles of the intellectual community, and put science in general in the public eye. As we have seen, philosophical essays and lectures, rather than contributions to the substance of physics, made N. A. Umov one of the most respected scientists in Russia during the two decades before the October Revolution.

The rapid modernization of physics made the inadequacies of the existing laboratory facilities even more apparent. "Until now," lamented the journal *Priroda* in 1915, "our country has made no serious effort to produce its own scientific and educational instruments and to free itself from the stranglehold placed on it by Germany."[52] Even where laboratories were satisfactory they were usually used primarily for teaching rather than research.[53]

Umov and several younger physicists advocated the establishment of privately endowed research institutes, which make scientific research independent of educational obligations and bureaucratic controls. Their initiative led to the founding of the Moscow Physical Institute, the first privately endowed modern scientific establishment in Russia.

Russian physicists were acutely aware that the almost complete separation of their science from industry did the country great harm, and they led the campaign to rectify this anomaly. V. A. Mikhel'son pointed out in 1916 that Russians might have been the first to discover several vital inventions if Russian industry and society had been willing to give financial, technical, and moral support to native talent. P. N. Iablochkov, said Mikhel'son, had found it necessary to go to Paris to demonstrate his electrical lamp, "giving a mighty stimulus to the development of electrical technology in the West."[54] In 1874, A. N. Lodygin received a prize from the St. Petersburg Academy of Sciences for his invention of incandescent lighting; but he found no industrialists who were interested in manufacturing his invention. In 1895, A. S. Popov, a professor at the Naval Torpedo School in Kronstadt, designed and constructed an instrument to detect and measure electrical oscillations in the atmosphere. Like the others, he received no support—though two years later the Italian Guglielmo Marconi turned an essentially identical instrument into the first practical radio receiver.

Mikhel'son was not trying to establish priorities in specific inventions; he merely wanted to emphasize his claim that the future development of science in Russia would depend on making the scientific laboratory an essential component not only of educational institutions but also of factories, specialized government agencies, and research institutions. If some industrial establishments could not afford their own laboratories, said Mikhel'son, several small industries of the same kind should establish joint research units. Noting that Russian industrialists and Russian scientists had traditionally been reluctant to cooperate with each other, he expressed some hope for the future: "The average German pursues science as a profitable craft—profitable not only for him personally, but also for the entire nation. Many Englishmen and Frenchmen pursue science as an interesting and noble sport, not giving a thought to its utility. Common among the Russians, and the Slavs in general, is an enthusiastic regard for science as the only expression of a tolerable though incomplete world view that emphasizes the search for truth as both an irresistible personal need and a duty to the nation and to humanity."[55] Mikhel'son did not intend to convey that the Russian view of science was the best, but merely that it was unique. The main point of his essay was that sheer enthusiasm alone would not raise

Russian science to the Western level: to do so would require the full cooperation of the government, the scientific community, and industry.

STRUCTURAL CHEMISTRY

V. L. Omelianskii, the noted microbiologist, observed at the beginning of the twentieth century that no natural science was more successful and more popular in Russia than chemistry.[56] The great Lomonosov had been one of the pioneers who uprooted the phlogiston theory and placed chemistry on scientific foundations. Hermann Hess had been "the first to undertake a systematic experimental investigation of the heat effects accompanying chemical change" and to make thermochemistry an important branch of science. A. M. Butlerov's name was associated with the emergence of structural chemistry. D. I. Mendeleev's periodic law of elements had unified the previously unintegrated experimental and classificatory data of inorganic chemistry. The English journal *Nature* noted in 1898 that N. A. Menshutkin's book on analytical chemistry was comparable to Mendeleev's *Principles* in importance; and it was the only book on analysis that R. W. Bunsen permitted in his laboratory.[57]

At the end of the nineteenth century Russian chemistry was a thriving discipline supported by an array of adequate though not outstanding laboratories, and by interest on the part of government, industry, and the other natural sciences in both the products of chemical research and the techniques of chemical experimentation. Yet many historians of Russian science are inclined to think that the great era of Russian chemistry that started in the 1860's had by this time run its course; and that during the 1890's a major reorientation took place, characterized by a massive adoption and experimental elaboration of the chemical advances made in Western Europe since the 1870's. During the 1860's and 1870's Russia had few competent chemists; but this small group produced a surprisingly large number of great scientists, who made theoretical contributions of revolutionary scope and formed "independent chemical schools in Russian universities that were in no way inferior to those existing in the West, and were in certain respects superior to them."[58] In the 1890's Russia had a relatively large number of competent chemists, but there were relatively few of international eminence. Mendeleev, for instance, was still alive, but the glory of his scientific contributions belonged to the preceding era.

The influence of Butlerov was decidedly stronger than the influence of Mendeleev, mostly because it was more concentrated: whereas Mendeleev covered many research areas, Butlerov devoted most of his time to the elaboration of his structural theory. An eminent Russian chemist wrote in 1887 that with a few exceptions the Butlerov school "included all contemporary Russian scientists"; and that, thanks to Butlerov, chemistry had risen to a higher position in Russia than in many nations with "long cultural histories."[59] At first Butlerov's theory had been rejected by Russia's most eminent authorities, including Menshutkin and Mendeleev, but by the 1890's it was widely accepted.[60]

Most Russian organic chemists were concerned with "chemical structure" or "chemical composition," by which they meant a regular and predictable distribution of the forces of chemical molecules; and most worked to realize Butlerov's prophecy that there would soon be only one formula for each chemical compound. The new structural formulas led many Russian chemists to the study of isomerism, which for the first time could be represented by diagrams.[61] However, although Butlerov's theoretical work encouraged further study of isomerism and more extensive experimental research in organic synthesis, it soon became a bastion of conservatism that hampered the normal diffusion of new ideas in chemistry. The negative role of this conservatism was most obvious in the late acceptance in Russia of the dramatic new ideas associated with stereochemistry.

Stereochemistry, originally advanced by J. H. van't Hoff, overcame the inadequacies of a two-dimensional diagrammatic representation of the distribution of valency bonds in an atom (the method used by Butlerov and Kekulé) by introducing a three-dimensional representation. Van't Hoff's new method was particularly effective in the study of isomerism and isomorphism; at first it was applied only to the carbon atom, but it was subsequently used to represent all chemical compounds. The development of stereochemistry is rightfully considered "one of the most significant and characteristic features of modern chemistry."[62]

Although Butlerov admitted the possibility of a spatial representation of molecular structure, he steadfastly refused to accept the full system of stereochemistry as advanced by van't Hoff and J. A. Le Bel.[63] He fully accepted Pasteur's idea of molecular asymmetry, which formed the basis of stereochemistry, but he refused to believe that the first could lead to the second. He even refused to admit that stereochemistry was an elaboration of his own structural theory. Butlerov's stubborn rejection of stereochemistry, in which he was supported by V. V. Markovnikov, the most influential of his disciples, greatly delayed the acceptance of van't Hoff's challenging ideas by Russian scientists.[64]

It was not until the 1890's, when N. D. Zelinskii, a professor of organic chemistry at Moscow University, gave it a paramount place in experiments in organic synthesis and in the theory of chemical bonds, that stereochemistry found a true home in Russia. By the beginning of the twentieth century, no Russian chemist challenged the superiority of stereochemistry to the structural theory of Kekulé and Butlerov. L. A. Chugaev spoke for the younger generation of Russian chemists when he noted in 1904 that stereochemistry not only explained many new series of isomers and served as a useful working hypothesis in explaining optically active compounds, but also made it possible to relate the optical activity of fluids to their molecular structure.[65] In 1912, a group of the more important younger chemists (notably Chugaev, F. Iu. Levinson-Lessing, and V. A. Kistiakovskii) began publishing a comprehensive survey entitled *New Ideas in Chemistry*; and van't Hoff's contributions to stereochemistry took up the bulk of the first volume.[66]

Two members of the Butlerov school, N. D. Zelinskii and A. E. Favorskii, achieved particularly notable success in organic chemistry.[67] Besides making tangible scientific contributions, they attracted many followers and founded their own schools in chemistry. Without abandoning their basic loyalty to Butlerov's theories, they helped introduce the new Western achievements in organic chemistry to Russia and synchronize them with the national tradition. Both lived well into the Soviet period, and were highly regarded among Soviet scientists.

A member of the landed gentry, N. D. Zelinskii was born in 1861 in a small Bessarabian town. In 1884 he graduated from Odessa University, and was promptly sent to the West to study modern laboratory techniques and new chemical theories. His work in two German chemical laboratories— J. Wislicenus's at Leipzig and Victor Meyer's at Göttingen—introduced him to the modern technique of studying stereoisomeric phenomena in saturated carbon compounds, and he wrote his doctoral dissertation on this topic. In his dissertation, Zelinskii made it clear that his primary interest was in developing the "dynamic aspects" of the structural theory.[68] He considered himself a member of Butlerov's school; but unlike Butlerov, he accepted the idea that the future development of chemical dynamics had to come from stereochemistry and physical chemistry. Zelinskii, in fact, was the first Russian chemist to adopt stereochemistry as a basic research tool.[69]

In 1888 Zelinskii was appointed private docent at Odessa University, and in 1893 he became associate professor of analytical and organic chemistry at Moscow University. His transfer to Moscow coincided with a rapid increase in the number of students enrolled in the Department of Physical and Mathematical Sciences, an expansion and modernization of university laboratories (rather slow until 1905), an intensification of the activities of learned societies, and a general broadening of the courses in applied science. Zelinskii was an enterprising organizer of complex research and a superior teacher, and had no difficulty in attracting promising young men to organic chemistry; eventually, his following was surpassed only by the gigantic school of the physiologist Ivan Pavlov.[70]

Together with his students, Zelinskii synthesized and described forty hydrocarbons of the alicyclic series. Subsequently, he discovered a simple method for the production of x-amino acids and conducted intensive research in the chemistry of Caucasian petroleum. During World War I, he developed a technique for the use of activated charcoal in gas masks, conducted extensive studies in catalytic hydrogenation and dehydrogenation, and discovered what he termed "irreversible catalysis." Also noted was his work on the catalytic hydrolysis of albuminous substances and on the electrical conductivity of salts and acids in methanol solutions.

The schools in organic chemistry founded by Butlerov and Zelinskii were quite different in many respects. Butlerov influenced his followers by the power of his theoretical ideas, Zelinskii by the challenge of his research projects. Butlerov's followers sought new applications for the theoretical ideas of their teacher; Zelinskii and his followers built on ideas imported from the West. Butlerov did not choose his disciples; they were attracted to his ideas, not to his personality. Zelinskii, following the model formulated by the French chemist Dumas, chose his disciples and carefully outlined their research assignments. Butlerov wrote all his scientific papers alone; Zelinskii published over 500 scientific papers, but in more than half of them he shared authorship. Butlerov founded a school based on the individual and independent research of his followers; Zelinskii's school emphasized collective, interdependent work. Zelinskii remarked: "I knew, and tried to convince my many students, that collective creativity is the guarantee of success. A scholar must be able to surround himself with a friendly, creative group and involve it in a common effort. Thus the success of one man increases the creativity of all the others. Important work is possible only on a group basis."[71]

Zelinskii made a concerted effort to explain the theoretical implications of modern chemical research to an audience reaching far beyond professional chemists. For this reason, he encouraged one of his graduate students to write and publish a general, semipopular study of stereoisomeric theories and their place in the general history of modern chemistry.[72] In his own popular lectures on Lavoisier and Pasteur, he outlined the salient points in the intellectual history of chemistry and offered a general background for the interpretation of stereochemistry.

By extending his activities far beyond the classroom and the laboratory, Zelinskii helped sustain the tradition established by Mendeleev and Butlerov. His biography is a good summary of the social activities, professional work, and ideological challenges with which most Russian scientists were involved during the two eventful decades preceding the October Revolution. He was one of the most active members of the Moscow Society of Naturalists, and participated extensively in the scholarly activities of the Society of Admirers of Natural Science, Anthropology, and Ethnography and the Russian Physical and Chemical Society. He was always present at the chemistry sessions of the national congresses of natural scientists. Under the sponsorship of the Finance Ministry, Zelinskii organized a special chemical laboratory in Moscow, where many leading chemists gained their initial research experience. He introduced organic chemistry courses and founded a laboratory at the Higher Courses for Women in Moscow, and helped to establish Shaniavskii University. In 1911, he was among the Moscow professors who resigned to protest the reign of terror introduced by L. A. Kasso, the Minister of National Education. During World War I, he instituted and guided the industrial production of gas masks. And in 1929, he was elected a member of the Soviet Academy of Sciences.

Zelinskii's most outstanding students achieved fame in research areas that escaped the attention of their teacher: L. A. Chugaev studied the complex compounds of metals of the platinum group; N. A. Shilov investigated adsorption and simultaneous reactions in oxidation; and S. S. Nametkin attempted to codify the chemistry of terpenes.

Zelinskii's prodigious output in synthetic chemistry was matched only by the work of A. E. Favorskii. Favorskii, who came from a priestly family, received his higher education at St. Petersburg University at a time when the chemistry staff associated with this institution included Mendeleev in inorganic chemistry, Menshutkin in analytical chemistry, and Butlerov in organic chemistry. He is best remembered for his research on the isomerization and polymerization of unsaturated hydrocarbons. Favorskii was trained by Butlerov, and he adhered closely to Butlerov's dictum that research in organic synthesis was almost useless unless it involved a systematic concern with chemical theory. He consistently emphasized the growing need for practical chemistry, but believed that only some new development in theory could increase the industrial applicability of chemical knowledge. In his lectures at St. Petersburg University, Favorskii emphasized the theoretical development of organic chemistry; at the Higher Courses for Women, he considered the contributions of organic chemistry to general education; and at the Artillery School and the Electrotechnical Institute, his attention was focused on chemical engineering.

Modern synthetic organic chemistry passed through three distinct stages of development. Before the 1860's, many chemists tried to synthesize new organic compounds, but their efforts were not guided by systematic theoretical considerations. During and after the 1860's, the various structural theories made organic synthesis an inextricable component of chemical theory. However, these early structural theories were concerned exclusively with the arrangement of atoms in molecules. The "electron" structural theory, the third phase in the evolution of synthetic organic chemistry, developed at the end of the century in the wake of the great discoveries that proved the divisibility of atoms; but it did not become theoretically integrated and methodologically advanced until much later.

Butlerov had urged his students to investigate the possibility of a physical and chemical fission of atoms, which would open new vistas in the development of the structural theory; but neither Zelinskii nor Favorskii took up his challenge. The electron structural theory originated not in Butlerovian "chemism"—according to which chemical phenomena could only be explained in chemical terms—but in the pioneering branches of the new physics, which opened the inner world of atoms to scientific scrutiny. Classical physical chemistry, inaugurated by J. H. van't Hoff and Svanté Arrhenius, provided the theoretical and experimental bridge that connected molecular structural chemistry with atomic chemistry.

### PHYSICAL CHEMISTRY

During the last quarter of the nineteenth century many Russian scientists became interested in the newly active field of physical chemistry, which eventually produced fundamental changes in both the theoretical and experimental aspects of almost every branch of chemistry. Physical chemistry is a general name for several disciplines, all of which apply the conceptual and experimental apparatus of physics to the study of chemical problems. Despite its long history, it did not come of age until the 1880's, when a series of significant discoveries in the United States, Germany, and Holland opened a new era in chemical research. At this time, the first physical chemistry journal—*Zeitschrift für physikalische Chemie, Stöchiometrie, und Verwandtschaftslehre*—came into existence to help publicize and coordinate the new research techniques and theoretical insights.

In the 1880's Russia already had a long but tenuous tradition in physical chemistry. In 1752–56, Lomonosov wrote and lectured on a new science, which he named "physical chemistry" and identified as the primary science for studying the structure of matter. In 1840, Hermann Hess formulated the law of constant heat summation and became the founder of thermochemistry, a basic branch of physical chemistry. During the early 1860's, Mendeleev expressed great faith in the future cooperation of physics and chemistry, and conducted research in the application of various physical techniques to the study of chemical problems. He discovered the phenomenon known as "critical temperature" (he called it "the absolute boiling point") eight years before Thomas Andrews arrived at it independently and made it a universally recognized law of modern chemistry.[73]

Mendeleev wrote in 1860: "The glamor of purely chemical discoveries has made modern chemistry a fully specialized science, separated from physics and mechanics. However, the time will come when chemical affinity will be treated as a mechanical phenomenon, just as light and heat are treated today. I have chosen to specialize in research that will speed up the coming of that time.... For many reasons, I have concentrated on the determinants of the cohesion of chemical compounds, a problem that requires a study of the capillarity, density, and expansion of bodies."[74]

N. N. Beketov went a step beyond Mendeleev: he not only advocated the introduction of physical research techniques into chemistry, but also offered a course in physical chemistry at Khar'kov University as early as 1864. However, Beketov soon turned to other fields, and he left no lasting imprint on the development of physical chemistry in Russia.

Wilhelm Ostwald, a Baltic German, earned his doctorate in chemistry from Dorpat University in 1878, and was appointed a professor of chemistry at the Riga Polytechnicum in 1881. In 1885–87, Ostwald published a two-volume chemistry textbook that was soon recognized as the first comprehensive survey of physical chemistry. (According to the German Nobel laureate W. H. Nernst, modern physical chemistry was definitely established as an independent discipline in 1885, when J. H. van't Hoff produced his osmotic interpretation of solutions and Ostwald published the first volume of his text.) In 1887, Ostwald left Russia to become a professor of physical chemistry at Leipzig University—the first such position to be established in any university. A great many of the younger Russian chemists took advantage of the hospitality of Ostwald's Leipzig laboratory when studying in Western Europe.

In spite of these promising historical antecedents, Russian scientists did not play an important role in the revolutionary development of physical chemistry between 1880 and 1900. The typical Russian chemist was too loyal to the strong national traditions, particularly in organic chemistry, to venture into the challenging areas opened by Western researchers. Moreover, modern research in physical chemistry demanded much more complex and sensitive laboratory equipment than the Russian universities could offer. The great names in Russian chemistry did nothing to help matters after 1870. Butlerov clung firmly to his assertion that the structural theory in organic chemistry was a purely chemical theory, with no need for any physical explanations. And in 1887, Mendeleev advanced a purely chemical theory of solutions at the very time when van't Hoff's physical-chemical, or osmotic, theory was making physical chemistry the most promising branch of modern chemistry outside Russia.

The main contributions of Russian physical chemists consisted of special elaborations or concrete adaptations of the ideas advanced by Western scientists. Russians were also quite successful in systematizing the rapidly growing knowledge in various branches of physical chemistry and in applying the new physical research techniques to isolated problems in both organic and inorganic chemistry. They were strongest in refining chemical theory and introducing mathematical methods into chemistry, and weakest in expanding the practical application of chemical knowledge.

In the 1890's, J. Willard Gibbs's "phase rule," which was concerned with chemical balances in heterogeneous systems and was expressed in very elaborate mathematical language, attracted the attention of several leading Russian chemists and stimulated lively theoretical and experimental work. Menshutkin actually undertook to study higher mathematics in an effort to fully understand the intricacies of modern thermodynamics, on which the phase rule was based. Mendeleev, however, claimed that Gibbs's theory did not explain the cause of chemical action but merely described its outward physical manifestations. Once again, Mendeleev defended the idea of "chemism" against the intrusion of physical explanations into chemistry.[75] He admitted, however: "The law of phases, by bringing complex instances of chemical reaction under simple physical schemes and graphic methods of representation, facilitates their study in detail and gives the means of seeking the simplest chemical relations dealing with solutions, dissociations, double decompositions, and similar cases, and therefore deserves serious consideration."[76]

Despite Mendeleev's protestations and the relative conservatism of Butlerov's immediate disciples, modern physical chemistry found active representatives in Russia. D. N. Konovalov studied the pressure of vapor solutions, developed a new experimental method based on the utilization of pressure as a thermodynamic function of phase equilibria, and arrived at new formulas for describing the autocatalysis of organic substances.[77] V. A. Kistiakovskii studied the mechanisms of various chemical reactions, concentrating on the speed of reactions and the electrical conductivity of aqueous solutions. L. V. Pisarzhevskii, working on similar problems, investigated the influence of solvents on the equilibria of reactions. Kistiakovskii and Pisarzhevskii were the first Russian advocates of Arrhenius's theory of ion dissociation. V. N. Ipat'ev's noted studies of catalytic reactions at high temperatures helped elucidate the nature of hydrogenation and made it possible to study many reactions from a kinetic standpoint.[78] N. A. Menshutkin carried the methods of chemical kinetics into the field of organic compounds. And N. S. Kurnakov distinguished himself by an elaborate physicochemical study of alloys, based on a skillful use of Gibbs's phase theory and an original topological handling and systematization of data. In Russia, physical chemistry was commonly referred to as theoretical chemistry because it combined complex experimental designs with modern conceptualization and a systematic search for mathematical expression. Certainly, its Russian practitioners provided ample proof that the practical applicability of modern chemistry grew proportionately with its theory.

Physical chemistry introduced new methods into chemical research and prompted the development of new types of laboratories, which required larger investments, the most modern engineering skills, and laboratory workers with a sensitivity to intricate, and often minute, developments in theory. The new polytechnical schools, unencumbered by the academic conservatism of the universities, were in a relatively favorable position to build laboratories to fit the needs of modern chemistry and the special interests of individual scientists. At the St. Petersburg Polytechnical Institute, for example, the very elaborate general chemistry laboratory had special sections for thermoanalysis, electrical measurement, physical measurement, and microphotography; all were usually engaged in the physicochemical study of alloys, the main interest of N. S. Kurnakov, the laboratory's director. The Mining Institute, the Electrotechnical Institute, and several other institutions of higher education acquired new chemical laboratories and increased the number of chemists on their staffs. But, as in the past, the fame of individual laboratories depended more on the achievements of the men who worked in them than on the quality of their equipment.

Russian scientists contributed greatly to the formation of new specialties by following the different leads offered by modern chemistry: N. A. Shilov and M. S. Tsvet worked in adsorption techniques, D. N. Prianishnikov in agrochemistry, A. Ia. Danilevskii in biochemistry, I. Plotnikov in photochemistry, and V. I. Vernadskii in geochemistry. In most of these areas, Russia differed from the advanced countries of the West less in the quality of her theoretical output than in her technical inability to put scientific discoveries to practical use. Close ties between theory and practice were much slower to develop in Russia than in the West. The Russian scientists who wrote in foreign languages were one major cause of this backwardness, for they were more interested in presenting their ideas to Western scientists than in making these ideas readily available for technological applications in their own country.

However, Russian chemists did make some efforts to popularize modern advances in chemistry, particularly in physical chemistry and its offshoots.[79] In a systematic analysis of the basic thermodynamic propositions in modern chemistry, the chemist I. A. Kablukov informed the readers of *Russian Thought*: "At the present time, in addition to descriptive chemistry, mathematical chemistry has a very promising future. . . . Chemistry has undergone a revolution that can be compared with the revolution in astronomy wrought by Newton's discovery of the law of universal gravitation."[80] And the physicist O. D. Khvol'son told the readers of *God's World* of the new branch of chemistry "based on thermodynamics and its powerful mathematical apparatus."[81]

### CHEMISTRY AND THE MODERN ATOMIC THEORY

When I. A. Kablukov wrote about the revolution set off by the introduction of the conceptual and mathematical apparatus of thermodynamics into chemistry, he was barely aware of the even greater revolution triggered by the discovery of X rays, radiation, atomic structure, and the quantum principle. As early as 1904, L. A. Chugaev lectured his students at the Moscow Technical School on the current challenges to the traditional notion of the unchanging nature and indivisibility of atoms. Perhaps, he said, the time would come when scientists could make "artificial atoms" by extrapolating from the atomic structures of existing elements.[82]

Mendeleev, however, who was by far the most influential voice in Russian chemistry, remained convinced of the physical indivisibility of atoms and the chemical discreteness of individual elements. This fundamental discrepancy between the new discoveries and Mendeleev's widely accepted interpretation made many Russian chemists extremely cautious in accepting new ideas in physics and chemistry; but there were other reasons for the slow progress of the new ideas in Russia. For one thing, the strongest Russian advocate of the new chemistry was N. A. Morozov, a man with no professional credentials who had just been released from the Schlüsselburg Fortress, where he had served a long prison term for illegal political activities. When asked to read one of Morozov's manuscripts, which offered sound, original arguments for the fundamental compatibility of the periodic law with the new atomic and radiation chemistry, the eminent chemist D. N. Konovalov commended Morozov's erudition and philosophical logic, but absolutely refused to endorse his ideas.

The Mendeleevian tradition did not actually turn Russian chemists against the revolutionary ideas of modern science; it merely delayed their "conversion." At the First Mendeleev Congress of Pure and Applied Chemistry, which met in 1907, the Academician N. N. Beketov argued that the periodic law of elements was fully compatible with the notion of the transmutability of elements, and that chemists had long anticipated the new discovery.[83] In 1909, L. A. Chugaev told his students at St. Petersburg University that the current research in radiation might confirm Prout's hypothesis (that all elements have a common origin) and might thus refute Mendeleev's view that the periodic law was incompatible with any theory of the evolution of heavier elements from a few basic elements of low molecular weight (e.g., hydrogen).[84] Beketov welcomed the "genetic" approaches to the structure of matter advanced by Sir William Crookes and N. A. Morozov. In 1910, V. I. Vernadskii predicted that the new radiation studies would be crowned by the discovery of previously untapped sources of energy "a million times larger than the most optimistic present-day estimates would indicate."[85] It was under his leadership that Russia began systematic surveys of her national resources in radioactive elements.

In 1913, the English physicist H. G. J. Moseley showed experimentally that the X-ray spectra of different elements corresponded to their places in the periodic table. By measuring the wavelengths of X rays of different elements, he established a full congruence between an atom's atomic weight and the number of electrons it contained. Essentially, Moseley placed modern electron physics behind Mendeleev's law, and opened the door for a much wider acceptance of the new ideas by Russian chemists.

In 1914, N. A. Shilov, an established research chemist, was sent to the University of Manchester to work in Sir Ernest Rutherford's laboratory and to purchase the basic instruments for setting up a projected radiological laboratory at the Institute of Commerce.[86] The ship carrying the equipment to Russia was sunk in the Baltic by German mines at the outbreak of World War I, and Russia did not begin experimental radiological studies until the Soviet era. However, Shilov had worked six months in Rutherford's laboratory—long enough to become familiar with the basic ideas and research techniques for the study of radioactivity and atomic structure; and when he returned to Russia in the autumn of 1914, a 1,000-seat hall at the Polytechnical Museum in Moscow proved too small to hold the crowds who gathered to hear him deliver four lectures on radioactivity.

## THE SOCIOLOGY OF PHYSICS AND CHEMISTRY

During the last three decades of the tsarist regime, Russian chemists were united in a self-contained community with its own ideology and *esprit de corps*. They differed from the physicists in several respects. To begin with, they were much more numerous: in most universities there were two or three chemists for each physicist; and in 1900, the Russian Physical and Chemical Society included 327 chemists and 134 physicists.[87] Similarly, the country had twice as many chemical laboratories as it had physical laboratories. The physicists represented a science that did not have a strong national tradition; chemistry, on the other hand, was generally regarded as a Russian specialty.

In facing the great crisis in physics at the turn of the century, Russian physicists were unencumbered by strong loyalties to the past and vested scientific interests; they were dedicated to visions of the future rather than traditions of the past. The chemists, by contrast, were concerned with blending the theories of the present with the legacy of the past. Unlike the physicists, they wrote extensively about the history of science; indeed, the first notable history of science in Russia dealt exclusively with chemistry.[88] The work of the great chemists, from Mikhail Lomonosov to N. A. Menshutkin, was treated in detailed biographical studies; the same attention was not accorded to the leading representatives of other sciences.

Steeped in the past, the Russian chemists were naturally conservative in their academic commitments. For example, they steered clear of the philosophical debate that attracted the attention of many great scientists in the West after 1880. During the same period, Russian physics produced men like A. G. Stoletov, N. A. Umov, and O. D. Khvol'son—men who sensed the profound meaning of the epistemological crisis in modern science and who set forth their own philosophies of science with great energy and precision. The chemists did not look beyond the direct requirements of their science, and paid no attention to the growing need for an integrated network of research organizations. The physicists looked beyond the imminent needs of their own science, and were concerned with modernizing the entire system of Russian research institutions.

Russian physics opened its doors to people of many different views and backgrounds. Both the philosophical base of its ideas and the socioeconomic background of its learned custodians reached far beyond traditional limits. Chemistry, by contrast, had only the meager skeleton of an unarticulated, pragmatic philosophy; and unlike physics, it was still dominated by men from the top rungs of the social ladder. In the chemical branch of the Russian Physical and Chemical Society, these older members, whose prestige was still great, safeguarded the stability of conservative thought by constantly rejecting the unorthodox ideas presented by their younger colleagues. Even Mendeleev was disposed to equate the daring new ideas and research techniques advanced by young chemists with sloppiness and lack of rigorous scientific discipline.[89]

In political ideology, too, the differences between chemists and physicists were pronounced. More physicists were willing to voice sharp criticism of the unfavorable conditions for scientific work in Russia, but more of them were also open supporters of the tsarist autocracy; the philosophical crusades of N. N. Shiller and O. D. Khvol'son, for example, were actually thinly veiled defenses of tsarist ideology against the mounting tides of scientific materialism. Russian chemists were steadier and more moderate in their political views. There were no outspoken critics of the existing political system among them, nor were there staunch supporters of tsarist ideology. To use a label employed by V. N. Ipat'ev, they were mostly "conservative liberals"—some more conservative and some more liberal. Generally, they were conservative because, as amply demonstrated by major figures like Mendeleev and Menshutkin, they opposed any revolutionary changes in the structure of the Russian polity and society. On the other hand, they were "liberal" because, with few exceptions, they maintained that the future prosperity of their country depended on fundamental democratic reforms in government, social relations, and the national economy. In their liberalism, the chemists were typical of the academic community; in the overwhelming uniformity of their political views, they were unique.

Physics and chemistry had one common feature: both were isolated from the national economy to a much greater degree than was usual in the West. The isolation of chemistry resulted primarily from the low development of the Russian chemical industry, which was still in its infancy at the beginning of World War I.[90] L. A. Chugaev observed in 1908: "Despite the limitless richness of our natural resources, and the overabundance of coal, petroleum, iron, and other useful ores, we hardly have a chemical industry. ... It is not the fault of Russian chemists that we pay so little attention to the scientific study of the natural resources of our country. The fault is in the general apathy with which the results of relevant scientific investigations are met—in the absence (with a few exceptions) of moral and financial support from the government and society at large."[91]

Very few chemists were fully isolated from the practical problems of the national economy. There were even examples of enterprising chemists who secured financial support from the government and established small plants to produce vital industrial chemicals. The agrochemist D. N. Prianishnikov, for example, was aided by both the Ministry of Agriculture and an industrial entrepreneur, and set up the first plant in Russia to produce superphosphate.[92] But this was an isolated case. The drastic curtailment of trade with Western countries during World War I made it clear that the poorly developed chemical industry was the main impediment to the full mobilization of industrial resources for national defense. Shortly after the declaration of war, for example, the military authorities discovered that the country had no reserves of toluene, a chemical indispensable to the manufacture of modern explosives.

In the military technology of World War I, chemical weapons were of unprecedented importance, and Russian industry was sadly unprepared to meet the challenge of modern warfare. Many vital industrial enterprises were owned by foreign concerns and run by foreign managers and engineers; they often relied on well-kept trade secrets, and had no reason to employ Russian scientists or engineers. The difficulties were compounded by Russia's staggering dependence on the importation of goods manufactured in Germany, including a long list of essential chemicals. Because of the traditional dependence on German industry, the government was not eager to invest large sums of money in systematic and thorough surveys of

Russia's own resources. The country did not even have a centralized agency entrusted with planning and coordinating the economic effort for national defense.[93]

To meet the demands of the war, the laboratories of research centers and educational institutions all over Russia were mobilized to produce vitally needed materials. The laboratory of the St. Petersburg Academy of Sciences produced a dozen chemicals never before produced in Russia. Special work-shops were established to fashion the most elementary instruments for chemical laboratories. For the first time, Russia mined and processed her own tungsten, iodine, nickel, and fluorine.[94] Aided by government funds, the Russian Physical and Chemical Society established a War Chemicals Committee and organized an experimental chemical plant for the production of high-priority chemical compounds.[95] This plant developed methods for producing potassium cyanide, arsenic, chromyl chloride, and many other military chemicals. It also worked to improve electrochemical techniques, which required complex equipment and involved procedures that were almost unknown in Russia. Eventually the plant was able to turn out electrolytically produced metallic sodium, potassium and sodium peroxides, and metallic magnesium.[96] Another research project initiated by the Physical and Chemical Society led to the production of the first Russian gas masks. The Society also played a leading role in organizing the production of the many pharmaceutical goods previously imported from Germany; and it established a special laboratory in Moscow to produce dyes for the textile industry. Finally, the war was responsible for the founding of the *Journal of Practical Chemistry* and the first efforts at the publication of a manual of chemical technology.

The upsurge in research brought on by the war had many long-range effects on Russian science: it stimulated the growth of research institutes free of educational obligations; it brought serious efforts to coordinate research on a national scale; it made scientific development a vital field of national policy; and it raised direct cooperation between scientific institutions and industry to unprecedented heights. Research in all the sciences contributed to these fundamental innovations, but the role of chemistry was by far the most important.

CHAPTER THIRTEEN

# The Earth Sciences

THE EMERGENCE OF MODERN GEOLOGY

Prior to the 1870's, Russia did not have a single geologist whose contributions were important enough to attract the attention of the international scientific community.[1] There was widespread interest in geology, but most of it was unsystematic, nontheoretical, and essentially amateurish. Until the middle of the 1860's, the Mining Institute was the only institution of higher education to offer geology as a regular part of the curriculum. The Academy of Sciences ignored the legacy of Alexander von Humboldt, Sir Roderick Murchison, and others who had conducted geological surveys in Russia and laid the groundwork for geological investigation based on modern methodology and theory. The Mineralogical Society, founded in 1817, showed no interest in the theoretical foundations of geology, and concentrated on gathering empirical data. The Geographical Society, founded in 1846, was interested in geological data only in connection with the overall geography of specific regions. The government sent survey teams only to areas that were known to have valuable mineral deposits; and according to the Academician G. P. Helmersen, these teams were usually made up of amateurs who lacked both zeal and technical competence.

Russian geology, as a separate discipline, was dominated by foreigners who, though competent in modern research techniques, carefully avoided any serious confrontation with the great theoretical ideas of modern historical geology, which conflicted with the Bible's account of the Creation. Native Russian geologists, on the other hand, were interested in geological knowledge more as one part of a versatile, natural-historical science of the earth's crust than as a special discipline with a unique area of inquiry and methodology. The two most competent researchers, S. S. Kutorga and G. E. Shchurovskii, regarded geology primarily as a descriptive discipline contributing to an integrated scientific picture of external nature.

After 1860, the trend toward modernization in the Russian economy and the proliferation of intellectual interests and challenges helped geology enter a period of rapid and versatile growth. The 1863 university charter made geology a part of the academic curriculum. The naturalist societies founded at all universities during this period expanded the institutional base of organized geological research and also facilitated a continuous exchange of ideas. The *Mining Journal*, a publication of the Department of Mines, began to print articles of a purely theoretical orientation, acquainting Russian readers with the major questions of contemporary geology. Sir Charles Lyell's *Principles of Geology* and *Antiquity of Man*, which compared the developmental notions of modern geology with the evolutionary theories of biology, were translated into Russian and were read by a wide and appreciative audience. The Mineralogical Society, which usually avoided sweeping or ambitious projects, put most of its resources behind the publication of a new series of monographs on Russian geology. And from the very beginning, the periodic national congresses of Russian scientists included special sessions on the earth sciences.[2]

The real turning point in the history of Russian geology was the founding of the Geological Committee in 1882 (exactly fifty years after its model, the British Geological Survey, had appeared). At first the Committee was an exceedingly small organization, with only seven members; but it did a great deal to coordinate and advance geological research in Russia.[3] Its major project was the preparation of a detailed geological map of European Russia; but it also undertook the first geological surveys of coal deposits in the Donets Basin and iron deposits in the Krivoi Rog area and the southern Urals, and it sponsored special expeditions to Novaya Zemlya and to the steppes of the Ural region. Its *Proceedings* became the most popular vehicle for the publication of monographs in geology, paleontology, and petrography. It also published the *Russian Geological Library*, which each year summarized all works on the geology of Russia published during the preceding year. The Committee grew rapidly, and it soon included, on an informal basis, all the St. Petersburg geologists working in the Academy of Sciences, in various government departments, and in the institutions of higher education. By 1897 it had 21 regular members.

The government's involvement in geological research also grew in scope and intensity. The Department of Mines conducted several field investigations in which geologists played a major role—e.g., surveys of the upper basins of the major rivers in European Russia. Special fieldwork of geological significance was also conducted by the Forestry Department, the

Section for Land Improvement, and the Soil Bureau—all agencies of the Ministry of Agriculture.[4] The Ministry of National Education founded geological research centers in Tomsk and Novaia Aleksandriia, and the Ministry of Communications sponsored geological research in the Caucasus and the Kirghiz steppe.

For the first time, private industrial and mining concerns employed geologists to help them discover new sources of wealth. Leading geologists, for example, were hired by privately sponsored teams of gold prospectors. After the 1860's, several prominent chemists received grants from private sources in order to study Caucasian petroleum; and a number of geologists worked for concerns interested in discovering new oil deposits. The building of the Trans-Siberian Railroad, started in 1891, provided geologists with a challenging opportunity to explore many fundamental questions in both the substantive and theoretical branches of geology. By 1898, various geological teams working with the railroad crews had gathered so much information that it was possible to prepare the first geological map of Siberia. The newly collected data showed that the largest part of North Asia, apart from the relatively young West Siberian plain, was very ancient, and that it had been covered by the sea during the Middle, and perhaps the Lower, Paleozoic era. This initial map of Siberia was far from complete: for example, vast areas were classified by their surface rocks or other external features, whereas paleontological remnants that might have offered some clue to the geological history of these areas were ignored.[5]

From 1880 on, geological research was one of the leading national concerns in Russian science. It branched out in many directions, met exacting methodological and philosophical challenges, opened new areas of research, and spilled over into neighboring disciplines. If all this research had any unifying theme, it was a consistent emphasis on the potential contributions of geology to the genetic view of nature. Russian geologists paid a great deal of attention to dynamic geology—i.e., to the existing, observable, and measurable causes of gradual change in the earth's crust, such as wind, precipitation, and the ecological adaptations of plants and animals. A knowledge of these causes, they felt, would lead to a fuller understanding of evolutionary changes in the earth's crust. As in the West, paleontology became the connecting link between geology and biology, both permeated by an evolutionary view.

During the first ten years of its existence, the Geological Committee was much concerned with theoretical issues, and particularly with integrating empirical data relevant to the geological past of Russia. Much effort was devoted to empirical studies of "parallel" or "synchronic" geological developments in Russia and Western Europe; and data collected by Russian geologists led to refinements or modifications of specific points in the geochronology established by the leading Western scholars. Several chapters of *Das Anlitz der Erde*—an elaborate encyclopedia of geological knowledge compiled by the German geologist Eduard Suess—relied heavily upon materials published by Russian scientists. Russian geologists were active participants in all the international geological congresses, and they joined Western scholars in compiling a uniform geological map of Europe and in standardizing geological periodization and nomenclature. The Seventh International Geological Congress met in St. Petersburg in 1897, providing an excellent opportunity for many leading Western geologists to become acquainted with the work of their Russian colleagues. Special geological excursions to the Caucasus, the Crimea, and Central Asia were organized for the members of the congress; and the Western delegates were, in general, much impressed with the status of their science in Russia.

At the turn of the century the Geological Committee was the de facto coordinator of the national effort in geological research. Through book exchanges with foreign institutions and private gifts, it acquired a large collection of modern geological literature, and its library became the major geological reference center in Russia. In 1897, the Committee built a versatile chemical analysis laboratory, which immediately acquired a wide reputation because of its important role in the first discovery of uranium deposits in Russia.

During the last three decades of the tsarist regime, geology rose from a weak, diffuse discipline to a flourishing science dominated by men who were as eager to enrich theory as they were to make practical contributions to the national economy. The institutional base of geological research was significantly expanded and diversified. When the Twelfth Congress of Russian Natural Scientists and Physicians met in Moscow in December 1909, the number of papers submitted in the earth sciences was so large that for the first time in the history of these congresses it was necessary to organize special subsections in geology, paleontology, applied geology, and mineralogy. The number of research geologists had more than doubled in the preceding thirty years, and the ratio of highly productive and original scientists among these was unusually high.

By the beginning of the twentieth century, the *Proceedings* and *Reports* of the Geological Committee could publish only a fraction of the acceptable papers submitted to them. The Academy of Sciences came to the rescue in 1906 by launching *Proceedings of the Geological Museum of the Academy of Sciences*; and during the next decade the *Mining Messenger* and *Surface and Depths of the Earth* were established. At the same time, the special publications of the Russian Geographical Society, the Russian Mineralogical Society, the Free Economic Society, and the university naturalist societies began to devote more space to the earth sciences in general.[6]

After the 1880's, geology was almost completely taken over by native Russians. This development had several important aspects. Geology became a complete science, with a rigid methodology, conceptual precision and unity, a technological orientation, a philosophical base, and ideological overtones. It united the practical research of many different groups: government agencies; metallurgical concerns; *zemstvo* activists who saw geological surveys as a preliminary phase in the systematic rehabilitation of agricultural land; and academic men of all descriptions. The tremendous accumulation of new geological information went hand in hand with an accelerated growth of industry and an increasing national concern with the economic potential of agricultural land. Finally, the victories of geological thought reinforced the widely accepted notion of evolution in both the organic and inorganic worlds, and strengthened the various modern ideologies based on a historical world view.

Russian geologists were among the leading critics of national policies that prevented a more rational study and exploitation of natural resources. Their persistent pressure finally made the government accept the view that without a vigorous study of the tectonic structure and stratification of individual regions there could be no sound basis for efficient and reliable surveys of the nation's mineral resources. Russian geologists were also among the leading advocates of a more solid and versatile natural-science curriculum in the high schools;[7] and they criticized the restrictive government policies in this and many other areas.

V. I. Vernadskii and A. P. Pavlov, both leading experts in the earth sciences, were the first to prepare a detailed plan for a national organization of Russian scientists on the model of the British Association for the Advancement of Science.[8] Their recommendation, which was rejected, repeated the earlier demands of scientists for more enlightened national policies regarding scientific work, and was part of a determined struggle against bureaucratic encroachments on the institutional domain of science. Quite frequently, this scientific concern extended to social conditions. The earth scientists, whose professional work took them to every corner of the vast Russian empire, were among the leading critics of the discriminatory government policies that perpetuated economic stagnation among the ethnic groups and nations of the Caucasus, Central Asia, and Siberia.

Vernadskii expressed the view of most of his colleagues when he stated that the government was as blind and anachronistic in its nationality policies as it was in its refusal to expand the scientific study of natural resources.[9]

In Russia, as in Western Europe, the period 1880-1920 was not one of grand theoretical concerns in geology; instead, researchers sought to refine and expand the more limited and practical theories. Although the grand scheme of organic and inorganic evolution was universally accepted, it was treated as an open idea requiring added precision and documentation. The modern paleontologist, typified in Russia by A. P. Pavlov, was involved in a double task: he conducted stratigraphic studies to unravel the intricacies of biological evolution, but he also used fossils as an essential aid in solving many problems of stratigraphic technique. Sometimes this dual approach produced surprising results. Pavlov was among the first Russian scientists to reject the idea of evolution as a unilineal process; his stratigraphic study of *Archaeopteryx* fossils demonstrated the existence of a separate evolutionary process parallel to the main trunk of evolutionary development.[10]

The professional concerns of Russian geologists were diverse. Some pursued comparative studies of Russian and West European deposits belonging to parallel geological periods. Pavlov, for example, accumulated impressive evidence to support his hypothesis of synchronic development of the Upper Jurassic and Lower Cretaceous deposits in the Volga Basin and Western Europe. Particularly in the 1880's and 1890's, most geologists were involved in fitting Russian tectonic, stratigraphic, and paleontological data into the established geochronological schemes, and in writing geological histories of Russia by following the internationally accepted periodization scheme. Many leading scientists dealt extensively with the systematic classification of geological specimens. This concern was exemplified by Pavlov's search for a "genetic" classification of fossils, A. P. Karpinskii's argument in favor of a mineralogical classification of rocks, and F. Iu. Levinson-Lessing's chemical classification of rocks.

In Russia, as in the West, geology was among the sciences least affected by the mounting criticism of the mechanistic orientation of Newtonian physics. Its orientation, being historical, had always had little connection with the essentially ahistorical approach of Newtonian mechanics. Moreover, geology, in contrast to classical physics, was primarily inductive and nonmathematical. Geologists relied on physics and chemistry only so far as these sciences helped them to understand changes in the earth's crust; they were not interested in the external harmony of the mechanistic model of the universe, but in a process of constant change. For decades geologists had disagreed on the nature of this change, some holding that it was a continuous evolution and others that it occurred in sudden, catastrophic spurts. But by the beginning of the twentieth century, even this controversy had died down, and most competent geologists agreed that the theories of gradualism and catastrophism were not mutually exclusive but supplementary.[11]

In the main, geology was a settled discipline, characterized more by a mushrooming of empirical research than by an inner battle between opposing theories. Russian activity in paleontology was especially impressive. Beginning in the 1890's, Russian scientists made a number of major finds, some dating from the Lower Cambrian. Several noncontiguous areas yielded significant Lower Silurian deposits. Of great theoretical and practical value were the Devonian deposits in Volynsk province and the Carboniferous or Permocarboniferous sediments in the Crimea and the northern Caucasus. Special teams of geologists discovered varied Triassic deposits in the Crimea, Jurassic deposits in the Donets Basin, and Upper Cretaceous deposits in Ufa province and on the eastern slopes of the Urals.[12]

A. P. Karpinskii, "the father of Russian geology," is generally considered the leading theoretician among modern Russian geologists; yet most of his theoretical ideas were stated in a few small studies. In 1887, he published an essay on "the physicogeographical changes in European Russia during various geological periods," in which he outlined and described the major trends that had transformed latitudinal sea basins into longitudinal ones. In a short paper published in 1894 and based on a paleogeographic analysis, he explained the major trends in the fluctuation of the earth's crust in Russia and presented the first tectonic map of the country. In subsequent essays, he discussed the effects of deep deformations of the central Russian geological platform. His original analysis of the dependence of the movement of shore lines on the motions of the earth made an especially strong impression on Western European scholars.[13] However, neither Karpinskii nor any of his colleagues tried to write a general treatise that would sum up modern geological knowledge of the entire earth.

Karpinskii's few empirical generalizations presented an overview of the geological processes that had molded the earth's crust in European Russia. Though limited, they proved that Russian geologists had accumulated enough solid data to be able to reconstruct the main developments in their country's geological past. This reconstruction was made relatively easy by the simplicity of the geological structure of the Russian platform, which had been formed by a succession of relatively mild geological events. European Russia, according to Karpinskii, had experienced only minor dislocations of strata, and thus had comparatively homogeneous sedimentary formations over wide areas.[14]

The general theoretical problems of geology reached a wider audience in two ways: through popular scientific journals, and through historical essays. Popular journals like *Priroda* published occasional articles outlining the substantive and theoretical contributions of modern geology and clarifying the place of geology in the family of natural sciences. Readers were acquainted with the grand succession of geological periods that made up the earth's history, and learned to appreciate the evolutionary view of nature. Even articles that were essentially travelogues made readers aware of the unique features of the geological approach.[15] The historical essays dealt either with the geological legacy of individual Russian scientists or with the main currents in the development of modern geological thought. In both cases, they presented geology as a vital part of modern intellectual history. These essays emphasized the continuity in Russian geological thought since Lomonosov had first expressed his views on the history of the earth,[16] and also illustrated the many research avenues that linked geology with the other natural sciences.

The rapid expansion of geological knowledge and research techniques led to the development of several important subdisciplines within geology. Tectonics, stratigraphy, paleogeography, petrography, regional geology, dynamic geology, and several other disciplines now emerged as distinct but complementary fields, each with its own body of knowledge and investigative techniques. At the same time, the traditional cooperation of geologists with mineralogists and crystallographers became closer and more systematic. The process of differentiation did not make geology itself obsolete, but merely transformed it from a general discipline to a specialized discipline concerned with the problems of theoretical and historical synthesis. Moreover, the differentiation of geology did not produce strict specialists, for every leading geologist was a "specialist" in several disciplines. Karpinskii, for example, was equally at home in tectonics, stratigraphy, paleogeography, and paleontology.

SOIL SCIENCE: A "NATIONAL SCIENCE"

The process of fission that produced so many autonomous disciplines within geology soon led to a new process of integration: the formation of new interdisciplinary specialties. In Russia, the most successful and popular of these "synthetic" sciences was soil science (or pedology), which owes its present position among the sciences to the continuing efforts of Russian researchers. Soil science combined several disciplines, but it developed most rapidly in the areas where geology overlapped various biological sciences and chemistry.

The great reforms of the 1860's stimulated a profound and critical reassessment of the values of Russian culture and the integrative principles of Russian society. Modernization, as well as the changes in demographic patterns and social dynamics, demanded the immediate solution of many economic and technical problems. The most acute of these problems was the improvement of agricultural land. Many emancipated peasants had been given land of the poorest quality and were justifiably angry. Even the *chernozem* areas, blessed with the earth's richest soil, were harassed by the whims of nature and suffered unpredictable harvest failures. Famine was a constant threat everywhere in Russia. The country's staggering ignorance of the physics, chemistry, and biology of soil eliminated any possibility of a rational struggle against the forces of nature and the crippling effects of a primitive technology.

Interest in rehabilitating the Russian soil was universal. After the late 1860's the government moved swiftly into action, founding several major agricultural schools to carry on both teaching and empirical research. Experimental farms sprang up in every part of European Russia. A rapidly growing number of scientists studied the specific effects of the various natural qualities of land on agricultural production and on prospects for more abundant harvests.

In a concise and stimulating study published in 1866, the biologist F. I. Ruprecht criticized theories that considered the Russian *chernozem* a mere geological formation—that is, a specific facies of some recent geological deposit. At about the same time, Mendeleev tackled the problem of Russian soil from a chemical vantage point. Under his influence, the Free Economic Society financed experimental studies of the effects of artificial fertilizers on the oat and rye harvests in Simbirsk and Smolensk provinces. Experts dispatched to conduct experimental research collected valuable information on the chemical composition of various types of agricultural land. Many enterprising landowners—most of them members of the Free Economic Society—established experimental farms on their estates.

Before the contributions of Ruprecht and Mendeleev, the Free Economic Society had been occupied primarily with determining the most productive varieties of cultivated plants for given types of Russian soil; now it began to seek ways of transforming the soil in order to obtain higher yields from the already acclimatized varieties. The origin of the different Russian soils became the point of departure for scholars who were trying to improve agricultural production. Geology became the backbone of the "agricultural sciences," and soil science emerged as the leading theoretical science of agriculture.

The creator of the new discipline was V. V. Dokuchaev, one of the very few Russian scientists of the nineteenth century whose work stimulated the formation of a truly national scientific school. According to one of his younger colleagues, "Only a few persons equaled the influence, depth, and originality of Dokuchaev's generalized thought."[17] At the Eighth Congress of Russian Naturalists and Physicians, which met in St. Petersburg in 1889, an expert in agriculture stated: "In reference to soil as the basic condition of agriculture, I must first of all mention the name of V. V. Dokuchaev, which is associated with the major achievements in geographical, natural-historical, and, particularly, economic studies of Russian soil during the last ten years. Dokuchaev's studies are characterized by a new methodology, an abundance of accumulated facts, and original and relevant conclusions. He has the great honor of having founded an entire school of soil scientists. ... Dokuchaev's investigations contribute not only to a better understanding of the types of soil and their geological, chemical, and physical characteristics, but also to soil cartography, which, together with climate cartography, could help yield answers to many general economic and special agricultural questions."[18]

In 1876 the Free Economic Society invited Dokuchaev to organize the first systematic study of the Russian *chernozem*, and specifically asked him to find scientific explanations for the structure, origin, and evolution of *chernozem*.[19] In essence, he was invited to determine two things: the geological nature of *chernozem*, and its geographical distribution. The new commission headed by Dokuchaev sought advice from a wide range of experts. For example, the soil samples it collected were subjected to a chemical and physical analysis by the most competent scientists in the laboratories of Dorpat University and the Academy of Forestry. Expert opinion was also solicited from the chemists Butlerov and Mendeleev. The final results of this effort appeared in Dokuchaev's classic *Russian Chernozem*, published in 1883.

Dokuchaev contended that most previous studies of soil had been too narrow and one-sided. He could not accept either Murchison's sweeping geological interpretation or F. I. Ruprekht's biological theories. He also rejected Liebig's and Mendeleev's exaggerated chemical views, and was equally unhappy with the physicists' interpretation, which treated soil in terms of temperature, moisture, and prevailing winds. To Dokuchaev, soil had to be studied as part of a specific geographical complex in which four factors were of primary significance: the relief of the surface, the parent rock, the character of vegetation, and the geological age of the land.[20] Comparing soil to an organism, he argued that each soil has its own physical and chemical qualities, a distinct origin, and a unique structure—all influenced by both geographical and biological conditions and all regulated by natural laws. The task of the scientist, according to Dokuchaev, was to study soil as a structured natural-historical body influenced by a multiplicity of geographical factors. His approach was structural and genetic, and he regarded soil as an integrated organic entity much more complex than the sum of its component parts. He focused his attention on the regularities in the dynamics of soil genesis and evolution. The structural views justified Dokuchaev's determination to make soil the subject of a special science; the historical views made Dokuchaev the founder of "genetic" soil science.

Soil is formed from its parent rock by the process of weathering, which reduces its content of certain substances (for example, carbon dioxide, or calcium and magnesium salts). At the same time, plant remnants enrich soil with humus and nitrogen and help to concentrate food substances like phosphoric acid. The changing chemistry of the soil inevitably leads to changes in the physics of the soil (e.g., in the effects of heat and water). The geology of a given area provides the base on which soil is built; and the vegetative cover, according to Dokuchaev, determines soil fertility. Dokuchaev treated vegetation as the main agent in the accumulation of humus and nitrogen, in the concentration of nourishing mineral substances, and, in general, in the development of all the physical and chemical qualities that determine the fertility of soil.[21]

Although Dokuchaev emphasized the role of vegetative cover in the formation of soil, he did not ignore the chemical results of weathering processes. He and many of his followers did much to clarify the chemical composition of the different horizons of soil, and worked to prepare a chemical typology of soils. However, it was usual for the Russian soil scientist of this time to think of rebuilding impoverished soil by enriching or diversifying its vegetative cover rather than by balancing its chemistry with the help of artificial fertilizers.

P. A. Kostychev, a very eminent and productive soil scientist, criticized Dokuchaev for overemphasizing the role of vegetation in the formation of the soil. The Academician V. R. Vil'iams disagreed, maintaining that not enough emphasis was placed on the role of vegetation; his theory eventually provided a scientific background for the policy of grassland agriculture instituted under Stalin. Actually, by overstressing the role of vegetation covers in the formation of soil, Dokuchaev and most of his followers were responsible for the rather slow development of Russian interest in chemical fertilizers.

If nothing else, the work of Dokuchaev and his school proved that the Russian learned societies could organize, administer, and finance national research undertakings of grand proportions. The Free Economic Society and the St. Petersburg Society of Naturalists were the chief sponsors of the complex expeditionary studies that made soil science so important in Russia. It was also through these societies that soil science became a harmonious blend of theoretical and practical interests.

The provincial *zemstvo* organizations, engaged in many activities aimed at raising the economic and cultural standards of rural life, generated a genuine and lively public interest in soil science, and provided organizational and financial support for many regional studies. After 1882, when the Nizhnii Novgorod provincial *zemstvo* invited Dokuchaev to help establish a set of objective criteria for the classification of local agricultural land in terms of fertility, research teams visited almost all the regions of European Russia and published an enormous volume of data. The brunt of financing these surveys fell on the *zemstvo* authorities, who also provided many enthusiastic local volunteers to help in the arduous business of gathering facts. These *zemstvo* activists, among other things, confronted modern science with folk wisdom that had traditionally explained the symbiotic relationship of man and land, often quite accurately. The *zemstva* did not limit their assistance to soil surveys; they were also eager to help survey teams trying to piece together a true table of Russia's geological past.

Although soil research was now the concern of a special science, it also attracted the attention of scholars from many other disciplines. Individual mineralogists, plant physiologists, botanists, geographers, and agrobiologists studied soil from the vantage points of their respective disciplines. The new specialists who acquired the label "geobotanists," for example, were less excited about the role of vegetation in the formation of soil than about the role of soil in the evolution of various plants.[22] Soil science, in whatever form, was a natural rallying point for many young scientists interested in the natural resources of their country.[23]

The utilitarian orientation in soil science received particularly strong encouragement in 1892, when Dokuchaev published *The Past and Present of Our Steppes,* in which he formulated a set of recommendations for a scientific campaign against the chronic droughts in the southeastern areas of European Russia. No previous study had made broader and more carefully elaborated recommendations for the improvement of Russian agricultural technology.

Dokuchaev's influence on the development of modern soil science, however, came less from his theoretical conceptions than from his talents for organizing collective research, and especially from the range of questions for which he demanded empirical answers as a precondition for sound and comprehensive theories. Powerful and influential as it was, the Dokuchaev school was made up of people united more by their enthusiasm for agricultural study than by a loyal adherence to any grand theory. By developing a synthetic, interdisciplinary science to meet the perennial desire of man for a more effective control over the land that feeds him, Dokuchaev made science a living part of society.

Dokuchaev was made famous not only by his followers but also by his critics, and he was respected by both. He contributed to both the unity of his own school and a refreshing diversity of thought in soil science outside it. He made geology the indispensable training ground and starting point for all the earth sciences; but to some of his most eminent students he gave only a general base from which they charted their own scientific careers. Three disciples of Dokuchaev became famous in their own right: K. D. Glinka stayed within the broad confines of soil science; F. Iu. Levinson-Lessing made major contributions to the development of modern petrography; and V. I. Vernadskii worked first in mineralogy and then in geochemistry.

K. D. Glinka first came to prominence in Dokuchaev's Poltava expedition of 1888, which produced fifteen volumes of detailed descriptions of local soils, geology, and vegetation. Among other things, the expedition established a definite correlation between the altitude of a locality and the specific features of its soil formation. Glinka applied the principles of Dokuchaev's genetic soil science in an effort to stake out a new subdiscipline, "paleopedology," which would study ancient soils. His reputation, however, rested on his extensive efforts to record the growth of the ideas that had produced modern soil science, to codify the main theoretical propositions of the Dokuchaev school, and to coordinate the achievements of various sciences in the study of soil.[24] He was the first to demonstrate the complementary relationship between Dokuchaev's theory of the role of vegetation in the formation of soil and S. N. Vinogradskii's microbiological explanation of the role of various bacteria in the nitrification of soil. Glinka belonged to a group of modern earth scientists who opposed the total domination of practical problems in their respective disciplines. Science, he believed, must be free to travel previously uncharted courses; and, besides responding to the needs of practical life, it must create new needs, and higher technology, through theoretical exploration.

F. Iu. Levinson-Lessing, who spent his scientific apprenticeship as a member of Dokuchaev's survey team in Nizhnii Novgorod province, became the most illustrious Russian petrographer of his time. In 1888, he published a voluminous study of the rocks of the Olonets diabase formation, in which he dealt mostly with such petrogenetic questions as the chemical origin and genetic classification of rocks. He also discussed the conditions determining the development of the entire magmatic formation, the underlying principles in the differentiation of the effusive and infusive facies of diabase, and several other questions of great theoretical interest. This study marked the first effort in Russia to make petrography a theoretically unified science.[25]

Intensive fieldwork in the central Caucasus and northern Urals supplied Levinson-Lessing with the empirical foundation for much of his theoretical thought. In *Researches in Theoretical Petrography* (1908), he presented a chemical classification of igneous rocks and formulated an intricate theory of the differentiation of primevally homogeneous magmatic fluids. In his research, he relied on a combination of tested geological techniques, modern chemical and physicochemical analysis, and a comprehensive critical scrutiny of modern literature. He also introduced the method of variational statistics into petrography. Eventually, his work raised the general standards of Russian petrography so high that no room was left for amateurs.

Levinson-Lessing thought that the traditional distinction between pure sciences and applied sciences was no longer as valid as it might have been in the past. In particular, he disapproved of the government's attempts to create a dual system of higher education: a university system dedicated to pure science, and a polytechnical system concerned exclusively with applied science. He himself felt that a unified system of higher education could be created by forming technical faculties in the universities and "university faculties" in the polytechnical institutes.[26] Like Glinka and many other scientists, Levinson-Lessing believed that the time had come to treat each science as a combination of pure and applied knowledge.

Earth scientists in general had begun to reject the idea that the response to practical needs should be the motive force in the growth of the earth sciences, feeling that theoretical exploration should not be bound by the contingencies of the day. At the beginning of the twentieth century, the intensified struggle for the independence of scientific theory was part of an acute struggle by the scientific community for academic autonomy. Most leading earth scientists did not want to isolate themselves from the pressing needs of national economic and social life; in their scientific work, however, they were attracted more to the vistas opened by the inner logic of theoretical development than to the satisfaction of external demands.

### V. I. VERNADSKII: FROM MINERALOGY TO GEOCHEMISTRY

V. I. Vernadskii was the philosopher among Russian earth scientists: he treated modern science as both a theoretically unified body of knowledge and an epistemologically elaborated branch of secular wisdom. As a pure philosopher, Vernadskii believed in the subjective origin and relativistic value of scientific knowledge. As a social philosopher and cultural historian, he treated science in the larger context of modern knowledge, considering it the major determinant of modern man's world view. As a social activist, he was in the forefront of the fierce struggle for the institutional autonomy of scientific inquiry. As a historian of science, he was concerned with the unique sociocultural determinants of scientific thought in Russia, especially in the earth sciences. And as a practical scientist, he specialized in mineralogy.[27]

Vernadskii's first mineralogical papers were published during the 1890's. Until they appeared, Russian mineralogy had been mostly a descriptive discipline that dealt with minerals in terms of their external qualities—crystalline form, size, color, hardness, and similar measurable attributes. Little attention was given to the internal structure of minerals or to the processes involved in their formation. Vernadskii, following in the footsteps of Dokuchaev, constructed an evolutionary mineralogy: according to him, minerals had to be studied as products of physicochemical processes that were regulated by, or conformed to, specific laws of nature. He may rightfully be considered one of the founders of modern geochemistry, a new science that "grew in the soil created by the new atomistics, the new chemistry, and the new physics." Vernadskii identified geochemistry as "the chemistry and history of the minerals of the earth's crust."

Using an evolutionary and structural approach, Vernadskii classified the chemical elements into eighteen "natural isomorphic groups"; all the elements within each group, he said, could replace each other in the formation of common minerals. He also established that these isomorphic groups could be modified by changes in temperature and pressure. Further research on isomorphism led Vernadskii to formulate a number of principles that were extremely useful in predicting the elements most likely to be found together in various geological situations.

Vernadskii's search for integrative theoretical principles in mineralogy led him into the field of modern crystallography. He treated crystals not as abstract geometrical systems but as real physical bodies. His major work on the subject, *The Foundations of Crystallography* (1904), was the result of a logically elaborate blend of modern mineralogical and crystallographical thought; it was also a bold effort to apply the theoretical and experimental tools of physical chemistry to the world of crystals. At one time, following Pierre Curie, he tried to introduce J. W. Gibbs's phase theory into crystallography, treating polymorphic varieties in crystals as different "phases" of the same chemical compound. Vernadskii's crystallographic ideas were really the scattered hunches of a brilliant and searching mind rather than organic components of a consistent overall theory. Nevertheless, his survey of the history of crystallographic thought was a most welcome addition to the growing literature on the history of the sciences.

The strong preoccupation with scientific history that appeared in Russia around the turn of the century was part of a massive scholarly endeavor with several objectives: to find a way out of the epistemological crisis in the physical sciences; to sum up the great intellectual achievements of the nineteenth century, "the century of natural science"; and to reaffirm the growing importance of science in modern culture. To K. A. Timiriazev, nineteenth-century science was the perfected end product of a grand intellectual tradition that had started in the seventeenth century; but to Vernadskii, it was only the prelude to even greater achievements. Thus Timiriazev indiscriminately resisted the newer developmental ideas in biology, which challenged the Darwinian legacy, whereas Vernadskii constantly worked on the advancing frontiers of science, opening new avenues of research and formulating new methods and scientific views.

Vernadskii was the first Russian earth scientist who fully appreciated the practical consequences of the discovery of radioactivity. In 1910 he stated that radioactivity would unleash energy "a million times more powerful" than the human mind could then imagine, and pleaded for a systematic survey of the Russian deposits of radioactive elements.[28] It was this interest in radioactivity that first stimulated Vernadskii's work on the chemistry of the earth's crust and made him the leader in Russian geochemistry. He conducted several spectroscopic studies of the earth's crust, concentrating on the rare elements selenium, lithium, rubidium, cesium, thallium, and bismuth. Of broader theoretical interest were his studies on the paragenesis and dispersion of elements and on the role of cyclical geochemical processes in the dynamics of the earth's crust. Vernadskii's efforts to collect modern geochemical ideas into a system of axioms and propositions, as well as most of his work on radioactivity, took place after the October Revolution. From the beginning, however, he was keenly interested in the effect of living organisms on the formation of minerals and the changing chemical profile of the earth's crust, a pursuit that made him a pioneer in biogeochemistry.

Most of Vernadskii's generalizations had a firm empirical basis. The progress of science, he believed, did not come from revolutionary negations of established scientific procedures and ontological premises, but from a gradual consolidation of the existing knowledge in all disciplines. He worked on the assumption that this consolidation could uncover valuable but neglected research areas, reveal new areas for interdisciplinary research, establish a more fruitful relationship between science and philosophy, and make science a far more powerful instrument of economic development. Vernadskii's skill as a scientific historian was a great help when he applied this approach to his own work; and he introduced most of his major studies by sketching the historical growth of the ideas under consideration and offering astute interpretations of established scientific traditions.[29] To him, the history of science was an important instrument for distilling the philosophical subtleties of scientific cognition, for explaining the changing relationship of science to other modes of inquiry, and for refining basic scientific concepts.

Vernadskii's interest in applied geochemistry was particularly strong during World War I, when the lack of reliable, systematic knowledge about Russia's mineral resources was seen to be the primary cause of the country's industrial weakness. The Commission for the Study of Natural Productive Forces (KEPS), founded at the Academy of Sciences on the initiative of Vernadskii and several of his close friends, was dominated by specialists in the earth sciences, who worked out emergency plans for systematic surveys of the minerals most vital to the war industry. Insufficient funds, disrupted communications, and general wartime hardships made the work of the Commission unsystematic, sporadic, and superficial. However, several research branches of the Commission became the nuclei of specialized research institutes that emerged after the war.

Vernadskii was the main spokesman of the KEPS, and the interpreter of its goals and philosophy. The alliance of science and industry, he argued, should not make science a slave to technology; on the contrary, science should make technology one of the many extensions of scientific work. Science is most effective and most versatile when it is most theoretical, and when practical studies are only one aspect of scientific endeavor. A study of the natural resources of Russia, therefore, would be most effective and profitable when it conformed to the canons of science rather than to the ephemeral needs of the day. After all, "Every advancement in geology, mineralogy, botany, and zoology increases our knowledge of the natural productive forces of Russia."[30] Despite his numerous pleas for a more extensive practical use of science, Vernadskii never abandoned his firm conviction that the true power of science was not in the extent of its concrete facts but in the depth of its abstractions. He opposed the official policies that favored the founding of new polytechnical institutes rather than an expansion of universities. Universities alone, according to him, could give Russia what she needed most: a respect for pure knowledge as the true source of personal enlightenment and national strength.

While collecting mineral specimens for the Mineralogical Museum of the Academy of Sciences, Vernadskii became aware of the serious lack of scientific studies of Russian natural resources. As a member of Dokuchaev's survey teams, he had learned to appreciate the urgent need for a scientific conservation and rehabilitation of soil; and as an active member of the Tambov *zemstvo*, he was aware that most rural activists were only too ready to accept scientific leadership in their agricultural programs. During his numerous Western travels, he spent much time working in university laboratories and libraries, observing the geological features of mining regions throughout Europe, and learning about the newest developments in mining technology. At the international geological congresses, he paid as much attention to the organizational aspects of scientific research and communication as he did to the content of scholarly papers. He gave much thought to the broader organizational and institutional aspects of the KEPS, and presented his conclusions in several papers.

Modern science, Vernadskii warned his colleagues, was a gigantic intellectual endeavor that required not only trained scholars but also an efficient institutional base. Since the traditional Russian scientific institutions (universities, learned societies, and periodic congresses) were not extensive enough to meet the challenge of the growing role of science in society, Vernadskii recommended the establishment of research institutes dedicated solely to the advancement of science and a rapid flow of scientific knowledge to the national economy. He made it clear, however, that any institutional base would be ineffective as long as the government did not have a definite policy toward science and did nothing to further the scientific study of national resources. As a historian and a philosopher of science in general, he had a healthy respect for the vitality of the scientific spirit in Russia; but his own work in mineralogy had shown him that there was very little cooperation between science and society at large.

Vernadskii's work ranged from simple trips through the countryside in search of soil samples to a serious involvement in the most abstract epistemological problems. He helped teach *zemstvo* activists—the intellectuals of the "third estate"—the most effective methods of collecting scientific specimens and statistical data. At the same time, he wrote treatises in mineralogy and crystallography that were model syntheses of modern scientific knowledge. No firm lines separated Vernadskii's many interests in scientific scholarship, social activities, and political life. His criticism of the institutional setting of Russian science, for instance, was only one part of a broader attack on the anachronistic features of the tsarist polity, which survived solely through police terror and political corruption. Vernadskii was the most eloquent spokesman of the large group of scientists who openly declared that the future welfare of Russia depended on advances in scientific thought, and that science could only develop after an extensive liberalization of political institutions.

Although he attacked the tsarist government's policies and institutions, Vernadskii wanted to preserve the continuity of Russian society and culture; he was a reformist, not a revolutionist. However, he firmly believed that the only system of values capable of sustaining a consistent and predictable program in science had to be based on democratic governmental institutions. He advocated a much broader participation of the government in the national effort in science; but he also made it very clear that government assistance would be beneficial only when it did not violate the scientific ethos or deny the right of scientists to be the only authoritative interpreters of the scientific legacy. To meet these conditions, the government had to support free scientific creativity rather than applied scientific technology; and it must not interfere with the freedom of any individual scientist.[31] Vernadskii argued that it was the government's duty to supplement a growing support for science throughout Russian society. An interest in science actually was growing among all segments of society, and this he saw as proof of "the democratization of social life." In 1913 he stated: "The democratization of social relations and the resulting respect for people of all stations are direct results of the triumphs of science."[32]

Since the very beginning of the nineteenth century, when V. M. Severgin had tried to explain the configurations of crystalline planes and angles in terms of R. J. Haüy's structural principles, Russian crystallography had been a thriving discipline. Toward the end of the tsarist era, the most eminent Russian crystallographer was Evgraf Stepanovich Fedorov, who did for his branch of science what men like Lobachevskii, Mendeleev, Mechnikov, and Pavlov had done in other areas.[33] In his famous *Introduction to the History of Mathematics in the Nineteenth Century*, Felix Klein recognized Fedorov as the first scientist to produce a consistent and complete mathematical integration of structural crystallography.[34]

Fedorov's path to professional eminence was most irregular. In the mid-1860's, he enrolled in a military gymnasium. At this time, under the influence of Pisarev and other Nihilists, countless informal student *kruzhoky* were dominated by fiery debates concerning the spirit and content of the natural sciences, and Fedorov soon learned to depend more on his own proclivities and ingenuity than on stale lecture materials. Unruly and independent, he left the gymnasium before graduating. In 1872 he graduated from a military technical school as a second lieutenant; but in 1874 he left the army in order to continue his education. Without a classical gymnasium diploma, he could not enter a university; however, a brilliant showing on the entrance examinations got him into the St. Petersburg Technological Institute.

Fedorov learned much about modern physics and chemistry at the Institute, and acquired valuable laboratory experience. But once again his personal engagement in science went far beyond the offerings and expectations of his formal studies. He also became involved in underground revolutionary work, and even went abroad for secret consultations with émigré leaders. He left the Technological Institute before graduation, and in 1880, at the age of 27, he was admitted to the Mining Institute in St. Petersburg, from which he finally graduated in 1883.

When Fedorov entered the Mining Institute, he had already completed a large study entitled *Elements of a Theory of Figures*, a novel exercise in pure geometry. "At the base of this study," he later remarked, "is the notion of the measurement of three-dimensional angles, just as the theorems of planimetry have a base in the notion of the measurement of plane angles."[35] Despite its geometrical orientation, Fedorov's study presented all the elements of the theory of figures that are now employed in modern crystallography. Referring to this study in an autobiographical note, Fedorov remarked that modern crystallographers had been forced by the advances in their science to venture into mathematics: because existing mathematical techniques did not always answer the needs of crystallography, crystallographers had often been compelled to invent their own mathematics.

The famous mathematician P. L. Chebyshev considered Fedorov's manuscript an exercise in useless mathematics; but A. V. Gadolin, the leading crystallographer of the time, recognized its intrinsic merits and recommended it for publication by the Mineralogical Society. Even before the publication of the *Elements*, Fedorov had gained some respect in professional circles with a number of papers on diverse topics—notably a general law of atomic weights, a "theory of twin crystals," and the geology of certain caves. In all these papers he sought out consistencies and regularities in the inner structure of rocks and minerals. Fedorov gave the clearest indication of his future scientific concerns in a paper delivered before the members of the Mineralogical Society in 1883. In it, he asserted that mineralogy had entered a new phase characterized by "a search for more abstract concepts with the help of mathematics."[36] He thought that mineralogy stood to gain most from the theory of "projective properties," a new geometry so far explored only by pure mathematicians.

Fedorov graduated from the Mining Institute in 1886. Although he was at the top of his class, the Institute made no effort to retain him for postgraduate studies. He had two handicaps: an unorthodox formal education and a liking for mathematical crystallography, which at the time had little support in the Russian scientific community. In order to support his family, he accepted an offer from the Department of Mines to conduct a geological survey in the northern Urals—a project that allowed him to spend the winter months in St. Petersburg and gave him valuable experience in geological cartography. It was at this time that Fedorov turned from pure geometry to the geometry of crystals and made crystallography his major scientific interest.

Among Fedorov's many crystallographic studies during this period, the most important is *The Symmetry of the Real Systems of Figures* (1891), which contains a complete algebraic derivation of 230 separate classes of symmetry, representing the basic "plans" of natural crystals. An essentially identical discovery was made at about the same time by the German crystallographer A. Schoenflies, and again a little later by the Englishman J. H. Barlow. The English crystallographer Harold Hilton stated in 1903: "Fedorov's and Schoenflies's work appeared about 1890; the former had a slight priority, but his work was published in Russian, and was, therefore, not so widely circulated as it might otherwise have been."[37] Both Schoenflies and Fedorov relied on mathematics to analyze the internal structure of crystals. However, Schoenflies relied primarily on the newly developed group theory, whereas Fedorov used algebraic geometry.

Fedorov's theories were confirmed in 1912, when the British physicists W. H. and W. L. Bragg developed a method for deciphering crystal structures by X rays. These techniques made it possible to unveil the atomic content and geometric forms of real crystals, allying crystallography with modern chemistry. Fedorov set forth 230 laws depicting the distribution of axes, surfaces, and points in uniform types of crystals, and thus provided a geometrical framework for the identification of specific arrangements of atoms or ions. In the words of a modern crystallographer, Fedorov, Schoenflies, and Barlow discovered the "different ways of arranging asymmetric groups of atoms . . . before the advent of X-ray methods made it possible to utilize the knowledge."[38] Fedorov, and others who later developed similar theories, made it possible to assign each natural crystal to a morphological group; the Braggs, depending on the established groups and on X-ray spectroscopy, made it possible to undertake a systematic study of the exact structure of each crystal. During the last years of his long career, Fedorov wrote a series of articles explaining recent discoveries in the application of X-ray spectroscopy to the study of crystal structures and heralding the emergence of "crystallochemistry," a new science that "shows the distribution of atoms by most reliable structural and stereochemical (i.e., spatial) formulas."[39]

From 1890 to 1895, Fedorov wrote a series of articles for the German periodical *Zeitschrift für Krystallographie*, clarifying and expanding his theory of the symmetry of the real systems of crystalline forms. Although Russia had a distinguished tradition in crystallography, Fedorov's ideas were so novel that he had to turn to Western scholarship for understanding and moral support.[40] In 1893, the St. Petersburg Academy of Sciences voted against admitting him; as in the case of Mendeleev, the learned custodians of the Academy considered his work both untested and highly speculative.

Fedorov once more took a job as a geological surveyor in the Urals, but he also continued his crystallographic work. In 1895, at the age of 42, he was appointed Professor of Geology at the Moscow Agricultural Institute, becoming for the first time a full member of the scholarly community. In

Russia his reputation grew slowly, and mostly as a result of the favorable acceptance of his work by Western crystallographers. In 1901, the Academy of Sciences elected him an "adjunct"; this dubious honor caused him endless irritation and made him a bitter critic of the estate system that dominated the Russian scientific community. At the beginning of the twentieth century, Fedorov joined the liberal group of scientists who lamented the absence of a private sector in higher education and who made merciless attacks on "government science" and the stultifying bureaucratization of scholarship. Like many of his colleagues, he thought that science could develop to its full potential only in societies that allowed a free and independent search for truth.[41] He was convinced that the Academy was responsible for the perpetuation of the caste system in Russian science, and that it prevented the formation of a modern network of research agencies. In 1905, Fedorov resigned from the Academy.[42]

As one result of the many temporary administrative reforms that came about after the 1905 outbursts, the academic councils of the institutions of higher education were allowed to choose school administrators. The professors' council of the Mining Institute immediately honored Fedorov by electing him director of their school. But when the Institute reelected him in 1910, the government voided the election, allowing him to serve only as a professor of mineralogy. During his five-year directorship, Fedorov founded the *Journal of the Mining Institute*, attempting to create a rallying point for Russian mineralogists and crystallographers who wanted to absorb the newest developments in physics, chemistry, and mathematics.

Fedorov was a member of the Bavarian Academy of Sciences, the Roman Academy of Sciences, the French Mineralogical Society, and the London Mineralogical Society; and he received honorary doctorates from Moscow University and Geneva University. His total scientific output went far beyond the theory of crystal structures. He was an accomplished "regional geologist" and petrographer. His work on an all-inclusive system of projective geometry was a marvel of combined aesthetics and geometry, impressive in both the harmony of its propositions and the depth of its mathematical elaboration; essentially, he constructed a uniform system of geometrical propositions designed to account for the theoretical multidimensionality of crystalline space. Fedorov was also an expert in the optical, or goniometric, analysis of minerals; and he invented a new goniometer and a universal stage for examining minerals, both of which are still in use.[43] With his contributions to *New Ideas in Chemistry* (1914), he tried to inform the general reader of the new scientific ideas emerging in the areas where crystallography met modern physics and chemistry; and in the post-humous *Realm of Crystals* (1920), he presented a comprehensive atlas of multiple projections designed to help determine the chemical composition of mineral crystals.

Fedorov was intensely interested in the general problems of science, and particularly in the inner logic of the growth of scientific thought and in the logical patterns of scientific explanations. The basic function of science, according to Fedorov, is to reduce the structure and dynamics of the universe —or a part of it—to a limited number of simple principles. To achieve this goal, science must find logical ways of linking the most abstract principles with generalizations based directly on empirical data. The scientist must strive to reach the highest possible level of abstraction; but he must never lose sight of the empirical base.

Fedorov viewed science as an indivisible whole. The boundaries between individual sciences, he said, are artificial; and if taken seriously they impede the growth of scientific thought. In word and deed, Fedorov showed that the most striking advances in modern science were made by scholars who ignored the boundary lines and worked in the areas where several sciences met.[44] In a lengthy essay published in 1906 in a biological journal, he combined the ideas of evolutionary biology and "modern physics" (particularly the second law of thermodynamics) to construct an interesting concept of universal evolution, in which he presented the periodic readjustments of natural phenomena to underlying conditions as the true motive force of natural history.[45] In a later article, he tried to apply this concept of evolution to a study of the dynamics of various national traditions in the institutionalization of science.[46]

The differences between various sciences, Fedorov argued, are expressed less in their fields of inquiry than in their varying degrees of methodological perfection; and the methodological perfection of each science depends on its use of mathematics. In this respect, the sciences can be divided into four groups: the mathematical sciences, which are thoroughly mathematicized and involve a minimum of observation and experimentation; the "exact" sciences (e.g., physics), which are essentially mathematical even though they are based on experiments; the "experimental" sciences, such as physiology, which are based on experiments closely related to observations and are mathematically underdeveloped; and the "observational" sciences, including all the social sciences and many natural sciences, such as botany, which have a poorly developed experimental base and almost no mathematical support.[47]

Fedorov was convinced that every scientist should work on the elaboration of mathematical technique in order to make it an efficient methodological tool in his own research. Individual sciences had to be adjusted to the rigorous methods of quantitative measurement; at the same time, mathematics must be adjusted to the specific needs of each science. Fedorov argued that sociology, for example, could become a dependable science only if sociologists directed their research toward collecting quantifiable data while mathematicians developed new procedures to process social data with a relatively low measurement potential.

### THE EARTH SCIENCES AND THE RUSSIAN ECONOMY

The Russian earth scientists formed a distinct community. By occupying key positions in the various technical institutes, they strengthened the bonds that joined the main institutions of higher education in the pursuit of science. Several disciplines connected with geology—particularly petrography, soil science, and crystallography—helped higher technical schools emerge as vital centers of scientific research. The ties between earth scientists of all specialties and the government were particularly strong and diversified. The chief task of the Geological Committee, in fact, was to regulate and coordinate these ties. At one time or another, every leading earth scientist participated in research sponsored by the Committee or some other government agency. This work gave earth scientists a certain unity of purpose, and strongly influenced their views on the utilitarian role of science and on the role of government in providing an institutional base for research.

More than other scholars, the earth scientists were given the opportunity to work for private enterprises, for there were always entrepreneurs eager to discover and exploit new mineral deposits. Russian geologists often worked on assignments in which the national welfare and economic development were subordinated to the predatory interests of private employers. Some of the larger businesses financed systematic geological studies conducted by leading experts in the field, and helped enrich geology as a body of theoretical knowledge and a source of practical information; but most relied on mining engineers, whose work was directed mostly toward a quick profit. By World War I, this situation was so out of hand that a group of noted geologists asked the scientific world to set forth some clear ethical guidelines for "expert counseling" in order to protect the integrity of their science and their own status as scientists.

In 1901, the Society of Mining Engineers decided to sponsor national congresses of experts in "practical geology."[48] These forums, held in 1903 and 1911, discussed the possibility of modernizing the search for new mineral deposits, demanded the establishment of separate geology departments in the polytechnical institutes, studied the economics of geological survey and prospecting activities, and recommended the enactment of laws that would define the legal responsibilities of prospectors working for private firms. The first one was opened by the Academician A. P. Karpinskii, who noted that this was the first joint meeting of theoretical and practical scientists to be held in Russia. He emphasized the interdependence of geological theory and practical prospecting; and he reminded his audience that the vision of the scientist must reach far beyond the practical demands of the day, even though the value of scientific knowledge is ultimately judged in terms of practical results.

Both "practical geology" congresses paid much attention to the conflict between the private and public domains in geological knowledge, condemning it as injurious to both the national economy and the science of geology. Several reporters were of the opinion that every earth scientist, in addition to providing expert knowledge in the search for useful minerals, must support a national campaign for the rational use and conservation of natural resources. These demands acquired particular urgency during World War I, when it became obvious that Russia's extensive dependence on foreign manufactures was responsible for the exceedingly slow transmission of geological knowledge to the national economy. The journals *Surface and Depths of the Earth* and *Mining Messenger*, both established in 1916, concerned themselves chiefly with the problems of scientific exploration and the economics of mineral resources.[49]

Although war encouraged the development of applied geology, it by no means discouraged the cultivation of geological theory. It was during the war that E. S. Fedorov made his first concerted efforts to look into the general laws of nature by using crystal structure as a point of departure.[50] It was also at this time that V. I. Vernadskii worked diligently on the theoretical foundations of geochemistry, while Iu. V. Vul'f undertook the first Russian X-ray studies of crystals.[51] In 1917, in the very midst of social and political chaos, Russian paleontologists organized a national association of their own, ending the traditional dependence of paleontology on geology and opening the way for much closer ties between paleontology and biology.

The congresses of applied geology had little impact on the Russian legal system, but they helped delineate the values that must guide the scientist as a custodian of his discipline, as a champion of economic rationality, and as a politically conscious citizen. They spelled out the great optimism of modern science and the sensitivity of scientists to the maze of values and institutions that regulate the life of modern man. Above all, they reaffirmed the idea that the future progress of Russia depended on a vigorous and concerted national effort in science.

CHAPTER FOURTEEN

# The Search for a Science of Society

THE BASIC PHILOSOPHICAL COMMITMENTS

The search for a science of society began in Russia during the 1860's, as part of the great popular preoccupation with schemes for a new society unencumbered by the vestiges of feudal institutions. It coincided with the emergence of Western European sociology, a discipline dedicated to formulating universal laws of social behavior; and most Russian sociological theories during the waning decades of the tsarist regime were either echoes or rebuttals of contemporary Western thought. Most of the pioneers in Russian sociology shared five philosophical commitments.

First, they sought a grand theory that would apply to all human societies. They sought to explain the quintessential features of Russian society not as relatively isolated historical phenomena but as integral parts of human society in general.

Second, Russian sociological ideas were more deeply embedded in dominant ideologies than was the case in Western Europe. Nihilists, Populists, Anarchists, and Marxists were the champions of distinct ideologies and at the same time the architects of the most widely debated sociological theories. M. M. Kovalevskii's "comparative historical" sociology was an organic part of an ideology that combined a belief in parliamentary democracy with a fervent dedication to social equality.

Third, with the exception of the Marxists, Russian thinkers made moral norms and values a central topic of sociological theory. They viewed morality as an index of social progress, a meeting ground of sacred culture and secular culture, and an indicator of social dynamics. Morality, they felt, was not a motive force of social evolution, but a result of cultural progress and a mechanism of social integration.

Fourth, a strong historicism was common to all the Russian pioneers in sociology. In Russia, sociology was generally defined as the study of universal laws of social development. The regularities assumed to be present in the historical process lured the early sociologists into reading broader meanings into the dim past and foretelling inevitable structural changes in the future. In most cases, sociology predicted a brighter future—a hope for the progressive triumph of humanity. The idea of progress as a good in itself was built into all the early Russian theories of social development. This historicism was perhaps best expressed by the philosopher N. I. Kareev when he claimed that the most reliable and productive scientific study of culture and society was one combining two contradictory ideas: the eighteenth-century idea that all historical changes result from individual creativity; and the nineteenth-century idea that social evolution is independent of human will and reason. Just such an intertwining of "objective" causality and subjective "purposiveness" dominated Russian sociology.[1]

Fifth, Russian sociology, with minor exceptions, was opposed to the basic tenets of the official ideology. The ideology of autocracy assumed complete harmony between society and the state; but all the major Russian sociological orientations were based on an implicit or explicit recognition of irreconcilable differences between the two. The official ideology was dedicated to perpetuating a social system that embodied the reigning values of the autocratic state; but the sociologists looked toward a future in which the state would be built on the reigning values of society. Official ideology interpreted society as an instrument of the state; but most leading sociologists regarded the ideal state as an instrument of society.

### NIHILIST AND POPULIST SOCIOLOGY

The Nihilists, led by D. I. Pisarev, concerned themselves a great deal with the problems of a scientific study of social phenomena.* Although their writing was undisciplined and full of contradictions, they deserve the major credit for making sociological thought an important part of Russian intellectual life. Combining the Comtean idea of progress (which goes back to the philosophies of Turgot and Condorcet) with the scientism of the German materialists Büchner and Vogt, the utilitarianism of John Stuart Mill, and the Darwinian idea of evolution, Pisarev formulated a grand theory of social change that met the needs and the mood of the 1860's. Social evolution, according to Pisarev, is tantamount to cultural progress, and cultural progress is best indicated by an increasing secularization of wisdom. The growth of rationality in the acquisition, appraisal, and application of knowl-

---

* The Nihilist and Populist sociologies are integral parts of the general philosophies of science adopted by these schools of thought, which are discussed in Chapter One.

edge produces several distinct lines of cultural and social progress: for example, an increased economy (or decreased waste) of intellectual effort; and a "realism of knowledge," i.e., an evaluation of knowledge in terms of its social usefulness.[2]

The purest and most exact expression of secular wisdom, according to Pisarev, is science. The age of science brings a complete victory of reason over superstition and a full recognition of the individual personality as the main agent of social change. In fact, the development of science hinges on the emancipation of human individuality, and is therefore an index of the growth of democracy. Societies become petrified unless their values and ethical norms are constantly challenged. Every man is both a person and an individual: as a person he reflects the dominant values of his society; but as an individual he challenges obsolescent values and institutions.

When Pisarev spoke of science, he was thinking primarily of the natural sciences. "Only the natural sciences," according to him, "are deeply rooted in living reality; only they are completely independent of speculation and fiction; only they are impervious to reactionary forces; only they form the sphere of pure knowledge, free of all tendentiousness; accordingly, only the natural sciences bring man face to face with living reality, unadorned with moral teachings, unstultified by political systems, and unaffected by the idle thought of philosophers."[3] Pisarev accepted Chernyshevskii's assertion that the "moral" or social sciences could develop only as ontological, logical, and methodological extensions of the natural sciences. Sociological knowledge assumes historical significance—that is, it becomes a mechanism of social change—only when it is part of natural-scientific knowledge. The laws of society are only a variety of the laws of nature, and the Darwinian "struggle for existence" is the supreme law of both nature and society. For Pisarev a "moral scientist," a historian, or a social activist cannot be effective unless he also knows differential calculus, chemistry, physiology, and anatomy.[4]

Pisarev built the foundations of a sociology, but not a complete system of sociology; nor did he make an effort to clarify the epistemological problems of sociology and elaborate a methodology of sociological inquiry. His theory of social change was as much a condemnation of the dogmatic, religious world view associated with tsarist autocracy as it was a positivist promise of a better society. His work was more important as a sociological codification of the problems, aspirations, and dreams of the intelligentsia of the 1860's than as a contribution to the conceptual tools of sociology. According to a contemporary writer, Pisarev wrote at a time when the Russian *avant garde* was convinced that "moral truths could no longer be accepted in their orthodox form"; that a scientific world view should replace the "supernatural and mythical world view"; and that the full rejuvenation of society depended on the triumph of "reason, science, and freedom."[5] Like many of his contemporaries, Pisarev stuck closely to the doctrines of positivism, which provided powerful arguments against the government's attempts to make use of idealistic philosophy as an ideological weapon of the autocratic system.[6]

In 1869, N. K. Mikhailovskii published a long essay entitled "What is Progress?"* In it, he criticized the sociology proposed by Herbert Spencer as a scientifically unfounded effort to extend the Darwinian notion of biological evolution to the study of social change. In the same year, P. L. Lavrov published his classic *Historical Letters,* which contained serious speculation on many philosophical questions related to science. In several respects both Lavrov and Mikhailovskii were in agreement with Pisarev. Like him, they subscribed to the idea of continuous progress, which justified a political opposition to autocratic institutions and identified universal history with a gradual realization of the ideals of justice, brotherhood, and equality. They saw the secularization of wisdom as a motive force of history and were sworn enemies of metaphysics. And they recognized the individual as the basic unit of society. The social theories advanced by Mikhailovskii and Lavrov are so closely intertwined and fundamentally similar that they should be treated as a single system.[7]

Mikhailovskii and Lavrov rejected the German materialist doctrines that had attracted Pisarev, and thus rejected every notion of an ontological basis for the unity of the sciences. Instead, they accepted the positivist epistemological argument: all sciences are united by the fact that they deal not with "the essence of things" but with "the interrelations between phenomena."[8] All knowledge, they argued, is subjective in its origin. However, the subjective knowledge dealt with by the social sciences differs from that dealt with by the natural sciences. Sociological knowledge, for example, is subjective not only in its origin but also in its orientation and goals. The social sciences in general involve a mixture of "objective" and "subjective" interpretations and methods of inquiry that is absent in the physical sciences. According to a follower of Mikhailovskii: "Only in the science of man and society, in which the investigating subject is also an object of inquiry, is there an imperative need for a harmonious blending of objective facts and

* See pp. 25–29.

subjective (psychological) interpretations."[9] According to Lavrov, the activities of individuals are the only source of the data dealt with by ethics, political science, and sociology; and to understand these activities, it is necessary to describe their objective manifestations in "social forms" and "historical events" and their subjective goals.[10] Lavrov and Mikhailovskii did not deny the existence of an objective base for the social sciences, but they consistently emphasized that these disciplines, particularly sociology, were made up entirely of subjective interpretations of objective data. From this basic proposition they derived several other essential characteristics of sociology.

First, any sociological interpretation combines an objective study of social causation and a subjective study of social teleology. Anticipating a subsequent trend in German sociology, this approach in sociology combined the methods of *Erklärung* and *Verstehen*. The complementarity of "external causality" and "inner purposiveness," or historical inevitability and personal motivation, is at the bottom of Populist sociology.[11]

Second, a profound sociological analysis must recognize the individual as the focal point of inquiry. The individual is neither a functional "organ" nor a structural "cell" in a society; he is the essence of society, and his actions are its moving force. He is not a mechanical product of society, but is formed by the harmonization of subjective individuality and objective social conditions. Society originates from the individual human need for "spiritual communication," and comes into being when a number of individual subjective perceptions are selected as a common normative system.[12]

Third, social change is equivalent to social progress, and social progress to an increasing harmonization of society and personality. Mikhailovskii interprets social progress as a dynamic balance between the heterogeneous division of labor in society and the homogeneous "wholeness" of personality, in which more advanced forms of cooperation are constantly replacing less advanced forms. Cooperation, in turn, is judged not by objective criteria but by subjective human ideals. According to Lavrov, social progress is based on the evolution of various forms of solidarity among "socially conscious individuals."[13] Lavrov also defined the general role of the concept of "progress" in historical writing: "Without a formula of progress, it is impossible to undertake a rational reconstruction of history. What should be made part of a historical study, and what should be ignored? What should stand on the first plane, and what on the second? What is the meaning of particular events, and what is the historical importance of particular men? All these questions can be answered only on the basis of the historian's view of progress. If a historian has clearly understood the need for the idea of progress and has truly understood the meaning of progress, then his work will make sense....If he has not constructed a conception of progress but has instead relied on ephemeral views...his work will have no scientific value."[14] The notion of progress in this context is to be deduced from the internal experience of man rather than from external conditions.

Fourth, since social development depends on a search for harmony between the individual and society, neither the Darwinian "struggle for existence" nor the Marxian "class struggle" can be seriously regarded as a key force of social change. The subjective elements in social dynamics render any monistic or deterministic interpretation of the historical process inadequate and simplistic.

Fifth, a sociological analysis, unlike a physical or biological analysis, must recognize a close interrelationship between the theoretical and practical aspects of knowledge. In the natural sciences, the difference between the theoretical and practical branches can be easily recognized; in sociology, this difference is not so clear, since human needs in specific social and historical situations are both the facts of theoretical inquiry and the criteria for selecting theoretical truths to be applied in practical fields.

Sixth, every sociological inquiry must include a moral appraisal. Mikhailovskii rejected Herbert Spencer's argument that sociology must be confined to a study of the laws of social change regardless of whether this change meant progress or regress from the viewpoint of the investigator. Spencer wanted sociology to rise above all ethical questions, treating social phenomena as a scientist treats physical or chemical phenomena. Mikhailovskii, however, wanted sociology to concentrate on the developments that contribute to the material and spiritual betterment of human collectivities, and natural-science methods alone could not do this.[15] The subject matter of sociology, according to Mikhailovskii, is described by the double meaning of the Russian word *pravda*: truth and justice. Truth denotes the objective aspect and justice the subjective aspect of sociology. The natural sciences are concerned exclusively with truth; but sociology and the other social sciences deal also with "justice," that is, with the moral side of social existence. Therefore, teleology and value judgments are integral parts of subjective sociology.[16] And subjective sociology itself is concerned not only with understanding the social world but also with changing it.

With these propositions, Mikhailovskii and Lavrov provided a broad theoretical scheme for sociology; but they did not translate their ideas into practical systems of concrete research. Accordingly, their "sociology" was more a statement of philosophical propositions than a useful tool for social inquiry. Nevertheless, they did provide the first systematic and critical surveys of Comtean and Spencerian sociology, laying the groundwork for the development of systematic sociological thought in Russia.[17] They knew that they had not established sociology as a full-fledged science, but they were certain that it could become one. In 1894, Lavrov wrote that sociology was still looking for sound scientific foundations, and that it still lacked the logical and methodological procedures necessary to extract laws of social development from diffuse ethnographic data.[18]

Mikhailovskii and Lavrov viewed sociology as a science of limited laws and extensive empirical generalizations. In 1879, for example, Mikhailovskii remarked that political economy (which had been established as a separate field by the work of the Englishman David Ricardo in the early nineteenth century) was too abstract and too removed from an empirical base of economic data.[19] He and Lavrov fought two kinds of enemies: Marxists, who made sociology a "natural science"; and the proponents of metaphysical idealism, who discarded sociology on the grounds that it did not have adequate conceptual and methodological tools to cope with the "absolute," "timeless," and "divine" attributes of human societies. The positivists made sociology part of an essentially democratic ideology, which opposed both the stationary view of society built into the tsarist ideology and the revolutionary view of society advanced by Nihilist and Marxist ideology.

Because of their ideological commitment, Mikhailovskii and Lavrov were not concerned with the divisive attributes of social classes and estates, but with the integrative functions of "the people." For this reason, they considered the Russian peasant—who made up 80 per cent of the Russian populace—to be the most basic topic of political and sociological debate.

Mikhailovskii and Lavrov formulated the basic principles of their sociology during the 1860's and early 1870's. Subsequently, their activities diverged in many directions; but they often came back to sociology, usually to define or elaborate their stand on the most influential new theories. In 1893 Mikhailovskii precipitated a bitter feud between the Populists and the Marxists by attacking the deterministic nature of economic materialism. He also undertook a detailed comparison of subjective sociology and Emile Durkheim's theory of the role of an increasing division of social labor in the development of "individuality" and "personality" as distinct sociological entities.[20]

The influence of subjective sociology on the Russian intelligentsia was enormous. According to one philosopher of modern Populism, this sociology satisfied the basic intellectual need of modern Russia for a concrete doctrine that was simultaneously a philosophy of reality and a philosophy of action. The same commentator adds: "The sociological doctrine that in the minds of all Russians is indissolubly linked with the names of P.

Mirtov [P. L. Lavrov] and N. K. Mikhailovskii reigned supreme over the minds and hearts of several generations of the most active Russian intelligentsia...because it appeared as an integrated and complete system satisfying both the theoretical and the practical needs of its adherents. It was an edifice chiseled out of a single piece of granite, and this determined the attitude of the reading public toward it. It was either completely accepted or completely rejected. The blending of the real and the ideal, the objective and the subjective, the theoretical and the practical—this was the bond that held together the entire architecture of this system, from the most general abstract propositions to the simplest concrete statements."[21]

One of the most erudite followers and elaborators of subjective sociology was Viktor Chernov. In a series of articles published during the 1890's, he distinguished himself not by the originality of his ideas but by his vast command of up-to-date philosophical and sociological knowledge, and by his skillful combination of subjective theory with modern Western epistemological and sociological thought. Indeed, he demonstrated that subjective sociology had in many respects anticipated some of the most influential developments in Western thought. For example, Chernov argued that Heinrich Rickert's views on the dichotomy of "nature" and "society" and the qualitative differences between the natural and social sciences were not essentially different from Mikhailovskii's and Lavrov's views on the unique features of objective and subjective realities and the specific methodological features of the natural and social sciences.[22] He also took a close look at Wilhelm Dilthey's classic *Introduction to the Cultural Sciences*, published in 1883, and saw no essential differences between the German philosopher's notion of *Geisteswissenschaften* and Mikhailovskii's and Lavrov's conception of subjective sociology. To all of these writers, "nature" is "external" to the inquiring mind, whereas society is part of its "inner" life. The sociologist, they say, must create special tools of social inquiry in order to take into account the fact that he, as a person, is not only a student but also a creator of social reality.

Chernov examined the theories of the German sociologist Georg Simmel in search of an answer to the most basic problem of subjective sociology: how the highly individualized content of personal experiences could allow for the formation of social thought, norms of behavior, and a common culture. He elaborated on Simmel's contention that truth is only a "relational concept," expressing an agreement on "the content of consciousness" that is shared by the majority of a group of interacting individuals. The statement that truth is a bias of the group and untruth a bias of the individual sums up Simmel's relativistic epistemology, which helped Chernov explain the psychological origins of human society and culture.[28] The same idea is expressed in Simmel's statement that the objective is a generalized version of the subjective, which Chernov found fully congruent with the basic ideas of Mikhailovskii's subjective sociology.

In his systematic search for modern philosophical support for subjective sociology, Chernov found himself in the unsettled waters of "scientific philosophy," as formulated by the German neopositivists (or "critical positivists") Alois Riehl, Carl Göring, Joseph Petzoldt, Ernst Mach, and Richard Avenarius. In the epistemological statements of these philosophers he found strong additional support for the basic principles of subjective sociology. However, in his preoccupation with finding support for Mikhailovskii's theses, Chernov overlooked the deeper philosophical meaning of the work of Mach and Avenarius, which also lent support to the notion of an epistemological, logical, and methodological unity of physics and psychology (including sociology). He accepted the idea that the knowledge of both physics and sociology is subjective in its origin; but he also argued that sociology, as a science of "the indivisible person," is doubly subjective, inasmuch as sociologists are both architects and investigators of social reality.

Subjective sociology was a unique combination of science and ideology. As a "science," it was founded on the view that human society could be fully understood only when its inner workings were subjected to scientific scrutiny. As an "ideology," it gave philosophically articulated support to the Populist view that the individual held the keys to history, which found many converts in Russia. Together with belief in the inevitability of social change and the secular nature of political institutions, it formed the creed of the Russian intelligentsia.

The Populists' interpretation of personality was based on their belief in the paramount historical role of harmonious relations between the individual and his society. It was a blend of the anti-individualism of the "repentant nobility" (the leaders of the "Going to the People" movement and the champions of the *narod*) and the ultra-individualism of the *raznochintsy* (who advocated uncompromising individual opposition to the existing institutions).[24] Both the repentant nobility and the *raznochintsy* attacked the pivotal institutions of tsarist autocracy. The *raznochintsy*, as represented by the Nihilists, did not think that conflict between the individual and the autocratic state could be softened or avoided. The repentant nobility, on the other hand, considered that the mass of the people, if united by the bonds of solidarity, could protect its individual members from the encroachments of the autocratic state. The Nihilists emphasized the individual as the destroyer of the established social system; the Populists saw the individual as the builder of a new and freer society. The subjective sociology of Mikhailovskii, Lavrov, and Chernov was not a theoretical platform for the Populist political program. On the contrary, it was an intricate derivation from Populist ideals—a unique effort to place the intellectual power of science behind the Populist dream of a democratic society.

BIOLOGICAL SOCIOLOGY

The idea of biological and social transformation (and progress) was staunchly supported by Russian writers of the most diverse interests and ideological bents. "Biological" sociology, however, which attempted to apply the Darwinian doctrine of a struggle for survival to social systems, found very few supporters indeed. Mikhailovskii and the other Populists attacked it on several grounds; and even the foremost champions of Darwinian biology among the natural scientists had no desire to extend Darwin's evolutionary ideas to social or moral reality.

The biological models produced two distinct types of sociology: "organismic" sociology, which equated society with organism; and evolutionary sociology, which applied the Darwinian concept of biological evolution to the study of social change. "Organismic" sociology dealt primarily with social statics, and evolutionary sociology concentrated on social dynamics.

The leading Russian pioneer of "organismic" sociology was Paul Lilienfeld, a graduate of the Aleksandrovsk Lycée in Tsarskoe Selo and a high government official unconnected with either academic life or the ideological ferment of the time. In 1872 he wrote a book on "the sociology of the future," which served as a basis for a five-volume presentation of organismic sociology published in German from 1873 to 1881. Though almost completely overlooked in Russia, this work was widely discussed, supported, and attacked in Western Europe. Lilienfeld viewed human society as a living organism, not in a figurative but in a real sense. "Human society," he wrote, "is a real being, like other natural organisms; it is nothing else but a continuation of nature and a higher expression of the fundamental natural forces."[25]

Unlike the proponents of subjective sociology, Lilienfeld claimed that the natural sciences and the social sciences were indistinguishable in both logic and methodology; but unlike the Nihilists, he conceded that human society, particularly in its ethical norms and values, was too complicated to be totally understood by scientific investigation. His model of society imposed drastic limitations on the scientific competence of sociology. Lilienfeld's *magnum opus* is remembered today as a monumental source of distorted information and misinterpreted illustrations of biological parallelism in human society.[26]

Jacques Novicow, a Russian who spent most of his life in France, made sociological Darwinism one of his main concerns, and acquired a wide reputation for his humanistic modifications of biological theories. At one time he was vice-president of the International Institute of Sociology. He, too, though unnoticed in Russia, received much attention in the West; and he was considered one of the more serious sociologists working with Darwin's ideas.

Evolution, according to Novicow, is a universal process. The great contribution of Darwin's theories was in replacing a static view of nature and society with a dynamic view. Although struggle is the mainspring of physical, biological, and cultural realities, it assumes many different forms. Biological struggle, for example, is based on a "physiological" principle: each animal can live only by destroying other living beings. Human societies, on the other hand, are engaged in several kinds of struggle, which Novicow categorized as physiological, economic, political, and intellectual struggles. These categories can be arranged on a scale of cultural progression: the most primitive societies depend extensively on physiological struggle; but the most advanced societies emphasize intellectual struggle, and the most successful of these are the societies that have the most efficient language, the most sublime literature, and the most universal philosophy.[27]

The more culturally advanced a society is, said Novicow, the more it seeks to form strong and lasting ties of cooperation with other societies. Although Novicow believed that "struggle" was the moving force of human social history, he contended that warfare would sooner or later cease to be an instrument of international relations. He did not see any conflict between the Darwinian "struggle for survival" and the existence of one peaceful community embracing all the nations of the world: "By pursuing its inexorable course, social progress will inevitably triumph in a federation of all mankind."[28] He devoted a good part of his *Critique du darwinisme social* to refuting the "false reasoning, sophistries, and contradictions" contained in the works of writers who treated war as the moving force of social and cultural evolution. According to him, "Harmony among men and the universal triumph of morality are one and the same thing."[29] In elaborating his basic proposition—a progressive affirmation of the supremacy of the intellectual struggle and a gradual elimination of the physical struggle—Novicow became a pioneer in the sociology of international relations.

Novicow's system of sociology stresses that the social and natural sciences are ontologically united, for society and nature are different parts of the same reality, and both are propelled by two ostensibly antithetical processes: association (cooperation) and struggle (conflict). From the constellations of stars to the alliances of states, there is, according to Novicow, a uniform reality, gradually changing its inner arrangement and seeking a balance between the forces of cooperation and the forces of struggle. The unity of the sciences also has an epistemological basis: neither the natural sciences nor the social sciences deal with absolute reality, but with artificial, logically constructed categorizations of the various components of the universe.

Novicow's recognition of the basic ontological and epistemological unity of the sciences did not prevent him from recognizing and emphasizing certain basic differences between the social and natural sciences. The physical world, he said, is made up of invisible atoms that require ultramicroscopic studies. Social phenomena, on the other hand, are of a macroscopic order: "One cannot see an atom; one can see all the social facts."[30] However, the exact sciences deal with microscopic but "countable" facts of nature, whereas the social sciences deal with macroscopic but uncountable social facts. In this uncountability—or imprecision—of social facts, Novicow saw the main reason for the relatively slow development of the social sciences. In Comtean terms, sociology has not yet entered the "positive" stage; it is still in the "metaphysical" stage because it has not yet established "a direct and immediate contact with concrete facts," and because it contains "vague theories" and "assertions as naïve as they are imprecise."[31]

Novicow agreed with the Populist assertion that the social sciences are "sciences" of a kind, and that Darwinian evolution cannot be applied to the study of society without certain major modifications and readjustments. He differed from the Populists in his heavy reliance on analogies between the workings of human society and the dynamics of the physical, chemical, and biological worlds; it is difficult to establish whether these analogies led him more to an anthropomorphic interpretation of nature or to a "naturalist" explanation of human society. Novicow also differed from the Populists in his notion of human society as a reality *sui generis,* which could not be reduced to the behavior patterns and activities of individuals.

Petr Kropotkin, the spiritual leader of the international Anarchist movement, agreed with Novicow that Darwinian biology provided the best model for a rigorous science of society. According to Kropotkin, Darwinism not only made biology a science but also offered the first dependable basis for a scientific study of human cultural history. "At the present time this history can be written without resorting to either the formulae of Hegelian metaphysics or to 'innate ideas' and 'inspiration from without'— without any of those dead formulae behind which, concealed by words as by clouds, was always hidden the same ancient ignorance and the same superstition. Owing on the one hand to the labors of the naturalists and on the other to those of Henry Maine and his followers, who applied the same inductive method to the study of primitive customs and laws that have grown out of them, it became possible in recent years to place the history of the origin and development of human institutions upon as firm a basis as that of the development of any form of plants and animals."[32]

As viewed by Kropotkin, the intellectual life of the nineteenth century had been dominated by the triumphs of scientific induction and deduction over metaphysical "dialectics." The scientific method had made it clear that the personal and social "spirit" of man was just as much a part of nature as is the growth of a flower or the social evolution of ants and bees. He saw no reason "for suddenly changing our method of investigation when we pass from a flower to man, or from a settlement of beavers to a human town."[33] Nature, in his opinion, was "the first ethical teacher of man."[34]

As the foremost ideologist of Anarchism, Kropotkin was not interested in personally applying "the scientific method of induction and deduction" to the study of human society; his interest was primarily in pointing out the compatibility of Anarchist ideology with the spirit and methods of modern science. However, he exercised no restraint in bending scientific knowledge to fit his political philosophy. Like most Russian interpreters of Darwin's legacy, he rejected the struggle for survival as a law of natural and social development; instead, he saw "mutual aid" as the most universal law of nature and society.

Kropotkin viewed social evolution as a continuous, progressive realization of social ideals, and he identified the most important of these ideals as the very values that autocratic Russia was most in need of: individuality in the interpretation of cultural tradition, self-government in politics, spontaneous cooperation in social life, and symbiotic interdependence in the relations between society and personality. The concept of mutual aid gives unity to these orientations, tying society to nature and sociology to the natural sciences. In sum, Kropotkin's sociological orientation lay somewhere between the scientism of the Nihilists and the scientific humanism of the Populists.

The first volume of *Das Kapital* was translated into Russian in 1872. Although it received wide attention, its ideas appealed more to the diffuse groups of revolutionaries on fringes of the Populist movement than to the scholars who were trying to build a scientific sociology. It was not until the early 1890's that a combination of apparently disconnected developments in the political and academic life of the country generated a serious interest in Marxism as a "scientific" theory of social structure and socioeconomic change.

Paramount among these developments was the growing scholarly interest in economic history, which had long been a purely descriptive discipline steeped in undigested statistics and lost in antiquarianism. In the late 1880's and early 1890's, an impressive number of younger historians introduced a new kind of economic history that combined a strong sensitivity for documentary detail with a systematic search for regularities in the development of economic institutions and for deeper sociological meanings in economic phenomena.[35]

The true pioneer of modern economic history in Russia was Maksim Kovalevskii, who transferred the problem of agricultural communalism (typified by the *obshchina*) "from the realm of sentiment to the realm of positive knowledge."[36] Kovalevskii acquired an international reputation as an economic historian of Russian feudal institutions, combining historical and ethnographic analysis with comparative historical sociology. He claimed that the study of economic institutions was the best way to discover the grand laws of social evolution, and that it provided the only sound empirical base for a comparative examination of analogous social institutions in various societies. Friedrich Engels incorporated Kovalevskii's thoughts on communal agriculture into his *Origin of the Family, Private Property, and the State.*

In 1892–94 Russian economic history entered a golden age, thanks to the publication of three works whose high quality attracted the attention of international scholarship. In 1892, in a classic study of Russian state finances in the early eighteenth century, P. N. Miliukov undertook a logically rigorous analysis of documentary information, most of which he obtained from previously ignored archives. From these materials, he sought to describe the structural ties between the various components of the state administration and the principal segments of the national economy. It was only through this "structural" approach that Miliukov was able to offer a comprehensive interpretation of Peter the Great's reforms and to draw a precise line between the continuities and discontinuities in the development of the Russian political system during the first quarter of the eighteenth century. In essence, his book was a study of the general "rationalist and organic" matrix of the broader "culture" of financial reforms.

In the same year, P. G. Vinogradov, a professor first at Moscow University and then at Oxford University, published in England his noted work *Villainage in England*. Vinogradov identified himself with those historians who searched for laws and generalizations that would describe "the complexity of human culture" as effectively as the natural sciences described the phenomena of nature.[37] Vinogradov identified his treatise as a history of "social arrangements," or recurrent patterns of social life that were similar enough to be compared. His statement that political economy was the only real "science" of society accurately expressed the prevalent opinion in the Russian scientific community at the beginning of the 1890's. A reviewer in the *Journal of the Ministry of National Education* devoted several pages to defending this thesis.

In 1894, M. I. Tugan-Baranovskii gave a vigorous boost to economic historiography by publishing an incisive study of the periodicity of industrial crises in England. The book attracted considerable attention in the Russian scholarly community and among the Populist economists, and was subsequently translated into German and French. It provided a theoretical basis for studying the social correlates and economic mechanisms of the capitalist transformation of Russia—a theme that attracted the attention of the intelligentsia far beyond academic institutions. Here, again, was an effort to approach economic history by examining regularities in the development of certain types of social behavior.

Tugan-Baranovskii combined historial induction with statistical and economic analysis, attempting to create a reliable pool of information from which empirical generalizations and universal social laws could be drawn. The development of the English national economy, according to him, was an important source of this information. "No matter how we look at the future of Russian capitalism, we cannot deny the real existence and rapid growth of a capitalist economy in Russia. For this reason, a study of the history of the English economy, in which the capitalistic system has reached its highest development, may be of interest to Russian economists."[38] Tugan-

Baranovskii may well have been "the father of the modern theory of crisis," as Werner Sombart called him;[39] but in Russia his primary contribution was in helping establish a new economics, the economics of capitalism, and a new sociology to deal with the "social attributes" of a capitalist economy.

The increase in scientific studies of economic history and institutions prompted the Russian Marxists to add a concern for economics to their traditional preoccupation with political work and ideological propaganda. Marxist ideas became part of the stock-in-trade of the radical intelligentsia, and the revolutionary movement could now boast a sizable nucleus of young intellectuals who were eager to arrive at a scientific explanation of the changing social and economic conditions of their country.[40]

Russian Marxist sociology came into its own in 1894–95. The basic postulates of economic materialism had been widely discussed in Russia for some time, but it was not until then that Russian Marxist social thought was presented as a complete system of general propositions. The work of integration was effected primarily by three men: Tugan-Baranovskii, G. V. Plekhanov, and P. B. Struve.[41] Tugan-Baranovskii was satisfied with a forthright presentation and endorsement of Marxist sociology. Plekhanov and Struve, however, chose a circuitous method, and attacked Populist "subjective sociology" from the vantage point of Marxist "objective sociology." By criticizing the basic propositions of Populist sociology and ideology, which had a large following, the Marxists not only sharpened and interrelated their sociological propositions but also gained a large following of their own.

Indeed, the new systematizers of Marxist theory did far more than simply presenting a unified picture of historical materialism. For example, taking a hint from Engels's *Anti-Dühring*, Plekhanov produced a detailed exposition of the roots of Marxist theory in the French materialism of the eighteenth century and the German idealism of the early nineteenth century as expressed in Hegelian philosophy. Struve bolstered his theoretical arguments by extensive excursions into contemporary neopositivist philosophy and sociology, notably the ideas of Alois Riehl and Georg Simmel. Plekhanov, Struve, and Tugan-Baranovskii all helped preserve Marxian orthodoxy; but they also endeavored to expand and modernize it. Familiarity with the epistemological and sociological ideas current in the West helped these and other Russian Marxists to add new details to the legacy of Marx and Engels; and extensive criticism by Populist leaders (which began to appear in the early 1890's) forced them to organize their thoughts into a system of sociological propositions.

As we have seen, the Populists claimed that the individual personality was both the architect and the quintessential material of human society and history. Plekhanov, Struve, and Tugan-Baranovskii responded by re-capitulating the Marxist axiom that "the mode of production and distribution" ultimately determined the architectural principles of every society; because of this, the workings of society resembled natural phenomena, and could be subjected to scientific inquiry. The Populists argued that an understanding of human personality would lead to an understanding of society, and that neither personality nor society could be fully explained by the methodological tools of the natural sciences. To rob sociology of its subjective element, according to Mikhailovskii, Lavrov, and Kareev, would remove the very essence of its competence as a scientific study of society. Marxist theory, however, asserted that sociology could totally ig-nore the individual, for studying the individual meant studying derivative rather than fundamental social phenomena; only by ignoring these deriva-tive phenomena could sociology hope to achieve the status of a natural science.

The "objectivism" of Marxian sociology produced two major ideas: it introduced the notion of society as an entity *sui generis*, both external to and independent of individuals; and it regarded society as a structured real-ity. The Marxists rejected the various "mechanistic," "atomistic" or "asso-ciationist" views of society, and regarded society as an integrated body of interacting structural and superstructural components. This objectivism, by limiting the legitimate content of sociology, helped make it more man-ageable as a science. In effect, the Marxists simply eliminated the burden-some problem of personal interaction and behavior, and equated sociology with political economy. The Populists, by contrast, would have deprived sociology of its status as a full-fledged "natural science" rather than nar-row its field of inquiry.

Social change, according to the Marxists, is objective, i.e., it results from forces outside the actions of individuals. Society is changed by variations in the "mode of production and distribution," and also by class struggle, which appears in all societies once they have passed through the initial phase of social development, a so-called primitive communism. According to Tugan-Baranovskii: "Social environment is determined primarily by economic relations. Philosophy, science, the arts, political institutions, cus-toms, and moral rules—all the most sublime manifestations of the human spirit—are rooted in economic conditions."[42]

In criticizing Populist sociology, Plekhanov argued that although individuals can influence the "fate" of a society, sometimes considerably, the nature and extent of this influence are always determined by the society's basic structure. If any single man, even an especially talented one, is to influence the course of events greatly, two conditions must exist. "First, his talent must enable him to identify himself with the social needs of a given epoch more thoroughly than others can.... Second, the existing social order must not stand in the way of a man possessing a talent that is needed."[43] In this view, the individual is not a shaper of history, but only a tool.

To the Populists, "freedom" meant a complete, critical expression of individuality in the search for better forms of social existence; to the Marxists, "freedom" meant knowing and obeying the objective laws of social development. To the Populists, freedom and necessity were incompatible; to the Marxists, they were almost identical. The Populist sociology, as a study of freedom, could not be based completely on the model of the natural sciences; the Marxist view of freedom did not in any way deny sociology the status of a natural science.

The Marxists identified class struggle as the basic instrument of social change. They identified classes by economic criteria, and interpreted capitalist society in terms of a rapidly growing class polarization. To them, the class struggle in a society at any given time was the best indicator of objective economic conditions in that society. The Populists, however, believed that history was moved by "critical individuals," who, in their search for the ideals of humanity, acted as an integrating social force. Social solidarity, not class antagonism, was the center of social life and social expectations. Moreover, it was not the proletariat that indicated the path of future social development, but the intelligentsia, whose members came from all the social classes; thus the basis of any future society, according to the Populists, would not be found in the class consciousness of the proletariat, but in the classless moral orientation of the intelligentsia.

The Marxists argued that the Russian intelligentsia was a product of contemporary economic conditions. The Populists, however, firmly believed that the ideology and sociocultural distinctiveness of the intelligentsia were solely products of critical thought and moral dedication. Russia, the Populists emphasized, provided the classic example of a country in which class struggle could not play a decisive historical role. In Russia the word "peasants" was synonomous with the word "people," for the peasants formed 80 per cent of the total population. Moreover, if the various estates existed to perform complementary social and economic functions in a total national system, then the Russian peasants were not an estate or class because they were socially and economically self-contained. Most interpreters of Populist theory agreed that the Populists' adherence to the old Slavophil view of Russia as a unique society and culture had probably prevented them from advancing a universal theory of social change. Marxists considered this one of the fundamental defects in the Populists' arguments.

The Populists contended that the unique configuration of Russia's dominant values freed her of any need to pass through a capitalist phase of social development. The Marxists, however, argued that the grand evolution of human society—i.e., "universal dialectics"—made capitalism an unavoidable stage in the development of modern Russian society. Plekhanov, for instance, was a consistent critic of capitalist economy; but he also saw in capitalism the basic instrument for elevating Russia to the higher levels of political and cultural life that he had seen in Western Europe.[44] Struve went so far as to assert that the sooner Russia absorbed the progressive spirit of capitalism the sooner it would join the family of civilized nations and place itself on the only path leading to socialism.[45] The same idea was adopted by Lenin, who debated six universal stages in the evolution of a nation's economy, from household crafts to heavy mechanized industry, and showed that Russia had already entered the stage of capitalism.[46]

Plekhanov recognized two types of concurrent changes in every society; he did not label them, but for the sake of convenience they can be identified as "structural" and "idiosyncratic."[47] Structural changes are changes in existing principles of social integration; they occur when quantitative changes in the "economic base" of a society become qualitative changes, and are uniform and predictable for all societies. In studying structural changes, sociology is a science indistinguishable from the natural sciences. Idiosyncratic changes are more limited: whereas structural changes unfold as part of a universal social evolution, idiosyncratic changes are confined to individual societies. Plekhanov noted: "Every society lives in its own particular historical environment, which may be, and often is in reality, very similar to the historical environment surrounding other peoples, but can never be, and never is, identical with it.... This introduces an extremely powerful element of diversity into the process of social development."[48] When Stalin later described the cultures of numerous Soviet nationalities as "socialist in content" and "national in form," he was applying new labels to characteristics that he identified as the structural and idiosyncratic aspects of individual societies. From the very beginning, Russian Marxists were ready to admit that the socioeconomic development of Russia was only analogous, not identical, to that of Western Europe.[49]

Because the Russian Marxists recognized that the structural and idiosyncratic characteristics of human societies were two different things, they combined their search for the universal aspects of social evolution with a study of the unique historical features of Russian society. Thus Plekhanov examined the history of Russian thought, searching for a continuous, but unique, development of a rationalist tradition; and Lenin undertook a detailed study of the emergent capitalist relations in Russia. Easily the most original Marxist examination of the historical individuality of Russian society was Tugan-Baranovskii's *The Russian Factory*, a meticulously documented study that described the evolution of Russian industry after the early eighteenth century and analyzed the economic, social, and political forces related to the emergence of Russian capitalism. The book reaffirms the Marxian rejection of the Populist model of peasant Russia as an alternative to "Western" industrial capitalism;[50] Struve called it a "scientific-sociological history of Russian industry."[51]

By the middle of the 1890's, Russian Marxism had reached its theoretical maturity, and had begun to fragment. Marxian orthodoxy was now seriously challenged by revisionists of one kind or another, as well as by persons who supported social philosophies totally alien to the Marxist theory.

Plekhanov and Lenin established themselves as the stalwarts of orthodox Marxism. Plekhanov worked more to preserve the pristine authenticity of the ideas of Marx and Engels than to link Marxist theory with the political practice of the Russian Social Democrats. Lenin, by contrast, introduced a pragmatic element by adapting the ideas of the masters to the practical needs of political action, which required a stable but flexible organization. In essence, however, both worked within the original Marxist theories. The division of the Russian Social Democrats into Bolsheviks and Mensheviks found Lenin and Plekhanov in opposite camps; however, the differences between the two camps were more in matters of organization and political tactics than in fundamental theory. After 1895, the orthodox Marxists in general concerned themselves more with practical politics and epistemology than with any general theory of social structure and social change.

In 1895, Struve stated that although Marxist social theory was essentially sound, it should not be viewed as a closed system of theoretical principles but must be constantly reexamined in the light of new facts.[52] Adhering to his own dictum, he gradually entered the camp of revisionism. In 1899, though not rejecting Marxism, he argued for several fundamental changes in Marxist social theory. The orthodox Marxist notion of social change by sudden "leaps," he said, was a relic of metaphysical thinking;

and he gave unqualified support to Kant's "law of continuity in all changes."[53] Struve argued that Marxist social theory was not an empirical science but a philosophical system permeated—though not fully sustained—by empirical data. Scientific socialism, in fact, was a mixture of scientific and utopian thought. Finally, Struve categorically rejected the Marxist blending of historical ("causal-genetic") postulates with practical politics.

Later, Struve abandoned his efforts to revise Marxism in accord with the currently popular neo-Kantian views on the sources and limitations of scientific knowledge. He joined the group of ex-Marxists who claimed that social reality was too complex to be comprehended by objective methods, and that only philosophy and subjective analysis could reveal the innermost depths of man's social existence. According to Struve, the revolutionary conflagration that had swept Russia since 1900 could be ended only if the exaggerated concern of the intelligentsia with the "external" conditions of social existence was effectively counterbalanced by a spiritual renaissance—a concentration on "internal" education guided by religion and the higher ideals of morality.[54] The "irreligious" ideology of the intelligentsia, in his opinion, was made up of empty "scientific" ideas and a rationalism without wisdom or common sense. In 1911, he viewed Marxism as a modern analog of medieval scholasticism—a theory with no real ties to social reality.[55]

Tugan-Baranovskii, unlike Struve, did not abandon all ties with the intellectual legacy of Marxism. However, he questioned the scientific validity of certain individual propositions of economic materialism. In 1900, he wrote that Marx's sociological conceptions were not only essentially correct but also a most original contribution to modern science. In Marx's economic conceptions, on the other hand, he now saw primarily a reworking of the ideas of Adam Smith and David Ricardo; he also claimed that in economics Marx was usually wrong when he was most original.[56]

Soon after 1900, Tugan-Baranovskii extended his criticism to Marxist sociology, which he discussed in several articles and books. *The Theoretical Foundations of Marxism* (1905) and *Modern Socialism in its Historical Development* (1906) were widely read in Russia, and were translated into several Western European languages. Although no match for his earlier historical studies of industrial crises in England and of the Russian factory, they showed the wide scope of his theoretical interests, combining the economic ideas of the classical English economists, the Austrian school, and Marx. In his earlier writings, he had viewed Marx's economic theory as a cogent synthesis of all previous writings on the subject; now he claimed that Marx had not originated the ideals of social-ism, but had borrowed them from utopian socialists.[57] Tugan-Baranov-skii's sociology, like that of most revisionists, sought to reconcile Marx-ism with neo-Kantianism and to relax the more rigid and scientifically un-supportable claims of Marxist theory.

A truly scientific study of society, according to Tugan-Baranovskii, had to go beyond the "genetic" and "explanatory" methods of the natural sci-ences and adopt critical and analytical methods that would approach man as a "goal" of social evolution, and not merely as a tool of history. Like many of his contemporaries, he viewed human society and its history as both a mechanical and a purposive process. The social scientist had to confront the unique historical conditions of social change and the uni-versal ethical conditions of human existence.[58] The value theory in eco-nomics, he now argued, must recognize that human desires were an important motive force in the economic process.[59] The study of social change and socialism, he claimed, must consider two components: ob-jective-scientific relations and ethical-legal norms. The first of these was "causal" and the second "teleological." At first, Tugan-Baranovskii thought that the neo-Kantian notion of moral purposiveness would give Marxism greater viability and more practical applicability; by 1911, however, he was convinced that a coalescence of Marxism and neo-Kantianism would produce a welcome "dissolution" of Marxism.[60]

Although Tugan-Baranovskii sought to construct a practical sociology that would combine Marxist objectivism and neo-Kantian subjectivism, he did not abandon his firm adherence to Lavrov's assertion that "the true sociology is socialism." To him, sociology as a science of social struc-ture and social change proved that socialism was a necessary higher stage in the development of modern society. His own theory of socialism, as evolved under neo-Kantian influence, was based on the premise that Marx-ism owed a great debt to utopian socialism and was only in part a scientific doctrine. He argued that true socialism combined the socialization of pro-duction with the freedom of the individual, and could therefore develop only in countries that combined a capitalistic mode of production with political democracy.

Tugan-Baranovskii rejected the Marxist theory of class struggle as a motive force in social change, and came close to accepting the Populist theory that the intelligentsia was above class distinctions. Marx, he thought, had not really been successful in identifying specific social classes in Western Europe, and had generally exaggerated the role of classes and class consciousness in modern societies. As human societies advance, he said, their dynamics are governed less by economic factors and more by ethical factors. In this respect, Marx had erred in not distinguishing between "class consciousness" as a centrifugal social force and "moral consciousness" as a centripetal social force.[61]

### A. A BOGDANOV'S SOCIOLOGY: A SYNTHESIS OF MARXISM AND MACHISM

One of the most active of the many Marxist doctrinaires, revisionists, and renegades was A. A. Bogdanov, whose philosophical position was the main target of Lenin's *Materialism and Empiriocriticism* (1909).[62] Bogdanov sought to modify the basic Marxist tenets in a number of ways, and he was particularly concerned with the Marxist approach to sociology.*

In 1897, having just completed a prison term for illegal activities connected with the national union of *zemliachestva* (regional student societies), Bogdanov published *A Short Course in Economic Science*, an elementary but comprehensive and rather original survey of Marxist sociology. The book reaffirmed the ideas expressed a few years earlier by Plekhanov, Struve, and Tugan-Baranovskii: that political economy is the only social science approaching the methodological rigor of the natural sciences; and that Marxist political economy is synonymous with Marxist sociology. In a review published in 1898, Lenin praised Bogdanov's "clear and correct" presentation of political economy as a science "concerned with the historical development of social relations in production and distribution."[63]

In 1899, Bogdanov published *Basic Principles of a Historical View of Nature*, in which he tried to reconcile the Newtonian static view of nature with the Darwinian dynamic view. He permanently rejected "dialectic" as a label for historical change, thus abandoning the very cornerstone of the Marxist theoretical edifice.[64] Bogdanov's "historical view" has three characteristics: first, it is universal in its application to both values and society; second, it is relative in that it recognizes that our knowledge is selective and incomplete; and third, it is causal and allows no room for any kind of teleology. Historical change, as subject to scientific analysis, is universal, relative, and causal.[65] In recognizing the relativity of historical knowledge, Bogdanov rejected the Marxian claim that the laws of historical development are absolute in their scientific

---

* "A. A. Bogdanov" was the pseudonym adopted by A. A. Malinovskii, who attached it to most of his political and philosophical writings. For a further discussion of Bogdanov's general philosophical orientation, see pp. 257–59.

validity. To orthodox Marxists, the facts of science were absolute epistemologically and relative historically; but to Bogdanov, they were relative in both cases. In *Basic Principles,* as in many subsequent studies,
Bogdanov was interested in saving Marxism not by protecting its canon-
ized orthodoxy but by bringing it into line with modern developments in
science and philosophy.

In *Knowledge from a Historical Viewpoint* (1902), Bogdanov introduced another radical deviation from Marxist theory: he accepted Wilhelm Ostwald's energeticism as the model for a new theory of knowledge,
which he presented as the best key to a scientific scrutiny of the historical
succession of social systems. He saw the main line of social progress in
the qualitative improvements in man's ability to generalize, and in social
selection as a distinct form of natural selection.[66] By identifying the
"thinking individual" as the basic social unit, he directly contradicted the
theory of Plekhanov and Struve that the individual is a product, rather
than a shaper, of history. This study marked the first step in Bogdanov's
prolonged search for a unified scientific approach to the study of both
nature and society.

Bogdanov soon conceded that his new philosophy was far removed
from dialectical materialism, and he made no effort to link the two.
He retained his Marxist faith in the forthcoming triumph of proletarian
civilization and the ultimate victory of socialism; and he fully accepted
the Marxist identification of the sociohistorical roots of ethical norms.
But all this did not prevent him from articulating an original system
of sociological thought with very little resemblance to orthodox Marxism. The more Bogdanov deviated from Marxist social theory, the more
he was attracted to the Russian Social Democratic party, which was inspired by the ideology of Marx and Engels. The best explanation of this
apparent contradiction was Bogdanov's sincere belief in the essential cor-
rectness of the Marxist legacy, which was coupled with an equally firm
conviction that this legacy needed extensive overhauling. He joined the
Bolshevik faction of the Social Democratic party, worked for a while as
an editor of *Pravda* and an elected official in the Bolshevik hierarchy,
made several trips abroad on Party assignments, and served a jail term
as a suspected revolutionary. Through all this, his search for a new philosophy and sociology continued with undiminished fervor. By 1905, any similarity between Bogdanov's ideas and those of Marx and Engels was purely
coincidental.

As early as 1902, Bogdanov tried to design a scheme of concepts and propositions treating human society as an integral part of nature, subject to self-adjusting natural processes and susceptible to precise mathematical measurement. He found inspiration and ample models in the "scientific" philosophies of Ernst Mach and Richard Avenarius. Essentially, Bogdanov was a politicized sociologist with a strong interest in the natural sciences;[67] and he was united with Mach and Avenarius not through common scientific interests but through a common theory of knowledge.

Nevertheless, Bogdanov treated Marx as the real founder of scientific sociology. He endorsed Marx's structural approach to the examination of social systems, accepting that "the mode of production in material life determines the spiritual process of life"; and like Marx, he believed that the social existence of men determined their consciousness.[68] He made it clear, however, that Marx's sociological theory suffered from serious shortcomings, most of them stemming from its failure to consider the avalanche of ideas unleashed by Darwinism and scientific philosophy. The Marxist idea of historical monism was incomplete. It did not explain the deeper meaning of social existence or the role of ideology in modern society; nor did it offer a precise explanation of what is meant by "economic structure." Worst of all, its propositions treated society as totally separated from the universal laws and processes of nature; for this reason, it could not take into account the heavy dependence of sociology on biology.

Social life, according to Bogdanov, is an extension of biological life, and the many differences between the two are overshadowed by basic similarities. Adaptation is the fundamental process of both nature and society, and selection is the primary force of adaptation. Social selection, in turn, depends chiefly on human social consciousness. Thus Bogdanov evolved the idea that human society is first of all a psychological phenomenon. "Social existence and social consciousness, in the strict meaning of these terms, are identical."[69] As the major vehicle of social adaptation, social consciousness expresses the purposiveness of human activity. Bogdanov called this purposive activity "social labor," and viewed it as the basic instrument in man's struggle for existence. He thus joined the many Russian thinkers who treated cooperation, rather than conflict, as the basic source of social progress (i.e., social adaptation).

Knowledge, to Bogdanov, is both the chief source and the most reliable index of social progress. As originally defined by Mach and Avenarius, knowledge derives solely from cognitive experience, which produces both psychical and physical "elements." Psychical elements consist of sense data and are basically "biological-physiological." They establish a link between an individual and the outside world; but they are completely subjective, since each man's experiences are unique to himself.[70] Physical elements are derived from psychical elements by a "collective synchronization," i.e., a long social distillation, of human experiences. They are biological inasmuch as they are derived from the primary sense data; they are social inasmuch as they are the basic part of the cultural legacy that makes social life possible; and they are objective inasmuch as they have a common meaning within human groups.[71] Physical elements, in essence, make up socially functional knowledge.

The notion of the derivation of physical elements from psychical elements led Bogdanov to identify his theory of knowledge as "historical monism," and he insisted that this theory differed appreciably from the epistemological "parallelism" of Mach and Avenarius and the materialistic ontology of Marxism. He conceded that the differences between psychical and physical experience had been adequately defined by Mach and Avenarius, but gave himself credit for having established precise causal ties between the two. In noting that objective, physical knowledge was produced by the socialization of subjective, psychical knowledge, Bogdanov gave credit to Marx for pointing out, though not pursuing, an important aspect of the modern sociology of knowledge; and he endorsed Marx's notion that only in social life could human experience become a reality.[72]

Knowledge based on physical elements appears, according to Bogdanov, in two basic forms: technology and ideology. These two forms apply to different areas of human activity (they are, in fact, two basic types of social processes), but both contribute to social adaptation by integrating and assessing accumulated experience and applying it to social labor.[73]

Bogdanov gave primacy to technical knowledge, that is, to technical forms of social adaptation. He argued that every ideology and every change in social forms ultimately derived from the technical process. By "technical process," Bogdanov meant the advancement of technology, or socially articulated practical knowledge. "Technology," as he defined it, was "neither the material environment nor the forces of nature, but the functioning of man in his influence on external nature."[74] The essence of sociotechnical adaptation is not expressed in the tools of production themselves, but in the fashioning and application of these tools.[75] As the primary matrix of social relations, techniques are reducible to knowledge, the very essence of human social existence. Science is the single most powerful component of the technical process; and it, too, is responsive to accumulated technical needs. "Every scientific advance originates in the sphere of man's direct relation to nature, that is, in the sphere of 'technical experience.' "[76] Ideology is "the entire sphere of social life outside the technical process." However, ideology is wholly derived from technology.[77]

Bogdanov made it clear that ideological elements, although they are secondary in origin and are determined by technical forms, are nevertheless very important for social development. Ideology plays a vital role in organizing the knowledge that forms the "material" and "conditions" of social development; the knowledge itself, however, is still basically a part of the technical process.[78] Science, the epitome of the modern age, is a bridge between technical and ideological processes, for it encompasses both practical knowledge and theoretical thought.

Ideological adaptations cannot develop by themselves, and each step of their progressive change has its starting point in the technical sphere. Technology is always progressive, for it is based on the continuous accumulation of practical experience. But ideology is not always progressive: powerful "ideological survivals," particularly in class-structured societies, often inhibit both historically necessary ideological adjustments and timely applications of new technical discoveries. Technical progress may provide the dynamic conditions for social change; but ideology determines the static conditions that regulate and modify technical innovations.

Behind Bogdanov's model of human society was an effort to integrate five distinct aspects of social systems. The first aspect is environmental, since the primary function of a society is to assure its own survival by working out a favorable adjustment to its physical environment. The second aspect comprises the biological foundations of society, which may be termed "social selection" and "social instinct." The third aspect is purely psychological: human society is essentially a psychological phenomenon based on the conscious interaction of individuals. The fourth aspect is technical: it is primarily through socially accumulated and articulated practical knowledge that the wheels of social history are put into motion and social progress is assured. The fifth aspect is ideology, which introduces order into collective technical knowledge. Bogdanov's sociology detailed all five categories of social data. In addition, he singled out adaptation, selection, and equilibration as the universal processes common to all five categories. These processes subordinate human society to the universal laws of nature, and give the study of society the precise and measurable conceptual instruments of natural science. Unfortunately, Bogdanov made no effort to apply his grand design to actual societies, and left it completely untested.

Bogdanov's search for an integrated social theory was focused on the relationship of technology to ideology, viewing each as a special system of socially functional knowledge. In working out the details of this relationship, he concentrated on two problems: the relationship of different social classes to knowledge, and the increasing sociocultural role of science.

Bogdanov readily admitted that the proletariat and the bourgeoisie were the two principal classes of modern society. However, although the relationship of the proletariat to the bourgeoisie was essentially that of one social class to another, the relationship of the proletariat to the technical intelligentsia was that of one professional group to another. Accordingly, the proletariat's role in the production process was only partly connected with its social class. Moreover, the relationship between the proletariat and the bourgeoisie was not necessarily dominated by conflict. The proletariat, according to Bogdanov, was the youngest class of present-day society; as such, it was inclined to borrow advantageous knowledge, attitudes, and values from other classes and make them part of its own ideology.

In production, the relationship of the proletariat to the technical intelligentsia is one of cooperation: the technicians organize industrial production, and the proletariat carries it out. Scientific knowledge is the basic capital of the modern technical intelligentsia, and manual skill is the basic capital of the proletariat. But the steady development of machine production demands increasing technical knowledge from the workers, who are gradually transformed from unskilled manual laborers to "intellectual" controllers of complex machinery. Their work becomes increasingly organizational and intellectual, and begins to resemble the work of the technical intelligentsia.[79] Bogdanov believed that a new society, dominated by the proletariat, would eventually arise; but he was convinced that the proletariat would triumph not by revolution but by absorbing the progressive traditions of the bourgeoisie and the technical intelligentsia. In fact, he regarded the leveling off of differences in the acquisition, modernization, and dissemination of technical and scientific knowledge as the main factor in the dynamics of social-class relations.[80]

The scientific philosophy of Mach and Avenarius, according to Bogdanov, is the basic ideology of the modern bourgeoisie and the technical intelligentsia. Moreover, it is fully compatible with the ideology of the proletariat, and is therefore the philosophy of the future. As the ideology of "the productive forces" of modern society, the philosophy of Mach and Avenarius falls completely within the scope of the natural sciences, which provide the most practical and socially useful knowledge. Like modern technology and science, this philosophy is positive and evolutionary and it can easily be applied to man's ceaseless search for gradual improvements in production techniques.[81] Philosophical materialism, according to Bogdanov, is too impractical to be of any use in the ideology of the modern technical intelligentsia. In the first place, it is too much involved in argument over the ontological primacy of "matter" or "spirit," which is far removed from the intellectual and technical needs of modern society. Mach and Avenarius, on the other hand, shift the emphasis from ontology to epistemology, and make experience, with all its practical derivations, the central topic of their philosophical work; rather than pursuing an impractical search for the origins of natural and social phenomena, they seek out the functions of these phenomena.

The "new philosophy" that Bogdanov develops from the ideas of Mach and Avenarius corresponds to the practical ideology of the technical intelligentsia. It demands that both philosophers and scientists abandon their traditional concern with the "explanation" of mechanically and causally intertwined phenomena and emphasize the "description" of pure forms of experience, which are reducible to mathematical expressions. The modern scientist, like the technical intellectual, values knowledge that is not only practical but economical—that is, knowledge that avoids circuitous and imprecise philosophical and logical procedures. The older causal-mechanical orientation in science, according to Bogdanov, corresponded to the seventeenth-century organization of social labor, which was essentially mechanical and custom-bound. The ideology of the new technical intelligentsia, elaborated by the new philosophy, responds to the historical reality of rapid technological advances; it minimizes the role of "sacred values" in industrial work and encourages a search for practical inventions. The new philosophy and the ideology of the technical intelligentsia are similar in another respect: both reject the notion that scientific laws have an independent existence. Instead, they regard scientific laws as transitional products of the human mind—special methods for meeting the challenge of practical social needs.[82]

Bogdanov's concern with the sociology of knowledge led him to formulate a new "science" that he called tektology. He envisioned this as a "universal organization theory" that would study those processes shared by all human and natural phenomena. Such processes, according to Bogdanov, take place in, and regulate, the organization of all systems of natural and social phenomena; therefore, the more universal aspects of both society and nature can be revealed by studying the laws of organization. Bogdanov noted that particular aspects of the universal theory of organization were studied by individual sciences: mathematics, for example, was concerned with "all kinds of complexes in a state of equilibrium." Bogdanov now proposed to develop a comprehensive science that could synthesize the knowledge accumulated by specialized disciplines. Tektology, he said, would "combine the abstract symbolism of mathematics with the experimental character of the natural sciences."[83] It was universal because it embraced the entire world of experience; yet it was primarily a sociohistorical science, since human society was the central problem of its inquiry.

Tektology grew out of Empiriomonism, Bogdanov's earlier philosophy: it is empirical inasmuch as it considers experience the only source of scientific knowledge; and it is monistic inasmuch as it assumes the operation of the same structural principles at every level of reality. (Dialectical materialism, said Bogdanov, is a "nonmonistic" theory, for it claims that nature and society are qualitatively different realities governed by different sets of laws.[84]) Tektology, like Empiriomonism, assumes that the world is a product of man's experience; and that the principles underlying the organization of human experience are models for the principles underlying the organization of the universe. "Human thought," according to Bogdanov, "is tektologically the same as the rest of nature."[85]

The tektological world view constructed by Bogdanov took him one more step away from Marxism. Marx and Engels, following Hegel, had envisaged a universe dominated by contending forces and sudden changes. Bogdanov tried to conceptualize a world in which contending forces are overshadowed by a general harmony, or complementarity, of universal processes, and in which all change is gradual. For example, he viewed "disorganization" as simply a special form of organization. Both of them follow the same patterns; the only difference is that organization is larger than the sum total of its individual components, whereas "disorganization" is smaller.[86]

Organization, as a universal attribute of nature, operates through two mechanisms: the regulative and the formative. The regulative mechanism, the most universal of all processes, selects the elements through which a system such as a society, a special class, an organism, or a planet maintains a working balance with the world outside it. The formative mechanism consists of the universal processes by which man's cognition integrates the elements of individual complexes into larger series. One such process is "ingression," which is based on the principle that close scrutiny can discover a link between any two complexes in nature or society. Ingression, according to Bogdanov, is the basic law of continuity in the universe.

Borrowing a thought from Marx, Bogdanov proclaimed that the intent of tektology was not merely to describe the overall structure of the world, but to reshape this structure entirely. His design for this tektological transformation of the world had a simple and unambiguous aim: the construction of models for a fuller understanding of human society. These models would express "the forms of our thought about organization combinations." They would be important not because they described specific areas of reality, but because they could help to reveal the basic structural principles of universal organization.[87]

Bogdanov may be counted among the pioneers of modern organization theory. He emphasized, correctly, that a discipline concerned with organization must be a special kind of science: it could not develop as an offshoot of any single existing science, but must draw its substance from several established branches of mathematics and the natural and social sciences. Bogdanov's real contribution lay in pointing out the necessity and the feasibility of such a science, rather than in developing a system of useful scientific propositions. His tektological formulation was vague when it tried to explain basic concepts, and its development from that point was unbalanced and logically imprecise. However, Bogdanov's ideas were bold, and his search for sociologically fruitful research models was a well-planned step in the right direction. He was one of the first to explore the epistemological domain where the social and natural sciences meet and where mathematical symbolism may be applied to the scientific study of social behavior.[88]

## ACADEMIC SOCIOLOGY

Most of the systematic sociological thought in Russia developed outside the academic community. To the intelligentsia, sociology was an ideological weapon whose main purpose was to chart the future development of Russian society—in other words, to offer a "scientific" solution to the grave problems of the existing social system. As spokesmen for the intelligentsia, most sociologists were critical of the existing political institutions and identified social and cultural progress with a gradual realization of democratic ideals. Regardless of their personal philosophies and inclinations, they believed that the study of society could become an exact science.

The development of academic sociology was exceedingly slow in Russia. Sociological theory, in the eyes of the government, was far too bound up with the bitter ideological controversies of the time; for this reason, it was excluded from the curriculum of the institutions of higher education. But despite all obstacles, modern sociological thought did find several outstanding representatives in Russian universities, chiefly among historians and law professors.

Most historians stuck closely to the traditional mode of history writing, sifting documentary sources for facts and meeting the standards of contemporary literary taste. An increasing number of historians sought to integrate data pertaining to specific themes or periods. Only a small number, however, were interested in the theory of history—i.e., in the scientific foundations of historical inquiry. Most of these treated sociology as the primary link between history and science, or as history transformed into a science.

N. A. Rozhkov, a professor of Russian history at Moscow University at the turn of the century, was one of the most notable "sociological" historians. He was a disciple of the eminent historian V. O. Kliuchevskii, who had guided him toward a study of Russian economic history and a search for broader interpretations of historical data. Rozhkov claimed that sociology, as an abstract study of the universal laws of social development, must obtain its data from history; and if history is to be a real aid to sociology in this process, historical data must be systematized in accordance with the laws of social causation and evolution. What zoology and botany are to general biology, history is to sociology.[89] Whether sociology operates on an "abstract" or a "concrete" level, according to Rozhkov, it must consider the regularities of social structure and social development; in view of these two concerns, sociology may be divided into social statics and social dynamics.

According to Rozhkov, historians must study "the equilibrium of all social processes" (which explains the structure of a society at one given time), as well as the interaction of the particular processes that produce structural changes. The sociological historian must recognize several "independent" processes that mold the structure of a society; but he must also recognize that all of these processes are not of equal importance for the study of social structure and social change. Rozhkov criticized the prevalent opinion in Russian political and legal scholarship which viewed the political process—that is, the growth of the state and the legal system—as the predominant process of Russian history. He was greatly influenced by the dominant trends in contemporary historiography, the upsurge of economic materialism as a social philosophy, and the emphasis on economic causes instilled in him by his mentor Kliuchevskii, and was therefore inclined to emphasize the social role of the economic process. In "The Origin of Estates in Russia" (1899), for example, he criticized the generally held notion that government policies had been the primary influence on the formation of the Russian estates, and presented evidence supporting his own theory that these segments of Russian society had been determined by economic processes.[90] Like Plekhanov, Rozhkov felt that although the basic laws of social development were universal, Russian social processes did have certain unique characteristics of their own.

As a university professor, Rozhkov did not wish to be considered a doctrinaire economic materialist. He claimed that certain psychological phenomena of social significance could not be explained in economic terms, and even wrote a series of articles on psychological themes connected with history and sociology.[91] Moreover, he stated that economic materialism was not supported by an integrated theory and was therefore open to conflicting interpretations, a situation best illustrated by the continual disagreements among Russian Marxists. He pointed out that economic materialism had never been tested in "practice," since it had never been fully and consistently applied to the study of economic history.[92] Nevertheless, Rozhkov believed that history had to adopt both economic and psychological approaches in order to be considered a true science. Thus he appreciated the metaphysically tinged writings of Hippolyte Taine and Georg Simmel as much as the materialism of the leading Marxists. Indeed, he was the only scholar whose articles were published in both the government's *Journal of the Ministry of National Education* and the Bolshevik *Pravda*.

Although Rozhkov's studies were clearly non-Marxian (for example, he had little use for the dialectical theory of natural and social change), he did pass through a brief phase of political identification with the Social Democratic party, and even served temporarily as a Bolshevik official; this activity earned him a prison term in Siberia. Subsequently, he flirted with neo-Kantian philosophy (particularly that of Heinrich Rickert), which earned him a scolding from Lenin. During the Soviet period he published *Russian History from a Comparative-Historical Perspective*, proclaiming himself an adherent of historical materialism but actually accepting neither the dialectical view of social change nor the rigid Marxist interpretation of social structure. Writing in 1922, the Soviet historian M. V. Nechkina stated categorically that Rozhkov, despite his "wanderings," was an economic materialist.[93] But the Soviet historians later changed their opinion of Rozhkov: in 1941, N. L. Rubinshtein wrote that Rozhkov was never a Marxist, and that he had never abandoned his "bourgeois views" and positivist philosophy.[94] Actually, Rozhkov was neither a Marxist nor a positivist. He made an earnest and original effort to raise the standards of historical scholarship by wedding history to sociology and sociology to the dominant currents in modern social philosophy and psychology.

P. N. Miliukov, then a professor at Moscow University, shared Rozhkov's views that the modern historian, in order to avoid the sterility of antiquarianism, must strive to increase the scientific rigor of historical inquiry.[95] The two agreed that sociology provided a means for elevating historical investigation to the level of the natural sciences. The basic difference between the two was that Miliukov, though satisfied with a considerably less elaborate system of sociological principles, was a superior historian and will be remembered more for his historical scholarship than for his efforts to combine history and sociology. However, his *Essays in the History of Russian Culture* were heralded by contemporaries as a happy combination of impeccable historical research, rigorous sociological analysis, and "clarity of thought."[96]

As a "sociologist," Miliukov was interested primarily in clarifying the fundamental principles of a general theory concerned with the inner structure of society, particularly with the interrelation of the "economic" and "cultural" systems. In this process, he rejected the two leading social theories in Russia at the end of the nineteenth century: the "subjective" sociology of the Populists, and the "objective" theory of the Marxists.

Populist sociology, said Miliukov, diverted scholars away from the objective criteria and logical precision of scientific inquiry and into the obscure areas of metaphysics. It did not separate the scientific-causal study of history from the philosophical-teleological use of history for guidance in practical action. Despite their emphasis on the primary role of personality in history, Populist sociologists showed little interest in social psychology, and made no effort to produce a coherent design for historical research. Finally, "subjective" sociology injected too much purposiveness into the historical process, and viewed all of history as an affirmation of the independence of the human will. Miliukov was unquestionably right when he asserted that not a single Russian scholar had based his "empirical" research upon Populist sociology as a theoretical guide, a source of research designs, or an interpretive mechanism.

Miliukov was somewhat less severe with Marxist sociology, and readily admitted that his own sociological orientation was much closer to economic materialism than to the "anthropocentric view" of the Populists.[97] In the first volume of his *Essays* he gave a prominent place to the "economic factor," and interpreted many aspects of the political system in terms of economic causation. However, he refused to carry economic determinism into spiritual culture, as the Marxists did, and omitted it from his sociological explanations of knowledge, religion, and ideology, which were collected in the second volume of the *Essays*.

Instead of reducing history to a unitary process, Miliukov concentrated on "parallel developments" in various branches of culture. He was convinced that in order to be scientifically fruitful such a study must be preceded by an extensive inquiry into the internal evolution of each individual branch of social and cultural life. This form of investigation was especially important because social evolution was producing a greater individualization of social life and looser ties between various components of culture. Miliukov himself concentrated primarily on individual branches of culture; but he made frequent references to parallel developments in the "economy" and in "culture," and tried to outline the interaction between the various components of the sociocultural system. In all of this, however, he firmly adhered to the principle that culture was not mechanically derived from any fixed social structure, and rejected every sociology that used historical material merely to illustrate preconceived propositions. In his own studies, Miliukov used a modest sociological scheme not to simplify the course of Russian cultural history but to detect its broader meanings without losing sight of the unique features of particular historical details.

In Miliukov's opinion, any serious historian had to reject every sociology that would divert him from a thorough, objective examination of documentary material. For the same reason, he was convinced that there was no meeting ground between historiography and any philosophy of history: the two could not be reconciled because the first depended on such criteria as objective examination and empirical verification and the second on subjective judgments and metaphysical concepts. Miliukov thought that Marxism, by wedding economic materialism to philosophical materialism, had committed the unpardonable error of identifying itself with a philosophy of history that sacrificed science to a monistic and metaphysical world view. Philosophical materialism, he contended, had given Marxist materialism a sociological view too deterministic and too narrow to be of much scientific value in the study of historical processes.[98]

Miliukov was equally critical of the Populist philosophy of history, which found its chief academic champion in N. I. Kareev, a professor of Western European history first at Warsaw and then at St. Petersburg. All existing sciences, according to Kareev, were either phenomenological or nomological: the former concentrated on the mere description of empirical data, and the latter sought to develop abstract laws of nature and society. But the time had come, he argued, to also develop "normative" sciences, which would be concerned with the "ideal world" of human values and with the "idea of progress" as expressed in the activities of individuals. In his opinion, a philosophy of history had to combine a nomological study of "cultural evolution" with a normative study of individual activities.[99] Miliukov regarded this effort to fuse subjective philosophy and objective science as a disruptive encroachment of ideology on science, and he criticized Kareev's arbitrary and superficial use of "scientific" concepts for nonscientific purposes. Kareev, he said, had totally ignored the basic incompatibility of the "practical" tenets of ideology and the "theoretical" abstractions of science.

In his search for a scientific-sociological basis for historiography, Miliukov also attacked the theorists who accepted the old Slavophil idea that Russia had a unique national character and pattern of development. He felt that these men had erred in several respects: in reserving to the Russian nation certain characteristics that were actually shared by all mankind; in overgeneralizing the sociocultural characteristics of individual periods in Russian history; and in habitually relying on sheer imagination and ideological bias rather than on historical data.[100] Miliukov did not underestimate the unique features of Russian history; but he argued that even these acquired a more profound meaning when viewed in light of the universal laws of social development. For example, only a general scientific theory of the emergence and the evolution of states could help a historian grasp the full meaning of the unique relationship between the state and society in Russian history. In the West, according to Miliukov, the state was a product of social evolution; in Russia, modern society had evolved under the state's supervision.

Miliukov did not particularly enrich sociological theory, but he was eminently successful in widening the base of historical inquiry by casting it within a broad sociological framework. He rigorously excluded ideological considerations from his scholarly work; and in that work he displayed an impressive mastery of historical research techniques. His early studies, particularly *The State Economy of Russia During the First Quarter of the Eighteenth Century* and *Essays in Russian Cultural History*, are among the best examples of Russian historical scholarship in the nineteenth century.

Miliukov and Rozhkov were the most important historians concerned with academic sociology. The second important academic effort to advance a scientific study of society came from scholars interested in the deeper meanings and development of legal norms. Most of these men were in active touch with the Moscow Juridical Society, which had been founded in 1863 and inspired by the reforming spirit of the 1860's. In effect, this organization inaugurated Russian efforts to systematically study the social causation and cultural evolution of law. The dominant figure of the Society was S. A. Muromtsev, a *zemstvo* organizer and a professor of law at Moscow University. In 1879 he became editor of the Society's *Juridical Messenger,* and promptly transformed it into a publication dedicated primarily to the philosophy and sociology of law.

Muromtsev's sociological ideas were presented in general pronouncements and explanations with theoretical implications rather than in a conceptually and methodologically integrated system of social thought. Without denying the usefulness of the traditional descriptive study of law as a system of norms enforced by state coercion, he advocated a search for universal regularities in the social history of legal norms, contending that law evolves not only through an impersonal development of regulative principles but also through an orderly communal search for more perfect ideas of justice.[101] Therefore, he argued, legal scholarship must not be limited to a search for regularities in the development of law, but must pay equal attention to the social origin of individual legal norms.

According to Muromtsev, law originates from the concerted effort of the entire society, "particularly legal experts," to find judicious solutions to conflicts between various social groups. Societies torn by social inequality and disharmony are faced with especially difficult conditions in promulgating and enforcing laws to sustain cooperation as the basic principle of social existence. Implicit in Muromtsev's studies was the belief that Russian society, in order to acquire just and workable laws, must first of all elucidate the nature, scope, and depth of all manifestations of social injustice and sources of social conflict. To achieve this goal, he argued in 1888 in his presidential address to the Juridical Society, it was necessary to begin with a broad program of political education for the Russian citizenry.[102] He also reminded his listeners that they as scholars must combine a comparative-historical study of legal norms with a careful investigation of the "folk creativeness" expressed in customary law. Law, in Muromtsev's opinion, is uniform in the grand outlines of its evolution; but it is national in its origin and social foundations.[103]

Although Muromtsev wrote in an inoffensive, scholarly tone, he was quickly identified as a critic of the Russian legal system and an advocate of social and political reforms. His attempts to make the impartial study of legal sociology an essential part of the information available to the country's lawmakers found no support in official circles. In 1884, he was dismissed from his position by a direct order of the Minister of National Education.[104] In 1892, the Moscow Juridical Society decided to terminate the publication of the *Juridical Messenger,* the stronghold of Muromtsev's influence on legal scholars. The decision was made in response to the government's order that the journal's contents be screened by the censorship authorities before each issue was published. In 1899, the government ordered that the Society terminate all its activities. This decision was a vindictive response to some remarks made when the Society gathered that year to commemorate the centennial of the birth of Aleksandr Pushkin: one of the speakers at the meeting stated that the great poet's most noble legacy was his lifelong ideal of freeing the individual spirit from the guardianship of the state. After this, the vigilance of the government prevented the emergence of another Muromtsev on the academic scene, and the questions he had raised could not be followed up.[105]

Muromtsev expressed two ideas that dominated most of Russian social thought. First, he treated cooperation of all kinds as the essence of social life and the basic problem that sociology had to elucidate in order to establish itself as a full-fledged science. Cooperation, according to him, explains not only social integration but also the basic processes in the development of personality.[106] Second, he viewed social evolution not as the mechanical unfolding of a grand, predetermined design, but as a process in which subjective purposiveness was combined with objective causation.[107] To him, the idea of purposiveness in social change was not a metaphysical concept but an empirical indicator of socially oriented deliberation aimed at improving the conditions of human existence; sociology, in other words, was both a system of knowledge and a design for action.

The fate of the *Juridical Messenger* prompted university scholars to avoid studying law as an instrument of social change or an embodiment of the libertarian idea of progress. A new type of legal academician emerged, characterized by deliberate detachment from the burning questions of existing social reality. These new theoreticians argued that the sociology of law provided only a very limited approach to the deeper cultural meanings of legal norms. P. I. Novgorodtsev, from Moscow University, was one of the leaders of this group.

Novgorodtsev attacked the sociology of law as totally inadequate. Law, as an embodiment of moral norms, was "self-governed," and could not be explained in terms of any kind of historicism or any scientific theory. He proposed not a scientific study based on "historicism" and rationalism, but a philosophical study grounded in morality and "will."[108] He replaced the sociological approach to law by a normative approach. Indeed, he substituted ethics for sociology; and, under the obvious influence of Wilhelm Windelband and Heinrich Rickert, he identified ethics as the science of "the norms of the will." Not sociology but "philosophical idealism," according to Novgorodtsev, would lead to a full understanding of law as an expression of humanity. He envisaged the individual, rather than society, as the basic instrument in the development of law. However, he viewed the individual not as a social unit but as a "cosmic" unit—a carrier of the absolute principle of morality. The individual was a product of moral ideals, and moral ideals were not sociohistorical phenomena but ramifications of an absolute principle independent of external influences. It was Kant who had imagined a sharp division between "existence," which was dealt with by science, and "duty," which was treated by moral philosophy. One of the most pressing tasks of the present generation, Novgorodtsev argued, was to establish a bridge between social existence and moral duty, and this could only be done by metaphysics.[109]

Novgorodtsev's critique was not merely a retreat into obscurantism in the face of mounting government pressure against any critical study of society; it also reflected the growing reaction of both scientists and philosophers to the use of mechanistic concepts in the study of society. Sociological "historicism," which Novgorodtsev criticized, came under fire from many scientific quarters as an extension of Newtonian mechanics to the study of social processes. At the time, the same mechanistic concepts were also under attack in physics, chemistry, and biology. Novgorodtsev's criticism, like that of many scientists, was probably valid, especially in view of the complex epistemological problems presented by the social sciences. However, by substituting metaphysical expediency for epistemological elaboration, he renounced any serious attempt to combine the philosophical and scientific study of law and morality. He claimed that the positivist and Marxist sociologies were doomed because they "undertook more than they could handle," were limited by their strict adherence to "moral relativism," and did not take advantage of the limitless potentialities of "philosophical idealism." Novgorodtsev accepted science only insofar as it recognized the comparatively narrow empirical scope of its inquiry and the relative value of its findings.[110]

Novgorodtsev was the editor of the well-known symposium *Problems of Idealism*, to which he contributed an essay on law and morality. His "philosophical idealism," as expressed in this volume, was viewed by his more critical contemporaries as a calculated flight into mysticism that had no connection with real existence and the widening crisis in the shaky structure of the autocratic polity.[111]

L. I. Petrazhitskii, a professor of law at St. Petersburg University, claimed that neither philosophy nor sociology offered a satisfactory way to uncover the fundamental principles of law. Instead, he developed an elaborate psychological theory of law, which attracted a great deal of attention in academic circles during the first two decades of the twentieth century. The sources of law, Petrazhitskii argued, are neither in reason nor in will, but in special emotions or emotionally charged instinctive states activated by stimuli from the motor nerves. The basic premise of this theory is that both law and morality result from "cultural adaptations of man's emotional endowments."[112] In the early history of human society, these adaptations were primarily "instinctive"; in later history, they were the result of deliberate actions by individuals or groups.

In "intuitive law"—which allows for individual discretion in applying legal norms to specific situations, and which depends not on deliberate legislative enactments but on the accumulated wisdom of court decisions and legal precedents—Petrazhitskii saw a meeting ground between the neuropsychological basis of "legal emotions" and the external cultural conditions that account for the social adaptability of law. And just as intuitive law is the most resourceful cultural base for legal norms, so "introspection" is the most productive method for gaining a scientific understanding of the evolution and structure of law.

Petrazhitskii's concept of intuitive law closely resembled Mikhailovskii's subjective sociology, which regarded the individual as the ultimate creator of all social norms and relations. Intuitive law, in the words of a contemporary interpreter, "has an individual and adaptive character, and is determined by the special conditions in the life of every person—his character, education, social status, profession, and acquaintances."[113] Individual experiences of common conditions produce the intuitive law of all social groups, from individual families to entire social classes; and this law reconciles the propensities of individuals with the needs of the various groups. By contrast, Petrazhitskii saw a minimum expression of individuality and legal flexibility in "customary law," which was the basic legal concept of rural Russia. Intuitive law was a reliable mechanism for cultural progress; customary law was the very antithesis of progress.

Like many other scholars in the age of crisis, Petrazhitskii sought refuge in a disciplined and logically elaborate search for the formal principles of the "human condition," and tried to discount the mounting turmoil around him. His theory stood above both society and history. It insulated itself by adopting an ontology that reduced human social experience and behavior to "legal emotions"—pure psychological states that were controlled by inner mechanisms. Petrazhitskii produced exciting ideas about the subjective aspects of legal consciousness, but he largely ignored the work of law as an objective reality molded by social and historical conditions.

Petrazhitskii may have avoided a critical analysis of contemporary Russian law, but he was in no way an apologist for the existing legal system. Behind his psychological orientation was a search for the universal principles of humanity that were expressed in legal norms. Although he limited his study primarily to the emotional foundations of law, almost adopting an evolutionary-biological orientation, he pointed out many aspects of legal behavior that invite sociological analysis.[114] His dedication to the formal aspects of law was really an attempt to discover abstract principles of legality that had logical, if not sociological and philosophical, autonomy. To the government policies that discouraged a sociological study of law, Petrazhitskii responded not by abandoning the search for a science of legal behavior but by shifting it to a more neutral ground. The ultimate task of the scientific study of law, according to him, was to replace the "unconscious and empirical adaptation" of man to changing social conditions with conscious efforts toward achieving the "grand ideals" of humanity.[115]

Although his substantive interests were primarily in the sociology of law and political institutions, B. A. Kistiakovskii acquired an enviable reputation by his contributions to the study of the epistemological foundations of sociology and the social sciences in general. In 1899, he published his dissertation *Society and the Individual* in Germany, where he had studied under Wilhelm Windelband and Heinrich Rickert.[116] The study attracted the attention of many leading social scientists, including Hans Kelsen and Max Weber, and it marked the beginning of Kistiakovskii's long concern with the epistemological foundations of the social sciences.[117] Kistiakovskii's orientation was essentially neo-Kantian—"idealistic" but "antimetaphysical"—and he concentrated on describing the state as a sociological category and law as the basic system of values. He differentiated between two aspects of his sociology: an empirical-causal theory concerned with social reality as a product of history and social dynamics, and a normative-teleological theory concerned with values that were independent of history and were guided by internal goals rather than by external causes.

As empirical studies (and only as empirical studies) the social sciences, according to Kistiakovskii, are methodologically and epistemologically similar to the natural sciences, for both are interested in causal relationships. Kistiakovskii rejected the usual claim that the sciences cannot attain the exactitude of the natural sciences because they cannot formulate universally applicable laws. Even in the natural sciences, he argued, universal laws are not objective reflections of external reality but internal "norms of the human mind." Not the universal "natural laws" but the much more limited laws of individual disciplines express the generalizing power of the natural sciences.[118] In order to become truly scientific, sociology must search not for universal laws but for limited and complementary general principles; and it must switch its interest from what is socially "desirable" to what is socially "inevitable." In Kistiakovskii's opinion, the Russian sociological tradition, particularly subjective sociology, dealt much more with the social desires and ideals of sociologists than with the inevitable results of cause-effect sequences.[119] However, he did feel that sociology had to go beyond causal study to some extent in order to examine social purposiveness.

It is clear, then, that to Kistiakovskii the natural and social sciences are neither completely identical nor completely different. Although the two have much in common, their differences are more profound than their similarities. The social sciences—particularly sociology—are essentially normative sciences. Whereas the natural sciences study regularities established by inflexible external determinants, the social sciences study the outward manifestations of internal human freedom as expressed in the moral code, the backbone of every social and legal system. Like most of his contemporaries, Kistiakovskii gave a negative definition of free will: the human will is free, according to him, only because it is independent of external influences. This approach to the normative sciences is more metaphysical than scientific; nonetheless, Kistiakovskii considered himself a champion of science, and he was certainly one of the most articulate Russian students of the idealistic foundations of the modern theory of scientific knowledge.

In Kistiakovskii's time, it was customary to consider the various orientations in social theory as mutually exclusive. His "two-faceted" theory of coexisting empirical and normative approaches was the first step toward investigating the complementary nature of different theories and methodologies in the study of law. Subsequently, Kistiakovskii expanded this theory to include four complementary approaches, which accounted for all the major orientations in Russian legal studies.[120]

Three of the approaches in Kistiakovskii's formulation were empirical. The formal-juridical orientation, which in Russia was the strongest, offered a logically precise presentation of the formal structure of legal institutions. The sociological orientation facilitated a systematic study of the interaction of law and society. The Russians, said Kistiakovskii, had been the first to stress the importance of studying law as a social phenomenon; he credited S. A. Muromtsev with laying the foundations of this study, and lamented the "external conditions" that hampered its continued development.[121] The psychological orientation (most successfully represented by Petrazhitskii) sought to develop a natural-scientific basis for determining the origins of law in human nature.

The normative orientation removed the scientific study of law and morality from the domain of empirical science and made it a unique science concerned with the values, moral goals, and intangible motivations of human existence. In his discussion of the normative sciences, Kistiakovskii allowed philosophy to reenter science, not only as a tool for assessing the formal (i.e., logical and methodological) aspects of scientific inquiry but also as a source of substantive assumptions and categorizations. His greatest efforts were in protecting the scientific study of law and morality from vicious attacks by mystical metaphysicists and in making epistemological debate an integral part of sociological theory.

In empirical sociology, Kistiakovskii was a true disciple of Georg Simmel: sociology, he argued, must not resort to any deterministic interpretations of social life, but must concentrate on the interrelations between various conditions of social existence and various forms of social behavior. Like Simmel, he saw the future of sociology not in a separation from philosophy but in an increasing cooperation of the two. According to Kistiakovskii, the function of philosophy was not only to clarify the epistemological nature of sociological knowledge but also to elucidate the ontological independence of the basic norms of morality, reducible to Kant's "categorical imperative." As the most consistent and erudite Russian neo-Kantian, he sought to combine the epistemological wisdom of Kant's *Critique of Pure Reason* with the metaphysical orientation of Kant's *Critique of Practical Reason*.

M. M. KOVALEVSKII: COMPARATIVE HISTORY AND GENERAL SOCIOLOGY

The historical and juridical currents of Russian academic sociology converged in the work of M. M. Kovalevskii, who is generally considered the most productive and erudite sociologist of modern Russia. According to the French sociologist René Worms, Kovalevskii was viewed in the West as Russia's most outstanding social scientist, and in his native country as an accomplished representative of "the best in Western thought."[122] Western scholars appreciated the actual data collected in Kovalevskii's studies, which were of great value to evolutionary ethnographers and comparative historians. Russian scholars were most impressed with his theoretical analyses of Russian society and culture; they also admired his ability to range over the entire spectrum of sociology, from personal fieldwork to the search for a grand theory of society.

After graduating from Khar'kov University's law school in 1873, Kovalevskii was invited by his professors to undertake graduate studies as a "professorial aspirant." He immediately went to Western Europe, spending most of his time in England; there he became personally acquainted with Karl Marx and Sir Henry Maine (one of the founders of the comparative-historical school in sociology). Kovalevskii's career advanced rapidly: in 1876, he published a monograph on the dissolution of communal agriculture in a Swiss canton; in 1877, he earned a magister's degree in law from Moscow University on the basis of a dissertation dealing with the history of police courts in premodern England; and in 1880, a study of the structure of English society at the end of the Middle Ages brought him a doctorate from Moscow University. In 1877 he was appointed a docent of constitutional law at Moscow University, and in 1880 he became a professor.

In the 1880's Kovalevskii spent several summers among the Ossets and other native groups in the Caucasus in order to gather ethnographic data on so-called "legal customs"—the unwritten or customary law sustained, mostly indirectly, by the coercive power of the state. At the same time, he became interested in the *obshchina*, the Russian rural community form praised by the Slavophils as the purest embodiment of the unique values of Russian culture. Kovalevskii declared that the time had come to abandon all sentimentality in the study of the *obshchina*, and to introduce a "positive" approach.[123] His criticism of the "theological" and "metaphysical" interpretations of the *obshchina* and his espousal of a positivist interpretation made it abundantly clear that he was under the spell of Comtean philosophy. He was interested not only in an objective critical study of rural communities and institutions, but also in refining and consolidating the scientific foundations of sociology. As a professor of constitutional and comparative law, Kovalevskii was much more interested in the social dynamics of law than in extracting general juridical patterns from the mass of legal norms. During the 1880's, the darkest period of governmental reaction, his sociological orientation brought him into direct conflict with the authorities; and in 1887 he was compelled to resign from his teaching position.

In the same year, at the invitation of Stockholm University, Kovalevskii delivered a series of lectures on the most recent achievements in comparative-historical studies of the origin of the family, the evolution of property concepts, and the patriarchal village community.[124] He accepted Lewis H. Morgan's notion of a unilinear evolution in which the patriarchal society

was preceded by a matriarchate and in which kinship bonds of social integration antedated territorial bonds. These lectures were extremely valuable
in making Russian ethnographic materials available to evolutionary ethnographers all over the world. During the following years, Kovalevskii lectured
at Oxford University, the Free College of Social Sciences in Paris, the Free
University of Brussels, and the University of Chicago, concentrating on the
description of traditional Russian institutions in the light of modern comparative history. He also studied the major trends of Western economic
development.

Kovalevskii spent most of his time in France, where he wrote two monumental studies: *The Origin of Modern Democracy* (4 vols., 1895–97), and
*The Economic Growth of Europe Prior to the Emergence of a Capitalist
Economy* (3 vols., 1898–1903).[125] The second work was most typical of his
scholarship during this period, and contained substantive information collected from a whole array of comparative historians, including Kovalevskii
himself. The theoretical position of the author was spelled out in an introductory chapter in order to help the reader recognize the more general social
and economic trends behind the maze of information presented. The classification of socioeconomic systems was placed into a logically integrated pattern, determined primarily by population density. However, Kovalevskii at
this time was more a social historian than a sociologist, and he did not allow
theoretical considerations to limit his selection or interpretation of substantive data. During this period he also wrote a detailed monograph on Russian economic institutions and a score of studies dealing with the ethnography of various national groups in the Caucasus.[126] His articles appeared
in French, English, and Russian journals.

Kovalevskii maintained personal contact with such leading French sociologists as Gabriel Tarde, Durkheim, and Worms. He was one of the
founders of the International Institute of Sociology, and in 1907 served as
its president. From all of this activity Kovalevskii developed a strong interest in social theory. By the turn of the century, he was strongly interested in
building a bridge between comparative history as an empirical, inductive
science and sociology as an abstract, deductive science.

In 1901 Kovalevskii played a leading role in founding the Russian School
of Advanced Social Studies in Paris, an institution that operated for five
years and reached hundreds of young Russians who came to Western Europe as either students or political refugees. Since the school's permanent
faculty included only a few persons, it relied heavily on visiting Russian
scholars and political leaders. Ilya Mechnikov, a leading member of the

Pasteur Institute in Paris, headed the list of guest lecturers, which also included Lenin, Struve, Tugan-Baranovskii, Timiriazev, Miliukov, and Chernov.[127] During the 1901–2 academic year the school had 13 lecturers and 320 regular students.[128] Heckled by rebellious students, annoyed by unnecessarily rigid surveillance by the Paris police, intimidated by the Russian secret service, and constantly threatened with financial disaster, Kovalevskii and his friends could not make the new school a stable institution with clear goals and balanced instruction. However, it was the only educational institution to offer a comprehensive survey of Russian social, economic, and political institutions from the standpoint of Western democratic ideologies.

The Paris school was the first "Russian" institution of higher education to offer courses in sociology. This job was entrusted to E. V. de Roberty, a Russian sociologist who had spent many years in France and had developed a rather rigid system of "neopositivist" sociology. He combined Comte's belief in the secularization of knowledge as the most trustworthy index of social progress with a firm conviction that sociology could never be reduced to the study of individual behavior. During the 1901–2 academic year, de Roberty delivered sixteen lectures on general sociology, concentrating on the comparative analysis of modern sociological thought. In 1903, the French authorities informed de Roberty that he would be allowed to reside in France only if he discontinued all relations with the Russian School. They took this action in response to a request from the Russian Minister of Internal Affairs, who had been informed by Russian agents in Paris that the school was "a seminar in revolution."[129] Resigning from the School, de Roberty left France, and was appointed a professor at the Free University in Brussels.

The 1905 revolution precipitated Kovalevskii's return to Russia. In the same year, the Khar'kov voters elected him to the First State Duma. In 1907 his candidacy was rejected by the same electorate, but he was given a post in the State Council as a representative of the academic community. The Academy of Sciences elected him to full membership, and St. Petersburg University and the Psychoneurological Institute appointed him to their respective faculties. At the Institute, he taught the first course in sociology offered at an institution of higher education in Russia. He worked on the staffs of several journals, and for several years edited the highly respected *Messenger of Europe*.

During this time, Kovalevskii's scholarly work proceeded with undiminished intensity, although he still made no effort to systematize his own sociological theory. His book *Modern Sociologists* (1905) was confined primarily to a critical analysis of the principal currents in modern sociological thought. In *Sociology* (1910), he limited his discussion primarily to the functional and conceptual bonds between sociology and the other social sciences, with lengthy excursions into the sociocultural origins of the various institutional complexes that were treated by so-called genetic sociology. To arrive at a general idea of Kovalevskii's own theoretical orientation, we must examine his studies in both comparative history and sociological theory.

Kovalevskii's early acceptance of comparative history as the most trustworthy source of empirical generalizations based on social and cultural data marked the beginning of his systematic search for a true science of sociology. However, he never identified comparative history with general sociology, but regarded it only as the most logical link between the descriptive social sciences and abstract sociology. Several distinct influences led him into the field of comparative history. From A. O. and V. O. Kovalevskii, K. A. Timiriazev, and I. I. Mechnikov, four of the greatest Russian naturalists, he learned the value of the comparative method in constructing scientifically verifiable generalizations.[130] From M. F. Miller, with whom he conducted joint ethnographic fieldwork in the Caucasus, he learned the generalizing value of comparative linguistics in reconstructing the cultural history of neighboring peoples; and in the work of Sir Henry Maine, he found the most impressive model for a comparative study of rural communities and their institutions and normative systems. Finally, Karl Marx impressed him with the great importance of a comparative study of economic institutions as agents of social progress. (Kovalevskii, in fact, had the distinction of having been called a "scientific friend" by Marx and an "ideological enemy" by Lenin.[131])

Gradually, Kovalevskii began to look for sociological abstractions that went beyond comparative history. The result was a combination of Comtean ideas and the principles advanced by evolutionary ethnologists, particularly L. H. Morgan and E. B. Tylor. Kovalevskii fully accepted Comte's idea that general sociology should deal with the laws of social order and social progress, and in 1913 he wrote that twentieth-century sociology could do no better than expand and refine the Comtean system. The modern stirrings in sociological thought, he was convinced, had not refuted Comte's ideas any more than similar stirrings in physics and biology had invalidated the accumulated wisdom of the Newtonian and Darwinian traditions.[132] Kovalevskii himself defined social order as an integration of the structural components of culture and society into a total pattern in which no specific set of conditions acted as primary causes. By social progress, he meant a regular, predictable transition of social orders to more "advanced" forms. Progress is the single most important concept in Kovalevskii's general sociology. He considered Condorcet the first codifier of the idea of progress, the first advocate of "social mathematics," and the true founder of sociology.[133] Following the dominant trend in Russian sociology, he measured social and cultural progress by the increasing interaction of individuals, groups, and societies.[134] In the theories of growing social solidarity advanced by Simmel and Durkheim, he saw only a reaffirmation and elaboration of Comtean humanistic philosophy.[135]

Kovalevskii defended the thesis that sociocultural evolution is not only progressive but unilinear; that is, all human societies must pass through the same phases of development. For this, Kovalevskii, like most of his preceptors, had only one explanation: the psychological unity of mankind. Since man's psychological constitution was the same everywhere, regardless of habitat and history, there could be only one main line of social progress. And thanks to the universality of this main line, there could be an abstract science of society—a general sociology comparable to physics and biology in the universality of its laws. Kovalevskii was skeptical of theories that considered the mind of primitive man "pre-logical" (notably the views expressed by the French philosopher Lucien Lévy-Bruhl), for he felt that these denied the psychological unity of mankind.[136]

The concept of progress and the principle of the psychological unity of mankind led Kovalevskii to endorse the evolutionary ethnologists' assumption that change in every human society is effected by internal forces rather than by external influences. In this view, independent invention (possible because of mankind's psychological unity) rather than a diffusion of cultural traits was the real mechanism of social evolution. This was the primary reason for Kovalevskii's uncompromising war against Gabriel Tarde's theory of imitation as the main source of change; on the same grounds, he attacked Ludwig Gumplowicz's theory of conquest and ethnic stratification as the major vehicle of social progress.

Kovalevskii had definite ideas about the internal dynamics of social change, particularly those of social progress. In several studies, he speculated that density of population probably determined the place occupied by individual societies on the evolutionary scale. Essentially, however, he was a critic of monistic causation. In his opinion, "All aspects of social life influence each other so much that it is impossible to talk about the priority of one over the other."[137] He firmly opposed economic determinism, Tarde's psychological interpretation of social change, and Paul Lilienfeld's biological models of social structure, since all were committed to a theory of key causes in social dynamics.[138] Social change, as viewed by Kovalevskii, is also gradual; and unlike the Marxists, he regarded revolutionary convulsions in human history as pathological aberrations.

General sociology, according to Kovalevskii, is the most abstract social science. Ethnography, statistics, jurisprudence, comparative history, and political science are all "concrete sciences" of society, and their relationship to sociology is reciprocal: they supply sociology with raw data and empirical generalizations, and they receive from sociology precise formulations of the laws of social development, which help them draw broader meanings from their data.

Kovalevskii made no effort to find a meeting ground between the *a priori* categories of sociology and the *a posteriori* generalizations of comparative history—i.e., between deduction and induction as methods of social inquiry. As a comparative historian, he accepted as valid only comparisons between societies that had been thoroughly investigated by competent scholars. But as an evolutionary sociologist, he felt that "uninvestigated" societies could be adequately explained in terms of "investigated" societies occupying the same position on the unilinear scale of evolutional development. For example, he saw no reason why Lewis H. Morgan's description of Iroquois social organization should not be applicable to other societies at the same stage of development. As a comparative historian, Kovalevskii relied on a careful analysis of historical and ethnographic data to provide empirical generalizations; as an evolutionary sociologist, he used selected historical and ethnographic data to illustrate the workings of preconceived laws of social development.

Kovalevskii's fame rests on his substantive work, and his substantive work was a product of comparative analysis. By a twist of irony, he embraced evolutionist sociology just as it was rapidly giving ground to newer sociological orientations that were less sweeping in their theoretical claims but more exact in describing the realities of modern society. The widespread controversy over the epistemological foundations of modern science in general, and sociology in particular, escaped him completely. Though eminently successful in connecting history and ethnography with comparative history, he failed to establish a working relationship between comparative history as an empirical sociology and general sociology as a theoretical system.

In his theoretical thought Kovalevskii never moved out of the nineteenth century. Why, then, was he treated by his learned countrymen as the dean of Russian sociologists? Why was the first national sociological association in Russia named after him, and why was he the first Russian sociologist to be elected to full membership in the St. Petersburg Academy of Sciences?

There are several answers to these questions. Kovalevskii was the first major Russian scholar to approach sociology as a complete science—a science with a logical framework, a theoretical base, and an empirical body. No other Russian scholar was as successful at integrating the diverse sociological theories of the nineteenth century. Moreover, his role as an ambassador of Russian scholarship in Western Europe and America added immensely to his stature in the Russian academic community. During his long years of foreign residence, his fellow emigrants regarded him as one of their most eminent representatives; indeed, after Ivan Turgenev's death he was considered the intellectual leader of the Russian expatriates. In Russia, Kovalevskii was an Academician, a member of the State Duma and the State Council, an editor and regular contributor for the *Messenger of Europe*, and a highly esteemed teacher and public speaker; in these roles, he was by far the most effective link between academic sociology and society at large.

Kovalevskii's gradualist sociology and his propensity to identify social progress with the inexorable affirmation of democratic principles produced a political philosophy that saw the future of Russia in a gradual democratization of political institutions and processes. But the deep-seated social and political crisis in his homeland eventually convinced him that Comte's definition of sociology as a science of social order and social progress was misleading. He learned from Russia's plight that every society does not necessarily exhibit order, and that every change is not necessarily synonymous with progress. However, when Miliukov asserted that Kovalevskii's sociological views were "strictly scientific," he acknowledged the academic community's appreciation of Kovalevskii's determination to keep sociology fully independent of ideological controls, regardless of immediate pressures. Mikhailovskii, by deliberately merging the two meanings of the word *pravda*—"truth" and "justice"—had merged sociology and ideology. By deliberately keeping *pravda*-truth apart from *pravda*-justice, Kovalevskii had acted in the best scientific spirit, seeking to advance sociology as a science of social laws rather than a code of good conduct.[139]

## CHAPTER FIFTEEN

# Conclusion

The emergence of great Russian scientists was one of the most impressive characteristics of the Reform era. The work of several youthful biologists showed conclusively that Russian scholars had entered the age of Darwinian evolutionism, and Russians were among the founders of evolutionary paleontology and comparative embryology. The work of P. L. Chebyshev and the St. Petersburg school in mathematics received recognition far beyond the Russian frontiers, and N. I. Lobachevskii's non-Euclidean geometry became widely known. A. M. Butlerov gave the first clear and comprehensive formulation of the structural theory in chemistry. I. M. Sechenov began the great neurophysiological tradition that reached its peak in the work of Ivan Pavlov. D. I. Mendeleev's periodic system of elements is considered one of the greatest chemical contributions of the nineteenth century. The foundations were laid for soil science as a Russian national science, and for the great contributions of Russian scholarship to a mathematically integrated system of crystalline forms.

The essential change during the 1860's was that science ceased to be a secondary intellectual force in Russian culture and became as important as the antirationalist tradition in understanding the full spectrum of Russian thought. After 1860, in fact, Russia produced most of its greatest scientists and champions of rationalism and most of its leading philosophical-religious thinkers.

From the Crimean War on, the social value of science was not seriously questioned in Russia; but thinkers in all branches of learning were deeply concerned about the real place of science in Russian culture. Was the historian T. N. Granovskii thinking of Russian culture when he praised Bacon's faith in the future victory of reason and in the contributions of science to the elimination of the evils rooted in ignorance? Did the physiologist Ivan Sechenov refer to Russian culture when he declared that "always and everywhere, science represents the culminating point of a people's spiritual

development and the cornerstone of cultural progress"? Was the plant physiologist K. A. Timiriazev correct when he asserted that science and realistic
literature were the two greatest Russian intellectual accomplishments of
the nineteenth century, and that both truly expressed the national bent of
the Russian mind? How representative of the Russian intellectual community was the physicist N. A. Umov when he boldly asserted that scientific
facts were the only source of the common weal?[1]

Dostoevskii, one of Russia's most renowned novelists, and Mendeleev, one of Russia's greatest scientists, expressed the two most typical
views on the place of science in Russian culture. Dostoevskii, representing
the antirationalist tradition, acknowledged the social value of science and
said that Russia should certainly take full advantage of scientific discoveries.
But he insisted that the true genius of Russian culture lay not in scientific
knowledge but in religious contemplation. He praised N. Ia. Danilevskii's
*Russia and Europe* as a careful assemblage of incontrovertible proofs for his
own contention that "the Russian Christ," as embodied in the Orthodox
Church, was the essence of Russian culture and the most powerful source
of Russian contributions to the good of humanity.[2] He told his countrymen
that science was one thing and enlightenment another. Russia had no choice
but to borrow science from Western Europe, "its only source." On the other
hand, enlightenment—the "spiritual light that shines upon the soul and
illumines the heart, that directs the mind and shows it the meaning of life"—
had "an absolute sufficiency" of sources in Russian spiritual thought, which
was not bound by the fetters of scientific "materialism" and the logical rigidity of the scientific method.

Mendeleev, by contrast, worked diligently to convince his compatriots
that science was actually the essential feature of modern enlightenment. Not
only did the natural sciences—"the power and the glory of our age"—give
Russia an honorable place in the family of civilized nations, but they were
a cultural asset fully compatible with the Russian national character. Realism, said Mendeleev, was a dominant trait in the Russian character, and
science was one of the more natural and effective forms of expressing realism; centuries of struggling to find a livelihood in the cold and monotonous
forests and steppes had made the Russian man a realist whose mind was
naturally suited to the exactitude of natural science. Mendeleev opposed the
traditional emphasis on classical studies in the gymnasiums on the ground
that such studies were alien to the realistic, scientific bent of the Russian
mind, and he lamented the continuing lack of adequate courses in the natural sciences.

The views of Dostoevskii and Mendeleev can easily be regarded as complementary rather than contradictory. Dostoevskii was essentially interested in the historical and cultural uniqueness of the Russian world view, that is, in the Russian soul; Mendeleev was most concerned with Russian secular wisdom, which was anchored in a rationalist tradition transcending national boundaries. In the terminology of Alfred Weber, Dostoevskii pondered the inner strengths of Russian culture and Mendeleev the measurable resourcefulness of Russian civilization. Because they and others like them disagreed, and because the resulting debates and polemics attracted representatives of all modes of intellectual inquiry, Russian intellectual culture acquired a far greater versatility, depth, and vitality.

Dostoevskii's uncomplimentary views of science should not be interpreted as a complete denial of science's social value, but rather as a refutation of Nihilist philosophy, which completely ignored the cultural import of aesthetic, ethical, and metaphysical views and modes of inquiry. Dostoevskii's intention was not to attack the work of modern scientists in general, but to deride those "unenlightened" scientists who lacked a broad humanistic background. For example, he acknowledged Ivan Sechenov's pioneering studies but was unhappy with the great physiologist's narrow intellectual and humanistic horizons.[3] Many historians of science would share Dostoevskii's unfavorable opinion of "unenlightened" scientists; but few would agree that Sechenov, a man of broad humanity and keen philosophical sense, fell into this category. Dostoevskii wanted his country to have more scholars of the type represented by Hermann Helmholtz and Claude Bernard—"men with universal minds" and philosophical competence. He no doubt agreed with Bernard's dictum that science and art complement each other and that the time would come when the poet, the philosopher, and the physiologist would all understand one another and work together.

At the beginning of the twentieth century, most of the leading Russian scientists accepted a synthesis of the ostensibly contrary views of Dostoevskii and Mendeleev. They abandoned the one-sided philosophy of scientism and acknowledged the vital role of nonscientific modes of inquiry. They extolled the extraordinary power of science in modern life, but they also recognized that an interaction of science with other cultural approaches could help man to expand, interpret, and systematize his knowledge about nature and society. Most scientists now recognized that the traditional conflict between Western and Slavophil interpretations of Russian culture was unfounded and intellectually sterile.

The consensus of modern scholarship was that Russian culture was a blend of internal creations and external influences, and that the integration of the two was the most critical problem in modern Russian society. The problem was a particularly complex one, not because the native Russian culture and the imported ideas were basically incompatible, but because the borrowing had been so random and so extensive. According to P. N. Miliukov, this borrowing from the West, intensified by the process of modernization after 1860, had made Russian culture "indeterminate."[4] The philosopher of history N. I. Kareev defined the values of the Russian intelligentsia as a synthesis of the ethos of Western European scholarship and the Russian "national spirit."[5] The poet Andrei Belyi thought that the label "Western East" best depicted the massive debt of modern Russian culture to both the Orient and the Occident. The historian A. S. Lappo-Danilevskii was convinced that extensive borrowing had forced Russian intellectual culture to search constantly for new principles of integration. The integrative work, he argued, was done by representatives of all the main currents of thought: leading scientists, philosophical-religious thinkers, great artists, and even the articulators of the materialistic world view.[6]

The leading codifier of modern views on the intellectual potentiality of science was Vladimir Vernadskii. An accomplished philosopher and historian of science, Vernadskii strove to arrive at a comprehensive sociological interpretation of the "scientific world view" and to trace its growth in Russian culture. However, he saw a number of profound differences between science in general and the scientific world view. Science, as viewed by Vernadskii, consists of all the "facts" examined by the scientific method and integrated into scientific theories. The scientific world view, on the other hand, is dominated by a relatively small number of basic scientific ideas, which introduce a hierarchy of values and unity of purpose into the world of science and define the relationship of science to other modes of inquiry. Science consists of accumulated positive knowledge; the scientific world view depends on the changing interpretation of dominant ideas within that knowledge.

According to the historian P. G. Vinogradov, the nineteenth-century scientific world view was dominated by two ideas: the idea of natural and social laws, and the idea of development. Modern science has proved that nature and society are tightly structured and subject to universal laws. By decoding the inner order of nature, science has given man a new means of controlling elementary forces, exploiting organic and inorganic resources, fighting disease, and improving morality. The idea of development—of gradual and continuous transformations in nature—has given man a scientific basis for his faith in progress. The idea of law has accelerated the development of modern technology; the idea of development has improved man's moral standards and ennobled his conscience.[7] Vinogradov saw the synthesis of Newtonian mechanicism and Darwinian historicism as the purest expression of the philosophical bent of nineteenth-century science. He did not anticipate the emergence of twentieth-century science as a world view antithetical to two basic thoughts that united Newtonianism and Darwinism: continuity and causality in the processes of nature.

Vernadskii notes that the scientific world view of every historical period is involved in a war with "alien" scientific ideas, which will eventually make up future world views.[8] His interpretation is graphically illustrated by the changes wrought by the revolution in science at the beginning of the twentieth century. This revolution did not deny the scientific facts accumulated by generations of scholars. Instead, it selected new notions to guide scientists in interpreting and integrating these facts. Some of these notions came from new experimental discoveries; others were the result of bold theoretical and philosophical deductions; and still others had existed for some time outside the mainstream of scientific thought. The scientific world view, to Vernadskii, is not a mechanical reflection of the cosmos; it is primarily an interpretation of the cosmos in terms of dominant scientific principles. The scientific world view is "a creation and an expression of the human mind," which, in turn, is a product of man's total culture.

The scientific propositions making up the scientific world view are not necessarily scientific facts. The Ptolemaic geocentric proposition was a central ingredient of the pre-Copernican world view, even though it was not a true expression of existing reality. It was part of the scientific world view because it did not contradict the principles of scientific inquiry: it was subject to scientific methodology, that is, to the scientific patterns of logical explanation and to the scientific value of objectivity.

The scientific world view changes not only in its internal configuration, but also in the importance it is given in a particular culture. In certain periods it may be subordinated to the philosophical mode of inquiry, and in others it may dominate not only philosophy but all other modes of inquiry. Therefore, the scientific world view is doubly relativistic: it depends both on the scientific propositions it selects for emphasis and on its relationship to religious doctrines, moral rules, technology, aesthetic appreciation and creativity, and other approaches to the study of man and nature.

At the root of Vernadskii's argument is the notion that the scientific world view is not isolated from other viewpoints and sources of wisdom.

Indeed, certain parts of the modern scientific world view have originated in "religious ideas, philosophy, social usage, or the arts"; their "transfer" to the realm of science has been possible after they meet the rigorous standards of scientific validation. Pythagoras, for example, made musical harmony a topic of mathematical study and in so doing aided the scientific search for a "harmony of nature"—an essentially aesthetic quality that is nevertheless expressible in mathematical terms.[9] According to Vernadskii, "It is difficult to say at the present time which is larger: the scientific study of areas previously dominated by religion and philosophy, or the new scope acquired by religion and philosophy thanks to the growth of the scientific world view."[10] Vernadskii felt that the years 1890–1910 were marked not only by a rapid expansion of the intellectual horizons of science but also by a rapid demise of scientism, which had underrated the nonscientific sources of wisdom. One could not appreciate the power of science, he said, until one understood and acknowledged its intrinsic limitations and its complementary relations to the religious, moral, philosophical, and aesthetic modes of inquiry. World War I, by involving scientists directly or indirectly in the job of designing weapons of destruction, taught them to search for the fundamental laws of humanity and morality outside of science.[11]

Vernadskii recognized the great contributions of Nihilism to the development of rationalist thought and science in modern Russia; but he was careful to emphasize that most scientists, influenced by the writings of the Nihilists in the 1860's to select science as a vocation, had gradually abandoned Nihilist scientism and adopted a more modest view of science as only one part of modern culture.[12] When such conservative writers as S. N. Bulgakov and N. A. Berdiaev attacked the "materialism" and intellectual imperialism of science in the early 1900's, they were under the erroneous impression that Russian science and scientists were still imbued with the spirit of Nihilism.

The conservatives were correct in one important respect: they sensed that in espousing the ethos of science the leading scientists were building a new ideology incompatible with the sacred values of autocracy. Vernadskii was the most eloquent spokesman of this formidable group, to which science was not only a body of factual knowledge but also a source of cultural values. In defending the paramount cultural role of modern science and spelling out the conditions that would favor its development, Vernadskii championed three great tenets of democracy: a critical attitude toward every authority, intellectual and otherwise; freedom for all modes of inquiry; and associative autonomy for the corporate groups engaged in the pursuit of specific vocational or other interests. He declared: "In its very foundations science is profoundly democratic; the power of human reason and the depths of human personality are its only sources."[13] Vernadskii argued that the best conditions for the development of science exist in societies that offer a maximum of freedom and open scientific work to every interested member of society. He was convinced that the growth of scientific thought since the seventeenth century had been the prime mover in the increasing democratization of social relations and political processes.

Vernadskii's views were shared by his contemporaries. The experimental method of science, according to another Russian scientist, is democratic because it is accessible to all persons. It is true that only a few men have the ability to discover general laws; but those who have learned to use the experimental method can at least collect scientific facts and contribute to the verification of existing hypotheses. Science, in fact, depends completely on the army of dedicated workers who collect the essential data underlying all scientific generalizations and explanations. Lakhtin asserted that during the formative age of modern science countries with a cultural predilection for the deductive method experienced much more difficulty in accumulating scientific knowledge than countries in which the inductive method was prevalent.[14] The physicist N. A. Umov saw in the gradual scientific conquest of the universe the noblest preoccupation of man. Science, according to him, is the most democratic of all modes of inquiry because it works in harmony with the progress of the ethical code, and because its guardians are "made," not "chosen." By unveiling the architecture of the universe and predicting the future course of its evolution, science increases man's adaptive power by giving him foreknowledge of the grand course of history; in the process, man also gains a sense of proportion and a feeling of intellectual modesty by realizing the infinitesimally small dimensions of the earth in the total configuration of the universe.[15]

In 1906, Vernadskii published a clear and forthright statement of his political philosophy, expressing the sentiments of a majority of the scholarly community. He scrutinized three possible ways out of the staggering crisis in Russian politics: a complete resurrection of the old autocratic institutions, supported by police terror; a socialist revolution led by the disgruntled segments of all social classes; and a triumph of representative government.[16] A staunch supporter of the third "solution," Vernadskii saw Russia's salvation in a complete, but gradual, democratization of the political system. He used the culture of science as a source of the values on which a new Russian polity could be built.

Vernadskii was a keen student of the history of Russian science. Proud of the great scientific achievements made by Russian scientists, he sought to determine and spell out the factors that had made the development of science appreciably slower in Russia than in the leading countries of Western Europe. In addition to such obvious "causes" as a comparatively late start in the pursuit of science, a belated industrialization, and a prolonged survival of feudal institutions, most scholars, including Vernadskii, emphasized three basic social, cultural, and political conditions that hampered a more impressive development of Russian science: government policy, the absence of a "scientific" class or estate in Russia, and Russia's dependence on the West.

In the 1900's, a rapidly increasing number of scholars began to voice the opinion that since the time of Peter the Great all science in Russia had been "government science." In the introductory remarks to his *History of Kazan University*, N. P. Zagoskin noted that the primary task of Russian universities was the training of government officials rather than the advancement and diffusion of scientific knowledge. After the February Revolution, the historian Mikhail Rostovtsev wrote, "In Russia, science ... can exist only insofar as it is under the direct protection of the state." The slow diffusion of scientific thought among the Russian masses was caused not only by the state monopoly of scientific research but also by the government's fear of closer ties between science and society at large. Rostovtsev added: "Official Russia supported science only as a showcase and not as a living organism requiring sustained assistance. Sorry was the state of the universities, which were assigned the task ... of producing only so many scientists as there were teaching positions in the schools of higher education. ... This clearly showed the government's consistent policy of supporting science only as a decoration and preventing it from reaching society at large."[17]

Because it controlled the university curriculum, the government was the sole authority in defining the social value of individual sciences. Neither the 1884 university statute nor the new draft statute prepared at the beginning of the twentieth century explicitly recognized the role of universities in the advancement of scientific knowledge. The 1884 statute, in fact, defined all university laboratories as educational auxiliaries; and in implementing it, the government overloaded the existing laboratories by introducing extensive practical exercises in an effort to give the students less time for political activities. "It can be said," Vernadskii argued, "that the research activities of university professors were carried out not according to but in spite of the will of the government."[18] The physicist P. N. Lebedev agreed with Vernadskii, and lamented the general absence of research centers that were unencumbered by teaching and uninterrupted by the chronic disorders common in university communities since 1860. Among other things, the educational overcommitment of university laboratories prevented a mutually beneficial interaction between industry and research institutions.

The basic complaint voiced by prominent professors was that the 1884 charter made them "government bureaucrats," with no freedom of action. The most serious blow came when the Ministry of National Education abrogated the traditional right of professors to administer examinations in their own classes; for by controlling examinations, the government sought to control the content of lectures.[19] Professors also lost the right to elect rectors, deans, and new members of the teaching staff. Moreover, they could not change the curriculum to meet the challenge of new disciplines or scientific orientations. The general feeling was that by losing a voice in university affairs academic scientists had also lost most of their power to defend the interests of science. Without academic autonomy and a genuine community of scholars, Russian scientists could not play an active role in advancing the culture of science and formulating national science policies.

After 1885 the salaries of individual professors depended on the number of students enrolled in their classes. This system of remuneration gave the highest salaries to professors who taught "required courses" in the more populous faculties and totally disregarded the professional accomplishments of individual professors.[20] It also discouraged leading scholars from offering highly specialized or experimental courses that would have attracted relatively small numbers of students. In essence, the new policy encouraged a mechanical review of noncontroversial substantive knowledge and discouraged the exploration of new theoretical and experimental challenges.

At the end of 1904, spurred on by the growing unrest in the country, Vernadskii published an essay on the urgent need for forming a national "union of professors" that would have some voice in formulating effective solutions to the acute problems of higher education and scientific work. The academic community took Vernadskii's article as a call to immediate action. In January 1905, the St. Petersburg professors and academicians issued the famous "Note of 342," so called because it was signed by 342 persons. Among the signatories were such well-known members of the St. Petersburg Academy of Sciences as the mathematician A. A. Markov, the historian A. S. Lappo-Danilevskii, and the plant physiologist A. S. Famintsyn.[21] The document was an open and sweeping attack on the existing system of higher education and its crippling effects on the national effort in science. It stated in part:

"A stream of government decisions and regulations has reduced professors and other instructors at the institutions of higher education to the level of bureaucrats, blindly executing the orders of higher government authorities. The scientific and moral standards of the teaching profession have been lowered. The prestige of educators has dwindled so much that the very existence of the institutions of higher education is threatened. Our school administration is a social and governmental disgrace. It undermines the authority of science, hinders the growth of scientific thought, and prevents our people from fully realizing their intellectual potentialities.

"Science can develop only when it is free, when it is protected from external interference, and when it is unhindered in its efforts to illuminate every aspect of human existence. . . .

"The tragic state of our educational system does not permit us to remain on the sidelines. It compels us to express our profound conviction that academic freedom is incompatible with the existing system of government in Russia. The present situation cannot be remedied by partial reforms but only by a fundamental transformation of the existing system. . . . Only a full guarantee of personal and social liberties will assure academic freedom—the essential condition for true education."[22]

The Note of 342 was heralded as a true expression of the academic community's sentiment; within a month the number of signatories rose to 1,800, including teachers from the secondary schools and several more members of the Academy of Sciences. In March, delegates from St. Petersburg gathered to plan a national organization of professors, and in early 1906 the contents of their proposed charter were made public. The government first procrastinated, and then refused to ratify the charter. The call for a national academic organization remained only a historical document, spelling out in bold and courageous terms the conflict between the autocratic system and the ideals of scholarship.

Ten years later, N. K. Kol'tsov summed up the basic grievances of the professors: "In our country, in contrast to Germany, the university staff, from professors to assistants, is not protected from the crudest treatment by all kinds of government officials. Although it takes decades of slow and arduous work to build scientific institutes and laboratories, it takes only a month for men like Magnitskii and Kasso to destroy them. Improvement in the legal status of our professors is an essential condition for the development of Russian science. Without legal protection for the university staff, no financial investments or laboratories will contribute to the development of our scientific thought."[23]

The government fought rebellious students in order to protect "government science," and it protected "government science" in a desperate move to stem the growing tide of dissatisfaction with the autocratic system. In combating student unrest, the government relied on blind and vindictive repression, the method it knew best. Many leading scholars were convinced that government reprisals did far more than student disorder to damage the universities as scientific institutions. P. G. Vinogradov expressed their sentiment when he asserted that the 1884 charter had been not an educational but a political measure.[24] A. S. Famintsyn criticized the government for regarding student unrest as the only problem in the universities and deliberately ignoring the many basic institutional problems generated by the urgent need for modernizing both instruction and research.[25] In fact the government habitually used student disorders as an excuse for uncompromising attacks on academic "republicanism."

The 1884 charter had turned both students and professors against the government. However, the students gravitated more toward political extremism, whereas the professors tended to prefer gradual, though fundamental, alterations within the existing political system.* Mendeleev's idea of "gradualism" in social development was an appropriate label for the political philosophy of most leading scholars. However, the number of professors who disapproved of the government's vindictive attitude toward student unrest and criticized the negative features of the 1884 charter was much larger than the number of professors openly engaged in political action.

Russian scholars recognized a second major reason for the comparatively slow development of science in their country. Russia did not have a single social class or estate on which it could depend in building a strong national tradition in science. Neither the gentry nor the clergy, the two relatively well-educated and financially secure estates, were reliable sources of scientific manpower; and few other estates could enter the classical gymnasiums or the universities.

A series of laws promulgated during the early 1860's had officially opened the institutions of higher education to all classes; but although the law sanctioned universal education, tradition and economic conditions kept the youth of peasant or lower-middle-class stock away from the institutional paths to higher education. And during the 1880's, the government once again adopted discriminatory laws controlling the admission of various

---

* A study of the political attitudes of the students enrolled in the St. Petersburg Polytechnical Institute in 1909–10 (the only systematic investigation of political behavior in the institutions of higher education undertaken in tsarist Russia) showed that 73.9 per cent of all students favored "leftist" parties and 5.5 per cent "rightist" parties; 20.6 per cent were not identified with any organized political group. Bernatskii, p. 16.

social strata to the state schools. The Ministry of National Education issued several orders that rendered classical gymnasiums virtually inaccessible to the lower classes.[26] Also, university tuition was raised, with the sole purpose of discouraging the enrollment of poorer students. Students whose police records showed any sign of illicit political activities were barred from the universities. Polish students were particularly discriminated against in the allocation of state stipends for study outside Russia, which virtually eliminated their chances of being selected as professorial aspirants.

Drastic limitations on the enrollment of Jewish students came just as Russia was developing a Jewish intellectual community imbued with values that encouraged scientific exploration and possessed of huge reserves of capable young people who were eager to obtain higher education. The geneticist N. K. Kol'tsov observed that one did not have to be a scholar to realize the injurious effects of these policies.[27] The academic community at large opposed the government's quota system, and used every opportunity to exceed the legal limits on Jewish enrollment in national universities. After the revolution of 1905, when academic autonomy was temporarily restored, the academic councils deliberately disregarded the still-extant *numerus clausus* and admitted Jews on the same basis as Christians. In St. Petersburg University, to take one example, the number of Jewish students jumped from 5.6 per cent of the total enrollment in 1905 to 12.5 per cent in 1907. But when the government eliminated the last vestiges of academic autonomy in early 1914, the Jews' share in the total enrollment was reduced to 3 per cent.

Even when discrimination in Russia slacked off, Jewish students faced many obstacles. In 1912 there were at least 8,000 Russian students in Western European universities, and Jews made up the bulk—according to some sources, 90 per cent—of this contingent. In 1913, swayed by a wave of anti-Semitism, the universities of Berlin, Breslau, Munich, Königsberg, and Bonn did not admit any Russian students. Many other universities applied various forms of limited discrimination; in Giessen, Tübingen, Vienna, and Prague, for example, only the medical faculties were closed to Russian students.[28] Hampered by the discriminatory practices of German universities, intensively involved in political work, and always troubled by shaky finances, many students, Jewish or not, could not complete their foreign studies. This was an especially severe blow to students in the natural sciences, for whom Western training was almost mandatory.

At the end of the nineteenth century, the Russian bourgeoisie, made up primarily of the commercial class, emerged as the first steady and politically acceptable source of scientific manpower. This new and relatively small class not only showed a healthy respect for scientific pursuits but also gave important financial aid to scientific institutions.[29] Even more significant was the bourgeoisie's role in financing a private system of research institutes and schools. Private interest in the welfare of science rose to new heights in the twentieth century, just before the October Revolution. One need mention only Kh. S. Ledentsov, whose donations established the Ledentsov Society for the Advancement of Exact Sciences and Their Practical Application, and A. L. Shaniavskii, who endowed a private university in Moscow. Shaniavskii University was an especially important undertaking, for it opened higher education to young people regardless of sex or religious, ethnic, and social background. This university and others like it offered curricula that were not prescribed by the government, and could thus adapt themselves quickly to the needs of the rapidly changing natural and social sciences.

The new bourgeoisie successfully challenged the nineteenth-century view that a person could be considered educated even though he did not have the least familiarity with the basic ideas and developments of modern science. Vernadskii was convinced that this "division of educated society" had so far stifled the natural sciences "because it helped create the idea of science as an ephemeral component of the modern world view and the knowledge of modern man."[30] The first decade of the twentieth century, according to Rostovtsev, produced an "intermediate group" of intellectuals who, though not professionally trained in science, dedicated themselves to defending the scientific world view and building a broader social foundation for scientific pursuits. Rostovtsev regretted that these new enthusiasts often lacked enough familiarity with science to give accurate interpretations of new theories or to be really trustworthy agents for popularizing scientific knowledge. In any case, they faced serious obstacles: "Over the abyss between the general population and science, inexcusable in a civilized society, the intelligentsia built frail, precarious little bridges, which were promptly destroyed by the state."[31]

Russia's third handicap in science was her disproportionate economic dependence on the West. Immediately after the outbreak of World War I, it became clear that Russia was unprepared to meet the challenge of modern warfare. Many vital industrial establishments were owned by foreign concerns and operated by foreign managers and engineers. The government could not effectively control and coordinate these industries, which often relied on trade secrets in their business and displayed little eagerness to tap Russian resources of scientific knowledge and engineering skills. The situation was aggravated by Russia's staggering dependence on the importation of goods manufactured in Germany. Moreover, because of its traditional dependence on German industry, the government had never been eager to invest large sums of money in systematic surveys of Russia's natural resources.

At a meeting of the St. Petersburg Academy of Sciences in 1915, Vernadskii summed up the economic causes of the national predicament:

"We have suddenly awakened to the inexcusable magnitude of our country's economic dependence on Germany. The experts have known about this dependence for a long time; now the entire nation knows about it. In peacetime this dependence was considered harmless and inconsequential; the current world crisis has unveiled the full range of its injurious and crippling effects.

"This dependence is undoubtedly behind many problems in our country. . . . One of these problems . . . is the glaring inadequacy of our knowledge of the productive forces that nature has given us. . . . Our dependence on foreign products . . . has kept us from searching for scientific answers to our economic needs. We do not even know whether some of the important natural resources are available to us, or in what quantities. . . . This is the present situation with regard to such metals as bismuth, antimony, molybdenum, cerium, lead, zinc, aluminum, nickel, barium, tungsten, tin, and vanadium."[32]

In their critical scrutiny of the political, social, and economic forces that worked against the promotion of scientific thought in Russia, Vernadskii, Rostovtsev, and their colleagues were extremely careful not to underestimate the real achievements of Russian scientific scholarship and the forces that did work in its favor. Whether they wrote about the glories of Lomonosov's scientific legacy or about Russian contributions to mathematics, crystallography, physiology, chemistry, and soil science, they recognized the powerful achievements of generations of Russian scholars. Whether they scrutinized the expanding cultural base of science during the 1860's or pondered the modern confrontation of "Russian science" and "Russian morality," they saw in science an instrument of universal progress and a guaranty for the growing welfare of their people. Science, one of them said, injected more humanity into both culture and conscience.

Though recognizing the symbiotic relationship of science with other modes of inquiry, Vernadskii and his peers did not hide their firm belief that science was the dominant feature of modern culture. "We see everywhere," Vernadskii said, "an infusion of science into all the components of our culture: science exercises a powerful influence on the religious consciousness of modern man; it precipitates changes in philosophical convictions; it penetrates deeply into the arts; and it dominates the entire technology ... way of life, and governmental processes of our age."[33] The scientific community in tsarist Russia, though laboring under many handicaps, had laid a solid foundation for the notable achievements of Soviet science.

*Notes*

# *Notes*

Complete authors' names, titles, and publication data
are given in the Bibliography, pp. 523–61.

CHAPTER ONE

1. Shelgunov, *Vospominaniia*, p. 82.
2. Shelgunov, *Ocherki*, p. 570. See also Bobrovskii, p. 82.
3. Markovnikov, *Izbrannye trudy*, pp. 680–81. See also Omelianskii, "Razvitie este-stvoznaniia," pp. 117–18.
4. Chicherin, *Vospominaniia*, p. 291.
5. Herzen, *Izbrannye stat'i iz "Kolokola,"* p. 248.
6. Chicherin, *Neskol'ko sovremennykh voprosov*, p. 26.
7. B. L. Modzalevskii, pp. 137–39. See also Golitsyn, pp. 238–39.
8. Grigor'ev, pp. 309–10.
9. *Ibid.*, p. 125.
10. Aleshintsev, pp. 65–66.
11. "Antonovich," pp. 668–69.
12. Andreevich, p. 195; Mechnikov, *Etiudy*, p. 5.
13. Andreevich, pp. 173–74.
14. Pisarev, *Sochineniia*, II, 21.
15. K. A. Timiriazev, "Probuzhdenie estestvoznaniia," pp. 27–28.
16. Leffler and Kovalewsky, p. 11.
17. Lemke, pp. 88–89.
18. As cited in Review of "Iz nauki," No. 4, p. 87.
19. *Ibid.*, p. 80.
20. *Ibid.*, No. 5, p. 56.
21. Iurkevich, No. 4, pp. 379–80. Despite his partial—and mostly tactical—concessions to philosophical realism, anchored in natural science and positivism, Iurkevich was remembered primarily as a founder of the modern Russian philosophy of irrationalism and mysticism. V. S. Solov'ev, VIII, 424–29; Aksakov, pp. 442–69.
22. Ikonnikov, *Opyt*, Vol. II, Pt. 1, p. 668.
23. E. R., "Russkie ratsionalisty: 3. Molokane; 4. Shtundisty," pp. 297–98. See also: N. M. Nikol'skii, pp. 282–83; "Krest'ianstvo i narodnicheskoe dvizhenie," p. 168.
24. E. R., "Russkie ratsionalisty: 3. Molokane; 4. Shtundisty," p. 314.
25. The teachings of the Shtundisty varied from province to province. N. M. Nikol'-skii (p. 288) groups all branches of the sect into two general categories: the utopian-communistic South Russian group—the so-called Spiritual Christians—and the political-evangelical group of Orel province and neighboring areas. See also Gumilevskii, pp. 11–19.
26. Shchapov, II, 156.
27. *Ibid.*, p. 157.

28. Sakulin, pp. 5–8, 139.

29. Serno-Solov'evich, pp. 190–91. The cited article, "Ne trebuet li nyneshnee sostoianie znanii novoi nauki?," was originally published in *Russkoe slovo*, 1865, No. 1.

30. Lavrov, *Filosofiia i sotsiologiia*, II, 22.

31. Tikhonravov, III, Pt. 2, p. 378.

32. Antonovich, *Literaturno-kriticheskie stat'i*, pp. 238–39.

33. Kavelin, "Filosofiia i nauka," p. 332.

34. Lavrov, *Filosofiia i sotsiologiia*, II, 54.

35. Mikhailovskii, *Sochineniia*, I, 88; III, 407–24.

36. For relevant discussions of the values emphasized by the Nihilists, see E. Solov'ev, *Ocherki*, pp. 243–57; and Skabichevskii, pp. 97–107. See also Rogers, "Darwinism," pp. 10–15.

37. Quoted in Dynnik *et al.*, IV, 23–24.

38. Dobroliubov, p. 195.

39. Chernyshevskii, *Antropologicheskii printsip*, p. 70.

40. Pisarev, *Sochineniia*, II, 226.

41. *Ibid.*, III, 126.

42. *Ibid.*, p. 76.

43. *Ibid.*, p. 78.

44. *Ibid.*, II, 11; Kornilov, *Obshchestvennoe dvizhenie*, p. 111.

45. For a critical survey of Pisarev's work in the popularization of science, see Coquart, pp. 333–41. For a perceptive but not very systematic study of Pisarev's views on the relation of science to the metamorphosis of the dominant values of Russian culture during the 1860's, see Bal'talon, Nos. 10–12.

46. Pisarev, *Selected Essays*, p. 305.

47. *Ibid.*, p. 304.

48. *Ibid.*, p. 309.

49. I. P. Pavlov, *Polnoe sobranie sochinenii*, VI, 441.

50. "Antonovich," p. 676.

51. Antonovich, "Dva tipa sovremennykh filosofov," p. 391.

52. *Ibid.*, pp. 385–86.

53. Antonovich, *Izbrannye filosofskie sochineniia*, p. 350.

54. Antonovich, "Dva tipa sovremennykh filosofov," p. 404.

55. "Antonovich," pp. 670–71.

56. Andreevich, *Opyt filosofii*, p. 233.

57. Mikhailovskii, *Sochineniia*, I, 50.

58. Lavrov, *Tri besedy*, p. 22.

59. Briullova-Shaskol'skaia, pp. 412–14.

60. Lavrov, *Zadachi pozitivizma*, p. 61.

61. Andreevich, *Opyt filosofii*, p. 223.

62. Ivanov-Razumnik, V, 101.

63. Mikhailovskii, *Sochineniia*, I, 132.

64. Lavrov, *Filosofiia i sotsiologiia*, II, 26.

65. An interesting discussion of Mikhailovskii's sociological views may be found in M. M. Kovalevskii, "N. K. Mikhailovskii," pp. 192–212. See also Kolosov, pp. 135–203.

66. Lavrov, *Filosofiia i sotsiologiia*, II, 24–26.

67. *Ibid.*, p. 20.

68. Mikhailovskii, *Sochineniia*, I, 778.

69. Nevedomskii, "80-ye gody," pp. 1–8.

70. Buckle, I, 837.

71. *Ibid.*, p. 840.
72. Mikhailovskii, *Sochineniia*, I, 904.
73. *Ibid.*, III, 284.
74. *Ibid.*, p. 293.
75. *Ibid.*, I, 908.
76. For information on the varied activities of young intellectuals in the country-side, see Kropotkin, *Memoirs*, p. 302.
77. Krasnosel'skii, "Mikhailovskii o religii," pp. 56–79.
78. Andreevich, *Opyt filosofii*, p. 264.
79. Kornilov, *Obshchestvennoe dvizhenie*, pp. 149–60.
80. For details on Danilevskii's social theory and philosophy of history, see Sorokin, *Modern Historical and Social Philosophies*, pp. 48–71; and Petrovich, pp. 72–77. For details on Danilevskii's effort to give his philosophy of history a scientific foundation, see Thaden, pp. 102–15.
81. Mikhailovskii, *Sochineniia*, III, 868–69.
82. N. Ia. Danilevskii, *Rossiia i Evropa*, pp. 139–40.
83. *Ibid.*, p. 141.
84. *Ibid.*, p. 151.
85. *Ibid.*, p. 163.
86. *Ibid.*
87. *Ibid.*, pp. 166–67.

CHAPTER TWO

1. I. N. Borozdin, pp. 189–90.
2. Pirogov, *Izbrannye pedagogicheskie sochineniia*, p. 54.
3. *Ibid.*, p. 73.
4. Ushinskii, III, 26–27; Pirogov, *Izbrannye pedagogicheskie sochineniia*, p. 22.
5. Tolstoi, *Pedagogicheskie sochineniia*, p. 215.
6. Pisarev, *Sochineniia*, II, 192–93.
7. *Ibid.*, p. 193.
8. *Ibid.*, p. 223.
9. Ovsianiko-Kulikovskii, p. 91.
10. "Materialy dlia istorii i statistiki nashikh gimnazii," p. 377.
11. Kovalenskii, "Sredniaia shkola," p. 170.
12. *Ibid.*, p. 155.
13. *Ibid.*, p. 146.
14. Aleshintsev, p. 86.
15. Dzhanshiev, p. 280.
16. Chicherin, *Neskol'ko sovremennykh voprosov*, p. 30.
17. Dzhanshiev, p. 281.
18. Miliukov, "Universitety v Rossii," p. 792.
19. Rozhdestvenskii, p. 358.
20. Dzhanshiev, p. 252.
21. I. N. Borozdin, p. 197.
22. Dzhanshiev, p. 253.
23. Pirogov, *Izbrannye pedagogicheskie sochineniia*, pp. 385–86.
24. Chicherin, *Vospominaniia*, p. 29.
25. Dzhanshiev, pp. 345–46.
26. Rodzevich, p. 104.

27. Nikitenko, II, 13. For details on student unrest, see: N. I. Kostomarov, pp. 249–66; Modzalevskii, "Iz istorii," pp. 162–70.

28. Nikitenko, II, 9.

29. Dzhanshiev, p. 242.

30. Rozhdestvenskii, pp. 414–19; I. Solov'ev, "Universitetskii vopros," p. 88.

31. Chicherin, *Vospominaniia*, p. 57.

32. Dzhanshiev, p. 281.

33. "Vnutrennee obozrenie," pp. 409–16.

34. Friche, p. 145. For additional criticisms, see Kapnist, No. 11, pp. 189–90.

35. Posse, p. 14.

36. Rozhdestvenskii, p. 419.

37. Sechenov, "Nauchnaia deiatel'nost'," pp. 334–36.

38. "Po povodu mer prinimaemykh Ministerstvom Narodnogo prosveshcheniia," p. 21.

39. *Ibid.*, p. 11. Before 1849, the universities had been allowed to select the students, but the supervision of training in Western universities was conducted directly by agents of the Ministry of National Education. After 1849, Russian students were not permitted to enroll in Western universities at all.

40. Sechenov, "Nauchnaia deiatel'nost'," p. 334.

41. Modestov, pp. 73, 79.

42. Korolivskii, p. 71.

43. Friche, p. 145.

44. Droshin, pp. 1–4. See also Kapnist, No. 11.

45. Korolivskii, p. 71.

46. Pokrovskii and Rikhter, p. 86.

47. Friche, pp. 160–61.

48. Satina, pp. 101ff.

49. Rodzevich, p. 107.

50. Ivanov-Razumnik, IV, 11.

51. Lemke, pp. 261–63.

52. Nikitenko, II, 234; Blagovidov, p. 902.

53. Shelgunov, *Ocherki russkoi zhizni*, p. 473.

54. Ikonnikov, p. 114.

55. Dzhanshiev, p. 257.

56. Aleshintsev, *Soslovnyi vopros*, p. 68.

57. Chicherin, *Neskol'ko sovremennykh voprosov*, pp. 87–89.

58. Kovalenskii, "Srednaia shkola," Granat-Ist., IV, 184–85.

59. Miliukov, "Universitety v Rossii," p. 704.

60. Aleshintsev, p. 71.

61. A. S., "Organizatsiia srednei shkoly v Rossii," pp. 102ff.

62. V. Z. Smirnov, p. 305.

63. Rozhdestvenskii, pp. 506–7.

64. Shelgunov, *Izbrannye pedagogicheskie sochineniia*, p. 339.

65. I. I. Mechnikov, *Stranitsy vospominanii*, p. 81.

66. M. M. Kovalevskii, "Moskovskii universitet," p. 185.

67. Miliukov, "Universitety v Rossii," p. 795. See Liubimov, No. 12, pp. 576–611; No. 1, pp. 111–62; No. 2, pp. 779–829; No. 3, pp. 190–239.

68. M. M. Kovalevskii, "Moskovskii universitet," p. 187.

69. Eimontova, p. 187.

70. M. M. Kovalevskii, "Moskovskii universitet," pp. 180–81.

71. Sechenov, "Nauchnaia deiatel'nost'," p. 342.
72. *Ibid.*, p. 339.


CHAPTER THREE

1. Rozhdestvenskii, p. 598.
2. Veselovskii, "Otchet . . . za 1865 god," p. 19.
3. E. Shmurlo, p. 462.
4. "Novye knigi," p. 919.
5. Veselovskii, "Otchet . . . za 1865 god," pp. 39–40.
6. "Otdel'nye zamechaniia na proekt ustava," p. 178.
7. "Proekt ustava," p. 164.
8. Timiriazev, "Probuzhdenie estestvoznaniia," p. 11.
9. Sechenov, "Nauchnaia deiatel'nost'," p. 334.
10. Gordeev, pp. 115, 124.
11. Bernard, p. 52.
12. Anuchin, *O liudiakh russkoi nauki*, p. 179.
13. Gnedenko, pp. 155–56.
14. Chebyshev, *Polnoe sobranie sochinenii*, V, 401.
15. Rozhdestvenskii, p. 600; Ferliudin, p. 21.
16. Banina, p. 116.
17. V. V. Grigor'ev, p. 419.
18. *Trudy I S'ezda russkikh estestvoispytatelei*, pp. 7–48.
19. Markevich, p. 724.
20. Pogozhev, *Dvadtsatipiatiletie estestvenno-nauchnykh s'ezdov*, p. vi.
21. Omelianskii, "Razvitie estestvoznaniia," p. 121.
22. Markovnikov, *Izbrannye trudy*, pp. 685–86. The Russian Physical Society had 33 members during the first year of its existence and 55 during the second year (A. T. Grigor'ian, p. 326).
23. Markovnikov, *Izbrannye trudy*, p. 682.
24. Timiriazev, *Nekotorye osnovnye zadachi*, p. 56.
25. Rozhdestvenskii, p. 478.
26. Khodnev, p. 278. See also Oreshkin, p. 33.
27. G. V. Bykov, *Butlerov*, pp. 158–59.
28. Oreshkin, pp. 37–38.
29. Berg, *Vsesoiuznoe Geograficheskoe obshchestvo*, pp. 185–86.
30. Kadek, p. 485.
31. Anuchin, *O liudiakh russkoi nauki*, p. 84.
32. *Ibid.*, pp. 83–84. For details on Przheval'skii's contributions to geography, see A. Kozlov, pp. 301–14.
33. Kropotkin, *Memoirs*, p. 333.
34. Hooson, pp. 258–59.
35. Karl Ritter, *Zemlevedenie Azii* (St. Petersburg, 1856–79).
36. Cherniavskii, pp. 29–30.
37. Semenov also enriched the historical literature on the Emancipation period by publishing a large volume on the work of these commissions (Volume IV of his *Memuary*).
38. "Koksharov," p. 332; Omelianskii, "Razvitie estestvoznaniia," p. 129.
39. Banina, p. 36; M. N. Bogdanov, p. 36.
40. *Trudy II S'ezda russkikh estestvoispytatelei*, I, 67.

41. Goier, p. 55.
42. Stoletov, *Izbrannye sochineniia*, p. 516.
43. Butlerov, *Sochineniia*, III, 128. For more details, see Kniazev, "D. I. Mendeleev i Imperatorskaia Akademiia," pp. 27–34.
44. For additional comments see Meilakh, p. 194.
45. Figurovskii, p. 194. When news of the Mendeleev affair reached the West, a French writer noted that the day would come when the St. Petersburg Academy would make the same admission that the Academie Française had made with regard to Molière: "Rien manque à sa gloire; il manquait à la nôtre." See A. B., "Notice," p. 908.
46. Butlerov, *Sochineniia*, III, 118–38; Pisarzhevskii, *Mendeleev*, pp. 296–306.
47. Mendeleev, "Kakaia zhe akademiia nuzhna," p. 184.
48. *Trudy V S'ezda*, I, 45–46.
49. Sechenov, "Nauchnaia deiatel'nost'," p. 339; Markovnikov, *Izbrannye trudy*, p. 647.
50. Eimontova, p. 185.
51. Zalkind, pp. 25–26.
52. Helmholtz, p. 385.
53. Du Bois-Reymond, "Über die Grenzen," p. 45.
54. A lengthy review of the essay in the *Messenger of Europe* acknowledged the philosophical challenge presented by Du Bois-Reymond's *ignoramus-ignorabimus* thesis, but was inclined to interpret *ignorabimus* as meaning that the scientific path to the full explanation of such ontological entities as "matter" and "force" would of necessity be long and arduous. The reviewer made it clear that in his opinion materialistic monism was the source of the triumphs of modern science. To him, the greatest contemporary scientist was Darwin, who had shown the scientific soundness of extending the mechanistic view of physical nature to the living world. (Lovtsov, pp. 816–17.)
55. V. O. Kovalevskii, *Paleontologiia loshadei*, p. 156.
56. Stern, p. 285; Pasteur, p. 215.
57. Gnedenko, p. 157.
58. Koshtoiants, *Sechenov*, p. 12. See also *Trudy III S'ezda russkikh estestvoispytatelei*, p. 57.
59. Markovnikov, *Izbrannye trudy*, pp. 646–67; Kablukov, "Markovnikov," p. 287.
60. Timiriazev, *Nekotorye osnovnye zadachi*, pp. 27–28.

CHAPTER FOUR

1. de Beer, p. 172.
2. Davitashvili, *V. O. Kovalevskii*, p. 105.
3. Antonovich, *Charlz Darvin*, p. 234. See also Rogers, "Charles Darwin," pp. 382–83; Mikulak, pp. 362–63.
4. A. N. Beketov, "Garmoniia v prirode"; Timiriazev, *Nasushchnye zadachi*, p. 119. Beketov's article, published in 1860, was written in 1859, before the publication of Darwin's classic.
5. "Poiavlenie cheloveka na zemle," pp. 1–9. See also Sobol', "Iz istorii."
6. The beginnings of Darwinism in Russia are discussed in: Sobol', "Iz istorii" and "Pervye soobshcheniia"; V. A. Alekseev, *Osnovy darvinizma*, pp. 341ff, and *Darvinizm: Khrestomatiia*, pp. 631ff; Antonovich, *Charlz Darvin*, pp. 232–39.
7. Svatikov, "Nikolai Dmitrievich Nozhin," p. 22.
8. K. N. Davydov, pp. 344ff; L. I. Mechnikov, pp. 819–20.
9. Kolosov, pp. 30–31, 161–66, 176–80.

10. Pisarev, *Selected Philosophical, Social, and Political Essays*, p. 304.
11. For a summary of A. O. Kovalevskii's work and its broader theoretical significance, see: Bliakher, *Istoriia embriologii*, pp. 11–12, 575–76; Gel'fenbein, pp. 59ff; K. N. Davydov, "Kovalevskii," pp. 326–63; Mikulinskii, pp. 306–10; Dogel', pp. 206–18; I. I. Mechnikov, *Stranitsy vospominanii*, pp. 14–44. See also: Lankester, pp. 394–96; Shimkevich, "A. O. Kovalevskii," pp. 107–14.
12. S. V. Kovalevskaia, *Vospominaniia i pis'ma*, p. 230.
13. I. I. Mechnikov, *Akademicheskoe sobranie sochinenii*, XIV, 13.
14. Charles Darwin, *The Descent of Man*, pp. 181–82.
15. Bliakher, "Kovalevskii," p. 161.
16. Omelianskii, "Razvitie estestvoznaniia," p. 137. For biographical data and summaries of Mechnikov's contributions to embryology, see: Zalkind, pp. 40–57; Bliakher, *Istoriia embriologii,* pp. 22–27; Novikov, pp. 427–77.
17. Lankester, p. 395.
18. I. I. Mechnikov, *Biologicheskie proizvedeniia,* pp. 9–238.
19. Gamaleia, V, 20.
20. Omelianskii, "Razvitie estestvoznaniia," p. 137.
21. For a systematic study of Mechnikov's basic work in biology, see Dogel' and Gasinovich, pp. 677–725.
22. A. O. Kovalevskii, "Otzyv," pp. 135–38. See also I. I. Mechnikov, *Akademicheskoe sobranie sochinenii*, III, 173–88.
23. I. I. Mechnikov, *Biologicheskie proizvedeniia,* p. 241.
24. *Ibid.,* pp. 267–70; Besredka, pp. 9–26.
25. I. I. Mechnikov, *Stranitsy vospominanii,* pp. 77–86.
26. *Ibid.,* p. 78.
27. Balfour's *Treatise* contains many references under appropriate headings.
28. Olga Metchnikoff, p. xiii.
29. "Zalenskii," pp. 298–305; Bliakher, *Istoriia embriologii*, pp. 74–75; 159–61; Balfour, *A Treatise on Comparative Embryology, passim.* Dawydoff's *Traité* contains details of Zalenskii's embryological contributions under appropriate headings.
30. Simpson, *Life of the Past,* pp. 142–43.
31. For a full list of translated works published by Kovalevskii, see Davitashvili, *V. O. Kovalevskii,* pp. 548–52.
32. *Ibid.,* p. 37.
33. Borisiak, *Kovalevskii,* pp. 68–69. For brief summaries of V. O. Kovalevskii's scientific work, see Borisiak, "Kovalevskii," pp. 27–46; Davitashvili, "Kovalevskii," pp. 23–32.
34. V. O. Kovalevskii, *Sobranie nauchnykh trudov,* I, 70.
35. W. Kowalewsky, pp. 154–55.
36. Simpson, *Horses,* pp. 87–88; Watson, p. 48.
37. Simpson, *Tempo and Mode in Evolution,* p. 103.
38. Osborn, p. 8.
39. Borisiak, *Kovalevskii,* p. 123.
40. Francis Darwin, III, 73.
41. The first volume of *Variation* appeared in a Russian translation in May 1867; the English original was published in January 1868.
42. I. I. Mechnikov, *Stranitsy vospominanii,* p. 49.
43. Shaternikov, p. xxiii.
44. Krylov, *Moi vospominaniia,* p. 27.
45. Sechenov, "Nauchnaia deiatel'nost'," p. 334.

46. For brief modern assessments of Sechenov's theory of the central inhibitory mechanism, see: Fearing, pp. 191–94; Livingston, pp. 58–60.

47. Sechenov, *Selected Works*, p. 176.

48. Rothschub, p. 120.

49. Sechenov, *Selected Works*, p. 334.

50. *Ibid.*, p. 34.

51. N. E. Vvedenskii, "Pamiati Sechenova," pp. 52–56.

52. I. I. Mechnikov, *Stranitsy vospominanii*, p. 46; Bogdanovich, pp. 421–38; Iaroshevskii, pp. 118–21.

53. Chicherin, *Vospominaniia*, pp. 124–25.

54. Mendeleev, *Sochineniia*, XXIV, 234.

55. Shaternikov, p. xxv.

56. Meek, p. 33.

57. For a summary of the basic criticisms of Sechenov's work, see Stadlin, pp. 834–82.

58. N. E. Vvedenskii, "Sechenov," pp. 77–78.

59. For a brief survey of Timiriazev's major scientific activities, see: Ivanov and Platonov, pp. 173–91; Beale, pp. 51–53.

60. Timiriazev, *Izbrannye raboty po khlorofillu*, pp. 7–16.

61. Rabinowitch, pp. 1142–43.

62. Krasheninnikov, pp. 1024–25.

63. Bogorad, p. 70.

64. Timiriazev, *Darvin i ego uchenie*, pp. 35–40.

65. Timiriazev, *Life of the Plant*, pp. 9–10.

66. *Ibid.*, p. 10.

## CHAPTER FIVE

1. Butlerov, *Sochineniia*, III, 86.

2. Mendeleev, "Voskresenskii," p. 244.

3. Val'den, *Ocherk istorii khimii*, pp. 429–30. For details on Engelhardt's activities, see Gerchikov, pp. 951–54.

4. Timiriazev, "Probuzhdenie estestvoznaniia," p. 11.

5. *Ibid.*

6. Mendeleev, *Sochineniia*, XVIII, 19.

7. Markovnikov, "Moskovskaia rech'," pp. 143–44.

8. Gustavson, "Butlerov," pp. 58–59.

9. Grigor'ev, pp. 355–56.

10. Markovnikov, "Moskovskaia rech'," p. 158.

11. Gustavson, "Butlerov," p. 59.

12. Butlerov, *Sochineniia*, III, 294.

13. Romanovich-Slavatinskii, p. 538.

14. Zaitsev, p. 28.

15. G. V. Bykov, *Butlerov*, p. 40; Partington, pp. 281, 316.

16. Leicester, "Butlerov," p. 208.

17. Butlerov, *Sochineniia*, I, 70; Kazansky and Bykov, pp. 5, 44–53.

18. *Ibid.*, pp. 73–74.

19. Hjelt, pp. 278, 281. According to Linus Pauling: "In 1861 the Russian chemist A. M. Butlerov used the term 'chemical structure' for the first time, and stated that it is essential to express the structure by a single formula, which should show how each

atom is linked to other atoms in the molecule of the substance. He stated clearly that all properties of a compound are determined by the molecular structure of the substance and suggested that it should be possible to find the correct structural formula of a substance by studying the ways in which it can be synthesized." (Pauling, p. 4.) According to O. T. Benfey, Butlerov "was probably the first to sense the full implications and potentialities of the structural theory of organic chemistry. He calculated the number of isomers of a given molecular formula, and used the theory as a guide to the synthesis of important classes of organic compounds. He used the term 'chemical structure' to designate 'the type and manner of the mutual binding of atoms in a compound substance' and insisted, contrary to the followers of the type theory, that there was only one structure for each compound." (Benfey, pp. 173–74.) See also: Leicester, "Contributions," pp. 328–29; G. V. Bykov, *Istoriia*, pp. 72–90.

20. Markovnikov, *Izbrannye trudy*, pp. 102–3; Kazansky and Bykov, pp. 102–10.

21. Leicester, "Contributions of Butlerov," pp. 328–29.

22. In 1885, eighteen months before his death, Butlerov had about thirty disciples, all trained in his Kazan and St. Petersburg laboratories and all interested in the experimental elaboration and amplification of the theory of chemical structure (M. L., "Butlerov," pp. 80–82).

23. Leicester, "Markovnikov," pp. 53–57. In "Contemporary Chemistry and Russian Chemical Industry," a speech delivered in 1880, Markovnikov asserted that Russian scientific institutions had far too little working contact with industry, and urged industrial firms to establish research laboratories. Toward the end of the century, many of his students were employed in industry. (Markovnikov, *Izbrannye trudy*, pp. 637–76; I. A. Kablukov, "Markovnikov," pp. 287–88.)

24. G. V. Bykov, "Zabytye izdaniia," pp. 74–84; S. F. Glinka, p. 195.

25. A. V. G., "Chetvertoe izmerenie i spiritizm," pp. 253–71; Butlerov, "Chetvertoe izmerenie," pp. 945–71, and "Mediumicheskiia iavleniia," pp. 300–348.

26. B. G., "Butlerov," p. 532.

27. Mendeléeff, *Principles*, II, 16.

28. Kedrov, "Otkrytie periodicheskogo zakona," p. 46. An interpretive review of Mendeleev's work leading to the discovery of the periodic law is given in Kedrov, *Den' odnogo velikogo otkrytiia*.

29. Mendeléeff, *Principles*, II, 24–25.

30. For a detailed discussion of the reception of the periodic law by Russian chemists, see Kedrov, *Filosofskii analiz*, pp. 239–49.

31. Izmailov, pp. 67–72.

32. Pisarzhevsky, *Dmitry Ivanovich Mendeleyev*, pp. 44–45. For a brief survey of main trends in the development of physical chemistry in Russia during the 1860's, see Iu. I. Solov'ev, *Ocherki po istorii fizicheskoi khimii*, pp. 42–52.

33. Mendeléeff, *Principles*, II, 419.

34. Vol'fkovich, p. 8.

35. Mladentsev and Tishchenko, I, 225.

36. Pogodin, "Otkrytie periodicheskogo zakona," p. 37.

37. Sechenov, *Avtobiograficheskie zapiski*, pp. 96–97.

38. For Mendeleev's description of this congress, see Mladentsev and Tishchenko, I, 250–58.

39. Mendeleev, *Rastvory*, pp. 381–82; Figurovskii, pp. 170–87; Pisarzhevskii, *Dmitrii Ivanovich Mendeleev*, pp. 253–68.

40. Mendeleev, *Sochineniia*, VIII, 44.

41. Rutherford, p. 635.

42. Thorpe, p. 195.
43. Mendeleev, *Problemy ekonomicheskogo razvitiia Rossii*, pp. 131–33.
44. Gusev, p. 560. Mendeleev's work on applied economics is discussed in Skvortsov, pp. 65–71.
45. There is no unanimity in the interpretation of Mendeleev's philosophy by Soviet scholars. To most of them, the periodic table as interpreted by Mendeleev is "dialectical" in a logical rather than a historical sense. The following is a typical Soviet summation of the "dialectical" elements in Mendeleev's thought: "In his scientific work Mendeleev employed many elements of dialectics. He recognized the qualitatively different motions of matter and the relations between them, and he criticized metaphysical efforts to reduce the diversity of the universe to a single primary matter. In the periodic law, he called attention to qualitative leaps in chemical transformations that depend on changes in mass or atomic weight. He pointed out the unity of contradictory properties in each element, and determined the place of each discrete element in a general pattern representing the unity of elements. He applied analysis and synthesis, induction and deduction, as parts of a dialectical unity.... However, he rejected any idea of change in individual chemical elements." (Karpovits and Makarenia, p. 386.) See also: Kedrov, *Filosofskii analiz*, pp. 105–6, 119–21; Ionidi, pp. 310ff. Some Soviet scholars admit that Mendeleev's scientific orientation was essentially alien to dialectical materialism. (Kuznetsov, *Ocherki istorii russkoi nauki*, pp. 94–95; Zabrodskii, p. 95.)
46. Mendeleev, *Sochineniia*, XXIII, 97–98.
47. In the words of a modern Russian chemist, Mendeleev was a philosopher in chemistry and physics and a scientist in philosophy and economics. Chugaev, *Mendeleev*, p. 16.
48. Mendeleev, *Sochineniia*, XV, 149.
49. Mendeleev, "Mirovozzrenie," p. 161.
50. Mendeleev, "Veshchestvo," p. 161.
51. Mendeleev, "Mirovozzrenie," pp. 161–62.
52. Mendeleev, *Sochineniia*, XXIII, 234–35.
53. *Ibid.*, p. 93.
54. Mendeleev, *K poznaniiu Rossii*, p. 50.
55. A. I. Mendeleeva, p. 56.
56. Mladentsev and Tishchenko, I, 259.
57. Mendeleev, *Sochineniia*, XX, 248.
58. *Ibid.*, XXIV, 18.
59. *Ibid.*, p. 14.
60. Mendeleev, *Problemy*, p. 102.
61. Mendeleev, "Voskresenskii," p. 243.
62. Mendeléeff, *Principles*, I, 17.
63. *Ibid.*, II, 17.
64. Mendeleev, *Zavetnye mysli*, p. 280.
65. Rutherford, p. 635. For a more personal assessment of Mendeleev as a man and a scholar, see the works by Trigorova-Mendeleeva and A. I. Mendeleeva, two members of his family.
66. Veselovskii, "Otchet ... za 1869 god," p. 4.
67. Prudnikov, p. 137.
68. *Ibid.*, p. 138.
69. Prudnikov, *P. L. Chebyshev*, M. 1950, p. 21.
70. Bertrand, 335ff, 512ff.
71. Todhunter, pp. 111–39, 350–52, 482.

72. Znamenskii, II, 88.
73. [P. L. Chebyshev], *Nauchnoe nasledie*, II, 72.
74. Chebyshev, *Polnoe sobranie sochinenii*, V, 247.
75. *Ibid.*, I, 15.
76. For an explanation of the law of large numbers, see: Keynes, 353–57; Gnedenko and Khinchin, pp. 93–99, 119; Vassilieff, pp. 36ff; A. D. Aleksandrov *et al.*, II, 238–47.
77. Uspensky, p. 13.
78. Posse, p. 13.
79. Schaeffer, p. 668.
80. Lobatchewsky, *Etudes géométriques* (Paris, 1866).
81. Hoüel, *Essai critique*.
82. Merz, II, 714.
83. Helmholtz, pp. 223–49.
84. Clifford, *Lectures and Essays*, I, 356.
85. Newman, I, 550–51.
86. Poincaré, *Foundations of Science*, p. 60.
87. *Ibid.*, p. 83.
88. Russell, p. 21. See also Clifford, *The Common Sense of the Exact Sciences*, p. xli.
89. Even many years later, A. M. Liapunov spoke on behalf of the St. Petersburg school of mathematics when he attacked Riemann's "pseudo-geometrical" ideas for their "total impracticality." (Liapunov, "Zhizn' i trudy P. L. Chebysheva," p. 20.)
90. Butlerov, "Chetvertoe izmerenie," pp. 945–71.
91. Ianishevskii, p. 55.
92. For a brief survey on Lobachevskii's influence on the mathematicians of Kazan University, see: Kiro, pp. 179–83; Kol'man, p. 99.
93. Nevskaia, p. 50.
94. Flammarion, pp. 524–25; Newcomb and Engelmann, pp. 448–52; Clerke, pp. 346–48.
95. Ball, p. 454.
96. Gadolin, *Abhandlung*.
97. Nikiforov, p. 189.
98. "Izvlechenie is protokolov zasedanii Akademii," pp. 51–52.
99. Shafranovskii, *Istoriia kristallografii*, p. 151.
100. Vernadskii, "Koksharov," p. 331; Veselovskii, "Otchet . . . za 1865 god," p. 16.
101. Vernadskii, "Pamiati Koksharova," pp. 506–10.
102. Kompaneets, *Mirovozzrenie A. G. Stoletova*, pp. 56–60; Omelianskii, "Razvitie estestvoznaniia," p. 126.

CHAPTER SIX

1. Bagalei *et al.*, pp. 239–40.
2. Friche, pp. 145–46. For the instructions given this commission, see Liubimov, No. 12, p. 607.
3. Friche, p. 148.
4. *Sbornik postanovlenii Ministerstva Narodnogo prosveshcheniia*, X (1894), 881.
5. Pazukhin, p. 25.
6. Kornilov, *Kurs*, III, 299.
7. Berdiaev, "Filosofskaia istina," p. 11.
8. For a semiofficial interpretation of the Statute, see "Novaia era," pp. 938–42.
9. For analytical details on various aspects of the Statute, see: Friche, pp. 151–52;

Omelianskii, "Razvitie estestvoznaniia," pp. 118–19; Rozhdestvenskii, pp. 615–22; M. N. Tikhomirov, I, 272–73; Glinskii, "Universitetskie ustavy," pp. 324–51, 718–42; Miklashevskii, pp. 1–20; Svatikov, "Opal'naia professura 80 gg."

10. Rozhdestvenskii, pp. 617–18.

11. "The university statute of 1884," wrote the historian A. A. Kizevetter, "brought some useful innovations, such as the institution of private docents, but it completely eliminated university autonomy; it brought to an end the independence of the academic councils, invalidated the right of professors to elect rectors and deans, and transformed the higher university officials into government bureaucrats. . . . The reactionaries were jubilant, for they saw in the new university statute an unmistakable symptom of the general orientation of government policies toward replacing all liberal influences with autocratic bureaucracy." Kizevetter, p. 133.

12. P. G. Vinogradov, "Uchebnoe delo," pp. 554–55.

13. Korolivskii et al., pp. 79–80.

14. Vitte, I, 302.

15. Lomonosovskii sbornik (Moscow), p. 7. See also: Glinskii, pp. 329ff; A. S., "Organizatsiia srednei shkoly," pp. 105–6; Famintsyn, "Nakanune universitetskoi reformy," pp. 238–55; P. G. Vinogradov, "Uchebnoe delo," pp. 537–73.

16. Friche, p. 153.

17. S. N. Trubetskoi, "Universitet i studenchestvo," p. 182. For a general account of the principal student groups, see Kapnist, No. 11, pp. 194–208.

18. "Khronika," p. 89.

19. Speranskii, pp. 115–16.

20. Timiriazev, Nauka i demokratiia, pp. 41–44.

21. Trubetskoi, Sobranie sochinenii, I, 140. See also N. Davydov, p. 31.

22. A. A. Tikhomirov, Ob'iasnitel'naia zapiska, pp. 1, 6–7.

23. Grimm, "Organizatsiia universitetskogo upravleniia," p. 65.

24. Korolivskii et al., p. 138.

25. M. N. Tikhomirov, I, 532.

26. From 1905 to 1911 the academic council of Moscow University ordered a temporary closing of the university on only two occasions. "Polozhenie del v Moskovskom universitete," p. 155.

27. Timiriazev, Nauka i demokratiia, p. 59.

28. Speranskii, p. 129.

29. Odinetz and Novgorodtsev, p. 151.

30. Bagalei, "Ekonomicheskoe polozhenie."

31. Vernadskii, "Vysshaia shkola v Rossii," pp. 311–12.

32. Timiriazev, Nauka i demokratiia, pp. 56–66.

33. For the educational philosophy and eventual fate of the projected charter, see Grimm, "Organizatsiia universitetskogo prepodavaniia," pp. 110–22. The charter's principles for university administration are set forth in Grimm, "Organizatsiia universitetskogo upravleniia," pp. 52–67.

34. Odinetz and Novgorodtsev, pp. 180–81.

35. I. Solov'ev, "Avtonomiia," p. 219.

36. Berdiaev, "Filosofskaia istina," p. 11.

37. Bagalei, "Ekonomicheskoe polozhenie," p. 222. See also Rostovtsev, "Nauka i revoliutsiia," pp. 4–5.

38. Omelianskii, "Razvitie estestvoznaniia," p. 143.

39. Modestov, p. 91; Timiriazev, Nasushchnye zadachi, p. 6.

40. *O-MU*, 1910, pp. 179–82; Bagalei, "Ekonomicheskoe polozhenie," pp. 222ff. The natural-science majors in Moscow University made up 27 per cent of the total enrollment in 1901, and 30 per cent in 1914. V. V. Danilevskii, pp. 385–86.

41. "Vysshee obrazovanie," pp. 508–9. These data, and similar figures in the following pages, cover not only state-supported institutions, but also many schools that depended largely on private donations (e.g., the Higher Courses for Women, which were located in all major cities of the empire). Rashin, p. 77.

42. Miliukov, "Universitety v Rossii," p. 799.

43. For data on the social origin of the students at St. Petersburg and Khar'kov Universities during the 1890's, see Miklashevskii, pp. 13–14. In 1904 at St. Petersburg, the most aristocratic of all the universities, 60.9 per cent of the students came from the families of the aristocracy and high government officials, and 19.5 per cent from the families of honorary citizens, entrepreneurial groups, and the clergy. Erman, p. 173. For general information on this subject, see Rashin, p. 78.

44. V. V. Bogdanov, p. 8.

45. *Ibid.*, p. 16.

46. *O-MU*, 1911, p. 293.

47. Markevich, p. 724.

48. *Obzor deiatel'nosti S. Peterburgskogo Obshchestva estestvoispytatelei*, pp. 14–17.

49. *Ibid.*, pp. 204–5.

50. Other leading societies of this type were the Khar'kov Mathematical Society (founded 1879), the St. Petersburg Mathematical Society (1890), and the Kazan Physical and Mathematical Society (1890).

51. Val'den, *Nauka i zhizn'*, I, 86.

52. A. T. Grigor'ian, *Istoriia estestvoznaniia*, II, 332.

53. Korolivskii *et al.*, p. 135. For similar information on St. Petersburg University in 1911, see *O-StPU*, 1911, pp. 47–49.

54. *O-StPU*, 1911, pp. 51–68.

55. Kovanov *et al.*, p. 32.

56. S. A. Fedorov, "Znachenie i trudy N. A. Umova," pp. 43–50; Bachinskii, "Zamechatel'nyi russkii uchenyi," pp. 31–32.

57. S. A. Fedorov, "Pamiati Ledentsova," p. 42.

58. "Deiatel'nost Obshchestva za pervuiu polovinu 1911 g.," p. 16.

59. Zagoskin, I, vi.

60. "Bibliograficheskii listok," p. 437.

61. Shpol'skii, *Sorok let sovetskoi fiziki*, p. 13; Shuleikin, *Petr Petrovich Lazarev*, p. 43.


CHAPTER SEVEN

1. "Anuchin," p. 2.

2. "Vernadskii," p. 152.

3. B. N. Menshutkin, p. 190; Ostrovitianov, II, 466; Kniazev, "Poritsanie akademikam," pp. 13–22.

4. *Ob otmene stesnenii malorusskogo pechatnogo slova*, p. 28.

5. *OAN*, 1905, pp. 6–7.

6. For a sample of the philosophically oriented studies written by Academy members, see: Vernadskii, "O nauchnom mirovozzrenii," and "Kant i estestvoznanie v XVIII stoletii"; N. N. Beketov, *Nauka i nravstvennost'*; I. P. Borodin, pp. 1–28;

Lappo-Danilevskii, "Osnovnye printsipi sotsiologicheskoi doktrini O. Konta," pp. 394–490, and *Metodologiia istorii*; Famintsyn, *Sovremennoe estestvoznanie i psikhologiia* (St. Petersburg, 1898).

7. *OAN*, 1913, p. 7.

8. Ostrovitianov, II, 658.

9. *MIAU*, I, 225–26.

10. *OAN*, 1906, pp. 11–12.

11. Vorontsov-Vel'iaminov, pp. 59–60.

12. *OAN*, 1905, pp. 5–6.

13. *MIAU*, I, 59.

14. Kniazev and Kol'tsov, pp. 65–66.

15. Vernadskii, *O blizhaishikh zadachakh*, p. 6. See also Vernadskii, "Ob ispol'-zovanii," p. 75.

16. Iu. I. Solov'ev and Zviagintsev, pp. 86ff.

17. For a comment by Academician A. N. Krylov, see Shimanskii, *Pamiati Krylova*, p. 136.

18. Vernadskii, *Ocherki*, I, 28–31.

19. Iu. I. Solov'ev and Zviagintsev, p. 91.

20. *Otchety deiatel'nosti Komissii po izucheniiu estestvennykh proizvoditel'nykh sil Rossii*, pp. 147–55.

21. *OAN*, 1915, pp. 11–12.

22. For a brief but pertinent review of the basic achievements and activities of the Geographical Society during the first fifty years of its existence, see A-v-s-v, "Russkoe Geograficheskoe obshchestvo," pp. 139–44. For a detailed report, see P. P. Semenov [Tian-Shanskii], *Istoriia*.

23. Popov, pp. 65–77; Obruchev, *Istoriia*, pp. 28–29.

24. W. G. Bogoras, *The Chukchee* (*Memoirs of the American Museum of Natural History*, Vol. XI, Parts 1–3, 1904–9); V. I. Jochelson, *The Koryak* (*ibid.*, Vol. VI, Parts 1–2, 1905–8) and *The Yukaghir and the Yukaghirized Tungus* (*ibid.*, Vol. XIII, Parts 1–3, 1910–26). For a brief survey of the role of Siberian exiles in the development of ethnography, see Tokarev, pp. 374–79.

25. Petri, pp. 329–40; A. Sokolov, pp. 294–328; Krotov, pp. 341–48. See also Berg, *Vsesoiuznoe Geograficheskoe obshchestvo*, pp. 195–99.

26. Esakov, p. 126.

27. A. I. Solov'ev, p. 42.

28. Berg, *Izbrannye trudy*, I, 198–203.

29. For biographical data on Berg and his relations to the Geographical Society, see: Berg, "Avtobiograficheskaia zapiska"; N. N. Sokolov, "Lev Semenovich Berg"; Gerasimov *et al.*, "L. S. Berg v Geograficheskom obshchestve"; Dobzhansky, Foreword to *Nomogenesis*, pp. xi–xii.

30. See V. V. Semenov-Tian-Shanskii, pp. 38–48.

31. Quoted in Berg, *Izbrannye trudy*, I, 235.

32. Anuchin, "Geografiia," p. 389.

33. For information on Anuchin's scientific activities, see: Levin, "Dmitrii Nikolaevich Anuchin"; Tolstov, "Anuchin—etnograf"; Kiselev, "Anuchin—arkheolog"; "Anuchin" (autobiographical note); A. A. Grigor'ev, "Dmitrii Nikolaevich Anuchin"; Berg, *Izbrannye trudy*, I, 225–48; Berg, *Istoriia*, pp. 233–63.

34. V. V. Kozlov, p. 303.

35. "Zapiski Russkogo Tekhnicheskogo obshchestva," pp. 535–37.

36. V. V. Kozlov, pp. 304–5.

37. *Ibid.*, p. 310.
38. For a quick survey of the Society's diverse activities, see V. M. Kostomarov, pp. 12–30.
39. "Obshchestva meditsinskie," pp. 621–22.
40. Kapustin, p. 98.
41. Ossipow *et al.*, pp. 126–27.
42. *Ibid.*, p. 138; Pogozhev, *Dvadtsat'piatiletie estestvennonauchnykh s'ezdov*, pp. 341–45.
43. Zabludovskii, p. 347.
44. Gran *et al.*, p. 152.
45. *Pirogovskii s'ezd po bor'be s kholeroi*, II, 210; Zabludovskii, p. 337; Dembo, p. 2.
46. *Deviatyi Pirogovskii s'ezd*, II, 81–83. See also: Kapustin, pp. 97–98; Mitskevich, pp. 290–94.
47. Berthelot, p. 139.

CHAPTER EIGHT

1. Mokievskii, p. 69. See also: A. I. Vvedenskii, *Filosofskie ocherki*, pp. 36–37; V. S. Solov'ev, VIII, 427.
2. Strakhov, *Iz istorii literaturnogo nigilizma*, pp. 123–24.
3. Chicherin, *Nauka i religiia*, p. 100.
4. *Ibid.*, p. vii.
5. *Ibid.*, p. 211.
6. *Ibid.*, p. 509.
7. Chicherin, *Mistitsizm v nauke*, pp. 180–82.
8. Chicherin, *Polozhitel'naia filosofiia*, pp. 139, 251, 317.
9. *Ibid.*, p. 272.
10. Evgenii Trubetskoi, pp. 656–57.
11. V. S. Solov'ev, I, 26–144.
12. *Ibid.*, pp. 143–44.
13. *Ibid.*, V, 87.
14. *Ibid.*
15. Lopatin, *Filosofskie kharakteristiki*, p. 126.
16. Evgenii Trubetskoi, pp. 651 52.
17. Radlov, "Solov'ev," p. x.
18. For a breakdown of the major orientations in Russian idealistic philosophy at this time, see Kudriavtsev, I, 79–81.
19. For a perceptive analysis of Berdiaev's switch from Marxism to mysticism, see Arthur Mendel, *Dilemmas*, pp. 194–212.
20. Vernadskii, *Ocherki*, I, 97.
21. S. N. Trubetskoi, *Sobranie sochinenii*, IV, 1.
22. Berdiaev, *Sub specie aeternitatis*, p. 4.
23. *Ibid.*, p. 6.
24. *Ibid.*, p. 31.
25. Berdiaev, "Gnoseologicheskaia problema," p. 289.
26. Bulgakov, p. 3. See also Berdiaev, "Bor'ba za idealizm," p. 12.
27. Berdiaev, *Sub specie aeternitatis*, pp. 155–56. S. Frank thought that "concrete idealism" became the most advanced philosophical orientation of modern time in Henri Bergson's *Creative Evolution*. Frank, p. 38.
28. Berdiaev, *Sub specie aeternitatis*, pp. 1, 197.

29. *Ibid.*, p. 137.
30. *Ibid.*, p. 219.
31. Berdiaev, "Filosofskaia istina," p. 12.
32. Berdiaev, "Vera i znanie," p. 232.
33. Berdiaev, *Sub specie aeternitatis*, pp. 218–19.
34. *Ibid.*, p. 131.
35. Berdiaev, "Eticheskaia problema," p. 103.
36. *Ibid.*, p. 107.
37. Vernadskii, *Ocherki*, II, 95–96; N. N. Beketov, *Rechi khimika*, pp. 164–65.
38. M. M. Rubinshtein, p. 2.
39. Kudriavtsev, I, 79–81.
40. Berdiaev, *Filosofiia neravenstva*, pp. 133–49.
41. *Ibid.*, p. 146.
42. Berdiaev, "Khomiakov," p. 22.
43. A. I. Vvedenskii, "Kritiko-filosofskii analiz," pp. 1–44, and "K voprosu o stroenii materii," pp. 18–65, 191–220.
44. A. I. Vvedenskii, "K voprosu o stroenii materii," pp. 2–3.
45. A. I. Vvedenskii, *Filosofskie ocherki*, pp. 157–213.
46. *Ibid.*, p. 96.
47. A. I. Vvedenskii, "K voprosu o stroenii materii," p. 204.
48. *Ibid.*, pp. 207–8.
49. *Ibid.*, p. 220.
50. Vvedenskii's attack on experimental psychology was supported by E. L. Radlov, who singled out the "naturalist epistemology" underlying I. M. Sechenov's physiological approach for a special attack. Radlov, "Naturalisticheskaia teoriia," pp. 682–93.
51. A. I. Vvedenskii, *Filosofskie ocherki*, pp. 30–32, and "K voprosu o stroenii materii," pp. 4–65.
52. Berdiaev, "Lange," pp. 251–52.
53. Iakovenko, pp. 62–70.
54. Lopatin, "Nauchnoe mirovozzrenie," p. 477.
55. Lesevich, "Filosofskoe nasledie," pp. 232–33. For a discusion of the positivist legacy and its role in the struggle against revived mysticism, see M. Filippov, "Kont i ego uchenie," pp. 552–95.
56. Lesevich, *Sobranie sochinenii*, I, 11–12.
57. Lesevich, "Chto takoe nauchnaia filosofiia?," 1889, No. 11, pp. 7, 15.
58. Lesevich, "Filosofskoe nasledie," pp. 232–33.
59. Chernov, "Sub'ektivnyi metod," No. 7, p. 234.
60. *Ibid.*, p. 236.
61. *Ibid.*, p. 242.
62. *Ibid.*, No. 8, p. 252.
63. *Ibid.*, No. 12, p. 124.
64. *Ibid.*, p. 125.
65. Mach, p. 243.
66. A. A. Bogdanov, "Ideal poznaniia," p. 189. See also A. A. Bogdanov, *Empiriomonizm*, I, 9–11.
67. A. A. Bogdanov, "Zhizn' i psikhika," p. 707.
68. A. A. Bogdanov, *Filosofiia zhivogo opyta*, p. 147.
69. For a brief clarification of Bogdanov's position between "the radicalism of Empiriocriticism" and "Plekhanov's opportunism," see A. A. Bogdanov, "Strana idolov," pp. 215–42, and *Padenie*, pp. 176–80.

70. A. A. Bogdanov, *Prikliucheniia*, p. 25.

71. *Ibid.*, p. 4.

72. See, for example: Bazarov, pp. 3–71; P. Iushkevich, pp. 162–214.

73. A. A. Bogdanov, *Iz psikhologii obshchestva*, pp. 38ff.

74. P. Iushkevich, pp. 206–9; A. A. Bogdanov, "Strana idolov," p. 242; Berman, pp. 219–26; Suvorov, pp. 62–70.

75. As cited in Gay, p. 142.

76. Lange, p. 360.

77. Gay, p. 29.

78. Bernstein, *Evolutionary Socialism*, pp. 223–24.

79. Bernstein, *Zur Geschichte und Theorie des Sozialismus*, pp. 338–66.

80. *Ibid.*, p. 297.

81. Haimson, p. 52.

82. *Ibid.*, p. 53.

83. Mach, p. 30.

84. Lunacharskii, *Otkliki zhizni*, p. vi.

85. For the first systematic Russian presentation of Avenarius's philosophy, see M. Filippov, "O filosofii chistogo opyta."

86. Lunacharskii, *Religiia i sotsializm*, I, 394–95.

87. Lenin, XIV, 117.

88. *Ibid.*, p. 39.

89. *Ibid.*, p. 268.

90. *Ibid.*, p. 248.

91. *Ibid.*, p. 299.

92. *Ibid.*, p. 294.

93. *Ibid.*, p. 295.

94. Plekhanov, *Izbrannye filosofskie sochineniia*, III, 67–88.

95. *Ibid.*, pp. 202–301. A third letter to Bogdanov, written in 1910, is also included.

96. Lenin, XXXIII, 206.

CHAPTER NINE

1. Mikulinskii, p. 438.

2. Bazilevskaia, p. 122.

3. K. E. von Baer, *Reden*, II, 235–479. For a brief summary of von Baer's attacks on Darwinism, see Raikov, pp. 393–412. Von Baer had begun by attacking specific aspects of Darwin's theory. Darwin himself, in his *Descent of Man*, had predicted that the work of the Russian embryologist A. O. Kovalevskii would eventually discover a probable link between the vertebrates and the invertebrates. Von Baer subjected Kovalevskii's studies of ascidians to relentless criticism; and in 1873 he categorically rejected any phylogenetic interpretation of them. He was particularly bitter toward the "dilettantes" who saw any connection between the ascidians and man.

4. N. Ia. Danilevskii, *Darvinizm*, Vol. I, Pt. 2, pp. 493–504.

5. Timiriazev, *Nasushchnye zadachi*, p. 187.

6. For additional details on Danilevskii's ideas, see: Raikov, pp. 14–21; V. A. Alekseev, *Osnovy darvinizma*, pp. 356–58.

7. N. N. Strakhov, "Polnoe oproverzhenie," p. 62.

8. *Ibid.*, p. 33.

9. A. Borozdin, p. 68.

10. *Ibid.*, p. 69.

11. V. S. Solov'ev, V, 130.

12. Timiriazev, "Oprovergnut li darvinizm?," p. 221.

13. *Ibid.*, pp. 277–79.

14. N. N. Strakhov, "Vsegdashniaia oshibka darvinistov," No. 12, p. 107.

15. *Ibid.*, p. 125.

16. Timiriazev, "Bessil'naia zloba antidarvinista," pp. 411–12.

17. Timiriazev, *Sochineniia*, VI, 3–237.

18. *Ibid.*, p. 235.

19. Timiriazev, *Nasushchnye zadachi,* p. 158. For a brief survey of Timiriazev's criticism of Mendel's theory, see Z. I. Berman *et al.*, pp. 275–76.

20. For a summary of antimechanistic arguments, see Rozanov, "Organicheskii protsess," pp. 1–22.

21. Korzhinskii, *Chto takoe zhizn'?*, p. 46.

22. *Ibid.*, p. 47.

23. Famintsyn, "Danilevskii i darvinizm."

24. *Ibid.*, p. 643.

25. *Ibid.*, pp. 635–37.

26. I. P. Borodin, "Protoplazma i vitalizm." See also Ognev, "Vitalizm," pp. 689–92.

27. Timiriazev, *Nekotorye osnovnye zadachi*, p. 267.

28. Timiriazev, *Nasushchnye zadachi*, p. 205.

29. Famintsyn, *Sovremennoe estestvoznanie*, p. 26. See also: Ognev, "Vitalizm," pp. 705–16; A. A. Borisiak, "Vitalizm."

30. Famintsyn, *Sovremennoe estestvoznanie*, pp. 74–75.

31. Mikulinskii, pp. 260–61; Ganin, "Iadro kletki."

32. Menzbir, "Glavneishie predstaviteli darvinizma," No. 12, p. 55.

33. Timiriazev, *Sochineniia,* VI, 265.

34. De Vries, p. 399.

35. Korzhinskii, "Geterogenezis i evoliutsiia," *ZAN*, pp. 1–3, and "Geterogenezis i evoliutsiia (predvaritel'noe soobshchenie)."

36. Shmal'gauzen, pp. 24–25.

37. Timiriazev, *Nauka i demokratiia*, pp. 156–61. For another analysis of Mendel's theory, see L. P. Kravets, pp. 721–44. A more conciliatory attitude is expressed in A. A. Gurvich, "Problemy nasledstvennosti," pp. 843–62, and "Problemy i uspekhi ucheniia o nasledstvennosti," pp. 371–94. In 1905, V. M. Shimkevich accepted both gradualist and mutationist explanations, but asserted that the gradualist theories were much more common. Shimkevich, "Teoriia mutatsii," pp. 16–28.

38. Timiriazev, *Nauka i demokratiia*, p. 138.

39. Timiriazev, *Sochineniia*, VIII, 78.

40. Timiriazev, *Nauka i demokratiia*, p. 160.

41. *Ibid.*, pp. 186–87; George Darwin, p. 547.

42. Plekhanov, *Izbrannye filosofskie proizvedeniia*, III, 149–50.

43. Skripchinskii, pp. 105–16.

44. Vavilov, "Immunity to Fungous Diseases."

45. Vavilov, *The Origin*, p. 75.

46. Vavilov, *Izbrannye trudy*, I, 23. For a brief summary of Vavilov's work and personal history, see Dobzhansky, "N. I. Vavilov," pp. 227–32.

47. Menzbir, "Ocherk uspekhov biologii," p. 91.

48. *Ibid.*, p. 92.

49. A. A. Tikhomirov, *Sud'ba darvinizma*, p. 3.

50. A. A. Tikhomirov, *Polozhenie cheloveka v prirode*, p. 5.

51. Chemen, p. 486. See also: Rumiantsev, "Darvinizm"; Glagolev, *O proiskhozhdenii*, pp. 275–76. For an interesting review of the Russian theological criticism of Darwinism, see G. L. Kline, "Darwinism."

52. Kapterev, "Teleologiia neolamarkistov."

53. Glagolev, "Botanika i darvinizm," pp. 71–72, and "Mendelizm."

54. Severtsov, *Sobranie sochinenii*, pp. 206–8. V. V. Zalenskii (pp. 665–91) adduced many examples from embryology in support of the thesis that evolution is actually an organic synthesis of "progress" and "regress" in the development of organisms.

55. Severtsov presented his general evolutionary ideas in his *Etiudy po teorii evoliutsii*, in which he set forth the principles that two decades later were incorporated in his "morphological theory of evolution." For an analysis of Severtsov's evolutionary theory before 1917, see L. B. Severtsova, pp. 330–36. For a modern view on Severtsov's theory, see Matveev, "Progress i regress."

56. Palladin, pp. xxxv, 13.

57. Review of R. G. Punnett, *Mendelizm*, p. 300.

58. Regel', "Selektsiia s nauchnoi tochki zreniia," p. 538; Berg, *Nomogenesis*, p. 69.

59. I. P. Pavlov, *Dvadtsatiletnii opyt*, pp. 205–6.

60. T. H. Morgan, p. 131. For details on Vavilov's comments on Morgan's theoretical orientation, see N. I. Vavilov, *Izbrannye trudy*, V, 727–32.

61. Chernyshevskii, *Polnoe sobranie sochinenii*, Vol. X, Pt. 2, pp. 42–43; Berg, *Nomogenesis*, pp. 64–65.

62. M. A. Antonovich, *Charlz Darvin*, pp. 100–101.

63. Plekhanov, *Development of the Monist View*, p. 274.

CHAPTER TEN

1. For an excellent brief biography of Pavlov, see Savich, "Ivan Petrovich Pavlov." There are other good biographies by Anokhin, Babkin, Babskii, and Frolov.

2. K. M. Bykov, "O tvorchestve I. P. Pavlova," p. 675.

3. I. P. Pavlov, *Polnoe sobranie trudov*, II, 33.

4. *Imperatorskii Institut*, p. 1.

5. Smolenskii, pp. 10–11; *Imperatorskii Institut*, pp. 1–3.

6. I. P. Pavlov, *Polnoe sobranie trudov*, II, 33–36.

7. Babkin, p. 214. For a detailed analysis of the contributions of the *Lectures*, see K. M. Bykov, " 'Lektsii o rabote glavnykh pishchevaritel'nykh zhelez,' " pp. 263–88.

8. Babskii, p. 25.

9. Frolov, *Pavlov and His School*, pp. 38–39.

10. I. P. Pavlov, *Polnoe sobranie trudov*, III, 37.

11. *Ibid.*, p. 228.

12. Maiorov, p. 100.

13. I. P. Pavlov, *Dvadtsatiletnii opyt*, p. 57.

14. Quoted in Samoilov, "Obshchaia kharakteristika," p. 118.

15. I. P. Pavlov, *Lektsii*, p. 174.

16. J. P. Pawlow, "Die äussere Arbeit," pp. 666–67. See also I. P. Pavlov, *Polnoe sobranie trudov*, II, 453–54.

17. I. P. Pavlov, "Reply," p. 102.

18. Ukhtomskii, "Velikii fiziolog," p. 673.

19. Orbeli, p. 74.

20. *Ibid.*, p. 38.

21. For detailed summaries of the work and contributions of Pavlov's followers,

see: Maiorov, *Istoriia ucheniia*; Kvasov and Fedorova-Grot, *Fiziologicheskaia shkola I. P. Pavlova.*

22. Koshtoyants, *Essays*, pp. 265–66; Koshtoiants, "Samoilov," pp. 4–5.

23. Samoilov, *Izbrannye stat'i i rechi*, p. 166; Samoilov, "Sovremennaia techeniia," pp. 51–52.

24. Samoilov, *Izbrannye stat'i i rechi*, p. 166.

25. N. A. Grigor'ian, "Samoilov," pp. 347–49. See also Fulton, p. 90.

26. N. A. Grigor'ian, *Samoilov*, p. 117.

27. For a summary of Vvedenskii's scientific work, see: L. L. Vasil'ev, pp. 3–20; Koshtoyants, *Essays*, pp. 241–54.

28. Koshtoyants, *Essays*, p. 252.

29. N. E. Vvedenskii, "O sovremennykh techeniiakh v fiziologii," pp. 575–77.

30. N. E. Vvedenskii, "Usloviia produktivnosti umstvennoi raboty," pp. 871–72.

31. Miasishchev, p. 597.

32. Bekhterev, *General Principles*, p. 428. For a summary of reflexological principles, see Bekhterev, "Ob obshchikh osnovakh refleksologii," pp. 1101–28.

33. For a typical Soviet interpretation of Bekhterev's contributions, see Budilova, pp. 327–39.

34. Bekhterev, *General Principles*, p. 7.

35. Dogel' and Gasinovich, p. 725.

36. *Ibid.*, p. 13. For a summary of Mechnikov's contributions to medicine and microbiology, see Tarasevich, pp. 707–24.

37. Mechnikov, "Darvinizm i meditsina," p. 114; Zalkind, pp. 76–78.

38. Elie Metchnikoff, *Lectures*, p. 1.

39. *Ibid.*, p. 193.

40. *Ibid.*

41. *Ibid.*, pp. 505–43. Mechnikov also provided an illuminating survey of the history of the scientific studies of immunity.

42. Mechnikov, *Izbrannye proizvedeniia*, pp. 348–58.

43. Elie Metchnikoff, *Nature of Man*, p. 302.

44. Elie Metchnikoff, *The Prolongation of Life.*

45. L. T., "2-e soveshchanie," p. 567.

46. Omelianskii, *Izbrannye trudy*, II, 46.

47. For a brief summary of Vinogradskii's contributions, see: Isachenko, pp. 285–86; Omelianskii, "O mikrobakh," pp. 1044–45.

48. Isachenko, p. 327.

49. Waksman, *Principles*, pp. 74–75, 92–96.

50. Gutina, p. 281.

51. Waksman, *Winogradskii*, pp. vii–viii.

52. Significant details of this odyssey are recounted in Waksman, *Winogradsky: His Life and Work*. See also: Omelianskii, *Izbrannye trudy*, pp. 166–72; Novikova, pp. 145–72.

53. Isachenko, p. 331; Omelianskii, *Izbrannye trudy*, II, 68–71.

54. Waksman, pp. 71–72.

55. Ivanovskii, p. 30.

56. Stanley, pp. 136–38. For more details on Ivanovskii's pioneering work, see: Ryzhkov, pp. 315–25; Maksimov, *Pamiati Ivanovskogo.*

57. Zechmeister and Cholnoky, pp. 1–2; Strain, p. 3. For a detailed analysis of Tsvet's scientific work and its influence, see: Dhéré, "Michel Tswett"; Krasnosel'skaia, "Mikhail Semenovich Tsvet." According to L. Zechmeister: "Tswett was well aware

of the importance of chromatography, the various applications of which he clearly foresaw in many fields, that of colorless substances included. He predicted the heterogeneity of plant xanthophyll and carotene and opened up new aspects for the study of the 'carotenoids'—a term used by him for the first time. But the best known early demonstration of his methods concerns chlorophyll. The coexistence of two native green pigments... which were later designated as 'chlorophylls *a* and *b*,' was claimed by him as early as in 1907, i.e., before the beginning of Willstätter's classic investigations." Zechmeister, "Mikhail Tswett," p. 109.

58. The work of many of these scientists is described in Mikulinskii, pp. 448–94.

59. Prianishnikov, *Vospominaniia*, pp. 201–2. Notable women in plant physiology were Kh. Karpetova, M. Sabashnikova, M. Korsakova, T. Krasnosel'skaia, and A. Petrushevskaia. Palladin, pp. 172–73, 176, 229.

CHAPTER ELEVEN

1. Whitehead, pp. 19–20.

2. For general surveys of the history of modern Russian mathematics, see: Iushkevich, "Matematika" and *Istoriia matematiki,* Chapters 15–26; Shtokalo *et al.,* *Istoriia*; Gnedenko, Chapters 11–20.

3. Wilder, p. 270.

4. For a brief analysis of the unique contributions of Russian mathematicians to probability theory, see Kolmogorov, pp. 53–64.

5. Aleksandrov *et al.*, II, 244.

6. Gnedenko and Khinchin, p. 119.

7. Dynkin, I, viii.

8. Poincaré, *Science and Hypothesis*, p. 186.

9. P. S. Aleksandrov, "Russkaia matematika," p. 14.

10. For a brief survey of Markov's mathematical contributions, see Pogrebysskii, "A. A. Markov." See also Gnedenko, pp. 125–32.

11. A. A. Markov (younger), pp. 604–13.

12. "Liapunov, Aleksandr Mikhailovich," p. 430.

13. For reviews of Liapunov's life and work, see: Chetaev, pp. 200–205; V. I. Smirnov, "Biograficheskii ocherk"; Moiseev, pp. 139–47.

14. Chebyshev, *Izbrannye matematicheskie trudy*, p. 20.

15. Poincaré, *The Value of Science*, p. 17, and "Sur le problème des trois corps," p. 26.

16. Mittag-Leffler, "Sophie Kovalewsky," p. 389.

17. Wentscher, p. 92.

18. S. V. Kovalevskaia, *Vospominaniia i pis'ma*, pp. 52–53.

19. *Ibid.*, p. 140.

20. Leffler and Kovalewsky, pp. 10–11.

21. For details on Weierstrass's role in the development of Sof'ia Kovalevskii's mathematical talents, see Mittag-Leffler, "Weierstrass et Sonja Kovalewsky."

22. At this time only one of the three papers was published: "Zur Theorie der partieller Differenzialgleichungen," in Crelle's *Journal für reine und angewandte Mathematik*, LXXX (1875), 1–32. The remaining two papers were: "Über die Reduktion einer bestimmten Klasse Abel'scher Integrale 3-ten Ranges auf elliptische Integrale," *Acta mathematica*, IV (1884), 393–414; and "Zusätze und Bemerkungen zu Laplace's Untersuchung über die Gestalt der Saturnringe," *Astronomische Nachrichten*, III (1885), 37–48.

23. Wentscher, p. 92.

24. Klein, I, 295.

25. Chebyshev, *Polnoe sobranie sochinenii*, V, 417–18, 434.

26. Mittag-Leffler, "Weierstrass et Sonja Kovalewsky," pp. 189–90.

27. Polubarinova-Kochina, p. 328.

28. Voting unanimously in favor of Kovalevskii's paper, the members of the selection committee "recognized in this work not only the power of an expansive and profound mind, but also a grand spirit of invention." *Séance publique annuelle,* p. 1036.

29. Polubarinova-Kochina, p. 334.

30. [A. V. Vasil'ev], "Vstupitel'naia rech'," p. 5; Kagan, *Ocherk geometricheskoi sistemy,* and *Zadacha obosnovaniia geometrii*; "Veniamin Fedorovich Kagan," pp. 224–25. For an attempt to make Lobachevskii's geometry acceptable to a wider audience, see Filippov, "Prostranstvo Lobachevskogo," *NO.,* 1894.

31. Iushkevich, "Matematika," p. 216.

32. Lopatin, "Filosofskie vzgliady V. Ia. Tsingera," p. 227; Tsinger, "Nedorazumeniia," p. 213.

33. Bobynin, *Filosofskoe, nauchnoe i pedagogicheskoe znachenie istorii matematiki,* pp. 1–16.

34. Bobynin, *Ocherki* and *Matematiko-astronomicheskie i fizicheskie sektsii.*

35. In *Opyty matematicheskogo izlozheniia logiki,* Bobynin describes the contributions of George Boole, Hermann Grassmann, and Ernst Schröder to mathematical logic.

36. See Singh, p. 150.

37. D. A. Grave, *Teoriia konechnyk grup.*

38. For a brief summary of Bugaev's work, see L. K. Lakhtin, pp. 19–26.

39. Nekrasov, *Moskovskaia filosofsko-matematicheskaia shkola,* p. 157.

40. The philosophy of arithmology is presented in Bugaev, "Matematika," pp. 697–717, and "Osnovnye nachala," pp. 26–44. For a general survey of the claims of arithmology, see the following studies by V. G. Alekseev: "Über die Entwicklung," pp. 73–99; *N. V. Bugaev i problemy idealizma; K voprosu o neobkhodimosti;* and *Matematika kak osnovanie kritiki.* See also: Nekrasov, "Filosofiia i logika," pp. 463–604; Lopatin, "Filosofskoe mirovozzrenie," pp. 172–95; Bachinskii, "Dukh beskonechno malykh," pp. 183–205.

41. Bugaev, "Matematika," p. 716.

42. Bachinskii, "Pis'ma: II," pp. 105–6. See also Bachinskii, "Dukh beskonechno malykh," p. 202.

43. Bachinskii, "Pis'ma: II," p. 100.

44. Bachinskii, "Dukh beskonechno malykh," pp. 202–3.

45. P. Tikhomirov, pp. 1–62. Tikhomirov gave Bugaev's ideas a theological endorsement, and particularly emphasized their close relationship to idealistic philosophy. S. S. Glagolev, a leading theologian, thought that Bugaev's ideas—particularly as elaborated by P. A. Nekrasov—proved conclusively that mathematics and theology were the most perfect sciences. P. Tikhomirov, p. 22. See also Kozhevnikov, III (1911), 714–15.

46. Lopatin, "Filosofskoe mirovozzrenie," p. 192.

47. Singh, p. 127.

48. Egoroff, pp. 244–46.

49. A. D. Aleksandrov *et al.,* III, 30.

50. Among Luzin's original students were the following stalwarts of Soviet mathe-

matics: A. Ia. Khinchin, D. E. Menshov, P. S. Aleksandrov, P. S. Uryson, M. A. Lavrent'ev, and A. N. Kolmogorov. See "Nikolai Nikolaevich Luzin," p. 226.

51. Khintchine, pp. 287–91; P. Alexandroff, pp. 323–25; D. Menchoff, pp. 433–36; M. Souslin, pp. 88–91. See also Lusin, "Analyse mathématique," pp. 975–78, and "Théorie des fonctions," pp. 91–94.

52. P. S. Aleksandrov, "O vazhneishikh predmetakh," p. 11. See also: Stepanov, p. 49; Sologub, pp. 437–43.

53. Delone, *Matematika*, p. 13; Bari, p. 342.

54. Singh, p. 127.

55. "Zasedanie Moskovskogo Matematicheskogo obshchestva," p. 540.

56. For an appreciation of Zhukovskii's ideas within the historical context of modern aerodynamics, see Giacomelli and Pistolesi, pp. 347–51. For additional information on Zhukovskii's scientific career, see: Stryzhevsky, *Nikolai Zhukovsky*; Kosmodem'ianskii, "Nikolai Egorovich Zhukovskii," pp. 169–77. For information on S. A. Chaplygin, see: Kosmodem'ianskii, "Osnovopolozhniki sovremennoi mekhaniki," pp. 105–28, and "Sergei Alekseevich Chaplygin," pp. 294–302.

57. V. I. Smirnov, "Raboty A. N. Krylova," p. 36. For details on Krylov's contributions to mathematics, see: Khanovich, pp. 118–60; V. I. Smirnov, "Matematicheskie raboty," pp. 13–23, and "Raboty A. N. Krylova," pp. 36–46.

58. Poincaré, *Science and Hypothesis*, p. 9.

59. Kryloff, "Comment on C. F. Monday," p. 87.

60. Kryloff, "A New Theory," pp. 326–59.

61. Monday, p. 80.

62. For details on the complexities involved in Krylov's translation, see Khanovich, pp. 161–68.

63. Krylov, *Vospominaniia i ocherki*, p. 198.

64. For more details on Krylov's life and work, see: Leibenzon and Markushevich, pp. 257–70; Shtraikh, "Kratkii ocherk," pp. 5–72; Shimanskii, "Krylov," pp. 734–43.

65. Krylov, *Vospominaniia i ocherki*, pp. 385–91.

CHAPTER TWELVE

1. Chicherin, *Polozhitel'naia filosofiia*, pp. 120–25, and *Sistema khimicheskikh elementov*, pp. 470–98.

2. Morozov, *Periodicheskie sistemy*, pp. vi–vii, 387, 437. See also Morozov, *Mendeleev*, pp. 11, 87.

3. Krukovskaia, p. 81; Morozov, "Vnov otkrytyia prevrashcheniia," p. 13.

4. Krukovskaia, p. 84.

5. Reingold, p. 268.

6. T. P. Kravets, *Ot N'iutona do Vavilova*, p. 205.

7. *MIAU*, I, 49; S. I. Vavilov, III, 508.

8. P. N. Lebedev, "An Experimental Investigation," pp. 177–78. The tests were completed in 1899, and not in 1901, as claimed by Max von Laue. Max von Laue, p. 89. See also Berry, p. 37.

9. Lazarev, "P. N. Lebedev i russkaia fizika," p. 74.

10. Lazarev, "Pamiati velikogo russkogo fizika," pp. 472–73.

11. According to the physicist V. A. Mikhel'son: "In P. N. Lebedev's laboratory our entire group of students was engaged primarily in studying electromagnetic and other waves and their various effects. The themes were divided and elaborated according to

a basic plan; and, as all of us know, the studies were inseparable from the work that brought Lebedev wide recognition." Mikhel'son, "Rasshirenie," p. 691.

12. A. K. Timiriazev, *Ocherki*, pp. 159–60.

13. T. P. Kravets, "Lebedev," pp. 291–92.

14. A. K. Timiriazev, "Nauchnye raboty P. N. Lebedeva," p. 89.

15. K. A. Timiriazev, *Nauka i demokratiia*, p. 77.

16. Zhukovskii, *Polnoe sobranie sochinenii*, IX, 259.

17. For the first systematic presentation of Planck's ideas in Russian, see Mikhel'son, "Obzor noveishikh issledovanii," pp. 188–207.

18. Eikhenval'd, "O nauchnykh rabotakh N. A. Umova," pp. 55–66.

19. Bachinskii, "Nikolai Alekseevich Umov," pp. 285–306, and "Zamechatel'nyi russkii uchenyi," pp. 26–34.

20. Umov, *Sobranie sochinenii*, III, 175.

21. Pasvolsky, pp. 113–15.

22. Umov, "Znachenie opytnykh nauk," pp. 25–26.

23. Umov, "Evoliutsiia atoma," p. 5.

24. *Ibid.*, p. 26.

25. These papers were published in 1910 and 1912 respectively. See Umov, *Izbrannye sochineniia*, pp. 492–502.

26. Zhukovskii, "Nikolai Alekseevich Umov," p. 54.

27. Bachinskii, "Pis'ma: I," p. 820.

28. According to Maxwell: "Shiller . . . ascertained the time of the electrical vibrations when a condenser is discharged through an electromagnet," which helped him establish "the values of dielectric coefficients of various substances." Maxwell, p. 109.

29. Shiller, "Znachenie poniatii o 'sile,' " p. 9.

30. *Ibid.*, pp. 71–72.

31. Shiller, "Proiskhozhdenie i razvitie poniatii o 'temperature,' " p. 12.

32. See, for example, Khvol'son, *Znanie i vera,* pp. 14–15, and *Gegel'*, pp. 8–16.

33. Khvol'son, "Printsip otnositel'nosti," p. 1316.

34. Shiller, "Proiskhozhdenie i razvitie poniatii o 'temperature,' " p. 11.

35. Bachinskii, "Pis'ma: I," pp. 813–14.

36. Khvol'son, *Znanie i vera*, pp. 15–16. The idea of "idealistic physics" was welcomed by theological writers. According to one such writer, Iakov Galakhov, the electron was "the purest nonmaterial principle whose place is in the kingdom of spirit, in the world of metaphysics." Modern physics, he said, had abandoned materialism by emphasizing force over matter as the ontological foundation of the world, rejecting the speed of light as an absolute norm for the determination of time, showing that absolute motion could not be isolated or measured, and assuming that no true understanding of physical phenomena could be achieved within the conceptual framework of the three-dimensional world. In the future, physics would be no more than a subsidiary of idealistic metaphysics. Galakhov, pp. 429–44. See also: Glubovskii, p. 467; Ern, "Priroda nauchnoi mysli."

37. Shilov, p. 207.

38. Frenkel', p. 30; Ioffe, *Moia zhizn'*, p. 18.

39. Frenkel', p. 28. For interesting comments on Ioffe's role in bringing modern physics to Russia, see S. Timoshenko, pp. 121–22.

40. *KOSVU*, 1898, p. 38; *KOSVU*, 1897, p. 53.

41. *O-MU*, 1916, p. 114.

42. *O-StPU*, 1910, p. 71.

43. *O-StPU*, 1915, p. 59.

44. Vernadskii, "Vysshaia shkola," pp. 324–25.
45. Ioffe, *Vstrechi*, p. 11; Sominskii, pp. 47–48.
46. Joffe, "Zur Theorie," pp. 534–52.
47. Sominskii, p. 513.
48. *Ibid.*, pp. 512–13; Ioffe, *Vstrechi*, pp. 40–42.
49. T. P. Kravets, *Ot N'iutona do Vavilova*, p. 348.
50. Ioffe, *Vstrechi*, p. 40.
51. Einstein, p. 215.
52. "Vvoz nauchnykh priborov," p. 610.
53. Lazarev, "Vzgliady P. N. Lebedeva," pp. 369–78.
54. V. A. Mikhel'son, "Rasshirenie," pp. 685–86.
55. *Ibid.*, pp. 697–98.
56. Omelianskii, "Razvitie estestvoznaniia," p. 127.
57. Smithells, p. 2.
58. Omelianskii, "Razvitie estestvoznaniia," p. 127.
59. Markovnikov, "Vospominaniia," p. 91. See also: Markovnikov, "Moskovskaia rech'," p. 168; N. A. Menshutkin, "Vospominanie," p. 11.
60. B. N. Menshutkin, pp. 316, 327.
61. For discussions of Butlerov's influence, see: Arbuzov, *Kratkii ocherk*, pp. 86–108; Petrov, "Peterburgskaia shkola."
62. Findlay, p. 68.
63. Esafov, pp. 135–74.
64. Val'den, *Ocherk*, pp. 528–29.
65. Chugaev, "Predmet," p. 128.
66. Chugaev, *Novye idei v khimii*.
67. For a brief description of their work, see Turkevich, pp. 15–16.
68. Zelinskii, *Sobranie trudov*, I, 277–78.
69. Nametkin, "Issledovaniia N. D. Zelinskogo," p. 23.
70. For detailed biographical data on Zelinskii, see: Nametkin, "Issledovaniia N. D. Zelinskogo" and "Nikolai Dmitrievich Zelinskii"; Nilov, *Zelinskii*; Balandin *et al.*, in Zelinskii, *Izbrannye trudy*, pp. 577–641.
71. Nilov, p. 68.
72. Bezredko, *Opyt*.
73. Val'den, *Ocherk*, pp. 561–62; Findlay, p. 74.
74. Quoted in Iu. I. Solov'ev, *Ocherki po istorii fizicheskoi khimii*, pp. 45–46.
75. Mendeléeff, *Principles*, I, 533.
76. *Ibid.*, II, 431–32.
77. Iu. I. Solov'ev and A. Ia. Kipnis, pp. 108–9.
78. Ipatieff, *Catalytic Reactions*, pp. iv–xxii.
79. See, for example: Khrushchov, *Vvedenie*; Kablukov, *Ocherki* and *Osnovnye nachala*; Kurilov, *Obshchii kurs*; Shchukarev, *Uchenie ob energii*; and Bezredko, *Opyt*.
80. Kablukov, "Kratkii istoricheskii ocherk," No. 9, p. 37.
81. Khvol'son, "Pozitivnaia filosofiia i fizika," p. 52.
82. Chugaev, "Predmet i zadachi sovremennoi khimii," pp. 128–29.
83. N. N. Beketov, "Znachenie periodicheskoi sistemy," pp. 33–35.
84. Chugaev, "Evoliutsiia veshchestva," p. 139; Ipatieff, *The Life of a Chemist*, p. 152.
85. Vernadskii, *Ocherki i rechi*, I, 37.
86. Ushakova, pp. 26–33.
87. "Otchet o deiatel'nosti Fizicheskogo otdeleniia," pp. iii, xiv–xv.

88. Val'den, *Ocherk istorii.*
89. Ipatieff, *The Life of a Chemist,* p. 35.
90. *Ibid.,* p. 188.
91. Chugaev, "Sovremennye zadachi," p. 171.
92. Prianishnikov, *Moi vospominaniia,* pp. 207–8.
93. Ipatieff, *The Life of a Chemist,* p. 190.
94. Vernadskii, *Ocherki i rechi,* I, 65.
95. Ipatieff, *The Life of a Chemist,* p. 216.
96. V. V. Kozlov, *Ocherki,* p. 79.

CHAPTER THIRTEEN

1. In "A Short Essay on the History of Geology" (1901), the paleontologist A. P. Pavlov did not mention a single Russian geologist as a contributor to the mainstream of geological thought. A. P. Pavlov, "Kratkii ocherk," pp. 55–78.
2. For the participation of the Russian Geographical Society in geological research, see Barkhatova, "Vklad," pp. 45–75.
3. For a detailed description of the committee's work, see Khabakov, "Deiatel'-nost'."
4. Karpinskii, *Sobranie sochinenii,* IV, 403.
5. Tikhonovich, "Vserossiiskie s'ezdy," p. 128.
6. The geological section of the Moscow Society of Admirers of Natural Science, Anthropology and Ethnography published a special geological journal. Gordeev, p. 191. During the first 25 years of its existence, the *Proceedings* of the St. Petersburg Society of Naturalists published 50 papers in the earth sciences and sponsored 140 expeditionary studies in European and Asian Russia. *Obzor deiatel'nosti S. Peterburgskogo Obshchestva estestvoispytatelei,* pp. 100–201.
7. A. P. Pavlov, *Dlia chego prepodavaet'sia estestvoznanie?,* p. 4.
8. A. P. Pavlov and Vernadskii, *Proekt Ustava,* p. 1.
9. Vernadskii, *Ocherki i rechi,* I, 154–57.
10. A. P. Pavlov's paleontological work is discussed in detail in Varsanof'eva, *A. P. Pavlov,* pp. 204–35.
11. A. P. Pavlov, "Kratkii ocherk," pp. 76–77.
12. Karpinskii, *Ocherki,* p. 22.
13. For an analysis of Karpinskii's scientific contributions, see: Shatskii, pp. 233–74, 322–33; Lichkov, *Karpinskii;* Mikulinskii, pp. 58–59; Borisiak, "K iubileiu A. P. Karpinskogo."
14. Karpinskii, "Ocherk fiziko-geograficheskikh uslovii," p. 4.
15. See, for example, Chernyshev, "Russkaia ekspeditsiia."
16. Vernadskii, "O znachenii trudov M. N. Lomonosova"; A. P. Pavlov, "Lomonosov kak geolog"; Nechaev, "Uspekhi geologii"; Andrusov, "O vozraste zemli."
17. Vernadskii, "Stranitsa iz istorii pochvovedeniia," pp. 5–6.
18. "Torzhestvennoe sobranie Imperatorskogo Vol'nogo ekonomicheskogo obshchestva," pp. 5–6.
19. A. N. Beketov, *Istoricheskii ocherk,* pp. 53–56.
20. Glinka, *Dokuchaiev's Ideas,* pp. 2–3; *Obzor deiatel'nosti St. Peterburgskogo obshchestva estestvoispytatelei,* pp. 198–99.
21. Mikulinskii, p. 224.
22. Kostychev, pp. 37–60.
23. Glinka, "O razvitii pochvovedeniia," pp. 30–39.

24. For interesting information on the history of soil science, see Glinka, *Pochvovedenie*, pp. 1–10. See also Polynov, pp. 935–42.

25. A. P. Lebedev, pp. 53–54.

26. Levinson-Lessing, *Edinaia vysshaia shkola*, p. 10.

27. Various phases of Vernadskii's many activities are discussed in: Gordeev, pp. 153–60; K. V. Vlasov, "Vladimir Ivanovich Vernadskii," pp. 135–57; Kozikov, pp. 66–76; A. P. Vinogradov, "The Scientific Legacy," pp. 1–8.

28. Vernadskii, *Ocherki*, I, 37.

29. See, for example: Vernadskii, *Iavleniia*, pp. 1–11, and *Osnovy kristallografii*, I, 1–36.

30. Vernadskii, *Ocherki*, I, 10.

31. *Ibid.*, p. 149.

32. Vernadskii, "Pis'ma," p. 3.

33. For biographical details on Fedorov, see: Shafranovskii, *Evgraf Stepanovich Fedorov*; Shafranovskii, *Istoriia*, pp. 325–56; Shafranovskii and Belov, pp. 341–50; N. V. Belov, "Velikii russkii kristallograf," pp. 580–86; V. V. Nikitin, "Evgraf Stepanovich Fedorov."

34. Klein, I, 344.

35. Shafranovskii, *Istoriia*, p. 337.

36. Quoted in *ibid.*, p. 329.

37. Hilton, p. 259.

38. Bunn, p. 267; Ewald, p. 29.

39. As cited by Shafranovskii, *Evgraf Stepanovich Fedorov*, pp. 210–11.

40. The same was done by a whole array of other contemporary Russian crystallographers. In his textbook, Fedorov advised readers who wanted to go beyond the basic principles of crystallography to read *Zeitschrift für Krystallographie und Mineralogie*, an "international journal" edited by P. Groth, the more so because among the contributors to this journal were, besides himself, the following Russian crystallographers: V. I. Vernadskii, Z. Veiberg, V. I. Vorob'ev, Iu. V. Vul'f, P. A. Zemiatchenskii, A. N. Karnozhitskii, B. Z. Kolenko, A. E. Lagorio, I. A. Morozevich, V. V. Nikitin, R. A. Prendel', P. P. Piatnitskii, Ia. V. Samoilov, and P. P. Sushchinskii. E. S. Fedorov, *Kurs kristallografii*, p. ii.

41. E. S. Fedorov, "Ob usloviiakh," p. 4.

42. For the full text of the resignation letter, see Shafranovskii, *Fedorov*, pp. 149–50.

43. For a detailed discussion of Fedorov's methods, see V. V. Nikitin, *Die Fedorow-Methode*.

44. E. S. Fedorov, "Priroda i chelovek," p. 425.

45. E. S. Fedorov, "Perfektsionizm."

46. E. S. Fedorov, "Priroda i chelovek," pp. 429–31.

47. *Ibid.*, pp. 426–27.

48. For a summary of the transactions of the congresses, see N. N. Tikhonovich, "Vserossiiskie s'ezdy."

49. Fersman, pp. 753–54.

50. E. S. Fedorov, "Stroenie veshchestva," pp. 779–88.

51. Shafranovskii, *Istoriia*, pp. 357–80.

CHAPTER FOURTEEN

1. Kareev, *Istoriko-filosofskie i sotsiologicheskie etiudy*, pp. 39–40.

2. Skabichevskii, p. 102.

3. Pisarev, *Sochineniia* (1894), III, 107; E. Solov'ev, *Ocherki*, pp. 243-45.

4. For more details, see: Kirpotin, pp. 53-110; Plotkin, pp. 216-28; Demidova, "D. I. Pisarev." For a critical survey of Pisarev's views on the role of science in modern culture, see Coquart, pp. 333-41.

5. Lesevich, *Sobranie sochinenii*, I, 11-12.

6. V. K., "Pozitivizm," No. 3, pp. 9-10.

7. Iu. Gardenin [V. M. Chernov], p. 1. The historian Ivanov-Razumnik concedes, however, that Mikhailovskii's sociological system is "complete" and "harmonious," whereas Lavrov's is "incomplete" and "elastic" (Ivanov-Razumnik, V, 14). According to N. I. Kareev, Mikhailovskii's sociology, too, lacks "overall unity" (Kareev, "Mikhailovskii," p. 4). Actually, the sociology of both Mikhailovskii and Lavrov shows a great deal of inner consistency without forming a tight and comprehensive system of propositions. In Lavrov's opinion, Mikhailovskii's early work suffered from "ethical relativism" and from an exaggerated emphasis on the incompatibility of "complete personality" with the "scientific specialization" in modern society (Gizetti, pp. 39-40). For a brief study of Lavrov's sociology, see Sorokin, "Lavrov kak sotsiolog," pp. 19-23.

8. Mikhailovskii, *Sochineniia*, I, 65.

9. Chernov, *Filosofskie i sotsiologicheskie etiudy*, p. 199.

10. Lavrov, *Zadachi pozitivizma*, p. 44.

11. This problem is explored in Krasnosel'skii, *Mirovozzrenie*, pp. 70-91.

12. Mikhailovskii, *Sochineniia*, I, 421-594; Lavrov, *Filosofiia i sotsiologiia*, II, 110-19; Chernov, *Filosofskie i sotsiologicheskie etiudy*, p. 13; Kareev, "Novyi istoriko-filosofskii trud," pp. 400-401.

13. Lavrov, *Zadachi istorii mysli*, pp. 25ff.

14. Chernov, *Filosofskie i sotsiologicheskie etiudy*, p. 238.

15. Mikhailovskii, *Sochineniia*, III, 376-77; *ibid.*, I, 142.

16. Chernov, *Filosofskie i sotsiologicheskie etiudy*, p. 220.

17. M. M. Kovalevskii, "Mikhailovskii," p. 192.

18. Lavrov, *Zadachi istorii mysli*, pp. 75-76.

19. Mikhailovskii, *Sochineniia*, VI, 288.

20. Mikhailovskii, *Polnoe sobranie sochinenii*, VIII, 595-631.

21. Chernov, *Filosofskie i sotsiologicheskie etiudy*, p. 6. For a detailed analysis of "subjective sociology," see Kablits, III, 1-56.

22. *Ibid.*, pp. 224-25. For a similar interpretation, see N. K., pp. 118-19.

23. Chernov, "Sub'ektivnyi metod," No. 7, p. 236, and *Filosofskie i sotsiologicheskie etiudy*, p. 13.

24. Ivanov-Razumnik, V, 34.

25. Lilienfeld, I, 2-26.

26. For more details on Lilienfeld's sociological theory, see: Barth, pp. 339-52; Coker, pp. 139-53; Bristol, pp. 47-49.

27. Novicow, *Les luttes*, pp. 64-111; Bristol, p. 272; Sorokin, *Contemporary Sociological Theories*, pp. 314-16.

28. Novicow, *Les luttes*, p. 744.

29. Novicow, "L'essence du progrès," p. 426.

30. Novicow, *Mécanisme*, p. 3.

31. Novicow, *Critique*, pp. 102, 163. See also Novicow, *Essai*, p. 2.

32. Kropotkin, *Modern Science* (1903), pp. 36-37.

33. *Ibid.*, p. 57.

34. Kropotkin, *Ethics*, p. 45. For a summary of Kropotkin's ideas, see Pipes, pp. 463-65.

35. Kareev, *Istoriko-filosofskie i sotsiologicheskie etiudy*, p. 236.
36. M. M. Kovalevskii, *Obshchinnoe zemlevladenie*, I, i.
37. Vinogradoff, pp. vi–vii.
38. Tugan-Baranovskii, *Promyshlennye krizisi*, p. 1.
39. Kindersley, p. 58.
40. Baron, "The First Decade," p. 330.
41. Plekhanov, *The Development of the Monist View*; Struve, *Kriticheskie zametki*; Tugan-Baranovskii, "Znachenie ekonomicheskogo faktora."
42. Tugan-Baranovskii, "Znachenie ekonomicheskogo faktora," p. 113.
43. Plekhanov, *Sochineniia*, VIII, 299. See also Tugan-Baranovskii, "Znachenie ekonomicheskogo faktora," p. 111.
44. Baron, "Legal Marxism," p. 123.
45. Struve, *Kriticheskie zametki*, I, 288.
46. Lenin, *Sochineniia*, III, 268–73, 328–31; Theodore von Laue, p. 39.
47. Plekhanov, *Sochineniia*, VII, 211.
48. *Ibid.*
49. Dan, p. 178.
50. Tugan-Baranovskii, *Russkaia fabrika*, pp. 410–24.
51. Struve, *Na raznye temy*, pp. 462–64. See also Filippov, "Sub'ektivizm i narodnichestvo."
52. Struve, *Kriticheskie zametki*, p. 46.
53. Struve, "Die Marxsche Theorie," p. 680. The metamorphosis of Marxian social theory in the 1890's is described in Struve, "Na raznye temy," pp. 12–23.
54. Struve, "Intelligentsia i revoliutsiia," pp. 170–74.
55. Struve, "Sovremennyi krizis," pp. 123–34.
56. Kindersley, p. 163.
57. Tugan-Baranovskii, *Modern Socialism*, p. 9.
58. Tugan-Baranowsky, *Theoretische Grundlagen*, pp. 238–39; Tugan-Baranovskii, *Modern Socialism*, pp. 11–14.
59. Tugan-Baranowsky, "Subjektivismus und Objektivismus," p. 564.
60. Tugan-Baranowsky, "Kritische Literatur," pp. 180–88.
61. Tugan-Baranovskii offered detailed criticisms of Marxian sociology in "Bor'ba klassov," "Chto takoe obshchestvennyi klass?," and "Intelligentsia i sotsializm." See also: Vorländer, pp. 200–206; Bernstein, "Tugan-Baranowsky als Sozialist."
62. For an autobiographical note, see "Bogdanov (Malinovskii), Aleksandr Aleksandrovich." See also Utechin, pp. 117–25. The most detailed study of Bogdanov's life and work is Grille, *Lenins Rivale*.
63. Lenin, *Sochineniia*, IV, 32.
64. A. A. Bogdanov, *Osnovnye elementy*, p. 18.
65. *Ibid.*, p. 206.
66. A. A. Bogdanov, *Poznanie*, pp. 107–18.
67. Grille, p. 113.
68. A. A. Bogdanov, *Iz psikhologii obshchestva*, p. 39; Marx, pp. 11–12.
69. A. A. Bogdanov, *Iz psikhologii obshchestva*, p. 57.
70. A. A. Bogdanov, *Empiriomonizm*, I, 38.
71. *Ibid.*, p. 250.
72. N. Verner [A. A. Bogdanov], "Nauka i filosofiia," p. 29.
73. A. A. Bogdanov, *Iz psikhologii obshchestva*, p. 77.
74. Vol'skii, No. 8, p. 3.
75. A. A. Bogdanov, *Empiriomonizm*, III, 59.

76. *Ibid.*, II, 66.

77. *Ibid.*, III, 48, 55.

78. *Ibid.*, pp. 83–84; A. A. Bogdanov, *Padenie velikogo fetishizma*, p. 180.

79. A. A. Bogdanov, "Filosofiia sovremennogo estestvoispytatelia," p. 98.

80. A. A. Bogdanov, *Kul'turnye zadachi nashego vremeni*, p. 55.

81. A. A. Bogdanov, "Filosofiia sovremennogo estestvoispytatelia," pp. 43–45.

82. *Ibid.*, p. 46.

83. A. A. Bogdanov, *Vseobshchaia organizatsionnaia nauka*, I, 38.

84. Shcheglov, p. 126.

85. A. A. Bogdanov, *Vseobshchaia organizatsionnaia nauka*, I, 217.

86. *Ibid.*, pp. 3, 11.

87. A. A. Bogdanov, "Taina nauki," p. 103.

88. For additional details on the basic principles of tektology, see Grille, pp. 190–200.

89. Rozhkov, "Sotsial'nyi materializm," p. 41, and *Obzor russkoi istorii*, I, 2.

90. Rozhkov, "Proiskhozhdenie soslovii."

91. *Ibid.*, p. 30; Rozhkov, *Istoricheskie i sotsiologicheskie ocherki*, I, 165–259.

92. Rozhkov, "Uspekhi," p. 27.

93. Nechkina, p. 82.

94. N. L. Rubinshtein, p. 575.

95. For a brief survey of Miliukov's historical training and academic career, see Riha, pp. 5–28.

96. P. B., "Neskol'ko zamechanii," p. 1.

97. Miliukov, *Ocherki*, II, 5.

98. *Ibid.*, pp. 3–4.

99. P. N. M[iliukov], "Istoriosofiia." For a brief summary of Kareev's views, see Kareev, *Sushchnost' istoricheskogo protsessa*, pp. 625–27. See also Hecker, pp. 174–202. For Kareev's endorsement and elaboration of "subjective sociology," see Kareev, *Osnovnye voprosy*, pp. 273–74, and *Istoriko-filosofskie i sotsiologicheskie etiudy*, pp. 114–34.

100. Miliukov, *Ocherki*, II, 7.

101. Shershenevich, p. 84.

102. Muromtsev, *Stat'i i rechi*, II, 25. See also M. M. Kovalevskii, "Sergei Andreevich Muromtsev," pp. 365–66.

103. Muromtsev's views on the social dynamics of law are presented briefly in his "Pravo i spravedl'ivost'," pp. 1–12.

104. Pospelov, p. 109. See also Svatikov, "Opal'naia professura," pp. 22–27.

105. B. A. Kistiakovskii, *Sotsial'nye nauki i pravo*, p. 339.

106. Muromtsev, "Sotsiologicheskie ocherki," pp. 1–32.

107. Chernov, *Filosofskie i sotsiologicheskie etiudy*, pp. 266–67. The American sociologist Lester Ward was particularly popular in Russia because of his interpretation of social evolution as an "active" process in which deliberate human action is the prime mover. See, for example: P. F. N., "Prikladnaia sotsial'naia teoriia," No. 11, p. 67; M. M. Kovalevskii, *Sotsiologiia*, I, 264–300.

108. Novgorodtsev, *Istoricheskaia shkola*, pp. 1–22.

109. Novgorodtsev, "Nravstvennyi idealizm," p. 296.

110. Novgorodtsev, "Znachenie filosofii," pp. 108–15.

111. Slonimskii, pp. 314–25; Review of P. I. Novgorodtsev, *Problemy idealizma*.

112. Gins, p. xxii; Gintsberg, p. 206.

113. Reisner, No. 2, p. 46.

114. *Ibid.*

115. Petrazhitskii, *Vvedenie*, p. viii. For a general appraisal of Petrazhitskii's theory, see B. A. Kistiakovskii, *Sotsial'nye nauki*, pp. 276–77, 323–24. See also: H. Babb, "Petrazhitsky: Theory of Law," *Boston University Law Review*, XVIII (1938), 511–78; H. Babb, "Petrazhitsky: Science and Legal Policy," *Boston University Law Review*, XVII (1937), 793–829; Gurvitch, *Le temps present et l'idée du droit social* (Paris, 1932), pp. 279–95; Timasheff, "Introduction," pp. xvii–xxxviii.

116. T. Kistiakowski, *Gesellschaft und Einzelwesen*, Berlin, 1899.

117. For an excellent summary of the principal ideas of Kistiakovskii's study, see Kelsen, pp. 106–13. See also von Beyme, pp. 42–46, 96–98. For relations between Kistiakovskii and Max Weber, see: Marianne Weber, p. 373; Mommsen, pp. 64–65.

118. T. Kistiakowski, p. 33. See also B. A. Kistiakovskii, *Sotsial'nye nauki*, p. 319.

119. B. A. Kistiakovskii, "Russkaia sotsiologicheskaia shkola."

120. B. A. Kistiakovskii, *Sotsial'nye nauki*, pp. 320–26.

121. *Ibid.*, p. 339.

122. Worms, p. 262.

123. M. M. Kovalevskii, *Obshchinnoe zemlevladenie*, I, i.

124. These lectures were published in French as *Tableau des origines et de l'évolution de la famille et de la propriété*; and the book was soon translated into Russian and Spanish.

125. *Economic Growth*, originally published in Russian, was subsequently translated into German and published in seven volumes as *Die ökonomische Entwicklung*.

126. M. M. Kovalewsky, *Régime economique de la Russie* and "The Origin and Growth of Village Communities in Russia."

127. Safronov, p. 28. See also "Russkaia shkola v Parizhe," pp. 3–4.

128. Verrier, p. 160.

129. Verrier, p. 162.

130. M. M. Kovalevskii, "Dmitrii Andreevich Dril'," pp. 427–28; M. G., "Parizhskii sotsiologicheskii kongress," p. 84.

131. M. M. Kovalevskii, "Dve zhizni," No. 7, p. 11; Safronov, p. 14.

132. M. M. Kovalevskii, "Sovremennye frantsuzskie sotsiologi," p. 369.

133. M. M. Kovalevskii, "Kondorse," No. 4, p. 494.

134. M. M. Kovalevskii, "Progress," p. 258, and "N. K. Mikhailovskii," pp. 206–7.

135. M. M. Kovalevskii, *Sovremennye sotsiologi*, pp. 135–64.

136. M. M. Kovalevskii, "Sovremennye frantsuzskie sotsiologi," pp. 361–62.

137. M. M. Kovalevskii, *Sotsiologiia*, I, 115.

138. *Ibid.*, pp. 115, 262. See also Kovalevskii's *Sovremennye sotsiologi*, pp. 53–54, and "Psychologie et sociologie."

139. P. N. Miliukov, "M. M. Kovalevskii," p. 139. For details on Kovalevskii's contributions to sociology, see: Kareev, "M. M. Kovalevskii," pp. 169–77; Kotliarevskii, pp. 121–35; Vagner, pp. 144–68; Sorokin, "Teoriia faktorov"; Kondrat'ev, "Rost naseleniia." P. B. Struve labeled Kovalevskii a "Cossack in science" because his scholarly work was so extensive. Kovalevskii, according to Struve, was essentially a historian; and as a historian, he did not have a single clear orientation. He ventured into economic history, but had little familiarity with economic theory. He wrote at length about legal usages and institutions, but he was not a trained jurist. He thoroughly investigated modern sociological theory, but had no consistent and elaborate theoretical view of his own. Struve, "M. M. Kovalevskii," pp. 98–100.

CHAPTER FIFTEEN

1. Umov, "Po povodu sbornika," p. 5.
2. Dostoevskii, *Pis'ma*, II, 181.
3. *Ibid.*, p. 259.
4. Miliukov, *Ocherki*, II, 7.
5. Kareev, "Mechta i pravda," p. 109.
6. Lappo-Danilevskii, "The Development of Science," pp. 215ff; Presniakov, p. 93.
7. P. G. Vinogradov, *Nakanune novogo stoletiia*, pp. 27–28.
8. Vernadskii, *Ocherki i rechi*, II, 34.
9. *Ibid.*, p. 15. See also Umov, "Znachenie opytnykh nauk," pp. 25–26.
10. Vernadskii, *Ocherki i rechi*, II, 23.
11. Vernadskii, "Ob ispol'zovanii khimicheskikh elementov," pp. 74–75.
12. Vernadskii, *Ocherki i rechi*, II, 49.
13. Vernadskii, "Pis'ma o vysshem obrazovanii," p. 4.
14. M. Iu. Lakhtin, pp. 754–55.
15. Umov, "Rol' cheloveka v poznavaemom im mire," p. 318.
16. Vernadskii, "Tri resheniia," p. 172.
17. Rostovtsev, "Nauka i revoliutsiia," p. 5.
18. Vernadskii, *Ocherki i rechi*, II, 46.
19. P. G. Vinogradov, "Uchebnoe delo," pp. 550ff.
20. Kol'tsov, *K universitetskom voprosu*, p. 81; Petrazhitskii, *Universitet i nauka*, I, 533–34.
21. Kniazev, "Poritsanie akademikam," p. 13.
22. B. N. Menshutkin, pp. 190–91. See also Syromiatnikov, p. 383.
23. Kol'tsov, "Natsional'naia organizatsiia nauki," p. 1034.
24. P. G. Vinogradov, "Uchebnoe delo," p. 540.
25. Famintsyn, "Nakanune universitetskoi reformy," pp. 239, 241.
26. *Sbornik postanovlenii Ministerstva Narodnogo prosveshcheniia*, X, 881.
27. Kol'tsov, "K universitetskom voprosu," p. 82.
28. Vernadskii, "Vysshaia shkola v Rossii," pp. 324–25.
29. Vernadskii, *Ocherki*, I, 46.
30. *Ibid.*, II, 44.
31. Rostovtsev, "Nauka i revoliutsiia," pp. 5–6.
32. Vernadskii, *Ocherki*, I, 4–6; II, 65ff.
33. Vernadskii, "Iz istorii idei," p. 125.

# Bibliography

This Bibliography includes only sources that have been consulted. The following abbreviations are used in the citations.

*AIIS*. Annales de l'Institut international de sociologie.

*BMOIP*. Biulleten' Moskovskogo Obshchestva ispytatelei prirody.

*Brockhaus-Efron*. Entsiklopedicheskii slovar'. F. A. Brockhaus and I. A. Efron, eds. 41 vols. St. Petersburg, 1894–1904.

*BSNM*. Bulletin de la Société Imperiale des naturalistes de Moscou.

*BS-StPU*. Biograficheskii slovar' professorov i prepodavatelei Imperatorskogo S. Peterburgskogo universiteta, 1869–1894. 2 vols. St. Petersburg, 1898.

*CR-AS-P*. Comptes rendus des séances de l'Académie des sciences, Paris.

*Chten*. Chteniia v Imperatorskom Obshchestve istorii i drevnostei rossiiskikh pri Moskovskom universitete.

*ERGO*. Ezhegodnik Imperatorskogo Russkogo Geograficheskogo obshchestva.

*Granat-Ents*. Entsiklopedicheskii slovar'. 53 vols. Moscow: Granat Institute, n.d.–1937 (7th edition).

*Granat-Ist*. Istoriia Rossii v XIX veke. 9 vols. Moscow: Granat Institute, n.d.

*IIAN*. Izvestiia Imperatorskoi Akademii nauk.

*IRGO*. Izvestiia Imperatorskogo Russkogo Geograficheskogo obshchestva.

*IV*. Istoricheskii vestnik.

*IZ*. Istoricheskie zapiski.

*KON-RU*. Kratkii otchet o sostoianii i deistviiakh Imperatorskogo Novorossiiskogo universiteta.

*KOSVU*. Kratkii otchet o sostoianii i deiatel'nosti Imperatorskogo Universiteta sv. Vladimira.

*LRN: Biol*. Liudi russkoi nauki: biologiia, meditsina, sel'skokhoziastvennye nauki. I. V. Kuznetsov, ed. Moscow, 1963.

*LRN: Geol*. Liudi russkoi nauki: geologiia, geografiia. I. V. Kuznetsov, ed. Moscow, 1962.

*LRN: Mat*. Liudi russkoi nauki: matematika, mekhanika, astronomiia, fizika, khimiia. I. V. Kuznetsov, ed. Moscow, 1961.

*MB*. Mir bozhii.

*MBS-AN*. Materialy dlia biograficheskogo slovariia deistvitel'nykh chlenov Imperatorskoi Akademii nauk. 2 vols. Petrograd, 1915-17.

*MIAU*. Materialy dlia istorii akademicheskikh uchrezhdenii za 1889–1914 gg. Vol. I. Petrograd, 1917.

*MS*. Matematicheskii sbornik.

*NN*. Nauchnoe nasledstvo.

*NO*. Nauchnoe obozrenie.

*NS*. Nauchnoe slovo.

*OIGZ*. Ocherki po istorii geologicheskikh nauk.

*O-MU*. Otchet o sostoianii i deistviiakh Imperatorskogo Moskovskogo universiteta.

*O-StPU*. Otchet o sostoianii i deiatel'nosti S. Peterburgskogo universiteta.

*RB*. Russkoe bogatstvo.

*RBS*. Russkii biograficheskii slovar'. 25 vols. St. Petersburg, 1896–1913.

*RM*. Russkaia mysl'.

*RV*. Russkii vestnik.

*TBPB*. Trudy Biuro po prikladnoi botanike.

*TIIE*. Trudy Instituta istorii estestvoznaniia.

*TIIE-T*. Trudy Instituta istorii estestvoznaniia i tekhniki.

*UZMU*. Uchenyi zapiski Moskovskogo universiteta.

*VAN*. Vestnik Akademii nauk SSSR.

*VE*. Vestnik Evropy.

*Vengerov-slovar'*. Kritiko-biograficheskii slovar' russkikh pisatelei i uchenykh. 6 vols. S. A. Vengerov, ed. St. Petersburg, 1889–1904.

*VFP*. Voprosy filosofii i psikhologii.

*VIE-T*. Voprosy istorii estestvoznaniia i tekhniki.

*VLU*. Vestnik Leningradskogo universiteta.

*VOL*. Vremennik Obshchestva sodeistviia uspekham opytnykh nauk i ikh prakticheskikh primenenii imeni Kh. S. Ledentsova.

*ZAN*. Zapiski Imperatorskoi Akademii nauk.

*ZFKhO*. Zhurnal Russkogo Fiziko-khimicheskogo obshchestva.

*ZMNP*. Zhurnal Ministerstva Narodnogo prosveshcheniia.

A. B. "Notice sur la vie et les travaux de Dmitrii Ivanowitch Mendeléeff," *Le Moniteur scientifique*, XXXIV (1889), 904–8.

Aksakov, A. N. "Mediumizm i filosofiia. Vospominaniia o professore Moskovskogo universiteta Iurkeviche," *RV*, 1876, No. 1, pp. 442–69.

Aksel'rod [Ortodoks], L. O "Problemakh idealizma." Odessa, 1905.

Aleksandrov, A. D., A. N. Kolmogorov, and M. A. Lavrent'ev, eds. Mathematics: Its Content, Methods, and Meanings. 3 vols. Tr. from the Russian by S. H. Gould. Cambridge, Mass.: M.I.T. Press, 1963.

Aleksandrov, P. S. "O vazhneishikh predmetakh vospitaniia," *Nauka i zhizn'*, 1967, No. 7, pp. 10–15.

———. "Russkaia matematika XIX i XX vv. i ee vlianie na mirovoiu nauku," *UZMU*, XLI (1947), 3–34.

Aleksandrov, P. S. *See also* Alexandroff, P.

Alekseev, V. A. Darvinizm: Khrestomatiia. Vol. I. Moscow, 1951.

———, ed. Osnovy darvinizma. Moscow, 1964.

Alekseev, V. G. N. V. Bugaev i problemy idealizma Moskovskoi matematicheskoi shkoly. Iur'ev, 1905.

———. K voprosu o neobkhodimosti dlia estestvoispytatelei izucheniia matematiki. Iur'ev, 1902.

———. Matematika kak osnovanie kritiki nauchno-filosofskogo mirovozzreniia. Iur'ev, 1903.

———. Osnovy simvolicheskoi teorii invariantov (dlia khimikov). Iur'ev, 1901.

Alekseev, V. G. *See also* Alexejeff, W.

Aleshintsev, I. Soslovnyi vopros i politika v istorii nashikh gimnazii v XIX veke. St. Petersburg, 1908.

Alexandroff, P. [P. S. Aleksandrov]. "Théorie des fonctions: Sur la puissance des ensembles measurables B," *CR-AS-P*, CLXII (1916), 323–25.

Alexejeff, W. [V. G. Alekseev]. "Über die Entwicklung der höheren arithmologischen Gesetzmässigkeit in Natur- und Geisteswissenschaften," *Vierteljahrsschrift für wissenschaftliche Philosophie und Soziologie*, XXVIII (1904), 73–92.

Andreevich [E. Solov'ev]. Opyt filosofii russkoi literatury. 2d ed. St. Petersburg, 1909.

Andrusov, N. I. "O vozraste zemli," *Priroda*, 1912, No. 3, pp. 393–465.

Anokhin, P. K. Ivan Petrovich Pavlov: Zhizn', deiatel'nost' i nauchnaia shkola. Moscow-Leningrad, 1949.

"Antonovich, Maksim Alekseevich," *Vengerov-Slovar'*, I (1889), 666–82.

Antonovich, M. A. Charlz Darvin i ego teoriia. St. Petersburg, 1896.

———. "Dva tipa sovremennykh filosofov," *Sovremennik*, LXXXVI (1861), Sect. 2, pp. 349–418.

———. Izbrannye filosofskie sochineniia. Moscow, 1945.

———. Literaturno-kriticheskie stat'i. Moscow-Leningrad, 1961.

———. "Predislovie," *Novoe obozrenie*, 1881, No. 1, pp. 227–46.

———. "Sovremennaia fiziologiia i filosofiia," *Sovremennik*, XCI (1862), Sec. 2, pp. 227–66.

"Anuchin, Dmitrii Nikolaevich," *MBS-AN*, I, 1–14.

Anuchin, D. N. "Geografiia," *Brockhaus-Efron*, VIII (1892), 377–90.

———. O liudiakh russkoi nauki i kul'tury. Moscow, 1952.

Arbuzov, A. E. Kratkii ocherk razvitiia organicheskoi khimii v Rossii. Moscow-Leningrad, 1948.

———, ed. Materialy po istorii otechestvennoi khimii. Moscow-Leningrad, 1950–53.

Arsen'ev, K., *et al*. Intelligentsia v Rossii: Sbornik statei. St. Petersburg, 1910.

—— *et al.* M. M. Kovalevskii: Uchenyi, gosudarstvennyi i obshchestvennyi deiatel' i grazhdanin. Petrograd, 1917.

A. S. "Organizatsiia srednei shkoly v Rossii v sviazi s usloviiami gosudarstvennoi i obshchestvennoi zhizni," *Obrazovanie*, 1903, No. 12, Sect. 2, pp. 84–108.

Avenarius, R. Kritika chistogo opyta v populiarnom izlozhenii A. Lunacharskogo. Moscow, 1905.

A. V. G. "Chetvertoe izmerenie i spiritizm," *VE*, 1879, No. 1–2, pp. 253–71.

A-v-s-v. "Russkoe Geograficheskoe obshchestvo i ego poluvekovaia deiatel'nost'," *RB*, 1896, No. 4, Sect. 2, pp. 139–44.

Babkin, B. P. Pavlov: A Biography. Chicago: University of Chicago Press, 1949.

Babskii, E. B. I. P. Pavlov: Zhizn' i deiatel'nost'. 2d ed. Moscow, 1959.

Bachinskii, A. I. "Chto takoe naturalisticheskii idealizm?," in Bachinskii *et al.*, pp. 71–85.

——. "Dukh beskonechno malykh ili o vozmozhnom vlianii matematicheskikh metodov na cherty nauchnogo miroponimaniia," in Bachinskii *et al.*, pp. 183–205.

——. "Kharakteristika N. A. Umova kak uchenogo, kak myslitelia i kak cheloveka," *BSNM* (New Series), XXIX (1916), Supplement, pp. 76–95.

——. "Nikolai Alekseevich Umov," *Priroda*, 1915, No. 2, pp. 285–306.

——. "Pis'ma po filosofii estestvoznaniia, Pis'mo I: Chto takoe naturalisticheskii idealizm?," *VFP*, 1903, No. 70, pp. 806–23.

——. "Pis'ma po filosofii estestvoznaniia, Pis'mo II: O vozmozhnom vlianii matematicheskikh metodov na cherty nauchnogo miroponimaniia (posviashchaetsia pamiati moego uchitelia N. V. Bugaeva)," *VFP*, 1905, No. 76, pp. 86–110.

——. "Zamechatel'nyi russkii uchenyi N. A. Umov," *RM*, 1916, No. 3, Sect. 2, pp. 26–34.

—— *et al.* Sbornik po filosofii estestvoznaniia. Moscow, 1906.

Baer, Karl Ernst von. Reden, gehalten in wissenschaftlichen Versammlungen und kleinere Aussätze vermischten Inhalts. Vol. II. St. Petersburg, 1876.

Bagalei, D. I. "Ekonomicheskoe polozhenie russkikh universitetov," *VE*, 1914, No. 1, pp. 222–53.

——. Kakovy dolzhny byt' shtaty Imperatorskogo Khar'kovskogo universiteta dlia udovletvoreniia ego neotlozhnykh nuzhd? Khar'kov, 1910.

——, N. F. Sumtsov, and V. P. Buzeskul. Kratkii ocherk istorii Khar'kovskogo universiteta za pervye sto let ego sushchestvovaniia (1805–1905). Khar'kov, 1906.

Baikov, A. A. Dmitrii Petrovich Konovalov. Leningrad, 1928.

Bakunin, A. I., ed. M. A. Bakunin. St. Petersburg, 1906.

Balandin, A. A., N. E. Zelinskii, and A. N. Zelinskii. "Zhizn' i nauchnaia deiatel'nost' N. D. Zelinskogo," in N. D. Zelinskii, Izbrannye trudy, pp. 577–641.

Balfour, Francis M. A Treatise on Comparative Embryology. 2 vols. London: Macmillan, 1880–81.

Ball, R. S. "Comets," *Nature*, XXX (1884), 454–57.

Bal'talon, V. "Pedagogicheskie vzgliady Pisareva," *Obrazovanie*, 1897: No. 10, pp. 1–29; No. 11, pp. 1–14; No. 12, pp. 20–33.

Banina, N. N. K. F. Kessler i ego rol' v razvitii biologii v Rossii. Moscow-Leningrad, 1962.

Bari, N. K. "Nikolai Nikolaevich Luzin," in *LRN: Mat.*, pp. 336–46.

Barkhatova, N. N. Geologicheskie issledovaniia Russkogo Geograficheskogo obshchestva, 1845–1917 gg. Moscow-Leningrad, 1955.

――――. "Vklad Vsesoiuznogo Geograficheskogo obshchestva v otechestvennuiu geolo-giiu," *OIGZ*, III (1955), 45–75.

Baron, Samuel H. "The First Decade of Russian Marxism," *American Slavic and East European Review*, XIV (1955), 315–30.

――――. "Legal Marxism and the 'Fate of Capitalism' in Russia," *American Slavic and East European Review*, XVI (1957), 113–26.

Barth, Paul. Die Philosophie der Geschichte als Soziologie. 2d ed., Vol. I. Leipzig, 1915.

Bazarov, V. "Mistitsizm i realizm nashego vremeni," in Bazarov *et al.*, pp. 3–71.

―――― *et al.* Ocherki po filosofii marksizma. St. Petersburg, 1908.

Bazilevskaia, N. A. "Sistematika i filogeniia v Rossii na rubezhe XX veka," *VIE-T*, X (1960), 119–24.

Beale, G. H. "Timiriazev, Founder of Soviet Genetics," *Nature*, CLIX (1947), 51–53.

Beketov, A. N. "Garmoniia v prirode," in Vasetskii and Mikulinskii, pp. 545–82.

――――. Istoricheskii ocherk dvadtsatiletnei deiatel'nosti Imperatorskogo Vol'nogo ekonomicheskogo obshchestva s 1865 do 1890 goda. St. Petersburg, 1890.

――――. Iz zhizni prirody. St. Petersburg, 1870.

Beketov, N. N. Nauka i nravstvennost'. St. Petersburg, 1903.

――――. Rechi khimika: Obshchedostupnye lektsii, stat'i, rechi i doklady—iz oblasti khimii i fiziki. St. Petersburg, 1908.

――――. "Znachenie periodicheskoi sistemy D. I. Mendeleeva," in "Trudy Pervogo Mendeleevskogo s'ezda," pp. 33–35.

Bekhterev, V. M. General Principles of Human Reflexology: An Introduction to the Objective Study of Personality. Tr. from the Russian by E. Murphy and W. Murphy. New York: International Publishers, 1932.

――――. "Ob obshchikh osnovakh refleksologii kak nauchnoi distsipliny," *Priroda*, 1917, No. 11–12, pp. 1101–28.

Belov, N. V. "Velikii russkii kristallograf i ego detishche," in E. S. Fedorov, *Simmetriia*, pp. 580–86.

Benfey, O. Theodor, ed. Classics in the Theory of Chemical Combination. New York: Dover, 1963.

Berdiaev, N. A. "Bor'ba za idealizm," *MB*, 1901, No. 6, Sect. 1, pp. 1–26.

――――. "Eticheskaia problema v svete filosofskogo idealizma," in Novgorodtsev, Problemy idealizma, pp. 91–137.

――――. "Filosofskaia istina i intelligentskaia pravda," in Berdiaev *et al.*, pp. 1–22.

――――. Filosofiia neravenstva. Berlin, 1923.

――――. "Gnoseologicheskaia problema (k kritike krititsizma)," *VFP*, 1910, No. 5, pp. 281–308.

――――. "A. S. Khomiakov kak filosof (k stoletiiu dnia rozhdeniia)," *MB*, 1904, No. 7, Sect. 2, pp. 17–22.

――――. "F. A. Lange i kriticheskaia filosofiia," *MB*, 1900, No. 7, pp. 224–54.

――――. Sub specie aeternitatis: Opyty filosofskie, sotsial'nye i literaturnye (1900–1906). St. Petersburg, 1907.

――――. "Vera i znanie," *VFP*, 1910, No. 102, pp. 198–234.

―――― *et al.* Vekhi: Sbornik statei o russkoi intelligentsii. 4th ed. Moscow, 1909.

Berdyshev, G. D., and V. N. Siplivinskii. Pervyi sibirskii professor botaniki Korzhinskii. Novosibirsk, 1961.

Berg, L. S. "Avtobiograficheskaia zapiska," in Murzaev, pp. 7–17.

――――. Istoriia russkikh geograficheskikh otkrytii. Moscow, 1962.

――――. Izbrannye trudy, Vol. I. Moscow, 1956.

――――. Nomogenesis, or: Evolution Determined by Law. Tr. from the Russian by J. N. Rostovtsev. Cambridge, Mass.: M.I.T. Press, 1969.

————. Vsesoiuznoe Geograficheskoe obshchestvo za sto let. Moscow-Leningrad, 1946.

Berman, Ia. Dialektika v svete sovremennoi teorii poznaniia. Moscow, 1907.

Berman, Z. I., A. L. Zelikman, and V. I. Polianskii. "Vozniknovenie i razvitie nauch-nykh techenii, napravlennykh protiv teorii Darvina," in V. I. Polianskii and Iu. I. Polianskii, pp. 236–85.

Bernard, Claude. An Introduction to the Study of Experimental Medicine. Tr. from the French by H. C. Greene. New York: Collier, 1961.

Bernatskii, M. V., ed. K kharakteristike sovremennogo studenchestva. 2d ed. St. Peters-burg, 1911.

Bernstein, Eduard. Evolutionary Socialism: A Criticism and Affirmation. Tr. from the German by E. C. Harvey. New York: Huebsch, 1911.

————. Zur Geschichte und Theorie des Sozialismus: Gesammelte Abhandlungen. Berlin-Bern, 1901.

————. "Tugan-Baranowsky als Sozialist," Archiv für Sozialwissenschaft und Sozial-politik, XXVIII (1909), 786–96.

Berry, A. J. From Classical to Modern Chemistry. New York: Dover, 1968.

Berthelot, M. Science et morale. Paris, 1897.

Bertrand, J. Traité de calcul différentiel et de calcul intégral. 2 vols. Paris, 1864–70.

Besredka, A. Histoire d'une idée: L'Oeuvre de E. Metchnikoff. Paris, 1921.

Beyme, Klaus von. Politische Soziologie im zaristischen Russland. Wiesbaden, 1965.

Bezredko, Sh. Opyt istorii razvitiia stereokhimicheskikh predstavlenii. Odessa, 1892.

B. G. "Butlerov, Aleksandr Mikhailovich," RBS, II (1903), 528–33.

"Bibliograficheskii listok," VE, 1913, No. 4, pp. 435–38.

Black, C. E., ed. The Transformation of Russian Society. Cambridge, Mass.: Harvard University Press, 1960.

Blagovidov, F. "Imperator Aleksandr II i tsenzurnye reformy 1860-kh godov," IV, XCIX (1905), 879–903.

Bliakher, L. Ia. "Aleksandr Onufrievich Kovalevskii," LRN: Biol., pp. 157–72.

————. Istoriia embriologii v Rossii XIX–XX vv.: Bespozvonochnye. Moscow, 1959.

————. "Nauchnye sviazi A. O. Kovalevskogo i I. I. Mechnikova s zarubezhnymi zoologami i embriologami," TIIE-T, XXIII (1959), 93–143.

Blin-Stoyle, R. J., et al. Turning Points in Physics. New York: Harper, 1961.

Bobrovskii, S. "Sud'ba estestvoznaniia v nashikh shkolakh i v obshchestve," Obrazo-vanie, 1898, No. 12, pp. 80–94.

Bobynin, V. V. Filosofskoe, nauchnoe i pedagogicheskoe znachenie istorii matematiki. Moscow, 1886.

————. Ocherki istorii razvitiia fiziko-matematicheskikh znanii v Rossii. 2 vols. Mos-cow, 1886–93.

————. Opyty matematicheskogo izlozheniia logiki. 2 vols. Moscow, 1886–94.

————, ed. Matematiko-astronomicheskie i fizicheskie sektsii pervykh deviati s'ezdov russkikh estestvoispytatelei i vrachei. Vol. I. Moscow, 1896.

Bogdanov, A. A. "Bogdanov (Malinovskii), Aleksandr Aleksandrovich," in Deiateli Soiuza Sovetskikh Sotsialisticheskikh Respublik i Oktiabr'skoi Revoliutsii: Avto-biografii i biografii, I, 29–33. Moscow, n.d. An autobiography.

————. Empiriomonizm: Stat'i po filosofii. 3 vols. Moscow, 1904–6.

————. "Filosofiia sovremennogo estestvoispytatelia," in N. Verner et al., pp. 35–142.

————. Filosofiia zhivogo opyta. Moscow, 1920.

————. " 'Ideal poznaniia' (Empiriokrititsizm i empiriomonizm)," VFP, 1903, No. 67, pp. 186–233.

————. Iz psikhologii obshchestva. 2d ed. St. Petersburg, 1906.

————. Kul'turnye zadachi nashego vremeni. Moscow, 1911.

——. Osnovnye elementy istoricheskogo vzgliada na prirodu. St. Petersburg, 1899.

——. Padenie velikogo fetishizma: Vera i nauka. Moscow, 1910.

——. Poznanie s istoricheskoi tochki zreniia. St. Petersburg, 1902.

——. Prikliucheniia odnoi filosofskoi shkoly. St. Petersburg, 1908.

——. Sotsializm nauki. Moscow, 1918.

——. "Taina nauki," in A. A. Bogdanov, Sotsializm nauki, pp. 64–104. This chapter was originally published in 1913.

——. Tektologiia: Vseobshchaia organizatsionnaia nauka. 3 vols. Berlin-Petrograd-Moscow, 1922.

——. Vseobshchaia organizatsionnaia nauka (tektologiia). 2 vols. St. Petersburg, 1913–17.

——. "Zhizn' i psikhika (empiriomonizm v uchenii o zhizni)," VFP, 1903: No. 69, pp. 682–708; No. 70, pp. 824–66.

Bogdanov, A. A. See also Verner, N.

Bogdanov, E. [A. A. Bogdanov]. "Strana idolov i filosofiia marksizma," in Bazarov et al., pp. 215–42.

Bogdanov, M. N. Karl Fedorovich Kessler. St. Petersburg, 1882.

Bogdanov, V. V. Piatidesiatiletie Imperatorskogo Obshchestva liubitelei estestvoznaniia, antropologii i etnografii, 1863–1913. Moscow, 1915.

Bogdanovich, T. A. Liubov' liudei shestidesiatykh godov. Leningrad, 1929.

Bogorad, Lawrence. "Photosynthesis," in Jensen and Kavaljian, pp. 35–70.

Borisiak, A. A. "K iubileiu A. P. Karpinskogo," Priroda, 1916, No. 12, pp. 1457–62.

——. V. O. Kovalevskii: Ego zhizn' i nauchnye trudy. Leningrad, 1928.

——. "Po povodu prazdnovaniia 150-letiia Gornogo Instituta," Priroda, 1926, No. 3–4, pp. 49–64.

——. "Vitalizm i teoriia poznaniia," NO, 1899, No. 4, pp. 793–99.

——. "Vladimir Onufrievich Kovalevskii," Priroda, 1918, No. 1, pp. 27–46.

Borodin, A. P., and A. M. Butlerov. "Nikolai Nikolaevich Zinin: Vospominaniia o nem i biograficheskii ocherk," ZAN, XXXVII (1880), Pt. 1, pp. 1–46.

Borodin, I. P. "Protoplazma i vitalizm," MB, 1894, No. 5, pp. 1–29.

Borodowsky, N. A. "Absorption of Beta Rays from Radium by Solutions and Liquids," Philosophical Magazine, XIX (1910), pp. 605–19.

Borozdin, A. "Danilevskii, Nikolai Iakovlevich," RBS, VII (1905), 67–72.

Borozdin, I. N. "Universitety v Rossii v epokhu 60-kh godov," Granat-Ist., IV, 185–212.

Borzenikov, Ia. "Istoricheskii ocherk napravlenii sushchestvovavshikh v zoologicheskikh naukakh v XIX stoletii," Rech' i otchet chitannye v torzhestvennom sobranii Imperatorskogo Moskovskogo universiteta 12-go ianvaria 1881 g., pp. 3–61. Moscow, 1881.

Botiashkov, F. "Zhenskii svobodnyi universitet," MB, 1903, No. 12, Sect. 2, pp. 1–13.

Bristol, L. M. Social Adaptation. Cambridge, Mass.: Harvard University Press, 1915.

Briullova-Shaskol'skaia, N. N. "Lavrov i Mikhailovskii," in Radlov et al., pp. 404–19.

Buckle, Henry Thomas. History of Civilization in England, 4th ed., Vol. I. London: Longmans, 1864.

Budilova, E. A. Bor'ba materializma i idealizma v russkoi psikhologicheskoi nauke. Moscow, 1960.

Bugaev, N. V. "Matematika i nauchno-filosofskoe mirovosozertsanie," VFP, 1898, No. 45, pp. 697–717.

——. "Osnovnye nachala evoliutsionnoi monadologii," VFP, 1893, No. 17, pp. 26–44.

Bulgakov, S. N. "Osnovnye problemy teorii progressa," in Novgorodtsev, Problemy idealizma, pp. 1–47.

Bunn, C. W. Chemical Crystallography: An Introduction to Optical and X-Ray Methods. 2d ed. Oxford: Clarendon, 1961.
Butlerov, A. M. "Chetvertoe izmerenie prostora i mediumizm," *RV*, 1878, No. 2, pp. 945–71.
———. "Mediumicheskie iavleniia," *RV*, 1875, No. 11, pp. 300–348.
———. Sochineniia. 3 vols. Moscow, 1953–58.
Bychkovskii, B. S. Sovremennaia filosofiia, Vol. I. St. Petersburg, 1911.
Bykov, G. V. Aleksandr Mikhailovich Butlerov. Moscow, 1961.
———. "Dva otzyva D. I. Mendeleeva ob A. M. Butlerove," *Uspekhi khimii*, XXII (1953), 115–18.
———. Istoriia klassicheskoi teorii khimicheskogo stroeniia. Moscow, 1960.
———. "Zabytye izdaniia lektsii A. M. Butlerova po khimii," *TIIE-T*, II (1954), 67–90.
Bykov, K. M. " 'Lektsii o rabote glavnykh pishchevaritel'nykh zhelez' I. P. Pavlova i ikh rol' v razvitii estestvoznaniia i meditsiny," in I. P. Pavlov, Lektsii, pp. 263–88.
———. "O tvorchestve I. P. Pavlova," in Sechenov *et al.*, IV, 674–84.

Campbell-Gamble, D. J. "Chromatographic Analysis (Correspondence)," *Chemistry and Industry*, LIX (1940), 598.
Chebyshev, P. L. Izbrannye matematicheskie trudy. Moscow-Leningrad, 1946.
———. Nauchnoe nasledie P. L. Chebysheva, Vol. II. Moscow-Leningrad, 1945.
———. Polnoe sobranie sochinenii. 5 vols. Moscow-Leningrad, 1946–51.
Chelpanov, G. "Ob otnoshenii psikhologii k filosofii," *VFP*, 1907, No. 4, pp. 309–23.
Chel'tsov, I. "Mendeleev, Dmitrii Ivanovich," *BS-StPU*, II, 17–21.
Chemen, I. A. Darvinizm: Nauchnoe issledovanie teorii Darvina o proiskhozhdenii cheloveka. Odessa, 1892.
Cherniavskii, V. I. P. P. Semenov-Tian-Shanskii i ego trudy po geografii. Moscow, 1955.
Chernov, V. M. Filosofskie i sotsiologicheskie etiudy. Moscow, 1907.
———. "Sub'ektivnyi metod v sotsiologii i ego filosofskie predposylki," *RB*, 1901: No. 7, pp. 231–56; No. 8, pp. 219–62; No. 10, pp. 107–56; No. 11, pp. 115–62; No. 12, pp. 123–75.
Chernov, V. M. *See also* Gardenin, Iu.
Chernyshev, F. N. "Russkaia ekspeditsiia na Shpitsbergen," *MB*, 1901, No. 2, pp. 256–86.
Chernyshevskii, N. G. Antropologicheskii printsip v filosofii. Moscow, 1948.
———. Polnoe sobranie sochinenii. Vol. X, Pt. 2. St. Petersburg, 1906.
Chetaev, N. G. "Aleksandr Mikhailovich Liapunov," *LRN: Mat.*, pp. 200–205.
Chicherin, B. N. Mistitsizm v nauke. Moscow, 1880.
———. Nauka i religiia. Moscow, 1879.
———. Neskol'ko sovremennykh voprosov. Moscow, 1862.
———. Philosophische Forschungen. Heidelberg, 1899.
———. Polozhitel'naia filosofiia i edinstvo nauki. Moscow, 1892.
———. I. Sistema khimicheskikh elementov. II. Zakony obrazovaniia khimicheskikh elementov. Moscow, 1911.
———. Vospominaniia: Moskovskii universitet. Moscow, 1929.
Chugaev, L. A. Dmitrii Ivanovich Mendeleev: Zhizn' i deiatel'nost'. Leningrad, 1924.
———. "Evoliutsiia veshchestva v mertvoi i zhivoi prirode," in Ipat'ev, Chugaev, pp. 137–52.
———. O khimicheskom stroenii. St. Petersburg, 1910.
———. "Predmet i zadachi sovremennoi khimii," in Ipat'ev, Chugaev, pp. 125–36.
———. "Sovremennye zadachi organicheskoi khimii," in Ipat'ev, Chugaev, pp. 153–71.

————, ed. Novye idei v khimii, Vol. I. St. Petersburg, 1912.

Chuprov, A. A. Ocherki po teorii statistiki. St. Petersburg, 1909.

[Chuprov, A. I.] "Studencheskie gody A. I. Chuprova (v pis'makh k V. M. Amfitea-trovu)," VE, 1912, No. 6, pp. 157–62.

Chwolson, O. D. [O. D. Khvol'son]. Lehrbuch der Physik. Vol. I. Tr. from the Russian by H. Pflaum. Braunschweig, 1902.

Clerke, Agnes M. A Popular History of Astronomy During the Nineteenth Century. 4th ed. London: Black, 1902.

Clifford, William Kingdon. The Common Sense of the Exact Sciences. New York: Dover, 1955.

————. Lectures and Essays. 2 vols. London: Macmillan, 1901.

Coker, F. W. Organismic Theories of the State: Nineteenth Century Interpretations of the State as Organism and as Person. New York: Columbia University Press, 1910.

Coquart, Armand. Dmitri Pisarev (1840–1868) et l'idéologie du nihilisme russe. Paris, 1946.


Dan, Theodore. The Origins of Bolshevism. Tr. from the Russian by J. Carmichael. New York: Harper, 1964.

Danilevskii, Aleksandr. "Zhivoe veshchestvo," VE, 1896, No. 5, pp. 289–336.

Danilevskii, N. Ia. Darvinizm: Kriticheskoe issledovanie. 2 vols. St. Petersburg, 1885–89.

————. Rossiia i Evropa. 3d ed. St. Petersburg, 1888.

Danilevskii, V. V. Russkaia tekhnika. Leningrad, 1948.

Darwin, Charles. The Descent of Man and Selection in Relation to Sex. New York: Clarke, 1874.

Darwin, Francis, ed. The Life and Letters of Charles Darwin. Vol. III. London: Murray, 1887.

Darwin, George. "The Genesis of Double Stars," in Seward, pp. 543–64.

Davitashvili, L. Sh. "Biografiia Vladimira Onufrievicha Kovalevskogo," in V. O. Kovalevskii, Sobranie nauchnykh trudov, I, 9–155.

————. V. O. Kovalevskii. 2d ed. Moscow, 1951.

————. "Vladimir Onufrievich Kovalevskii," LRN: Geol., pp. 23–32.

Davydov, K. N. "A. O. Kovalevskii kak chelovek i kak uchenyi (vospominaniia uchen-ika)," TIIE-T, XXXI (1960), 326–63.

Davydov, N. "Iz proshlogo: Kniaz S. N. Trubetskoi," Golos minuvshego, 1917, No. 1, pp. 5–34.

Dawydoff, C. [K. N. Davydov]. Traité d'embriologie comparée des invertébrés. Paris, 1928.

de Beer, Sir Gavin. Charles Darwin: A Scientific Biography. New York: Doubleday, 1965.

"Deiatel'nost' Obshchestva za vtoruiu polovinu 1910 g.," VOL, 1911, No. 1, pp. 5–17.

"Deiatel'nost' Obshchestva za pervuiu polovinu 1911 g.," VOL, 1911, No. 2, pp. 5–21.

Delone, B. N. Matematika i ee razvitie v Rossii. Moscow, 1948.

————. Peterburgskaia shkola teorii chisel. Moscow-Leningrad, 1947.

Dembo, G. E., ed. Desiatyi s'ezd russkikh vrachei v pamiat' N. I. Pirogova—Moskva, 25 aprelia–2 maia 1907 goda. St. Petersburg, 1907.

Demidova, N. V. "D. I. Pisarev i nigilizm 60-kh godov," VLU: Seriia ekonomiki, 1965, No. 1, pp. 54–65.

Deviatyi Pirogovskii s'ezd. 3 vols. St. Petersburg, 1903–4.

De Witt, Nicholas. "Scholarship in the Natural Sciences," in Black, pp. 385–405.

de Vries, Hugo. "The Evidence of Evolution," *Science* (New Series), XX (1904), 395–401.

Dhéré, Charles. "Michel Tswett: Le créateur de l'analyse chromatographique par adsorption. Sa vie, ses travaux sur les pigments chlorophylliens." *Candollea*, X (1943), 23–73.

Dnevnik IX s'ezda russkikh estestvoispytatelei i vrachei. 10 vols. Moscow, 1894.

Dnevnik X s'ezda russkikh estestvoispytatelei i vrachei v Kieve. 10 vols. Kiev, 1898.

Dnevnik XI s'ezda russkikh estestvoispytatelei i vrachei v S. Peterburge. 11 vols. St. Petersburg, 1902.

Dnevnik XII s'ezda russkikh estestvoispytatelei i vrachei v Moskve. Moscow, 1910.

Dnevnik XIII s'ezda russkikh estestvoispytatelei i vrachei v Tiflise. 10 vols. Tiflis, 1913.

Dobroliubov, N. A. Izbrannye filosofskie proizvedeniia. Vol. I. Moscow, 1948.

———. Sochineniia. Vol. I. St. Petersburg, n.d.

Dobzhansky, Theodosius. "Foreword to Paperback Edition," in Berg, *Nomogenesis*, pp. vii–xii.

———. "N. I. Vavilov, A Martyr of Genetics," *Journal of Heredity*, XXXVIII (1947), 227–32.

Dogel', V. A. "Embriologicheskie raboty A. O. Kovalevskogo v 60-kh–80-kh godakh XIX v.," *NN*, I (1948), 206–18.

———, and A. E. Gasinovich. "Osnovnye cherty tvorchestva I. I. Mechnikova kak biologa," in I. I. Mechnikov, Izbrannye biologicheskie proizvedeniia, pp. 677–725.

Dokuchaev, V. V. Russkii chernozem. 2d ed. Moscow, 1952.

Dorovatovskii, S., and A. Charushnikov, eds. Ocherki realisticheskogo mirovozzreniia. 2d ed. St. Petersburg, 1905.

Dostoevskii, A. A., ed. Petr Petrovich-Tian-Shanskii. Leningrad, 1928.

Dostoevskii, F. M. Pis'ma. Edited by M. S. Dolinin. 4 vols. Moscow-Leningrad, 1928–59.

Doviner, D. V. "Pioner otechestvennoi fiziologii," *Priroda*, 1953, No. 12, pp. 66–70.

Drentel'n, N. "Mirovozzrenie fizika-filosofa," *RM*, 1917, No. 7–8, Sect. 2, pp. 119–28.

Droshin, P. "Studencheskaia zhizn'," *Otechestvennye zapiski*, 1879, No. 1, Sect. 2, pp. 1–30.

Du Bois-Reymond, Emil. Über die Grenzen des Naturerkennens: Die Sieben Welträtsel. Leipzig, 1882.

Duff, J. D., ed. Russian Realities and Problems. Cambridge, Eng.: Cambridge University Press, 1917.

Dvadtsatpiat' let, 1859–1884: Sbornik izdannyi Komitetom Obshchestva dlia posobiia nuzhdaiushchimsia literatoram i uchenym. St. Petersburg, 1884.

Dvukhsotletie pamiati N'iutona (1687–1887). Moscow, 1888.

Dynkin, E. B. Markov Processes. Tr. from the Russian by J. Fabius *et al.* 2 vols. Berlin, 1965.

Dynnik, M. A., *et al.*, eds. Istoriia filosofii. Vol. IV. Moscow, 1959.

Dzhanshiev, G. Epokha velikikh reform. 8th ed. Moscow, 1900.


Egoroff, D. Th. "Analyse mathematique: Sur les suites des fonctions mesurables," *CR-AS-P*, CLII (1911), 244–46.

Eikhenval'd, A. A. "O nauchnykh rabotakh N. A. Umova po fizike," *BSNM* (New Series), XXIX (1916), Supplement, pp. 55–66.

Eimontova, R. G. "Universitetskaia reforma 1863 g.," *IZ*, LXX (1961), 163–96.

Einstein, Albert. Out of My Later Years. New York: Philosophical Library, 1950.

E. R. "Russkie ratsionalisty: 1. Subbotniki; 2. Dukhobortsy," *VE*, 1881, No. 2, pp. 650–89.

——. "Russkie ratsionalisty: 3. Molokane; 4. Shtundisty," *VE*, 1881, No. 7, pp. 272–323.

Erman, L. K. "Sostav intelligentsii v Rossii v kontse XIX i nachale XX v.," *Istoriia SSSR*, 1963, No. 1, pp. 161–77.

Ern, V. F. "Priroda nauchnoi mysli," *Bogoslovskii vestnik*, I (1914), 154–73, 342–68.

Esafov, V. I. "Materialy k istorii voprosa o vozniknovenii stereokhimicheskogo ucheniia i ob otnoshenii k nemu A. M. Butlerova i nekotorykh sovremennykh emu zapadno-evropeiskikh khimikov," *TIIE-T*, XXX (1960), 143–74.

Esakov, V. A. D. N. Anuchin i sozdanie russkoi universitetskoi geograficheskoi shkoly. Moscow, 1955.

Ewald, P. P., ed. Fifty Years of X-Ray Diffraction. Utrecht, 1962.


Famintsyn, A. S. "N. Ia. Danilevskii i darvinizm," *VE*, 1889, No. 2, pp. 616–43.

——. "Nakanune universitetskoi reformy," *MB*, 1903, No. 1, Sect. 1, pp. 238–55.

——. Sovremennoe estestvoznanie i psikhologiia. St. Petersburg, 1898.

Fearing, Franklin. Reflex Action: A Study in the History of Physiological Psychology. New York and London: Hafner, 1964.

Fedorov, E. S. Kurs kristallografii. 3d ed. St. Petersburg, 1901.

——. "Ob usloviiakh nauchnoi deiatel'nosti v nashem obshchestve (pis'mo v redak-tsiiu)," *Russkie vedomosti*, 1903, No. 253.

——. "Perfektsionizm," *Izvestiia S. Peterburgskoi biologicheskoi laboratorii*, 1906: No. 1, pp. 25–65; No. 2, pp. 9–67.

——. "Priroda i chelovek," *Priroda*, 1917, No. 4, pp. 423–32.

——. Simmetriia i struktura kristallov. Moscow, 1949.

——. "Stroenie veshchestva i zakon N'iutona," *Priroda*, 1916, No. 7–8, pp. 779–88.

Fedorov, S. A. "Pamiati Khristofora Semenovicha Ledentsova," *VOL*, 1911, No. 1, pp. 35–43.

——. "Znachenie i trudy N. A. Umova v Obshchestve sodeistviia uspekham opyt-nykh nauk i ikh prakticheskikh primenenii (imeni Kh. S. Ledentsova)," *BSNM*, XXVI (1916), 43–50.

Ferliudin, P. Istoricheskii obzor mer po vysshemu obrazovaniiu v Rossii. Vol. I. Sara-tov, 1894.

Fersman, A. E. "Novyi zhurnal, posviashchennyi izucheniiu i metodam ispol'zovaniia estestvennykh bogatstv Rossii," *Priroda*, 1916, No. 5–6, pp. 753–54.

Figurovskii, N. A. Dmitrii Ivanovich Mendeleev. Moscow, 1961.

Filippov, M. "Darvinizm na russkoi pochve," *NO*, 1894: No. 32, pp. 993–1005; No. 33, pp. 1025–43; No. 34, pp. 1057–71; No. 35, pp. 1089–1105.

——. "Kont i ego uchenie," *NO*, 1898, No. 3, pp. 552–95.

——. "O filosofii chistogo opyta," *NO*, 1898: No. 5, pp. 924–37; No. 6, pp. 1054–69.

——. "Prostranstvo Lobachevskogo i mnogomernoe prostranstvo," *NO*, 1894: No. 15, pp. 450–59; No. 19, pp. 577–83; No. 22, pp. 679–87; No. 24, pp. 749–55; No. 25, pp. 769–76; No. 27, pp. 833–41; No. 28, pp. 865–72.

——. "Sub'ektivizm i narodnichestvo," *NO*, 1897, No. 12, pp. 114–30.

Findlay, Alexander. A Hundred Years of Chemistry. London: Duckworth, 1937.

Fischer, George. Russian Liberalism: From Gentry to Intelligentsia. Cambridge, Mass.: Harvard University Press, 1958.

Flammarion, Camille. Popular Astronomy. Tr. from the French by J. E. Gore. New York: Appleton, n.d.

Frank, S. "Krizis sovremennoi filosofii," *RM*, 1916, No. 19, Sect. 2, pp. 33–40.

Frenkel', V. Ia. Iakov Il'ich Frenkel'. Moscow, 1966.

Friche, V. M. "Vysshaia shkola v kontse veka," *Granat-Ist.*, IX, 145–63.

Frolov, Iu. P. Ivan Petrovich Pavlov: Vospominaniia. Moscow, 1949.

———. Pavlov and His School. Tr. from the Russian by C. P. Dutt. London: Kegan Paul, 1938.

Fulton, J. F. Muscular Contraction and the Reflex Control of Movement. Baltimore: Williams, 1926.


Gadolin, Axel. Abhandlung über die Herleitung aller krystallographischer Systeme mit ihren Unterabteilungen aus einem einzigen Prinzipe, in Ostwald's *Klassiker der exakten Wissenschaften*, No. 75 (1896).

Galakhov, Iakov. "Znachenie fiziki i matematiki v voprosakh religiozno-filosofskogo poriadka," *Vera i razum*, III (1913), 429–44.

Gamaleia, N. F. Sobranie sochinenii. Vol. V. Moscow, 1953.

Ganin, M. S. "Iadro kletki kak organ nasledstvennosti (kriticheskii analiz 'nuklearnoi teorii')," *NO*, 1894: No. 28, pp. 872–80; No. 29, pp. 897–905; No. 30, pp. 929–37.

Gardenin, Iu. [V. M. Chernov]. Pamiati N. K. Mikhailovskogo. St. Petersburg, 1901.

Gay, Peter. The Dilemma of Democratic Socialism: Eduard Bernstein's Challenge to Marx. New York: Columbia, 1952.

Gel'fenbein, L .L. Russkaia embriologiia vtoroi poloviny XIX veka. Khar'kov, 1956.

Gerasimov, I. P., *et al.* "L. S. Berg v Geograficheskom obshchestve," in Murzaev, pp. 61–66.

Gerchikov, M. G. "Pamiati zabytogo russkogo khimika," *Priroda*, 1932, No. 10, pp. 951–54.

Geronimus, Ia. L. Ocherki o rabotakh korifeev russkoi mekhaniki. Moscow, 1952.

Giacomelli, R., and E. Pistolesi. "Historical Sketch," in W. F. Durand, ed., Aerodynamic Theory: A General Review of Progress (2d ed.), I, 305–94. Pasadena: California Institute of Technology, 1943.

Gins, G. K. L. I. Petrazhitskii: Kharakteristika nauchnogo tvorchestva. Kharbin, 1931.

Gintsberg, V. Ia. "Uchenie L. I. Petrazhitskogo o prave i ego predposylki," *VFP*, 1909, No. 2, pp. 204–60.

Gizetti, A. "P. L. Lavrov i N. K. Mikhailovskii," in Vitiazev, pp. 39–41.

Glagolev, S. "Botanika i darvinizm," *Vera i razum*, 1907, No. 1, pp. 49–72.

———. "Mendelizm," *Bogoslovskii vestnik*, III (1913), 250–85, 476–505, 725–37.

———. "Novoe miroponimanie," *Bogoslovskii vestnik*, I (1911), 1–42.

———. O proiskhozhdenii i pervobytnom sostoianii roda chelovecheskogo. Moscow, 1894.

———. "Otsustvie religioznogo obrazovaniia v sovremennom obshchestve," *Bogoslovskii vestnik*, 1912, III, 273–96.

———. "Vzgliad Vasmanna na proiskhozhdenie cheloveka," *Bogoslovskii vestnik*, 1911: I, 621–42; II, 1–16, 417–50; III, 233–64.

Glinka, K. D. Dokuchaiev's Ideas in the Development of Pedology and Cognate Sciences. Leningrad, 1927.

———. "O razvitii pochvovedeniia kak samostoiatel'noi nauchnoi distsiplini," *Izvestiia Dokuchaevskogo Pochvennogo komiteta*, 1913, No. 1–2, pp. 30–39.

———. Pochvovedenie. St. Petersburg, 1908.

Glinka, S. F. "A. M. Butlerov v chastnoi i domashnei zhizni," *TIIE-T*, XII (1956), 182–99.

Glinskii, B. B. "Universitetskie ustavy (1755–1884 gg.)," *IV*, XXI (1910), 324–51, 718–42.

Glubovskii, M. "Mechty estestvoznaniia," *Vera i razum*, 1891, No. 11, Sect. 2, pp. 466–82.

Gnedenko, B. V. Ocherki po istorii matematiki v Rossii. Moscow-Leningrad, 1946.

———— and A. Ya. Khinchin. An Elementary Introduction to the Theory of Probability. Tr. from the Russian by L. F. Boron. New York: Dover, 1962.

Goier, G. F. "O znachenii prakticheskikh nauchnykh uchrezhdenii," in Trudy V S'ezda, I, 48–57.

Golitsyn, V. M. "Moskovskii universitet v 60-kh godakh," *Golos minuvshego*, 1917, No. 11–12, pp. 173–240.

Gonikman, S. "Teoriia obshchestva i teoriia klassov Bogdanova," *Pod znamenem marksizma*, 1929, No. 12, pp. 27–62.

Gordeev, D. I., ed. Istoriia geologicheskikh nauk v Moskovskom universitete. Moscow, 1962.

Gran, M. M., Z. G. Frenkel', and A. I. Shingarev, eds. Nikolai Ivanovich Pirogov i ego nasledie Pirogovskie s'ezdy. St. Petersburg, 1911.

Grigor'ev, A. A. "Dmitrii Nikolaevich Anuchin," *LRN: Geol.*, pp. 508–15.

Grigor'ev, V. V. Imperatorskii S. Peterburgskii universitet v techenie pervykh piatidesiati let ego sushchestvovaniia. St. Petersburg, 1870.

Grigor'ian, A. T., ed. Istoriia estestvoznaniia v Rossii. Vol. II. Moscow, 1960.

Grigor'ian, N. A. "Aleksandr Filippovich Samoilov," *LRN: Biol.*, pp. 345–54.

————. Aleksandr Filippovich Samoilov. Moscow, 1963.

Grille, Dietrich. Lenins Rivale: Bogdanov und seine Philosophie. Köln, 1966.

Grimm, E. "Organizatsiia universitetskogo prepodavaniia po proektu novogo ustava," *RM*, 1916, No. 4, Sect. 2, pp. 109–22.

————. "Organizatsiia universitetskogo upravleniia," *RM*, 1916, No. 5, Sect. 2, pp. 52–67.

Gubkina, N. Ia. Semeinaia khronika i vospominaniia o D. I. Mendeleeve. St. Petersburg, 1908.

Gumilevskii, N. Kratkaia istoriia i oblichenie novykh ratsionalisticheskikh sekt. Kiev, 1910.

Gurvich, A. G. "Problemy i uspekhi ucheniia o nasledstvennosti: Uchenie o chistykh liniiakh i Mendelizm," *Priroda*, 1912, No. 3, pp. 371–94.

————. "Problemy nasledstvennosti," *Priroda*, 1914, No. 7–8, pp. 843–62.

Gusev, N. N. Letopis' zhizni i tvorchestva L'va Nikolaevicha Tolstogo, 1891–1910. Moscow, 1960.

Gustavson, G. G. "Aleksandr Mikhailovich Butlerov kak predstavitel' shkoly," *ZFKhO*, XIX (1887), Supplement, pp. 58–68.

————. "D. I. Mendeleev i organicheskaia khimiia," in "Trudy Pervogo Mendeleevskogo s'ezda," pp. 50–57.

Gutina, V. N. "Sergei Nikolaevich Vinogradskii," *LRN: Biol.*, pp. 274–87.


Haimson, Leopold H. The Russian Marxists and the Origins of Bolshevism. Cambridge, Mass.: Harvard University Press, 1955.

Hecker, Julius F. Russian Sociology. New York: Columbia, 1915.

Helmholtz, Hermann. Popular Lectures on Scientific Subjects. Tr. from the German by S. Atkinson. New York: Appleton, 1873.

Herzen, A. I. Izbrannye stat'i iz "Kolokola." Geneva, 1887.

——. Polnoe sobranie sochinenii i pisem. Vol. XII. M. K. Lemke, ed. Petrograd, 1919.
Hilton, Harold. Mathematical Crystallography and the Theory of Groups of Movements. New York: Dover, 1963.
Hjelt, Edv. Geschichte der organischen Chemie von ältester Zeit bis zur Gegenwart. Braunschweig, 1916.
Hooson, J. M. David. "The Development of Geography in Pre-Soviet Russia," *Annals of the Association of American Geographers*, LVIII (1968), 250–72.
Hoüel, G. J. Essai critique sur les principes fundamentaux de la géométrie élémentaire. Paris, 1867.

Iakovenko, B. "Chto takoe filosofiia?," *Logos* (Russian edition), 1911–12, No. 2–3, pp. 27–104.
Ianishevskii, E. Istoricheskaia zapiska o zhizni i deiatel'nosti N. I. Lobachevskogo. Kazan, 1868.
Iarilov, A. A. Nauka o pochve—russkaia nauka. Voronezh, 1916.
Iaroshevskii, M. G. Ivan Mikhailovich Sechenov, 1829–1905. Leningrad, 1968.
Ikonnikov, V. S. Opyt russkoi istoriografii. 2 vols. Kiev, 1891–1908.
——. "Russkie universitety v sviazi s khodom obshchestvennogo obrazovaniia," *VE*, 1876, No. 11, pp. 73–132.
Illeritskii, V. E., and I. A. Kudriavtsev, eds. Istoriografiia istorii SSSR. Moscow, 1961.
Imperatorskii Institut Eksperimental'noi Meditsiny (1890–1910). St. Petersburg, 1911.
Ioffe, A. F., ed. Fiziko-matematicheskie nauki. Moscow-Leningrad, 1945.
——. Moia zhizn' i rabota. Moscow-Leningrad, 1933.
——. Vstrechi s fizikami. Moscow, 1960.
Ioffe, A. F. *See also* Joffe, A.
Ionidi, P. P. Mirovozzrenic D. I. Mendeleeva. Moscow, 1959.
Ipat'ev, V. N., ed. L. A. Chugaev: Sbornik. Leningrad, 1924.
Ipatieff, V. N. [V. N. Ipat'ev]. Catalytic Reactions at High Pressures and Temperatures. New York: Macmillan, 1936.
——. The Life of a Chemist. Tr. from the Russian by V. Haensel and R. H. Lusher. Stanford: Stanford University Press, 1946.
Isachenko, B. L. Izbrannye trudy. Vol. II. Moscow-Leningrad, 1951.
Isakova, O. V., *et al.*, eds. Nikolai Ivanovich Vavilov. Moscow, 1962.
Iurkevich, P. D. "Iazyk fiziologov i psikhologov," *RV*, 1862: No. 4, pp. 912–34; No. 5, pp. 373–92.
Iushkevich, A. P. Istoriia matematiki v Rossii. Moscow, 1968.
——. "Matematika," in A. T. Grigor'ian, pp. 41–221.
Iushkevich, P. "Sovremennaia energetika s tochki zreniia empiriosimvolizma," in Bazarov *et al.*, pp. 162–214.
Iuzhakov, S. N. "Sotsiologicheskaia doktrina N. K. Mikhailovskogo," in Na slavnom postu, pp. 352–69.
Ivanov, L. A., and G. V. Platonov. "Kliment Arkad'evich Timiriazev," in *LRN: Biol.*, pp. 173–91.
Ivanov-Razumnik. Istoriia russkoi obshchestvennoi mysli. 5th ed., Vols. IV and V. Petrograd, 1918.
Ivanovskii, Dmitrii. "Concerning the Mosaic Disease of the Tobacco Plant," in Phytopathological Classics, No. 7, pp. 27–30. Tr. from the German by J. Johnson. Ithaca: American Phytopathological Society, 1942.
Izgoev, A. S. "Krizis vysshei shkoly: Nebyvalyi razgrom," *RM*, 1911, No. 3, pp. 135–47.

Izmailov, N. A. "Rukovodstvo po fizicheskoi khimii 'Fiziko-khimiia' N. N. Beketova," in Arbuzov, Materialy po istorii otechestvennoi khimii, pp. 67–72.

"Izvlechenie is protokolov zasedanii Akademii," *ZAN*, XXVI (1876), Pt. 2, pp. 37–58.

Jensen, William A., and Leroy G. Kavaljian, eds. Plant Biology Today: Advances and Challenges. Belmont, Calif.: Wadsworth, 1963.

Jepsen, Glenn L., George Gaylord Simpson, and Ernst Mayr, eds. Genetics, Paleontology, and Evolution. New York: Atheneum, 1963.

Joffe, A. [A. F. Ioffe]. "Zur Theorie der Strahlungserscheinungen," *Annalen der Physik*, Series 4, 1911, No. 36, pp. 534–52.

Joravsky, David. Soviet Marxism and Natural Science: 1917–1932. New York: Columbia University Press, 1961.

Kablits, I. [I. Iuzov]. Osnovy narodnichestva. 2d ed., 2 vols. St. Petersburg, 1888–93.

Kablukov, I. A. "Kratkii istoricheskii ocherk razvitiia ucheniia o khimicheskom srodstve," *RM*, 1909: No. 8, pp. 31–46; No. 9, pp. 22–37.

———. Ocherki iz istorii elektrotekhniki za XIX v. Moscow, 1901.

———. Osnovnye nachala fizicheskoi khimii. 3 vols. Moscow, 1900–1910.

———. "Vladimir Feodorovich Luginin," *O-MU*, 1911, pp. 92–121.

———. "Vladimir Vasil'evich Markovnikov (biograficheskaia svedeniia i kratkii ocherk nauchnykh rabot)," *ZFKhO*, XXXVI (1905), Pt. 1, pp. 247–303.

Kadek, M. G. "Nikolai Mikhailovich Przheval'skii," *LRN: Geol.*, pp. 479–87.

Kagan, V. F. Ocherk geometricheskoi sistemy Lobachevskogo. Odessa, 1900.

———. Osnovaniia geometrii. 2 vols. Odessa, 1905–7.

———. Zadacha obosnovaniia geometrii v sovremennoi postanovke. Odessa, 1908.

Kapnist, P. A. "Universitetskie voprosy," *VE*, 1903: No. 11, pp. 167–218; No. 12, pp. 465–518.

Kapterev, P. N. "Teleologiia neolamarkistov," *Bogoslovskii vestnik*, 1914, I, 84–115, 561–91.

Kapustin, M. Ia. Osnovnye voprosy zemskoi meditsiny. St. Petersburg, 1889.

Kapustinskii, A. F. Ocherk po istorii neorganicheskoi i fizicheskoi khimii v Rossii. Moscow-Leningrad, 1949.

———, and Iu. I. Solov'ev. "Termokhimicheskie raboty G. I. Gessa i ikh vlianie na russkikh termokhimikov vtoroi poloviny XIX veka," *TIIE-T*, VI (1955), 214–28.

Kareev, N. I. Istoriko-filosofskie i sotsiologicheskie etiudy. St. Petersburg, 1895.

———. "M. M. Kovalevskii kak istorik i sotsiolog," in Arsen'ev et al., Kovalevskii, pp. 169–79.

———. "P. L. Lavrov kak sotsiolog," in Radlov et al., pp. 193–248.

———. "Mechta i pravda o russkoi nauke," *RM*, 1884, No. 12, Sect. 2, pp. 100–135.

———. "N. K. Mikhailovskii kak sotsiolog," *Russkie vedomosti*, 1900, No. 318, pp. 3–4.

———. "Novyi istoriko-filosofskii trud," *VFP*, 1898, No. 45, pp. 388–415.

———. Osnovnye voprosy filosofii istorii. 3d ed. St. Petersburg, 1877.

———. Starye i novye etiudy ob ekonomicheskom materializme. St. Petersburg, 1896.

———. Sushchnost' istoricheskogo protsessa i rol' lichnosti v istorii. St. Petersburg, 1890.

———. "Teoriia kul'turno-istoricheskikh tipov," *RM*, 1889, No. 9, Sect. 2, pp. 1–32.

Karpinskii, A. P. "Ocherk fiziko-geograficheskikh uslovii Evropeiskoi Rossii v minuvshie geologicheskie periody," *ZAN*, LV (1887), Supplement 8.

———. Ocherki geologicheskogo proshlogo Evropeiskoi Rossii. Moscow-Leningrad, 1947.

———. Sobranie sochinenii. Vol. IV. Moscow-Leningrad, 1949.

Karpovits, E., and A. Makarenia. "Mendeleev, Dmitrii Ivanovich," in Filosofskaia entsiklopediia, III, 386–87. Moscow, 1964.

Kavelin, K. D. "Filosofiia i nauka v Evrope i u nas," in Dvadtsatpiat' let, pp. 319–36.

———. Sobranie sochinenii. 3 vols. St. Petersburg, 1897–99.

"Kavkazskii Otdel Imperatorskogo Russkogo Geograficheskogo obshchestva," Priroda, 1915, No. 2, pp. 321–23.

Kazansky, B. A., and G. V. Bykov, eds. Centenary of the Theory of Chemical Structure. Moscow, 1961.

Kedrov, B. M. Den' odnogo velikogo otkrytiia. Moscow, 1958.

———. Filosofskii analiz pervykh trudov D. I. Mendeleeva o periodicheskom zakone (1869–1871). Moscow, 1959.

———. "Kratkie svedeniia o zhizni i nauchnoi deiatel'nosti D. I. Mendeleeva i o ego rabote nad periodicheskim zakonom," in D. I. Mendeleev, Periodicheskii zakon, pp. 746–70.

———. "Otkrytie periodicheskogo zakona D. I. Mendeleevym," in Iu. I. Solov'ev, Ocherki po istorii khimii, pp. 36–80.

Keller, B. M. "Russkie geologi na mezhdunarodnykh geologicheskikh kongressakh (I–XII sessii)," OIGZ, I (1953), 137–52.

Kelsen, Hans. Der soziologische und der juristische Staatsbegriff. Tübingen, 1922.

Keynes, John Maynard. A Treatise on Probability. London: Macmillan, 1957.

Khabakov, A. V. "Deiatel'nost' Geologicheskogo komiteta v Rossii (1882–1917 gg.)," TIIE-T, XXVII (1959), 146–77.

Khanovich, I. G. Aleksei Nikolaevich Krylov. Leningrad, 1967.

Khintchine, A. "Théorie des fonctions: Sur une extension de l'intégrale de M. Denjoy," CR-AS-P, CLXII (1916), 287–91.

Khodnev, A. I. Istoriia Imperatorskogo Vol'nogo ekonomicheskogo obshchestva. St. Petersburg, 1865.

Kholodkovskii, N. A. "Teoriia Darvina, eia kritika i ee dal'neishee razvitie," RB, 1888: No. 1, Sect. 2, pp. 123–47; No. 4, Sect. 2, pp. 37–64.

"Khronika," Obrazovanie, 1901, No. 5–6, Sect. 2, pp. 81–96.

Khrushchov, P. D. Vvedenie k izucheniiu teorii khimicheskikh ravnovesii. Khar'kov, 1894.

Khvol'son, O. D. Gegel', Gekkel', Kossut i dvenadtsataia zapoved. St. Petersburg, 1911.

———. "Pozitivnaia filosofiia i fizika," MB, 1898, No. 5, pp. 41–58.

———. "Printsip otnositel'nosti," Priroda, 1912, No. 11, pp. 1275–1316.

———. Znanie i vera v fizike. Petrograd, 1916.

Khvol'son, O. D. See also Chwolson, O. D.

Kindersley, Richard. The First Russian Revisionists: A Study of "Legal Marxism" in Russia. Oxford: Clarendon Press, 1962.

Kipnis, A. Ia. Razvitie khimicheskoi termodinamiki v Rossii. Moscow-Leningrad, 1964.

Kiro, S. N. "N. I. Lobachevskii i matematika v Kazanskom universitete," in Shtokalo et al., pp. 151–83.

Kirpotin, V. Radikal'nyi raznochinets D. I. Pisarev. Leningrad, 1929.

Kiselev, S. V. "Dmitrii Nikolaevich Anuchin—arkheolog," Trudy Instituta etnografii (N.S.), I (1947), 22–24.

Kistiakovskii, B. A. "Ideia ravenstva s sotsiologicheskoi tochki zreniia," MB, 1900, No. 4, Sect. 1, pp. 160–69.

———. "Russkaia sotsiologicheskaia shkola i kategoriia vozmozhnosti pri reshenii sotsial'no-eticheskikh problem," in Novgorodtsev, Problemy idealizma, pp. 297–393.

———. Sotsial'nye nauki i pravo: Ocherki po metodologii sotsial'nykh nauk i obshchei teorii prava. Moscow, 1916.

———. "V zashchitu nauchno-filosofskogo idealizma," VFP, 1907, No. 1, Sect. 1, pp. 57–109.

Kistiakowski, T. [B. A. Kistiakovskii]. Gesellschaft und Einzelwesen. Berlin, 1899.

Kizevetter, A. A. Na rubezhe dvukh stoletii. Prague, 1929.

Klein, Felix. Vorlesungen über die Entwicklung der Mathematik im 19. Jahrhundert. 2 vols. Berlin, 1926.

Kline, George L. "Darwinism and the Russian Orthodox Church," in Simmons, pp. 307–28.

Kniazev, G. A. "D. I. Mendeleev i Imperatorskaia Akademiia," VAN, 1931, No. 3, pp. 27–34.

———. "Poritsanie akademikam za uchastie v 'Zapiske 342 uchenykh,'" VAN, 1931, No. 4, pp. 13–22.

———, and A. V. Kol'tsov. Kratkii ocherk istorii Akademii nauk SSSR. 3d ed. Moscow-Leningrad, 1964.

Kobell, Franz von. Geschichte der Mineralogie von 1650–1860. Munich, 1864.

Koch, Sigmund, ed. Psychology: A Study of a Science. Vol. IV. New York: McGraw-Hill, 1962.

Kodis, Zh. D. "Empiriokrititsizm." Tr. from the Polish by V. V. Lesevich. RM, 1901, No. 9, Sect. 2, pp. 1–28.

"Koksharov, Nikolai Ivanovich," MBS-AN, I (1915), 329–38.

Kol'man, E. Velikii russkii myslitel' N. I. Lobachevskii. Moscow, 1956.

Kolmogorov, A. N. "Rol' russkoi nauki v razvitii teorii veroiatnostei," UZMU, XCI (1947), 53–64.

Kolosov, E. E. Ocherki mirovozzreniia N. K. Mikhailovskogo. St. Petersburg, 1912.

Kol'tsov, N. K. K universitetskom voprosu. Moscow, 1909.

———. "Natsional'naia organizatsiia nauki," Priroda, 1915, No. 7–8, pp. 1017–40.

Kompaneets, A. I. Bor'ba N. A. Umova za materializm v fizike. Moscow, 1954.

———. Mirovozzrenie A. G. Stoletova. Moscow, 1956.

Kondrat'ev, N. D. "Rost naseleniia kak faktor sotsial'no-ekonomicheskogo razvitiia v uchenii M. M. Kovalevskogo," in Arsen'ev et al., Kovalevskii, pp. 196–217.

Konni, A. F. Ocherki i vospominaniia. St. Petersburg, 1906.

Korkunov, N. M. General Theory of Law. Tr. by W. G. Hastings. Boston: Boston Book Co., 1909.

Kornilov, A. Kurs istorii Rossii XIX veka. 2d ed., Vol. III. Moscow, 1918.

———. Obshchestvennoe dvizhenie pri Aleksandre II (1855–1881). Paris, 1905.

Korolivskii, S. M., et al., eds. Khar'kovskii Gosudarstvennyi universitet im. A. M. Gor'kogo za 150 let. Khar'kov, 1955.

Korzhinskii, S. I. Chto takoe zhizn'? Tomsk, 1888.

———. "Geterogenezis i evoliutsiia," ZAN, IX (1899), 1–94.

———. "Geterogenezis i evoliutsiia (predvaritel'noe soobshchenie)," IIAN, X (1899), 255–68.

Koshtoiants, Kh. S. "Aleksandr Filippovich Samoilov," in Samoilov, Izbrannye stat'i, pp. 3–12.

———. Sechenov. Moscow-Leningrad, 1945.

Koshtoyants [Koshtoiants], Kh. S. Essays on the History of Physiology in Russia. Tr. from the Russian by D. P. Boden, K. Hanes, and N. O'Brien. Washington, D.C.: American Institute of Biological Sciences, 1964.

Kosmodem'ianskii, A. A. "Nikolai Egorovich Zhukovskii," in *LRN: Mat.*, pp. 169–77.
———. "Osnovopolozhniki sovremennoi aeromekhaniki: N. E. Zhukovskii i S. A. Chaplygin," *UZMU*, XCI (1947), 105–28.
———. "Sergei Alekseevich Chaplygin," in *LRN: Mat.*, pp. 294–302.
Kostinskii, S. K. "Bredikhin, Fedor Aleksandrovich," *Vengerov-Slovar'*, V (1897), 279–90.
———. "Pamiati Bredikhina (k desiatiletiiu so dnia ego konchiny)," *Priroda*, 1914, No. 4, pp. 411–20.
Kostomarov, V. M. Iz deiatel'nosti Russkogo Tekhnicheskogo obshchestva v oblasti mashinostroeniia. Moscow, 1957.
Kostychev, P. A. "Sviaz mezhdu pochvami i nekotorymi rastitel'nymi formatsiiami," in Vos'moi S'ezd, Sect. 4, pp. 37–60.
Kotliarevskii, Nestor. "Ocherki iz istorii obshchestvennogo nastroeniia shestidesiatykh godov," *VE*, 1912: No. 11, pp. 268–94; No. 12, pp. 229–56.
Kotliarevskii, S. "M. M. Kovalevskii i ego nauchnoe nasledie," in Arsen'ev *et al.*, Kovalevskii, pp. 121–35.
Kovalenskii, M. N. "Sredniaia shkola," *Granat-Ist.*, IV (n.d.), 128–85.
———. "Sredniaia shkola," *Granat-Ist.*, VII (n.d.), 170–202.
Kovalevskaia, S. V. Nauchnye raboty. Moscow, 1948.
———. Vospominaniia i pis'ma. Moscow, 1961.
Kovalevskaia-Chistovich, V. A. "Aleksandr Onufrievich Kovalevskii," *Priroda*, 1926, No. 7–8, pp. 5–20.
Kovalevskii, A. O. "O deiatel'nosti nashikh s'ezdov," in Trudy III S'ezda, pp. 55–58.
———. "Otzyv o sochinenii I. I. Mechnikova Embriologische Studien an Meduzen," *ZAN*, LXVIII (1892), 135–38.
Kovalevskii, M. M. "Dmitrii Andreevich Dril'," *VE*, 1910, No. 12, pp. 427–36.
———. "Dve zhizni," *VE*, 1909: No. 6, pp. 495–522; No. 7, pp. 5–23.
———. "Kondorse," *VE*, 1894: No. 3, pp. 99–144; No. 4, pp. 469–507.
———. "N. K. Mikhailovskii kak sotsiolog," *VE*, 1913, No. 4, pp. 192–212.
———. "Moskovskii universitet v kontse 70-ikh i nachale 80-ikh godov proshlogo veka," *VE*, 1910, No. 5, pp. 178–221.
———. Obshchinnoe zemlevladenie: Prichiny, khod i posledstviia ego razlozheniia. Vol. I. Moscow, 1877.
———. "Progress," *VE*, 1912, No. 2, pp. 225–60.
———. "Sergei Andreevich Muromtsev (opyt ego kharakteristiki)," *VE*, 1910, No. 11, pp. 363–68.
———. Sotsiologiia. 2 vols. St. Petersburg, 1910.
———. "Sovremennye frantsuzskie sotsiologi," *VE*, 1913, No. 7, pp. 339–69.
———. Sovremennye sotsiologi. St. Petersburg, 1905.
———, and E. V. de Roberty, eds. Novye idei v sotsiologii. 2 vols. St. Petersburg, 1913–14.
———, *et al.* Pamiati Darvina. Moscow, 1910.
Kovalevskii, M. M. *See also* Kovalevsky, M., *and* Kovalewsky, M.
Kovalevskii, V. I., ed. Rossiia v kontse XIX veka. St. Petersburg, 1900.
Kovalevskii, V. O. Paleontologiia loshadei. Moscow, 1948.
———. Sobranie nauchnykh trudov. Vol. I. Moscow, 1950.
Kovalevskii, V. O. *See also* Kowalewsky, W.
Kovalevsky, M. [M. M. Kovalevskii]. "The Origin and Growth of Village Communities in Russia," *Archaeological Review*, I (1888), 266–73.
———. "Survivals of Iranian Culture Among Caucasian Highlanders," *Archaeological Review*, I (1888), 313–31.

Kovalewsky, M. [M. M. Kovalevskii]. "Psychologie et sociologie," *AIIS*, X (1904), 247–64.

———. Régime économique de la Russie. Paris, 1898.

———. Tableau des origines et de l'évolution de la famille et de la propriété. Stockholm, 1890.

Kovanov, V. V., *et al.*, eds. Ocherki po istorii I. Moskovskogo ordena Lenina Meditsinskogo instituta imeni I. M. Sechenova. Moscow, 1959.

Kovrov, A. "Iz byta russkikh uchashchikhsia za granitsei," *Obrazovanie*, 1897, No. 10, pp. 1–29.

Kowalewsky, W. [V. O. Kovalevskii]. "On the Osteology of the Hyopotamidae," *Proceedings of the Royal Society of London*, XXI (1878), 147–65.

Kozhevnikov, B. A. "Preobladanie nauchnogo somneniia v sovremennom neverii," *Bogoslovskii vestnik*. 1911: II, 113–34, 336–60; III, 1–42, 265–77, 688–717. 1912: I, 119–46.

Kozikov, I. A. Filosofskie vozzreniia V. I. Vernadskogo. Moscow, 1963.

Kozlov, A. "Nikolai Mikhailovich Przheval'skii," *IRGO*, XLIX (1915), 301–14.

Kozlov, V. V. Ocherki istorii khimicheskikh obshchestv SSSR. Moscow, 1958.

Krasheninnikov, F. N. "Kliment Arkad'evich Timiriazev," *Priroda*, 1913, No. 9, pp. 1021–32.

Krasnosel'skaia, T. A. "Mikhail Semenovich Tsvet," *LRN: Biol.*, pp. 374–80.

Krasnosel'skii, A. I. "N. K. Mikhailovskii o religii," *RB*, 1907, No. 4, Sect. 1, pp. 56–79.

———. Mirovozzrenie gumanista nashego vremeni: Osnovy ucheniia N. K. Mikhailovskogo. St. Petersburg, 1900.

"Kratkii otchet o sostoianii i deiatel'nosti Imperatorskogo universiteta Sv. Vladimira v 1897 godu," *Universitetskie izvestiia*, 1898, No. 3, Sect. 1, pp. 23–86.

"Kratkii otchet o sostoianii i deiatel'nosti Imperatorskogo universiteta Sv. Vladimira v 1898 godu," *Universitetskie izvestiia*, 1899, No. 3, Sect. 1, pp. 1–22.

Kravets, L. P. "Nasledstvennost' v cheloveka," *Priroda*, 1914, No. 6, pp. 721–44.

Kravets, T. P. "P. N. Lebedev i sozdannaia im fizicheskaia shkola," *Priroda*, 1913, No. 3, pp. 283–92.

———. Ot N'iutona do Vavilova. Leningrad, 1967.

"Krest'ianstvo i narodnicheskoe dvizhenie," in *Granat-Ist.*, VI (n.d.), 162–200.

Kriloff, A. [A. N. Krylov]. "Comment on C. F. Monday's 'On the Advantages of Using Tchebycheff's Rule in Association with the Integrator to Obtain Cross Curves of Stability,'" *Transactions of the Institution of Naval Architects*, XLI (1899), 86–87.

———. "On Stresses Experienced by a Ship in a Seaway," *Transactions of the Institution of Naval Architects*, XL (1898), 197–209.

———. "Die Theorie des Schiffes," in Felix Klein, ed., *Enzyklopädie der mathematischen Wissenschaften*, IV (1903), Pt. 3, pp. 517–62.

———. "Théorie generale des oscillations du navire sur une mer houleuse," *Bulletin de l'Association technique maritime*, 1898, No. 8, pp. 19–49.

———. "Über die erzwungenen Schwingungen von gleichformigen elastischen Stäben," *Mathematische Annalen*, 1905, No. 61, pp. 211–34.

Kropotkin, Peter. Ethics: Origin and Development. Tr. from the Russian by L. S. Friedland and J. R. Piroshnikov. New York: Dial, 1924.

———. Memoirs of a Revolutionist. London: Swan, 1906.

———. Modern Science and Anarchism. Tr. from the Russian by D. A. Modell. Philadelphia: Social Science Club, 1903.

———. Mutual Aid: A Factor of Evolution. New York: McLure Phillips, 1903.

Krotov, P. I. "Zadachi nauchnoi geografii i postanovka ee prepodavaniia v Imperatorskom Kazanskom universitete," *ERGO*, II (1892), 341–68.

Krukovskaia, L. N. A. Morozov: Ocherk zhizni i deiatel'nosti. Moscow, 1912.

Kryloff, A. [A. N. Krylov]. "A New Theory of the Pitching Motion of Ships on Waves, and of the Stresses Produced by this Motion," *Transactions of the Institution of Naval Architects*, XXXVII (1896), 326–59.

———. "Théorie du tangage sur une mer houleuse," *Bulletin de l'Association technique maritime*, 1896, No. 6, pp. 129–34; 1897, No. 7, pp. 5–42.

Krylov, A. N. Izbrannye trudy. Moscow, 1958.

———. Moi vospominaniia. Moscow-Leningrad, 1942.

———. Vospominaniia i ocherki. Moscow, 1956.

Krylov, A. N. *See also* Kriloff, A., *and* Kryloff, A.

Kudriavtsev, P. Absoliutizm i reliativizm. Vol. I. Kiev, 1908.

Kurbatov, V. Ia. "K voprosu ob efire," *ZFKhO*, XL (1908), 1468–71.

Kurilov, V. V. Obshchii kurs khimii na sovremennykh osnovakh. Warsaw, 1910.

Kuznetsov, B. G. Lomonosov, Lobachevskii, Mendeleev. Moscow-Leningrad, 1945.

———. Ocherki istorii russkoi nauki. Moscow-Leningrad, 1940.

Kvasov, D. G., and A. K. Fedorova-Grot. Fiziologicheskaia shkola I. P. Pavlova. Leningrad, 1967.


Labedz, Leopold, ed. Revisionism: Essays on the History of Marxist Ideas. New York: Praeger, 1962.

Lakhtin, L. K. "Nikolai Vasil'evich Bugaev," *NS*, 1904, No. 2, pp. 19–26.

Lakhtin, M. Iu. "Metod polozhitel'nogo znaniia," *Priroda*, 1912, No. 6, pp. 737–56.

Lange, Friedrich Albert. The History of Materialism and Criticism of Its Present Importance. 3d ed. Tr. from the German by E. C. Thomas. New York: Harcourt, 1925.

Lankester, E. Ray. "Alexander Kowalevsky," *Nature*, LXVI (1902), 394–96.

Lappo-Danilevskii, A. S. "The Development of Science and Learning in Russia," in Duff, pp. 153–229.

———. *Metodologiia istorii*. Vol. II. St. Petersburg, 1913.

———. "Osnovnye printsipi sotsiologicheskoi doktriny O. Konta," in Novgorodtsev, Problemy idealizma, pp. 394–490.

Laue, Max von. History of Physics. New York: Academic Press, 1950.

Laue, Theodore von. "Legal Marxism and the 'Fate of Capitalism in Russia,'" *Review of Politics*, XVIII (1956), 23–46.

Lavrov, P. L. Istoricheskie pis'ma. 5th ed. Petrograd, 1917.

———. Filosofiia i sotsiologiia: Izbrannye proizvedeniia. 2 vols. Moscow, 1965.

———. Tri besedy o sovremennom znachenii filosofii. St. Petersburg, 1861.

———. Zadachi istorii mysli: Podgotovlenie cheloveka. Geneva, 1894.

———. Zadachi pozitivizma i ikh reshenie. Teoretiki sorokovikh godov v nauke i verovaniiakh. St. Petersburg, 1906.

Lazarev, P. P. "P. N. Lebedev," *RM*, 1912, No. 6, Sect. 2, pp. 137–52.

———. "P. N. Lebedev i russkaia fizika," *VOL*, 1912, No. 2, pp. 65–78.

———. "Pamiati velikogo russkogo fizika (P. N. Lebedev)," *Priroda*, 1917, No. 4, pp. 465–76.

———. Sochineniia. Vol. I. Moscow-Leningrad, 1957.

———. "Vzgliady P. N. Lebedeva na organizatsiiu nauchnykh issledovanii," *Priroda*, 1917, No. 3, pp. 369–78.

Lebedev, A. P. "Glavneishie etapy v razvitii petrografii v dorevoliutsionnoi Rossii," *OIGZ*, V (1956), 47–70.

Lebedev, P. N. "An Experimental Investigation of the Pressure of Light," *Annual Re-*

*port of the Board of Regents of the Smithsonian Institution for the Year Ending June 30, 1902,* pp. 177–78. Washington, D.C., 1903.

———. Sobranie sochinenii. Moscow, 1963.

Leffler, Anna Carlotta, and Sonia Kovalewsky. *Sonia Kovalewsky: Biography and Autobiography.* Tr. by L. von Cossel. New York: Macmillan, 1895.

Leibenzon, L. S., and A. I. Markushevich. "Aleksei Nikolaevich Krylov," in *LRN: Mat.,* pp. 257–70.

Leicester, Henry M. "Alexander Mikhailovich Butlerov," *Journal of Chemical Education,* XVII (1940), 203–9.

———. "Contributions of Butlerov to the Development of Structural Theory," *Journal of Chemical Education,* XXXVI (1959), 328–29.

———. The Historical Background of Chemistry. New York: Wiley, 1956.

———. "Vladimir Vasil'evich Markovnikov," *Journal of Chemical Education,* XVIII (1941), 53–57.

Lemke, M. Epokha tsenzurnykh reform, 1859–1865 godov. St. Petersburg, 1904.

Lenin, V. I. Sochineniia. 4th ed., 45 vols. Moscow, 1941–67.

Lesevich, V. V. "Chto takoe nauchnaia filosofiia," *RM,* 1888: No. 1, Sect. 2, pp. 1–26; No. 2, Sect. 2, pp. 1–16; No. 11, Sect. 2, pp. 1–20; No. 12, Sect. 2, pp. 13–24. *RM,* 1889: No. 1, Sect. 2, pp. 58–75; No. 3, Sect. 2, pp. 1–16; No. 10, Sect. 2, 1–17; No. 11, Sect. 2, pp. 1–17.

———. "Filosofskoe nasledie XIX veka," *RB,* 1896, No. 12, pp. 229–68.

———. Sobranie sochinenii. 3 vols. Moscow, 1915–17.

Levchenko, V. "Krizis universitetskoi zhizni," *RM,* 1908, No. 5, pp. 111–21.

Levin, M. G. "Dmitrii Nikolaevich Anuchin," *Trudy Instituta etnografii* (N.S.), I (1947), 3–17.

Levinson-Lessing, F. Iu. Edinaia vysshaia shkola, II. Dal'neishee razvitie Politekhnicheskogo Instituta. Petrograd, 1915.

———. "Zhenshchiny-geologi," *MB,* 1901, No. 6, Sect. 1, pp. 65–83.

"Liapunov, Aleksandr Mikhailovich," in *MBS-AN,* I (1915), 430–33. An autobiographical note.

Liapunov, A. M. Sobranie sochinenii. Vol. I. Moscow, 1954.

———. "Zhizn' i trudy P. L. Chebysheva," in Chebyshev, Izbrannye matematicheskie trudy, pp. 3–25.

Lichkov, B. L. Karpinskii i sovremennost'. Moscow-Leningrad, 1946.

Lilienfeld, Paul. Gedanken über die Sozialwissenshaft der Zukunft. 5 vols. Mitau, 1873–81.

Linitskii, P. "Filosofiia nashego vremeni," *Vera i razum,* 1891, No. 19, Sect. 2, pp. 297–304.

Lipshits, S. Iu. Moskovskoe Obshchestvo ispytatelei prirody za 135 let ego sushchestvovaniia: 1805–1940. Moscow, 1940.

Liubimov, N. A. "Universitetskii vopros," *RV,* 1876: No. 12, pp. 576–611. 1877: No. 1, pp. 111–62; No. 2, pp. 779–829; No. 3, pp. 190–239.

Livingston, Robert B. "How Man Looks at His Own Brain: An Adventure Shared by Psychology and Neurophysiology," in Koch, pp. 51–99.

Lomonosovskii sbornik: Materialy dlia istorii razvitiia khimii v Rossii. Moscow, 1901.

Lomonosovskii sbornik: 1711–1911. St. Petersburg, 1911.

Lopatin, L. M. Filosofskie kharakteristiki i rechi. Moscow, 1911.

———. "Filosofskoe mirovozzrenie N. V. Bugaeva," *VFP,* 1904, No. 72, pp. 172–95.

———. "Filosofskie vzgliady V. Ia. Tsingera," *VFP,* 1908, No. 93, pp. 219–27.

———. "Nauchnoe mirovozzrenie i filosofiia," *VFP,* 1903, No. 5, 475–96.

Lovtsov, S. "Predely poznaniia prirody," *VE*, 1873, No. 4, pp. 800–817.

L. S. Z. "Novyi trud M. M. Kovalevskogo," *RB*, 1898, No. 11, Sect. 2, pp. 110–19.

L. T. "2-e soveshchanie po bakteriologii i epidemiologii (Moskva, 28 marta–1 aprelia)," *Priroda*, 1912, No. 4, pp. 567–70.

Lunacharskii, A. V. Etiudy kriticheskie i polemicheskie. Moscow, 1905.

———. Otkliki zhizni. St. Petersburg, 1906.

———. Religiia i sotsializm. 2 vols. St. Petersburg, 1908.

Lunacherskii, V. [A. V. Lunacharskii]. "Ateisty," in Bazarov *et al.*, pp. 107–61.

Lusin, N. "Analyse mathematique: Sur la recherche des fonctions primitives," *CR-AS-P*, CLXII (1916), 975–78.

———. "Théorie des fonctions: Sur la classification de M. Baire," *CR-AS-P*, CLXIV (1917), 91–94.

Luzin, N. N. *See* Lusin, N.


Mach, Ernst. The Analysis of Sensations and the Relation of the Physical to the Psychical. Tr. from the German by S. Waterlow. New York: Dover, 1959.

Maiorov, F. P. Istoriia ucheniia ob uslovnykh refleksakh. Moscow-Leningrad, 1954.

Maksimov, N. A., ed. Pamiati Dmitriia Iosifovicha Ivanovskogo. Moscow, 1952.

Malinin, I. "Makh, Ernst," *Granat-Ents.*, XXVIII (n.d.), 347–49.

Markevich, A. I. Dvadtsatipiatiletie Imperatorskogo Novorossiiskogo universiteta. Odessa, 1890.

Markov, A. A. (elder). Izbrannye trudy: Teoriia chisel. Teoriia veroiatnostei. Moscow, 1951.

Markov, A. A. (younger). "Biografiia A. A. Markova," in A. A. Markov (elder), Izbrannye trudy, pp. 599–613.

Markov, K. K., and Iu. G. Saushkin, eds. Geografiia v Moskovskom universitete za 200 let: 1755–1955. Moscow, 1955.

Markovnikov, V. V. "Istoricheskii ocherk o Moskovskom universitete," in Lomonosovskii sbornik (1901), pp. 1–281.

———. Izbrannye trudy. Moscow, 1955.

———. "Moskovskaia rech' o Butlerove," *TIIE-T*, XII (1956), 134–81.

———. "Vospominaniia i cherty iz zhizni i deiatel'nosti A. M. Butlerova," *ZFKhO*, XIX (1887), Supplement, pp. 69–96.

Marx, Karl. A Contribution to the Critique of Political Economy. Tr. from the second German edition by N. J. Stone. New York: International Library, 1904.

"Materialy dlia istorii i statistiki nashikh gimnazii," *ZMNP*, CXXI (1864), Sect. 2, pp. 129–71, 355–90, 493–571.

Materialy VI-oi Konferentsii po istorii nauki v Pribaltike. Vilna, 1965.

Matveev, B. S. "Progress i regress v evoliutsii," *Priroda*, 1967, No. 5, pp. 71–78.

Maximoff, G. P., ed. The Political Philosophy of Bakunin: Scientific Anarchism. Glencoe, Ill.: Free Press, 1953.

Maxwell, James Clerk. The Elementary Treatise on Electricity. Oxford: Clarendon Press, 1888.

Mazurmovich, B. N. "A. O. Kovalevskii v Kieve (po neopublikovannym materialam)," *TIIE-T*, XVI (1957), 34–48.

Mechnikov, I. I. Akademicheskoe sobranie sochinenii. Vol. III. Moscow, 1955.

———. "Antropologiia i darvinizm," *VE*, 1875, No. 1, pp. 159–95.

———. "Darvinizm i meditsina," in M. M. Kovalevskii *et al.*, pp. 112–16.

———. Etiudy optimizma. Moscow, 1964.

———. Izbrannye biologicheskie proizvedeniia. Moscow, 1950.

———. Izbrannye proizvedeniia. Moscow, 1956.

———. O darvinizme. Moscow-Leningrad, 1943.

———. Sorok let iskaniia ratsional'nogo mirovozzreniia. Moscow, 1913.

———. Stranitsy vospominanii. Moscow, 1946.

Mechnikov, I. I. *See also* Metchnikoff, Elie, *and* Metchnikoff, Elias.

Mechnikov, L. I. "M. A. Bakunin v Italii v 1864 godu," *IV*, LXVII (1897), 807–34.

Meek, Walter J. "Carl Ludwig," *The Gamma Alpha Record*, XXIII (1933), 31–43.

Meilakh, B. "Posleslovie," *Novyi mir*, 1966, No. 12, pp. 191–98.

Menchoff, D. "Théorie des fonctions: Sur l'unicité du développement trigonomé-
trique," *CR-AS-P*, CLXIII (1916), 433–36.

Mendel, Arthur P. Dilemmas of Progress in Tsarist Russia: Legal Marxism and Legal
Populism. Cambridge, Mass.: Harvard University Press, 1961.

———. "N. K. Mikhailovskii and His Criticism of Russian Marxism," *American Slavic
and East European Review*, XIV (1955), 331–45.

Mendel, Gregor. Opyty nad rastitel'nymi gibridami. Tr. from the German by K. Fliaks-
berger. St. Petersburg, 1910.

Mendeléeff, D. [D. I. Mendeleev]. The Principles of Chemistry. 2 vols. Tr. from the
5th Russian edition by G. Kamensky. London: Longmans, 1891.

[Mendeleev, D. I.]. Arkhiv D. I. Mendeleeva. Vol. I. Leningrad, 1951.

Mendeleev, D. I. "Kakaia zhe akademiia nuzhna v Rossii," *Novyi mir*, 1966, No. 12,
pp. 176–91.

———. "Khimicheskaia i neftianaia promyshlennost'," in V. I. Kovalevskii, pp. 309–18.

———. K poznaniiu Rossii. 5th ed. St. Petersburg, 1907.

———. "Mirovozzrenie," *NN*, II (1948), 157–62.

———. Periodicheskii zakon. Moscow, 1958.

———. Problemy ekonomicheskogo razvitiia Rossii. Moscow, 1960.

———. Rastvory. Moscow, 1959.

———. Sochineniia. 25 vols. Moscow-Leningrad, 1934–54.

———. "Veshchestvo," *Brockhaus-Efron*, VI (1892), 151–61.

———. "Voskresenskii (Aleksandr Abramovich)," *Brockhaus-Efron*, VII (1892),
243–44.

———. Zavetnye mysli. St. Petersburg, 1904.

Mendeleeva, A. I. Mendeleev v zhizni. Moscow, 1928.

Men'shov, D. E. *See* Menchoff, D.

Menshutkin, B. N. Zhizn' i deiatel'nost' Nikolaia Aleksandrovicha Menshutkina. St.
Petersburg, 1908.

Menshutkin, N. A. Razvitie khimicheskikh vozzrenii. St. Petersburg, 1888.

———. "Vospominanie ob Aleksandre Mikhailoviche Butlerove," *ZFKhO*, XIX
(1887), Supplement, pp. 13–57.

Menzbir, M. A. "Glavneishie predstaviteli darvinizma v Zapadnoi Evrope," *RM*, 1900:
No. 1, Sect. 2, pp. 60–76; No. 2, Sect. 2, pp. 45–57; No. 6, Sect. 2, pp. 1–17; No. 12,
Sect. 2, pp. 39–57.

———. Istoricheskii ocherk vozzrenii na prirodu. Moscow, 1896.

———. "Ocherk uspekhov biologii v XIX stoletii," *RM*, 1901, No. 1, Sect. 2, pp. 75–92.

Merz, John Theodore. A History of European Thought in the Nineteenth Century.
4 vols. Edinburgh and London: Blackwood, 1907–14.

Metchnikoff, Elias. [I. I. Mechnikov]. Lectures on the Comparative Pathology of Inflammation. Tr. from the French by F. A. Starling and E. H. Starling. London:
Kegan Paul, 1893.

Metchnikoff, Elie. [I. I. Mechnikov.] Immunity in Infective Diseases. Tr. from the
French by F. G. Binnie. Cambridge, Eng.: Cambridge University Press, 1905.

———. The Nature of Man. Tr. from the French by B. C. Mitchell. New York: Putnam, 1909.

———. The Nature of Man: Studies in Optimistic Philosophy. New York: Putnam, 1903.

———. The Prolongation of Life: Optimistic Studies. New York: Putnam, 1908.

Metchnikoff, Olga. Life of Elie Metchnikoff, 1845–1916. Boston: Houghton-Mifflin, 1921.

M. G. "Parizhskii sotsiologicheskii kongress," *RB*, 1895, No. 3, Sect. 2, pp. 82–91.

Miasishchev, V. N. "Vladimir Mikhailovich Bekhterev," in *LRN: Biol.*, pp. 592–604.

Mikhailovskii, N. K. "Literatura i zhizn'," *RB*, 1903, No. 1, Sect. 3, pp. 84–108.

———. Polnoe sobranie sochinenii. Vol. VIII. St. Petersburg, 1914.

———. Sochineniia. 6 vols. St. Petersburg, 1896–97.

Mikhel'son, V. A. "Obzor noveishikh issledovanii po termodinamike luchistoi energii," *ZFKhO*, XXIV (1902), Sect. 2, pp. 157–207.

———. "Rasshirenie i natsional'naia organizatsiia nauchnykh issledovanii v Rossii," *Priroda*, 1916, No. 5–6, pp. 679–98.

Miklashevskii, I. "K voprosu o professorskom gonorare," *Obrazovanie*, 1897, No. 12, pp. 1–20.

Mikulak, M. W. "Darwinism, Soviet Genetics, and Marxism-Leninism," *Journal of the History of Ideas*, XXXI (1970), 359–76.

Mikulinskii, S. R., ed. Istoriia estestvoznaniia v Rossii. Vol. III. Moscow, 1962.

M[iliukov], P. N. "Istoriosofiia g. Kareeva," *RM*, 1887, No. 11, Sect. 2, 90–101.

Miliukov, P. N. Iz istorii russkoi intelligentsii. 2d ed. St. Petersburg, 1908.

———. "M. M. Kovalevskii kak sotsiolog i kak grazhdanin," in Arsen'ev *et al.*, Kovalevskii, pp. 136–43.

———. Ocherki po istorii russkoi kul'tury. Vol. I, 5th ed., St. Petersburg, 1904; Vol. II, 4th ed., St. Petersburg, 1905; Vol. III, 2d ed., St. Petersburg, 1903.

———. "Universitety v Rossii," *Brockhaus-Efron*, LCVIII (1902), 788–800.

Ministerstvo Narodnogo prosveshcheniia: Proekty i predlozheniia v Gosudarstvennuiu Dumu. St. Petersburg, 1909–13.

Mitskevich, S. I. Revoliutsionnaia Moskva: 1888–1905. Moscow, 1940.

Mittag-Leffler, G. "Sophie Kovalevsky: Notice biographique," *Acta mathematica*, XVI (1892–93), 385–92.

———. "Weierstrass et Sonja Kowalewsky," *Acta mathematica*, XXXIX (1923), 133–98.

M. L. "Butlerov (Aleksandr Mikhailovich)," *Brockhaus-Efron*, V (1891), 79–82.

Mladentsev, M. N., and V. E. Tishchenko. Dmitrii Ivanovich Mendeleev: Ego zhizn' i deiatel'nost'. Vol. I. Moscow-Leningrad, 1938.

Modestov, V. I. "Russkaia nauka v poslednie dvadtsatpiat' let," *RM*, 1890, No. 5, pp. 73–91.

Modzalevskii, B. L. "Iz istorii Peterburgskogo universiteta, 1857–59 gg.," *Golos minuvshego*, 1917, No. 1, pp. 135–70.

———, ed. Perepiska L. N. Tolstogo s N. N. Strakhovym. St. Petersburg, 1914.

Moiseev, N. D. "A. M. Liapunov i ego trudy po teorii ustoichivosti," *UZMU*, XCI (1947), 129–47.

Mokievskii, P. "Lavrov kak filosof," in Radlov *et al.*, pp. 29–72.

Mommsen, Wolfgang J. Max Weber und die deutsche Politik, 1890–1920. Tübingen, 1959.

Monday, C. F. "On the Advantages of Using Tchebycheff's Rule in Association with the Integrator to Obtain Cross Curves of Stability," *Transactions of the Institution of Naval Architects*, XLI (1899), 80–86.

Morgan, Thomas Hunt. The Scientific Basis of Evolution. 2d ed. New York: Norton, 1932.

Morozov, N. A. D. I. Mendeleev i znachenie ego periodicheskoi sistemy dlia khimii budushchego. Moscow, 1907.

———. Periodicheskie sistemy stroeniia veshchestva: teoriia obrazovaniia khimicheskikh elementov. Moscow, 1907.

———. "Vnov' otkrytyia prevrashcheniia emanatsii radiia s tochki zreniia evoliutsionnoi teorii stroeniia atomov," *Izvestiia S. Peterburgskoi Biologicheskoi laboratorii*, IX (1908), 6–13.

"Moskovskoe Iuridicheskoe obshchestvo v 1891–92 g.," *Iuridicheskii vestnik*, XI (1892), 494–534.

Muromtsev, S. A. "Pravo i spravedlivost'," *Sbornik pravovedeniia i obshchestvennykh znanii*, II, 1–12. St. Petersburg, 1893.

———. "Sotsiologicheskie ocherki," *RM*, 1889, No. 1, Sect. 2, pp. 1–32.

———. *Stat'i i rechi*. 5 vols. Moscow, 1910.

Murzaev, E. M., ed. Pamiati akademika L. S. Berga. Moscow-Leningrad, 1955.

Nametkin, S. S. "Issledovaniia N. D. Zelinskogo v oblasti organicheskogo sinteza i khimii nefti (1884–1934)," *UZMU*, 1934, No. 3, pp. 21–26.

———. "Nikolai Dmitrievich Zelinskii (biograficheskii ocherk)," *UZMU*, 1934, No. 3, pp. 7–20.

Na slavnom postu, 1860–1900: Literaturnyi sbornik, posviashchennyi N. K. Mikhailovskomu. St. Petersburg, 1901.

Naturalist'. "Strannoe napadanie na darvinizm," *RB*, 1889, No. 2, Sect. 2, pp. 230–51.

Navashin, S. G. Edinitsy zhizni. Kiev, 1900.

———. Izbrannye trudy. Vol. I. Moscow-Leningrad, 1951.

Nechaev, A. V. "Uspekhi geologii," *Priroda*, 1912, No. 2, pp. 159–75.

Nechkina, M. V. Russkaia istoriia v osveshchenii ekonomicheskogo materializma. Kazan, 1922.

Nekrasov, P. A. "Filosofiia i logika nauki o massovykh proiavleniiakh chelovecheskoi deiatel'nosti (peresmotr osnovanii sotsial'noi fiziki Ketle)," *MS*, XXIII (1902), 463–604.

———. Moskovskaia filosofsko-matematicheskaia shkola i ee osnovateli. Moscow, 1904.

Nevedenskii, S. Katkov i ego vremia. St. Petersburg, 1888.

Nevedomskii, M. "80-ye i 90-ye gody v nashei literature," *Granat-Ist.*, IX (n.d.), 1–116.

———. "N. K. Mikhailovskii (opyt psikhologicheskoi kharakteristiki)," *MB*, 1904, No. 4, Sect. 2, pp. 1–32.

Nevskaia, N. I. Fedor Aleksandrovich Bredikhin. Moscow-Leningrad, 1964.

Newcomb, S., and R. Engelmann. Populäre Astronomie. 6th ed. Leipzig, 1921.

Newman, James R., ed. The World of Mathematics. Vols. I–IV. New York: Simon and Schuster, 1956.

Nikiforov, P. M. "Gadolin, Aksel' Vil'gel'movich," *MBS-AN*, I (1915), 187–93.

Nikitenko, A. V. Zapiski i Dnevnik (1804–1847 gg.). 2 vols. St. Petersburg, 1905.

Nikitin, A. I., ed. Materialy po istorii otechestvennoi khimii. Vol. III. Moscow-Leningrad, 1954.

Nikitin, V. V. "Evgraf Stepanovich Fedorov," *Izvestiia Geologicheskogo komiteta*, XXXVIII (1919), 429–67.

———. Die Fedorow-Methode. Berlin, 1936.

"Nikolai Nikolaevich Luzin (k shestidesiatiletiiu so dnia rozhdeniia)," *Uspekhi matematicheskikh nauk*, I (1946), Pt. 1, pp. 226–28.

Nikol'skii, B. V. Nikolai Nikolaevich Strakhov: Kritiko-biograficheskii ocherk. St. Petersburg, 1896.

Nikol'skii, N. M. "Raskol' i sektanstvo," Granat-Ist., V (n.d.), 228–92.

Nilov, Evgenii. Zelinskii. Moscow, 1964.

N. K. "Istoriko-teoreticheskie vzgliady Chernyshevskogo, Lavrova i Mikhailovskogo," Nauchnyi istoricheskii zhurnal, I (1913), 113–24.

"Novaia era v universitetskoi zhizni," RV, 1887, No. 8, pp. 938–42.

Novgorodtsev, P. I. Istoricheskaia shkola iuristov: Ee proiskhozhdenie i sud'ba. Moscow, 1896.

——. "Nravstvennyi idealizm v filosofii prava," in Novgorodtsev, Problemy idealizma, pp. 237–96.

——. "Znachenie filosofii," NS, 1903, No. 4, pp. 108–15.

——, ed. Problemy idealizma. Moscow, 1903.

Novikov, P. A. "I. I. Mechnikov kak zoolog," NN, I (1948), 427–77.

Novikova, V. N. "Otkrytie S. N. Vinogradskim vozbuditelei protsessa nitrifikatsii," TIIE-T, XXXII (1960), 145–72.

Novicow, Jacques. La critique du darwinisme sociale. Paris, 1910.

——. Essai de notation sociologique. Paris, 1895.

——. "L'essence du progrès," AIIS, XIV (1913), 415–40.

——. Les luttes entre sociétés humaines et leur phases successives. Paris, 1893.

——. Mécanisme et limites de l'association humaine. Paris, 1912.

——. Théorie organique des sociétés. Paris, 1899.

——. War and Its Alleged Benefits. Tr. from the French by Thomas Seltzer. New York: Holt, 1911.

"Novye knigi," VE, 1871, No. 2, pp. 917–22.

Ob otmene stesnenii malorusskogo pechatnogo slova. St. Petersburg, 1905.

Obler, P. C., and H. A. Estrin, eds. The New Scientist. New York: Doubleday, 1962.

Obruchev, V. A. Istoriia geologicheskikh issledovanii Sibira (period tret'ii: 1851–1888 gg.). Leningrad, 1934.

——. Istoriia geologicheskogo issledovaniia Sibira (period chetvertyi: 1889–1917 gg.). Moscow-Leningrad, 1937.

——. "Zametki sibirskogo geologa," OIGZ, II (1953), 5–19.

"Obshchestva meditsinskie v Rossii," Brockhaus-Efron, XXI (1897), 621–22.

Obzor deiatel'nosti S. Peterburgskogo Obshchestva estestvoispytatelei za pervoe dvadtsatipiatiletie ego sushchestvovaniia: 1868–1893. St. Petersburg, 1893.

Odinetz, D. M., and P. J. Novgorodtsev. Russian Schools and Universities in the World War. New Haven: Yale University Press, 1929.

Ognev, I. F. "Rechi E. diu-Bua-Reimona i ego nauchnoe mirovozzrenie," in Bachinskii et al., pp. 42–70.

——. "Vitalizm v sovremennom estestvoznanii," VFP, 1900, No. 54, pp. 686–730.

Omelianskii, V. L. Izbrannye trudy. Vol. II. Moscow, 1953.

——. "O mikrobakh sviazyvaiushchikh svobodnyi azot atmosferi," Priroda, 1913, No. 9, 1041–48.

——. "Razvitie estestvoznaniia v Rossii v poslednuiu chetvert veka," Granat-Ist., IX (n.d.), 116–44.

—— and L. A. Orbeli, eds. Sbornik posviashchennyi 75-letiiu akademika Ivana Petrovicha Pavlova. Moscow-Leningrad, 1924.

O proekte ustava i shtatov Imperatorskoi Sankt'-Peterburgskoi Akademii nauk: Doklad Komissii Soveta Moskovskogo universiteta i otdel'nye zamechaniia odnogo iz chlenov komissii. Moscow, 1865.

Orbeli, L. A. Vospominaniia. Moscow-Leningrad, 1966.

Oreshkin, V. V. Vol'noe ekonomicheskoe obshchestvo v Rossii: 1765–1917. Moscow, 1963.

Origanskii, I. "Universitetskii vopros i 'Proekt universitetskogo ustava,'" VE, 1906, No. 1, pp. 5–50.

Osborn, H. The Age of Mammals in Europe, Asia, and North America. New York: Macmillan, 1910.

Ossipow, E., I. Popow, and P. Kourkine. La medicine du zemstvo en Russie. Moscow, 1900.

Ostrovitianov, K. V., ed. Istoriia Akademii nauk SSSR. Vol. II. Moscow-Leningrad, 1964.

"Otchet o deiatel'nosti Fizicheskogo otdeleniia Russkogo Fiziko-khimicheskogo obshchestva za 1900 g.," ZFKhO, XXXIII (1901), Sect. 1, pp. xiv–xv.

"Otchet o deiatel'nosti Otdeleniia khimii Russkogo Fiziko-khimicheskogo obshchestva," ZFKhO, XXXIII (1901), Sect. 1, pp. iii–xiii.

Otchety o deiatel'nosti Komissii po izucheniiu estestvennykh sil v Rossii, Vol. VIII. Petrograd, 1917.

"Otdel'nye zamechaniia na proekt ustava i shtatov Peterburgskoi Akademii nauk odnogo iz chlenov komissii," Chten., 1865, No. 2, Sect. 4, pp. 166–92.

Ovsianiko-Kulikovskii, D. N. Istoriia russkoi intelligentsii. Vol. II. Moscow, 1907.

Ozarkovskaia, O. E. D. I. Mendeleev. Moscow, 1929.


Palladin, Vladimir I. Plant Physiology. 3d ed. Philadelphia: Blakiston, 1926.

Partington, J. R. A Short History of Chemistry. 3d ed. New York: Harper, 1960.

Pasteur, Louis. Oeuvres. Vol. VII. Paris, 1939.

Pasvolsky, Leo. "Nicholai Alexeyevich Oumov," Science (n.s.), XLII (1915), pp. 113–15.

Pauling, Linus. The Nature of the Chemical Bond. 3d ed. Ithaca: Cornell University Press, 1960.

Pavlov, A. P. Dlia chego prepodavaetsia estestvoznanie. Moscow, 1916. A reprint from Vestnik vospitaniia, 1916, No. 7.

——. "Kratkii ocherk istorii geologii," MB, 1901: No. 10, pp. 1–33; No. 11, pp. 55–78.

——. "Lomonosov kak geolog," in Prazdnovanie dvukhsotletnei godovshchiny rozhdeniia M. V. Lomonosova, pp. 69–94.

——. Polveka v istorii nauki ob iskopaemykh organizmakh. Moscow, 1897.

Pavlov, I. P. Dvadtsatiletnii opyt ob'ektivnogo izucheniia vysshei nervnoi deiatel'nosti (povedeniia) zhivotnykh: Uslovnye refleksy. 5th ed. Leningrad, 1932.

——. Lectures on Conditioned Reflexes. Vol. I. Tr. from the Russian by W. H. Gantt. New York: International Publishers, 1967.

——. Lektsii o rabote glavnykh pishchevaritel'nykh zhelez. Moscow, 1949.

——. Polnoe sobranie sochinenii. Vols. II and III. Moscow, 1946–49.

——. Polnoe sobranie sochinenii. 2d ed., 6 vols. Moscow-Leningrad, 1951–52.

——. Polnoe sobranie trudov. Vol. II. Moscow, 1946.

——. "The Reply of a Physiologist to Psychologists," The Psychological Review, XXXIX (1932), 91–127.

——. Selected Works. Moscow, 1955.

Pawlow, J. P. [I. P. Pavlov]. "Die äussere Arbeit der Verdauungsdrüsen und ihr Mechanismus," in W. Nagel, ed., Handbuch der Physiologie des Menschen, II, 666–743. Braunschweig, 1907.

——. The Work of the Digestive Glands. Tr. from the German by W. H. Thompson. London: C. Griffin, 1902.

Pazukhin, A. Sovremennoe sostoianie Rossii i soslovnyi vopros. Moscow, 1886.
P. B. "Neskol'ko zamechanii ob 'Ocherkakh po istorii russkoi kul'tury' g. Miliukova," *RB*, 1898, No. 8, Sect. 2, pp. 1–21.
"Peterburgskoe Biologicheskoe obshchestvo," *Priroda*, 1915, No. 4, pp. 614–15.
Petrazhitskii, L. I. Universitet i nauka. 2 vols. St. Petersburg, 1907.
Petrazycki, Leon [L. I. Petrazhitskii]. Law and Morality. Tr. by H. W. Babb. Cambridge, Mass.: Harvard University Press, 1955.
Petri, E. "Geografiia kak predmet universitetskogo prepodavaniia," *ERGO*, II (1892), 329–40.
Petrov, A. D. "Peterburgskaia shkola A. M. Butlerova," *TIIE-T*, XXXV (1961), 197–211.
Petrovich, Michael B. The Emergence of Russian Panslavism: 1856–1870. New York: Columbia University Press, 1956.
Peunova, M. N. Mirovozzrenie M. A. Antonovicha. Moscow, 1960.
P-ev, A. "Tret'ii s'ezd russkikh vrachei v Peterburge," *VE*, 1889, No. 2, pp. 849–56.
P. F. N. "Prikladnaia sotsial'naia nauka i teoriia progressa," *RM*, 1889: No. 11, Sect. 2, pp. 53–78; No. 12, Sect. 2, pp. 92–108.
P. G. "K kharakteristiki nashego filosofskogo razvitiia," in Novogorodtsev, Problemy idealizma, pp. 72–90.
Pipes, Richard. "Kropotkin, Petr," *International Encyclopedia of the Social Sciences*, VIII (1968), 463–65.
Pirogov, N. I. Izbrannye pedagogicheskie sochineniia. Moscow, 1953.
———. Rechi k studentam i evreiam. St. Petersburg, 1906.
———. Sochineniia. 2 vols. St. Petersburg, 1910.
Pirogovskii s'ezd po bor'be s kholeroi. 2 vols. Moscow, 1905.
Pisarev, D. I. Selected Philosophical, Social, and Political Essays. Moscow, 1958.
———. Sochineniia. Vol. III. St. Petersburg, 1894.
———. Sochineniia. 4 vols. Moscow, 1955–56.
Pisarzhevskii, O. N. Dmitrii Ivanovich Mendeleev. Moscow, 1959.
———. Dmitry Ivanovich Mendeleyev: His Life and Work. Moscow, 1954.
Platonov, G. V. Kliment Arkadyevich Timiryazev. Tr. from the Russian by Gannushkin. Moscow, 1955.
———. Mirovozzrenie K. A. Timiriazeva. Moscow, 1952.
Plekhanov, G. V. The Development of the Monist View of History. Tr. from the Russian by A. Rothstein. Moscow, 1956.
———. Izbrannye filosofskie sochineniia. 5 vols. Moscow, 1956–58.
———. Sochineniia. Vols. VII and VIII. Moscow-Petrograd, 1923.
Plotkin, L. A. Pisarev i literaturno-obshchestvennoe dvizhenie shestidesiatykh godov. Leningrad-Moscow, 1945.
"Po povodu mer prinimaemykh Ministerstvom Narodnogo prosveshcheniia s 1862 goda dlia prigotovleniia kandidatov k professorskomu zvaniiu," *ZMNP*, CXXIX (1866), Sect. 4, pp. 1–28.
Pogodin, S. A. "Otkrytie periodicheskogo zakona D. I. Mendeleevym i ego bor'ba za pervenstvo russkoi nauki," *Nauka i zhizn'*, 1949, No. 3, pp. 37–40.
———. "Vystuplenie russkikh khimikov—Zinina, Butlerova, Mendeleeva i Engel'gardta—protiv natsionalizma i shovinizma v nauke," *Uspekhi khimii*, XV (1946), 633–43.
Pogozhev, A. V. Dvadtsatipiatiletie estestvenno-nauchnykh s'ezdov v Rossii: 1861–1886 g. Moscow, 1887.
———. Pervyi s'ezd Moskovskogo-Peterburgskogo obshchestva vrachei. Moscow, 1886.

Pogrebysskii, I. B. "A. A. Markov," in Shtokalo *et al.*, II, 328–39.

"Poiavlenie cheloveka na zemle," *ZMNP*, 1860, No. 1, Sect. 7, pp. 1–9.

Poincaré, Henri. The Foundations of Science. Tr. from the French by G. B. Halsted. New York: Science Press, 1913.

————. "Sur le problème des trois corps et les équations de la dynamique," *Acta mathematica*, XIII (1890), 1–270.

————. Science and Hypothesis. New York: Dover, 1952.

————. The Value of Science. Tr. from the French by G. B. Halsted. New York: Dover, 1958.

Pokrovskii, V., and D. Rikhter. "Rossiia, II: Naselenie," *Brockhaus-Efron*, XXVII (1899), 75–128.

Polianskii, Iu. I., ed. Pis'ma A. O. Kovalevskogo k I. I. Mechnikovu (1866–1900). Moscow-Leningrad, 1955.

"Polozhenie del v Moskovskom universitete," *RM*, 1911, No. 3, pp. 154–64.

Polubarinova-Kochina, P. Ia. "Sof'ia Vasil'evna Kovalevskaia (ocherk nauchnoi deiatel'nosti)," in Kovalevskaia, Nauchnye raboty, pp. 313–42.

Polynov, B. B. "Akademik Konstantin Dmitrievich Glinka," *Priroda*, 1927, No. 12, pp. 935–42.

Popov, I. I. "Dmitrii Aleksandrovich Klements (biograficheskii ocherk)," *Izvestiia Vostochno-Sibirskogo Otdela Imperatorskogo Russkogo Geograficheskogo obshchestva*, XLV (1916), 65–77.

Pospelov, I. "Iz zhizny nashei shkoly," *Vestnik vospitaniia*, 1914, No. 4–6, pp. 98–114.

Posse, K. "Chebyshev, Pafnutii L'vovich," *Vengerov-Slovar'*, VI (1904), 1–23.

Prazdnovanie dvukhsotletnei godovshchiny rozhdeniia M. V. Lomonosova Imperatorskim Moskovskim universitetom. Moscow, 1912.

Predvoditelev, A. S. "Pervootkryvatel' svetogo davleniia," *Priroda*, 1966, No. 3, pp. 48–60.

Presniakov, A. E. Aleksandr Sergeevich Lappo-Danilevskii. Peterburg, 1922.

Prianishnikov, D. N. Izbrannye sochineniia. Vol. IV. Moscow, 1955.

————. Moi vospominaniia. Moscow, 1957.

"Proekt Ustava i shtatov Imperatorskoi Akademii nauk v S. Peterburge i sostoiashchikh pri nei muzeev v Sovete Imperatorskogo Moskovskogo universiteta," *Chten.*, 1865, No. 2, Sect. 5, pp. 142–65.

Protokoly VII S'ezda russkikh estestvoispytatelei i vrachei. Odessa, 1883.

Prudnikov, V. E. P. L. Chebyshev: Uchenyi i pedagog. Moscow, 1950.


R. "Krizis vysshei shkoly: Sostiazanie sil," *RM*, 1911, No. 3, pp. 147–54.

Rabinowitsch, Eugene I. Photosynthesis and Related Processes. Vol. II, Pt. 1. New York: Interscience Publishers, 1951.

Radlov, E. L. "Naturalisticheskaia teoriia poznaniia (po povodu statei prof. I. M. Sechenova)," *VFP*, 1894, No. 5, pp. 682–93.

————. "Vl. S. Solov'ev: Biograficheskii ocherk," in V. S. Solov'ev, IX, i–lv.

———— *et al.* P. L. Lavrov: Sbornik statei. Peterburg, 1922.

Raikov, B. E. "Iz istorii darvinizma v Rossii," *TIIE-T*, XVI (1957), 3–33.

————. Karl Ber: Ego zhizn' i trudy. Moscow-Leningrad, 1961.

Rashin, A. G. "Gramotnost' i narodnoe obrazovanie v Rossii v XIX i nachale XX v.," *IZ*, XXXVII (1951), 28–80.

Rechi i protokoly VI-go S'ezda russkikh estestvoispytatelei i vrachei. 2 vols. St. Petersburg, 1880.

Regel', R. "Ot redaktsii," *TBPB*, 1910, No. 1, pp. 1–6.

——. "Selektsiia s nauchnoi tochki zreniia," *TBPB*, 1912, No. 11, pp. 425–540.

Reingold, Nathan, ed. Science in Nineteenth-century America. New York: Hill and Wang, 1964.

Reisner, M. "Sovremennaia iurisprudentsiia L. I. Petrazhitskogo," *RB*, 1908: No. 1, Sect. 2, pp. 27–55; No. 2, Sect. 2, pp. 26–59.

Review of P. D. Iurkevich, Iz nauki o chelovecheskom dukhe, in *RV*, 1861: No. 4, Sect. 2, pp. 79–105; No. 5, Sect. 2, pp. 26–59.

Review of P. I. Novgorodtsev, ed., Problemy idealizma, in *VE*, 1902, No. 3, pp. 371–78.

Review of R. G. Punnett, Mendelizm, in *Priroda*, 1913, No. 4, pp. 389–91.

Review of A. Vvedenskii, Opyt postroeniia teorii materii na printsipakh kriticheskoi filosofii, *RB*, 1888, No. 9, Sect. 3, pp. 198–206.

Rickert, Heinrich. Die Grenzen der naturwissenschaftlichen Begriffsbildung. Tübingen and Leipzig, 1902.

Riha, Thomas. A Russian European: Paul Miliukov in Russian Politics. Notre Dame, Ind.: University of Notre Dame Press, 1969.

Rikhter, D. "Zemskaia statistika," *VE*, 1904, No. 4, pp. 315–42.

Rodzevich, N. "Otstavka E. P. Kovalevskogo," *IV*, XCIX (1905), 98–129.

Rogers, James A. "Charles Darwin and Russian Scientists," *Russian Review*, XIX (1960), 371–83.

——. "Darwinism, Scientists, and Nihilism," *Russian Review*, XIX (1960), 10–23.

Romanenko, V. I. Mirovozzrenie N. A. Serno-Solov'evicha. Moscow, 1954.

Romanovich-Slavatinskii, A. V. "Moia zhizn' i akademicheskaia deiatel'nost'," *VE*, 1903, No. 4, pp. 527–66.

Rostovtsev, M. "Mezhdunarodnoe nauchnoe obshchenie," *RM*, 1916, No. 3, Sect. 2, pp. 74–81.

——. "Nauka i revoliutsiia," *RM*, 1917, No. 9–10, Sect. 2, pp. 1–16.

Rothschuh, K. E. Geschichte der Physiologie. Berlin, 1953.

Rozanov, V. I. "Organicheskii protsess i mekhanicheskaia prichinnost'," *ZMNP*, CCLXIII (1889), Sect. 2, pp. 1–22.

——. Priroda i istoriia. St. Petersburg, 1900.

——. "Vopros o proiskhozhdenii organizmov," *RV*, 1889, No. 5, pp. 311–16.

Rozhdestvenskii, S. V. Istoricheskii obzor deiatel'nosti Ministerstva Narodnogo prosveshcheniia, 1802–1902. St. Petersburg, 1902.

Rozhkov, N. Istoricheskie i sotsiologicheskie ocherki: Sbornik statei. Vol. I. Moscow, 1906.

——. "Nauchnoe mirosozertsanie i istoriia," *NS*, 1903, No. 1, pp. 105–12.

——. Obzor russkoi istorii s sotsiologicheskoi tochki zreniia. 2d ed., Vol. I. Moscow, 1905.

——. "Proiskhozhdenie soslovii v Rossii," *Obrazovanie*, 1899, No. 7–8, pp. 13–30.

——. "Sotsial'nyi materializm," *RB*, 1899, No. 11, pp. 31–43.

——. "Uspekhi sovremennoi sotsiologii v ikh sootnoshenii s istoriei," *Obrazovanie*, 1898, No. 12, pp. 17–36.

Rubakin, N. A. "Literatura sovremennogo nauchno-filosofskogo mirosozertsaniia," *Priroda*, 1912, No. 6, pp. 803–28.

Rubinshtein, M. M. "Genrikh Rikkert," *VFP*, 1907, No. 1, Sect. 2, pp. 1–61.

Rubinshtein, N. L. Russkaia istoriografiia. Moscow, 1941.

Rumiantsev, N. "Darvinizm (kriticheskoe issledovanie)," *Vera i razum*, 1895, No. 1, Sect. 2, pp. 1–31.

Russell, Bertrand. The Analysis of Matter. London: Kegan Paul, 1927.

"Russkaia shkola v Parizhe," *Russkie vedomosti*, 1904, No. 326, pp. 3–4.

"Russkoe Obshchestvo mirovedeniia v 1914 godu," *Priroda*, 1915, No. 4, pp. 619–20.

Rutherford, Ernest. "The Periodic Law of Elements and Its Interpretation: Mendeléef Centenary Lecture," *The Journal of Chemical Society*, 1934, Pt. I, pp. 635–42.

Rybnikov, K. A., *et al.*, eds. Voprosy istorii fiziko-matematicheskikh nauk. Moscow, 1963.

Ryzhkov, V. L. "Kratkii ocherk istorii izucheniia virusov," *TIIE-T*, XXXVI (1961), 315–25.

Safronov, B. G. M. M. Kovalevskii kak sotsiolog. Moscow, 1960.

Sakulin, P. N. Iz istorii russkogo idealizma. Kniaz V. F. Odoevskii: Mylitel'-pisatel'. Vol. I, Pt. 1. Moscow, 1913.

Samoilov, A. F. Izbrannye stat'i i rechi. Moscow-Leningrad, 1946.

———. "Obshchaia kharakteristika issledovatel'skogo oblika I. P. Pavlova," in Sechenov *et al.*, I, 118–30.

———. "Sovremennaia techeniia v fiziologii," *NS*, 1904, No. 5, pp. 42–57.

Satina, Sophie. Education of Women in Prerevolutionary Russia. Tr. from the Russian by A. F. Poustchine. New York: Satina, 1966.

Savich, V. V. "Ivan Petrovich Pavlov," in Omelianskii and Orbeli, pp. 3–25.

Sbornik postanovlenii Ministerstva Narodnogo prosveshcheniia. 17 vols. St. Petersburg, 1864–1904.

Schaeffer, Clemens, ed. Briefwechsel zwischen Carl Friedrich Gauss und Christian Ludwig Gerling. Berlin, 1927.

"Séance publique annuelle du lundi 24 Décembre 1888," *CR-AS-P*, CVII (1888), 1031–38.

[Sechenov, I. M.]. Avtobiograficheskie zapiski Ivana Mikhailovicha Sechenova. Moscow, 1945.

Sechenov, I. M. "Nauchnaia deiatel'nost' russkikh universitetov po estestvoznaniiu za poslednee dvadtsatipiatiletie," *VE*, 1883, No. 11, pp. 330–42.

———. Selected Works. Moscow-Leningrad, 1935.

———, I. P. Pavlov, and N. E. Vvedenskii. Fiziologiia nervnoi sistemy. Edited by K. M. Bykov. 5 vols. Moscow, 1952.

Semenov, Iu. "2-i Vserossiiskii vozdukhoplavatel'nyi s'ezd," *Priroda*, 1912, No. 4, pp. 571–73.

Semenov [-Tian-Shanskii], P. P. Istoriia poluvekovoi deiatel'nosti Imperatorskogo Russkogo Geograficheskogo obshchestva (1845–1895). St. Petersburg, 1895.

Semenov-Tian-Shanskii, P. P. Memuary, Vol. IV: Epokha osvobozhdeniia krest'ian v Rossii (1857–1861). 7th ed. Petrograd, 1916.

Semenov-Tian-Shanskii, V. Gorod i derevnia v Evropeiskoi Rossii. St. Petersburg, 1910.

Serno-Solov'evich, N. A. Publitsistika, pis'ma. Moscow, 1963.

Severtsov, A. N. Etiudy po teorii evoliutsii. Kiev, 1912.

———. Sobranie sochinenii. Vol. III. Moscow-Leningrad, 1945.

Severtsova, L. B. Aleksei Nikolaevich Severtsov. Moscow-Leningrad, 1946.

Seward, A. C., ed. Darwin and Modern Science. Cambridge, Eng.: Cambridge University Press, 1909.

Shafranovskii, I. I. Evgraf Stepanovich Fedorov. Moscow-Leningrad, 1963.

———. Istoriia kristallografii v Rossii. Moscow-Leningrad, 1962.

——— and N. V. Belov. "E. S. Fedorov (1853–1919)," in Ewald, pp. 341–50.

Shakhovskii, D. I., ed. Sergei Andreevich Muromtsev. Moscow, 1911.

Shaternikov, M. N. "The Life of I. M. Sechenov," in Sechenov, Selected Works, pp. vii–xxxvi.

Shatskii, N. S. Izbrannye trudy. Vol. IV. Moscow, 1965.

Shchapov, A. P. Sochineniia. 3 vols. St. Petersburg, 1906–8.

Shchedrin, N. [M. E. Saltykov]. Polnoe sobranie sochinenii. Vol. X. Leningrad, 1936.

Shcheglov, A. V. Bor'ba Lenina protiv bogdanovskoi revizii marksizma. Moscow, 1937.

Shchipanov, I. Ia., ed. Iz istorii russkoi filosofii. Moscow, 1952.

Shchukarev, A. N. "Problema materii i teoriia poznaniia," in Bachinskii et al., pp. 27–41.

————. Uchenie ob energii i ego prilozheniiakh k zadacham khimii. Moscow, 1900.

————. "Zakony prirody i zakony obshchestva," in Bachinskii et al., pp. 86–103.

Shchurovskii, G. "Ob obshchedostupnosti ili populiarizatsii estestvennykh nauk," in Trudy I S'ezda, pp. 7–17.

Shelgunov, N. V. Izbrannye pedagogicheskie sochineniia. Moscow, 1954.

————. Ocherki russkoi zhizni. St. Petersburg, 1895.

————. Vospominaniia. Moscow-Petrograd, 1923.

Shershenevich, G. F. "S. A. Muromtsev kak uchenyi," in Shakhovskii, pp. 80–90.

Shiller, N. N. "Proiskhozhdenie i razvitie poniatii o 'temperature' i o 'teple' (kritiko-gnoseologicheskii ocherk)," Universitetskie izvestiia, 1899, No. 7, Sect. 2, pp. 1–53.

————. "Znachenie poniatii o 'sile' i o 'masse' v teorii poznaniia i v metafizike," Universitetskie izvestiia, 1898, No. 2, Sect. 2, pp. 1–91.

Shilov, N. A. "V nedrakh atoma," Priroda, 1915, No. 2, pp. 179–207.

Shimanskii, Iu. A. "Aleksei Nikolaevich Krylov: Kratkii ocherk zhizni i deiatel'nosti," in A. N. Krylov, Izbrannye trudy, pp. 734–43.

————, ed. Pamiati Alekseia Nikolaevicha Krylova. Moscow-Leningrad, 1958.

Shimkevich, V. M. "A. O. Kovalevskii (nekrolog)," Obrazovanie, 1901, No. 11, Sect. 1, pp. 107–14.

————. "Teoriia mutatsii," NS, 1905, No. 5, pp. 16–28.

Shmal'gauzen, I. F. O rastitel'nykh pomesiakh: Nabliudeniia iz peterburgskoi flory. St. Petersburg, 1874.

Shmurlo, E. "Pekarskii, Petr Petrovich," RBS, XIII (1902), 462–63.

Shpol'skii, E. V. Sorok let sovetskoi fiziki. Moscow, 1958.

Shtokalo, I. Z., et al., eds. Istoriia otechestvennoi matematiki. Vol. II. Kiev, 1967.

Shtraikh, S. Ia. Aleksei Nikolaevich Krylov. Moscow-Leningrad, 1944.

————, ed. Bor'ba za nauku v tsarskoi Rossii. Moscow-Leningrad, 1931.

————. "Kratkii ocherk zhizni i deiatel'nosti A. N. Krylova," in A. N. Krylov, Vospominaniia i ocherki, pp. 5–72.

Shubnikov, A. V. "Iurii Viktorovich Vul'f," Priroda, 1926, No. 1–2, pp. 5–8.

Shubnikova, O. M. "V. I. Vernadskii kak mineralog i ego shkola v Moskovskom universitete," OIGZ, III (1955), 130–59.

Shuleikin, V. V. Petr Petrovich Lazarev. Moscow, 1960.

Simmons, Ernest J., ed. Continuity and Change in Russian and Soviet Thought. New York: Russell and Russell, 1967.

Simpson, George Gaylord. Horses. New York: Oxford University Press, 1951.

————. Life of the Past: An Introduction to Paleontology. New Haven: Yale University Press, 1953.

————. Tempo and Mode in Evolution. New York: Columbia University Press, 1944.

Singh, Jagjit. Great Ideas of Modern Mathematics: Their Nature and Use. New York: Dover, 1959.

Skabichevskii, A. M. Istoriia noveishei russkoi literatury: 1848–1908 gg. 7th ed. St. Petersburg, 1909.

Skripchinskii, V. V. "O razlichii vo vzgliadakh I. V. Michurina i T. D. Lysenko na nekotorye iz osnovnykh problem genetiki," *BMOIP*, Biological Section, LXX (1965), 105–16.

Skvortsov, A. I. "D. I. Mendeleev kak ekonomist," *RM*, 1917, No. 2, Sect. 2, pp. 65–71.

Slonimskii, L. "Noveishie idealisty," *VE*, 1903, No. 5, pp. 313–25.

Smirnov, V. I. "Biograficheskii ocherk," in Liapunov, Sobranie sochinenii, pp. 5–15.

——. "Matematicheskie raboty A. N. Krylova," *TIIE-T*, XV (1956), 13–23.

——. "Raboty A. N. Krylova po matematicheskoi fizike i mekhanike," in Shimanskii, Pamiati A. N. Krylova, pp. 36–46.

Smirnov, V. Z. Reforma nachalnoi i srednei shkoly v 60-kh godakh XIX v. Moscow, 1954.

Smithells, Arthur. "Analytical Chemistry," *Nature*, L (1898), 1–3.

Smolenskii, P. O. Novoe meditsinskoe uchrezhdenie. St. Petersburg, 1890.

Sobol', S. L. "Iz istorii bor'by za darvinizm v Rossii," *TIIE-T*, XIV (1957), 195–226.

——. "Pervye soobshcheniia o teorii Ch. Darvina v russkoi pechati," *BMOIP* (New Series), Biological Section, L (1945), 128–38.

Sokolov, A. "Uchebnaia geografiia dlia poslednie piat' let," *ERGO*, II (1892), 294–328.

Sokolov, N. N. "Lev Semenovich Berg (nekotorye biograficheskie dannye)," in Murzaev, pp. 18–60.

Sologub, V. S. "Moskovskaia shkola teorii funktsii," in Shtokalo *et al.*, pp. 437–43.

Solov'ev, A. I. "Geografiia v Moskovskom universitete v dorevoliutsionnoe vremia," in Markov and Saushkin, pp. 23–46.

Solov'ev, E. A. Ocherki iz istorii russkoi literatury XIX veka. St. Petersburg, 1903.

Solov'ev, I. "Avtonomiia vysshei shkoly i poslednii proekt universitetskogo ustava," *Vestnik vospitaniia*, 1917, No. 4–5, pp. 218–37.

——. "Universitetskii vopros v shestidesiatykh godakh," *Vestnik vospitaniia*, 1913, No. 9, pp. 56–96.

Solov'ev, Iu. I. Ocherki po istorii fizicheskoi khimii. Moscow, 1964.

——, ed. Ocherki po istorii khimii. Moscow, 1963.

—— and A. Ia. Kipnis. Dmitrii Petrovich Konovalov, 1856–1929. Moscow, 1964.

—— and O. E. Zviagintsev. Nikolai Semenovich Kurnakov: Zhizn' i deiatel'nost'. Moscow, 1960.

Solov'ev, N. M. "O neobkhodimom verovanii, lezhashchem v osnove matematicheskogo myshleniia," in Bachinskii *et al.*, pp. 158–82.

[Solov'ev, S. M.]. Zapiski Sergeia Mikhailovicha Solov'eva. St. Petersburg, n.d.

Solov'ev, V. S. Sobranie sochinenii. 9 vols. St. Petersburg, 1902–7.

Sominskii, M. S. Abram Fedorovich Ioffe. Moscow-Leningrad, 1964.

Sorokin, Pitirim A. Contemporary Sociological Theories. New York: Harper, 1928.

——. "P. L. Lavrov kak sotsiolog," in Vitiazev, pp. 19–23.

——. Modern Historical and Social Philosophies. New York: Dover, 1963.

——. "Teoriia faktorov M. M. Kovalevskogo," in Arsen'ev *et al.*, Kovalevskii, pp. 180–95.

Souslin, M. "Théorie des fonctions: Sur une définition des ensembles mesurables *B* sans nombres transfinis," *CR-AS-P*, CLXIV (1917), 88–95.

Spektorskii, E. "Kovalevsky, Maksim Maksimovich," *Encyclopedia of the Social Sciences*, VIII (1932), 595–96.

——. Problema sotsial'noi fiziki v XVII stoletii. Vol. I. Warsaw, 1910.

Speranskii, N. Krizis russkoi shkoly. Moscow, 1914.

Stadlin, A. Ts. " 'Refleks' pred sudom refleksii," *RV*, 1874, No. 11, 834–82.

Stanley, W. M. "Soviet Studies in Viruses," *Science*, XCIX (1944), 136–38.

"Starye Bogi i novye Bogi," *RV*, 1861, No. 2, pp. 891–904.

Stepanov, V. V. "Moskovskaia shkola teorii funktsii," *UZMU*, XCI (1947), 47–52.

Stern, Alfred. "Science and the Philosopher," in Obler and Estrin, pp. 280–301.

Stoletov, A. G. Izbrannye sochineniia. Moscow-Leningrad, 1950.

——, N. E. Zhukovskii, and P. A. Nekrasov. Sof'ia Vasil'evna Kovalevskaia. Moscow, 1891.

Strain, Harold H. Leaf Xanthophylls. Washington, D.C.: Carnegie Institution, 1938.

Strakhov, N. N. Bor'ba s zapadom v nashei literature. 3d ed., 3 vols. Kiev, 1897.

——. Filosofskie ocherki. St. Petersburg, 1895.

——. Iz istorii literaturnogo nigilizma, 1861–1865. St. Petersburg, 1890.

——. O metode estestvennykh nauk i znachenii ikh v obshchem obrazovanii. St. Petersburg, 1865.

——. "Polnoe oproverzhenie darvinizma," *RV*, 1887, No. 1, pp. 9–62.

——. "Vsegdashniaia oshibka darvinistov," *RV*, 1887: No. 11, pp. 66–114; No. 12, pp. 98–129.

Strakhov, P. S. "Atomy zhizni," *Bogoslovskii vestnik*, I (1912), 1–29.

Strannoliubskii, A. "Zhenskoe obrazovanie v Rossii," *Obrazovanie*, 1894, No. 10, Sect. 2, pp. 320–44.

Strashun, I. "Pirogovskoe obshchestvo: s'ezdy," in *Bol'shaia meditsinskaia entsiklopediia*, XXIV (1962), 443–62.

Struve, P. B. "Intelligentsia i revoliutsiia," in Berdiaev *et al.*, pp. 156–74.

——. "M. M. Kovalevskii," *RM*, 1916, No. 4, Sect. 2, pp. 98–101.

——. Kriticheskie zametki k voprosu ob ekonomicheskom razvitii. Vol. I. St. Petersburg, 1894.

——. "Die Marxsche Theorie der sozialen Entwicklung: Ein kritischer Versuch," *Archiv für soziale Gesetzgebung und Statistik*, XIV (1899), 658–704.

——. "Na raznye temy," *MB*, 1901, No. 6, Sect. 2, pp. 12–27.

——. Na raznye temy (1893–1901 gg.): Sbornik statei. St. Petersburg, 1902.

——. "Sovremennyi krizis v politicheskoi ekonomii," *Logos*, 1911, No. 1, pp. 123–44.

Stryzhevskii, S. Nikolai Zhukovsky: Founder of Aeronautics. Moscow, 1957.

Suvorov, S. "Osnovy filosofii zhizni," in Dorovatovskii and Charushnikov, pp. 1–113.

Svatikov, S. G. "Nikolai Dmitrievich Nozhin," *Golos minuvshego*, 1914, No. 10, pp. 1–36.

——. "Opal'naia professura 80-ykh gg.," *Golos minuvshego*, 1917, No. 2, pp. 5–78.

Syromiatnikov, B. "Moskovskii universitet," in *Granat-Ents.*, XXXIII (n.d.), 373–86.

Tarasevich, L. A. "Raboty I. I. Mechnikova v oblasti meditsiny i mikrobiologii," *Priroda*, 1915, No. 5, pp. 707–24.

Thaden, Edward C. Conservative Nationalism in Nineteenth-Century Russia. Seattle: University of Washington Press, 1964.

Thorpe, T. E. "Dmitrii Ivanowitsh Mendeleef," *Nature*, XL (1889), 193–97.

Tikhomirov, A. A. Nashe universitetskoe delo. Moscow, 1906. A reprint from *Moskovskie vedomosti*, 1906, Nos. 306 and 307.

——. Ob'iasnitel'naia zapiska po proektu novogo ustava universitetov. St. Petersburg, 1907.

——. Osnovnoi vopros evoliutsionizma v biologii. St. Petersburg, 1911.

——. Polozhenie cheloveka v prirode. Moscow, 1906.

——. Sud'ba darvinizma. St. Petersburg, 1907.

Tikhomirov, M. N., ed. Istoriia Moskovskogo universiteta. Vol. I. Moscow, 1955.

Tikhomirov, P. "Matematicheskii proekt reformy sotsiologii na nachalakh filosofskogo idealizma," *Bogoslovskii vestnik*, 1903, No. 2, pp. 1–62.
Tikhonovich, N. N. "S'ezdy russkikh estestvoispytatelei i vrachei," *IOGZ*, I (1953), 95–119.
———. "Vserossiiskie s'ezdy deiatelei po prakticheskoi geologii i razvedochnomu delu," *OIGZ*, II (1953), 114–42.
Tikhonravov, N. S. Sochineniia. Vol. III, Pt. 2. Moscow, 1898.
Tilden, Sir William A. Chemical Discovery and Invention in the Twentieth Century. London: Routledge, 1916.
Timasheff, N. S. Introduction, in Petrazycki, pp. iii–xlvi.
Timiriazev, A. K. "Nauchnye raboty P. N. Lebedeva," *TIIE-T*, XXVIII (1959), 79–90.
———, ed. Ocherki po istorii fiziki v Rossii. Moscow, 1949.
Timiriazev, K. A. "Bessil'naia zloba antidarvinista," in K. A. Timiriazev, Darvin, pp. 297–414.
———. Charlz Darvin i ego uchenie. 3d ed. Moscow, 1894.
———. Istoricheskii metod v biologii. Moscow-Leningrad, 1943.
———. Izbrannye raboty po khlorofillu i usvoeniiu sveta rasteniem. Moscow, 1948.
———. Nasushchnye zadachi sovremennogo estestvoznaniia. 3d ed. Moscow, 1908.
———. Nauka i demokratiia: Sbornik statei, 1904–1919 gg. Moscow, 1963.
———. Nekotorye osnovnye zadachi sovremennogo estestvoznaniia. Moscow, 1895.
———. "Oprovergnut li darvinizm?," in K. A. Timiriazev, Darvin, pp. 221–96.
———. "Probuzhdenie estestvoznaniia v tret'ei chetverti veka," *Granat-Ist.*, VII (n.d.), 1–30.
———. Sochineniia. 10 vols. Moscow, 1937–40.
Timiriazeff, C. A. [K. A. Timiriazev]. The Life of the Plant. Tr. from the Russian by Anna Chermeteff. London: Longmans, 1912.
Timoshenko, S. Vospominaniia. Paris, 1963.
Tishchenko, V. E. "Dmitrii Ivanovich Mendeleev: Kratkii biograficheskii ocherk," in "Trudy Pervogo Mendeleevskogo s'ezda," pp. 8–32.
——— et al. A. M. Butlerov, 1828–1928. Leningrad, 1929.
Todhunter, I. A History of the Progress of the Calculus of Variations. Cambridge, Eng.: Macmillan, 1861.
Tokarev, S. A. Istoriia russkoi etnografii: Dooktiabr'skii period. Moscow, 1966.
Tolstoi, L. N. Pedagogicheskie sochineniia. Moscow, 1948.
———. Works. Vol. XII. New York: Crowell, 1899.
Tolstov, S. P. "Dmitrii Nikolaevich Anuchin—etnograf," *Trudy Instituta etnografii* (N.S.), I (1947), 18–21.
"Torzhestvennoe sobranie Imperatorskogo Vol'nogo ekonomicheskogo obshchestva i chlenov s'ezda," in Vos'moi S'ezd, General Section, pp. 96–118.
Trirogova-Mendeleeva, O. D. Mendeleev i ego sem'ia. Moscow, 1947.
Trubetskoi, Evgenii. "Vladimir Solov'ev i ego delo," *VFP*, 1910, No. 4, pp. 637–60.
Trubetskoi, S. N. Sobranie sochinenii. Vol. IV. Moscow, 1906.
———. "Universitet i studenchestvo," *RM*, 1897, No. 4, pp. 182–203.
Trudy I S'ezda russkikh estestvoispytatelei v S. Peterburge. St. Petersburg, 1868.
Trudy II S'ezda russkikh estestvoispytatelei v Moskve. Moscow, 1871.
Trudy III S'ezda russkikh estestvoispytatelei v Kieve. Kiev, 1873.
Trudy IV S'ezda russkikh estestvoispytatelei v Kazani. Vol. I. Kazan, 1874.
Trudy V S'ezda russkikh estestvoispytatelei i vrachei v Varshave. Vol. I. Warsaw, 1877.
"Trudy Pervogo Mendeleevskogo s'ezda po obshchei i prikladnoi khimii," *ZFKhO*, LXI (1909), Pt. I, Supplement.

Tsetlin, L. S. Iz istorii nauchnoi mysli v Rossii (nauka i uchenye v Moskovskom universitete vo vtoroi polovine XIX veka). Moscow, 1958.

Tsinger, V. Ia. "Nedorazumeniia vo vzgliadakh na osnovaniia geometrii," *VFP*, 1894, No. 22, pp. 199–213.

Tugan-Baranovskii, M. I. "Bor'ba klassov kak glavneishee soderzhanie istorii," *MB*, 1904, No. 9, Sect. 1, pp. 242–59.

——. "Chto takoe obshchestvennyi klass?," *MB*, 1904, No. 1, Sect. 1, pp. 64–72.

——. "Intelligentsia i sotsializm," in Arsen'ev *et al.*, Intelligentsia, pp. 235–58.

——. "Kritische Literatur Uebersicht: Kant und Marx," *Archiv für Sozialwissenschaft und Sozialpolitik*, XXXIII (1911), 180–88.

——. Modern Socialism in Its Historical Development. Tr. from the Russian by M. I. Redmount. London: Sonnenschein, 1910.

——. "Promyshlennye krizisi," *Sbornik pravovedeniia i obshchestvennykh znanii*, V (1895), 69–87.

——. Promyshlennye krizisi v sovremennoi Anglii, ikh prichiny i vlianie na narodnuiu zhizn'. Vol. I. St. Petersburg, 1894.

——. Russkaia fabrika. 6th ed. Moscow-Leningrad, 1934.

——. "Subjektivismus und Objektivismus in der Wertlehre," *Archiv für Sozialwissenschaft und Sozialpolitik*, XXII (1906), 557–64.

——. Teoreticheskie osnovy marksizma. St. Petersburg, 1905.

——. Theoretische Grundlagen des Marxismus. Leipzig, 1905.

——. "Znachenie ekonomicheskogo faktora v istorii," *MB*, 1895, No. 12, Sect. 1, pp. 101–18.

Turchenko, Ia. I. Nikolai Nikolaevich Beketov. Moscow, 1954.

Turkevich, John. Chemistry in the Soviet Union. New York: Van Nostrand, 1965.

Ukhtomskii, A. A. Sobranie sochinenii. Vol. V. Leningrad, 1954.

——. "Velikii fiziolog (pamiati I. P. Pavlova)," in Sechenov *et al.*, IV, 669–73.

Umov, N. A. "Evoliutsiia atoma," *NS*, 1905, No. 1, pp. 5–27.

——. Izbrannye sochineniia. Moscow-Leningrad, 1950.

——. "Po povodu sbornika," in M. M. Kovalevskii *et al.*, pp. 1–7.

——. "Rol' cheloveka v poznavaemom im mire," *Priroda*, 1912, No. 3, pp. 310–32.

——. Sobranie sochinenii. Vol. III. Moscow, 1916.

——. "Voprosy poznaniia v oblasti fizicheskikh nauk," *VFP*, 1894, No. 2, pp. 214–29.

——. "Znachenie Dekarta v istorii fizicheskikh nauk," in Bachinskii *et al.*, pp. 1–26.

——. "Znachenie opytnykh nauk," *NS*, 1903, No. 1, pp. 13–26.

Ushinskii, K. D. Sobranie sochinenii. 11 vols. Moscow-Leningrad, 1948–52.

Uspensky, J. V. Introduction to Mathematical Probability. New York: McGraw-Hill, 1937.

Utechin, S. V. "Philosophy and Society: Alexander Bogdanov," in Labedz, pp. 117–25.

Uzhakova, N. N. Nikolai Aleksandrovich Shilov. Moscow, 1966.

Vagner, Vladimir. "M. M. Kovalevskii kak sotsiolog," in Arsen'ev *et al.*, Kovalevskii, pp. 144–68.

Val'den, P. I. Nauka i zhizn'. 3 vols. Petrograd, 1918–22.

——. Ocherk istorii khimii v Rossii. Odessa, 1917.

Varsanof'eva, V. A. Moskovskoe Obshchestvo ispytatelei prirody i ego znachenie v razvitii otechestvennoi nauki. Moscow, 1955.

——. A. P. Pavlov. Moscow, 1941.

Vasetskii, G. S., and S. R. Mikulinskii, eds. Izbrannye proizvedeniia russkikh estestvoispytatelei pervoi poloviny xix veka. Moscow, 1959.

Vasetskii, G. S., *et al.* Ocherki po istorii filosofii v Rossii (vtoraia polovina XIX i nachalo XX veka). Moscow, 1960.

Vasil'ev, A. V. Nikolai Ivanovich Lobachevskii. Kazan, 1894.

[Vasil'ev, A. V.]. Vstupitel'naia rech' predsedatel'ia Fiziko-matematicheskogo obshchestva A. V. Vasil'eva v torzhestvennom zasedanii Obshchestva 22 oktiabria 1897 g. Kazan, 1897.

——, ed. Novye idei v matematike. 2 vols. St. Petersburg, 1913.

Vasil'ev, A. V. *See also* Vassilieff, A.

Vasil'ev, L. L. Znachenie fiziologicheskogo ucheniia N. E. Vvedenskogo dlia nevropatologii. Moscow, 1953.

Vassilieff, A. [A. V. Vasil'ev]. P. L. Tchébychef et son oeuvre scientifique. Turin, 1898.

Vavilov, N. I. "Gibrid obyknovennoi pshenitsy," *TBPB*, 1913, No. 1, pp. 1–19.

——. "Immunity to Fungous Diseases as a Physiological Test in Genetics and Systematics, Exemplified in Cereals," *Journal of Genetics*, IV (1914), 49–68.

——. Izbrannye trudy. Vol. V. Moscow-Leningrad, 1965.

——. Izbrannye trudy v piati tomakh. Vol. I. Moscow-Leningrad, 1959.

——. The Origin, Variation, Immunity and Breeding of Cultivated Plants. Tr. from the Russian by K. S. Chester. Waltham, Mass.: Chronica Botanica, 1951.

Vavilov, S. I. Sobranie sochinenii. Vol. III. Moscow, 1956.

Velichkin, V. G. Rasskazy o russkikh samouchkakh. Moscow, 1874.

"Veniamin Fedorovich Kagan (k semidesiatipiatiletiiu so dnia rozhdeniia)," *Uspekhi matematicheskikh nauk*, I (1946), Pt. 1, 224–25.

Veniukov, M. "Ob uspekhakh estestvoistoricheskogo izucheniia Aziatskoi Rossii v sviazi s geograficheskimi otkrytiiami v etoi strane za poslednie 25 let," in Trudy I S'ezda, pp. 49–58.

Verkhunov, V. M. "N. I. Lobachevskii i teoriia otnositel'nosti," in Rybnikov *et al.*, pp. 295–306.

"Vernadskii, Vladimir Ivanovich," in *MBS-AN*, I (1915), 146–56. An autobiography.

Vernadskii, V. I. Iavleniia skol'zheniia kristallicheskogo veshchestva. Moscow, 1897.

——. "Iz istorii idei," *RM*, 1912, No. 10, Sect. 2, pp. 125–38.

——. "Kant i estestvoznanie v xviii stoletii," *VFP*, 1905, No. 76, pp. 36–70.

——. "Koksharov, Nikolai Ivanovich," *MBS-AN*, I, 1915, 329–38.

——. O blizhaishchikh zadachakh Komissii po izucheniiu proizvoditel'nykh sil Rossii. Petrograd, 1915.

——. "O nauchnom mirovozzrenii," *VFP*, 1902, No. 65, pp. 1409–65.

——. "O znachenii trudov M. V. Lomonosova v mineralogii i geologii," in Lomonosovskii sbornik: Materialy, pp. 11–34.

——. "Ob ispol'zovanii khimicheskikh elementov v Rossii," *RM*, 1916, No. 1, Sect. 2, pp. 73–88.

——. Ocherki i rechi. 2 vols. Petrograd, 1922.

——. Osnovy kristallografii. Vol. I. Moscow, 1904.

——. "Pamiati N. I. Koksharova i A. V. Gadolina," *BSNM*, VI (1893), 506–10.

——. "Pis'ma o vysshem obrazovanii v Rossii," *Vestnik vospitaniia*, 1913, No. 5, pp. 1–17.

——. "Stranitsa iz istorii pochvovedeniia (pamiati V. V. Dokuchaeva)," *NS*, 1904, No. 6, pp. 5–26.

——. "Tri resheniia," *Poliarnaia zvezda*, 1906, No. 13, pp. 163–73.

——. "Vysshaia shkola v Rossii," Ezhegodnik gazety Rech' na 1914 godu, pp. 302–25. Moscow, 1915.

Vernadsky, W. I. [V. I. Vernadskii]. "Problems of Biochemistry, II." Tr. from the

Russian by George Vernadsky. *Transactions of the Connecticut Academy of Arts and Sciences*, XXXV (1944), 483–517.

Verner, N. [A. A. Bogdanov]. "Nauka i filosofiia," in N. Verner *et al.*, pp. 9–33.

—— *et al.* Ocherki filosofii kollektivizma. Vol. I. St. Petersburg, 1909.

Verrier, René. Roberty: Le positivisme russe et la foundation de la sociologie. Paris, 1934.

Veselovskii, K. S. Istoricheskoe obozrenie trudov Akademii nauk na pol'zu Rossii v proshlom i tekushchem stoletiiakh. St. Petersburg, 1865.

——. "Otchet Imperatorskoi Akademii nauk po Fiziko-matematicheskomu i Isto-riko-filologicheskomu otdeleniiam za 1865 god," *ZMNP*, CXXX (1866), Sect. 2, pp. 1–40.

——. "Otchet Imperatorskoi Akademii nauk po Fiziko-matematicheskomu i Isto-riko-filologicheskomu otdeleniiam za 1869 god," *ZAN*, XVII (1870), 1–24.

Vilenskii, D. G. Istoriia pochvovedeniia. Moscow, 1958.

Vinogradoff, Paul [P. G. Vinogradov]. Villainage in England. Oxford: Clarendon Press, 1892.

Vinogradov, A. P., ed. Chemistry of the Earth's Crust: Proceedings of the Geochemical Conference Commemorating the Centenary of Academician V. I. Vernadskii's Birth. Vol. I. Tr. from the Russian by N. Kaner. Jerusalem: Israel Program for Scientific Translations, 1966.

——. "The Scientific Legacy of V. I. Vernadskii," in Vinogradov, Chemistry of the Earth's Crust, I, 1–8.

Vinogradov, P. G. Nakanune novogo stoletiia. Moscow, 1902.

——."Uchebnoe delo v nashikh universitetakh," *VE*, 1901, No. 10, pp. 537–73.

Vitiazev, P., ed. Sbornik statei posviashchennykh pamiati Petra L. Lavrova. Petrograd, 1920.

Vitte, S. Iu. Vospominaniia. 3 vols. Moscow, 1960.

V. K. "Pozitivizm v russkoi literature," *RB*, 1889: No. 3, Sect. 2, pp. 3–41; No. 4, Sect. 2, pp. 116–40.

Vlasov, K. V. "Vladimir Ivanovich Vernadskii," *LRN: Geol.*, pp. 135–57.

"Vnutrennee obozrenie," *Sovremennik*, 1863, No. 10, Sect. 2, pp. 359–418.

Vodzinskii, E. I. "Russkoe neokantianstvo protiv nauki," *VLU: Seriia ekonomiki, filosofii i prava*, 1964, No. 4, pp. 46–54.

Vol'fkovich, S. I., ed. Dmitrii Ivanovich Mendeleev: Zhizn' i trudy. Moscow, 1957.

Vol'skii, M. "Ekonomicheskii materializm v ponimanii A. Bogdanova," *Zavety*, 1913: No. 8, Sect. 2, pp. 1–23; No. 9, Sect. 2, pp. 1–22.

Vorländer, Karl. Kant und Marx. 2d ed. Tübingen, 1926.

Vorontsov-Vel'iaminov, B. A. "Istoriia astronomii v Rossii v XIX stoletii," *TIIE*, II (1948), 26–70.

Vos'moi S'ezd russkikh estestvoispytatelei i vrachei v S. Peterburge ot 28 dekabria 1889 g. do 7 ianvaria 1890 g. St. Petersburg, 1890.

Vvedenskii, A. I. Filosofskie ocherki. Prague, 1924.

——. "K voprosu o stroenii materii," *ZMNP*, CCLXX (1890), Sect. 2, pp. 18–65, 191–220.

——. "Kritiko-filosofskii analyz massy i sviaz vysshikh zakonov materii v zakone proportsional'nosti," *ZMNP*, CCLXII (1889), Sect. 2, pp. 1–44.

——. Opyt postroeniia teorii materii na printsipakh kriticheskoi filosofii. St. Petersburg, 1888.

——. Psikhologiia bez vsiakoi metafiziki. St. Petersburg, 1914.

Vvedenskii, N. E. "Ivan Mikhailovich Sechenov," in Sechenov *et al.*, I, 59–81.

———. "O sovremennykh techeniiakh v fiziologii," in Sechenov *et al.*, I, 575–77.
———. "Pamiati Ivana Mikhailovicha Sechenova," in Sechenov *et al.*, I, 52–56.
———. "Usloviia produktivnosti umstvennoi raboty," in Sechenov *et al.*, III, Pt. 2, pp. 865–76.
"Vvoz nauchnykh priborov v Rossiiu," *Priroda*, 1915, No. 4, pp. 610–11.
"Vysshee obrazovanie," *Bol'shaia Sovetskaia Entsiklopediia* (2d ed.), IX, 508–9. Moscow, 1951.

Waksman, Selman A., *Principles of Soil Microbiology*. Baltimore: Williams, 1927.
———. *Sergei N. Winogradsky: His Life and Work*. New Brunswick, N.J.: Rutgers University Press, 1953.
Watson, D. M. S. "The Evidence Afforded by Fossil Vertebrates on the Nature of Evolution," in Jepsen *et al.*, pp. 45–63.
Weber, Alfred. "Prinzipielles zur Kultursoziologie (Gesellschaftsprozess, Zivilisationsprozess und Kulturbewegung)," *Archiv für Sozialwissenschaft und Sozialpolitik*, CLVII (1920–21), 1–49.
Weber, Marianne. Max Weber: Ein Lebensbild. Heidelberg, 1950.
Wentscher, P. "Weierstrass und Sonja V. Kowalewsky," *Jahresbericht der deutschen Mathematiker-Vereinigung*, XVIII (1909), 89–93.
Whitehead, Alfred North. "Mathematics as an Element in the History of Thought," in R. W. Marks, ed., *The Growth of Mathematics*, pp. 7–24. New York: Bantam Books, 1964.
Wilder, R. L. Introduction to the Foundations of Mathematics. New York: Wiley, 1952.
Worms, René. "Maxime Kovalewsky," *Revue internationale de sociologie*, XXIV (1916), 257–63.
Wurtz, A. Histoire des doctrines chimiques depuis Lavoisier jusqu'à nos jours. Paris, 1868.

Zabludovskii, P. E. Istoriia obshchestvennoi meditsiny. Part I: Period do 1917 goda. Moscow, 1960.
Zabrodskii, G. Mirovozzrenie D. I. Mendeleeva. Moscow, 1917.
Zagoskin, N. P. Istoriia Imperatorskogo Kazanskogo universiteta za pervye sto let ego sushchestvovaniia: 1804–1904. Vol. I. Kazan, 1902.
Zaitsev, Aleksandr. "Aleksandr Mikhailovich Butlerov (materialy k biografii ego i ocherk ego eksperimental'nykh rabot)," *ZFKhO*, XIX (1887), Supplement, pp. 13–57.
Zaitseva, L. L., and N. A. Figurovskii. Issledovaniia iavlenii radioaktivnosti v dorevoliutsionnoi Rossii. Moscow, 1961.
"Zalenskii, Vladimir Vladimirovich," *MBS-AN*, I (1915), 298–305. Autobiographical note.
Zalenskii, V. V. "Embriologiia i evoliutsiia," *Priroda*, 1915, No. 5, pp. 665–91.
Zalkind, S. Ilya Mechnikov: His Life and Work. Moscow, 1956.
"Zasedanie Moskovskogo Matematicheskogo obshchestva," *MS*, XXI (1900), 537–51.
Zechmeister, L. "Mikhail Tswett—The Inventor of Chromatography," *ISIS*, XXXVI (1946), Pt. 2, 108–9.
——— and L. Cholnoky. Principles and Practice of Chromatography. Tr. from the German by A. L. Bacharach and F. A. Robinson. New York: Wiley, 1944.
Zelinskii, N. D. Izbrannye trudy. Moscow, 1968.
———. Sobranie trudov. 4 vols. Moscow, 1954–60.
Zelinskii, O. "Universitetskii vopros v 1906 godu," *ZMNP*, 1906, No. 8, Sect. Sovremennaia letopis', pp. 111–59.

Zhukovskii, N. E. "Nikolai Alekseevich Umov kak matematik," *BSNM* (New Series), XXIX (1916), Supplement, pp. 50–55.

———. "O trudakh S. V. Kovalevskoi po prikladnoi matematike," in Stoletov *et al.*, pp. 19–31.

———. Polnoe sobranie sochinenii. Vol. IX. Moscow-Leningrad, 1937.

———. Sobranie sochinenii. Vol. VII. Moscow-Leningrad, 1950.

Znamenskii, P. Istoriia Kazanskoi dukhovnoi akademii. 2 vols. Kazan, 1891–92.

# Index

Asterisks indicate membership in the
St. Petersburg Academy of Sciences
prior to October 1917